THE ORAL TRADITION
FROM ZHANG-ZHUNG

THE
ORAL TRADITION
FROM ZHANG-ZHUNG

An Introduction to the Bonpo Dzogchen Teachings of the Oral Tradition from Zhang-zhung known as the *Zhang-zhung snyan-rgyud*

by

John Myrdhin Reynolds

Vajra Publications
Thamel, Kathmandu

Published by
Vajra Publications
Jyatha, Thamel (Hotel Norling),
P.O. Box: 21779, Kathmandu, Nepal
Tel/Fax: 4220562
e-mail: bidur_la@mos.com.np
www.vajrabooks.com.np

Distributed by
Vajra Book Shop
Jyatha, Thamel (Hotel Norling),
P.O. Box: 21779, Kathmandu, Nepal
Tel/Fax: 4220562
e-mail: bidur_la@mos.com.np
www.vajrabooks.com.np

ISBN 99946-644-4-1

Printed on acid-free paper
Printed in Nepal

Table of Contents

Foreword by
Lopon Tenzin Namdak

Foreword to the Translation into the English Language of Some Selected Texts from the Zhang-zhung Nyan-gyud.

When the precious teachings of the Victorious One, Tonpa Shenrab Miwoche, were first established in the country of Zhang-zhung, and subsequently spread and flourished there, the transmission of the Zhang-zhung Nyan-gyud was originally kept very secret. Merely examining of the candidate in order to see whether or not he was a suitable vessel to receive the teachings and then giving him permission to practice them was not felt to be a sufficient reason for explaining these Dzogchen teachings publicly. Therefore, the master transmitted the Dzogchen precepts orally and in private to one disciple only in his lifetime, in what was known as the single transmission lineage (gcig brgyud) Only with the advent of Je Tapihritsa in the 8th century of our era, who transmitted the precepts of Dzogchen to his disciple, Gyerpung Nangzher Lodpo, were these teachings given to more than one disciple at a time. Moreover, the master gave permission for him to write down the text of the precepts for the first time in the Zhang-zhung language. Nangzher Lodpo was succeeded by the six Mahasiddhas from Zhang-zhung and in the next century, Ponchen Tsanpo, the last native-born Zhang-zhung master in this lineage, translated the texts of the Experiential Transmission (nyams brgyud) deriving from earlier masters into the Tibetan language for the benefit of his two Tibetan speaking disciples, Lhundrub Muthur and Shengyal Lhatse. However, the Precepts Transmission (bka' brgyud) was not given to these Tibetan masters. Rather, it was later transmitted by Ponchen Tsanpo to other masters in Guge in Western Tibet. In the 10th century, Yangton Chenpo Sherab Gyaltsan of Dolpo received the complete Experiential Transmission from his master, Orgom Kundrol, who had committed the entire corpus to memory. Thereupon, Yangton Chenpo, together with two men from Kham in Eastern Tibet, set down the texts of the Experiential Transmission in writing and organized them into their present form. At a later time, from Togmed Zhigpo, a hermit living in a cave in Lo Mustang, Yangton received the texts of the Precepts Transmission. These two transmission lineages having been reunited by Yangton Chenpo, the Zhang-zhung Nyan-gyud has passed down in an unbroken transmission until our own time.

Moreover, at the time of explaining this particular scripture to disciples, it was thought necessary by various masters to measure and weigh matters by conveying the teaching in terms of four transmissions. These four transmissions (brgyud-pa bzhi), are as follows:

1. the transmission of the words which produce knowledge and where there exist no interpolations from other texts;
2. the transmission of the meaning which cuts off doubts and where there exist no adulterations or additions to the original small text;
3. the transmission of the upadeshas representing the experiences of the meaning and where there is no alteration of the words; and
4. the transmission of the authenticity which realizes belief and where there are no alterations due to the Rudra demons (of personal egotism and spurious interpretations).

A disciple who is a proper vessel for receiving the instructions of Dzogchen and who has definitively decided to cut his ties with the worldly life may then finally proceed to the actual practice in terms of making retreats of whatever length, beginning with the dark retreat. Eventually, such a dedicated practitioner will come to realize the signs of the understanding of the Natural State of the Nature of Mind. In this way, in the future, just as in the past, there will surely come forth many successful practitioners who, at the end of their lives, will realize the Rainbow Body ('ja'-lus) and dissolve their polluted material body into pure radiant light.

Furthermore, in terms of the four great sytems of instruction for Dzogchen found in the Bonpo tradition, where, in the past such signs of realization frequently came forth, there now exist many scriptures for teaching the completely perfect corpus of Dzogchen, the teaching of some parts of it, teaching the integrating of Tantra with Dzogchen, and so on, as well as the general exposition of the view. These four great scriptures coming from the Teacher, Tonpa Shenrab, are as follows:

1. *Zhang-zhung snyan-rgyud,*
2. *sPyi-rgyud ye-khri mtha'-sel,*
3. *rDzogs-pa chen-po bsgrags-pa skor gsum,*
4. *rDzogs-pa chen-po gab-pa dgu skor,*

together with the requisite commentaries of the *Sems smad sde dgu.*
With regard to the Zhang-zhung Nyan-gyud in particular, if one exemplifies and illustrates it with the biographies of the various great masters in the lineages of transmission, we find that, due to the great blessing of its successive and uninterrupted transmission from the Primordial Teacher Kuntu Zangpo, who represents the original source of the transmission, down until the present time, there have been an extraordinary number of masters who have attained the Rainbow Body of the Great Transfer ('ja'-lus 'pho-ba chen-po). This, indeed, is very remarkable.

In general, when one realizes the view of Dzogchen, coming to see that all appearances are merely empty forms, one will have the capacity to carry on along the spiritual path, bringing about a harmonious unification of action and result without mistakes. We can rejoice with devotion at such practitioners who come forth from this path of intelligence and wisdom, possessing both analytical discrimination and the virtuous qualities of understanding born of their meditation practice. Therefore, both the study of the scriptures embodying the Dzogchen view and regular meditation practice become united in the same individual.

Nevertheles, in terms of the view of Dzogchen, even though there exist good reasons for explaining many technical terms, such as clarity (gsal-ba), emptiness (stong-pa nyid), inseparability (dbyer-med), primordial purity (ka-dag), spontaneous perfection (lhun-grub), and so on, arriving at an agreement of the words and the meaning, it must be asserted here that the view of Dzogchen is truly beyond conceptual thought and expression in words. For that reason, it is more especially exalted than the views of the Tirthikas, or non-Buddhists, and it cannot fail to contend and strive with the greater and lesser vehicles of the Insiders, the Buddhists and the Bonpos. Indeed, it transcends the objects of thought among ordinary beings and possesses virtuous qualities that are inconceivable. Therefore, even though meditation practice is extremely important, the correct understanding of the view of Dzogchen, both in itself and in relation to and compared with the views found in other teachings, is equally important.

Here in this present volume by the translator John Myrdhin Reynolds, who is not only a scholar of Buddhism and Tibetan, but a long time practitioner of Dzogchen, there will be found translations into English, in a clear and concise fashion, of some selected texts of the oral tradition from Zhang-zhung. These translated texts include, not only the biographies or hagiographies (rnam-thar) of the principal early masters in the lineages of transmission, but also the very words that the enlightened master Ponchen Tapihritsa addressed to his disciple, Nangzher Lodpo, when they first met at the Darok Lake in Northern Tibet. This is followed by translations of the Guru Yoga for Tapihritsa and other preliminary practices for entering into the gateway of this ancient tradition of Dzogchen. These latter texts are taken from the *sNyan-brgyud rgyal-ba phyag-khrid*, which was composed by another master in the lineage, Druchen Gyalwa Yungdrung, the Abbot of Yeru Wansakha monastery, who flourished in the 13th century. We are happy to see the translations of these precious texts, as well as the lives of the masters, presented to a Western audience, and we pray that the Dharma of the Buddha, Tonpa Shenrab, known as Yungdrung Bon, will continue to benefit and inspire sentient beings at the present time and in the future generations to come.

Yongdzin Lopon Tenzin Namdak
Triten Norbutse Bonpo Monastery
Kathmandu, Nepal
January 2003

Preface

I began the study of the Zhang-zhung Nyan-gyud Cycle of Bonpo Dzogchen teachings in 1987 under the inspiration of Namkhai Norbu Rinpoche. Although not a Bonpo Lama himself, being a Drugpa Kagyudpa Tulku and educated in the Sakyapa traditions of Derge Gomchen in Eastern Tibet, nevertheless, he was greatly interested in the ancient pre-Buddhist religious culture of Tibet known as Bon. Earlier, while in New Delhi, India, in 1971, I had purchased a copy of this collection of Tibetan texts from Dr. Lokesh Chandra at his International Academy of Indian Culture. The original block-prints had been brought out of his homeland by Lopon Tenzin Namdak, at present the most knowledgeable Bonpo Lama living outside of Tibet. He had obtained them from his own monastery of Tashi Menri in Tsang Province, the foremost Bonpo monastery and academic center in Central Tibet. In collaboration with Dr. Chandra, the collection was published as *History and Doctrine of Bon-po Nispanna-Yoga*.

Although I had this copy in my possession for some years, it was not until 1987, at the urging of Martin Bugter of Deventer, the Netherlands, who also provided some sorely needed financial sponsorship at the time, that I began to undertake the translations of these texts. The following year, a young Bonpo Geshe and scholar, Tenzin Wangyal Rinpoche, came to visit and teach at Merigar in Italy. With his help I translated a number of key texts in the collection. In 1989, I finally met Lopon Tenzin Namdak in person when he came to visit the Tsegyalgar community at Conway, Massachusetts. We began working on the translations of other texts in the cycle, together with those from the *Phyag-khrid* or Practice Manual, including the preliminary and principal practices. The result of this collaboration with the Lopon in San Francisco and Los Angeles that same year, and later in Bischofshofen, Austria, and South Devon, UK, was a series of edited transcripts of the Lopon's teachings privately published as the Bonpo Translation Project (1992). In 1994, I was able to return to

Nepal and visit the Lopon at his new monastery of Tridan Norbutse near Swayambhu Hill. Although our work together now mainly focused on the Bonpo Mother Tantra cycle, the *Ma rgyud thugs-rje nyi-ma*, I also managed to translate the remainder of the texts in the collection, some of which are included here.

Historically speaking, Dzogchen appears to have originated somewhere in Central Asia outside of both India and Tibet as Upadesha (man-ngag), or secret oral instructions, communicated privately from a realized master to a disciple. At least, that is the Tibetan tradition. In the Buddhist tradition, this mysterious region was designated as Uddiyana (O-rgyan), which appears to be identifiable as Eastern Afghanistan before the Muslim era. In my previous book, *The Golden Letters*, I have dealt with the question of the origins of Dzogchen as presented in the Nyingmapa school of Tibetan Buddhism. In this present work, I shall consider the Bonpo account of the origin of these same teachings. According to the Bonpos, their own Dzogchen tradition, known as the *Zhang-zhung snyan-rgyud*, "The Oral Transmission from Zhang-zhung," comes from two masters, Tapihritsa and Gyerpung Nangzher Lodpo, who lived in the then independent kingdom of Zhang-zhung in Western and Northern Tibet in the seventh and eighth centuries of our era. These Dzogchen precepts, exceedingly brief in form, were originally oral, but Tapihritsa gave permission for his disciple to write them down in *Zhang-zhung smar-yig*, the writing and language of Zhang-zhung. Later, in the following century, these same precepts were said to have been translated from the Zhang-zhung language into Tibetan by Ponchen Tsanpo for his Tibetan disciples. Like the famous Tibetan Yogin Milarepa, these early masters of the Zhang-zhung tradition were not educated monks residing in monasteries, but solitary hermits and ascetics living in remote mountain caves in the wilds of Northern Tibet. Thus, this tradition, like the early Nyingmapas before the eleventh century, gives us much insight into the evolution of Dzogchen as a mystical and spiritual transmission existing outside the more familiar monastic context.

In both traditions, the Nyingmapa and the Bonpo, Dzogchen (rdzogs-pa chen-po), "the Great Perfection," focuses on the Nature of Mind. This Nature of Mind (sems-nyid) must be distinguished from the mind (sems) that represents the ordinary thought process. This Nature of Mind is identified with the Bodhichitta or Natural State (gnas-lugs), a state of total primordial purity (ka-dag chen-po) discovered by way of contemplation (khregs-chod), and this contemplation is then developed through the practice of vision (thod-rgal), also known as the practice of the Clear Light ('od-gsal).

The core of the material in this book was originally presented as a paper entitled "The Concepts of *Kun-gzhi, Rig-pa,* and *rTsal* in the Bonpo Dzogchen Teachings of the *Zhang-zhung snyan-rgyud,*" at the Sixth Seminar of the International Association for Tibetan Studies, in Fagerness, Norway, in August of 1992. That paper focused on the concept in Dzogchen of "Space," which is both the state of Shunyata (stong-pa nyid) and the basis of everything (kun-gzhi), on the concept of "Awareness" (rig-pa), which is clear luminosity (gsal-ba), and on the concept of "Energy" (rtsal), which is creative and unceasing (ma 'gag-pa), and how their inseparability (dbyer-med) characterizes the Natural State of the Nature of Mind (sems-nyid gnas-lugs) or the Primordial Base (ye gzhi) of the individual. That state is both primordially pure (ka-dag) in terms of its own nature and spontaneously perfected (lhun-grub) in terms of the manifestations that emerge or unfold out of it. Also, in that paper comparisons were made of the Dzogchen approach with the understanding of these concepts in the Madhyamaka and Chittamatra philosophies as they are explicated in the Bonpo sources. The textual material translated in this book has been is drawn from the *Zhang-zhung snyan-rgyud* collection in the New Delhi edition, originally compiled and printed at Menri Monastery in Tibet, and from a commentary on the practice of Dzogchen in the same Zhang-zhung tradition, namely, the *sNyan-rgyud rgyal-ba phyag-khrid,* by the thirteenth century Bonpo Dzogchen master, Druchen Gyalwa Yungdrung.

Here I have arranged the material from the Zhang-zhung tradition into a series of translations. This present volume provides a general introduction to the different Dzogchen traditions found within Bon and their relationship to Tibetan Buddhism. This includes a survey of the lineages for the Zhang-zhung tradition and the hagiographies of the various masters of this tradition in the early period. A future volume will focus on the philosophical aspects of the view of Dzogchen from the Bonpo perspective, while another future volume will focus on some of the associated practices, especially the practice of contemplation. A further prospective volume would contain certain additional translations from the tradition known as the Experiential Transmission (nyams rgyud). Each of these volumes may be read independently of the others. The first book in the series presented here, entitled *The Oral Tradition from Zhang-zhung: An Introduction to the Bonpo Dzogchen Teaching,* is divided into two parts as follows:

Within Part One, "The History and Lineages," the Introduction compares the Bonpo and Nyingmapa Buddhist traditions of Dzogchen and suggests their common origin in the country of Uddiyana in Central Asia, which can probably be identified with Eastern Afghanistan. The traditional Bonpo account of the Zhang-zhung lineages, namely, the Mind Transmission of the Buddhas (rgyal-ba'i dgongs brgyud) and the Oral Transmission of the Siddhas (grub-thob snyan-brgyud), is briefly examined, as well as the careers of the first two unquestionably historical figures in the the lineage of transmission, Tapihritsa and Gyerpungpa, who both appear to have flourished in the lake region to the west of Mt. Kailas in the country of Zhang-zhung in Northern Tibet in the early and middle eighth century of our era. In this context, here we present the translations of two texts relating to the history of the lineages and the origin of the Dzogchen teachings:

1. *The Small Text concerning the Nine-fold Transmission of the Mind* (dGongs rgyud dgu'i yig-chung) and
2. *The Hagiographies of the Masters of the Lineages* (brGyud-pa'i bla-ma'i rnam-thar).
Thereafter are presented translations of two further texts recounting the face-to-face encounters of the Dzogchen master Tapihritsa with his chief disciple Gyerpung Nangzher Lodpo:
3. *The Prophetic Sayings of the Lord Tapihritsa* (rJe ta-pi-hri-tsa'i lung-bstan) and
4. *The Intermediate Advent and Encounter* (mJal thebs bar-ma).
The final translation in this section recounts the legendary conflict between the Mahasiddha Gyerpeungpa and the great Buddhist king of Tibet Trisong Detsan, which occurred after the assassination of the last native king of Zhang-zhung in the mid eighth century, namely,
5. *The Reasons why the Bon did not Decline* (Bon ma nub-pa'i gtan-tshigs).

This is followed by a survey of the lineages of transmission after the time of Gyerpungpa in both Zhang-zhung and Tibet until the end of the thirteenth century.

In Part Two, "The Literature of the Zhang-zhung Nyan-gyud Cycle," the contents of the Zhang-zhung Nyan-gyud cycle in general and particularly the collection or anthology used here are outlined, as well as that of the associated practice manual for this collection, known as the *rGyal-ba phyag-khrid*

These two sections are followed by the three Appendices. Appendix One discusses the Guru Yoga, the practice of which is essential for Dzogchen. This meditation is then placed in relationship to the principal practice of Dzogchen, namely, contemplation. Appendix Two provides an introduction to and a translation of the basic Ngondro or preliminary practices text found in the practice manual. Before one can be properly introduced, in terms of Dzogchen, to the Natural State of the Nature of Mind by a qualified master, the individual mind-stream must be purified by way of these nine preliminary practices. Appendix Three presents the two guardian deities of this tradition, Nyipangse and Menmo, and provides a translation of the ritual texts used for their propitiation. The former figure has been incorporated into the Buddhist tradition as the guardian deity Tsangpa Karpo. Appendix Four provides the biography of Lopon Tenzin Namdak, the greatest living Bonpo Dzogchen master outside of Tibet and the foremost Bonpo scholar alive today, to whom this volume is dedicated..

The texts found in this collection entitled the *Zhang-zhung snyan-rgyud* belong both to the Experiential Transmission (nyams brgyud) of the Mahasiddhas, the realized masters of the past, and to the scriptural Transmission of the Precepts (bka' brgyud). In general, the commentarial tradition of both Buddhism and Bon in Tibet relates directly to spiritual experience (nyams) realized by way of meditation practice. Therefore, citations of scripture are largely employed as back-up support (rgyab rten) to something that is realized first by way of experience in meditation. In the Buddhist tradition, the teachings found in scripture (lung gi chos, bstan-pa'i chos) are distinguished from the teachings, which originate from a direct understanding (rtogs-pa'i chos) deriving from the individual master's personal meditation experience. These two, however, Agama, or scripture (lung), and Avabodhi, or direct understanding (rtogs-pa), are considered to be complimentary in the traditions of both Buddhism and Bon. The understanding of the master's own realization or enlightenment experience (nyams rtogs) is transmitted to the disciple in a personal context through the master's instructions and the disciple's own meditation practice and experience. In terms of Dzogchen, this type of transmission represents a practice lineage (grub brgyud) in contrast to an exposition lineage (bshad brgyud), which is of a more scholarly nature and focuses on the transmission and hermeneutics of scripture. Both types of transmission are found within the Zhang-zhung tradition. It may be true that the permission, or scriptural authorization (lung), in the form of the master reading aloud the text to the disciple, does, in the traditional view, connect the reader to an unbroken lineage of realized masters who have studied and memorized the texts in the past. However, the mere transmission of scripture or texts (lung) without the oral explanation (khrid) of a master who has attained a certain degree of realization in practical terms in that tradition is held to be one that is incomplete. Many Tibetan Lamas, to whom I have posed the question, have asserted that the empowerment (dbang), the scriptural authorization (lung), and the oral explanation (khrid) regarding the practice must all be present. Otherwise, although one may receive the blessings (byin-rlabs), the transmission itself is not complete.

This suggests two lines of inquiry with regard to these ancient texts: first, the philological one, that is to say, treating the text as a purely historical document and focusing on the preparation of a critical edition, placing the text historically in the development of a literary tradition; and second, the hermeneutical one, that is to say, the philosophical interpretation of the meaning of the text: what it means in the tradition and what it tells us about meditation experience from the viewpoint of the practitioner. I do not mean to play down the importance of basic philological work: the preparation of critical editions and the presenting of a supposedly objective account of the text, the determining of its date, authorship, and original structure, as well as placing the text in the development of the history of ideas. All of this and the accompanying critical apparatus are very useful. But this does point up a difference between the modern Western academic approach, which attempts to be scientific, objective, and strictly historical, as against the traditionalist approach in both Buddhism and Bon, which is more concerned with what the text means in terms of individual practice and experience in meditation. There is something to be said for both approaches.

Personally, I am more concerned here with the hermeneutical and philosophical dimension of these ancient texts from Zhang-zhung and Tibet, that is to say, with how their meaning is to be understood and interpreted within a living spiritual tradition. For this reason, in my exposition I have mainly relied on the oral explanations (khrid) of an accomplished master of this Bonpo tradition, Lopon Tenzin Namdak. In terms of the exposition of Dzogchen in general, I am more concerned with how this ancient tradition, whether Buddhist or Bonpo, deals with both mind and the Nature of Mind. This is more a question of Gnosis than of speculation regarding supposed historical origins. It is more a question of our origin, our true identity, and our spiritual destiny as human beings, and I believe that the Dzogchen perspective can do much to illuminate our present crisis of self-identity and our existential predicament at the threshold of the new millennium. Clearly, the fundamental question of our time is not what we should do or what course of action we should follow, but "Who am I?" and "What does it mean to be conscious and aware and human?" The light that Buddhism in general and Dzogchen in particular shed on these fundamental existential questions of human subjectivity and self-identity, which plague us in the post-modern world, opens before us like a new dawn.

First of all, and most importantly, I wish to thank Lopon Tenzin Namdak himself for his great patience and generous help in translating these texts. These translations were only made possible by his vast and comprehensive knowledge of the Bonpo tradition and its archaic and specialized terminology, indeed, a knowledge almost unique among the Bonpos inside and outside of Tibet. The Lopon was encouraged to make the Dzogchen teachings contained in these texts available, not only to his many Tibetan students in Dolanji, India, and later in Nepal, but also to Western practitioners and students, because of the vision that had come to his own teacher, Jongdong Sangye Tenzin, the former Abbot at Dolanji. The goddess and Bonpo guardian Sidpa Gyalmo had appeared to this master and warned him that if the Dzogchen teachings were not made more widely available, they would indeed die out within a generation. Since the goddess Sidpa Gyalmo is the principal guardian and protector of the Bon tradition and of the Bonpo Dzogchen precepts in particular, it is with her specific authority that these teachings are now made available.

Since that time, a Tibetan student of the Lopon, Tenzin Wangyal Rinpoche, and his Ligmincha Institute of Charlottesville, Virginia, have been transmitting these teachings belonging to the Experiential Transmission widely in Europe and America. Lopon Tenzin Namdak himself, over the course of a number of visits to Europe and America, has also transmitted these teachings and practices of the Zhang-zhung Nyan-gyud to an ever-growing audience, especially in England, Austria, the Netherlands, France, Italy, Germany, Denmark, Poland, and the United States. In France, the Association Yungdrung Bon was formed some years ago to present the Lopon and his teachings and to establish a center for his activities in the West known as Shenten Dargyeling. I also want to thank for their help over the years, in one way or another, in relation to this project: Martin Bugter who first encouraged me in this endeavor, Tim Walker, Ken Rivad, Des and Paula Barry, Dennis Waterman, Michael Canter, Fred Wingert, Jim

Casilio, Bob Kragen, Gerrit Huber, Florens van Canstein, Lee Bray, Bruce Bennett, Stephanie Denyer, Benny Friis Gunno, Jens Rasmussen, Gerd Manusch, Toni Winzer, Else Marie Kaasboel, Robert Anger, Sodis Vita, Sebastien Doerler, Dorothea Mihm, Larry Spiro, Eckhart Volmar, Reinhold Jacob, Christine Daniels, and especially Michael Taylor for his aid in editing the contents of the present work. I also wish to thank again Ken Rivad and Molly Thoron-Duran for the use of photographs of the initiation cards depicting some of the masters in the Zhang-zhung lineages. And I want especially to thank John Vincent Bellezza for his permission to use some of the photographs he took of the Darok lake and its environs while making an archaeological survey of that region in Northern Tibet, as well as the sketch map he made of the area.

For my own part, I have continued, as a part of the Bonpo Translation Project, to publish and privately circulate a number of translations from the Bon tradition, but in an unaffiliated, independent, and non-sectarian manner. My own view is that what is really important here are the Dzogchen teachings themselves, which represent the quintessential teaching of all the Buddhas, and it does not matter whether these come through a Buddhist lineage of Indian origin or a Bonpo lineage of Central Asian or indigenous Tibetan origin. Even the Nyingmapa tradition of Tibet asserts that Dzogchen did not originate in India, but came originally from Uddiyana in Central Asia. The essence of the teachings in terms of contemplation and vision practice are more or less the same in both traditions, the Buddhist and the Bonpo, and that would appear to indicate a common source in the distant past. Even in its own terms, Dzogchen is not something to be limited by any narrow-minded sectarianism, for it pertains directly to the Nature of Mind, which, in its own terms, is unbiased and transcends all cultural limitations and conditioning, not only among humanity, but among all sentient life-forms on this planet and elsewhere in the universe. Dzogchen belongs to all humanity and to all life.

As author and translator, it is my hope that this present volume will serve to make the ancient Bon tradition better known and understood in the West, to counter a number of erroneous and intolerant remarks made regarding Bon in the past, and to give some insight into the vastness and profundity of the Dzogchen tradition within Bon and within Tibetan culture generally.

MU-TSUG SMAR-RO!

John Myrdhin Reynolds (Vajranatha)
Dortmund, Germany, June 2003

PART ONE

THE HISTORY AND LINEAGES

CHAPTER 1

The Bonpo and Nyingmapa Traditions of Dzogchen

Introduction

In general, the Dzogchen teachings are found only in the old, unreformed Tibetan schools of the Buddhist Nyingmapas and the non-Buddhist Bonpos. In both cases, these teachings are substantially the same in meaning and terminology, and both traditions claim to have an unbroken lineage coming down to the present time from the eighth century and even before. Both of these schools assert that Dzogchen did not originate in Tibet itself, but had a Central Asian origin and was subsequently brought to Central Tibet by certain masters known as Mahasiddhas or great adepts. There thus would appear to exist two ancient and authentic lineages for the Dzogchen teachings, the Buddhist and the Bonpo. As I have previously discussed the Nyingmapa Buddhist tradition of the origin of Dzogchen in my book *The Golden Letters*, here I shall present a preliminary survey of the Bonpo tradition of Dzogchen known as the Zhang-zhung Nyan-gyud. This Bonpo tradition is especially important for research into the historical origins of Dzogchen, because it claims to represent a continuous oral tradition (snyan-rgyud) from the earliest times coming from Zhang-zhung in Western Tibet. [1]

Although some medieval and modern Tibetan histories written by cloistered Buddhist monks portray the ancient pre-Buddhist religion of Tibet called Bon as a nefarious mixture of sorcery, black magic, shamanism, and bloody sacrifices, this appears to be just so much anti-Bonpo propaganda providing a melodramatic effect. The principal aim of these Buddhist historians was to glorify the role of Indian Mahayana Buddhism in Tibetan history, suggesting that there was no culture or civilization in Tibet before the coming of Indian Buddhism to Central

Tibet in the seventh century of our era. India, the birthplace of the Lord Shakyamuni Buddha, was looked upon, not only as the source of all genuine religion and spirituality, but as the source of civilized culture generally, and even the lineage of Tibetan kings was traced back to an Indian origin by such native Tibetan historians as Go Lotsawa, Buton, and others. [2]

Another problem is that the Tibetan term *bon*, probably deriving from the old verb form '*bond-pa*, meaning "to invoke the gods," [3] has two different cultural referents. In the first usage, Bon does indeed refer to the indigenous pre-Buddhist shamanistic and animistic culture of Tibet, a culture that possessed many characteristics in common with other shamanistic tribal cultures of Central Asia and Siberia. Although these cultures involved various types of religious practice and belief, the central role was occupied by a practitioner known as a shaman. The activity of the shaman was definitively characterized as entering into an altered state of consciousness by way of chanting, drumming, dancing, and so on, whether this altered state of consciousness or "ecstasy" was understood to be soul-travel, as an out-of-the-body experience, or a form of spirit possession. [4] The principal social function of such a practitioner was healing. A traditional form of Central Asian shamanism involving spirit possession continues to be practiced widely in Tibet even today among both Buddhist and Bonpo populations, as well as among Tibetan refugees living elsewhere in Ladakh, Nepal, and Bhutan. Such a practitioner is known as a *lha-pa* or *dpa'-bo*. [5] Elsewhere on the borders of Tibet in the Himalayas and along the Sino-Tibetan frontiers, among certain Tibetan speaking and related peoples, there exist shamanic practitioners known as Bonpos, as for example among the Na-khi in China [6] and among the Tamangs in Nepal. [7]

But there exists a second type of religious culture also known as "Bon" whose adherents claim to represent the pre-Buddhist civilization of Tibet. These practitioners of Bon assert that at least part of their religious tradition was not native to Tibet, but was brought to Central Tibet sometime before the seventh century from the previously independent country of Zhang-zhung, west of Tibet, and more remotely from Tazik (stag-gzig) or Iranian speaking Central Asia to the northwest. [8] This form of Bon is known also as Yungdrung Bon (g.yung-drung bon), "the Eternal Teaching," a term which could be reconstructed into Sanskrit as "Svastika-dharma," where the swastika, or sun-cross, is the symbol of the eternal and the indestructible, corresponding in almost every respect to the Buddhist term vajra, or diamond (rdo-rje). In addition to ritual texts relating to shamanic and animistic practices, this ancient tradition possesses a large corpus of texts, also claiming to be pre-Buddhist in origin, relating to the higher teachings of Sutra, Tantra, and Dzogchen (mdo rgyud man-ngag gsum).

The Bonpo Lamas, instead of looking back to the North Indian prince, Siddhartha Gautama, as their Buddha and as the source of their higher teachings of Sutra, Tantra, and Dzogchen, look back even further in time to another prince, Shenrab Miwoche (gShen-rab mi-bo-che), born in Olmo Lungring ('Ol-mo lung-ring) in remote Central Asia, as their Buddha (sangs-rgyas) and as the source of their teachings. Hence, the latter is given the title of Tonpa or Teacher (ston-pa), literally "the one who reveals." Modern scholars may question the historicity of this figure, and Tonpa Shenrab is indeed given a rather fabulous date by the Bonpo tradition, asserting that he flourished some eighteen thousand years ago. [9] Furthermore, he is given a hagiography in Bonpo sources in no way inferior to that of Shakyamuni Buddha, as found, for example, in the *Lalitavistara*. [10] Along with the fabulous hagiographies of Padmasambhava found in the extensive literature of the Nyingmapa school, such as the *Padma bka'-thang* and the *bKa'-thang gser-phreng*, the career of Tonpa Shenrab represents one of the great epic cycles of Tibetan literature. [11]

To the outsider, this Yungdrung Bon nowadays appears little different from the other schools of Tibetan Buddhism in terms of their higher doctrines and monastic practices. Contemporary Bon possesses a monastic system much like the Buddhist one and a Madhyamaka philosophy fully comparable with the other Tibetan Buddhist schools. According to the Bonpo Lamas themselves, the main difference between Bon and the Buddhist schools is one of lineage rather than of teaching or doctrine, because the Bonpos look to Tonpa Shenrab as their founder and the Buddhists look to Shakyamuni. Indeed, both of these numinous figures are manifestations of Buddha enlightenment in our world, an epiphany that is technically known as the Nirmanakaya (sprul-sku). H.H. the Dalai Lama has now recognized Bon as the fifth Tibetan religious school, along side the Nyingmapas, the Sakyapas, the Kagyudpas, and the Gelugpas, and has given the Bonpos representation on the Council of Religious Affairs at Dharamsala. [12]

The Historical Development of Bon

Some Tibetan historians and scholars, on the other hand, were aware of this distinction between the two kinds of Bon referred to above [13], and certainly the Bonpo Lamas themselves were aware of it. According to one leading native-born Bonpo scholar, Lopon Tenzin Namdak [14], the history of the development of Bon may be divided into three phases:

1. **Primitive Bon** was the indigenous shamanism and animism of Tibet and adjacent regions in ancient times. Indeed, according to Bonpo tradition, some of these practices such as invoking the gods (lha gsol-ba) and rites for exorcising evil spirits (sel-ba) were actually taught by Tonpa Shenrab himself when he briefly visited Kongpo in Southeastern Tibet in prehistoric times. [15] Such rites were later incorporated into the classification of the teachings and practices of Bon known as the nine successive ways or vehicles (theg-pa rim dgu). These shamanistic types of practices are now known as "the Causal Ways of Bon" (rgyu'i theg-pa). Teaching and practice found in the Causal Ways are considered to be dualistic in their philosophical view, that is, the gods (lha), representing the forces of light and order called *Ye,* and the demons (bdud), representing the forces of darkness and chaos called *Ngam,* have an independent existence, and the concern of the practitioner is principally with the performing of rituals that invoke the positive energies of the gods and repel the negative influences of the demons and evil spirits (gdon). [16] An examination of the ritual texts in question reveals them to be largely of non-Indian origin. [17] However, like Buddhism generally, Yungdrung Bon is totally opposed to the practice of blood sacrifice (dmar mchod), for the origin of such practices is attributed to the cannibalistic Sinpo (srin-po) demons and not to Tonpa Shenrab. Thus, Bonpo Lamas are loath to identify even the Causal Ways of Bon with the shamanism of the Jhangkris or shamans still flourishing in the mountains of Nepal who continue even today to perform blood sacrifices. [18]

2. **Old Bon** (bon rnying-ma), or Yundrung Bon (g.yung-drung bon) as such, consists of the teachings and the practices attributed to Shenrab Miwoche himself in his role as the Teacher or the source of revelation (ston-pa), and, in particular, this means the higher teachings of Sutra, Tantra, and Dzogchen. He revealed these teachings to his disciples in Olmo Lungring on earth, as well as elsewhere in a celestial realm in his previous incarnation as Chimed Tsugphud ('Chi-med gtsug-phud). [19] These teachings of Tonpa Shenrab, already set down in writing in his own time or in the subsequent period, are said to have been brought at a later time from Olmo Lungring in Tazik to the country of Zhang-zhung in Western and Northern Tibet where they were translated into

the Zhang-zhung language. Zhang-zhung appears to have been an actual language, distinct from Tibetan, and apparently related to the West Himalayan Tibeto-Burman dialect of Kinnauri. Thus, it was not some artificial creation fabricated by the Bonpos in order to have an ancient source language corresponding to the Indian Sanskrit of the Buddhist scriptures. [20]

Beginning with the reign of the second king of Tibet, Mutri Tsanpo, it is said that certain Bonpo texts, in particular the Father Tantras (pha rgyud), were brought from Zhang-zhung to Central Tibet and translated into the Tibetan language. [21] Thus, the Bonpos assert that Tibetan acquired a system of writing at this time, based on the *sMar-yig* script used in Zhang-zhung, which, therefore, would have been ancestral to the *dbu-med* script now often used for composing Tibetan manuscripts, especially among the Bonpos. [22] The Bonpos subsequently experienced two persecutions in Central Tibet, the first under the eighth king of Tibet, Drigum Tsanpo, and later the second under the great Buddhist king of Tibet, Trisong Detsan in the eighth century of our era. According to the tradition, on both occasions, the persecuted Bonpo sages concealed their books in various places in Tibet and adjacent regions such as Bhutan. These caches of texts were rediscovered beginning in the tenth century. Thus, they are known as rediscovered texts or as "hidden treasures" (gter-ma). [23] Certain other texts were never concealed, but remained in circulation and were passed down from the time of the eighth century in a continuous lineage. These are known as s*nyan-rgyud*, literally "oral transmission," even though they are usually said to have existed as written texts even from the early period. One example of such an "oral tradition" is the *Zhang-zhung snyan-rgyud*, which, in the eighth century, the master Tapihritsa gave permission to his disciple Gyerpungpa to write down in the form of his pithy secret oral instructions (man-ngag, Skt. upadesha). Or else, the texts were dictated during the course of ecstatic visions or altered states of consciousness by certain ancient sages or certain deities to Lamas who lived in later centuries. One such example of this was the famous lengthy hagiography of Tonpa Shenrab known as the *gZi-brjid*, dictated to Lodan Nyingpo (bLo-ldan snying-po, b.1360) by the ancient sage Tangchen Mutsa Gyermed (sTang-chen dMu-tsha gyer-med) of Zhang-zhung. [24] This classification is rather similar to the Nyingmapa classification of its canon of scriptures into *bka'-ma* and *gter-ma*. [25] This form of Old Bon flourished in Western and Central Tibet down to our own day.

The teachings of Bon revealed by Tonpa Shenrab are classified differently in the three traditional hagiographical accounts of his life. In general, Tonpa Shenrab was said to have expounded Bon in three cycles of teachings:

I. The Nine Successive Vehicles to Enlightenment (theg-pa rim dgu);
II. The Four Portals of Bon and the fifth, which is the Treasury (sgo bzhi mdzod lnga); and
III. The Three Cycles of Precepts that are Outer, Inner, and Secret (bka' phyi nang gsang skor gsum).

These Nine Ways or Nine Successive Vehicles to Enlightenment are delineated according to three different systems of hidden treasure texts (gter-ma) that were said to have been put into concealment during the earlier persecutions of Bon and were rediscovered in later centuries. These hidden treasure systems are designated according to the locations where the concealed texts were discovered.

1. The System of the Southern Treasures (lho gter lugs): These were the treasure texts rediscovered at Drigtsam Thakar ('brig-mtsham mtha' dkar) in Southern Tibet and at Paro (spa-gro) in Bhutan. Here, the Nine Ways are first divided into the Four Causal Ways, which contain many myths and magical shamanistic rituals and which are principally concerned with working with energies for worldly benefits. Then, there are the five higher spiritual ways known as the Fruitional Ways. Here, the purpose is not gaining power or insuring health and prosperity in the present world, but realization of the ultimate spiritual goal of liberation from the suffering experienced in the cycles of rebirth within Samsara. The final and ultimate vehicle found here in this nine-fold classification is that of Dzogchen. [26]

2. The System of the Central Treasures (dbus gter lugs): These treasure texts were rediscovered at various sites in Central Tibet, including the great Buddhist monastery of Samye (bsam-yas). In general, this classification of the Bonpo teachings is rather similar to the system of the Nine Vehicles found in the traditions of the Nyingmapa school of Tibetan Buddhism. Some of these Bonpo texts are said to have been introduced from India into Tibet by the great native-born Tibetan translator Vairochana of Pagor, who translated works from both the Buddhist and the Bonpo traditions. [27]

3. The System of the Northern Treasures (byang gter lugs): These treasure texts were rediscovered at various locations north of Central Tibet. However, according to Lopon Tenzin Namdak, not much is currently known regarding this system. [28]

The Four Portals of Bon and the Treasury which is the fifth (bon sgo bzhi mdzod lnga) represent another and probably independent system for the classification of the Bonpo teachings into four groups known as the Four Portals (sgo bzhi), together with an appendix known as the Treasury (mdzod). These groups or classes of teachings are as follows:

1. The Bon of "the White Waters" containing the Fierce Mantras (chab dkar drag-po sngags kyi bon): This collection consists of esoteric Tantric practices focusing the recitation of wrathful or fierce mantras (drag sngags) associated with various meditation deities. Within this class are included the Chyipung cycle or "General Collection" (spyi-spungs skor), that is to say, the practices associated with the Father Tantras (pha rgyud). [29]

2. The Bon of "the Black Waters" for the continuity of existence (chab nag srid-pa rgyud kyi bon): This collection consists of various magical rituals, funeral rites, ransom rites, divination practices, and so on, necessary for the process of purifying and counteracting negative energies. This collection would seem to correspond, by and large, to the Four Causal Ways described above. Here the term "black" refers not to the practitioner's intention, but to the expelling of negativities, which are black in color symbolically.

3. The Bon of the Extensive Prajnaparamita from the country of Phanyul ('phan-yul rgyas-pa 'bum gyi bon): This collection consists of the moral precepts, vows, rules, and ethical teachings for both monks and ordained lay people. In particular, the focus is on the philosophical and ethical system of the Prajnaparamita Sutras, which are preserved in the Bonpo version in sixteen volumes known as the *Khams chen*. This collection basically represents the Sutra system, whereas the *Chab dkar* above represents the Tantra system. [30]

4. The Bon of the Scriptures and the Secret Oral Instructions of the Masters (dpon-gsas man-ngag lung gi bon): This collection consists of the oral instructions (man-ngag) and the written scriptures (lung) of the various masters (dpon-gsas) belonging to the lineages of transmission for Dzogchen.

5. The Bon of the Treasury, which is of the highest purity and is all-inclusive (gtsang mtho-thog spyi-rgyug mdzod kyi bon): This collection contains essential material from all Four Portals of Bon. The Treasury, which is the fifth (mdzod lnga), is described in the *gZer-myig*: "As for the highest purity (gtsang mtho-thog), it extends everywhere. As insight, it belongs to the Bon that is universal (spyi-gcod). It purifies the stream of consciousness in terms of all four Portals." [31]

The Three Cycles of Precepts that are Outer, Inner, and Secret (bka' phyi nang gsang skor gsum) are as follows:

1. The Outer Cycle (phyi skor) contains the Sutra system of teachings (mdo-lugs) relating to the Path of Renunciation (spong lam).
2. The Inner Cycle (nang skor) contains the Tantra system of teachings (rgyud-lugs) relating to the Path of Transformation (sgyur lam), otherwise known as the Secret Mantras (gsang sngags).
3. The Secret Cycle (gsang skor) contains the Upadesha teachings (man-ngag) relating to the Path of Self-Liberation (grol lam), otherwise known as Dzogchen, the Great Perfection.

3. New Bon (bon gsar-ma) arose since the fourteenth century, relying upon the discoveries of a different Terma system than the above. As a whole, this system is quite similar to the Nyingmapa one, and here Padmasambhava is also regarded as an important figure. Indeed, some Tertons, such as Dorje Lingpa, discovered both Nyingmapa and Bonpo Termas. In a text such as the *Bon-khrid*, rediscovered by Tsewang Gyalpo, it is asserted that Padmasambhava went to Uddiyana and received the Dzogchen teachings directly from the Sambhogakaya Shenlha Odkar (gShen-lha 'od-dkar) himself. Later he transmitted these teachings in Tibet, concealing many of them as Termas meant for the use of the future generations of Bonpos. According to Shardza Rinpoche also, the New Bon Movement began in the fourteenth century and continues until today. The Termas revealed to such masters as Lodan Nyingpo, Mizhik Dorje (otherwise known as Dorje Lingpa), Kundrol Dragpa, Dechen Lingpa, Sang-ngag Lingpa, Khandro Dechen Wangmo, and so on, are all considered Tersar (gter-gsar) or recent treasure text discoveries. The New Bon has flourished mainly in Eastern Tibet. [32]

The Origin of Dzogchen

Just as in the case of the Nyingmapas among the Tibetan Buddhists, the Bonpo tradition possesses as its highest teaching the system of contemplation known as Dzogchen, "the Great Perfection," (rdogs-pa chen-po). These teachings reveal in one's immediate experience the Primordial Base (ye gzhi) of the individual, that is to say, the individual's inherent Buddha-nature or Bodhichitta, which is beyond all time and conditioning and conceptual limitations. This Natural State (gnas-lugs) is spoken of in terms of its intrinsic primordial purity (ka-dag) and its spontaneous perfection in manifestation (lhun-grub). Both the Buddhist Nyingmapas and the Bonpos assert that their respective Dzogchen traditions were brought to Central Tibet in the eighth century, the Nyingmapa transmission from the Mahasiddha Shrisimha living in Northern India and the Bonpo transmission from a line of Mahasiddhas dwelling around Mount Kailas and the lake country of Zhang-zhung to the west and north of Tibet. Thus there appear to exist two different historically authentic lineages for the transmission of these teachings.

Subsequently, the Nyingmapa transmission of the Dzogchen precepts was brought to Central Tibet principally due to the activities of three teachers: the great Tantric master Padmasambhava from the country of Uddiyana, the Mahasiddha and Mahapandita Vimalamitra from India, and the native-born Tibetan translator Vairochana of Pagor. According to tradition, the latter came originally from a Bonpo family. [33] It is said that the latter and Vimalamitra were responsible for the first translations of the texts belonging to the Semde (sems-sde) or "Mind Series" and the Longde (klong-sde) or "Space Series" of Dzogchen teachings. However, some scholars, both Tibetan and Western, dispute that Vairochana actually made the many translations attributed to him. [34] Moreover, some contemporary scholars assert that the Dzogchen Tantras, which represent the literary sources for the Dzogchen teachings, were actually fabricated in the tenth century by certain unnamed unscrupulous Bonpo and Nyingmapa Lamas who then anachronistically attributed them to earlier numinous figures like Padmasambhava and Tapihritsa in order to win their acceptance as authentic scriptures. They therefore represent a kind of Buddhist and Bonpo Apocrypha and Pseudepigrapha. Modern critics cite the fact that, with the exception of two short Dzogchen texts, the *Rig-pa'i khu-byug* and the *sBas-pa'i sgum-chung*, the texts of the Dzogchen Tantras have not been found in the Tun Huang library on the borders of

Western China, which had been sealed in the tenth century. But simply noting that these texts were not discovered at Tun Huang does not prove that they did not exist elsewhere at the time or that they must have been composed after the closing of that library. On the basis of the extant evidence and in view of the lack of a thorough analysis of all the texts in question, it would appear that this conclusion is unwarranted. [35]

It has also been asserted by some scholars that Padmasambhava, although he may have been an actual historical figure, certainly did not teach Dzogchen, but only the Tantric system of the *sGrub-pa bka' brgyad*, the practices of the eight Herukas or wrathful meditation deities. This system forms the Sadhana Section (sgrub-sde) of Mahayoga Tantra. [36] However, eminent Nyingmapa Lama-scholars, such as the late Dudjom Rinpoche, reply that although Padmasambhava may not have taught Dzogchen as an independent vehicle to enlightenment, he did indeed teach it as an Upadesha (man-ngag), or secret oral instruction, to his immediate circle of Tibetan disciples. This private instruction concerned the practice of Dzogchen and the interpretation of the experiences arising from this practice of contemplation. In the context of the system of Mahayoga Tantra, Dzogchen is the name for the culminating phase of the Tantric process of transformation, transcending both the Generation Process (bskyed-rim) and the Perfection Process (rdzogs-rim). In this context, Dzogchen would correspond in some ways to the usage of the term Mahamudra in the New Tantra system (rgyud gsar-ma) of the other Tibetan schools. An old text, the *Man-ngag lta-ba'i phreng-ba*, traditionally attributed to Padmasambhava himself, does not treat Dzogchen as an independent vehicle (theg-pa, Skt. yana), but only as part of the system of the Higher Tantras. [37] When taught as an independent vehicle, Dzogchen practice does not require any antecedent process of Tantric transformation of the practitioner into a deity, and so on, before entering into the state of even contemplation (mnyam-bzhag). [38] So it would appear that, according to the Nyingmapa tradition at least, Dzogchen originated as an Upadesha that elucidated a state of contemplation or intrinsic Awareness (rig-pa) that transcended the Tantric process of transformation alone, both in terms of generation and of perfection. Therefore, it became known as the "great perfection," that is to say, the state of total perfection and completion where nothing is lacking.

According to Nyingmapa tradition, the Dzogchen precepts were first expounded in our human world by the Nirmanakaya Garab Dorje (dGa'-rab rdo-rje, Skt. *Prahevajra) in the country of Uddiyana and were later propagated in India by his disciple Manjushrimitra. The latter transmitted them to his disciple Shrisimha who, in turn, conferred them upon Padmasambhava, Vimalamitra, and Vairochana the translator. These three brought the precepts to Tibet in the middle part of the eighth century. Thus, this teaching was originally a secret oral instruction restricted to a small group of Tantric initiates. The tradition claims that it originally came from the mysterious country of Uddiyana located somewhere to the northwest of India. Therefore, it appears most likely that it is to the Indo-Tibetan borderlands of the northwest that we should look for the origins of Dzogchen. [39]

This seems equally true for the historical origins of Bonpo Dzogchen, for this second authentic lineage of the Dzogchen teachings also did not originate in India proper, but was brought to Central Tibet in the ninth and tenth centuries from Zhang-zhung in Northern Tibet by the disciples descending from Gyerpung Nangzher Lodpo. [40] Until the eighth century, the country of Zhang-zhung had been an independent kingdom with its own language and culture. It lay in what is now Western and Northern Tibet and the center of the country was dominated by the majestic presence of the sacred mountain of Gangchen Tise or Mount Kailas. Examining the available evidence, it now appears likely that before Indian Buddhism came to Central Tibet in the seventh and eighth centuries, Zhang-zhung had extensive contacts with the Buddhist cultures that flourished around it in Central Asia and in the Indo-Tibetan borderlands. Just to the west of Zhang-zhung once existed the vast Kushana empire that was largely, although not exclusively, Buddhist in its religious culture. This was an area in which Indian Buddhism interacted with various strands of Iranian religion— Zoroastrian, Zurvanist, Mithraist, Manichean, as well as Indian Shaivism and Nestorian Christianity. This was also true of the oasis cities of the Silk Route to the northeast of Zhang-zhung, such as Kashgar. Some scholars have seen this region beyond India as playing a key role in the development of certain aspects of Mahayana Buddhism, and later also in the development of Tantric form of Buddhism known as Vajrayana. [41] For example, the revelation of the *Guhyasamaja Tantra* is said to have occurred to king Indrabhuti in Uddiyana and was later brought to India proper by the Mahasiddhas Saraha and Nagarjuna. [42] Moreover, the *Kalachakra Tantra* is said to have been brought from Shambhala in Central Asia to Nalanda in India in the tenth century by the Mahasiddha Tsilupa. [43] The Bonpos came to identify this Shambhala with Olmo Lungring itself. [44] All this suggests that certain trends within Yungdrung Bon, rather than being later plagiarisms and imitations of Indian Buddhism concocted in the tenth century, actually do go back to a kind of syncretistic Indo-Iranian Buddhism that once flourished in the independent kingdom of Zhang-zhung before it was forcibly incorporated into the expanding Tibetan empire in the eighth century. This "Buddhism," known as *gyer* in the Zhang-zhung language and as *bon* in the Tibetan, was not particularly monastic but more Tantric in nature, and its diffusion was stimulated by the presence of various Mahasiddhas in the region, such as the illustrious Tapihritsa and his predecessors, dwelling in caves about Mount Kailas and about the lakes to the east in Northern Tibet. Even into this century, Kailas remained an important site of pilgrimage drawing Hindu sadhus and yogis from India. [45]

Such a mixed "Buddhist" culture, being both Tantric and shamanic, was suppressed in the eighth century when, at the instigation of the Tibetan king Trisong Detsan, the last king of independent Zhang-zhung, Ligmigya, was ambushed and assassinated when he left his castle of Khyung-dzong on the Dang-ra lake in Northern Tibet. Zhang-zhung and its people were absorbed into the Tibetan empire, and this ancient kingdom disappeared as an independent entity. The Zhang-zhung-pas were pressed into the service of the Tibetan army as it expanded westward into Ladakh and Baltistan. [46] Today the Zhang-zhung-pas survive as the nomad people of Western and Northern Tibet, often possessing the same ancient clan names. Having been converted to the Drigung Kagyudpa school of Buddhism, they have forgotten their ancient heritage. The old caves, once the dwelling places of the Bonpo Mahasiddhas, are now thought to be the domain of ghosts, places to be shunned and avoided. Yet ancient ruins, believed to antedate the Tibetan empire, are still to be seen at Khyung-lung (Khyung-lung dngul-mkhar) west of Kailas and on the shores of the Dang-ra lake to the east in Northern Tibet. [47]

In response to the urgings of the Indian Buddhist monk-scholar Bodhisattva, who thoroughly rejected these Bonpo heretics, [48] and failing to recognize the ties of doctrine and practice between the "Buddhism" of Zhang-zhung known as Gyer or Bon, with the monastic Buddhism recently imported from India into Central Tibet, the Tibetan government actively suppressed the indigenous religious culture of Zhang-zhung. Moreover, the persecution of the Bonpos by the Tibetan king Trisong Detsan may have had a political motive and not just a religious one. At that time, the Bonpos in Tibet were certainly not organized into a rival church or sect that could effectively oppose the Indian monks financially supported by the Tibetan government. This picture was a later anachronism created in the accounts of the medieval Buddhist historians. Rather than a conflict of rival religious doctrines, a parallel might be the suppression and subsequent annihilation of the Druids by the Romans in Gaul and Britain, where the Druids represented an ever-present source for Celtic nationalism and a rallying point for resistance against Roman rule. In the same way, the Bonpos may also have been suppressed because they represented a possible source of Zhang-zhung-pa rebellion against the rule of the Yarlung dynasty of Tibet. Just as the Druids were accused of making human sacrifices and the Romans used this accusation as an excuse to exterminate them, so the Bonpos were accused of making blood sacrifices and this represented another excuse for expelling them from Tibet.

The Three Traditions of Bonpo Dzogchen

In general, within the Bon tradition, there exist different lines of transmission for the Dzogchen teachings, which are collectively known as *A rdzogs snyan gsum*. The first two of them represent Terma traditions based on rediscovered treasure texts, whereas the third is an oral tradition (snyan brgyud) based on a continuous transmission through an uninterrupted line of realized masters. These three transmissions of Dzogchen are as follows:

1. *A-khrid*

The first cycle here of Dzogchen teachings is called *A-khrid* (pronounced A-tri), that is, the teachings that guide one (khrid) to the Primordial State (A). The white Tibetan letter A is the symbol of Shunyata and of primordial wisdom. The founder of this tradition was Meuton Gongdzad Ritrod Chenpo, who was frequently just known as Dampa, "the holy man." [49] He extracted these Dzogchen precepts from the *Khro rgyud* cycle of texts. Together with the *Zhi-ba don gyi skor*, these texts formed part of the *sPyi-spungs yan-lag gi skor* cycle of teachings that belong to the Father Tantras (pha rgyud), originally attributed to Tonpa Shenrab in his celestial pre-existence as Chimed Tsugphud ('Chi-med gtsug-phud). To this collected material, Meuton added his own mind treasure (dgongs gter) and organized the practice of the cycle into eighty meditation sessions extending over several weeks. This was known as the *A-khrid thun mtsham brgyad-cu-pa*. The instructions were divided into three sections dealing with the view (lta-ba), the meditation (sgom-pa), and the conduct (spyod-pa). Upon a successful completion of the eighty session course, one received the title of Togdan (rtogs-ldan), that is, "one who possesses understanding."

The system was later condensed by his successors. In the thirteenth century Aza Lodro Gyaltsan [50] reduced the number of sessions to thirty and subsequently in the same century Druchen Gyalwa Yungdrung wrote a practice manual in which the number of sessions in retreat (thun mtsham) was further reduced to fifteen. This popular practice manual is known as the *A-khrid thun mtsham bco-lnga-pa.* [51] And in the present century, the great Bonpo master Shardza Rinpoche wrote extensive commentaries on the *A-khrid* system, together with a commentary on the practice of the associated dark retreat (mun mtshams). [52] The *A-khrid* tradition, where the practice is very systematically laid out in a specific number of sessions, in many ways corresponds to the *rDzogs-chen sems-sde* of the Nyingmapa tradition. [53]

2. *rDzogs-chen*
Here the term *rDzogs-chen* does not mean Dzogchen in general, but the reference is to a specific transmission of Dzogchen whose root text is the *rDzogs-chen yang-rtse'i klong-chen*, "the Great Vast Expanse of the Highest Peak which is the Great Perfection," rediscovered by the great Terton Zhodton Ngodrub Dragpa in the year 1080. This discovery was part of a famous cycle of treasure texts hidden behind a statue of Vairochana at the Khumthing temple at Lhodrak. This root text is said to have been composed in the eighth century by the Bonpo master known as Lishu Tagring. [54]

3. *sNyan-rgyud*
The third cycle of transmission of the Dzogchen teachings within the Bon tradition is the uninterrupted lineage of the oral transmission from the country of Zhang-zhung (Zhang-zhung snyan-rgyud), which is the subject of the present study. Because this tradition has a continuous lineage extending back to at least the eighth century of our era and so does not represent Terma texts rediscovered at a later time, it is of particular importance for research into the question of the historical origins of Dzogchen.

CHAPTER 2

The Primordial
Buddha Kuntu Zangpo

The Primordial Buddha

According to traditions of Bon, just as is the case with the Nyingmapa tradition of Buddhism, the ultimate source for the revelation of the Dzogchen teachings is the Adibuddha, or Primordial Buddha (thog-ma'i sangs-rgyas), who exists beyond time and history, dwelling in eternity at the center of existence. Both of these old, unreformed schools, the Bonpo and the Nyingmapa, designate the Primordial Buddha in their scriptures by the name of Kuntu Zangpo (Kun tu bzang-po, Skt. Samantabhadra). On the other hand, in the New Tantra system (rgyud gsar-ma) of the later Tibetan schools, namely, the Sakyapa, the Kagyudpa, and the Gelugpa, the Primordial Buddha is known as Vajradhara (rDo-rje 'chang). [1] This Adibuddha in the Old Tantra system (rgyud rnying-ma) should not be confused with the great Bodhisattva of the same name, Samantabhadra. Unlike a Bodhisattva, this Primordial Buddha has never had to attain enlightenment and liberation from Samsara because He has been fully and perfectly enlightened from the very beginning. He has never even entered into the delusions of Samsara in the first place. He has nothing to attain or realize; He simply is what He is from the very beginning and never otherwise. This Primordial Buddha is called the entirely (kun tu) good (bzang-po) because He has never been afflicted with ignorance and the negative emotional defilements, nor mixed up in the rounds of Samsara. Therefore, He represents "the ultimate good" that transcends the relativities of good and evil, which belong to Samsara.

Kuntu Zangpo, the Primordial Buddha, the Buddha from all eternity, has been awake and enlightened from the very beginning by virtue of possessing the full understanding of the Natural State of the Nature of Mind (sems-nyid gnas-lugs). He is, therefore, like a clear mirror that can reflect whatever is set before it, whether beautiful or ugly, light or dark, good or evil, without having its nature in any way changed or modified thereby. The Primordial Buddha knows and reflects all of existence, but He has never been touched nor changed nor corrupted by the kleshes or emotional defilements that represent the actual causes of the Samsara that is cyclical existence. He has never been touched nor moved by a sense of ego identity (bdag-'dzin) nor caught up in entanglements with the illusions of Samsara, that mode of cyclical existence exemplified by historical time and by the thought process itself. Kuntu Zangpo is beyond mind and its operations. Therefore, He represents a state of total primordial purity (ka-dag chen-po) and is the very embodiment of the Dharmakaya (bon-sku), the ultimate aspect of Buddhahood and enlightenment. [2]

Like the Buddhists, the Bonpos also use the Tibetan term *sangs-rgyas*, which translates the Sanskrit Buddha, "the enlightened one," "the awakened one," for both the historical and the transcendent sources of their respective traditions. This term is also used in both schools to designate the principle of enlightenment that is immanent within every individual sentient being. Literally, a Buddha (sangs-rgyas) is an individual who has purified (sangs-pa) the mind-stream and awakened to the nature of Reality, thereby coming to unfold and expand (rgyas-pa) one's innate potentialities that manifest as the qualities of enlightenment. This unfolding may be compared to a lotus blossom opening its petals when touched by the rays of the sun in the early morning. As the aspect of total enlightenment known as the Dharmakaya, Kuntu Zangpo is without boundaries, without limitations, without definitions, without any divisions, being like the infinity of the sky. He is totally all-pervading and all-encompassing, like the nature of space itself. Never having undergone the evolution and the morphogenesis we know as rebirth in Samsara, Kuntu Zangpo has been the Dharmakaya from the very beginning and never otherwise. He embodies, therefore, the very principle of enlightenment itself. [3]

Although Kuntu Zangpo represents the Primordial Buddha in the transcendent sense of being completely enlightened from the very beginning (ye nas sangs-rgyas-pa) and never having been mixed up in Samsara, He is, nevertheless, equally present in the heart of and at the core of every single sentient being as the Primordial Base (ye gzhi) or the Primordial State of the individual (kun-bzang dgongs-pa). Thus, this name Kuntu Zangpo is also employed to designate the principle of enlightenment, or the Buddha-nature as such, that is immanent within every individual stream of consciousness and is synonymous, in the Dzogchen context, with the Bodhichitta. Therefore, the Primordial Buddha is simultaneously transcendent and immanent, as paradoxical as this may seem to common sense.

Metaphorically, the texts appear to speak of Kuntu Zangpo as a particular Buddha, as if He were a person or an individual personality. Although one may speak of Him as a Buddha, He did not need to work His way up like the other Buddhas through the ranks of the Bodhisattvas over the course of countless aeons in order to attain realization of Buddhahood, but had been enlightened from the very beginning. Therefore, He is called the Adibuddha or "the primordially enlightened one" who has been awake and enlightened from the very beginning. [4] However, it should be understood that this way of speaking is only symbolic and metaphorical, in the same way that the iconography of Kuntu Zangpo is symbolic and not something actual. This anthropomorphic representation is only a concession to a limited human understanding. [5] The name Kuntu Zangpo indicates the transpersonal dimension of enlightenment, which has been beyond Samsara or cyclical existence from the very beginning. Nor is Kuntu Zangpo a substance, not even an imperishable divine substance, because all phenomena lack inherent existence and are, therefore, empty and impermanent. The Primordial State of Kuntu Zangpo (kun-bzang dgongs-pa) represents a transpersonal state of being, the Primordial State of the individual, which lies beyond personality and the transitory operations of the mental processes called mind. At the same time, this transcendent state is perfectly immanent as the very ground and matrix (gzhi) for the activities of the individual mind-stream and thought process.

Indeed, the very thought process itself, the multifarious operations of the discursive mind, manifest the nature of Samsara, even creating it and bringing it into visible manifestation, wherein everything is conditioned by time and causality. In contrast to this process, the name Kuntu Zangpo indicates not the mind (sems), but the Nature of Mind (sems-nyid), and this should always be understood as embodied within an individual stream of consciousness. Just as the mirror is not the reflections that appear in it, so Kuntu Zangpo is not the mind or the thoughts that arise in it. Nevertheless, without the presence of this Nature of Mind, there would be no awareness or consciousness at all in the universe, just as, without the presence of the sun in the sky, the world would lie below in total darkness. Therefore, one must carefully distinguish between these two, the mind and the Nature of Mind. This distinction is crucial to the understanding of Dzogchen. However, the designation Kuntu Zangpo usually refers to the Dharmakaya in a more general and universal sense, that is to say, the Dharmakaya as representing the aspect of dimension or spaciousness (dbyings-cha) and the aspect of emptiness (stong-cha) in terms of the Nature of Mind and, therefore, it is compared to the vast, open, limitless space of the sky.

It is said in the Dzogchen texts that this Dharmakaya is the same in essence wherever it is found, whether in an enlightened being or in an ignorant sentient being, even a lowly worm. It is the same empty space found inside each of the clay vessels set in a row. The only difference in the quality of the space is the individual shape imposed by the form of each clay vessel. Break these clay vessels and it is all the same space. Indeed, the Dharmakaya has been primordially present within the mind-stream of each and every sentient being as the Nature of Mind itself. Not only the Dharmakaya, but also the entire Trikaya, or the three supreme aspects of Buddhahood, have been equally present from the very beginning, without any increase or decrease, in both the enlightened Buddha and the deluded sentient being. Just as the nature of the mirror is neither altered nor changed by any of the images it reflects, so the Nature of Mind is neither increased by enlightenment nor decreased by delusions. Nirvana and Samsara are merely reflected images. [6]

But if everyone, every sentient being, has been Buddhas from the very beginning, why is it necessary to practice the Path? Here the Dzogchen texts have been speaking only from the standpoint of the Base. Yes, Buddhahood has been wholly present from the very beginning, but this Buddhahood has gone unrecognized and is not yet manifest. This primordial enlightened nature has gone unrecognized because it has been obscured by ignorance, delusion, and karmic traces, just as the face of the sun in the sky may be totally obscured by the thick layers of clouds. The sun has been there all the time, present in the sky above, but its radiant face has gone unseen and unrecognized because of the persistence of the heavy clouds. It is the same with the Bodhichitta, one's inherent Buddha-nature. Therefore, it is necessary to practice the path in order to purify and remove the thick layers of obscurations, both emotional and intellectual, [7] so that the face of one's Buddha-nature comes clearly into view. The practicing of the path is like the winds dissipating the clouds that conceal the face of the sun.

The Base, the Path, and the Fruit

As already pointed out, Kuntu Zangpo is identified in the Dzogchen texts, as well as in the Old Tantras of the Nyingmapa and Bonpo traditions generally, as being the Dharmakaya (chos-sku, bon-sku). These texts assert that Kuntu Zangpo is the single Adibuddha or Primordial Buddha who has been enlightened from the very beginning and has never, at any time, been mixed up in the rounds of Samsara nor tainted by the kleshas, or the negative emotional defilements. This represents the transcendent aspect of Primordial Buddhahood. Nevertheless, paradoxically, this same Primordial Buddha Kuntu Zangpo is embodied as the Bodhichitta or Buddha-nature inherent within the mind-stream of every individual sentient being inhabiting the universe. This represents the immanent aspect of Primordial Buddhahood. Although, in terms of the Dharmakaya, the spaciousness and emptiness aspect is emphasized, the Dzogchen texts generally speak of the Dharmakaya as being without form or limitations like the infinity of space, yet Kuntu Zangpo represents the state of the primordial enlightenment of the individual where this spaciousness is inseparable from luminosity and awareness from the very beginning (ye nas gsal stong dbyer-med).

Therefore, there exist two sides to this single reality of Primordial Buddhahood: the Essence, or the side of emptiness (stong-cha), which is the Dharmakaya that is formless and invisible, on the one hand, and the Nature, or the side of Awareness (rig-cha) which is the Rupakaya that is manifest and visible, on the other. In terms of examples or images (dpe), Shunyata is said to be like the vast open dimension of the sky, whereas Awareness, or clear luminosity, is said to be like the radiant face of the sun high in the sky. [8] The presence of a single sun in the sky symbolizes the individuality of the Sambhogakaya, whereas the rays of the sun refer to the multiplicity of Nirmanakaya manifestations. The sky and the sun are only symbols or images. The infinite dimension of all existence has space or room enough for the presence of an infinite number of Sambhogakaya suns. Enlightenment will never become overcrowded nor congested. Therefore, the individuality of a Buddha persists and continues even after enlightenment in just this aspect of the Rupakaya or Form Body, which is comprised of the single Sambhogakaya and the multiplicity of Nirmanakayas, these being like the single sun in the sky and the multiplicity of its rays of light. This visible manifestation of enlightenment signifies and embodies the concrete expression of compassion, whereas the Dharmakaya signifies Shunyata in the universal sense. Indeed, the very term Rupa (gzugs) implies individuality. Therefore, the Dzogchen texts suggest that from the emptiness side, one may speak of the universal aspect of Buddhahood, while from the clarity or Awareness side, Buddhahood remains individual. According to the Buddhist way of thinking, the universal and the individual or particular are not contradictory and do not exclude each other. Rather, they are complimentary, being the two sides of a single non-dual reality called the *thig-le nyag-gcig* or the Unique Sphere.

To be more precise, this Natural State (gnas-lugs) or the Primordial Base (ye gzhi), which has been present all of the time since the very beginning, is, in this context, termed the Trikaya of the Base (gzhi'i sku gsum). It represents Primordial Buddhahood (ye sangs-rgyas-pa), even though, at the present time, this Buddhahood is not visibly manifest and, therefore, goes unrecognized while the stream of consciousness of the individual sentient being is still caught up in the delusions of Samsara. Nevertheless, it fully embodies the unmanifest potentiality for enlightenment that is latent within each individual sentient being from the very beginning. This Buddhahood, already present, but which is progressively becoming manifest (mngon sang-rgyas-pa) as one practices the spiritual path and purifies one's obscurations and karmic traces, is designated the Trikaya of the Path (lam gyi sku gsum).

However, simply the presence of the Base or Primordial Buddhahood within the individual stream of consciousness from the very beginning is not sufficient for this Buddhahood to become manifest. Its manifestation does not just happen fortuitously or automatically. Enlightenment does not happen of itself or as the result of an inevitable, progressive evolution that requires individuals to make no exertions in this regard. The deluded, discursive consciousness, on its own account, will not automatically shed its delusions and evolve into the enlightenment of a Buddha, neither in terms of the individual stream of consciousness nor in terms of the evolution of the human race as a whole. The presence of certain secondary causes, as represented by the Path, the processes of purification, are necessary in order to bring about the transformation of deluded discursive consciousness into the enlightened awareness of a Buddha. Therefore, the mere presence of a Primordial Buddhahood in the individual sentient being does not abrogate the necessity for practicing the spiritual path in order to attain its realization. [9]

When the Dzogchen texts speak of the Primordial Base that has been ever-present from the very beginning, they do so in terms of its Essence, its Nature, and its Energy, where these three aspects of gnosis, or primordial awareness (ye-shes gsum), are understood to indicate the Trikaya of the Base, that is, the Dharmakaya, the Sambhogakaya, and the Nirmanakaya. This is the Trikaya as potential, as the Base, in contrast to the Trikaya becoming manifest on the Path and the Trikaya fully realized and visible as the Fruit. In this context, the Essence (ngo-bo) means Shunyata, or emptiness, the state of primordial purity (ka-dag), whereas the Nature (rang-bzhin) indicates Awareness (rig-pa) or luminous clarity (gsal-ba), which represents the condition of spontaneous perfection (lhun-grub) where each form or manifestation arising out of the Base or Natural State is complete and perfect just as it is. Energy, literally compassion (thugs-rje), represents the inseparability (dbyer-med) of emptiness, or space, and luminosity, or Awareness, from the very beginning (ye nas rig stong dbyer-med). This Energy, or compassion, is characterized as being unceasing and uninterrupted (ma 'gag-pa). But here the texts are speaking only from the side of enlightenment, and at the present moment, this primordial enlightenment is concealed and obscured in the mind-stream of deluded sentient beings. It is merely latent and potential in the individual stream of consciousness. From the side of the individual practitioner, this primordial enlightenment is clouded over and goes unrecognized and, therefore, the practice of the Path is necessary in order to bring it into view or into visibility. That visibility, or manifestation, represents the Fruit.

The entering onto the spiritual path, from the perspective of Dzogchen, begins with the discovery, within one's own immediate experience, of the Natural State of the Nature of Mind by way of a direct introduction (ngo-sprod) from someone who has previously had the experience of it. A direct introduction is like the pointing out of the presence of the sun in the sky between the clouds by an adult to a small child who has never been outdoors before. Thereafter, the entire course of the spiritual path (lam) is a process of purifying these various layers of obscurations, both gross and subtle, the clouds, so to speak, that have been accumulated from previous lifetimes beyond counting. These obscurations represent not only the individual's past karma, but also all impulses, emotional reactions, and egoistic tendencies, as well as the obsessive ideas and the habitual conceptions that continuously afflict the thought process. This includes even the subtle thought constructions that structure reality itself within the stream of consciousness for the individual. This path or process of purification may be compared to the winds dissipating the clouds in the sky, so that the azure vault of heaven comes into view as clear and unobstructed. In total, this process represents the Trikaya of the Path (lam gyi sku-gsum) and the Buddhahood that is in the process of becoming manifest (mngon snags-rgyas).

From the standpoint of the ultimate result, or the Fruit ('bras-bu), the Trikaya is not manifest as such as an ordinary sentient being, although it is latently present, because the layers of obscurations, both emotional and intellectual, conceal its face. This is like the face of the sun in the sky being obscured by the clouds, or again, like having a bright golden Buddha image inside a temple where the doors are closed so that it cannot be seen from outside. When the clouds are dispersed by the winds, however, the face of the sun will be clearly seen. When the temple doors are opened at dawn, the Buddha image within will be fully revealed. The sun and the Buddha image have been present all along, but now their vision or appearance has become clearly visible to all. Once the clouds, which are the obscurations both emotional and intellectual, have finally been dissipated, they do not arise again because the causes that had engendered them have been annihilated. The face of the sun, which is one's own Rigpa or intrinsic Awareness, is clearly revealed and remains visible in the sky thereafter, whereupon the entire dimension of one's existence is brilliantly illuminated. This condition is known as the Trikaya of the Fruit ('bras-bu'i sku-gsum) and represents the Perfection of Buddhahood (rdzogs sangs-rgyas-pa). Thus, the individual comes to the ultimate self-recognition that is the attainment of Buddhahood. [10]

The Iconography of the Primordial Buddha

Because the Dharmakaya is totally devoid of and in no way limited by conceptions or discursive thoughts, Kuntu Zangpo is represented iconographically as a nude male Buddha figure, with cropped hair and lacking any ornaments or adornments. Sitting in meditation posture in the center of the infinity of space, He is entirely nude and unadorned because He embodies the Nature of Mind in all its unadorned nakedness, the primordial Natural State devoid of all discursive thoughts (rtog-pa med-pa), much like the clear open sky devoid of clouds. His body color is a deep azure blue because he represents the Dharmakaya and the state of Shunyata, being like the vast, open, empty, infinite daytime sky. He is sitting cross-legged in meditation position with His hands on His lap in samadhi-mudra, the gesture of equipoise, because He is perpetually dwelling in samadhi, the state of pure contemplation, which transcends and lies beyond the workings of the mind and its conceptual limitations. He is surrounded by an aura of rainbow lights because He embodies the inherent light of intrinsic Awareness or Rigpa in its visible aspect as the lights of the five gnoses or primal cognitions. The sphere of rainbow light (thig-le) surrounding Him represents the purified aspect of the elements. He sits suspended in the middle of infinite space, without any physical support, resting upon an immaculate lotus blossom, because He totally transcends all the limitations of Samsara and, therefore, He embodies the state of total, primordial purity (ka-dag chen-po) that is Shunyata. Yet He manifests Himself in a clear, empty, translucent form, like a rainbow appearing in the sky, because He expresses a total spontaneous self-perfection (lhun-grub chen-po). This Dharmakaya is beyond all limitations of form and conception, being without any perceptible form whatsoever in reality. But this conventional form of the formless Dharmakaya is presented here only as an aid to human understanding. Although the Dharmakaya in itself is totally inconceivable by the finite intellect and inexpressible in words (blo 'das brjod-med chen-po), nevertheless, the name Kuntu Zangpo is grammatically masculine in gender and so He is conventionally depicted as a solitary male figure seated in serene contemplation in the midst of the clear, open, infinite sky. The Primordial Buddha is represented in human form because, within our world system of the Sahalokadhatu, a precious human existence (mi lus rin-po-che) presents the maximum opportunity for the attaining of enlightenment. [11]

However, gender does not define the essence of the Dharmakaya. The Primordial Buddha may also be depicted in both Nyingmapa and Bonpo thangka paintings as being in sexual union (yab yum) with His consort, the Primordial Wisdom Kuntu Zangmo (kun tu bzang-mo, Skt. Adiprajna Samantabhadri). She is the Primordial Wisdom or Holy Perfection of Wisdom that is the Mother of all the Buddhas who have appeared throughout the three times of past, present, and future. Indeed, it is said in the Sutras that a Buddha only becomes a Buddha by virtue of this Perfection of Wisdom, just as a son cannot be born without a mother. [12] Being the embodiment of the Prajnaparamita, or the Perfection of Wisdom, She is known as Sherab Jyamma (Shes-rab byams-ma) in the Bon tradition. [13] She is also identified with the

Great Goddess of Zhang-zhung, *Sa-trig Er-sangs*. [14] Both goddess figures, when standing alone, are depicted as being golden in color. They are considered to be Sambhogakaya forms of the Great Goddess, corresponding to the male figures of Vajrasattva in Buddhism and Shenlha Odkar in Bon. But as the Dharmakaya, either alone or in union with the Primordial Buddha, She is also shown as nude, but as being white in color. Thus, the two sides or aspects of the enlightened awareness of Buddhahood, Skillful Means and Discriminating Wisdom, are expressed in human terms by these two nude male and female figures of Kuntu Zangpo and Kuntu Zangmo in sexual union (kun-bzang yab-yum). This sexual union is not something pornographic, but a sacred symbol of unification and integration (zung-'jug, Skt. yuganaddha) at the highest spiritual level of meaning. It is an iconic representation of the Ultimate Reality in the bliss of a timeless eternity, which is actually inexpressible in words. This union also indicates the primordial inseparability of luminous clarity and emptiness (gsal stong dbyer-med) that constitute the Natural State of the Nature of Mind, the primordially enlightened state of the individual (kun-bzang dgongs-pa). In general, when the Dharmakaya or Ultimate Reality is depicted iconographically as a male and female in ecstatic union, Kuntu Zangmo signifies Shunyata (stong-pa nyid), whereas Kuntu Zangpo signifies Awareness (rig-pa) and luminous clarity (gsal-ba), these representing the two sides of the single non-dual state of enlightenment. [15]

The Dialogue in Eternity

In the Dzogchen Tantras, for example, those found in the *rNying-ma'i rgyud 'bum* collection [16], the Primordial Buddha is depicted as the Dharmakaya,dwelling in eternity beyond time and history, whereupon He reveals the essence of Dzogchen directly by way of the mind-to-mind transmission (dgongs brgyud), without any recourse to words, to the Sambhogakaya Vajrasattva (rDo-rje sems-dpa') who is the chief among the five Jinas or Dhyani Buddhas (rgyal-ba rigs lnga). [17] The revelation of the teachings in the Dzogchen Tantras is presented in the form of a dialogue between a spiritual master and his disciple. It has always been the custom, in the Buddhist tradition in both the Sutras and the Tantras, to present the teachings of the Dharma, in their original form always oral, in the form of a dialogue between the teacher and the disciple, and so the Dzogchen scriptures follow suit, even though it is no longer the historical Buddha who is speaking here. This dialogue, although inspired by the Sutra model, is not a real dialogue spoken between real persons. Indeed, no words were spoken at all. The transmission was direct, mind-to-mind, instantaneous and telepathic. In essence, the dialogue is only a literary device employed to make the transmission manifest and comprehensible to human understanding. The commentaries explain that the Teacher (ston-pa) who expounds the Dharma and his audience ('khor) who listens to it are actually the same and identical. It is a dialogue in heaven between the Father and his spiritual Son. But the latter is really an emanation (sprul-pa) of the former, manifested here so that a dialogue may occur in the sequence of time and events. It is like the same actor simultaneously playing two roles. It does not mean that there are actually two persons present, only the appearance of such. [18]

In the Bonpo Dzogchen Tantras also, the revelation of the Dzogchen teachings is presented in the form of a dialogue. The Teacher (ston-pa) is the Primordial Buddha Kuntu Zangpo, but in this case His audience and disciple ('khor) is not called Vajrasattva, but the Sambhogakaya Buddha Shenlha Odkar (gShen-lha 'od-dkar), "the Shen god, white light." [19] He appears attired in the full raiment and symbolic ornaments of the Sambhogakaya, possessing the thirty-two marks and the eighty characteristics and all symbols of the inexhaustible richness and effulgence of the Sambhogakaya. According to the commentaries, this occasion of revelation possesses five certainties (nges-pa lnga), or five supreme aspects (phun-tshogs lnga):

(1) The supreme place (gnas) is always Mahakanishtha ('og-min chen-po), the highest plane of existence at the center.
(2) The supreme Teacher (ston-pa) is always the Dharmakaya Kuntu Zangpo (kun-bzang bon-sku).
(3) The supreme audience ('khor) is always the Sambhogakaya (rdzogs-sku).
(4) The supreme doctrine (bon) that is revealed is always the teaching of the highest vehicle to enlightenment, namely, Dzogchen.
(5) The supreme time (dus) for the revelation is eternity, a state beyond time and history. [20]

The Four Peaceful Deities

It was the Dharmakaya Buddha that first revealed the Dzogchen precepts to the Sambhogakaya Buddha. Thereupon, He taught to the

Sambhogakaya "the twelve indestructible verses." [21] Thus began the process of revelation by way of dialogue.

However, according to Bonpo cosmology, in each kalpa, or cycle of time, there exist four manifestations of the principle of enlightenment which possess both cosmogonic and soteriological functions. These represent offices or functions in the cosmic scheme of things, and these offices are occupied by different individuals during the different cycles of time. [22] In Akanishtha ('og-min), the highest plane of existence, there appears the Sambhogakaya (rdzogs-sku) known as the God of Wisdom (ye-shes lha); for our own aeon this is Shenlha Odkar (gShen-lha 'od-dkar) himself. At the same level of being manifests his consort, the Holy Perfection of Wisdom or Prajnaparamita, the Great Mother Sherab Jyamma (yum-chen Shes-rab byams-ma). Then in the heavens below there manifests the Creator God and World-Ruler (srid-pa); for this present aeon this is Sangpo Bumtri (Sangs-po 'bum khri), corresponding to the Indian creator god Brahma Prajapati. Then, on earth, for the sake of saving humanity and guiding all sentient beings to enlightenment and liberation from Samsara, there appear in our auspicious aeon (bskal-pa bzang-po) fully one thousand and two Nirmanakaya Buddhas. Each of them is a "Savior" and "Teacher" (ston-pa) who reveals the truth: the gnosis or knowledge that saves, representing the path to liberation and enlightenment. According to the Bon tradition, there have already occurred within this cycle the advent of seven Nirmanakaya Buddhas; the last in this lineage of saviors was Tonpa Shenrab Miwoche (Ston-pa gShen-rab mi-bo-che) who appeared in Olmo Lungring in Central Asia some 18,000 years ago. In the indefinite future there will come the advent of the future Buddha, Tonpa Thangma Medron (sTon-pa Thang-ma me-sgron), whom the Bonpos generally equate with the Buddhist future savior Maitreya (Byams-pa). These four luminous figures, namely, Shenlha Odkar, Sherab Jyamma, Sangpo Bumtri, and Tonpa Shenrab, collectively known as the Four Peaceful Deities (zhi-ba'i lha bzhi), all have their soteriological functions, but in the ancient Bonpo treatise dealing with cosmology called the *Srid-pa'i mdzod-phug*, the first three are also given cosmogonic functions. [23]

CHAPTER 3

The Mind-to-Mind
Transmission of the Buddhas

The Nine-Fold Mind Transmission of the Sugatas

In the hagiographies of the masters of the lineage that prefaces the published version of the Zhang-zhung Nyan-gyud, a series of lineages are given for the transmission (brgyud-pa) of the Dzogchen teachings. [1] The ultimate source of the revelation and the transmission is the Dharmakaya (bon-sku), the Primordial Buddha Kuntu Zangpo. This initial line of transmission is transcendental and transmundane. The transmission occurs not on earth, nor in time and history, but under the light of eternity on the highest plane of existence. It represents the direct Mind Transmission of the Sugatas, or Buddhas (bder-gshegs dgongs brgyud). This Mind Transmission (dgongs-brgyud) is so-called because it represents a direct mind-to-mind communication without any words or symbolic expressions intervening. This transmission is immediate, intimate, and direct. It is nine-fold (dgongs-rgyud dgu) because it consists of nine luminous figures who are transcendent rather than historical. This lineage of transmission is as follows:

1. The Teacher in Eternity (ye-nyid kyi ston-pa), the Dharmakaya Kuntu Zangpo (bon-sku kun-tu bzang-po);
2. The Teacher who is Compassion, (thugs-rje'i ston-pa), the Sambhogakaya Shenlha Odkar (rdzogs-sku gshen-lha 'od-dkar);
3. The Teacher who is an Emanation, (sprul-pa'i ston-pa), the Supreme Nirmanakaya, the celestial prototype for the great Shenrab (gshen-rab chen-po);
4. The Teacher who is Intrinsic Awareness (rig-pa'i ston-pa), Tsadmed Oddan (tshad-med 'od-ldan), "the immeasurable light," an emanation of Shenrab;

5. Trulshen Nangdan ('phrul gshen snang-ldan), the divine father of Chimed Tsugphud;
6. Barnang Khujyug (bar-snang khu-byug), Shenrab in the form of a sky-blue cuckoo bird;
7. Zangza Ringtsun (bzang-za ring-btsun), the mother of Chimed Tsugphud;
8. Chimed Tsugphud ('chi-med gtsug-phud), the heavenly pre-existence of Tonpa Shenrab; and
9. Sangwa Dupa (gsang-ba 'dus-pa), the chief disciple of Chimed Tsugphud.

Shardza Rinpoche in his *Legs-bshad mdzod* gives an account of the the history of the revelation and the transmission of both the Secret Mantras (gsang-sngags), or Tantras, and of Dzogchen. [2] According to this text, both systems were first taught in this present cycle of manifestation by Chimed Tsugphud ('Chi-med gtsug-phug), the celestial pre-existence of Tonpa Shenrab before he descended from above and incarnated on earth as the savior and world-teacher (ston-pa). According to the middle length hagiography of Shenrab, the *gZer-myig*, in his pre-existence in the heaven-world of Sidpa Yesang (srid-pa ye-sangs), "the world of primordial purity," he was known as Salwa (gsal-ba) whose name means "clarity." However, the relationship between Salwa and Chimed Tsugphud is not made clear here. In any event, Shenrab descended from an even higher plane of existence in the form of a heavenly blue cuckoo bird (bya khu-byug) and alighted on the right shoulder of the goddess-princess Zangza Ringtsun (bZang-za ring-btsun) while she was taking her leisure and her bath beside a celestial lake. An immaculate conception occurred and later the goddess gave birth to a precocious and luminously miraculous child as a virgin birth. Ashamed of bearing a child without a father, she built a small shelter on the golden sands beside the lake and left him there for nine days before returning. When she did, the infant recognized her and smiled at her lovingly, whereupon she was overwhelmed by his great beauty, especially the knot of hair bound up on top of his head. Therefore, she gave him the name of the immortal one ('chi-med) with the top-knot (gtsug-phud). Later he received the Dzogchen precepts directly from Shenlha Odkar himself when he ascended to a higher plane of existence. [3]

According to Lopon Tenzin Namdak, Trulshen Nangdan, the turquoise-colored cuckoo bird, and Chimed Tsugphud himself were all emanations of the Supreme Nirmanakaya who later revealed himself on earth and in history as Tonpa Shenrab Miwoche, whereas the

princess Zangza was actually an
emanation of the Great Goddess
Sherab Jyamma (yum-chen Shes-rab
byams-ma). [4] She was the
embodiment of the Prajnaparamita,
the Holy Perfection of Wisdom, who
is the Mother of all the Nirmanakaya
Buddhas appearing in the three times.
Moreover, his chief disciple in that
heaven-world, Sangwa Dupa (gSang-
ba 'dus-pa), to whom he revealed the
Tantras and also the Dzogchen
precepts, was none other than the
previous incarnation of Shakyamuni
Buddha. Thus the Bonpos believe
that Buddhism, the Dharma of India,

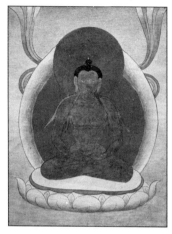

1. Kuntu Zangpo

was but another later version of the Primordial Revelation represented
by Yungdrung Bon and previously revealed by Chimed Tsugphud to
Sangwa Dupa. [5]

According to the *sPyi-spungs skor,* the cycle of the Bonpo Father
Tantras (pha rgyud), this sage Sangwa Dupa was born on earth to king
Zhiwadan (zhi-ba-ldan) and queen Lhajyindze (lha-sbyin-mdzes) in the
region of ancient Iranian-speaking Central Asia known as Tazik (stag-
gzig). When he reached maturity, he ascended in his physical body to
the heaven-worlds and listened to the Tantric and Dzogchen teachings
directly from the mouth of Chimed Tsugphud himself. Thereafter, this
sage practiced the teachings in nine different locations, and at each
place he subdued a specific violent deity (dregs-pa pho rgyud) and
erected a temple at each site to commemorate his victories. [6]

Introduction to the Translations

In order to give a little of the sense of this history as experienced by
Bonpo practitioners, we present here a number of translations of the
hagiographical texts found in the collection of the Zhang-zhung nyan-
gyud brought from Menri monastery in Central Tibet and reprinted in
New Delhi. [7] The first text, *The Small Text of the Nine-fold Lineage
of the Mind* (dGongs rgyud dgu'i yig-chung, ff. 245-246), is called a
small text (yig-chung), and briefly describes the exalted individuals,
all of them enlightened beings known as Sugatas or Buddhas, found
within the Mind-to-Mind Transmission of the Jinas (rgyal-ba dgongs

2. Shenlha Odkar

brgyud), extending from the Primordial Buddha Kuntu Zangpo down to Sangwa Dupa. [8]

The second text, *The Hagiographies of the Masters of the Lineages for the Oral Transmission from Zhang-zhung for the Great Perfection Teachings* (rDzogs-pa chen-po zhang-zhung snyan-rgyud kyi brgyud-pa'i bla-ma'i rnam-thar, ff. 1-130), presents the hagiographies (rnam-thar) that provide a history of the lineages of transmission and is placed at the beginning of the entire collection. This larger hagiographical text covers this Mind Transmission in much more detail, as well as the Oral Transmission of the Siddhas (grub-thob snyan-brgyud), including the later masters in the lineages from Gyerpungpa in Zhang-zhung down to the Tibetan author of the this text, Patsun Tangyal Senge Zangpo, who composed it in the year 1299. [9] A similar history of the masters in the lineage was composed by Druchen Gyalwa Yungdrung somewhat earlier in the same century, but there is no space to include a translation of that text here. [10] In any event, only the major portion of the translation of the hagiography text is included below, omitting some of the later Tibetan masters in the lineage.

Translation of "The Small Text of the Nine-Fold Transmission of the Mind": *dGongs rgyud dgu'i yig-chung*

Here is contained "The Small Text concerning the Nine-fold Transmission of the Mind" (dGongs rgyud dgu'i yig-chung bzhugs-so).

Homage to Kuntu Zangpo who represents uninterrupted compassion! [11]

1. Kuntu Zangpo— The Teacher in Eternity

In the Akanishtha of the all-pervading and all-encompassing Dimension of the Ultimate Reality, the inexpressible Dharmakaya, the Teacher in Eternity, from the uncreated state of self-originated primordial purity, expounded the teachings of Dzogchen in the center of the Mind of the Teacher of Compassion. [12] Thereupon, the latter contemplated the real meaning of these teachings, which was inexpressible in words from the very beginning. [13]

2. Shenlha Odkar— The Teacher of Compassion

In the Akanishtha of the all-pervading and all-encompassing Dimension that is unmoving, the Teacher of Compassion Kuntu Zangpo, from the state of this unmoving Mind itself, expounded the Dzogchen teachings in the center of the Mind of the Teacher who is an Emanation. Thereupon, the latter contemplated the real meaning these teachings as being like the sky that pervades everything. [14]

3. Shenrab Chenpo— The Teacher who is an Emanation

In the Akanishtha of the all-pervading and all-encompassing Dimension that is Spontaneous Perfection, the Sambhogakaya, from a state that does not move (from that condition), by means of magical apparitions that moved about everywhere, having all their marks and characteristics with respect to the Dharmakaya completely perfect, displayed these various different divine forms that subdued and converted everyone everywhere. Thereupon, Shenlha Odkar, the Teacher who is also an emanation, from the state of the infinite blessings of the Great Compassion, expounded the Dzogchen teachings in the centers of the Minds of these divine forms, which were Nirmanakayas, and they emanated everywhere (throughout time and space). Each of them possessed a core (or heart) of light that was without center or end, and these Nirmanakayas contemplated the real meaning of these teachings as being like the sun rising in the sky. [15]

4. Tsadmed Oddan— The Teacher of Awareness

In the Akanishtha of the Abhasvara Devas, the Gods of the Clear Light, which is the intermediate divine realm, the Teacher of Awareness known as Tsadmed Oddan, from the state of the total self-arisen primordial awareness, expounded the Dzogchen teachings in the center of the Mind of Trulshen Nangdan. Thereupon, he contemplated the real meaning of these teachings as being like sunlight and the rays of the sun. [16]

5. Trulshen Nangdan— The Teacher of the Great Means

In the Akanishtha which is the golden heaven of the realms of the Chya gods who are noble protectors, the Teacher of the Great Means known as Trulshen Nangdan, from the state of the inherent clear luminosity of Self-Awareness that is without any obscurations, expounded the Dzogchen teachings in the center of the Mind of the

Teacher (who dwelt in the intermediate spaces) of the atmosphere. Thereupon, the latter contemplated the real meaning of these teachings as being like the moon reflected on the water. [17]

6. Barnang Khujyug— The Teacher in the Intermediate Spaces

In the Akanishtha of the Trayatrimsha Devas, the realm of the Thirty-Three Gods, Barnang Khujyug, the Teacher who was an emanation, from the state where Wisdom and Means are inseparable in their manifestations, expounded the Dzogchen teachings in the center of the Mind of the Secret Consort (Zangza Ringtsun). Thereupon, she contemplated the real meaning of these teachings as appearances being without any inherent existence. [18]

7. Zangza Ringtsun— The Mother of Wisdom

In the Akanishtha that is the heavenly evergreen forest of jewels and turquoise, Zangza Ringtsun, who is the Mother of Wisdom, from the state of emptiness where Dimension and Gnosis are inseparable, expounded the Dzogchen teachings in the center of the Mind of her son Chimed Tsugphud. Thereupon, the latter contemplated the real meaning of these teachings as being the inseparability of clarity and emptiness. [19]

8. Chimed Tsugphud— The Teacher who Emanated in the Sky

In the Akanishtha that is the secret crystal cave in the turquoise valley, Chimed Tsugphud, the Teacher who emanated into the space of the sky, having connected the meaning with the words found in the Tantras, the Agamas, and the Upadeshas, expounded this ultimate nectar of the Primordial State in the center of the Mind of the Teacher who is the source of the Oral Transmission Lineage. Thereupon, the latter contemplated the real meaning of these teachings, condensing them into the secret Upadeshas. [20]

9. Sangwa Dupa— The Teacher who is the Source of the Lineage

In the Akanishtha of the visible intermediate divine realm, Sangwa Dupa, who condensed the meaning of the Dzogchen teachings into Upadeshas and expounded this root of the Tantras and Agamas that represents the highest peak of the vehicles to enlightenment, transmitted them from his Mind by means of scripture and reasoning to the Devas, to the Nagas, and to human beings, such as the Twenty-Four August Persons. [21] Thereafter, those persons, who were actually emanations, taught it to practitioners who possessed good karma.

Moreover, having thus far guided fortunate disciples along the path to liberation, until the end of this aeon, may there be no decline in their accomplishing the benefit of beings! SAMAYA!

Translations from "The Hagiographies of the Masters of the Lineage": *brGyud-pa'i bla-ma'i rnam-thar*

Here is contained "The Hagiographies of the Masters of the Lineage for the Oral Transmission from Zhang-zhung for the Great Perfection Teachings" (rDzogs-pa chen-po zhang-zhung snyan-rgyud kyi brgyud-pa'i bla-ma'i rnam-thar bzhugs-so).

3. Shenrab Chen-po

Here is presented that which is called "The Clear Mirror," which is a complete explanation of the Oral Transmission Lineage from Zhang-zhung for the Great Perfection Teachings. [22]

Preface

Homage to the Buddha and to the Hosts of Bodhisattvas!

I do homage to the Victorious Ones, together with the Lineages of Masters who possess the compassion that bestows Buddhahood upon us within this present lifetime. Meditating upon them seated above the crown of my head, with a single-pointed faith I pray to them fervently. By merely hearing their names with my ears, all fear and terror of Samsara, as well as all the afflictions of the evil destinies, are removed. Consequently, from the vast ocean of their virtuous qualities, I need only explain here a few drops of water concerning them.

The Divisions of the Text

Here, within this Oral Transmission from Zhang-zhung for the Great Perfection Teachings, there exist three principal parts:

1. the General Topics that represent the Preliminary Section (spyi don sngon du 'gro),
2. the Teaching of the Instructions that represent the Principal Section (dngos-gzhi gdams-pa bstan-pa), and
3. the Recognizing of the Methods of the Traditional System for the facilitating conditions of the meditation practice (cha rkyen mdzad srol gyi lag-len ngos bzung-ba). [23]

Part I: The Preliminary Section
Within the first part, there exist two sections:

1. the Divisions of the Portals to Bon entered by way of the Initiation (bon sgo dbang gis dbye-ba) and
2. the Teaching on the History and Origin of Bon (lo-rgyus byung-khungs bstan-pa).

Entering into the Portals of Bon
Within this first section, the Divisions of the Portals to Bon entered by way of the Initiation, there are three subdivisions, namely,

4. Tsadmed Oddan

1. Externally, there is the entering into the Mandala possessing visible characteristics (phyi mtshan bcas kyi dkyil-'khor la 'jug-pa) pertaining to the meditation deity Meri who is the one that guards the Scriptures for the Rites of the Peaceful and Wrathful Deities (me-ri zhi khro'i cho-ga'i gzhung bsgrub),
2. Internally, there is the receiving of the blessings deriving from the Transmission Lineage of the August Persons by way of the stages of the Initiation (nang dbang gi rim-pas gang-zag gi rgyud byin gyis brlab), and
3. Secretly, there is the receiving of the direct introduction (to the Natural State) by way of the examples that illustrate it, this representing the symbolic method of the Singular Initiation Lineage (gsang-ba dbang gcig brda thabs mthon-pa'i dpe la ngo-sprad-pa). [24]

The Origin and History of Bon
Second, as for the teaching on the origin and history (of the Dzogchen teachings), there are two considerations:

1. the systematically setting down of what should be explained regarding the nature of Bon (bshad-bya bon gi rang-bzhin gtan la phab-pa) and
2. the manner of the Advent of the Teachers who were the Original Expositors of the Dzogchen teachings ('chad mkhan ston-pa'i byon tshul).

Explanation concerning the Nature of Bon

First, when one comes to recognize just (the nature of) Bon in general, according to the *kLu-'bum*, it is said, "Everything that can be known within all phenomenal existence is termed Bon. There is nothing encompassed within all phenomenal existence that is not Bon. " [25] "As space, it pervades everything everywhere; therefore, it is difficult to measure it or evaluate it by the mind." "The full measure of its pervasion extends throughout and fully pervades the vessel of the universe. Moreover, the realms of this universe are inconceivable as multiple enumerations." "Just as there exist many enumerations of worlds, so also the numbers of sentient beings who are their inhabitants are inconceivable. [26] As for those sentient beings which are seen with the eye of gnosis, [27] we might ask how many enumerations can be made of the atoms of the earth?" "Just as there are so many of them, the actions (karma) of sentient beings are as many enumerations, but even these karmic actions of sentient beings are inconceivable in terms of their multiple enumerations." "The worlds of this universe that should be converted are extensive; therefore, the sentient beings who are the inhabitants of these worlds represent multitudes of enumerations. Moreover, the doctrines (bon) expounded by the Sugatas who are the subduers (that convert living beings) are inconceivable to the mind. Even the Precepts of the Teachers are inconceivable and represent a multitude of enumerations."

That "Bon," which was expounded by the Teachers, is twofold, namely,

1. entering into the word "bon" (bon kyi sgra gang la 'jug-pa) and
2. recognizing the real meaning of Bon on that occasion (skabs don gyi bon ngos bzung-ba).

Entering into the Word Bon

First, when entering into any of the words expressing the doctrine, one engages them in terms of the five objects:

1. the virtues which should be known (shes bya dge-ba),
2. Nirvana, the transcending of sorrow (myang 'das),
3. the thoughts of Bon (bon scms),
4. the samadhi that is without divisions (dbye ru med-pa'i ting-nge-'dzin), and
5. the object (yul). [28]

One engages (the real meaning) in terms of these five.

Furthermore, according to the *dBal-mo las thig*, [29] "Gradually those doctrines that should be known were collected." According to the

Sutra, "There is no Bon other than Bon." (What does this mean?) With regard to Bon, according to the same text, it is said that its words are stable and unshifting. It is called *g.yung* because it is undistracted with regard to the real meaning. It is called *drung* because it is unchanging with regard to the sign or indication. It is called *bon* because the Nature of Mind is a vast expanse that is all-encompassing. According to the *bsDud-pa*, it is called Mind and Dharma. [30]

Recognizing the Real Meaning of Bon

Second, in terms of recognizing the real meaning of Bon on that occasion, there are three considerations, which are, according to the Sutra:

1. the essential characteristic of Bon (mtshan-nyid),
2. the meaning of the word Bon (sgra don), and
3. the divisions of Bon (dbye-ba).

First, as for the essential characteristic, it is what was enunciated in the actual teachings of the Sugatas. Second, as for the meaning of the word, because Bon was listened to by all those in the various retinues when it was expounded by the Teachers, it came to be called Bon, that is, the Dharma. Third, as for the divisions, these have been enumerated in the *Khro-bos byas-pa*. [31]

As the innermost among all these divisions, in particular there exists the *rDzogs-pa chen-po zhang-zhung snyan-rgyud*. According to the *gZer-bu*, "This teaching is the highest peak among all the vehicles and represents the culmination of the Portals of Bon. It is the heart of the Tantras and overflows as the core of the Agamas. This instruction on Dzogchen is a most excellent Upadesha that is like the eyes (of the body)." Truly, Dzogchen is the highest peak of the Nine Vehicles and the culmination of the eighty-four thousand gateways to Bon. It is the physical heart of all the Tantras and the heart-essence of all the Agamas. [33] Among all secret instructions, it is similar to the eyes of the body.

Having briefly discussed how to recognize the various sections of Bon that need to be explained, one should look into the *Khro-bos byas-pa* for an extensive enumeration of them. Now I shall proceed to explain how the Advent of the Teachers came about. [34]

The First Teachers of Dzogchen

Second, with regard to the manner of the Advent of the Teachers who were the Original Expositors (of the Secret Doctrine of Dzogchen) ('chad mkhan ston-pa'i byon tshul), there exist two divisions, namely:

1. the Unoriginated Transmission of the Long Lineage (ring rgyud ma chags su rgyud-pa) and

2. the Directly Occurring (in history) Transmission of the Short Lineage (nye rgyud thog babs su rgyud-pa).

The Long Lineage

First, within the Long Lineage itself there are two subdivisions:

1. the Lineage of the Direct Mind-to-Mind Transmission of the Jinas (rgyal-ba dgongs-pa'i rgyud-pa) and

5. Trulshen Nangdan

2. the Lineage of the Oral Transmission of the Siddhas (grub-thob snyan khung gi rgyud-pa).

The Mind Transmission of the Jinas

As for the first, (the Lineage of the Direct Mind-to-Mind Transmission of the Jinas), according to the *gZer-bu*, it is said, "In what is called the Mind Transmission of the Primordial State, there exist nine (enlightened beings), [35] namely,

1. the Teacher in Eternity (Ye nyid ston-pa),
2. the Teacher of Compassion (Thugs-rje'i ston-pa),
3. the Teacher who is an Emanation (sPrul-pa'i ston-pa),
4. Tsadmed Oddan (Tshad-med 'od-ldan),
5. Trulshen Nangdan ('Phrul-gshen snang-ldan),
6. Barnang Khujyuk (Bar-snang khu-byug),
7. Zangza Ringtsun (bZang-za ring-btsun),
8. Chimed Tsugphud ('Chi-med gtsug-phud), and
9. Sangwa Dupa (gSang-ba 'dus-pa)."

1. The Teacher in Eternity: Kuntu Zangpo

With respect to the first of them, the Teacher in Eternity, there are two considerations: the Supreme Place and the Supreme Teacher.

First, as for the Supreme Place, according to the *Yig-chung*, it is said, "In the Akanishtha which is the Dimension of the all-pervading and all-encompassing Ultimate Reality." That which is called the

6. Barnang Khujyug

realm of the great all-pervading and all-encompassing Ultimate Reality is not created by any antecedent primary causes or secondary conditions; it does not originate in the world or among its inhabitants, and it is not created with any color or shape. It does not abide at the center nor at the periphery, nor in any cardinal or intermediate direction. [36]

Second, as for the Teacher, He is the Kuntu Zangpo that is totally devoid of a self. Moreover, He is untouched by any limitations whatsoever that pertain to Samsara or Nirvana. Not even the names "Buddha" or "sentient being" may be applied to Him. He is spontaneously perfected Buddhahood from the very beginning (existing in eternity), but He is inexpressible (in words and indefinable in concepts) because He is completely free of the eight extremes that represent conceptual elaborations. In terms of His outer aspect, He is just existence or being as such. However, in terms of His inner aspect, having already abided as the Kunzhi, the basis of everything, which represents total primordial purity, then as Rigpa, or intrinsic Awareness, adopting the guise of the self-arisen Teacher, He confers the blessings of compassion upon the retinues of the mind that represent the thought process and the functional mind. [37]

According to the *Sems kyi gnad drug*, "The Kunzhi is the Bodhichitta. Being all-pervading and all-encompassing and completely lacking in partialities, it represents the Dharmadhatu, the dimension of the Ultimate Reality. And when that state abides, Self-Awareness remains in total primordial purity and the Dharmakaya arises of itself." [38]

From that state and its power, because the dimension of space is connected from the very beginning with the manifest universe and Awareness is connected from the very beginning also with those sentient beings who are its living inhabitants, the external universe and its internal inhabitants of the six realms come into being from the five elements. [39]

2. The Teacher of Compassion: Shenlha Odkar

Second, with respect to the Teacher of Compassion, there exist three considerations: the Supreme Place, the Supreme Teacher, and the method of the Mind-to-Mind Transmission.

First, as for the Supreme Place, according to the *Yig-chung*, it says, "In the Akanishtha of the all-pervading and all-encompassing Dimension of the unmoving state." Even though it may be called the celestial palace that does not pass beyond Akanishtha, within it there exists no soil or stones or mountains or rocks. Verily, this immeasurable celestial palace of light is a magical apparition; it was created from the self-manifestations of gnosis. [40]

Second, as for the Teacher, according to the *Khu-byug rang-'grel*, it is said, "The Teacher is Shenlha Odkar. He is the Sovereign of Compassion who possesses the eyes of gnosis. The rays of light of his compassion pervade everywhere." From the light rays of that (supreme) deity originate multitudes (of enlightened beings), such as Kunnang, both chief and retinue. Since he is the root deity (and the source) of all the Shenrab deities, his three aspects comprise the Supreme Place, the Supreme Teacher, and the Supreme Retinue." [41]

Even though, in his outer aspect, he simply exists in that way, in his inner aspect, (as the Sambhogakaya), he dwells in the heart of each sentient being, for as it says in the *sGron-ma*, "The physical heart is a maroon-colored pavilion of cornelian, having projections of crystal. This immeasurable celestial palace of light, which is luminously clear and visible, is, in reality, the Supreme Place of Mahasukha Akanishtha. In that place, these three, namely, the sounds, the lights, and the rays, manifest in their spontaneous perfection to the primal cognitions of inherent Awareness. Thus, everything within Samsara and Nirvana is complete in its spontaneous perfection, and the Sambhogakaya arises by itself." [42]

Third, as for the method of the Mind-to-Mind Transmission: At that time, the Teacher of Compassion, Shenlha Odkar himself, presented to the Teacher in Eternity, Kuntu Zangpo, an inconceivable puja offering by means of his samadhi. Because the former requested the transmission of the essential practice, the inexpressible Dharmakaya who is the Teacher in Eternity, from the state that is self-originated and unborn, expounded upon the four aspects of the precious Transmission of the Precepts in the center of the heart of the Teacher of Compassion. Thus, he came to contemplate the real meaning, which was inexpressible in words from the very beginning. This has been expounded in the *Yig-chung*. [43]

3. The Teacher who is the Emanation: Shenrab Chenpo as the Turquoise Cuckoo

Third, with respect to the Teacher who is the Emanation, there are three considerations, namely, the Supreme Place, the Supreme Teacher, and the method of the Mind-to-Mind Transmission.

First, as for the Supreme Place: According to the *dGongs rgyud*, "In the Akanishtha of the world of the Gods of the Pure Abodes." Beginning with the seventeen levels of the Rupadhatu, it is the first (and highest) among the five Pure Abodes.

Second, as for the Supreme Teacher: The Great Shenrab, who is the guide of all living beings, departed from the realm of the Tushita Gods and descended to the human realm of this world in order to reveal (Dzogchen to human beings). Having emanated himself in the divine form of the king of birds, the turquoise-colored cuckoo, by his will power alone, he descended to alight upon a stupa of light in order to become the supreme guide for living beings. Thus, this came to be called the stupa where the Teacher had descended from the realm of the Gods. [44]

Then, while the Mother Zangza Ringtsun performed circumambulations of this luminous stupa, he emanated a single dark azure-colored syllable OM and caused it to enter into her womb. After some nine or ten months of pregnancy, on an island of clear light, within a beautiful grove of flowers in the presence of evergreen trees, on the eighth day of the first month of spring, the lunar mansion being the Pleiades (smin-drug) and the planet was the sun (that is, Sunday), at the first hour at daybreak, she gave birth to a son. Thereafter, he expounded the *Khams brgyad 'bum* (the Sutras of the Prajnaparamita, or Perfection of Wisdom) on the peak of the highest summit of the divine mountain of light. He was active from that beginning of that year, of that month, of that day, of that lunar mansion, and of that hour as the king of birds, thereby accomplishing many deeds (for the benefit of beings)." That is the significance of what was said (in the text).

That Shenrab, who was perfect in every way, ultimately realized the benefit of beings by way of sixty deeds. Finally, at the time when he prepared to depart into the dimension of the sky, in the evening he subdued the demons, at midnight he entered into a state of even contemplation, and at daybreak he attained Buddhahood in the dimension of Reality. [45]

In terms of his outer aspect, he existed in the way described. However, in terms of his inner aspect, according to the *sGron-ma*, "The place is the three channels and the six chakras, together with the trunk, the branches, and the lesser limbs. These exist as a field comprising a complete circle of letters. In that place, with regard to the primal cognitions of inherent Awareness, the energies having arisen as the six consciousness aggregates and the six sense objects; there are accomplished the various activities of the three gates (of Body, Speech, and Mind). Thus, the Nirmanakaya arises of itself." [46]

7. Zangza Ringtsun

Third, as for the method of the Mind-to-Mind Transmission: It is said that this Teacher presented an unsurpassed puja offering (whereupon the Dzogchen precepts were conferred upon him). This is expounded in the *dGongs rgyud yig-chung* as follows: "The Teacher of Compassion, Shenlha Odkar, from the state of the unmoving Mind, expounded the teaching in the center of the heart of the Teacher who is an Emanation, whereupon the latter contemplated its real meaning as being like the all-pervading sky." [47]

4. The Teacher of Awareness: Tsadmed Oddan

Fourth, with regard to Tsadmed Oddan, there are also three considerations, namely, the Supreme Place, the Supreme Teacher, and the method of the Mind-to-Mind Transmission.

First, as for the place, it is said in the *dGongs rgyud*, "In the Akanishtha of the realm of the Gods of the Clear Light, which is the intermediate Deva realm." Among the Sudarshana Devas of the seventeen levels of the Rupadhatu, there exists one place called the Realm of the Clear Light of the Intermediate Gods. [48]

Second, as for the Teacher, according to the *Rig-'dzin thugs rgyud*, "From the emanating of turquoise light into the sky, there occured extensive agitation of both heat and cold, and from the agitation of light, sounds, winds, and clouds, (there arose) the Man of the Mind, as well as the horse of the functional mind. The former possessed the nature of compassion and loving thoughts. Without having the name of "man" attached to him (by any human agency), nevertheless, this name came to be attached to him from the spaces of the sky. He was the great man of the spaces of the sky, and his immeasurable compassion was

8. Chimed Tsugphud

without partiality or one-sidedness. He became as a man who had emanated from the light, and therefore, he was called the indestructible divine form possessing immeasurable light."

Thereafter, Tsadmed Oddan, in the intermediate realm of the Gods of the Clear Light, brought those Bodhisattvas, who were established in the higher stages and who had purified their obscurations to knowledge, to obtain the ultimate stage of transcending all suffering, which is Nirvana itself. [49]

Third, as for the method of the Mind-to-Mind Transmission: Then because that Teacher (Tsadmed Oddan) emanated, by way of his samadhi, an unsurpassed puja offering and presented it to the Teacher who is the Emanation, Shenrab Miwo, from the state of the blessings of the great compassion, the latter expounded the Dzogchen teachings in the middle of the heart of this fortunate, divine form who possessed a heart of light that was without center or end. Thereupon, he contemplated that its meaning was like the rising of the sun in the sky." [50]

5. The Teacher of the Great Means: Trulshen Nangdan

Fifth, also with respect to Trulshen Nangdan, there are the three considerations of the Supreme Place, the Supreme Teacher, and the method of the Mind-to-Mind Transmission.

First, as for the place, according to the *dGongs rgyud*, "In the golden heaven of the Akanishtha of the Chya gods who are the noble protectors." This is said to be a city of the Gontsun Chya gods who are among the races of Sudrisha Devas inhabiting the Five Pure Abodes.

Second, as for the Teacher: "From the rays of light emanated from the Dharmakaya Kuntu Zangpo, there came forth effulgently a deity who possessed the nature of compassion without any discursive thoughts. From this emanation of His Mind, there emanated a divine form from these unchanging rays of light (of compassion); this was the Shen of Realization who possessed the appearance of a magical Shen." Because it was expounded thus in the *dGongs rgyud*, it is clear that he was a direct emanation of the Mind of Kuntu Zangpo. Thereupon, he purified all the obscurations to knowledge of those Intermediate Gods belonging to the Realm of the Clear Light and in general accomplished the benefit of beings. [51]

Third, as for the method of the Mind-to-Mind Transmission: With respect to that, Tsadmed Oddan, the Teacher of Awareness, from the state of the total Clear Light which is Gnosis, [52] expounded the Dzogchen teachings in the center of the heart of Trulshen Nangdan; the latter contemplated that their meaning was like sunlight and the rays of the sun. This was explained according to the *dGongs rgyud yig-chung*.

6. The Teacher of the Intermediate Spaces: Barnang Khujyuk

Sixth, with respect to Barnang Khujyuk, there are also three considerations, namely, the place, the Teacher, and the method of the Mind-to-Mind Transmission.

First, as for the place, according to the *dGongs rgyud*, it is "in the Akanishtha of Light in Trayatrimsha." Among the six Devalokas belonging to the Kamadhatu, there exists the place of the thirty-two Upendras with Shatakratu (their king Indra) as the thirty-third. [53]

Second, as for the Teacher, according to the *Khu-byug rang-'grel*, "From the Speech Emanations of the Teachers Kunzang and Shenlha, there came forth the Turquoise Cuckoo, the king of birds, who possessed a color similar to green turquoise. From the status of the Ultimate Reality, he appeared in the various places of the world among sentient beings of the nine stages in the Samsara of the three worlds. Nonetheless, he abided perpetually in the great bliss of the Dharmadhatu. Therefore, he is called the Teacher in the Intermediate Spaces. [54]

Third, as for the method of the Mind-to-Mind Transmission: With respect to that, Trulshen Nangdan, the Teacher of the Great Means, from the state of the self-arising of the inherent Awareness that is without obscurations, expounded the Dzogchen teachings in the center of the heart of this Teacher of the Intermediate Spaces. He thereupon contemplated the meaning of this as being like the moon reflected on the water. So it was expounded in the *dGongs rgyud yig-chung*.

7. The Teacher who is the Mother: Zangza Ringtsun

Seventh, with respect to the Mother Zangza Ringtsun, there are also three considerations, namely, the place, the Teacher, and the method of the Mind-to-Mind Transmission.

First, as for the place, according to the *dGongs rgyud yig-chung*, it was "in the Akanishtha of the forest of the jewel-like evergreen trees."

With regard to this crystal cave in the turquoise valley, there extends all about it a forest of jewel-like evergreen trees and various different flowers that illuminate everything with rainbow lights.

Second, as for the Teacher, according to the *bSen-thub*, "From the Mind where originate the nine vast spaces, there comes forth the existence of thinking and that which is created by memories. With respect to that, it represents existence as knowledge and as intellect. As for these two, thinking and memory, from their emanating into the great ocean of the nine vast spaces, there came into existence a single Goddess." [55]

The body color of this Goddess is golden. Her marks and characteristics are entirely complete. The hair of her head twists to the right and is tied up on top with a white lotus. Her body is adorned with water-born blue utpala blossoms. In her right hand she holds a golden vase and with her left hand she turns a golden rosary. Her own name, which she attached to herself, is Zangza Ringtsun.

Third, as for the method of the Mind-to-Mind Transmission: "With respect to that Mother, Barnang Khujyuk, the Teacher who is an Emanation, from the state which manifests the inseparability of Means and Wisdom, expounded the Dzogchen teachings in the center of the heart of the Secret Mother. Thereupon, she contemplated its meaning, namely, that all appearances are without any inherent existence." [56] So it was expounded in the *dGongs rgyud yig-chung*.

8. The Teacher who is the Son: Chimed Tsugphud

Eighth, with respect to Chimed Tsugphud, there are also three considerations, namely, the place, the Teacher, and the method of the Mind-to-Mind Transmission.

First, as for the place, it was called the Akanishtha of the crystal cave in the turquoise valley. On a golden mountain there were six peaks of crystal, and in front of that there were nine islands in a turquoise lake. He was born there (on one of those islands) upon an udumbara flower in that place that was beautiful and exceedingly delightful.

Second, as for the Teacher, the turquoise-colored cuckoo bird that had come flying to her descended on to the right shoulder of the Mother Zangza Ringtsun; this contact produced in her a gentle sensation of heat. After the time of one year, a son was born to her. Thereupon, she contemplated that mysterious event, saying, "Alas! There has been born to me a son without a father— what a shame!" She put him into a little box made of slabs of stone, having already spread in it a comfortable bed of white smooth raw silk. Having selected a garment of white silk to keep him warm, she let him remain there. But then, when she went to look for him after nine days, her son had emanated into the dimension of the sky; he remained suspended there, radiant and translucent. Thereupon, his mother realized that he was indeed a Nirmanakaya. Having accepted him thus, she gazed upon him and discovered that on this male figure of turquoise color there had come forth on his head a miraculous hair tuft of crystal. Since he did not die after remaining there for nine days, she realized that, indeed, he was immortal. Because a top-knot

9. Sangwa Dupa

of crystal existed upon his head, this head-crest led to his being called "the immortal head-crest," or Chimed Tsugphud. [57]

Third, as for the method of this Mind-to-Mind Transmission, Chimed Tsugphud, the Teacher who emanated into the dimension of the sky, skillfully connecting the meanings with the words in the Tantras, the Agamas, and the Upadeshas, expounded these Dzogchen teachings in the middle of the heart of the Teacher of the Oral Transmission Lineage (who was known as Sangwa Dupa). Condensing these extensive meanings of the Secret Upadeshas, the latter contemplated them thoroughly. So it was expounded according to the *dGongs rgyud yig-chung*. [58]

9. The Teacher of the Oral Transmission Lineage: Sangwa Dupa

With respect to Sangwa Dupa there are three considerations: the place, the Teacher, and the method of the Mind-to-Mind Transmission.

First, as for the place, he descended from the place called the Devaloka of the Akanishtha of the Intermediate Gods of the Clear Light into the country of Shodma Serteng and into the castle located on the peak of Langlingbang.

Second, as for the Teacher, he was born the son of those two, his father, the king Zhiwadan, and his mother, the queen Lhajyindze. He possessed all the requisite marks and characteristics. However, from the state of peacefulness, he emanated as a wrathful form, whereupon he condensed in his heart the meanings of the Nine Vehicles. He was born as one who had obtained all the Dharani-mantras of the Secret Mind. Therefore, he had bestowed upon him the name of Sangwa Dupa, meaning "he who condenses the secrets." [59]

Third, as for the method of the Mind-to-Mind Transmission: He transmitted the Dzogchen teachings to the three (Bodhisattva sages)— the Deva, the Naga, and the human. All of these Upadeshas had been condensed by Sangwa Dupa, and this compendium represented the highest peak of all the vehicles and the root of both the Tantras and the Agamas.

With regard to those Bodhisattvas, the three, Deva and Naga and human, from his mind, he (Sangwa Dupa) transmitted the Dzogchen teachings by means of both scripture and reasoned arguments. [60] So it was expounded according to the *dGongs rgyud yig-chung*.

Furthermore, as for the above transmissions, because they were transmitted by means of the methods of Rigpa, or intrinsic Awareness, and by way of magical power or apparitional displays, this became known as the Mind Transmission of the Jinas. [61]

CHAPTER 4

The Oral Transmission of the Siddhas

The Transmission Lineages in General

Following this Nine-fold Direct Transmission of the Mind of the Sugatas (bder-gshegs dgongs brgyud dgu), there come the lineages for the Oral Transmission of the Siddhas (grub-thob snyan khung gi brgyud-pa). [1] According to Shardza Rinpoche in his *Legs-bsad mdzod*, "Second, with regard to the Perfection Process, there exist two considerations,

1. the historical process of how the *Ma rgyud* spread and
2. the historical process of how the Oral Transmission of Dzogchen spread...." [2]

"Secondly, with regard to the Dzogchen teachings: In general, even though the gateways to the Bon of Dzogchen (rdzogs-chen bon sgo) are inconceivable in their numbers, when one condenses them, one may speak of three, namely,

1. the Four Cycles of the Transmission of Precepts (bka'-brgyud skor bzhi),
2. the Three Cycles of Revelation (bsgrags-pa skor gsum), and
3. the Nine Lower Sections of Mind Teachings (sems smad sde dgu)." [3]

"As for the first among them, namely, the Four Cycles of the Transmission of the Precepts (from Zhang-zhung), these cycles are four in number:

1. *Phyi lta-ba spyi-gcod*, the general exposition of the view, which is the external teaching;

2. *Nang man-ngag dmar-khrid*, the secret oral instructions presenting the vital explanations, which is the internal teaching;

3. *gSang-ba rig-pa gcer mthong*, intrinsic Awareness seeing nakedly, which is the secret teaching; and

4. *Yang gsang gnas-lugs phugs chod*, definitively deciding upon the Natural State as the source, which is the exceedingly secret teaching." [4]

" Moreover, with regard to them, (there exist three distinct types of transmissions involved, namely,)

1. the Longer Lineages of Transmission (ring brgyud),

2. the Shorter Lineages of Transmission (nye brgyud), and

3. the Combination of these Transmissions (brgyud-pa rkang 'dril)."

The Interrupted Transmission Lineages

"In terms of the Longer Lineages of Transmission, there exist two types:

1. the disturbed or interrupted transmission ('khrug-can) and

2. the undisturbed or uninterrupted transmission ('khrug-min).

Furthermore, from Chimed ('Chi-med gtsug-phud), the Teacher who is the ultimate source of this transmission, and from (his disciple) Sangwa Dupa, there were, in brief, three equivalent modes of transmission that came down to the great Gyerpungpa.

"As for the Shorter Lineages of the transmission, Tapihritsa transmitted them directly to Gyerpungpa." [5]

These Longer Lineages are divided and subdivided in the large hagiography text as follows. First there are the disturbed or interrupted transmissions (rgyud-pa 'khrug-can):

1. the Transmission from the heat-born Chimed Tsugphud (drod-skyes 'chi-med gtsug-phud nas brgyud-pa),

2. the Transmission from the egg-born Yeshe Tsugphud (sgong-skyes ye-shes gtsug-phud nas brgyud-pa), and

3. the Transmission from the apparitionally-born Sangwa Dupa (rdzus-skyes gsang-ba 'dus-pa nas brgyud-pa).

This first set of lineages, the interrupted transmissions, presumably represented intermittent revelations by these three initial numinous figures given from time to time to those sages listed. For example, Chimed Tsugphud appeared in a vision and transmitted the Dzogchen precepts to the renowned scholar Horti Chenpo, who appears to be an actual historical figure in Zhang-zhung in the early seventh century. He transmitted the precepts to his disciple Kunkhyen Dondrub, also known as Donkun Drubpa, who in turn transmitted them to Tsepung Dawa Gyaltsan, the teacher of both Tapihritsa and Gyerpungpa in the eighth century. Each of these Mahasiddhas practiced meditation at known sites, usually caves, in the Mount Kailas region and in the lake-district stretching to the east

10. Lhabon Yongsu Dagpa

in Northern Tibet. Thereby they attained remarkable siddhis or psychic and spiritual attainments, including the Rainbow Body. It therefore appears likely that Horti Chenpo, Dawa Gyaltsan, and the rest mentioned here, were all actual historical persons, Mahasiddhas living in Zhang-zhung in Western and Northern Tibet in the early period. Some figures such as Horti Chenpo and Sadnagau also appear to have been scholars and translators as well, and not just solitary yogins.

Chimed Tsugphud, as said above, represented the celestial pre-existence of Tonpa Shenrab, wherein he revealed the esoteric teachings of Tantra and Dzogchen, especially to Sangwa Dupa. According to Lonpon Tenzin Namdak, Yeshe Tsugphud is another emanation of Tonpa Shenrab. [6] However, much more research needs to be done in the Bonpo historical texts before any more can be said about these individual figures and their historical character, as well as the authenticity of these lineages in general. Like the lineages of the Indian Mahasiddhas who were associated with revelations of the Buddhist Tantras, these lineages are confused and at times appear in a contradictory state. Many figures appear to be contemporaries rather than successors of each other. Nevertheless, these Mahasiddhas flourished in the period from the sixth to the eighth century when the spiritual culture of independent Zhang-zhung was at its height.

The Uninterrupted Transmission Lineages

The second set of lineages represents the undisturbed or uninterrupted transmissions (rgyud-pa 'khrug-med), which has four divisions:

11. Lubon Banam

1. the Symbolic Transmission of the Bodhisattvas (sems-dpa' brda'i brgyud-pa),
2. the Awareness Transmission of the Vidyadharas (rig-'dzin rig-pa'i brgyud-pa,
3. the Oral Transmission of individual August Persons (gang-zag snyan-khungs kyi brgyud-pa), and
4. the Transmission through Learned Scholars and Translators (mkhas-pa lo-pan gyi brgyud-pa).

With regard to this, Shardza Rinpoche goes on to say: "As for the undisturbed transmission: From Sangwa Dupa, who was the last of the Nine belonging to the Mind Transmission, it was transmitted to the three Shenpos among the Devas, the Nagas, and the humans and thereafter it was transmitted successively to the twenty-four Shenpos." [7] But in the hagiography text translated below, Tonpa Shenrab himself is made the source of this lineage of transmission rather than Sangwa Dupa.

The Lineage of the Twenty-Four August Persons

The lineage of masters between Tonpa Sherab and Tapihritsa are known as the Twenty-Four August Persons (gang-zag nyi-shu rtsa bzhi) and all of them were said to have attained the Rainbow Body of Light ('ja' lus) by virtue of their practice of Dzogchen. In each case the complete Dzogchen precepts were transmitted by the master to only a single chief disciple (gcig brgyud) and not to any others. This lineage of transmission is presented in the large hagiography text as follows:

A. The Symbolic Transmission of the Bodhisattvas:
(sems-dpa' brda'i brgyud-pa)

From Tonpa Shenrab the transmission went to

1. Lhabon Yongsu Dagpa (Lha-bon Yongs-su dag-pa),
2. Lubon Banam (kLu-bon Ba-nam),
3. Mibon Tride Zambu (Mi-bon Khri-lde zam-bu),
4. Banam Kyolpo (Ba-nam skyol-po),
5. Trisho Gyalwa (Khri-sho rgyal-ba),

B. The Awareness Transmission of the Vidyadharas: (rig-'dzin rig-pa'i brgyud-pa)

6. Rasang Samdrub (Ra-sangs bsam-grub),

12. Mibon Tride Zambu

7. Darma Sherab (Dar-ma shes-rab),
8. Darma Bodde (Dar-ma 'bod-de),
9. Zhangzhung Triphan (Zhang-zhung khri-'phan),
10. Muye Lhagyung (Mu-ye lha-rgyung),
11. Mashen Legzang (rMa-gshen legs-bzang),

C. The Oral Transmission of the August Persons: (gang-zag snyan-khungs kyi brgyud-pa)

12. Gyershen Taglha (Gyer-gshen stag-lha),
13. Rasang Yungdrungse (Ra-sangs g.yung-drung gsas),
14. Rasang Yungphan (Ra-sangs g.yung-'phan),
15. Gephar Dondrub (dGe-'phar don-grub),
16. Gyerpung Gephen (Gyer-spungs dge-'phen),
17. Gegyal (dGe-rgyal),
18. Zhangzhung Namgyal (Zhang-zhung rnam-rgyal),
19. Mugyung Karpo (dMu-rgyung dkar-po),
20. Horti Chenpo (Hor-ti chen-po),

D. The Transmission of the Learned Scholars and Translators: (mkhas-pa lo-pan gyi brgyud-pa)

21. Donkun Drubpa (Don-kun grub-pa),
22. Rasang Phan-gyal (Ra-sangs 'phan-rgyal),
23. Gurib Sega (Gu-rib gsas-dga'),
24. Tsepung Dawa Gyaltsan (Tshe-spungs zla-ba rgyal-mtshan).

13. Banam Kyolpo

In some texts, Lhashen Yongsu Dagpa, the first in the lineage of twenty-four, received the transmission for Dzogchen from Tonpa Shenrab himself, while in other sources he received it from Sangwa Dupa, the disciple of the former and the last of the Nine Sugatas or enlightened beings in the transcendent Mind Lineage. The first few figures in this lineage of Mahasiddhas appear to be fabulous. The Lhashen or Lhabon Yongsu Dagpa was a Bonpo or Shen among the Devas or celestial gods. [8] The second figure, Banam, belonged to the race of chthonic serpentine water spirits or Nagas, who dwell in the Nagaloka underworld beneath the earth, where he was a Bonpo among the Nagas (klu yi bon-po). The third figure, Tride Zambu, is the first human sage in the lineage, being a Bonpo among humans (mi yi bon-po). Traditionally it is held that he was a prince born in Tazik in Central Asia. Thus, the three races inhabiting the three zones of the ancient Bonpo cosmology, namely, the celestial Devas (lha) who inhabit the Meru mountain and the heavens, the chthonic Nagas (klu) who inhabit the Underworld, and the human beings who inhabit the surface of the earth, all received the Dzogchen transmissions which descended from a transcendent realm of being.

The next figure in the lineage, Banam Kyolpo, is said to be the first native-born Zhang-zhung-pa in the list. Several among the succeeding masters belonged to the Rasang and the Gurib (or Gurub) clans, which survive even until this day in Northern Tibet and Northwestern Nepal. [9] Horti Chenpo, belonging to the generation preceding Tapihritsa and Gyerpungpa in the eighth century, was held to have been the greatest scholar in Zhang-zhung in his time in terms of all areas of Bon. The last figure in this lineage of twenty-four, Tsepung Dawa Gyaltsan (Tshe-spungs zla-ba rgyal-mtshan) appears almost certainly to be historical. It is said that he collected all of the teachings and expanded what his masters had given him. He was the teacher of both the Mahasiddha Tapihritsa and his disciple and successor Gyerpungpa, both of whom probably flourished in Zhang-zhung in the late seventh and the early eighth centuries.

Shardza Rinpoche gives some additional biographical material on a number of these Mahasiddhas, tracing the revelation of the Dzogchen precepts back to Sangwa Dupa:

"As for the combined transmissions: This occurred when the disturbed lineage and the undisturbed lineage combined with the short lineage of transmission and became five-fold. From Gyerpungpa this was transmitted upward to the present

14. Trisho Gyalwa

time. We have already shown how the lineage was transmitted from Sangwa Dupa, who belonged to the Nine-fold Lineage of the Mind Transmission, to the three Shenpos among the Devas, the Nagas, and the humans. [10] But here, in terms of the disturbed lineage, we shall expand a little on how the masters who preceded Gyerpungpa attained realization.

"From Chimed Tsugphud the precepts were transmitted to Ponchen Horti (dPon-chen Hor-ti). From him they were transmitted to Kunkhyen Dondrub (Kun-mkhyen don-grub). And both of them, having come to dissolve external appearances, their internal thoughts, and even their own physical bodies into the dimension of space, they became liberated directly into the Primordial Base. [11]

"The disciple of Kunkhyen (Dondrub) was Tsepung Dawa Gyaltsan (Tshe-spungs zla-ba rgyal-mtshan). Having meditated for nine years at the site of Dragmarshad (brag-dmar shad), he purified both his outer and inner impurities into translucency and dissolved his physical body into the light of the rainbow.

"His disciple was Rasang Lugyal (Ra-sangs klu-rgyal). Having meditated at the site of Pomar (spo-dmar), he thereby arrived at the full measure of the four stages of vision.

"His disciple was Ponchen Tapihritsa (dPon-chen Ta-pi-hri-tsa) (who was the son of the preceding master). Having meditated for nine years at the lion rock of Tagthab Sengedrak (stag-thabs seng-ge'i

15. Rasang Samdrub

brag), he thereby attained the Body of Perfect Gnosis.

"His disciple was Rasang Kumaradza (Ra-sangs ku-ma-ra-dza). Having meditated for nine years at the site of Nering (ne-ring), he definitively decided that the visions encountered upon the path (of his practice) represented the Trikaya.

"His disciple was Rasang Sodtse (Ra-sangs bsod-rtse). Having meditated for thirteen years in solitude, he realized the stage of the overthrowing and exhausting of Reality .

"His disciple was Sadnagau of Zhang-zhung (Zhang-zhung gi Sad-na-ga'u). Having meditated for sixteen years in a rock cave, the elements of his physical body dissolved into their own original condition.

"His disciple was Gurub Lhajyin (Gu-rub lha-sbyin). Having meditated for eleven years at the site of Jyatsang (bya-tshang), without ever visiting any town or other inhabited place, he became liberated into the Body of Light.

"His disciple was Gurub Palzang (Gu-rub dpal-bzang). Having practiced the precepts while dwelling in the mountains, he liberated his polluted physical body into the unpolluted state.

"His disciple was Rasang Trine (Ra-sangs khri-ne). Having practiced in the valley of Chanrong (gcan-rong) in the south, he obtained both the ordinary and the supreme siddhis.

"His disciple was the Bonpo of Sumpa, Abadong (Sum-pa'i bon-po A-ba-ldong), and his disciple, in turn, was Gyabon Salwa Odchen (rGya-bon gsal-ba 'od-chen). The two of them transmitted the precepts in Sumpa and in China respectively. And as for the disciple of Gyabon, there came forth one called Jagrong Sekhar ('Jag-rong gsas-mkhar). Moreover, the three of them, having exhausted the visions of materiality, became Bodies of Radiance.

"The latter had taught the instructions to Drubpa Gyaltsan (Grub-pa rgyal-mtshan), who was the middle son among the three sons of this Jagse. [12] Having meditated for eight years at Dragmar Tagtsang (brag-dmar stag-tshang), he became liberated from all materiality, both external and internal.

"His disciple was Khyungpo Tragyal (Khyung-po bkra-rgyal). Having meditated for twenty-one years in the cave of Sati in Zhang-zhung (zhang-zhung sa-ti'i phug), he obtained the body that is without pollutions.

"His son and disciple was Leggon (Legs-mgon). Having meditated for eight years on an island in the lake of Riti (mtsho ri-ti'i do), he dissolved his appearant materiality into light.

16. Darma Sherab

"His disciple was Mahor Tagzig (Ma-hor stag-gzig). Even though he meditated for twelve years on Gang Tise (Mount Kailas), still he was unable to find belief and so he returned again to his master. He offered his master ten measures of gold and inquired, 'Even though I have practiced the precepts for just these twelve years, still I did not find belief (or the confidence that comes from the realization of the practice). Therefore, I request from you further instructions.' The master replied, 'I do not want your gold.' Nevertheless, he gave him the instructions. Having meditated for another six years, with patience he attained realization.

"Furthermore, everyone in these two equivalent lineages of transmission (the disturbed and the undisturbed) from Sangwa Dupa onward, and also among those Mahasiddhas who appeared among the twenty-four masters who received the transmission from the source in terms of the undistubed lineage onward to Gyerpungpa himself, all became Jalupas or Rainbow Bodies of Light. Tapihritsa, the master of Gyerpungpa, also became a Jalupa...... In brief, there is no need to boast about the profundity of Bon as it is evident that (so many practitioners of Dzogchen) became Jalupas." [13]

The Transmission Lineages according to "The Three Revelations": *bsGrags-pa skor gsum*

The cycle of Dzogchen teachings known as the *bsGrags-pa skor gsum*, has its own lineage, but also speaks of the transmissions of the

Dzogchen precepts to the Shenpos
among the Devas, the Nagas, and
the humans:

17. Darma Bodde

1. the upper division: the
    cycle of revelations in the
    realm of the Devas (steng
    lha yul du bsgrags-pa'i
    skor),
2. the intermediate division:
    the cycle of revelations in
    the human realm (bar mi
    yul du bsgrags-pa'i skor),
    and
3. the lower division: the
    cycle of revelations in the
    realm of the Nagas ('og
    klu yul du bsgrags-pa'i
    skor).

The three Revelations or Promulgations of the teachings (bsgrags-
pa gsum) into which the texts of this collection are divided are precisly
those given to the Shen of these three races—Devas, the Nagas, and
the humans (lha klu mi gsum). But here they receive the teachings
directly from Chimed Tsugphud himself, rather than from his disciple
Sangwa Dupa. The beginning of the lineage is as follows:

1. Shenlha Odkar (gShen-lha 'od-dkar), the Sambhogakaya,
2. Gyalwa Rig-nga (bder-gshegs rgyal-ba rigs lnga), the Five
    Dhyani Buddhas,
3. Chimed Tsugphud ('Chi-med gtsug-phud), the Nirmanakaya,
    the heavenly pre-existence of Shenrab,
4. Lhashen Yongsu Dagpa (Lha-gshen Yongs su dag-pa), the
    Shen of the Lha or Devas,
5. Milu Samlek (Mi-lus bsam-legs), the human Shen, a prince of
    Tazik,
6. Lushen Yeshe Nyingpo (kLu-gshen Ye-shes snying-po), the
    Shen of the Lu or Nagas,
7. Odzer Pagmed ('Od-zer dpag-med), a sage of Tazik,
8. Munpa Kunsal (Mun-pa kun-gsal),
9. Trulshen Nangdan ('Phrul gshen snang-ldan), an emanation of
    Shenrab,

10. Sangwa Dupa (gSang-ba 'dus-pa). [14]

Transmission Lineages from India and from Zhang-zhung

Elsewhere, the *Legs-bshad mdzod* of Shardza Rinpoche distinguishes two separate lineages of transmission for Dzogchen:

18. Zhangzhung Triphan

1. the Teachings that come by way of India (rgya-gar gyi bon): This refers to the Dzogchen precepts that reached Tibet by way of India, but which came originally from Central Asia or Tazik;

2. the Teachings that come from Zhang-zhung (zhang-zhung gi bon): These are the Dzogchen precepts that reached Tibet from Zhang-zhung, but which also originated in Tazik in Central Asia. [15]

Here Shardza Rinpoche is suggesting that both the Nyingmapa and the Bonpo represent authentic lineages of Dzogchen and that they had a common source in Central Asia. Lopon Tenzin Namdak also points out that a name, given without any biographical details, which occurs in the Disturbed Lineage coming from Sangwa Dupa, namely Zhang-zhung Garab (Zhang-zhung dga'-rab), may be identical with the mysterious Garab Dorje (dGa'-rab rdo-rje), the Mahasiddha dwelling in Uddiyana to the west of Tibet, who is regarded as the source of the Nyingmapa lineage for the Dzogchen teachings. Zhang-zhung and Uddiyana appear to be adjacent regions, and Garab Dorje was most probably an actual historical figure who flourished in the sixth century. [16]

Below is presented the translation of the next section from the *brGyud-pa'i bla-ma'i rnam-thar,* which gives some of the flavor of these transmissions.

Translations from "The Hagiographies of the Masters of the Lineage": The Lineages of the Oral Transmission

Second, as for the Lineages of the Oral Transmission of the Siddhas (grub-thob snyan-khung gi rgyud), according to the *gZer-bu*, "They were transmitted orally by way of words." [17] And with respect to this, here there are two divisions:

1. the interrupted or discontinuous transmission (rgyud-pa 'khrug-can) and
2. the uninterrupted or continuous transmission (rgyud-pa 'khrug-med).

19. Muye Lhagyung

The Interrupted Transmissions

First, among the interrupted or discontinuous transmissions, there are found three lineages:

1. the lineage of transmission from the heat-born Chimed Tsugphud (drod skyes 'chi-med gtsug-phud nas rgyud-pa),
2. the lineage of transmission from the egg-born Yeshen Tsugphud (sgong skyes ye-gshen gtsug-phud nas rgyud-pa), and
3. the lineage of transmission from the apparitionally-born Sangwa Dupa (rdzus skyes gsang-ba 'dus-pa nas rgyud-pa). [18]

A. The Transmission from the heat-born Chimed Tsugphud

1. Shen Horti Chenpo

As for the first, from the heat-born Chimed Tsugphud the teachings of Dzogchen were transmitted directly to the Shen Horti Chenpo (gShen Hor-ti chen-po) (by way of revelation in a vision).

2. Kunkhyen Dondrub

Because he knew all the Nine Vehicles of Bon thoroughly, [19] he was requested by his disciple Kunkhyen Dondrub (Kun-mkhyen don-grub) to expound the Dzogchen teachings. The latter inquired as follows:

"As for the Bon of the Causes and the Essential Characteristics (rgyu mtshan-nyid gyi bon), the basis is renunciation (gzhi spong-ba). Furthermore, there exist great difficulties to be found here and there comes forth little benefit. As for the Bon of the Mantras with its Generation Process and its Perfection Process, the basis is transformation (gzhi bsgyur-ba). However, there are also great difficulties to be found here and again little benefit. But with regard to this Bon that transcends the duality of cause and effect (rgyu 'bras gnyis-med la zla-ba'i bon), its basis is the blessings (of the

20. Mashen Legzang

Guru). Here there is to be found little difficulty and there comes forth great benefits. Therefore, I request this latter." [20]

To this request the great Horti Chenpo replied, saying, "The Bon that should be thoroughly known and then abandoned is the first. The Bon that should be thoroughly known and then set aside is the second. The Bon that should be thoroughly known and then accepted in its entirety is the third. These are the three [21] and it is said that it is necessary to know all of them thoroughly. But having once learned philosophy (mtshan-nyid), one must come to abandon it. Moreover, this Bon of the Mantras, which encompasses both the Generation Process and the Perfection Process (sngags bskyed rdzogs kyi bon) is like so many illusions or like images reflected in a mirror, or like even like the disc of the moon reflected in the water. One should know thoroughly (these Tantric meditations) and then leave them aside. But within this Bon (which is Dzogchen) that goes beyond cause and effect (rgyu 'bras la zla-ba'i bon), there exist many great modes of transmission, such as,

1. transmission by way of verbal instructions (gdams-pa'i rgyud-pa),
2. transmission in terms of realization (grub-pa'i rgyud-pa),
3. transmission by way of samaya vows (dam-tshig gi rgyud-pa),
4. transmission by way of empowerments (dbang gi rgyud-pa),

5. transmission by way of the speech of the master (bla-ma'i zhal gyi rgyud-pa),
6. transmission in terms of confident belief (yid-ches-pa'i rgyud-pa),
7. transmission in terms of results ('bras-bu'i rgyud-pa), and
8. transmission by way of verbal explanations (bshad-pa'i rgyud-pa).

These are the eight kinds of transmissions."

Thereupon Dondrub became very knowledgeable in the Nine Vehicles of Bon without any

21. Gyershen Taglha

confusion. And having come to know everything in the Bon of Characteristics (mtshan-nyid kyi bon) and everything in the Lower Vehicles (theg-pa 'og-ma) as well, he set them aside. But the Bon of the Mantras (sngags kyi bon) and especially the Unsurpassed Bon of Dzogchen (bla na med-pa'i bon) he wholly accepted and retained in their entirety. Thereupon he realized both ordinary and supreme siddhis. [22]

3. Tsepung Dawa Gyaltsan

Because Ponchen Tsepung Dawa Gyaltsan (dpon-chen Tshe-spungs zla-ba rgyal-mtshan) had requested the transmission from the master Kunkhyen Dondrub, the latter taught him whatever there was of the previous Bon (that had come down from Horti Chenpo). Thereupon the master addressed him, saying, "In terms of the methods of this Bon (of Dzogchen), its unmistakenness is, for example, like a snake easily entering into its hole without any hesitation. Therefore, you should practice it!" Because Dawa Gyaltsan practiced the teachings for nine years at the site of Dragmar Chadsik (brag-dmar chad-gsig), he could boast of having attained siddhis both ordinary and supreme.

4. Rasang Lugyal

Because Rasang Lugyal (Ra-sangs klu-rgyal) [23] had requested the transmission from the master Tsepung Dawa Gyaltsan, the latter taught to him unceasingly all of the Bon of Cause and Effect. [24] The master addressed him as follows, "This teaching (of Dzogchen) is like a wish-granting jewel; it is very difficult to find." Thereafter Ponchen Rasang practiced for seven years at Pomar (spo-dmar) and eventually he could boast of having attained siddhis both ordinary and supreme.

5. Ponchen Tapiratsa

Then Ponchen Tapiratsa (dpon-chen Ta-pi-ra-tsa, i.e., Tapihritsa) requested the transmission from his father, the master Rasang Lugyal. The latter taught him everything without exception from the Bon of Cause and Effect. Whereafter the master said to him, "This Bon (of Dzogchen) is similar to the milk of the lioness. It is very rare and when

22. Rasang Yungdrungse

one finds it, it is difficult to drink. Therefore, you should practice it!' Retiring to the lion rock of Tagthab (stag-thabs seng-ge'i brag), he practiced diligently for nine years, whereupon he realized siddhis both ordinary and supreme. And when he attained Buddhahood, he left no remainders of his material body behind. [25]

6. Rasang Kumaratsa

Because his son Rasang Kumaratsa (Ra-sangs ku-ma-ra-tsa) [26] requested the transmission from the master Tapiratsa, the latter said to him, "Indeed, this Bon (of Dzogchen) is like the milk of the lioness. But the individual who is a bad vessel will not be able (to receive the Teachings). So do not teach it to just anyone! [27] Indeed, it is very rare like the water on a dry arid mountain. Because it is very difficult to find it like the egg of the Garuda, you should not waste or squander it!"

Thereafter (having received the instructions), Kumaratsa practiced for nine years and could boast of having realized siddhis both ordinary and supreme.

7. Rasang Samdrub

Because his brother Rasang Samdrub (Ra-sangs bsam-grub) had requested the transmission from the master Rasang Kumaratsa, the Lama said to him, "This Bon is similar to a great stone lying at the bottom of the sea; it is very difficult to find. It is similar to a rainbow in the sky; therefore, it is difficult to examine closely. It is similar to a

23. Rasang Yungphan

rock rolling down the steep side of the mountain and so it is very difficult to catch. And it is similar to the stone in a river; it is very slippery. So, you must be careful!" Thereafter (having received the instructions), he practiced for three years without attaching himself to any particular place, being like a child of the mountains. Thereby he could boast of having attained siddhis both ordinary and supreme.

8. Zhang-zhung Sadnegau

Sadnegau of Zhang-zhung (Zhang-zhung Sad-ne-ga'u) requested the transmission from the master Rasang Samdrub. However, the former said that he did not seek to acquire the Causal Bon (rgyu yi bon). Thus the master replied, saying, "Maybe you do not need it personally. But nevertheless, it is necessary for you to know it, because otherwise it will not become known to any individuals belonging to future generations." Therefore, he studied everything.

Again the master said, "This Bon (of Dzogchen) is like a Garuda chick or a lion cub that emerge complete in every respect. [28] Or again, it is similar to a vast treasury filled with precious jewels. Kept for one's own benefit alone, it will not increase the benefit of others. But if one shares it, it will never become exhausted!"

Because he practiced the teachings for six years at the site of a rock cave, he could boast of having realized siddhis both ordinary and supreme.

9. Gurib Lhajyin

Because Gurib Lhajyin (Gu-rib lha-sbyin) requested the transmission from Lama Sadnegau of Zhang-zhung, that master said to him, "This Bon (of Dzogchen) is similar to a wish-granting jewel; it is exceedingly difficult to find. But once having found it, one should place it on the crown of one's head and recite the prayers of aspiration, [29] so that one comes to realize whatever one needs or desires!"

(Having received the instructions), he practiced meditation uninterruptedly for eleven years without speaking and without going out into the country side or into any village. And because he practiced in this way, he soared in the sky like a bird and he swam in the water like a fish. When he attained Buddhahood, no remainders of his material body left behind.

10. Gurib Palzang

Having requested the transmission from his master Gurib Lhajyin, Gurib Palzang (Gu-rib dpal-bzang), wandered about in the mountains without being attached to any particular place. But mainly he did meditation practice at the rock of Drotsachan (sgro-rtsa-can). When he attained Buddhahood, no remainders of his material body were left behind.

24. Gephar Dondrub

11. Rasang Trinnekhod

Rasang Trinnekhod (Ra-sangs khrin-ne-khod) requested the transmission from the master Gurib Palzang. Thus the master said to him, "It is said that one should purify one's mind as a learned scholar and consider one's morality as a monk." [30] Thereupon he granted him everything in terms of the Bon of Cause and Effect. Then the master said to him, "After having obtained the instructions, one should become detached toward all experiences, just like the ewe abandoning her lamb. Otherwise, this Bon (of Dzogchen) would be wasted. Be careful and go practice!"

Thereafter Trinnekhod used to go about mounted on a man-eating tiger among the valleys and the gorges of the mountain of Chentrong in the south. [31] He was able to walk on the surface of the water without a boat and he exhibited many other signs of realization.

Lama Trinnekhod transmitted (the instructions) to Abadong, the Bonpo of Sumpa, and he, in turn, transmitted them to Salwa Odchen, the Bonpo of China. It was these two who transmitted the instructions to Sumpa and China respectively. [32]

12. Jagrong Sekhar

Then (Rasang Trinnnekhod) gave the instructions to Jagrong Sekhar (Jag-rong gsas-mkhar). Furthermore, the master bestowed upon him three kinds of instructions:

1. the instructions by way of the speech of the master (bla-ma'i zhal rgyud-pa'i gdams-pa),
2. the instructions deriving from personal practice (nyams su blangs-pa'i gdams-pa), and
3. the instructions in terms of confident belief (yid-ches-pa'i gdams-pa). [33]

25. Gyerpung Gephen

The master Jagrong said at one time, "In terms of the practice of the yogin, there exist three methods for staying in the practice ('dug-tshul). There is the yogin who is like a lion. He turns away from all attachments to appearances. He is like the ewe who does not want her lamb. Then there is the yogin who is like a king. He is able to move among appearances without attachments. He is like a Garuda soaring in the sky. Finally, there is the yogin who is like Duntse Dungna. He apprehends all appearances as being like a dream and is thereby freed of all attachments and desires for them. It is certainly appropriate to be one of these three." [34] He was a householder Lama who had many children. But principally, he gave the instructions to the middle one among his three sons. When he attained Buddhahood, no remainders of his material body were left behind.

13. Khyungpo Abadong

Khyungpo Abadong (Khyung-po a-ba-ldong) requested the transmission from the master Jagrong Sekhar. The master told him, "Either wander about the countryside like someone who is courageous and persevering although suffering from a chronic disease, or roam about the glacial peaks and the slate mountains like a lion searching for its prey, or just be humble like a king who has lost his country!" Thereafter (having received the instructions), he practiced for eight years at Gadmar Tagtsang (gad-dmar stag-tshang) and eventually he could boast of having realized siddhis both ordinary and supreme.

14. Khyungpo Tashi Gyaltsan

Khyungpo Tashi Gyaltsan (Khyung-po bkra-shis rgyal-mtshan) requested the transmission from the master Khyungpo Abadong. The master said to him, "Like a bird flying from the top of a rock without leaving any footprints behind, or like a lightning bolt descending in the sky with nothing to impede it, or like a mirage in the atmosphere that is without substance, or like a Garuda chick who soars in the sky without fear— if you do not know matters in this way, you will not understand the Bon (of Dzogchen)!" (After having received the instructions), he practiced in the Sati cave in the country of Zhang-zhung for some twenty-one years. There he used to

26. Gegyal

milk the wild deer and the wild predatory beasts would bring him food and drink. Thereupon he could boast of having realized siddhis both ordinary and supreme.

15. Khyungpo Leggon

His son Khyungpo Leggon (Khyung-po legs-mgon) requested the transmission from his father, Lama Khyungpo Tashi Gyaltsan. The master said to him, "Having once systematically established oneself in Rigpa, one realizes an indestructible unchanging Body (or state of being). This unmodified awareness is like a nugget of precious gold. Moreover, like the sky flower, it does not originate anywhere. Like the rainbow in the atmosphere, it does not abide anywhere. And like the sky itself, it is free of any middle or end. If one does not understand all phenomena in this way, it is like loosing again a precious jewel that one has found previously." [35]

(Having obtained the instructions), because he practiced for eight years on the island of Tsori (mtsho ri'i do la), he could boast of having attained siddhis both ordinary and supreme.

16. Mahor Tagzik

Mahor Tagzik (Ma-hor stag-gzig) [36] requested it from the master Khyungpo Leggon. The master said to him, "External appearances and internal awareness do not exist as two (different orders of reality). You should realize that they are one! Either they are not separate and thereby cut the snare, or they are without any substance in themselves

27. Zhangzhung Namgyal

and should be left as you like, or they are uncertain (in their occurrences) and should just be left as they are." [37]

Even though he practiced for twelve years at Mount Kailas (gangs ti-se), he gained no confident belief (regarding the Natural State) and so he was forced to return again. He presented his request to Khyungpo Leggon, saying, "O master! Although I have practiced for all these years, at present I cannot even fixate my mind. Therefore, I seek more instructions from you." Because he offered ten measures of gold when he made this request, the master replied, "I do not desire your gold!" Thereupon he scattered it into the sky. Then he agreed to give the necessary instructions. Mahor said, "The total understanding of one's own mind, as one's real wealth, is of greater value than a mountain of gold or a mound of turquoises. Even by offering that, I could not repay your kindness!" Thereafter he practiced for six more years without meeting any people and thus attained realization.

Then Gurib Nangzher Lodpo requested the instructions from the master Mahor Tagzik and they were taught to him.

However, there does not exist a total chronology for the transmission of the above instructions. Well then, it might be objected, if there does not exist an original source for the transmission of these instructions, [38] how then may this be distinguished as Bon? The original source of any transmission is exceedingly important! We answer that, with regard to this original source, it was transmitted from Horti Chenpo (who is a reliable source). So, this transmission, which has become divided and fragmented, still has a single foot (which is the great Horti). For the reason (that it has become fragmented), it is called "the discontinuous transmission" (rgyud-pa 'khrug-can). One may know by an investigation whether the instructions of the masters were obtained or not obtained authentically. With regard to the Bon of Dzogchen in question here, there exist three kinds of transmission:

1. the Bon which has actually been transmitted directly from the speech of the master (bla-ma'i zhal nas rgyud-pa'i bon),
2. the secret instructions that derive from the practice of individual masters (nyams su blangs-pa'i gdams-ngag), and
3. the secret instructions that were given by the masters to the non-human spirits (ma ma yin la gnang-ba'i gdams-ngag).

28. Mugyung Karpo

But elsewhere, all those things which may be found agreeable, but which are merely idiosyncratic creations of the mind (and one's personal fancy), are just empty and poverty-stricken. However, we may say that all those great mediators, even when they were without instructions (traditionally given for meditation practice), are actually cairns on the tops of mountains.

B. The Transmission from the egg-born Yeshen Tsugphud

Second, Yeshen Tsugphud, [39] the egg-born Teacher who is the source of this transmission, transmitted (the Dzogchen instructions)

1. to Dondrub Legpa, the son of the Naga (Don-grub legs-pa klu'i sras);
2. He, in turn, taught them to Zhang-zhung Tranya Tagdro (Zhang-zhung khra-snya stag-sgro);
3. He taught them to Zhang-zhung Yulo (Zhang-zhung g.yu-lo);
4. He taught them to Zhang-zhung Tripa (Zhang-zhung khri-pa);
5. He taught them to Khyungpo Leggon (Khyung-po legs-mgon),
6. He taught them to Mahor Tagzik (Ma-hor stag-gzig);
7. He taught them to Gurib Shinglagchan (Gu-rib shing-slag-can);
8. And he taught them to Gyerpung Nangzher Lodpo (Gyer-spungs snang-bzher lod-po).

C. The Transmission from the apparitionally-born Sangwa Dupa

Third, Sangwa Dupa, the apparitionally-born Teacher who could emanate anywhere, [40] taught (the Dzogchen instructions)

29. Horti Chenpo

1. to Lhabon Thodkar (Lhabon thod-dkar);
2. He, in turn, taught them to Yeshen Samdrub (Yegshen bsam-grub);
3. He taught them to Gyerpung Legdrub (Gyerspungs legs-grub);
4. He taught them to Gyungyar Tsadpo (rGyung-yar btsad-po);
5. He taught them to Trese Gyalpo (Khre-sras rgyal-po);
6. He taught them to Zhang-zhung Garab (Zhang-zhung dga'-rab); [41]
7. He taught them to Rasang Sodnamtsek (Ra-sangs bsod-nams brtseg);
8. He taught them to Zhang-zhung Tashi Gyaltsan (Zhang-zhung bkra-shis rgyal-mtshan);
9. And he taught them to Gyerpung Nangzher Lodpo (Gyerspungs snang-bzher lod-po).

The Uninterrupted Transmission

Second, within the uninterrupted or continuous transmission belonging to the Unoriginated Transmission of the Long Lineage (rgyud-pa 'khrug-med ring rgyud ma chags su rgyud-pa), there are four divisions:

1. the Symbolic Transmission of the Bodhisattvas (sems-dpa' brda'i rgyud-pa),
2. the Awareness Transmission of the Vidyadharas (rig-'dzin rig-pa'i rgyud-pa),
3. the Oral Transmission of the August Persons (gang-zag snyan-khung gi rgyud-pa), and
4. the Transmission of the Learned Scholars and Translators (mkas-pa lo-pan gyi rgyud-pa).

A. The Symbolic Transmission of the Bodhisattvas

1. Lhabon Yongsu Dagpa

First, Shenrab, the Teacher who is the Emanation born from the human womb, transmitted (these Dzogchen teachings) to the Deva Bonpo, Lha-bon Yongsu Dagpa (Lha-bon yongs su dag-pa), the son of Lharab-od (Lha-rab-'od). [42] Moreover, that master, because his contemplation was pure like the sky, came to realize the ordinary siddhis, such as soaring aloft in the heavens. By means of extending his hook-like tongue, he was able to produce flowers upon the earth. And in terms of the supreme

30. Donkun Drubpa

siddhi, he attained Buddhahood in a state where Means and Wisdom were without duality.

2. Lubon Banam

He then transmitted (the Dzogchen teachings) to the Naga Bonpo Lubon Banam (kLu-bon ba-nam), the son of the Brahman Lujyindze (Lha-byin-mdzes). [43] That master also, because his contemplation was completely unmoving like the dimension of space, came to realize the ordinary siddhis, such as actually appearing to the Nagas without sinking into the water. And in terms of the supreme siddhi, his body having emanated rays of light, he attained Buddhahood.

3. Mibon Tride Zambu

He then transmitted the teachings to the human Bonpo, Mi-bon Tride Zambu (Mi-bon khri-lde zam-bu), the son of king Tride-od (Khri-lde-'od). [44] That master also, because the state of his contemplation was free of conceptual elaborations, came to realize the ordinary siddhis. He was able to cause rainfalls of flowers to descend from the sky and was able to burn up wrong views with the fire of his samadhi. And in terms of the supreme siddhi, his body having dissolved into the pollutionless dimension, he attained Buddhahood.

4. Banam Kyolpo

He then transmitted the teachings to Banam Kyolpo (Ba-nam skyol-po). That master also, because his contemplation abided in a vast

31. Rasang Phan-gyal

expanse of space without thoughts, came to realize the ordinary siddhis, such as invoking the gods and controlling their food, so as to bring all the noxious spirits under his power. And in terms of the supreme siddhi, he realized non-duality with the God of Wisdom. [45]

5.Trisho Gyalwa

He then transmitted the teachings to his son Trisho Gyalwa (Khri-sho rgyal-ba). That master also, because his contemplation arose as energy in manifestation, came to realize the ordinary siddhis, such as eating his samadhi as food, so it was not necessary for him to take any other nourishment to maintain his health. And in terms of the supreme siddhi, he attained Buddhahood without any duality of appearance and emptiness. [46] The life spans of the physical bodies of these above masters are uncertain for they had realized their complete independence of birth and death. Indeed, they had become visible in this world as emanations of the Victorious One.

B. The Awareness Transmission of the Vidyadharas

6. Rasang Samdrub

Second, as for the Awareness Transmission of the Vidyadharas, Trisho Gyalwa transmitted the Dzogchen teachings to Rasang Samdrub (Ra-sangs bsam-grub). That master also, because his contemplation was like the sky, came to realize the ordinary siddhis, such as reversing upward the courses of rivers and he was able to mount on gigantic boulders like they were his horses. And in terms of the supreme siddhi, he attained Buddhahood in a Body of Light.

7. Darma Sherab

He then transmitted the teachings to Darma Sherab (Dar-ma shes-rab). That master also, because his contemplation was unmoving like a vast expanse of space, came to realize the ordinary siddhis, such as enslaving the Sadak, the Nagas, and the Nyen spirits as his servants. [47] Moreover, he was able to emanate himself as various bodies and divine forms. And in terms of the supreme siddhi, his physical body having dissolved in the dimension of blazing fire, he attained Buddhahood.

8. Darma Bodde

He then transmitted the teachings to Darma Bodde (Dar-ma 'bod-de).

32. Gurib Sega

That master also, because his contemplation remained in the original condition of the spontaneously perfected Trikaya, came to realize the ordinary siddhis, such as hurling magical missiles of gold dust and being able to transmute poison into medicine. And in terms of the supreme siddhi, having dissolved his physical body into light, he attained Buddhahood. [48]

9. Zhang-zhung Triphan

He then transmitted the teachings to Zhang-zhung Triphan (Zhang-zhung khri-'phan). That master also, because his contemplation possessed the Dharani-mantras without them being perceived, came to realize the ordinary siddhis. [49] He was able to cure someone of leprosy simply by looking at them with his eyes and he was able to live upon samadhi as his food. And in terms of the supreme siddhi, he attained Buddhahood when his physical body dissolved into a rainbow in the sky.

10. Muye Lhagyung

He then transmitted the teachings to Muye Lhagyung (Mu-ye lha-rgyung). That master also, because his contemplation abided in a state free of any root, came to realize the ordinary siddhis, such as enslaving the gods and demons as his servants. And he was able to actually liberate (that is, slay) the evil Theurong spirits. [50] And in terms of the supreme siddhi, no longer abiding in the limited conditions of a physical body, he went to traverse the sky.

11. Mashen Legzang

He then transmitted the teachings to Mashen Legzang (rMa-gshen legs-bzang). That master also, because his contemplation was pure

33. Tsepung Dawa Gyaltsan

without any faults, came to realize the ordinary siddhis. He was able to hang his robes on sunbeams and to bring forth water from barren mountains. And in terms of the supreme siddhi, he became inseparable from his Yidam or meditation deity.

These masters in the lineage above, having completed their accomplishing the benefit of living beings, at the time of their passing into Nirvana, they attained Buddhahood as the nature of light without abandoning the condition of a physical body. [51]

C. The Oral Transmission of the August Persons

12. Gyershen Taglha

Third, as for the Oral Transmission of the August Persons, Mashen Legzang transmitted the Dzogchen teachings to Gyershen Taglha (Gyer-gshen stag-lha). That master also, because his contemplation completely understood birth and cessation without duality, came to realize the ordinary siddhis. He was able to emanate various bodies and divine forms and he was able to travel about the four continents after having mounted upon the rays of the sun. And in terms of the supreme siddhi, he remained with the original condition (of the Natural State) without birth or death. [52]

13. Rasang Yungdrungse

He then transmitted the teachings to Rasang Yungdrungse (Ra-sangs g.yung-drung-gsas). That master also, because his contemplation became manifest, came to realize the ordinary siddhis, such as being able to load burdens on to wild yaks. And in terms of the supreme siddhi, he abided in the state of the unmoving Ultimate Reality. [53]

14. Rasang Yungphen

He then transmitted the teachings to his son Rasang Yungphen (ra-sangs g.yung-'phen). That master also, because his contemplation understood the totality of non-meditation, [54] came to realize the ordinary siddhis, such as being able to wrap up the sea in the lap of his skirt and to hurl mountains as weapons. In terms of the supreme siddhi, he attained Buddhahood instantly without having to traverse the paths and stages.

15. Gephar Dondrub

He then transmitted the teachings to Gephar Dondrub (dGe-'phar don-grub). That master also, because his contemplation was free of the extremes of emptiness and clarity, came to realize the ordinary siddhis. Having perfected the energies of clairvoyance, he knew the thoughts of those who were at a distance and he contemplated various different things that were concealed. [55] In terms of the supreme siddhi, he remained unmoving in the state of Primordial Buddhahood.

16. Gyerpung Gephen

He then transmitted the teachings to Gyerpung Gephen (Gyer-spungs dge-'phen). That master also, because his contemplation understood the sameness of everything, came to realize the ordinary siddhis. He was able to hurl red magical missiles like they were arrows and he was able to enslave the gods and demons as his servants. In terms of the supreme siddhi, he attained Buddhahood while in a state completely devoid of concepts. [56]

17. Gegyal

He then transmitted the teachings to his son Gegyal (dGe-rgyal). That master also, because in his contemplation the Ultimate Truth became manifest, came to realize the ordinary siddhis, such as being able to pass unimpeded through solid rock, earth, and mountains. And in terms of the supreme siddhi, ultimately arriving at the Two Truths, he attained Buddhahood.

18. Zhang-zhung Namgyal

He then transmitted the teachings to Zhang-zhung Namgyal (Zhang-zhung rnam-rgyal). That master also, because his Self-Awareness became manifest, came to realize the ordinary siddhis and so, he was confident in his ability at Tsalung (the yoga of the channels and the winds) and obtained self-control over the Bindus. [57] And in terms of the supreme siddhi, coming to understand that Samsara and Nirvana are inseparable, he attained Buddhahood

19. Mugyung Karpo

He then transmitted the teachings to Mugyung Karpo (dMu-rgyung dkar-po). That master also, having destroyed the delusions of subject and object, came to realize the ordinary siddhis. Hence, he was able to project and diffuse inconceivable numbers of emanations from his body, speech, and mind. In terms of the supreme siddhi, while in a state that was totally inexpressible, he attained Buddhahood.

20. Horti Chenpo

He then transmitted the teachings to Horti Chenpo (Hor-ti chen-po). That master also, because he was confident of his learning and realization, came to realize the ordinary siddhis, such as possessing the Dharani-mantras without forgetting them and knowing the Nine Vehicles exceedingly well. In terms of the supreme siddhi, without experiencing birth or death he accomplished the benefit of living beings by roping them in from afar. [58]

Because the above masters all appeared as Nirmitas or emanations in order to benefit beings, they concretely manifested the virtuous qualities of wisdom and love of the Buddha and the various signs of realization. And moreover, they diffused their magical apparitions into the ten directions. Because they were all actual Vidyadharas who had especially severed the roots of Samsara, they passed beyond suffering (and entered into Nirvana) without abandoning the condition of a physical body. [59] They transcended existence by means of their magical powers.

D. The Transmission by the Learned Scholars and Translators

21. Donkun Drubpa

Fourth, as for the Transmission of the Learned Scholars and Translators, the great Horti Chenpo transmitted the Dzogchen teachings to his disciple Donkun Drubpa (Don-kun grub-pa). [60] The latter master understood the view (of Dzogchen) that is free of every root.

22. Rasang Phangyal

He, in turn, transmitted the teachings to Rasang Phangyal (ra-sangs 'phan-rgyal). That master was confident of his ability to meditate in terms of emptiness and clarity.

23. Gurib Sega

Then, he transmitted the teachings to Gurib Sega (Gu-rib gsas-dga'). That master guarded his conduct in terms of the Same Taste. [61]

24. Tsepung Dawa Gyaltsan

And he transmitted the Dzogchen teachings to Dawa Gyaltsan (Zla-ba rgyal-mtshan). That master remained in the original condition of the Ultimate Reality. [62]

Moreover, these four masters who represent the head-ornament (of the lineage), realized the ordinary siddhis, including such unimpeded deeds as walking upon the water without sinking, flying through the sky, riding upon boulders as their horses, and reversing uphill the courses of rivers. In terms of the supreme siddhi, a state of being totally beyond thoughts having become manifest in them, they all attained Buddhahood. [63]

All of these instructions for the Dzogchen teachings were transmitted in an uninterrupted manner from the divine Bonpo Lhabon Yongsu Dagpa down to Dawa Gyaltsan. The culmination of these instructions resided within Nangzher Lodpo. Accordingly, none of these twenty-four (masters listed above) recorded the teachings (of Dzogchen) in writing, but they transmitted them only in spoken words. However, their virtuous qualities were inconceivable. They thoroughly purified all the seeds of the obscurations that tend to conceptualize everything and they directly perceived the truth by means of discriminating wisdom. [64] They rose above the conditions of Samsara. They surpassed the stages of the Svastikayana itself. [65] They flew through the sky like birds and moved through the water like fish. They passed unimpeded through solid rock, soil, stones, and mountains.

During some sixteen hundred years, at first for durations of one hundred years, afterwards changing into durations of sixty years, eventually they each displayed the method of dying and transferring consciousness in order to benefit living beings. But even though they actually abided for many kalpas, they remained ever youthful, without really dying or transferring consciousness. They served as regents for the Sambhogakaya (Shenlha Odkar) and for the Supreme Nirmanakaya (Shenrab Miwoche). By means of their methods, that is, by way of emanating innumerable bodies and by immeasurable actions in countless fields, it is explained in various places (in the texts) that they actually accomplished the benefit of immeasurable numbers of sentient beings. [66]

CHAPTER 5

The Masters Tapihritsa and Gyerpungpa

The Mahasiddha Tradition in Zhang-zhung

The *Zhang-zhung snyan-rgyud* is of particular interest to the history of the development of Dzogchen in Tibet because it is not a Terma, as are the other cycles of Bonpo Dzogchen texts such as the *bsGrags-pa skor gsum* and the *Gab-pa dgu skor*, but represents a *snyan-rgyud*, or "oral transmission." It is asserted in the Bon tradition that these teachings have been passed down in a continuous unbroken lineage of transmission of master to disciple since before the eighth century. Therefore, in this context *snyan-rgyud* corresponds to the Nyingmapa classification of a text as *bka'-ma*, or "a continuous tradition". The transcendental origin of Dzogchen according to the Bon tradition has been described in the previous chapter. However, in strictly historical terms, it may be asserted that this Zhang-zhung Nyan-gyud derived from the oral precepts of a kind of Bonpo Mahasiddha known by the name of Gyerpung Nangzher Lodpo (Gyer-spungs snang-bzher lod-po), the disciple of another mysterious Mahasiddha, Tapihritsa, whom he encountered in a series of visionary experiences. This Gyerpungpa, who is almost certainly historical, was a contemporary of the great Buddhist king of Tibet, Trisong Detsan (742-797) and of the Buddhist master from Uddiyana, Guru Padmasambhava, who established the Tantric form of Buddhism known as Vajrayana in Tibet. [1] Thus, Gyerpungpa and his master probably lived in the axial period of the eighth century to which the Nyingmapas equally look back to as the Golden Age for the establishing in Tibet of the teachings of their own tradition deriving from India, which also included Dzogchen. Gyerpungpa was not a Central Tibetan however, but a Zhang-zhung-

34. Tapihritsa

pa, a native of the then independent kingdom of Zhang-zhung that included the nomad country of Northern Tibet where he lived. Having received the permission of his master to write down the Dzogchen precepts in the Zhang-zhung language, it appears that either Gyerpungpa or his immediate successors did so and one of them, Ponchen Tsanpo (dPon-chen bTsan-po) in turn translated them into Tibetan in the ninth or tenth century. Moreover, Ponchen Tsanpo is portrayed in these accounts as having been bilingual, speaking both Tibetan and his native Zhang-zhung dialect. [2] In the tradition it is clearly stated that it was Gyerpungpa who first wrote down the Dzogchen precepts and made them available to more than one disciple, whereas previously they had only been privately transmitted in an oral fashion from the master to a single disciple alone (gcig brgyud). Indeed, this had been the case from the time of Yongsu Dagpa, the disciple of Tonpa Shenrab and of Sangwa Dupa, until the advent of Tapihritsa in the historical period. From Gyerpungpa, an unbroken lineage of transmission can be traced down to the present day. [3]

Some modern scholars have cast doubts on the historical existence of Gyerpungpa and his master, but the eminent Tibetologist David Snellgrove, who has studied the material, writes: "There is no serious reason for doubting the existence of the Bon sages who come within the historical period, and at the same time there is no doubt of the Indian Buddhist origin of their philosophical theories and meditation practices." [4] Again, he writes of Tapihritsa: "He belongs to one of the several lines of meditating hermits who seem to have established themselves in Western Tibet from the seventh century on, and possibly even earlier." [5] Elsewhere, Snellgrove speculates about Tapihritsa possibly being of Indian origin because of the appearance of his name, which might have been originally *tapiraja*, probably meaning a prince or lesser king. [6] However, Lopon Tenzin Namdak adamantly asserts that Tapihritsa was not an Indian traveler, but a native Zhang-zhung-pa and that his name derives from the Zhang-zhung language. [7] In any event, Snellgrove sees no real reason to doubt the historical existence of a Zhang-zhung-pa Mahasiddha, such as Gyerpungpa, living in the caves above the western end of the Darok lake in Northern Tibet in the eighth century.

The historical existence of Tapihritsa is less certain than that of Gyerpungpa, but it appears that he was an actual Mahasiddha, living in Zhang-zhung or Northern Tibet, who flourished in the late seventh and early eighth centuries. In the recorded accounts, Tapihritsa's encounters with his disciple Gyerpungpa appear to be somewhat of the nature of visionary experiences, where he manifested to the latter in the guise of a miraculous youth. Certainly one is encountering here the archetype of the wise child. But this is no more fanciful than the encounters of Naropa with his own mysterious master, the Mahasiddha Tilopa. [8] Modern scholars do not question the real historical existence of these two masters, Naropa and Tilopa. So we need not dismiss Tapihritsa out of hand as a later myth or literary fabrication, even though, according to the tradition, he reappeared to his disciple in a rather miraculous fashion after the former had attained enlightenment. [9]

The Life of Tapihritsa

Not much is known of the life of Tapihritsa, as was the case also with his predecessors in the Zhang-zhung lineage. He was, however, born in Zhang-zhung or Northern Tibet sometime in the seventh century when Zhang-zhung was still an independent kingdom. At this time the provinces of Central Tibet (dbus-gtsang) were already under the rule of the Yarlung dynasty of Tibet. It is widely recorded in later Tibetan histories, but also in the Tun Huang documents, that the first Buddhist king of Tibet, Songtsan Gampo (627-649), conquered Ligmigya, the king of Zhang-zhung, apparently making him into a vassal without permanently occupying the country. Then it is reported that, over a century later, during the reign of the greatest Buddhist king of Tibet, Trisong Detsan, the Tibetans killed in ambush the last Ligmigya king of Zhang-zhung and the Tibetan armies moved into occupy the country to the west. Thereupon the native Zhang-zhung-pas were pressed into service as porters for the Tibetan forces as they moved further westward into Baltistan and Gilgit and northward into Central Asia. [10]

It was especially from the master Tsepung Dawa Gyaltsan (Tshe-spungs zla-ba rgyal-mtshan) [11] that Tapihritsa received all four cycles of precepts from the Zhang-zhung Nyan-gyud, and, in particular, the Experiential Transmission (nyams-rgyud) from the twenty-four previous masters. [12] According to the tradition, it is said that some portions of the Four Cycles of Precepts (bka'-rgyud bzhi skor) may be taught to any suitable disciple or group of disciples, but certain other exceedingly secret instructions and Upadeshas are restricted in their disclosure to a single disciple within the master's lifetime. This latter is known as the Single Transmission Lineage (gcig brgyud).

The master examined the marks of his young disciple, which were outer, inner, and secret, over the course of a three year probationary period in order to determine whether or not he was a suitable vessel for the full and complete transmission. Moreover, the permission of the guardian deities of the tradition had to be sought by the master by way of divination, omens, dreams, and visions, before the transmission could be granted. Otherwise, there might be dire consequences. Then, when the transmission did actually occur, the master whispered the secret oral instructions of Upadesha (man-ngag) into the ear of his disciple through a long bamboo tube, so that the local spirits and deities in the vicinity might not inadvertently overhear these instructions. When both the requisite signs have appeared and there existed the permission of the guardian deities, then there remained no excuse for the disciple not to enter into retreat. Going into such a closed retreat (mtshams-bcad), cutting oneself off from the rest of the world, the disciple practiced there in an isolated site, such as a cave or rock shelter, until the signs of success (grub rtags) in practice appeared.

Having received the transmissions for both the Four Cycles of Precepts and for the Meditation Experiences of the previous masters, Tapihritsa retired to a cave at the mountain of the lion rock of Tagthab (stag-thabs seng-ge'i brag) that lay to the east of Mount Kailas in Northern Tibet. Most of his twenty-four predecessors in the lineage had also made their retreats in this same region. [13] Living alone in this cave, Tapihritsa practiced in silence for nine years. Finally, through his practice of the Clear Light, otherwise known as Thodgal, he attained the Rainbow Body of the Great Transfer, leaving no remnant of his material body behind in the cave. His later miraculous appearances to his disciples, such as Gyerpungpa and Yungdrung Gyaltsan, were due to the fact that he had realized this Rainbow Body of the Great Transfer, and so he possessed the capacity to manifest to his disciples, or to anyone else, in whatever form was suitable to the circumstances. [14]

Translation from "The Hagiographies of the Masters of the Lineage"

According to the brief hagiography found in the text by Paton Tangyal, only few details of the life of Tapihritsa are known.

The Direct Occurrence of the Shorter Lineages for the Transmission
Second, there are the direct occurring (in history) of the Shorter Lineages for the Transmission that have benefited living beings by way of Emanations (nye rgyud thog babs/ rnam-sprul 'gro don gyi rgyud-pa). [15] Here there are found six divisions:

1. the Two Nirmanakayas displaying great kindness (sprul-sku drin-can gnyis),
2. the Six Mahasiddhas of Zhangzhung Mar (zhang-zhung smar gyi grub-chen drug),
3. the Five Masters of the System of Lower Zhangzhung (smad lugs kyi bla-ma lnga),
4. the Six Masters of the System of Upper Zhangzhung (stod lugs kyi bla-ma drug),
5. the Nine Masters of the Northern Lineage (byang rgyud kyi bla-ma dgu), and
6. the Eleven Masters of the Southern Lineage (lho rgyud kyi bla-ma bcu-gcig).

The Two Nirmanakayas possessing Great Kindness
The Nirmanakyas displaying great kindness were

1. Ponchen Tapihritsa (dPon-chen Ta-pi-hri-tsa) and
2. Gyerpung Chenpo Nangzher Lodpo (Gyer-spungs chen-po snang-bzher lod-po).

The Hagiography of Ponchen Taphritsa
Firstly, with respect to the history of the great master Tapihritsa who was the disciple of the previous master (Tsepung Dawa Gyaltsan), there are five considerations: [16]
First, his father was Rasang Lugyal (Ra-sangs klu-rgyal) and his mother was Shcrigsal (Shes-rig-gsal). When he was born as their son, he was given the name of Tapihritsa, which means "king" in the Zhan-zhung language just as the word *rgyal-po* does in the Tibetan language. [17]
Second, because he possessed both ripened karma and good fortune, he met masters who would show him great kindness. He requested the Bon teachings from his father Rasang Lugyal and then from the great master Ponchen Rasang. In particular, when he came into contact with the Lineage of the Twenty-Four August Persons, he requested the

complete Experiential Transmission, as well as the Transmission of the Precepts for Dzogchen from Tsepung Dawa Gyaltsan.

Third, he resided for some time relying upon a very special place (for the practice of meditation). In particular, he practiced ascetic conduct at the lion rock of Tagthab (stag-thabs). [18] For nine years he practiced there uninterruptedly without speaking to anyone.

Fourth, as for the signs of his realization and his virtuous qualities that he attained during his lifetime, having realized all siddhis without exception, those which were both ordinary and supreme, he ultimately attained Buddhahood in the Body of Light without leaving any remainder of his material body behind. [19]

Fifth, an understanding (of the Natural State) that was extraordinary became manifest within him. The realization of the Dharmakaya having become manifest for his own benefit, he thereupon emanated himself in the form of the one called Tapiradza in the Zhang-zhung language, that is to say, as a Nirmanakaya he acted for the benefit of others. He emanated himself in the guise of a young boy who embodied the Gnosis of Omniscience (for the benefit of his disciple Gyerpungpa) and, moreover, he emanated various different divine forms or bodies in an unpredictable manner elsewhere. Thereby he brought about immediately liberation in the mind-streams of his fortunate disciples and they in turn came to manifest various virtuous qualities. [20] (This brief account is all we are told about the life of Tapihritsa.)

His Disciple Gyerpung Nangzher Lodpo

The chief disciple of the master Tapihritsa was the great Gyerpung Nangzher Lodpo. He was also born in Zhang-zhung, in the lake district of Darok in Northern Tibet. He began to study the Nine Ways of Bon became very proficient in all of these practices. Then at the age of forty-seven, he met Tsepung Dawa Gyaltsan who had previously been the master of Tapihritsa. He made offerings of an abundance of wealth to the master and especially asked for the transmissions and teachings associated with the Tantric meditation deities Zhang-zhung Meri and Gekhod. He also received many teachings for Dzogchen, especially the Experiential Transmission in its extensive, medium, and abridged forms. However, although he had received many of the teachings of Yungdrung Bon, he was not granted the Single Transmission (gcig-brgyud) for the Zhang-zhung Nyan-gyud by the master. When he asked the master if he could transmit the teachings he had received from him to others, Dawa Gyaltsan replied that this would be appropriate in the case where a suitable disciple appeared, or even if there be as many as one hundred of them, but it would not be appropriate to teach anything to one who was not a suitable vessel. After he had received all of these teachings for Tantra and for Dzogchen from his master Tsepung Dawa Gyaltsan, he went to the northeast of the Darok lake to the Drajye valley, retiring into a ravine among the white rocks, where he especially engaged in the practices for the Tantric deity Zhang-zhung Meri. Eventually came to realize many siddhis, especially the power of Tswo, that is to say, the dispatching of magical missiles against one's enemies, which is the magical practice particularly associated with that deity. [21]

Then, one winter Gyerpungpa went to the fresh water lake of Darok, which had become covered with ice. Here there was an island with a rock shelter located on it and he decided to make another retreat there for a year. Walking across the lake on the ice to the island, he took with him one attendant to do his cooking and enough food supplies to last for a year. But when the next winter season did come, it was a bit warmer and no ice formed to cover the surface of the lake. Thus the master and his servant found themselves trapped on the small island and faced with starvation. The story of what occurred on this island during the retreat and how he and his attendant escaped from the island is told in the translation below.

These and other events are said to have occurred in the time of the great Tibetan king Trisong Detsan and when Ligmigya still reigned as king over Zhang-zhung. Gyerpungpa became famous as a great scholar learned in the Nine Ways of Bon and as a great Tantric magician. And because he had developed a great many siddhis and magical powers and people were always coming to him asking for his blessings, he became very proud of his learning and his attainments. Furthermore, he came to be appointed the personal sacrificial priest to the king of Zhang-zhung. [22]

The Encounters of Gyerpungpa with His Master

But despite his realization of the practice of Tantra, in terms of Dzogchen, he did not practice properly and so his pride nearly destroyed his understanding of the Natural State. Thereupon, by virtue of his own clairvoyant powers, Tapihritsa became aware of this situation and thus he emanated himself in the form of a young boy and came to Merchyugpo Yungdrung Gyaltsan, the wealthy nomad chieftain who was the patron of Gyerpungpa and who lived in an encampment in the Drajye valley north of the Darok lake. At that time, Gyerpungpa was staying in a retreat at the heritage of the deer-faced

35. Gyerpung Nangzher Lodpo

rock (brag sha-ba dgong gi dgon-pa). [23]

At the door of this patron's tent in the valley, the young boy suddenly appeared. He asked to be taken in and allowed to work as a servant, explaining that he was an orphan without family. He asserted that he could do whatever was needed in the nomad encampment. He did so well at first, while looking after the patron's large herds of yaks and sheep, that the patron came to call him "the well-found young boy." [24] Then one day, the boy went to collect firewood and neglecting his herdsman duties, the animals scattered into the hills. Carrying a large bundle of firewood on his back he came to the entrance of the rock cave where Gyerpungpa was meditating, its entrance partly concealed by a number of small bushes. Setting down his load of wood, the boy eloquently uttered nine kinds of praises to the master. [25] However, Gyerpungpa doubted the authenticity of the learned and eloquent speech of this ragged young boy. He therefore set about to interrogate him, asking five questions: "Who is your master, what do you study, how do you meditate, what is your burden, and why do you labor as a servant?"

The precocious answers of the young boy at first astonished Gyerpungpa and then he became a bit angry. The master haughtily proposed that the next day they would go before the king of Zhang-zhung residing in the Khyung-dzong castle, make their offerings, and engage in a public debate. If the boy won, the master would become his disciple, placing the boy's foot on his head. But if the master won, the boy would be severely punished by the order of the king. Gyerpungpa felt challenged and tested by this young boy. Upon hearing this proposal, the boy merely laughed three times and refused, saying, "All debate is just blind play, all Tantrikas just create illusions in the mind, all scholars only speak words— but all of these words are empty and make no sense! It is not worthwhile to engage in this!" [26]

But Gyerpungpa became overwhelmed by these further sagacious replies and realized that the ragged young boy must be a Siddha or realized being. He fell silent and could not reply. But when he looked up, he no longer saw a ragged little orphan boy, but the glorious vision of a beautiful sixteen year old youth sitting within a rainbow sphere of light suspended in the sky above him. This youth was pure white like crystal, translucent, and naked, completely devoid of all ornaments. [27] When Gyerpungpa offered him gold for his teachings, the rainbow vision replied, "I am Tapihritsa. If you offer gold to the birds, do they take it?" Gyerpungpa pleaded again and Tapihritsa agreed that he would teach him to be free of action, leaving no traces behind, like the birds soaring in the sky. [28]

Just then the patron, in search for his lost animals, came to the entrance of the cave and asking what had happened to them, Gyerpungpa announced that they both must have accumulated many negative karmic causes, but this boy was indeed an emanation of the Dharmakaya. The patron was astonished at this vision in the sky and fell silent. Both of them made offerings to the master and requested teachings, whereupon Tapihritsa expounded "the Four Good Things." [29] At the conclusion of his teaching, Tapihritsa admonished them to keep his teaching secret and announced, "I am Tapihritsa. If you do not forget me, we shall meet again." He then rose up into the sky and disappeared from view. Thus, Gyerpungpa overcame his arrogant pride and all his previous conceptions regarding the nature of reality. This was the first encounter of Gyerpungpa with his master Tapihritsa. The full story of this encounter between master and disciple is told in the translation presented in the following chapter, entitled "The Prophetic Sayings of the Lord Tapihritsa.".

Five years after this first encounter, when Gyerpungpa was in retreat on the island in the Darok lake, at midday on the fifteenth day of the first month of summer, he had his second encounter with the master Tapihritsa which became known as "the Intermediate Advent and Encounter." [30] The youthful Tapihritsa again appeared to him in a blaze of light, seated naked in the middle of a rainbow sphere suspended in the sky. Gyerpungpa prostrated to him and made three circumambulations. Thereupon Tapihritsa taught Gyerpungpa how to see in the ultimate sense, transmitting to his disciple the teachings regarding the Six Lamps. [31]

Sometime later, Gyerpungpa had his third encounter with the master Tapihritsa while he was meditating again on an island in the Darok lake. Tapihritsa again manifested in front of him in his

Nirmanakaya form. [32] Tapihritsa then addressed him, saying, "You have been led to the Primordial Base. Now I will teach you the profound and secret oral instructions for Dzogchen. This will be my final teaching to you and it represents the highest teachings of Bon and the heart of the Tantra teaching. It is like the eye of the body." These teachings had originally come from the Dharmakaya Himself and had been transmitted by way of the celestial and the terrestrial lineages to Tapihritsa. The master gave his permission and at his command Gyerpungpa wrote down these brief teachings with blue ink on white paper. Thus he recorded "The Upadesha in Eight Chapters." Then Tapihritsa taught him "The Twenty-One Little Nails," which belonged to the exceeding secret cycle. [33] This was their third and final encounter. [34]

Translation from "The Hagiographies of the Masters of the Lineage"

The Hagiography of Gyerpung Chenpo Nangzher Lodpo

With respect to the history of the great Gyerpung Nangzher Lodpo who was the principal disciple of that master (Tapihritsa), there exist five considerations:

First, as for the history of his parents from whom he obtained a pure human body, he belonged to the clan of Gurib, his father being Gurib Bumme (Gu-rib 'bum-me) and his mother was Mangorza Dronne (Mang-'or-za sgron-ne). [35]

Second, because he possessed both ripened karma and good fortune, he met various masters who showed him great kindness. And when he reached the age of thirteen years old, he entered into the gateway of Bon. At the age of forty-seven, at the time when he had cut off the limitations of conceptual elaborations, he offered an abundance of enjoyable things, mainly consisting of food, to Tsepung Dawa Gyaltsan. Then, in a ravine of white rocks lying in the direction west of Mamik (to the northwest of the Darok lake), this master expounded the instructions for the five direct introductions (to the Natural State). [36] Thereafter the great Gyerpungpa inquired, "May I teach this to anyone?" Thereupon, from the mouth of the master came this reply, "If there come forth some suitable vessels, then you may teach them, indeed, even if there are as many as one hundred."

Third, then for a time he depended upon a certain special place for practice and he resided there continuously. This site was in the country of Darok where there was located a medicine lake (with fresh waters) where both human beings (nomads) and non-human spirits assembled. [37]

Then, as for how he engaged himself in ascetic conduct at that site (on an island in that lake): [38] For one year the master and his disciple who attended him resided below a rock on the island in the lake (of Darok), together with sufficient food and provisions to sustain their bodies (for one year). Gyerpungpa put the left-overs of their meals into a small food container. When the lake thawed (the ice melting in the spring), the left-overs in the food container became soft. The master and the disciple ate the sediments and grounds of these soft left-overs, and he left the droppings from what they ate on the rock which served as his pillow.

Again the lake remained unfrozen (throughout the following year). Having scraped the soft sediments of the droppings of food from the face of the rock, he put them into water (in order to make a soup) and they ate that. This procedure continued for three years. Whereupon his attendant thought to himself, "We two, master and disciple, if we stay here on this island any longer, we will surely starve and die!" And he thought to jump from the cliffs and make himself into a corpse.

Thus he came and asked Gyerpungpa what he thought about using the body of a dead creature for food. The latter replied, "Certainly we could make a soup out of that!"

"How can I make such a soup?" his attendant asked.

"Well, go around this large rock and see for yourself what is there!"

Doing as he was told, the attendant went there and discovered the corpse of a wild ass (rkyang). But, regarding this, the master said, "Because we must rely on the different types of purities, we cannot take this as food!"

Then after some days had passed, the attendant found the corpse of a woman (washed up on the beach) who had died of a bad case of goiter. And since he inquired again, the master replied, saying, "I will not listen to eating the flesh of such a one with undivided hooves! And I will not touch a human corpse either!" [39]

Gyerpungpa thought to himself, "What is to be done?"

Then early one morning, the attendant thought that there was no place else to go on the island and he became terrified (at the prospect of starvation). So Gyerpungpa told him to hold tight to his hand and close his eyes. They went walking along for a long time, when the attendant remembered (that he had forgotten to bring with them) the flint and steel (used for making fire). Opening his eyes, he looked back behind him. Thereupon he saw a young woman, wearing ornaments and robes, who was rolling up a long white woolen cloth. And looking before him, he saw that there was a similar young woman (unrolling this same cloth). Both the master and the disciple were walking along on top of that single white woolen cloth. And because he was looking at this miraculous sight with his physical eyes, immediately (the two young woman vanished and) that woolen cloth was withdrawn and no part of it went anywhere anymore. And then they were flung down into the waters of the lake and barely managed to climb out of the frigid waters on to the farther shore. [40]

There they found themselves surrounded by many householders (who were nomads from Zhang-zhung). When they were asked who they were, the master replied, "I am Gyerpungpa."

But their flesh had become so emaciated and their hair had so grown long that they were not recognized.

Thereupon the chief (of the nomads) said, "Gyerpungpa has died many years ago. You are most certainly not him!"

But when he explained their previous history, the nomads came to believe them. At first they were given water mixed with ashes. Later they were given the milk of a white female yak mixed with that of a white goat. [41] Then, after some days, they requested the full measure of food for their meal and in this way the full measure of their bodies came to be restored. As for the full extent of the life span that supported him, Gyerpungpa is said to have remained alive for five hundred and seventy-three years.

Fourth, in terms of the signs of his realization and his virtuous qualities that were both ordinary and immediate, (that is, pertained to this present life): His powers were truly beyond conception. If he recited mantras over gold dust weighing an ounce (spu-byang), he could destroy with it the entire country of Tibet. Dividing this into fractions of an ounce (khyung), if he recited mantras for three months over the gold dust, with it he could destroy the entire entourage of the king. However, having received offerings and the urgent request from the queen Khyungza Tsogyal (Khyung-za mtsho-rgyal) and perfecting the display of his magical powers, he recited mantras over one full measure (zho) of gold dust in a ritual called *rngub*. [42] Thereupon he practiced (the mantras in this way) for seven days. Then at dusk, he hurled a one-third portion (of the gold dust as a magical missile toward Yarlung in Tibet), thereby drying up the entire lake in Yarlung and subduing its Nagas. At midnight he hurled the next one-third portion, which killed the deer upon the mountain of Yarlung Pungperi (yar-lung spungs-pa'i ri), leaving the other five deer senseless on the mountain. And at daybreak, he hurled the remaing one-third portion (of the mantra-infused gold dust), whereafter the king of Tibet, Trisong Detsan, fell terminally ill. Because the king later accepted the master's foot upon the crown of his head (submitting to Gyerpungpa), the king was brought under the latter's power (and cured of his affliction). Subsequently, practicing in accordance with those precepts, namely, the Dzogchen Zhang-zhung Nyan-gyud and the Tantric Rites of Gekhod and Meri, (the king promised not to persecute them in the future). And after the king offered the full measure (of his repentance), he erected a memorial representation of the murdered king Ligmigya, as well as a golden stupa as a memorial monument, at the neck of the soul-mountain of Gang Tise. [43] Moreover, those Bon doctrines (expounded by Gyerpungpa) would be permitted to remain individually diffused throughout Tibet and the men of the clan of Gurib would sit in the row on the right-hand side of the king and would not be subject to his taxes. The Tibetan king Trisong Detsan solemnly promised all this. And so, even until this present day, the Bon of the Zhang-zhung Nyan-gyud did not decline into the status of becoming a hidden treasure. Moreover, by virtue of his great blessings, this tradition remains even today the highest spiritual science (gtsug-lags) and will come to spread even more in the future.

Then Gyerpungpa, having decided to seek out a guardian deity for the precepts of this profound Bon, walked to the nose of a cliff, and there performed the practice for the magical missile, whereupon he gathered under his power all the races of the male spirits of existence. At that time, the king of great power Nyipangse offered his heart's prana and promised that he would accomplish all those deeds not yet realized by Gyerpungpa. Moreover, he promised to be the Guardian of the teachings (of the Zhang-zhung Nyan-gyud). Then Gyerpungpa brought under his power all the female spirits of existence, whereupon Menmo Kumaradza offered her heart's prana to him. These two Guardians of the teachings have continued to accomplish those deeds that had not yet been realized. [44] Moreover, Gyerpungpa emanated himself everywhere in uncertain and unpredictable divine forms, such as emanating himself as a crystal antelope horn that radiated lights. [45]

Fifth, his extraordinary understanding (of the Natural State) became manifest. His doubts were cut off by listening to many learned practitioners such as Tsepung Dawa Gyaltsan, and so on. He impressed upon his mind the teachings of the Nine Vehicles of Bon, he purified his mind with learning, and he guarded his morality with noble conduct. Moreover, since he practiced the *Me-ri this-las* rites, he came to possess magical powers and telekinetic abilities. He engaged in many ascetic practices and he was appointed as the chief sacrificial priest by king Ligmigya. [46]

But at that time, because he did not perceive the supreme attainment, but, rather, thought only of himself, there being excessive pride in his thinking, "I am great!", the Nirmanakaya, Lord Tapihritsa or Tapiradza, came to him as an emanation. And the latter subdued the fierce pride of those two, the fortunate priest and his patron, and he revealed to them the Natural State, which is intrinsic Awareness. Having cut them loose from their fetters, which represented the full measure of their bonds, they overflowed upon the level plain (like water released from a dam) and for both of them, Rigpa came to remain in its own original condition. Thereafter the Precepts, the Tantras, and the Agamas, which eventually came to exist as scriptures, were given out gradually (by Tapihritsa to Gyerpungpa). Having produced simultaneously the realization of understanding, he accomplished the benefit of beings equal to that of the Nirmanakaya (Tapihritsa). Eventually he became like an omniscient Buddha. [47]

Persecution and the Decline of Bon

The events recorded above in the translation are thought to have occurred in the seventh century of our era. Then in the following century, Trisong Detsan became king of Tibet and the Tibetan empire expanded to its farthest extent. As the Tibetan king acquired more territories to administer, he was forced to expand his advisors from three to thirty ministers. According to the traditional histories, his power now extended to Tokharia in the north and even to the Roman Empire in the west. [48] All of these nations paid homage and tribute to the mighty Tibetan king. However, although a vassal state, the kingdom of Zhang-zhung had retained an internal autonomy that was now swiftly brought to an end.

In his history of Bon, the *Legs-bshad mdzod*, Shardza Rinpoche presents an account of how the teachings of Bon declined (bon bstan nub tshul) on two occasions:

1. First, in the time of the seventh Tibetan king Drigum Tsanpo, a persecution was launched against Bon, expelling the Bonpo priests from the kingdom because the king feared their growing power. [49]
2. And second, in the time of the great Buddhist king of Tibet, Trisong Detsan, who was certainly historical and the

contemporary and patron of Guru Padmasambhava. He can probably be dated as living 742 to 797, having ascended the throne upon the death of his father in 754 and founding Samye (bSam-yas), the first Buddhist monastery erected in Tibet in c. 779. [50] He is said to have also launched a persecution of Bon because he had come under the influence of Indian Buddhist monks, such as the great monk-scholar Shantirakshita who became the first Abbot of Samye monastery. The latter, in particular, did not recognize the authenticity of Bon as Buddha Dharma. Moreover, it is also said that the king had made a vow in a previous lifetime to establish the Buddhist religion in Tibet in view of the fact that Bon was in decline. [51]

As the *Legs-bshad mdzod* says, referring to this second persecution: "Second, with respect to this process of decline (nub lugs), there exist three considerations, namely,

1. the lands where it declined, '
2. in the time of which king and which Shen it declined, and
3. the manner in which it declined. [52]

"First, as for the countries (in which the teachings of Bon declined due to persecution), it declined in Zhang-zhung and it declined in U-Tsang of Tibet (that is, Central Tibet). As it says in the *rNam-'byed,* 'It declined in the reign of (the Tibetan king) Trisong Detsan.' [53] And according to the *Zhang-zhung snyan-rgyud,* 'As for the kings (in whose reigns the Bon teachings declined), this occurred at the time when Ligmigya reigned in Zhang-zhung, Pantalikha was king in Mon, and Trisong Detsan reigned as king in Tibet.' [54]

"As for the Shenpos (who flourished at that time), according the *Yang-rtse klong-chen,* 'In the lifetimes of Lachen Dranpa Namkha (bla-chen Dran-pa nam-mkha') and Nya Lishu Tagring (sNya li-shu stag-ring), it declined during the later part of the reign of the sovereign Trisong Detsan.' [55]

"Again, according to the *Zhang-zhung snyan-rgyud,* 'Those Siddhas who were learned and eminent scholars preserved the teachings and those practitioners who were their regents apprehended and realized those teachings. Those who possessed magic and great powers guarded the teachings. In both Zhang-zhung and in Tibet, there existed only Bon and no one even spoke of Buddhism. At just that time, in Zhang-zhung, among the many Siddhas (who attained realization there) there lived the Siddha Tsomi Gyerchen (Tso-mi gyer-chen), whereas in Tibet among many Siddhas there lived the four learned men, such as Pa Jitrom Karpo (sPa ji-phrom dkar-po) and Tonggyung Thuchen (sTong-rgyung mthu-chen), and so on. And at that time there also dwelt there the great master Lachen Dranpa Namkha." [56]

To account for the cause of this decline in the fortunes of Bon in both Zhang-zhung and Tibet, Shardza Rinpoche quotes from another Bonpo historical text, the *Srid-rgyud*. According to the story found there, long ago there lived three beggars in India (actually Nepal) who collected alms and, making wise investments, they later became very rich. They thereupon conceived the good intention to erect a great stupa in gratitude for their good fortune. Thus they began building the stupa of Jyarung Khashor (jya-rong kha-shor), now known as the Baudhanath stupa in the village of Baudha, east of Kathmandu in the country of Nepal. But they grew old and died before they could complete their work. Thus, they made the vow to be reborn in the future in order to complete this pious task. The first vowed to be reborn as the architect, the second as the patron for its construction, and the third as the workman. Thereafter they were reborn as they had vowed and completed the building of the great stupa. But before he died the next time, the patron expressed the aspiration to be reborn as a powerful king in Ngari (West Tibet) and the architect vowed to be reborn as a Buddhist emissary. But worn out by his arduous labors, the third man vowed to be reborn in Tibet as a Bon-suppressing translator. Later attaining rebirths just as they had vowed, the architect became the lotus-born Guru Padmasambhava and the patron became the king Trisong Detsan. But the builder and workman was reborn as Bodhisattva, whom some identify as the scholar-monk Shantirakshita. The latter, however, was reborn as the son of a servant belonging to an inferior family because of the hostile prayers that he had made before his death in Nepal where he vowed to destroy Bon. [57] And according to the *Gri-shad*, there were also the effects of the curses uttered centuries before by the king Drigum Tsanpo, which now came to fruition at this time.

Moreover, according to the *Srid-rgyud*, because of his earlier prayers made in a previous lifetime, the king Trisong Detsan was more attracted to the Indian form of Buddhism than he was to Bon. And because he neglected the rites of Bon, various natural disasters befell the land. Ghosts and demons engaged in soul stealing. Plagues, lightning, and hail storms afflicted Lhasa. The king consulted a Bonpo diviner by the name of Pe Negu (sPe ne-gu). [58] He advised the king that the calamities were all due to the incestuous birth of an individual who exercised great magical powers. After a prolonged investigation and search, a fifteen year old boy was identified as this star-crossed child and he was expelled from the land. Sitting on an ox, together with the appropriate ransoms, he was dispatched to the southwest where eventually he reached India. There the boy studied Indian Buddhism and eventually became a learned scholar possessing magical powers. He received the name of Anda Bodhisattva. Recalling the prayers made in his previous lifetime, where he promised to destroy Bon, he wrote a letter to the king of Tibet, intending to take revenge on those Bonpos who had caused him to be sent away from his homeland as a scapegoat. His letter reawakened the king's faith in Indian Buddhism. Also the king received reports at that time of a prophetic dream that had come to Pantalikha, the king of Mon.

Shardza Rinpoche continues, saying that during the lifetimes of Tonggyung Thuchen, Pa Jitrom Karpo, Nangzher Lodpo, Dranpa Namkha, and Lishu Tagring, although the teachings of Bon had spread widely, still there were many people whose behavior was immoral and perverse. Many monks had broken their vows and had allowed the moral disciple to deteriorate. Priests and magicians practicing Tantric rites became arrogant and proud of their magical powers. Many shrines and pilgrimage sites were neglected or even destroyed. Therefore, the king considered carefully what the Buddhist monk Bodhisattva had proposed to him and also the portents that appeared in the dream of the king of Mon. Therefore he decided that the time had come to suppress Yungdrung Bon and import spiritual teachers from India.

Then Shardza Rinpoche proceeds to describe the process for the decline of Bon in both Zhang-zhung and Tibet: "Second, with regard to the process of the decline of Bon, there are two considerations, namely,

1. the actual process of decline and
2. the manner of the concealing (the texts of the teachings) as treasures. [59]

"With regard to the first, there was the process of the decline in Zhang-zhung and the process of the decline in Tibet. As for the first of them, according to the *Zhang-zhung snyan-rgyud*, [60] 'During the time of the reign of Trisong Detsan, there were at his court ten ministers for external affairs, ten ministers for internal affairs, and ten ministers who acted as liaisons (that is, ministers for intelligence gathering), there being a total of thirty in all. Moreover, this king became very powerful. He subdued the wealthy king of Tazik and thereafter he concluded with him a very favorable trade agreement. The latter promised to construct wooden bridges over the great rivers that cut through (the country and inhibited trade). Furthermore, he subdued king Gesar of Trom [61] who promised to construct easily traveled roads along the four borders. He also subdued the Dharmaraja, the Buddhist king of India, who promised to establish with Tibet the relationship of patron and priest. [62]

"It was not because of his military power alone that he absorbed and brought under his rule so many kingdoms, but because of his previous karma. And because he had brought them under his power, he became very proud and he recalled his plan to subdue the king of Zhang-zhung."

Again, according to the same text, "At the time when there lived Ligmigya, the king of Zhang-zhung, the country of Zhang-zhung had an army consisting of nine hundred and ninety thousand soldiers. [63] And in addition, Zhang-zhung exercised authority over the country of Sumpa where it kept a small regiment. Whereas Tibet had only forty-two thousand soldiers, plus a small regiment in reserve, making a total of not more than forty-three regiments in all. The king of Tibet saw that he would be unable to subdue the king of Zhang-zhung by means of a direct attack. Therefore, the king of Tibet, because he was of an evil disposition in his heart at that time, he remembered a useful stratagem to subdue the latter by way of trickery and deceit.

"At that time, the king of Zhang-zhung had three wives as his queens, and the youngest queen was called Nangza Dronlek (sNang-bza' sgron-legs). She was only eighteen years old. Thereupon the chief minister for intelligence gathering, named Nannam Legdrub (sNan-nam legs-grub), who was evil-minded and ill-willed, but who possessed great cunning (and was a skillful talker), was sent (to the Khyung-dzong castle above the shores of the Dang-ra lake) on a diplomatic mission, carrying with him the horn of a wild yak filled with gold dust. [64] Coming into the presence of Nangza Dronlek, he spoke softly to her as follows:

"'O Nangza Dronlek! Alas, that one like you are only a lesser queen to the king of Zhang-zhung. We Tibetans are greatly discontented with this. Also the king of Tibet has lost his patience with this situation. Is there no way to put an end to this disgrace? If there is, the king of Tibet would make you his principal wife and grant to you two-thirds of the realm of Tibet.'

"To this Dronlek replied: 'The king of Zhang-zhung has an army that could cover the earth, whereas the king of Tibet has an army that could not even cover the mid-part of a cow's hide. So he will not be able to conquer him by way of a direct attack. But the mighty king of Zhang-zhung can be subdued (and vanquished) by means of cunning and trickery. Next month, he, together with his entourage of attendants, will travel from the country of Zhang-zhung to attend an assembly that has been summoned to Langgi Gyimshod (glang gi gyim-shod) in Sumpa (to the east of Zhang-zhung). Lie there in waiting and then kill him when the opportunity presents itself. That is the means and I will send a message in advance.'

"Then (the following month) the king of Tibet and his ministers came there with many regiments of soldiers. The king and Nannam Legdrub, having arrived at the top of the aforementioned pass (where there was a cairn or pile of rocks), looked about him. Inside of an iron bowl filled with water (placed there as a message), they found three things: a small piece of gold, a small piece of conch shell, and a poisoned arrow-head.

"Interpreting these signs, the king said: 'The full bowl of water means that they will come to this pass on the full moon of next month. The small piece of gold and the small piece of conch shell indicate that our army should camp and lie in waiting at the gold cave (gser phug) and at the conch cave (dung phug) at the Dang-ra lake. And the poisoned arrow-head means that, after due deliberation, (the king of Zhang-zhung) should be surreptitiously killed there (with an arrow)'

"And so, they waited there in concealment. When the two kings finally met, the king of Zhang-zhung was struck down by the Tibetan soldiers. Thereupon Zhang-zhung, which had a hundred thousand communities, was defeated, while Tibet, which had only ten thousand, was victorious."

Thereafter, Trisong Detsan summoned together all of his ministers and commanded that Buddhist teachers be invited to Tibet. Even though his ancestor Drigum Tsanpo had proceeded to suppress Bon and thereby his life was cut short, being killed at the age of thirty-six, and his great grandfather Songtsan Gampo, who had nearly suppressed Bon, also died at the age of thirty-six, the king did not hesitate in this course of action. According to the *Srid-rgyud*, the king sent a translator to India in order to invite Padmasambhava and the monk Anda Bodhisattva to bring Indian Buddhism to Tibet. As the result of their activities in Tibet, some five hundred Bonpo priests converted to Indian Buddhism.

Because conflicts had increased in the kingdom, the king decided to hold a contest of magic between the Buddhists and the Bonpos in order to show who was the more powerful. At the red rock of Dragmar Dringzang (brag-dmar 'gring-bzang), a large cotton tent was erected. The sage Dranpa Namkha was appointed the chief advocate for the Bon and Bodhisattva was made the advocate for Buddhism. When the contest began, Tonggyung Thuchen rode on his drum down the river and flew up into the air. However, Padmasambhava hung his cloak over its rays when the sun rose in the morning. Dranpa Namkha struck the sun and the moon together like a pair of cymbals in the sky. But Bodhisattva threw a thunderbolt into the sky, which stayed there suspended for a day. Se Shari Uchen went to lake Mapang near Mount Kailas and bestrode a water-horse, he flew up into the sky. But Nub Namkhai Nyingpo left his rosary suspended in space. Chetsa Karbu of Me-nyag made the river flow backwards. But Lang Palgyi Nyingpo drew rainbow figures in space. De Gyimtsa Maching loaded wild beasts with burdens and drove them ahead like tame cattle. But Dre Palgyi Lodro caught wild animals and milked them. Ku Gyimthang Mawo made his drum and bell emit flames. But Lang Tsugtor Rinchen trained deer, wild asses, and antelopes so that they became domestic animals. Khyungpo Tagdra Dontsuk made tigers, leopards, bears, and brown bears into animals as tame as dogs. But Ma Atsara Rinchen sat cross-legged suspended in space. Nya Lishu Tagring transformed himself into a vulture and flew through the sky. But Kawa Paltsek cut off his head and put it back on again. Pe Negu evoked gods into visible appearance. But Ba-gor Vairochana displayed swift-footedness equal to that of a bird. Mabon Thugkar crossed the river Ma (rma-chu) in only three steps. But Nyanpa Paljyin stood on a vase suspended in space. Choza Bonmo tied three knots in a sword. But Landro Konchok Jyungne sat in the midst of a great fire without being burned. The king and his ministers were very pleased at these miraculous displays. [65]

In this way, the Bonpos and the Buddhists continued to display their skills in magic, even bringing a dead man back to life. They also engaged, it is said, in philosophical debate. But because the Bonpos were in no way defeated, neither in this magical contest nor in debate, the king could do nothing overt to suppress them. Yet because of the prayers of aspiration he had made in his previous life, he ardently desired to practice Buddhism and he felt that, since the Tibetans were no longer genuinely practicing Yungdrung Bon, as had been the case in ancient times, the time had truly come to supplant it with the

Buddhism from India. Thus, the great temples at Lhasa came to be built and the first Buddhist monastery at Samye was erected. Then summoning the Bonpo leaders into his presence, the king urged them to convert to Buddhism and to abandon Bon. He offered them the choice of following Buddhism and remaining in Tibet, or otherwise to face banishment if they remained obstinate in their continued adherence to Bon. A number of the Bonpos thus converted, at least outwardly. Even the great Dranpa Namkha shaved his head and made a show of converting to Indian Buddhism. Thus facing the prospects of conversion or banishment, the Bonpo priests made copies of their scriptures, which they presented to the king who, in turn, had them concealed and sealed up at various sites, including Samye monastery itself. It is also said, according to the *Srid-rgyud*, that the Mind Teachings of Bon were transformed into the *Sems lung phyogs* of Buddhism, that is to say, the Dzogchen teachings in general. In this way, it came about that many texts that were originally Bonpo were rewritten and made to appear Buddhist in format with their titles changed. [66]

At that time the goddess Madud Sidpa Gyalmo became offended and appeared to the king in a dream in the guise of a fierce black woman with iron locks for hair, with three red eyes that burned, and with a grimace having her canine teeth bared, entirely naked in a scanty cloak of peacock feathers, carrying a sword and a skull cup. [67] She said to the king, "Give me my texts and their commentaries for the Four Portals of Bon and the Treasury which is the fifth. [68] If you do not turn them over to me immediately and try to destroy them, you will surely die and sink to the bottom of hell after sunrise tomorrow, without time to practice any religion!" She then disappeared. The king became terrified at this and dared neither to transform nor to destroy Bon texts after having that dream of the goddess.

Nevertheless, certain Bonpos flew up in the sky on their drums and went elsewhere. Others loaded their texts on the backs of wolves, tigers, and leopards and departed to China, Mongolia, and Yunan. [69] Some other Bonpos transformed themselves into vultures and wild geese and departed. Apart from the Shen Dranpa Namkha, Lishu Tagring, and a few others, all of the Bonpo priests departed into different directions, each taking a few texts with them. [70]

Again, according to the *Srid-rgyud* and the *bsGrags-byang*, after the departure of these Bonpos, the Tibetan Dranpa Namkha came to the king, petitioning him as follows, "I still request you not to suppress

Yungdrung Bon entirely, but allow it to be concealed for a time." The king replied that Dranpa Namkha had done well to take ordination as a Buddhist monk and, in turn, he gave his permission for the texts of Bon that remained behind to be recopied and then concealed underground, to be accompanied with the appropriate prayers of aspiration. Thereupon Dranpa Namkha and his nine assistants classified all the extant Bon texts into the categories of the *gZungs 'bum* (the collection of Dharani-mantras), the *mDo 'bum* (the collection of Sutras), the *rGyud 'bum* (the collection of Tantras), and the *Shes-rab 'bum* (the collection of the Prajnaparamita). In turn these texts were concealed in various sites in Tibet, Sumpa, Zhang-zhung, and Bhutan, and in particular, at Samye monastery itself. [71]

In one of the texts found in the Zhang-zhung Nyan-gyud collection, the *Bon ma nub-pa'i gtan-tshigs*, "the Reason why the Bon Teaching did not Decline," [72] the story is told of how the Tibetan king Trisong Detsan conspired to arrange for the assassination of Ligmigya, the last native king of independent Zhang-zhung, at the time when the latter departed from his castle of Khyung Dzong, "the Garuda castle", on the shores of the Dang-ra lake in Northern Tibet. [73] This account goes on to say that Khyungza Tsogyalma, the chief queen of the murdered Zhang-zhung king, craved revenge and commissioned Gyerpung Nangzher Lodpo to dispatch a Tswo (btswo) or golden magical missile against the Tibetan king who was residing in his castle of Chyingwa in the Yarlung valley. [74] Becoming thus afflicted by an incurable illness, the king repented his evil actions and besought Gyerpungpa not to take his life. In gratitude, the king agreed to suspend the persecution of the followers of Gyerpungpa and not to suppress the Dzogchen texts of the Zhang-zhung transmission, as well as to make gifts of restitution to the grieving queen. For this reason, the lineage of the transmission for the Zhang-zhung Nyan-gyud remained uninterrupted despite the government persecution of the Bonpos in general in the late eighth century.

Following this account of the decline and suppression of Bon (bon bstan nub tshul) at the time of the Tibetan king Trisong Detsan, in his *Legs-bshad mdzod* Shardza Rinpoche gives an account of the retribution (dbu-yog byung tshul) that occurred because of the actions of this king: "Third, with regard to how the Retribution came forth, there are two considerations, namely,

1. the explanation according to the *Zhang-zhung snyan-rgyud* and
2. the explanation according to the Northern Treasures (byang gter). [75]

"As for the first, because the king of Zhang-zhung had been killed at the instigation of Trisong Detsan, the tens of thousands of people in Zhang-zhung became separated and cut off from each other and the thousands in Sumpa also became isolated. When Zhang-zhung fell into little pieces, the primary wife of the king of Zhang-zhung, who was called Khyungza Tsogyalma, hatched a conspiracy in her heart against the king of Tibet. Having invited Gyerpung Nangzher Lodpo into her presence, she made a request of him. [76]

"'O honorable Great Shen! My Lord Ligmigya has been killed at the orders of Trisong Detsan, the king of Tibet. He has destroyed the silken knot of the law of Bon and broken the golden yoke of the law of the king. He has caused the teachings of Yungdrung Bon to decline. Since there has come forth such an evil time as this, I request you to please grant what I have deliberated in my heart with regard to this matter.'

"And when she had made this request, from the mouth of Gyerpungpa (came this reply:) 'I have a ritual called Pu. If I should perform it for three years with one full measure of gold, certainly it would be able to crush the four horns of Tibet. If I should perform the ritual called Khyung for three months with half a measure of gold, it would be able to crush Trisong Detsan and his entire entourage in the valley of Yarlung. But if I should perform the ritual called Ngub, having practiced it for only seven days with one full gram of gold and, if I hurl it as a magical missile, it will kill only the king himself. Which among these rites shall I perform?' he asked. [77]

"But because Khyungza Tsogyalma was one who possessed Bodhichitta, she replied, saying, 'It is not the fault of the people of Tibet. It is the fault of the king alone. Therefore, I request that you perform only the Ngub ritual!'

"And because she had requested this (having made many offerings), the great Gyerpungpa retired to an island in the lake of Darok where he set up a white silk tent having the pattern of mountain deer upon it. And having seated himself upon a silken cushion, he practiced the ritual for a full week with one full gram of gold. Then he divided the measure of gold dust into three parts and at sunset he hurled one third of it (in the direction of Yarlung in Tibet) and since this hit seven female deer who were lying on the mountain of Sogkhai Phungpori, two of them were killed and the other five became paralyzed. For this reason, nowadays that mountain is called Yarlung Shawareng, the mountain of the rigidly paralyzed deer of Yarlung. [78]

"Then at midnight, he hurled the second third (of the gold dust) and because it struck a lake on the side of the Yarlung Shampo mountain, that lake dried up and its Nagas fled. So, nowadays it is called Yarlung Tsokam (yar-lung mtso skam), the dry lake of Yarlung. And finally, at daybreak he hurled the last third (of the gold dust) and since it struck the castle of Chyiwa Tagtse (byi-ba stag-rtse), this castle caught fire and the king was struck down with illness.

"At that time, from the mouth of that intelligent king there came forth the expression of a realization, namely, 'The king of Zhang-zhung who had protected Bon has been killed and the teachings of Yungdrung Bon have been caused to decline. Now at daybreak, because of the way in which a Dzwa (a magical missile of gold) has come upon us, it is clear that there is much anger in the heart of the great Gyerpungpa. Therefore, he must be propitiated!'

"Having said this, and giving them a large amount of gold dust, he dispatched one hundred horsemen into the presence of Gyerpung Nangzher Lodpo. Arriving at the valley of Drajye, [79] the delegation presented some gold dust to a man of Zhang-zhung and inquired where Gurub Nangzher Lodpo resided.

"The man replied, saying, 'The great Gyerpungpa dwells now on an island in the lake of Darok. Since the form of his body is uncertain and he can surely emanate anywhere, you should pray to whatever appears (to you on that island) and he will surely show his face.'

"Then they crossed the lake in a boat and when they arrived at the island, (they found the white tent and inside it) on a silken cushion there appeared a crystal antelope horn that emanated many lights. Having realized that this must be Gyerpungpa, they made prostrations and offered the gold dust to it. And since they narrated the history (of recent events) and made supplications, the crystal antelope horn transformed into the form of Gyerpungpa. [80]

"Showing his face to them, he announced, 'The king who protected Bon has been killed and Yungdrung Bon has been caused to decline (in Zhang-zhung and Tibet). However, a consideration had been produced among my thoughts that if the physical body of the king of Tibet were killed, then the entire kingdom of Tibet would fall into ruin. Still, this would be proper!'

"(The envoys replied,) 'Indeed, the king of Tibet has fallen seriously ill and this has caused the people of Tibet to suffer. But the punishment of Bon and Shen has come forth in such a way (so as to fall upon innocent people). Now we have been sent here to invite you to become the priest of our lord, the king.'

"Because they had made this request, he replied, 'Well then, (in order for me to rescind my curse) there are three conditions that are necessary. First, the king shall erect a stupa of gold to enclose the body of the dead king of Zhang-zhung. Second, no taxation by priests or ministers shall be imposed upon the people of the Gurub clan when they come to Yarlung Sogkha. And third, none of the three hundred and sixty sections of Bon, which are practiced by me, shall be suppressed by the king. These are my conditions and they are non-negotiable!'

"The three ministers who were envoys promised to abide by this and Gyerpungpa was invited (to become the king's priest). The king of Tibet, as well as his ministers and subjects, made prostrations (when Gyerpungpa arrived) and listened to whatever he said. Then Gyerpungpa performed the mantras of the *gSang-this* rite, [81] whereupon many pieces of gold, which were like the hairs of a horse tail, were expelled from the king's body. Thus, the king recovered from his illness and also the people of Tibet were relieved of their suffering."

Moreover, according to the Bonpo accounts, it was not so much the king himself who was irreconcilably hostile to the Bon teaching, but the monk-scholar from Zahor in India, Shantirakshita, who became the first Abbot of the newly established Samye monastery, the first Indian Buddhist monastery in Tibet. [82] Shantirakshita was an eminent scholar, the author of such polemical philosophical works as the *Tattvasamgraha*, but also a monk of exemplary conduct who ordained the first native-born Tibetan monks and established the Vinaya of the Mulasarvastivadin school in Tibet as the norm for monastic discipline. [83] But he was hostile to native forms of religious practice, some of which, no doubt, in those days involved blood sacrifice (dmar mchod). It was said that the king was attracted to Indian Buddhism because of a vow he made in a previous incarnation, but it was the Indian monk Bodhisattva who persuaded the king to suppress the native Bonpos. Thus Trisong Detsan decided to hold a magical contest between the Buddhists and the Bonpos at Dragmar Drinzang (Brag-dmar 'grin-bzang), as recounted above, in order to determine which party was the more powerful. The Bonpos managed to hold their own, but again at the urging of Bodhisattva, the king admonished them to forsake their ancestral ways and convert to the practice of Indian Buddhism. The Bonpo priests were given the choice of conversion, or otherwise suicide or exile. The Shen practitioner Dranpa Namkha [84] considered the matter, thinking to himself: "Ultimately, the wise make no distinction between Bon and

Buddhism; but the king is mighty and the Indian Buddhist monks are jealous. Therefore, I will convert!" It is said that the Tibetan Dranpa Namkha thereupon became a disciple of the Buddhist Tantric master Padmasambhava. The king and the ministers within his government then set about to suppress Bon. [85]

Nevertheless, at this time many old Bonpo texts were copied and concealed in various places, including at Samye monastery itself and in other Buddhist temples as well. [86] The Bonpos were accused by the later medieval Buddhist historians of plagiarism and even of making Bonpo texts over into Buddhist ones. In particular, the *Semsphyogs* (Dzogchen) of the Bon was supposedly transformed into the *rDzogs-chen sems-sde* of the Nyingmapas and the translation of these texts was subsequently attributed to Vairochana of Pagor. The *rGyud kun-byed rgyal-po*, the principal Tantra of the *Sems-sde* or Mind Series in the *rNying-ma'i rgyud 'bum*, the Nyingmapa collection of the Old Tantras generally excluded by Buton Rinpoche from the Kangyur or canon of Buddhist scriptures, is also said to be one example of an original Bon work made over into a Buddhist one. [87] Some Bonpo shrines were destroyed; others were converted into Buddhists shrines. [88] Apart from Shen Lishu Tagring and Shen Dranpa Namkha, all of the Bonpo priests were scattered into the different directions of the earth, taking their precious texts with them. [89]

Again, according to the *bsGrags-pa skor gsum*, [90] a curse was put on Trisong Detsan and his whole dynasty by the Bonpo sage Lishu Tagring. For this reason, the Tibetan empire disintegrated in the ninth century after the assassination in 842 of king Langdarma by the former Buddhist Abbot of Samye monastery, Lhalung Palgyi Dorje. Thereafter followed a dark age for almost a century where almost nothing is known to later historians of events in Central Tibet. But just prior to this disintegration, the ascension of Langdarma to the throne was accompanied by a reaction against the excesses of monastic Buddhism. The large numbers of monks and the many shrines and monasteries generously supported by the pro-Buddhist kings of the Yarlung dynasty put a severe strain on the state treasury, especially under the religious king Ralpachan (815-836). This led to a successful coup in 836 where Ralpachan was assassinated and his brother Langdarma was set on the throne. A systematic government persecution then closed the monasteries and defrocked the monks in Central Tibet, but this appears to have left the Tantric practitioners, who were largely married Lamas with families, such as Nubchen Sangye Yeshe (sNubs-chen sangs-rgyas ye-shes), largely untouched and free to carry on with their non-monastic Buddhist activities. Nubchen was a practitioner of Mahayoga Tantras, as well as of Dzogchen, and he continued with his religious and scholarly activities unrestricted by the government. [91] So it would seem that this persecution did not seek to persecute Buddhism for doctrinal reasons, but merely to eliminate the monastic institutions that were such a great financial burden on the government. However, this reaction against monastic Buddhism did not lead to the reinstatement of Bon as an official religion. Rather, the government and its authority disintegrated altogether in Central Tibet and the once far-flung empire of the Tibetans collapsed.

However, this "Dark Age" appears to have been a fertile period for the development of both the Nyingmapa and Bonpo traditions among married Lamas who transmitted their teachings and practices in family and clan lineages before these traditions re-emerged full blown into the light of history in the eleventh century. At that time the practitioners of the old ways, whether Buddhist or Bonpo, came to define themselves against the Buddhist New Tantra schools (gsar-ma-pa) [92] then in the process of formation. The first of these schools was the Kadampa, to be followed by the Sakyapa and the Kagyudpa, all of which generally rejected the Old Tantras (rgyud rnying-ma) in favor of the Tantras from India newly translated into Tibetan by Rinchen Zangpo (985-1055) and his successors. This century was a time of renewed contacts with India, new translations were being made of Sanskrit texts, and a full-scale revival of monastic Buddhism began in the kingdom of Guge in Western Tibet, and spread to Central and Eastern Tibet.

The precepts that were transmitted from Tapihritsa to Gyerpungpa in the eighth century form the core of the Zhang-zhung Nyan-gyud cycle and appear to have been much elaborated later in the period from the ninth to the eleventh century by such masters as Ponchen Tsanpo, Orgom Kundul, and Yangton Sherab Gyaltsan that is, until they attained their present form. The Tibetan language of these texts, occasionally interspersed with Zhang-zhung words, appears old, simple in syntax, without the elaborations and embellishments and ornate style that characterized the scholastic prose of later centuries. The present form of the texts is certainly later than the spelling reform of the ninth century, but this does not mean that the Zhang-zhung Nyan-gyud texts were simply fabricated *ex nihilo* in the tenth or eleventh century. [93] It is likely that later copyists would have automatically corrected the earlier archaic spellings to bring them into conformity with current usage. So we should not expect to find in these texts the archaic orthography that is found, for example, in the Tun Huang documents that were sealed up in the mid-tenth century. [94] According to Lopon Tenzin Namdak, it was Ponchen Tsanpo, the sixth successor of Gyerpungpa in the lineage, living in the next century, who translated the Dzogchen precepts into Tibetan that form the core of the Zhang-zhung tradition. And it would appear that it is to this Zhang-zhung master and especially to his Tibetan successors, Orgom Kundul and Yangton Chenpo Sherab Gyaltsan, that we must look for the expanded content and structure of the contents of the Zhang-zhung Nyan-gyud. [95]

Shawadong (sha-ba-gdong lha-khang) or shrine at the deer-faced cave, at the Darok
Lake (da-rog mtsho), where Gyerpungpa made retreats and encounterd his master
Tapihritsa. Courtesy of John Vincent Bellezza.

However, it was just at that time that the teachings of Yungdrung
Bon declined. The process of this decline may be fully known from the
transmission of the history, such as is found in the *Kha-byang*.

Again, at just that time, the great Gyerpung Nangzher Lodpo, by
virtue of the power of purification, realized many ordinary siddhis and
consequently within his mind-stream there was produced a fierce pride
that asserted, "I am the greatest!" The various enumerations of all
essential characteristics (that is to say, philosophy), [11] were known to
him and he impressed upon his mind all of the vehicles (to
enlightenment found within Yungdrung Bon). He knew the words of all
of these instructions. Since the king of Zhang-zhung had elevated him
to the position of chief sacrificial priest, [12] there was readily
produced within his mind-stream a sense of overwhelming pride that
thought only about "I !" Thus having become obscured with respect to
the supreme siddhi, he continued to exist in just that way for some time.

Again, at just that time, dwelling in the river valley of Drong
Drajye in the yak-hair tent of a householder of Zhang-zhung, there
lived a wealthy man known as Merchyugpo Yungdrung Gyaltsan. And
it happened that a young boy who was really an emanation came to
him (at this tent) and made a request for work. [13]

The rich man Merchyugpo inquired, "Are you able to do any kind
of work?"

And since he asked that, the young boy replied, "I am able to
work, but I am without any taskmaster, (since I am an orphan with no
family)."

Image of Tapihritsa made in clay at the Lhakhang Marchak (lha-lhang dmar-chag) at the Darok Lake (da-rog mtsho), c. 1000 CE (?). Courtesy of John Vincent Bellezza.

Thereupon the rich man said, "Then you may stay here and belong to me!"

So the boy remained there, now belonging to the rich man (as a servant) and he proved to be very useful to the former. In consequence, he was given the name Khyeu Nyedlek, "the well-found young boy." [14] And it came about that he performed all kinds of tasks both indoors and outdoors.

One day, this young boy, (having been sent to collect firewood), allowed the cattle he was watching to scatter into the mountains. When he had returned from hauling a bundle of wood as his burden, he went into the fruit bushes at the foot of the rock cave in the river valley of Drajye Dunglung where the great Gyerpung Nangzher Lodpo was dwelling in retreat, and thus they met face to face.

Thereupon the young boy offered many polite expressions (together with his prostrations), [15] as well as some long disparaging remarks. Gyerpungpa cultivated a suspicious thought within his mind and said, "Your thoughts seem to be informed with philosophical tenets. [16] So, who is your master? What is your practice? On what meditation do you meditate? What is your burden? And what is this strange activity that you are doing in this way?"

Since he had asked this, the young boy replied, saying, "My teacher is normal vision just as it is. My practice is to be without discursive thoughts. My meditation encompasses the full measure of all the visible things in the three worlds. I carry discursive thoughts as my burden. And my activity is to labor as a servant for an ordinary living being." [17]

Because he had spoken in this way, Gyerpungpa queried skeptically, "If your teacher is normal vision just as it is, then you are without any kind of real teacher. If your practice is to be without thoughts, then no food or clothing should be necessary for you. If your meditation encompasses the full measure of all the visible things in the three worlds, then you have no need of meditation in order to attain Buddhahood. If discursive thoughts represent your burden, then your desires are not yet exhausted. And if your activity is to labor as a servant for an ordinary living being, then you are not yet beyond suffering."

Thereupon the young boy, who was an emanation, replied to this master, saying, "All normal visions are my teacher. If you do not know normal vision as your teacher, then who was it that taught Kuntu Zangpo? [18] My practice is to be without discursive thoughts. Because no thoughts should be created with respect to the Base, those visions that are connected with discursive thoughts do not represent the real practice. My meditation encompasses the full measure of all the visible things of the three worlds. But the real meaning of the Ultimate Reality is without partialities. If partiality comes forth in one's mind (and thus one comes to make judgments), this would not represent the real meditation. I carry discursive thoughts as my burden. When one's desires become exhausted, there will be no more discursive thoughts and everything will be known to be merely an illusion. My activity is to labor as a servant for an ordinary living being. Because all happiness and sorrow have come to have the same taste [19] for me, my conduct is to behave equally towards all."

When he had said that, Gyerpungpa became rather annoyed and replied irritably, "If you are really so learned as just this, tomorrow we shall go into the presence of the king and we two shall debate before him. If you are victorious, you will become my master. But if I am victorious, you shall be sentenced to punishment by the command of the king."

The young boy who was an emanation laughed loudly, "Ha ha!" shaking all his extremities, and replied, "Those who cling to notions of cause and effect have their heads wrapped up in confusion. For those who are great meditators, discursive thoughts are indeed their jailers. Those with the full measure of words are caught in a net of darkness. These essential characteristics of things are merely appellations that are no more than words. For those following the Secret Mantras, the mind is also the manufacturer of thoughts. [20] For those who are learned scholars, their knowledge is without purpose. Those with the view and the meditation, (are addicted to mere words, and so) only babble and speak non-sense. For all of them, there is no real meaning regarding the Natural State. However, the real meaning of the Natural State cannot be fabricated by discursive thoughts. Rather, one should follow the natural path where there is no necessity for the purification of anything whatsoever. Indeed, this self-originated primal knowledge is without obscurations. In terms of the state of genuine understanding, there is no recourse to the making of calculations (by the mind). When one superimposes these faults upon everything, the imposer himself becomes crazy!" [21]

When he had spoken thus, the great Gyerpungpa thought to himself in astonishment, "Probably he really is an emanation!" Thereupon the great Gyerpungpa went into something resembling a faint and fell into a stunned silence.

When he saw this, the young boy, who indeed was an emanation, just sat there in the sky. [22] Thereupon Gyerpungpa, having become aware that this young boy was indeed a Nirmanakaya who knew all aspects, accepted his foot upon the crown of his head. He confessed his various obscurations of speech to the Nirmanakaya and he requested some instructions regarding his actual meditation experiences during the present period of his life. [23]

Becoming distressed on that occasion (because his cattle had disappeared), the rich man Merchyugpo came looking for his cattle and the three of them met together (at the mouth of the rock cave). The rich man asked the young boy, "What are you doing here? And where did my cattle go?"

Since he demanded an answer, Gyerpungpa replied to his patron, saying, "Alas, my patron, he is truly a Nirmanakaya! Having already confessed to him each of my obscurations of action, I am now confessing my obscurations of speech."

Becoming himself astonished upon hearing that, the rich man also thought to himself, "Alas! How many obscurations do I have to confess?" And he went into a near faint and fell into a stunned silence.

Then at that time, the young boy who was an emanation said, "Now that the time has occurred for the converting of you two, since I have already come here, rise up from your faints and listen to my instructions! Furthermore, having already praised the lofty and sublime knowledge within this foremost among the vehicles to enlightenment (which is Dzogchen), you should listen to these instructions with your minds in an undistracted manner!"

When he had spoken to them in that way, the two of them listened attentively with undistracted minds, together with fervent feelings of repentance and devotion.

The young boy who was an emanation expounded the instructions concerning the four good things: "When (appearances) are not grasped at (by the mind), these visions will all self-liberate of themselves. So let your intrinsic Awareness (rig-pa), which in itself is without any partialities (or judgments) whatsoever, release them with a benign neglect. Just letting them go in that way is the first good thing. When the process of meditation is without concepts (or judgments), just that alone preserves a state of inherent clarity and thereby you guard yourself against uncontrolled experiences, so that they do not remain (and cause distractions). Just guarding yourself (against distractions) represents the second good thing. When your conduct is without any attachments (or desires), and yet you are alertly relaxed, then the visions that may occur anywhere at anytime are straightway cut off (from judgments and conceptual elaborations, being left just as they are). Just cutting off immediately (of judgments and conceptions) represents the third good thing. When the fruit or result is not sought after (or burdened with expectations), everything arises naturally and spontaneously by itself, just as it is. The characteristics of both expectation and anxiety (regarding what may arise in the future) are allowed to liberate of themselves into their own original condition (which is the state of emptiness). Just the process of (self-) liberation represents the fourth good thing. You should look closely into these topics here (regarding the view, the meditation, the conduct, and the fruit) in order to see whether they represent the path of clarity or of non-clarity!" He stated this and remained there (sitting suspended in the sky). [24]

Each of them remained silent for a time, then again the young boy spoke after a short while: "You cannot exhaust (or diminish in any way) the Ultimate Reality no matter how much you may practice. Because there exists nothing at all substantial or material in (this Ultimate Reality) which can be exhausted or diminished, therefore, you should practice, while just keeping your mind in that same condition of non-substantiality (which is its empty nature). You can never know the Dharmakaya by way of any cognitive mental activities. Because there exist no primary causes or secondary conditions in relation to it, therefore, you should practice while just keeping your mind in a condition beyond all causes and conditions. You cannot find your mind when you search everywhere for it. Because there exists no inherent existence to be found anywhere, therefore, you should apply this also to your mind. Because there is a lack of any inherent existence to be found anywhere, therefore, you should practice while just fixating your mind on this lack of any inherent existence. You cannot change the Natural State by means of any modifications. Because there exist no changes in it due to modifications, therefore, you should practice while just keeping your mind in this unchanging nature. You should look closely into these topics here in order to see whether or not they should be applied to your mind!" [25]

For a moment each of them remained silent. Then again, the young boy who was an emanation spoke after while: "Because there does not exist any partiality or one-sidedness (such as the distinction between "I" and "other") within the Natural State, is it not so that (appearances and the visions) also arise without any partialities? Therefore, you should practice without either partiality or one-sidedness with regard to anything. Because there does not exist any desire (within the Natural State) to grasp at external objects, is it not so that external objects also liberate of themselves into non-existence? Therefore, you should practice without either trying to bind them or to liberate them, (but just let them be as they are in themselves). Because there does not exist any birth or death with respect to the Mind (that is, the Nature of Mind), is it not so that (appearances and the visions) abide and remain in a condition that is not produced by anything? Therefore, you should practice without either trying to decrease them or to increase them, (but just let them be as they are in themselves). Because (the Natural State) is inexpressible in words (and ungraspable by concepts), is it not so that (appearances and the visions that arise) just abide and remain within that vast expanse of space in an inexpressible manner? Therefore, you should practice without either trying to emphasize anything or to obscure anything. Because (appearances and the visions) have never been separate from the Natural State from the very beginning, is it not so that these visions do not need to be linked to it? Therefore, you should practice without either trying to separate them from it or to link them to it. You should look closely at these topics in order to see whether (appearances) arise from the Mind or do not arise from it!" [26]

For a time they each remained silent. Then again, the young boy who was an emanation spoke: "Because the mind does not rely upon long sessions for meditation practice where the opportunities for meditation sessions are fleeting (and circumstantial), therefore, you should remain (in the Natural State) just as you are and bind yourself to training directly in your natural disposition (which is the state of contemplation) and practice without being distracted. Because there exist no distractions within the vast dimension of the Great Bliss, therefore, you should remain (in the Natural State) just as you are and bind yourself to training directly in that natural disposition (which is the state of contemplation) and practice without making any separation (between bliss and emptiness). Because being unconditioned is the real meaning of the Natural State, produced by the power of the inseparability (of appearances and emptiness), therefore, you should remain (in the Natural State) just as you are and bind yourself to training directly in that natural disposition (which is the state of contemplation). Because there does not exist any birth or death (any origination or cessation) within the Essence itself (which is the Natural State), abiding in a condition that is not produced by anything, therefore, you should remain (in the Natural State) just as you are and bind yourself to training directly in that natural disposition (which is the state of contemplation). You should look closely at these topics in order to see whether or not you have obtained stability or not attained it!" [27]

For a time each of them remained silent. Then again, after a short while, (the miraculous child) spoke: "When you come to understand that (the Natural State) is without any substantial existence, then you will have the confidence to come to a single definitive decision regarding everything. When you come to understand that (appearance and emptiness) are inseparable (from the very beginning), then you will have the confidence that everything has just a single taste. When ou come to understand that (the Natural State) is without partialities (or judgments), then you will have a confidence that it is free of all limitations. When you possesses these three confidences, you may then truly call yourself a yogin or practitioner of Dzogchen!" [28]

Finally, from the mouth of the master, it was said, "These instructions are not (for those unrealized individuals) who listen only a little, who have only small experiences, who become panic-stricken and terrified, and who flee into ordinary thoughts. But these experiences in contemplation [29] of the industrious yogin should be kept concealed very secretly as a treasure in the mind."

Then he proclaimed, "I am Tapihritsa. Do not forget me! And if you remember me, we shall always meet again. But if you do not remember me, at no time shall we meet again." [30]

And having said this, the master ascended into the sky and vanished like the rainbow.

With these four good things, the four applications to the mind, the five practices, the four trainings directly related to the natural disposition, and the three kinds of confidence, the teaching of these instructions of the master was completed. [31] Virtue!

Translation of "The Intermediate Encounter": *mJal-thebs bar-ma*

Here is contained "The Intermediate Advent and Encounter" (mjal thebs bar-ma).

Then the great Gyerpungpa went to make a three year retreat at the hermitage of the deer-faced rock at Drak Shawadong [32] and he remained there in that isolated place. And after a short time, he again met the Nirmanakaya in the innermost recesses of his heart. [33] Even though, when they had met for the first time, Gyerpungpa had been given many instructions, he thought to obtain similar instructions that would go into other topics. Thinking to meet his master once more, by every means possible, Gyerpungpa felt great devotion. In the evening, he prayed to the Guru and sat in contemplation [34] Then, early the next morning at daybreak, in a ray of sunlight that arose above the horizon, he saw the Lord Tapihritsa sitting there, suspended in the sky before him, as an immaculate body like translucent white crystal. This Body of Self-Originated Awareness [35] was nude and without adornments. Feeling immeasurable faith and devotion, he circumambulated and made prostrations.

Whereupon, from the mouth of the Lord, this speech was uttered: "O fortunate son of a noble family! [36] You possess the ripened karma of purification from your previous lifetimes. I shall teach to you the certain meaning, [37] so listen now with stable and undistracted senses! In order to guide those fortunate disciples of future generations along the unmistaken path, I shall teach to you the instructions of the profound Upadesha. This represents the innermost essence of the eighty-four thousand doctrines (or dharmas of the Buddhas). Verily, this ultimate Great Perfection is the highest peak of Bon. It represents the root of all the Tantras and the heart of all the Agamas. It represents the Primordial State of all the Buddhas. [38] It is the innermost source of all the views and the heart's essence of all instructions. Truly, it is the essence of all the Buddhas. This Nature is the Unique Sphere of the Bodhichitta. These three aspects — the outer, the inner, and the secret — are systematically established with aspects that are exceedingly secret. [39] They represent the heart's nectar of the Nine-fold Transmission of the Mind of the Victorious Ones and of the Oral

Transmission of the Twenty-Four August Persons. [40] These teachings on the instructions of the essential points of the great Perfection should be kept very secretly in the center of your heart!" So it was said.

Translation of "The Nine Respectful Polite Speeches": *Zhe-sa dgu-phrug*

Here is contained "The Nine Respectful Polite Speeches" (zhe-sa dgu phrug).

The Lord Tapihritsa (in the guise of a wise young boy, uttered the following) respectful polite speeches to Gyerpung Chenpo (upon first meeting him):

"Your body is immaculate, your speech is completely pure, and your mind is exceedingtly knowledgeable. O my precious Lama, your presence is similar to a (wish-granting) jewel on the crown (of my head). I come before you similarly." And having said this, he offered his prostrations (to the Lama).

"I have completed my accumulations and have purified my obscurations. But because we have stayed for a time in different countries, therefore, we have not met for some time (in this present life). Neverthess, on this auspicious occasion when we meet, I am glad to see that your precious body is in good health and not attired in any further troubles. Now at the present time, I am very delighted to meet and see your face that (is radiant) like the sun and the moon. On this occasion when we meet, your Mind surely remains clear." Again the boy offered three prostrations.

"O Shenrab Lama,you are the sovereign possessing great compassion. Therefore, please explain the Precepts to me, as well as for the sake of living sentient beings. With regard to your exceedingly precious principal practice, surely it has been leader successively among all the great activities of your mind. Last night and this morning has not your health and your well-being been excellent?" And again the boy offered three prostrations.

"And again, with respect to your precious principal practice, has not your mind become tired and weary? Indeed, are you comfortable in your body and feeling well?" And once again the boy was pleased to offer (to the Lama) three prostrations.

At this time during his retreat near the Darok lake, Gyerpungpa was largely engaged in Tantric sadhana, that is to say, the practice of his tutelary meditation deity Zhang-zhung Meri, the exceedingly wrathful form of Walchen Gekhod, the patron deity of the Zhang-zhung kingdom. In general, Gyerpungpa was primarily a Tantric practitioner with many accomplishments and siddhis, or psychic and magical powers, and not very much a practioner of Dzogchen. In this context, Mind (dgongs-pa) refers to this Lama's practice of contemplation, consequent upon the dissolution of his visualization of his meditation deity. The boy Tapihritsa, as the wise child, is ironically greeting the Lama and inquiring after his bodily health and mental disposition in relation to his precious principal practice (thugs-dam rin-po-che), which is Tantric sadhana.

The Primordial Buddha Kuntu Zangpo and his consort Kuntu Zangmo in union (yab-yum).

CHAPTER 7

The Reasons Why
the Bon did not Decline

Introduction to the Translation

The final text in the section of "historical texts", "The Reasons why the Bon did not Decline" (Bon ma nub-pa'i gtan-tshigs), places Gyerpungpa directly in the context of the history of his time. In the mid eighth century of our era, the great Buddhist king Trisong Detsan ruled over the vast Tibetan empire. The undefeated Tibetan armies were expanding into Western Tibet and into Central Asia, as well as fighting successfully against the Chinese armies of the T'ang dynasty in the east. Gyerpungpa, and a number of other Bonpo sages, such as Tsomi Gyerchen, Pa Jitrom Karpo, Tonggyung Thuchen, Zhang-zhung Tashi Gyaltsan, Gurub Tagwer Shinglak, Mahor Tagzik, and Tsepung Dawa Gyaltsan lived in Zhang-zhung or Northern Tibet as the contemporaries of this Tibetan king. To the south, king Pantalikha ruled over Mon in Nepal or Bhutan. Zhang-zhung still maintained some sort of independence under the last of the Ligmigya kings. However, the Tibetan king and his ministers plotted the death in ambush of Ligmigya in order to complete the annexation of Zhang-zhung and its vassal state of Sumpa into the growing Tibetan empire. When the king left his castle of Khyung-dzong, "the Garuda castle," on the shores of the Dang-ra lake, Ligmigya was met in ambush while traveling eastward on a state visit to Sumpa. After his assassination, both Zhang-zhung and Sumpa were incorporated into the Tibetan empire.

Sometime thereafter, the Zhang-zhung queen enlisted the aid of the Mahasiddha Gyerpungpa, who at an earlier time had been closely connected with the royal family and even served as the chief sacrificial priest to the Zhang-zhung kings. Thus she requested him to exercise his considerable magical powers on her behalf against the mighty Tibetan king, who had her husband killed and who now sought to suppress Bon on the advice of certain ministers and the Indian monk-scholar Bodhisattva. The latter especially, bore a great deal of personal animosity against the Bonpos. The great Gyerpungpa proceeded to subdue the distant Tibetan king by means of his magical missiles. And the king, now threatened with death, repented his misguided actions and agreed to Gyerpungpa's demands, including not forcing the Zhang-zhung Nyan-gyud into concealment, as was the case with the other text cycles of Bon teaching and practice. Thus, the work we have here provides us with the reason (gtan-tshigs) why the Bon of Zhang-zhung never declined (bon ma nub-pa) in Tibet nor were these texts ever concealed and rediscovered in later centuries as hidden treasure texts (gter-ma).

How much of this account is actual history and how much is later pious legend is not clear. The story of the encounter between Gyerpungpa, the Zhang-zhung sage and Mahasiddha, and the Tibetan king Trisong Detsan is not found in the Buddhist sources. But one would not expect to find it there because this Bonpo version casts the Tibetan king, one of a triad of numinous religious heroes in early Tibetan history along with Guru Padmasambhava and the Abbot Shantirakshita, in a rather bad light, making him responsible for the actual persecution of the Bonpos. However, the real villain in the piece is not the king, who received some bad advice, but the Indian Buddhist monk-scholar Bodhisattva, otherwise known as Shantirakshita, who became the first abbot of Samye monastery. In any event, he and the other Buddhist monks of Indian origin did not recognize the Bonpos as their co-religionists and fellow practitioners of the Dharma. Even so, elsewhere it is indicated that the Tibetan king did not proscribe Bon for doctrinal reasons, but actually permitted, even encouraged, the recopying and concealing of Bonpo texts, not only in remote places like Paro in Bhutan, but at Samye monastery itself. The king is even said to have sponsored the translation into Tibetan of certain Bonpo texts from Zhang-zhung, such as the famous *kLu-'bum*, "the Book of the Hundred Thousand Nagas." This translation work was actually done at Samye monastery itself. [1]

In this early period of the seventh, eighth, and ninth centuries, the relationship between Bon and Indian Buddhism was a very complex one, and both traditions interpenetrated and mutually influenced each other. Indian Buddhism, especially in its Tantric form, although loyally

View across the Darok Lake (da-rog mtsho) at the island in the lake (mtsho'i gling), middle left, where Gyerpungpa made retreats, encountered Tapihritsa and also the Tibetan soldiers sent by the Tibetan king, Trisong Detsan. The pennisula on the far left contains many old ruins. Courtesy of John Vincent Bellezza.

adhering to the higher principles of the Dharma, ceased in these early centuries to be something purely Indian and became assimilated and acclimatized to the indigenous culture of Tibet, which, since the earliest times, was so closely associated with Bon and the indigenous North Asian shamanism.

Translation of "The Reason Why the Bon did not Decline": *Bon ma nub-pa'i gtan-tshigs*

Here is contained "The Reasons why the Bon of the Dzogpa Chenpo Zhang-zhung Nyan-gyud did not Decline. (rDzogs-pa chen-po zhang-zhung snyan-rgyud bon ma nub-pa'i gtan-tshigs bzhugs-so).

As for the teaching regarding the initial spreading and then the subsequent decline of the Teachings: At first the teachings of the Yungdrung Bon, having been apprehended and realized, initially spread and increased everywhere. Those Siddhas, who were learned and faithful, preserved the teachings and those who were practitioners, as well as their regents, held and retained the teachings. Those who possessed the Upadeshas of great power guarded these teachings. Both in Zhang-zhung and in Tibet, there existed only Bon and no one even spoke of "Buddhism."

At just that time, in Zhang-zhung there was the Siddha Tsomen Gyerchen, whereas in Tibet there were the Siddhas Pa Jitrom Karpo and Tonggyung Thuchen. Furthermore, there were four learned men, such as Dranpa Namkha who was in the latter part of his life. As for the four Nirmanakayas, they were Zhang-zhung Tashi Gyaltsan, Gurub Tagwer Shinglag, Mahor Tagzik and Tsepung Dawa Gyaltsan. [2] At that time also there dwelt in Zhang-zhung the great Gyerpung Nangzher Lodpo who had received the ordinary teachings from the master Tsepung Dawa Gyaltsan and the supreme instructions (for Dzogchen) from Tapihritsa. But then, because of the power of the Wheel of Time it came about that Yungdrung Bon began to decline. [3] As for the kings, in Zhang-zhung, there was the king Ligmigya, whereas the king of Mon was Panraling and at the same time Trisong Detsan reigned as king of Tibet. [4] Before the time of the latter's birth, each of the kings (of Zhang-zhung, Mon, and Tibet) had only three ministers—one minister for external affairs, one minister for internal affairs, and one minister who acted as a liaison. [5] However, Trisong Detsan, having become very powerful as a king, increased in his own time the number of ministers to thirty—ten ministers for external affairs, ten ministers for internal affairs, and ten ministers serving as liaisons (that is, for intelligence gathering and spying).

The king of the wealthy country of Tazik, [6] having been brought into submission, made various favorable trade agreements with Tibet. But because the rivers at the border of Tibet were large, he had a number of long wooden bridges constructed and he promised to protect the life of the king of Tibet.

At that same time when Ligmigya reigned over Zhang-zhung as king, the mighty country of Zhang-zhung possessed an army of great military strength consisting of many thousands of soldiers, amounting to nine hundred and ninety thousand units, whereas Sumpa was much smaller, possessing only a thousand subject soldiers. Tibet, on the other hand, in terms of its regiments, had forty-two thousand soldiers, plus one small group, making forty-three in all. [7] Thus, the king of Tibet was unable to overcome and conquer the king of Zhang-zhung openly in battle. Therefore, the Tibetan king deliberated in his heart and thought, "I shall overcome him by nefarious trickery!"

At just that time, the king of Zhang-zhung had three queens and the youngest among them was named Gurubza Nangdron Legma. [8] She was only eighteen years old. So the chief minister for intelligence gathering advised the king of Tibet that, "She is angry and evil-minded. Her inner disposition is poisonous."

There was an agent who was clever at speech and who moved around much, one named Namnam Legdrub, and he was dispatched to her, carrying with him the horn of a wild yak filled with gold dust.

Having presented this to the young queen Nangdron Legma, he delivered the following speech (full of flattering words):

"O Nangdron Legma, you are beautiful, but you are only the lesser wife of the king of Zhang-zhung. Alas for you! However, the king of Tibet has no tolerance for this situation. So, there does exist a means to reverse these circumstances and, if that event should occur, you could become the senior wife of the mighty king of Tibet. And he would give to you fully two-thirds of his domain (and the wealth) of Tibet."

When he had addressed her thus, Nangdron Legma replied, "The king of Zhang-zhung has an army that covers the land, whereas the king of Tibet, since he does not have an army worth mentioning even as a joke, cannot openly subdue and conquer the king of Zhang-zhung. But if we use this devilish method, he can easily be overthrown and subdued (by means of trickery). Next month, the king of Zhang-zhung will depart from the country of Zhang-zhung and will travel (eastward) to the border of Sumpa. He will ride in front, accompanied by his attendants, and he may easily be killed at this point. He should be slain upon his arrival there and I will send a message before that time."

In the mind of the girl, however, she desired not to be seen doing this, so she said, "Before the time of that date, I will send a sign indicating his coming to the border and will put it at the foot of the cairn on the mountain pass between Zhang-zhung and Tibet."

Thereupon the chief minister of the king of Tibet dispatched an army of many thousands of men. At their head came the king himself, accompanied by Namnam Legdrub, and having come to the foot of the cairn (at the summit of the pass), they looked about. There they saw that inside of an iron bowl filled with water, there were three things: a small piece of gold, a small piece of conch, and an arrow-head.

From the mouth of the king of Tibet there proceeded the following interpretation, "The iron bowl filled with water means that he will come next month on the day of the full moon. The small piece of gold and the small piece of conch refer to two small valleys where are located the golden cave of Dangri [9] and the conch cave. Our army is to await his arrival there. And as for the arrow-point, it indicates that we are to kill him upon his arrival."

So saying, they went to that place where the two kings were to meet. On the full moon day, as instructed, the men in the Tibetan army killed the king of Zhang-zhung from ambush, and in that way the Tibetan king with his tens of thousands of Tibetan soldiers managed to defeat and conquer the hundreds of thousands of Zhang-zhung-pa soldiers.

Just at that same time, in the place called Lhasa in Central Tibet, an illegitimate child was born into the family of a householder. A diviner by the name of Pe Negu was summoned (to the royal palace) and his advice was sought by (the king and his ministers) in terms of the casting of divinations. [10] The diviner replied when asked, saying, "Do not accept such a one as this (illegitimate boy) who will eventually destroy your household! This boy is without a father, but he is the product of incest." When no one admitted to doing this incestuous deed (with the boy's mother), Pe Negu made the prediction that "When this boy becomes fifteen years old, he will cause great disturbances. There will be this to consider!" Then he advised, "For the sake of benefiting (your whole community), fifteen Bonpos, who are not related to this family, should perform a great rite of exorcism. [11] The boy should be set on the back of an ox which faces into the west and he should be banished to a country where everyone speaks a different language than people do here. This surely would be of benefit to all!"

Thus, it came about that the boy was banished to Kashmir which, at that time, was the country of the Vaibhashika Buddhists. [12]

Moreover, this young boy, being one who possessed ripened karma, became a student of the Buddha Dharma while he was residing in India and eventually he became an excellent translator and received the name of Bodhisattva. [13]

But because he had been banished (from his homeland in Central Tibet) at the insistence of the Bonpo priests and diviners, (he wrote letters to certain ministers of the king of Tibet). Thus, these ministers of the king came to utter slanders against Bon, declaring that, "Bon is surely declining and, therefore, we should now practice the Dharma (of Indian Buddhism). The true precepts are only those of the Holy Dharma coming from India. If this Bon remains high and powerful, the state and the kingdom will surely be harmed. Therefore, it is very necessary to bring about a decline of Bon here in Tibet!"

Even though they spread about this propaganda, the king did not listen to these slanders, but said, "Well then, even the sun and the moon must decline; this is what occurs in time. So, it is possible that Bon will also decline. But even so, it is not proper to cause Bon to decline deliberately."

However, just at that time, there came forth a sign in a dream to the king of Mon, Pantalikha, wherein even the light of the sun and the moon were extinguished. Even though, in his dream, there arose at midday fully three thousand golden suns, they subsequently sank into the depths of the earth. Having dreamed this, he elucidated his dream to the king Halayaga and he in turn explained it with some difficulty, indicating that the minister would die. This account of the dream having been listened to, one after the other, it eventually came into the hearing of the king of Tibet himself.

Having pondered upon this matter in his heart, he said to his minister, "Since he (this boy called Bodhisattva) was banished from our kingdom, he has been like a child of unknown parentage. Not having died despite the high bridges, the narrow passages, and the dangerous fevers of Nepal in the south, it came about that he has been taught the Buddhist Dharma in the country of India. And having become very learned in it, does he now cast slanders upon my person? Is he now proclaiming that because the king of Tibet is a practitioner of Bon, he should be killed? Is he the light that was a sign in the dream of the king of Mon?" And having proclaimed that the precious Yungdrung Bon was likely to decline, he himself became the cause for its decline.

At that time Zhang-zhung had upward to ten thousand soldiers and Sumpa had downward to one thousand, but Tibet went its own way separately (growing in might and power). The chief queen of the former king of Zhang-zhung, Khyungza Tsogyalma, [14] having conceived in her heart a conspiracy for revenge with regard to the king of Tibet, she invited Gyerpung Nangzher Lodpo into her presence. She prepared for him a seat of nine stacked silken cushions inside a tent and canopy of white silk embroidered with deer designs. She invited him to partake of rice wine and offered him many delicious foods and desirable things. Having shed many passionate tears that were like drops of blood, she implored him, saying, "The king of Zhang-zhung, who was the protector of Bon, was treacherously murdered. The moral law of Bon is a knot of silk and the law of the king is a golden yoke, yet they are no longer sufficient! The country of Tibet grows only a little (in power), but the teachings of Yungdrung Bon are now declining. Because such an evil time like this has now come upon us, please deliberate upon this matter in your heart and grant my request!"

Because she had spoken thus, Nangzher Lodpo replied, "Practicing mantras for three full years upon a gram (srang) of gold dust during the rite called *Ral-spu*, if I then dispatch it (as a magical missile in the direction of Tibet) the entire country of Tibet will be entirely carried away by the winds. However, practicing for only three months upon half a gram of gold during the rite called *Khyung*, if I then dispatch it, it will destroy both the Yarlung valley and the king

Trisong Detsan. But if I just practice for only seven days upon one small measure (zho) of gold dust during the rite called *rNgub*, and then dispatch it as a magical missile, only the king himself will be killed." [15]

When he had announced that, from the mouth of Tsogyalma came the reply, "Grant the performing it with *rNgub*!"

And because the queen had requested that, the great Gyerpungpa retired to an island in the lake of Darok (in Northern Tibet) and he resided there, seated on nine successive silk cushions in the middle of a tent and canopy made white silk and embroidered with designs of prancing deer. Having practiced the requisite mantras for seven days, and dividing a single measure of gold dust into three parts, he hurled the first one-third into the direction of Tibet at dusk and the magical missile struck the lake at the foot of the Yarlung Shampo mountain. Thereupon the lake dried up and the Nagas who dwelled there were reduced to his power. For this reason, thereafter it was called "the dry lake of Yarlung." Then at midnight he hurled toward Tibet the second one-third, half beyond and half hither, and having struck seven sleeping deer on the Khapunpo mountain, two of them died instantly and the remaining five were totally paralyzed. For that reason, this site is now called "the mountain of the paralyzed deer." Then at daybreak, he hurled toward Tibet the last one-third of the gold dust and having struck the Batagtse peak where the king's castle was located, thereupon the king fell grievously ill. [16]

From the mouth of this intelligent king (after due consideration) there came forth the following reflection, "The killing of the king of Zhang-zhung, who had protected Bon, has now caused the teachings of Yungdrung Bon to decline. By means of the arrival of a magical missile at daybreak, [17] I have been fatally stricken because I have angered the heart of the mighty Gyerpungpa. Therefore, I shall send him the horn of a wild yak filled with gold dust, and muster one hundred horses and men to take it to him. Surely Gyerpungpa has some method to heal me! If I have not now died upon this seat, still it certainly feels very much like dying!" he exclaimed.

Then, those one hundred horsemen, having arrived at the valley of Drajye, [18] made inquiries of some nomad shepherds from Zhang-zhung, saying, "Due to a conspiracy having overflowed from the heart of Gyerpungpa, the king of Tibet has now fallen ill. So, the king would now make offerings to this great Gyerpungpa in order to appease him. Tell us, where does he reside?"

The herdsmen replied, "Down below at the foot of a white rock on that island in the lake, there is erected a white silken tent decorated with deer designs. However, his own form is uncertain and he can emanate anywhere (turning himself into any shape)."

Having dispatched a boat to the island, the delegation arrived at that spot and found that, inside the tent, on top of a seat of nine successive silken cushions, there indeed was a crystal antelope horn which was an emanation. They offered to it the horn of the wild yak filled with gold dust, and then circumambulated the crystal antelope horn and made prostrations to it. Thereupon this antelope horn made of crystal transformed and the master resumed his human form, saying to them, "The king of Zhang-zhung who has protected Bon has been treacherously murdered. Therefore, the teachings of Yungdrung Bon have been caused to decline. Having duly considered in my heart that· the king of Tibet should also die because of this crime, I have proceeded to arrange this by means of my powerful magic and this will indeed destroy the entire country of Tibet. But if I rescind this curse, will you promise to do what I ask?"

The ministers deliberated and made this request of him, saying, "From the mouth of the Lord Trisong Detsan himself, he said that it was not his crime alone that Yungdrung Bon was caused to decline. Rather, it was due to the urging of Bodhisattva [19] and those scholars from India who accompanied him, together with certain ministers in the court, all of whom uttered the slanders against Bon. Truly, it was just like that!"

Because they had presented this proclamation, the great Gyerpungpa replied, saying, "Well then, I will present my four demands: These three hundred and sixty sections of the Bon from Zhang-zhung, which represent my personal practice, shall not be caused to decline. That is my first demand. Those among the people belonging to my Gurub clan, even though they have previously paid tribute to the country of Yarlung, shall henceforward serve as priests and ministers without having to pay taxes and shall sit in the row to the right (of the king). That is my second demand. As a memorial to the Lord Ligmigya, there shall be erected a golden stupa, one full fathom in height, and adorned with a swastika. That is my third demand. And in the presence of the queen Kyungza Tsogyalma, reparations shall be paid to her (in terms of gold weighed against) the twelve parts of the king's body with the addition of the thirteenth part for his head. That is my fourth demand." [20]

Thereupon these three ministers promised compliance with his demands. Then Gyerpungpa went by magical means into the presence of the Lord (Trisong Detsan) and there performed the nine-fold cycle of Sangti Pharma, which is a rite for afterwards reversing a magical attack. [21] Whereupon from the nine orifices of the Lord, he vomited up golden threads, each of which was just like tangled silken cords. And because these weighed in total one gram (srang), he had vomited up one half of the gold. Following that, he extracted from the king's body many substances such as blood, spit, and pus (in large quantities), so that the king was cured of his affliction.

Moreover, the king was exceedingly grateful and so those sections of the Bon from Zhang-zhung did not decline in Tibet. The people of the Gurub clan, when they were in the country of Sog-kha, remained in a row on the right hand side of the king. The memorial monument for the king of Zhang-zhung was erected and the thirteen parts of the reparations payment were made in the presence of the queen. [22]

Thereupon, at the time when Gyerpungpa resided there, Yungdrung Bon spread and increased in influence. It was from this custodian of the blessings of the precepts (of the Zhang-zhung Nyan-gyud) that the learned scholar and Siddha Tonggyung Thuchen requested the Portals of Bon which were inconceivable. These have been elucidated in the *Kha-byang rgyas-pa*. [23]

This represents the condensed history, the teaching just in outline, entitled "The Reasons Why the Bon did not Decline."

SARVA MANGALAM. Virtue!

CHAPTER 8

The Experiential Transmission and the Precepts Transmission

The Revival of Bon and the Terma Discoveries

Like Buddhism in general, Bon also enjoyed a revival, even a renaissance, in the eleventh and twelfth centuries. This revival began in the late tenth century with the rediscovery of Terma texts, texts that are said to have been hidden in the time of the persecutions of the eighth century, if not before according to Bon tradition. Thus, Bon shares with the Nyingmapa tradition the idea of Terma or rediscovered texts. The Nyingmapas, however, ascribe most of these Termas to the activities of Padmsambhava in the eighth century, whereas the Bonpos attribute their Termas to a number of ancient sages, such as Dranpa Namkha, Lishu Tagring, and others. The Nyingmapas assert that the reason why Padmasambhava did not make these Terma teachings (gter chos) available in his own time was that the Tibetan people were not yet spiritually mature enough to receive them, or else, that the times were not yet ripe and that these teachings were more suited to some future age. [1] However, according to the Bonpos, the reason for concealing the Terma texts were actually the persecutions launched by the Tibetan kings Drigum Tsanpo and Trisong Detsan. Nowadays the Bonpo canon or Kangyur (bka'-'gyur) consists of both these Terma (gter-ma) texts and those that have been passed down orally or in writing in a continuous transmission (snyan-rgyud) from early times. [2]

The Six Mahasiddhas from Zhang-zhung Mar

As successors in the lineage for the transmission of the Zhang-zhung Nyan-gyud after Tapihritsa and Gyerpungpa, there first came the Six

Mahasiddhas of Zhangzhung Mar (Zhang-zhung smar gyi grub-chen drug) who, according to the tradition, were all natives of Zhang-zhung, and who preserved the Dzogchen precepts in the written language of Zhang-zhung known as *Zhang-zhung smar*, hence their designation. [3] These Six Mahasiddhas were as follows:

1. Phawa Gyalzik Sechung (Pha-ba rGyal-gzigs gsas-chung),
2. Mushen Tsogge (dMu-gshen Tsog-ge),
3. Mu Gyershen Tsotong (dMu Gyer-shen Tso-stongs),
4. Mu Shodtram Chenpo (dMu Shod-tram chen-po),
5. Mu Gyalwa Lodro (dMu rGyal-ba blo-gros),
6. Ponchen Tsanpo (dPon-chen btsan-po).

Shardza Rinpoche in his *Legs-bshad mdzod* provides some biographical details regarding these six Mahasiddhas who were the immediate successors of Gyerpungpa: [4]

"Tapihritsa, the master of Gyerpungpa, also became a Jalupa or Rainbow Body of Light. He had meditated for nine years at the site of the lion rock of Tagthab Senge Drak. [5] Gyerpungpa himself lived to the advanced age of five hundred and seventy-three years. After having been graciously granted the instructions (from Tapihritsa in a vision) for the *Man-ngag le'u brgyad-pa*, "The Upadesha in Eight Chapters," Gyerpungpa realized the Body of the Great Transfer, and having thereupon accomplished infinite benefits for living beings, he entered into the equanimity of the Dimension of the Base. [6]

"His disciple was Gyalzik Sechung. Having meditated at the site of Melagyung, he attained the Primordial State of the Dharmakaya. Having lived for three hundred and seventeen years, he passed away into the dimension of space. [7]

"His disciple was Mu Tsogge. Having practiced for a long time, he purified the impurities of his gross physical body. And having lived for one hunderd and seventy-three years, he passed away like a bird flying up into the sky. [8]

"His disciple was Mu Tsotong. Having meditated at the place of practice called Shang-shelrong, the elements (of his gross physical body) were purified into their original condition. And after having lived for one hundred and thirteen years, he passed away like a Garuda soaring into the sky. [9]

"His disciple was the great Mu Shodtram. Having meditated at (the wild glacier of) Gang-nyan Targo, he attained the Body of Perfect Gnosis. And after having lived for one hundred and seventeen years, he passed away like a lion leaping into the sky. [10]

"His disciple was Mu Gyalwa Lodro. Having meditated at the site of Zangzang Lhadrak, he arrived at the full measure of the four stages of vision. And after having lived for two hundred and seventy years and having extensively accomplished the benefit of infinite numbers of sentient beings, he attained Buddhahood like the wind becoming calm in the atmosphere. [11]

"His disciple was Pongyal (v. Ponchen) Tsangpo. Having meditated at the site of the Shangdrak mountain in Yeru, he attained the Primordial State of the Victorious One. Having remained alive for one thousand and six hundred years in order to benefit living beings, he transformed himself into a turquoise cuckoo bird and thereupon flew away to the southwest in order to subdue the Rakshasa demons." [12]

Translations from "The Hagiographies of the Masters of the Lineage"

More details regarding the lives of these six Mahasiddhas are provided in the hagiography text by Paton Tanggyal found in the Zhang-zhung Nyan-gyud collection from Menri Monastery and we translate this section here: [13]

1. Phawa Gyalzik Sechung

Within the history of Phawa Gyalzik Sechung (Pha-ba rgyal-gzigs gsas-chung) who was the disciple of that master (Gyerpungpa), there are five considerations:

First, as for his history, his father Ya-ngal Segyal (Ya-ngal gsas-rgyal) (who belonged to the famous Ya-ngal clan) was a minister and a priest in the service of the great Tibetan king Tri Ralpachan. His mother was Thodkar Menkyid (Thod-dkar sman-skyid). Their son eventually became the great Lama known as Gyalzik Sechung. [14] At a later time (long after Gyalzik Sechung

36. Phawa Gyalzik Sechung

had grown to maturity), the great Gyerpung Nangzher Lodpo was conducting his search among the people of the kingdom of Zhang-zhung in order to discover a suitable vessel (to receive the transmission of his Dzogchen teachings). He found (two possible candidates:) Mu Tsogge (dMu Tsog-ge), who was then only a small child of three years, and Phawa Gyalzik Sechung who was at that time seventy-three years old.

This latter individual, Gyalzik Sechung was very learned in all philosophical systems (relating to Bon) without in anyway becoming confused thereby, and he was also knowledgeable in all branches of learning concerning the accumulation of merit (especially the performing of rituals). [15] He went to reside (at various wild and remote places where he was considered to be) the son of a Masang spirit, or the son of a flesh-eating Rakshasa demon, or the son of a Deva who was like a rock of melted bronze. In terms of his power and capacity, even the king of the Sadak earth spirits was unable to move or change him in any way. [16] And even the beautiful daughters of the Devas, with all their deceitful charms, were not able to disturb his meditations or tempt him. Moreover, he was largely able to abandon all substances (for food and nourishment) and lived there like one possessing a wish-granting gem.

Second, because he possessed both ripened karma and good fortune, he came to meet with the great kindness of his teachers. (Perceiving that Gyalzik Sechung possessed all the requisite qualities making him a suitable vessel for the transmission of the precepts), the great Gyerpung Nangzher Lodpo, having secured his boundaries from the outside world in order to make a retreat for five years, thereupon transmitted the Dzogchen teachings by way of his contemplation into the hearing of his disciple, doing so by projecting the form of his face through the hole in a piece of birch bark (that is to say, by speaking into a hollow tube made of birch bark set into the wall of his hermitage). [17] Thereafter Lama Gyalzik ignored his wife Rogshudza Gema (Rog-shud-za dge-ma), as well as his son and daughter, and regarded these three without attachments.

Third, in terms of the special places where he stayed (and practiced meditation), principally there was the site called Megyud Karnak (me-rgyud dkar-nag). [18] He remained in that place of great blessings for a long time. Then in terms of his life span while relying upon that site, he lived to be fully three hundred and seventy years old.

Fourth, as for the signs of his realization and his virtuous qualities that were both ordinary and immediate: His physical body (and countenance) came to be characterized by a special radiance and he favorably impressed the minds of others with his pleasing appearance. His special quality of speech possessed the power of a voice where others listened to and heeded his commands (especially the local nature spirits). And in his mind he became especially realized with regard to the Mantrayana in terms of *gSang-sngags, This-sngags,* and *Rigs-sngags.* [19] (That is to say, he principally practiced the sadhanas for Zhang-zhung Meri and became very accomplished in them.) The signs of his realization became very evident and thereby indicated that he had attained siddhis both ordinary and supreme.

Fifth, his extraordinary understanding (of the Natural State) then became manifest. Having received the Upadeshas of the Experiential Transmissions (of the previous masters) from his own master Gyerpungpa, after only one year his understanding came to have no expectations of attaining Buddhahood by moving upward spiritually and no feverish anxieties of becoming once more an ordinary sentient being through falling downward (into rebirth in Samsara). [20] (Thereafter he manifested the Rainbow Body.)

2. Mu Tsogge

Within the history of Mu Tsogge (dMu Tsog-ge) who was the disciple of that previous master, there are five considerations:

First, as for the history of his parents and how he obtained a pure human body: He belonged to the Gurib clan. His father was Gurib Gyergyung (Gu-rib gyer-rgyung) and his mother was called Nyamo Chamchik (sNya-mo lcam-gcig).

Second, because he possessed both ripened karma and good fortune, he met with a master who showed him great kindness. Having encountered Phawa Gyalzik Sechung in person when he was

37. Mushen Tsogge

nineteen years old, he requested and received all the instructions (for the practice of Dzogchen and for the Secret Mantras of Zhang-zhung Meri).

Third, as for the special places where he resided: It was principally at a place called Phawa Taglagchan (pha-ba stag-lag-can), a site where those Siddhas who had subdued the Yenkham gods gathered. [21] He resided at that place of great blessings and in terms of his life span while he relied upon that site, he lived for some one hundred and seventy-one years.

Fourth, in terms of the signs of his realization and his virtuous qualities, which were both ordinary and immediate, he became the equal in every way to his benevolent master.

Fifth, his extraordinary understanding became manifest. Having received the Upadeshas of the Experiential Transmissions (of the previous masters) from his own master, after only five months he realized confidence (in the Natural State) and renounced Samsara entirely. In his mind he perfected the Primordial State of Buddhahood. (He entered into Nirvana and realized the Rainbow Body without leaving any sign of his physical body behind.)

3. Mu Tsotang

Within the history of Mu Tsotang (dMu tso-stangs) who was the disciple of that previous master, there are five considerations:

First, as for the history of his parents and how he obtained a pure human body: His clan was also Gurib. His father was Gurib Tonpa Gyung-nge (Gu-rib ston-pa rgyung-nge) and his mother was called Rogshudza Aloman (Rog-shud-za a-lo-sman). [22]

Second, because he possessed both ripened karma and good fortune, he met with a master who showed him great kindness. Having encountered Lama Mu Tsogge in person at the age of

38. Mu Gyershen Tsotong

forty-seven, he requested and was given the instructions (for the practice of Dzogchen).

Third, as for the special places where he resided, he stayed principally at a place of great blessings called the crystal valley of Shang Shel-rong (shangs shel-rong). [23] In terms of his life span while he relied upon that site, he lived for fully one hundred and thirteen years.

Fourth, in terms of the signs of his realization and his virtuous qualities that were both ordinary and immediate, he realized a powerful confidence with regard to both the ordinary and the supreme siddhis.

Fifth, his extraordinary understanding became manifest. Having received the Upadeshas (from this master), for four days he wandered about hither and thither, and after one month, due to his complete understanding (of the Natural State), he became liberated.

4. Mu Shodtram Chenpo

Within the history of Mu Shodtram Chenpo (dMu shodtram chen-po) the disciple of that previous master (Mu Tsotang), there are five considerations:

39. Mu Shodtram Chenpo

First, as for the history of his parents and how he obtained a pure human body: He also belonged to the Gurib clan. His father was Gurib Trogyal (Gu-rib khro-rgyal) and his mother was Ramo Lugu (Ra-mo lu-gu).

Second, because he possessed both ripened karma and good fortune, he met with a master who showed him great kindness. The father of Mu Shodtram was indeed the brother of Lama Mu Tsogge. Furthermore, having abandoned attachments (to the worldly life as a farmer and householder) at the age of forty, he went and offered five measures of the produce of his fields to Lama Tsotang. And when he requested the Upadeshas for Dzogchen, he received them and preserved them in his heart, (retaining them in memory).

Third, as for the special place where he resided: It was at a place of great blessings called the great glacial mountain of Gang Targo, [24] at the left face of the sunny side of the valley. He stayed there in front of a huge boulder. In terms of his life span while he relied upon that site, he lived for one hundred and seventeen years.

Fourth, in terms of the signs of his realization and his virtuous qualities that were both ordinary and immediate, the signs of his realization were inconceivable.

Fifth, his extraordinary understanding became manifest. Having then received the Upadeshas for the Dzogchen teachings, after only seventeen days, he cut off the roots of birth and death. And his understanding having become manifest, he became the equal of the Buddha.

40. Mu Gyalwa Lodro

5. Mu Gyalwa Lodro

Within the history of Mu Gyalwa Lodro (dMu rgyal-ba blo-gros) who was the disciple of that previous master, there are five considerations:

First, as for the history of his parents and how he obtained a pure human body: He belonged to the Gurub clan; however his father was a poor man. [25]

Second, because he possessed both ripened karma and good fortune, he met with a master who showed him great kindness: In the early part of his life, he labored only as a poor shepherd. (At one time he found himself living in a cave that had good grass nearby for his sheep. But one night a wolf came and killed many of the sheep and the next day the crows came to pluck their intestines. Then the wolf came again and killed more sheep and his remaining sheep ran away. He went to look at his dead sheep and thought that his own life was impermanent just like this. Then he remembered his kinsman who had been practicing meditation all that time in another cave.) So, when he was forty-five years old, he went to the great glacial mountain of Gang-chen Targo (gangs-chen rta-sgo) where he came into the presence of Shodtram Chenpo. For nine years he served as an attendant of that master. And when he requested the instructions for Dzogchen, he received them and preserved them in his heart (as memories without any mistake or error).

Third, as for the special places where he resided: In the earlier part of his life, he stayed at that place of great blessings (in the Darok region) called the cave of Rogchag-phuk (rog-lcag phug). And in the latter part of his life he resided at the place of great blessings called Zangzang Lhadrak (zang-zang lha-brag). [26] As this was a site closely connected with the realization of practice, there came forth for him many blessings and spiritual attainments. He remained in that place where both human beings and non-human spirits gathered.

Fourth, in terms of the signs of his realization and his virtuous qualities that were both ordinary and immediate, he came to possess a very great many siddhis (including visions of his tutelary deity Zhang-zhung Meri).

Fifth, his extraordinary understanding became manifest. Having received the Upadeshas of the Experiential Transmissions (of the previous masters) from his own master, within just one year he became liberated from being tethered to the words that denote things and within another year he became liberated from being tethered to examples, meanings, and texts. Then, within one month, because he meditated with understanding upon the Upadeshas of his master, his body and his mind everywhere remained untouched by either the conditions of Samsara or of Nirvana. Thus, he became equal to the Primordial State of Buddhahood. [27]

6. Ponchen Tsanpo

Ponchen Tsanpo (dPon-chen btsan-po) was the last of the native Mahasiddhas from Zhang-zhung. Moreover, he was considered a very important master in this lineage for the transmission because, according to Lopon Tenzin Namdak, he was the key individual who translated the Dzogchen precepts from the Zhang-zhung language into the Tibetan language for the benefit of his Tibetan disciples. He is also said to have written down the description of the yantras or yoga positions associated with the Zhang-zhung Nyan-gyud, whereas

41. Ponchen Tsanpo

previously they had only been given orally. [28] As it says in the translation:

Within the history of Ponchen Tsanpo (dPon-chen btsan-po) who was the disciple of that previous master, there are five considerations:

First, as for the history of his parents and how he obtained a pure human body: Among the rocky mountains in the country of Darok (west of that lake), he was born into the Thoglha clan. His father was Kushen Thoglha Tsemo (sku-gshen Thog-lha rtse-mo) and his mother was Mangwerza Gyanchungma (Mang-wer-za rgyan-chung-ma). [29] Previously, for a duration of twelve years, his parents were without a son. Then one day, three women came to his future mother and she confided her desire to them. They prophesied that she would find her child in a casket. Then that night, in a visionary experience (or dream), she beheld a miraculous child who indeed was an emanation, having all of his marks complete, emerge from inside a shining casket of precious jewels that sat amidst the white boulders of the rock valley in the western direction. And just as it had happened in her dream, within one year a son was born to her and this was Pon Tsanpo. [30]

Second, because he possessed both ripened karma and good fortune, he met with a master who showed him great kindness: When he was seven or eight years old, he performed many virtuous deeds. When he was twelve years old, at Zangzang Lhadrak (zang-zang lha-brag) where there lived Mu Gyalwa Lodro, he met and came into the presence of the master. And when he had requested the instructions for Dzogchen, he received them and preserved them in his heart (without forgetting a single word). And in gratitude, he made many offerings of food to his master.

Third, as for the special places where he resided at the time he was relying upon them: Departing from the village of his parents, he lived roaming about the mountain peaks of Yeru Shang (g.yas ru shangs). He was a yogin who was like a king of wild birds. [31] And at the time he relied upon that site, because he had realized the Vidyadhara stage of the power of long life, (thereby prolonging his life indefinitely) he came to complete some sixteen hundred years (of his life span). And because he possessed the inherent power to do so (because of his greatly extended life span), he was able to produce greatly the benefit of others. During the time that he was training his disciples, it is said that there did not occur any visible manifestations of either him dying or being reborn (because he continued in that same physical body for that entire period). [32]

Fourth, as for the signs of his realization and his virtuous qualities that were both ordinary and immediate: Because he had exhausted his pollutants in terms of his physical body, his constitution, and birth condition (or sphere of rebirth), it was no longer necessary for him to take food to nourish his health. [33] And transforming his physical body into that of a turquoise cuckoo bird, he went to Tazik (where he subdued the Tirthikas and even the non-human spirits made offerings to him). Thereafter, he departed into the southwest direction in order to accomplish the suppression of the Rakshasa demons (on an island in the great southern ocean). Indeed, he continuously manifested various signs of realization such as these. [34]

Fifth, his extraordinary understanding became manifest. Having received the instructions for Dzogchen, after only seven days an understanding (of the Natural State) arose within him and there came forth for him a confidence, a realization, and a pride (that was extraordinary) and he became non-dual with the Nirmanakaya itself." [35]

The Experiential Transmission

Again, according to the *Legs-bshad mdzod* of Shardza Rinpoche: [36] "Second, with respect to the Mantras and to the Mind Teachings, there are three considerations, namely,

1. the Cycle of Bon from Zhang-zhung,
2. the Cycle of Bon from India, and
3. the Cycle of Bon for Yong Luk. [37]

"As for the Cycle of Bon from Zhang-zhung: The textual cycle known as the Zhang-zhung Nyan-gyud is the most important among the three hundred and sixty cycles of Bon belonging to the Zhang-zhung tradition. [38] The king of Tibet Trisong Detsan promised not to bring about their decline by means of deliberately suppressing them because he was brought under the power of Zhang-zhung Nangzher Lodpo by way of the latter dispatching a magical missile of gold. [39] The mode of the transmission of both the Mantras and the Mind Teachings from Gyerpungpa up to Pongyal Tsanpo has already been explained above. From Pongyal Tsanpo (the transmission of the Zhang-zhung Nyan-gyud) separated into two: the Upper Lineage and the Lower Lineage.

"As for the Upper Lineage of the Transmission (stod brgyud): Pongyal Tsanpo taught the *bKa' brgyud skor bzhi* (the Four Cycles for the Transmission of the Precepts of the Zhang-zhung Nyan-gyud) [40] to his disciple Guge Sherab Lodan (Gu-ge shes-rab blo-gros). From the Six Ascetics who possessed Understanding (rtogs-ldan 'khrul-zhig drug) it spread into the upper country (westward) and so it became known as the Upper System for the Oral Transmission (snyan-brgyud stod lugs).

"As for the Lower Lineage of the Transmission (smad brgyud): Pongyal Tsanpo taught the Experiential Transmission to Khyungjyid Muthur of Shang (Shang gi Khyung-byid mu-thur), in its extensive, intermediate, and condensed versions, [41] as well as the oral transmission of the Mantras, including both the long and the short rites for Meri. [42] From the five Mahasiddhas who were Emanations (rnam-sprul grub-chen lnga) it spread into the lower countries (eastward) and so it became known as the Lower System of the Oral Transmission (snyan-brgyud smad lugs).

"Then, from these two: Togmed Zhigpo of the Upper System (stod lugs kyi rTog-med zhig-po) and Olgom Kundul of the Lower System (smad lugs kyi 'ol-sgom kun-'dul), all of the Upadeshas in their perfection were taught to Yangton Chenpo [43] And although there were many transmissions that derived from the great Yangton, they all may be condensed into two:

1. the Southern Lineage (lho brgyud) and
2. the Northern Lineage (byang brgyud).

"As for the Southern Lineage, it went from (his son and disciple) Dampa Bumje (Dam-pa 'bum-rje) up to Chigchod Dadshe (Cig-chod dad-shes). And as for the Northern Lineage, it went from Lunggom Togmed (Lung-sgom rtog-med) up to the great Namdrol Mutowa (rNam-grol mu-lto-ba chen-po). Although these two, the Upper and the Lower, together with the Southern and the Northern, make four (lineages in all), having looked at the particular countries where these masters lived in terms of being places that were higher or lower (geographically speaking)— it may be concluded that it should be explained in that way.

"As for just a brief enumeration of the masters in these lineages of transmission, we find

1. the Six Ascetics who possessed Understanding (rtogs-ldan 'khrul-zhig drug),
2. the Five Mahasiddhas who were Emanations (rnam-sprul grub-chen lnga),
3. the Nine Gurus who possessed the Sources (khungs-ldan bla-ma dgu),
4. the Five Gurus of the Mantras and the Mind Teachings (sngags sems bla-ma lnga),
5. the Nine Vidyadharas of the Transmission of the Precepts (bka' brgyud rig-'dzin dgu),
6. the Eight Sovereigns of the Profound Path (zab lam mnga'-bdag brgyad),
7. the Two Protectors of Living Beings ('gro-ba'i mgon-po gnyis).
8. the Three Gurus who possessed the Transmission (brgyud-ldan bla-ma gsum), and
9. the Eight possessing Unequaled Courage (mnyam-med gdengs-ldan brgyad).

"Up until the present time, both the Transmission of the Precepts and the Experiential Transmission have been linked together as a pair. [44] Moreover, some of these masters attained the Body of Light, leaving no remainder behind, whereas others attained liberation afterwards in the Bardo or in a pure field into which they emanated naturally. [45] As the signs of their Buddhahood becoming manifest, such as mysterious sounds and lights, movements of the earth, and the appearances of letters, and so on, these are described in the *rNam-thar chen-mo*."

The Five Masters of the System of Lower Zhang-zhung

According to this latter text, the hagiographies by Paton Tan-gyal found in the Zhang-zhung Nyan-gyud collection, after the time of Pongyal Tsanpo, the last of the six Mahasiddhas from Zhang-zhung, the transmission lineage split into two separate lines:

1. the Experiential Transmission (nyams brgyud), also known as the Lower Transmission (smad rgyud), and
2. the Precepts Transmission (bka' brgyud), also known as the Upper Transmission (stod rgyud).

"Thus we have demonstrated above the history with regard to the virtuous qualities of the six Mahasiddhas from Zhang-zhung. Thereafter, from Pongyal Tsanpo, the last among these six Mahasiddhas from Zhang-zhung, the transmission divided into two lines. There came into existence both the Lower Transmission (smad rgyud) and the Upper Transmission (stod rgyud). The first is so-called because it was transmitted from the lower country. Thus, Pon Tsanpo while residing in the lower country (of Northern Tibet) transmitted the Dzogchen teachings to two individual (Tibetans), namely, Lhundrub Muthur and Shengyal Yungdrung Lhatse. That Lower Transmission came into being as just what is called the Experiential Transmission, namely,

1. Ponchen Lhundrub Muthur (dPon-chen lhun-grub mu-thur),
2. Shengyal Lhatse (gShen-rgyal lha-rtse),
3. Lhagom Karpo (Lha-sgom dkar-po),
4. Ngodrub Gyaltsan Ringmo (dNgos-grub rgyal-mtshan ring-mo), and
5. Orgom Kundul ('Or-sgom kun-'dul)

"Here we have elucidated the histories of the five Mahasiddhas of Bon." [46]

With regard to the first of these lineages of transmission, Ponchen Tsanpo, while residing in the eastern or lower part of Zhang-zhung (sa smad du) transmitted the precepts to Lhundrub Muthur and to Shengyal Yungdrung Lhatse. In this way, there originated the Experiential Transmission that represents the Lower Transmission (smad rgyud de nyams rgyud). The hagiographies of the Five Masters of the Lower System (smad lugs kyi bla-ma lnga) are as follows:

1. Ponchen Lhundrub Muthur

Ponchen Lhundrub Muthur (dPon-chen Lhun-grub mu-thur) was a Tibetan rather than a Zhang-zhung-pa by birth. He belonged to the Khyungpo clan and was born in the country of Raring (yul ra-ring). His father was called Khyungjyid Drubpai Gyalpo (Khyung-byid Grub-pa'i rgyal-po) and his mother was Gyerloza Nangsidgyan (Gyer-lo-za sNang-srid rgyan). [47] Because his good karma had ripened and he possessed good fortune, he came to meet with the great kindness of his master.

At one time Lama Ponchen Tsanpo was dwelling on the mountain of Shang (shangs kyi ri). While mounted on the back of a yak that had lost its way, the young boy Lhundrub Muthur came to the cave in the Long Valley of Slate (g.ya' lung ring-mo'i phug). When he went into this cave out of curiosity, he was astonished to see a small man wearing a blue hermit's hat and a tattered blue robe. [48] However, his feet remained bare. Into the half open mouth of the book bag slung by a strap over his shoulder, he had stuffed a number of small manuscripts. In his hands he carried a ladle and a small plate, both of which were made from iron, designed for making water offerings. [49]

Having encountered such a strange apparition, the boy eagerly inquired where the mysterious hermit had come from. To this the Lama replied enigmatically, "O my son, I do not come from anywhere at all."

And asked again by the astonished boy where he was going, he replied, "O my son, I do not go anywhere at all" And asked finally where he was staying at the present, the Lama replied, "O my son, I do not stay anywhere in particular."

"Sir, are you a Mahasiddha?" the boy inquired politely. And to this the Lama replied with a shrug, "I have accomplished nothing whatsoever!"

Having noticed that his robe was blue, the boy asked, "Sir, are you a Bonpo?" The Lama replied, saying, "I am not even recognizable as such!."

"Sir, there are no shoes on your feet. Will you put on my shoes?" the boy inquired. Having declined to put on the boy's shoes, the Lama said, "Whatever I wear now is just enough for me."

At that point the boy decided that the hermit must be a Bonpo sage and developed very great faith in the master. He went to fetch an animal hide to serve as a seat and offering it to the master, he requested initiation, saying, "May I make a request for empowerment?" [50]

Then the Lama observed, "You already have a hat suitable for the initiation and the hair for initiation. Are you a Bonpo?"

42. Lhundrub Muthur

"Yes, I am a Bonpo."

"If you are a Bonpo, how many other Bonpos are there where you come from?"

"We are all Bonpos. My parents are Bonpos also. I know only the virtuous practice that is Bon."

"Indeed, your parents are known to me, so then your request is proper!"

The boy then asked, "How did you actually come to meet my parents?"

"Your parents are known to me clairvoyantly, even though there does not exist the physical connection of meeting them in person. So, I will confer the initiation upon you in secret. But you must fetch the required items that are necessary for this."

The boy asked what these required items he needed to fetch might be. "You must fetch here a fresh sample of wine, a fresh sample of food, flowers of gold and silver, and some pieces of silk."

The boy Lhundrub Muthur returned the next day, bringing him the items required for the initiation ceremony, and entered again into the presence of the venerable Lama. Thereupon the master conferred the complete initiation upon him for Zhang-zhung Meri and gave him the instructions for the practice of the Secret Mantras. Thus, in this way, it came about that these marvelous instructions for the practice of Meri were preserved in the Tibetan language. Then, during the month of the horse, the two of them performed a Ganapuja and thereafter the Lama in the tattered blue robe mysteriously departed. [51]

But when Ponchen Lhundrub Muthur grew old, he expressed that he had three regrets. First, in his youth he was too easily satisfied with the teachings from his master Ponchen Tsanpo and regretted that he did not request more advanced teachings in detail (regarding Dzogchen), for which reason he was lacking the Precepts Transmission. Second, he did not spend more time in his youth practicing Dzogchen, the Upadeshas of Experience, rather than Tantra, and he regretted this lack. And third, he had only Tantric experiences of realization, having practiced the This-sngags, but his realization of the Natural State in terms of Dzogchen practice was not stable. Therefore, he did not realize the Rainbow Body of Light at the end of his life. Moreover, the duration of his life span is not told anywhere and the date of his death is unknown.

Then Muthur travelled to Yeru in Shang and also to the mountains of Yonpo where he practiced the teachings of the master. These were the special places where he resided. [52] In terms of the signs of realization and his virtuous qualities that were both ordinary and immediate, he was especially a practitioner of the Tantric deity Zhang-zhung Meri and because of this Tantric practice, he came to realize many siddhis. Thus, he became famous throughout the region as a Tantrika and a magician. Even the guardian deity Gyalpo Nyipangse and the lady Menmo became his servants while he lived alone in the mountains. He dedicated a white goat in honor of Nyipangse, which was an emanation of that deity, and so it was no longer necessary for him to follow the livelihood of a shepherd with regard to his goats and sheep. And because he raised a white female yak in honor of the goddess Menmo or Men Kuma (sMan ku-ma), it was no longer necessary for him to be a herdsman with regard to his yaks. The goat and the female yak looked after his herds of goats and yaks on the mountain side and so he had no need for human servants. [53]

He also held the lineage for the practice of Tswo or magical missiles of several kinds and he was known to be very powerful with regard to this practice. Moreover, he could shoot red magical missiles into the sky like they were arrows. [54] Indeed, he manifested various signs of realization such as these. However, he never showed his precious secret bTswo-dpe, or grimoire text, to anyone, but kept it safely hidden in a small silver tube tied up in the knot of hair on the crown of his head. Because he did not sufficiently practice Dzogchen in order to realize the Rainbow Body, when he died, his body was cremated according to custom of the country and inadvertently the magical text he wore in his hair was destroyed in the funeral fire. In this way, the practice lineage for Tso (btswo), or magical missiles, came to an end and is no longer performed today.

And in terms of his extraordinary understanding which ultimately became manifest, even though he had received the Upadeshas for the Experiential Transmission of the previous masters from his own master Ponchen Tsanpo, he principally practiced the Secret Mantras. Because of the fierce intensity of his practice, his own body assumed the form of his meditation deity, which at times became visible to all, and it was said that he became non-dual with the Sambhogakaya. [55]

2. Shengyal Yungdrung Lhatse

Shengyal Yungdrung Lhatse (gShen-rgyal g.yung-drung lha-rtse) was not only the disciple of the preceding master, Lhundrub Muthur, but his good spiritual friend and fellow disciple under their master Ponchen Tsanpo. [56] He also was a native-born Tibetan, as were those who came after him in this lineage in Northern Tibet. His father was Shen Barwa Langnak (gShen 'bar-ba glang-nag); however, his mother died when he was only a small child. His new step-mother was very cruel to him, so at the age of thirteen, the boy ran away from home and thought to seek out some sort of magic by which he could destroy her. He traveled about the countryside in Northern Tibet, living by begging for his food. Then one day, while playing dice with some other boys, he heard about the great Tantrika and magician named Lhundrub Muthur. He asked where he might find this Tantric sorcerer from whom he wanted to learn black magic. One of the boys pointed to a high mountain valley, saying that the Tantric Lama lived there. They told him in hushed tones that this Lama possessed very great magical powers (mthu-che). For example, he owned a great white yak who tended his herds without any need for a human herdsman. His flocks of sheep and goats were similarly tended by a white goat. Moreover, he was able to shoot down his enemies with a red magical missile that flew straight like an arrow. [57] But when the boy decided to seek out this Tantric sorcerer, the other boys refused to go with him out of fear. They warned him that in the valley above lived two gigantic Tibetan dogs, which kept everyone away because of the danger of being killed and eaten by them. They advised him to wait in hiding where the Lama would fetch water at the spring.

Doing so, the runaway boy met a beautiful nomad woman who had indeed come there to fetch water. She asked the boy who he was

43. Shengyal Lhatse

and he, in turn, asked if he could work for her as her servant. The woman took him home to her hut on the mountain where he worked very hard and conscientiously for her for a long time, cleaning up the yak dung and carrying it on his back to the fields for manure. But he never came to meet the mysterious Tantrika Lhundrub Muthur. He knew this woman was somehow connected with the Lama. When he asked, she told him that the Lama was up on the mountain where he was practicing meditation and performing rituals together with his own master.

Because his good karma had ripened, he came to meet with the kindness and benevolence from both of his masters. Ponchen Tsanpo knew about the presence of this boy on the same mountain because of his powers of clairvoyant vision and he knew of the boy's intention to learn black magic in order to wreck vengeance upon and destroy his wicked step-mother. Lhundrub Muthur replied to the inquiry of his master that it would be easy to teach the boy the techniques of the magical missile in order to accomplish his aims. But Ponchen Tsanpo allowed the boy to work for the woman awhile longer because he understood that this boy was indeed a suitable vessel for the precepts of Dzogchen. Finally Lama Lhundrub returned to this woman and addressed the young boy who was serving her, "What is it you want of me?" The boy replied that he wanted to learn magic in order to destroy his evil stepmother who had caused him so much suffering. The Lama told him, "Your troubles with your stepmother are like the mixing of our yaks with the herd of our neighbor. So it will be no problem."

When the boy inquired where the master of this Lama was living, Lhundrub replied that he did not wish to speak of that as yet. But he told the boy that Lama Tsanpo possessed the Vidyadhara power of long life [58] and that he would meet him again in the month of the horse. At that time he would bring the boy with him because Ponchen Tsanpo had previously prophesied that Lhundrub Muthur would meet a Tibetan boy interested in magic and said that he should bring him along with him because he would be a suitable vessel (snod-ldan) to receive the instructions for Dzogchen.

When the horse month arrived, the Tantrika took the young boy to meet his master. Ponchen Tsanpo told the boy that he possessed a method that would turn his evil stepmother into his good friend and thereafter he gave the empowerment for Zhang-zhung Meri to the boy and bestowed upon him the special precepts for the Nyams-rgyud or Experiential Transmission. The boy practiced enthusiastically and diligently for a long time, thinking that he was doing magic. When he came to realize stability in the practice of contemplation that is the Natural State, the master asked him what he was thinking. He replied, "Nothing at all." The master explained to him that this was indeed very powerful magic for thereby he could destroy in his mind the concept of his evil stepmother. In this way, the boy Shengyal came to forget all about his original intention of vengeance. So, in this way it came about that the great Dzogchen master Ponchen Tsanpo had two principal Tibetan disciples, one a Tantric sorcerer and the other a runaway boy.

Ponchen Tsanpo delivered several more prophesies regarding this boy and, in particular, he foretold that in the future a patron would come to construct a hermitage for him and that would serve for the benefit of sentient beings generally. The master said, "You will find your hermitage at the mountain with the name of Yungdrung Lhatse and your patrons will be named Kyidbar (skyid 'bar) or the three Kyid brothers." [59] He also told the boy that he should always practice in the wild mountains and avoid going into the villages.

Then Ponchen Tsanpo explained his instructions concerning Dzogchen as follows, "In terms of Dzogchen, there are three considerations: One point is to recognize the existence (of the Natural State) that is the real meaning of the Great Perfection. One point is to just abide· in that condition of existence alone (which is contemplation). And one point is not to take the side either of its existence or non-existence. With regard to recognizing the existence (of the Natural State), this same instruction has been given by all the realized Siddhas of the past. With regard to abiding just in that condition of existence (which is the state of contemplation), this indeed is what is indicated by all the profound Precepts Transmissions that are found in the treasure texts. And with regard to not abiding in the existence nor non-existence (of the Natural State and thereby avoiding the two extremes), this is elucidated by way of the activities of the mind (that is, by way of research and investigation). When one speaks of the Base and the Path without reference to the Oral

The Targo mountain range (rta-sgo gangs ri) seen from across the Dangra Lake (dang-ra g.yu mtsho). Courtesy of John Vincent Bellezza.

Transmission, this speaking aloud about the Base is like the buzzing of small insects and this speaking aloud about the Path is like the chattering of a Jyati bird searching for its nest. But when one speaks about the experiences in meditation of the Siddhas, that is like having in one's hand a polished nugget of gold!" [60]

With that the master Ponchen Tsanpo transformed himself before the very eyes of the astonished boy into the form of a turquoise-colored cuckoo bird and departed through the clear empty sky to the distant country of Tazik where he set about to subdue the Rakshasa demons who resided there. [61]

As his understanding matured, Shengyal realized the illusory nature of all appearances and abandoned all attachments to worldly concerns. He wandered about the rocks of Shang Shelrong (shangs shel-rong gi brag), practicing intensively over the course of three years. Thus, he came to realize non-duality with regard to friends and enemies and came to experience everything as having but a single taste. [62] At that time he came to compose a song regarding his experiences. [63]

Then one day, a herdsman with many animals met the boy as the latter was wandering about in the wild mountains. The herdsman noticed that the boy had no shoes. Thus, he offered the boy his own shoes. And recognizing that this boy was a disciple of the Ponchen, he generously offered to supply him with food and clothes. The following day the herdsman invited the boy to a small chapel (mchod khang), which he had previously erected and offered to serve him food there. But the boy refused, claiming that he was sick. When the herdsman

Targo Gegar (rta-sgo dge-gar), the highest peak in the Targo range. Courtesy of John Vincent Bellezza.

offered to fetch a doctor, the boy claimed he had an incurable leprosy. In this way, day after day the boy kept making excuses and avoided coming for a meal. The wealthy herdsman did not believe these excuses and, gathering his kinsmen, he came with them and caught the wild boy, taking him by force to the chapel he had prepared. The boy tried to run away again, but he failed because he was well guarded at all times day and night by the herdsman and the members of his clan. Finally the wild boy acquiesced to this enforced hospitality when he realized that this wealthy herdsman and his brothers were the patrons that his master had foretold in the prophecy. Eventually his patrons, the three Kyidbar brothers, built him a larger hermitage at Ombo on the eastern shores of the Dang-ra lake at the foot of the mountain of Yungdrung Lhatse. For this reason the boy Shengyal became known as Shengyal Yungdrung Lhatse and his hermitage bore the same name. [64] All this coincided perfectly with the prophesies made by his master Ponchen Tsanpo. Shengyal lived there for a long time, supported by the donations of the people of the village who were his patrons.

In the tenth century, Shengyal was also the contemporary of the great Buddhist master and scholar of the Nyingmapa school, Zurpoche Shakya Jyungne (Zur-po-che Shakya 'byung-gnas). This master had been wandering about Western and Northern Tibet in search of obscure lineages and fragments of the Dzogchen teachings. One night he came secretly to Shengyal in his hermitage at Yungdrung Lhatse and, after making prostrations and presenting offerings, he requested the transmission of the Dzogchen teachings that he had been unable to obtain from any other source. In time the two masters became great friends. But there was some bad talk locally about a Buddhist scholar taking teachings from a Bonpo Lama, and so Zurpoche asked permission to change the proper names occurring in the teachings, although he would preserve the real meaning of the texts without distortions. The Bonpo master readily agreed to this. Therefore, in this way, these Dzogchen teachings of Ponchen Tsanpo came to receive the name of Rig-pa'i khu-byug, because that master had transformed himself into the form of a turquoise blue cuckoo bird and disappeared into the sky. And instead of citing the Bonpo master Ponchen Tsanpo as the source, he gave to these teachings an Indian Buddhist background to make this Dzogchen transmission acceptable to the Buddhists generally. Thereby he disguised the identities of both Pochen Tsanpo and Lama Shengyal. From Zurpoche, the transmission went to his kinsman Zurchungpa, to the latter's son Drobugpa, and finally to Rangzom Pandita, the great Nyingmapa scholar. Thus, it is asserted by the Bonpos that the Dzogchen teachings of the Zhang-zhung master Ponchen Tsanpo became part of the Dzogchen transmission of the Nyingmapa school of Tibetan Buddhism as well. [65]

Shengyal Yungdrung Lhatse lived to the advanced age of one hundred and thirteen years, exhibiting many signs of his realization, which were both ordinary and extraordinary. In terms of his immediate and ordinary attainments, the obtained the blessing of the Siddhas of the past without effort and he was attended by all the races of the female spirits of existence, such as Kongtsun Demo and Menmo Kuma, as his servants. Moreover, all of the races of the male deities of existence attended him as well, such as Tise Lagring, the king of the northeast direction, who promised to perform those actions of the master concerning the teachings that had not yet been realized. [66] The four castes among the black Nagas equally promised to perform those actions he had not yet realized. It was said that just a minute piece of his garment could prevent infant deaths (sri'u) at home and equally preserve beer and yogurt from not rising properly. Soil or small pebbles from a place where he had stayed could prevent hail-storms and diseases. He could drink poisoned water like it was beer and he could dispatch golden magical missiles like arrows. [67] Indeed, he displayed such signs of realization (grub rtags) as these. And having received the Upadeshas of the experiences of the past masters, at the time when he gained understanding of the Natural State, he simultaneously realized liberation.

3. Lomting Lhagom Karpo

Lomting Lhagom Karpo (Lom-ting lha-sgom dkar-po) was the son of Lomting Atsara who belonged to the Or clan and who was very learned in the Bon of Causes and Appellations. [68] He began practicing with his father at a young age the rituals of a village priest, performing rituals that aimed at securing immediate worldly benefits. But when he was eight years old, he announced to his father that he no longer wanted to learn the worldly rituals of the village, which he called the Bon of dogs (khyi bon grong chog). Angered at this, his father cuffed

44. Lhagom Karpo

him on the cheek and told him that the performance of these rituals would give him the power of a king. But if the boy did not want to practice the Bon of the village (grong bon), then he could practice the Bon of the tigers (stag bon).

Thereafter he studied diligently with other teachers for thirteen years and by the age of twenty-three he had become very learned. At that time he loaded two horses with raw sugar and went to one of his patrons at Na-re. Along the way he stayed for the night with an old couple and at daybreak, the old man said to his wife, "He is leaving. Give him some beer and let him go to Yungdrung Lhatse and make some offerings." The young man, now curious, asked who was the Lama that resided on that mountain and the old man replied that the Lama was also called Yungdrung Lhatse and that he was a Nirmanakaya. Just by hearing this name, the flesh of the young man began to tingle and he developed a passionate faith in that Lama. Coming into the presence of the master at the latter's hermitage, he made some polite expressions and presented him with offerings of a seat made of two rolls of cloth and a large turquoise. In addition, he offered the two horses and the load of raw sugar.

The Lama inquired what he wanted and the young man requested an initiation. The Lama entered for a moment into the state of samadhi and saw that indeed this was a disciple who was a suitable vessel for the teachings. Thereupon the Lama announced, "The master who possesses the nectar (which is the understanding of the Natural State) should bestow this upon a disciple who is the proper vessel. Therefore, I shall perform the ritual for conferring upon you the empowerment for the Mahamudra!" And so saying, he waved his hand three times over the head of the young man. [69] During the course of the next three years, the master bestowed upon Lhagom all the instructions for both the Secret Mantras and Dzogchen. Then the Lama said to him, "According to the scriptural system for this teaching, there are five examinations of the disciple to be made: the examination of the marks on his flesh, the examination of his name, the examination of the complexion of his flesh, the examination of his conduct, and the examination of his dreams. You now possess in their perfection all five of these characteristics." [70] Therefore, the Lama agreed to bestow upon Lhagom all of the secret instructions that he possessed. Thereupon Lhagom offered whatever he had to his Lama. Having now reached the age of thirty, Lomting Gomchen entered into his own hermitage for retreat, supported by his parents.

It was said that thereafter Lhagom, having contemplated that the meaning of Shunyata, or emptiness, does not abide anywhere with partiality, mostly wandered about the country side without partiality. [71] But for his special place of practice, he went to live in isolation at the white slate mountain of Hakhyu Yakya (hag-khyu g.ya'-skya). And because of the strength of the promise made in the presence of his master, he also resided for a time at the lion cave of Paro Taktsang (spa-gro stag-tshang) in Bhutan and at the rock cave where the stone staircase ascends to the sky near the Dang-ra lake in Northern Tibet. [72]

Externally he displayed the signs of his realization such as gathering the five elements under his power, controlling them perfectly so as to assume all manner of appearances. And internally, he showed the signs of his realization by gathering both human beings and non-human spirits under his power. He subdued the worldly gods and the demons, both the males and the females, commanding them as his servants, [73] and they listened to him preach Bon like they were human children. And having received the instructions from his Lama concerning the experiences of the previous masters, at the lion cave of Paro Taktsang he attained liberation and an unchanging understanding with regard to the Primordial State of Buddhahood. [74] At the narrow gorge of the female red dog (Khyi-mo dmar-mo'i 'phrang), having attained the age of ninety-seven, he passed away into Nirvana.

4. Ngodrub Gyaltsan Ringmo

Ngodrub Gyaltsan Ringmo (dNgos-grub rgyal-mtshan ring-mo) was the second among the four sons of Or-bon Lhabum ('Or bon lha-'bum), also known as Lomting Lhatse (Lom-ting lha-rtse), and of Menmo Chosse (Men-mo chos-se). [75] At a very young age he displayed evidence of a keen interest concerning the practical instructions from the cycle of teachings for the meditation deity Meri (me-ri'i gdams-pa). Moreover, he was motivated by a good disposition toward others and because of that, the local patrons showed him their respect. He rid

45. Ngodrub Gyaltsan Ringmo

himself of all attachments to appearances and requested from his father the instructions to permit him to transcend birth and death.

But his father was displeased with him and replied, "The definitive character of my wife is one load of buckwheat grain, whereas the definitive character of you, my son, is to be possessed by a malignant Gongpo spirit! It will be difficult for you to attain Buddhahood in this present life. So I will not give you what you ask. It will be better for you to practice according to the instructions of the Mantras. I have performed divination with scapula. I know what will occur to you by way of scapula and skrying. You will have horsemen and cattle that are white, red, and multicolored standing at your gate. That is your study!" [76]

But the young man protested, "You are the only Lama who has this oral transmission of Bon. If you will not give it to me, I will seek out and request the oral transmissions from the Buddhists!" [77] Thereupon his father reluctantly gave him the two measures of gold that he had received from Gomchen Rinchenbar (sGom-chen rin-chen 'bar) for performing a ceremony and arrogantly dismissed his son.

The young man went home and sold his family's field, giving three measures of gold and a load of wool to his wife. He told her that he was leaving in order to pursue his studies and that she would have to carry on with the farm and look after their child. Coming into the presence of Gyaphugpa [78] he studied Buddhist logic and epistemology. And in the presence of Chechungwa, the Shangpa of Zhathak, he listened to the Buddhist teaching known as the *rDzogs-pa chen-po nam-mkha'-che.* [79]

At that time, his father Lama Lhagom reconsidered the matter and thought to re-examine the marks of his son in order to see if he truly was a suitable vessel to receive the Dzogchen transmission. He instructed the latter's wife and son to seek out Ngodrub Gyaltsan. She shaved the head of her son and she donned a yellow robe so that they might resemble the Buddhists. However, the old Lama gave her his own blue robe (sngo bem) as a sign that now he would grant the instructions to his son that had been originally requested.

The mother and son went to various Buddhist monasteries in Central Tibet in search of him. At one such monastery they saw a group of monks making prostrations and they recognized that one of them was Ngodrup Gyaltsan. When confronted, he inquired after his father and was told that now he would grant the instructions he sought because the time had come for this. They showed him the blue robe as proof and now believing them, he returned home.

Arriving there, the Lama and his son had some philosophical discussions, but the son was not able to overcome his father in debate. Lama Lhagom replied, "What you have now is only partial. Therefore, it is of little benefit. You are not able to overcome me in debate. I have asked a question that you cannot answer. Anger has subdued you and the fool has no reply!"

Thereupon all of the instructions for Dzogchen according to the Zhang-zhung tradition were bestowed upon him. Lama Lhagom once explained, "When I made an examination of Ngodrub Gyaltsan, externally he was smooth, but internally he was tense and rigid. Nevertheless, he was intelligent and he had little desire. He was diligent in his studies and he had the capacity to concentrate. His discursiveness was small, but his analytical abilities were great. Although he appeared to be at leisure, he possessed great diligence. Therefore, he was a suitable vessel for the teachings!" Even his name reflected this character.

However, in order to avoid the envy of others, they retired together into the mountains. Arriving at a level place beside a gray slate boulder, [80] the father and his son resided there in separate small huts. During the day his father extensively instructed his son in the teachings of Bon, but during the night the Lama expounded the secret teachings to a multitude of assembled non-human spirits. This privilege accorded to these non-human spirits elicited the jealousy of his human disciple and Ngodrub hid himself in order to listen to the teachings.

But the Lama discovered his son's deception and irritably confronted him in the morning, telling him that the spirits had complained that a human had been listening the previous night. The Lama told his son to bathe and purify himself and thereafter he permitted his son to listen to the nocturnal teachings. One day when the snow had fallen on the mountainside, the Lama sang a song concerning Dzogchen (rdzogs-chen gyi mgur) and Ngodrub Gyaltsan immediately realized the full measure of understanding.

In the wake of that experience, the Lama sent his son into an isolated retreat at the cave of Rongjya Lagtsang, [81] where he cultivated realization over the course of seven months and within him there arose a special full measure of understanding of the Natural State. Then Ngodrub Gyaltsan wandered about the country side, practicing at different sites in the region, and brought great benefits to the local people who were his patrons. Because the intensity of his practice, the virtuous qualities of his purification of mind and the full measure of his extraordinary understanding in meditation became manifest. And having received the oral instructions from his Lama, he said regarding the Kunzhi which is the Nature of Mind (kun-gzhi sems), "However people may see me, I have happiness of mind!"

At the end of his life, he entered into the Primordial State of Buddhahood [82] and thereupon, by way of the instructions for the Unification of the Four Cognitions (ye-shes bzhi sbyor gyi gdams-pa), he separated his Awareness from the materiality of his body. [83] He died at the age of seventy-three.

5. Orgom Kundul

As for Orgom Kundul ('Or-sgom kun-'dul), his father was Or-bon Tonpa Gyalwase ('Or-bon ston-pa rgyal-ba gsas), who belonged to the Or clan, (gdung-rus 'or) and his mother was Khyungjyidza Jyangchubdron (Khyung-byid-za Byang-chub sgron). When he was thirteen years old, he studied the Mantras (sngags) and the Mind Section or Dzogchen (sems-phyogs) under the master Lharje Menyak (Lha-rje me-nyag). Then at the age of nineteen, because was the nephew (dbon-po) of that Lama, he met Ngodrub Gyaltsan and received the instructions for the Oral Transmission from Zhang-zhung. He listened to these from the beginning of the spring and by the end of the autumn, he had completed his studies and integrated the meaning of all the words into his mind-stream without error. For some time he continued to reflect upon them.

46. Orgom Kundul

At one time he was meditating in the burrow of a marmot [84] were he engaged himself in these reflections, when the non-human spirits came upon him and caused disturbances by not showing the heads of their bodies. They tried to test him in this way, but he showed no fear. Then, when he and his Lama were performing a Ganapuja, he sang the song of his experiences, [85] which delighted the heart of his master who thereupon exclaimed, "I have taught to you all of the meanings of the words that I know! Now it is up to you whether to practice or not. You have your own self-knowledge!" [86]

He lived for a time and practiced in a small chapel (mchod khang) and later in the hermitage Rangthang Kyurmo (Rang-thang skyur-mo) where his meditation practice benefited his patrons. In particular, he practiced and perfected within himself the Tantric teachings of the Mantras for Zhang-zhung Meri and the Mind Teachings of Dzogchen. [87] However, there were not many Bonpos who came to him for teachings. A Buddhist scholar named Geshe Terawa listened to him expound the Dzogchen teachings in secret and also Marmen Kunne (Mar-sman kun-ne), the Buddhist nun, followed his teachings. A Buddhist yogin from Rutod offered him flowers similar to gold and followed him, requesting the teachings. But all of them were Buddhists [88]

At a later time, two Khampas from Dokham or Eastern Tibet came to him and requested the texts of the teachings. To this request the master replied, saying, "In terms of the transmission of the real meaning (of Dzogchen) that cuts through all doubts, since it has not been contaminated previously by being set down in writing, it has not yet been written down. But because this has been already requested by Yangton, he and I have written down some notes from memory. Apart from these notes, we have no texts, not even as much as the tongue of a dog." [89]

Thereupon the three scribes (bris-mkhan gsum), Yangton and the two men from Kham, began to write down what the master explained orally and within twenty days they had set down in writing some one hundred and twenty folia, each page containing thirteen lines. Previously, Orgom had retained all of these Upadeshas as oral texts in this memory without forgetting any of them. Later Yangton transmitted these texts to his sons and his grandson. And so, these instructions, but only in part, were transcribed and written down by Yangton Sherab Gyaltsan.

As for Orgom himself, he displayed all the signs of being a Nirmanakaya. His ordinary siddhis, his virtuous qualities, and the signs of his realization were various and he realized extraordinary meditation experiences. In particular, he displayed manifest realization of both Dzogchen and the Mantras of Zhang-zhung Meri. [90] His life flowed without hindrances and he ultimately realized the benefit of beings. Being unattired in any adventitious taints, his clairvoyance and his mental state were clear and without obstructions. [91] Having received the Upadeshas for the meditation experiences of the previous masters, he realized within himself the essence of Buddhahood. [92] He became a yogin who was literally liberated into the sky. In this way, Orgom lived to eighty years of age.

The Transmission of the Precepts: The Six Masters of the System of Upper Zhang-zhung

Ponchen Tsanpo translated the Dzogchen teaching of the Experiential Transmission from the Zhang-zhung language into the Tibetan language in order to transmit them to his two Tibetan disciples, the Tantric magician Lhundrub Muthur and the runaway boy Shengyal Lhatse. Then afterwards the line of the transmission split for a time into two separate lineages. The former had taught only the Experiential Transmission to his Tibetan disciples in Lower Zhang-zhung, the lake country in Northern Tibet. Then, while the master resided in the upper country of Western Tibet near Mount Kailas, in the districts of Guge and Puhrang, he transmitted the Four Cycles of the Precepts Transmission (bka' brgyud skor bzhi), but not the Experiential Transmission (nyams brgyud). This second lineage, became known as the System of Upper Zhang-zhung (stod lugs) and was represented by six masters (stod lugs kyi bla-ma drug), who were as follows:

1. Guge Sherab Lodan (Gu-ge shes-rab blo-ldan),
2. Purang Kunga Ringmo (Pu-hrang kun-dga' ring-mo),
3. Naljyor Sechok (rNal-'byor gsas-mchog),
4. Khyungjyid Muthur (Khyung-byid mu-thur),

5. Tsi Dewa Ringmo (rTsi bde-ba ring-mo),
6. Rong Togmed Zhigpo (rTog-med zhig-po).

1. Guge Sherab Lodan

Sherab Lodan (Shes-rab blo-ldan) was born in Nangkong in the region of Guge in Western Tibet and belonged to the Nyel (snyel) clan. [93] In his youth, he spent his days working as a goat-herder and during this time he frequently experienced a cuckoo speaking to him in his visions and dreams. [94] Then one day, he actually saw a cuckoo come to earth nearby and with his curiosity aroused, he went to investigate. There he met a mysterious yogin in a tattered blue robe wearing a hermit's blue hat. This was none other than Ponchen Tsanpo. Because this boy displayed all the requisite signs,

47. Guge Sherab Lodan

the master gave him initiation and the instructions for the Precepts Transmission. The master said to the boy, "If you leave everything just as it is, you will go to where there is happiness. I have not found anything other than that. You should examine and investigate this!" [95] Thereafter the master transformed himself into a turquoise blue cuckoo bird and departed once more into the southwest direction, amidst a great display of sounds and lights, in order to subdue the Rakshasa demons who lived on an island in the great southern ocean.

Sherab Lodan practiced meditation in the villages and retreat places of Guge. Being exceedingly intelligent and aware, he swiftly attained enlightenment through the practice of the Dzogchen teachings of his master.

2. Puhrang Kunga Ringmo

Kunga Ringmo (Kun-dga' ring-mo) was born in the Puhrang district of Western Tibet and he belonged to the Tongpa clan. [96] Even from an early age, he was inclined toward the practice of Bon and he learned to read and write. From Guge Sherab Lodan he obtained the instructions of the Precepts Transmission. The master said to him, "Without emanating or re-absorbing anything (in terms of thoughts), leave everything just as it is in its original condition; that is the practice!" [97] Practicing in this way for only a month, he attained realization. He dwelt mainly around the great glacial mountain of Tise (Mount Kailas) and the two lakes of Ma-pang and Lag-ngar, [98] as well as at Rin-khung in western Puhrang. His place of practice among the rocks on the glacial mountain of Nag-nyel-gang (nag-snyel-gangs) can still be seen.

48. Purang Kunga Ringmo

3. Naljyor Sechok

Because he was a Nirmita or emanation, it is said that the yogin Sechok (rNal-'byor gsas-mchog) possessed neither parents nor an actual place of birth. Some sources identify him as an aspect of Tsewang Rigdzin, the great sage of ancient Zhang-zhung, who realized the power of long life (tshe-dbang) and, therefore, it is said that, even until this very day, he has not died.

Nevertheless, he obtained the Precepts Transmission from Kunga Ringmo. The master said to him, "All things both external and internal will eventually dissolve into self-liberation; I have definitively decided that it is just like that." [99] Naljyor Sechok meditated on this assertion for eighty-five days and thereby gained full confidence in his own understanding of the Natural State. He never resided at any particular place, but mysteriously wandered about everywhere, displaying many miraculous signs. Finally he just disappeared without dying.

49. Naljyor Sechok

4. Khyungjyid Muthur

Khyungjyid Muthur (Khyung-byid mu-thur) came from Droshod (Gro-shod) and belonged to the Khyungpo clan. [100] When he met Naljyor Sechok, the master said to him, "By examining the real meaning and not making any deliberate efforts of body, speech, or mind, I came to understand that discursive thoughts could not disturb my contemplation!" [101] Khyungjyid Muthur heard this and developed a confident belief that was without any traces of doubt in

50. Khyungjyid Muthur

it. Therefore, he had perfect confidence in his own understanding of the Natural State. He became a great yogin without any particular place of practice.

5. Tsi Dewa Ringmo

Tsi Dewa Ringmo (rTsi bde-ba ring-mo) also came from Droshod and belonged to the Khyungpo clan as well. When he met his master, the latter said to him, "Because I know that appearance and emptiness are inseparable, I can subdue both of them!" [102] Dewa Ringmo immediately understood this and entering into the practice and thereby he realized a total confidence. [103] He mostly lived at the Gangzang (gang-bzang) mountain in the upper direction of the west.

51. Tsi Dewa Ringmo

6. Rong Togmed Zhigpo

Rong Togmed Zhigpo (Rong rtog-med zhig-po) came from the upper or western part of Lo and he belonged to the Rongpo clan. [104] When he met his master, the latter imparted to him the Precepts Transmission. The master said to him, "When I gazed into the radiance of my own intrinsic Awareness, without fixating the mind on it, I came to a definitive decision with regard to its existence!" [105] Togmed Zhigpo immediately understood the meaning of these words and, continuing in his meditation, he gained full confidence in his understanding. For most of his life he lived in the cave of Bonkhor in the valley of Yezur in Upper Lo, without emerging from retreat. [106] He developed clairvoyant vision as a sign of his realization.

It was the great achievement of Yangton Sherab Gyaltsan to reunite these two lineages and his story is told in the next chapter.

52. Rong Togmed Zhigpo

CHAPTER 9

The Later History of the Transmission

The Northern Lineage and the Southern Lineage

As was said, these two lineages of the Experiential Transmission (nyams rgyud) and the Precepts Transmission (bka' brgyud) were reunited in the person of Yangton Chenpo Sherab Gyaltsan. But immediately after Yangton Chenpo, the transmission divided again, this time into the Northern Lineage (byang brgyud) and into the Southern Lineage (lho brgyud). The Northern Lineage begins with his disciple Lunggom Togmed, whereas the Southern Lineage begins with the names of his two sons Dampa Bumje and Tashi Gyaltsan and with that of his grandson Yeshe Gyaltsan. [1]

Yangton Chenpo Sherab Gyaltsan

His father was Ya-ngal Sungrabkyab (Ya-ngal gsung-rab skyabs) and his mother was Nyimo Chokyid (sNyi-mo chos-skyid). Moreover, he possessed four names. Because his father died only thirty days after his birth, he was called Tsabma (Tshab-ma), which means regent or representative. Because he belonged to the Ya-ngal clan, which could be abbreviated as Yang, he later became known as Yangton Chenpo (Yang-ston chen-po), which means the great teacher from the Ya-ngal clan. [2] Because it had been predicted in a prophecy that he would be the reincarnation of the ancient Bonpo sage Pangla Namshen (sPang-la nam-gshen), he was also called by this name. But his actual name was Sherab Gyaltsan (Shes-rab rgyal-mtshan).

Until the age of twenty, he studied under a number of very learned practitioners (mkhas grub) such as Druchen Yungdrung Lama (Bru-chen g.Yung-drung bla-ma), the first abbot of the famous Bonpo

53. Yangton Chenpo Sherab Gyaltsan

monastery of Yeru Wensakha (Ye-ru'i dben-sa-kha), and Meuton Lhari Nyenpo (rMe'u-ston Lha-ri gnyen-po), a very important master for the diffusion of the teachings of *A-khrid* system of Dzogchen. [3] Sherab Gyaltsan also studied Pramana, Madhyamaka, and Prajnaparamita under the celebrated Buddhist master Bari Lotsawa. [4] He used to sit in the midst of the Buddhist monks and debate with them. But because they were not able to defeat him, they used to say, "This Bonpo has a sharp tongue, but we cannot accept what he says!" [5] At the age of twenty-seven, he took two wives, but did not have any children by them. He practiced intensively various Bonpo Tantric teachings and, as a consequence, he became renowned for the power of his magic and for his blessings. He became very learned in the Termas containing the instructions for the transmission of the explanations. [6] And it is said that at that time he interiorized the complete teachings of thirteen cycles of revealed treasure texts. [7] Thereby he lost all attachments to the reality of worldly appearances and understood that they merely represented illusions that were false displays. He looked upon these appearances as being just mirages. He was drawn very much to the ascetic life and would go up into the mountains alone and do vision practice, gazing into the vast spaces of the sky. At that time, he had many extraordinary visions and experiences. In particular, he had clear visions of Ponchen Tsanpo who actually spoke to him. He received numerous instructions and prophesies from that master which he kept secret at the time.

Then at one time he entered into a conversation with Sebon Trogyal (Se-bon khro-rgyal) and they discussed the teachings in terms of the real meaning of the thirteen essential points contained in thirteen chapters. [8] Yangton Sherab Gyaltsan was astonished at this and inquired from where he had acquired the texts of these chapters. The Lama replied that he got them from another Lama holding a lineage of divine origin whose name was Orbon Kundul. [9] Thinking that this Lama possessed what he himself lacked, without much delay Sherab Gyaltsan went into the presence of Lama Orgom, but the master said to him, "If you are not satisfied with the ocean, how can you be satisfied with only the eyes of a fish?" But Shesrab Gyaltsan persisted and the Lama recognized that in his future awakening this man would have a great capacity for the Tantric practice of Zhang-zhung Meri. The master bestowed upon him the principles of Dzogchen with a symbolic gesture, saying, "The Mother Garuda and the Child Garuda fly together in the sky; they are not supported by anything whatsoever and they do not touch anything with their wings." The master employed a number of other skillful methods by way of direct introduction to the Natural State. The latter perfectly integrated the words of Orgom Kundul into his stream of his consciousness. First the master conferred upon him the Lower System for the Oral Transmission (snyan-rgyud smad lugs) and then the Upper System for the Oral Transmission (snyan-rgyud stod lugs), both of which had been inaugurated by Ponchen Tsanpo. [10] Thus, over the course of three and a half months, he wrote down whatever he heard of the extensive and the condensed versions of the Experiential Transmission. [11]

His Lama then uttered a prophecy, saying that he should go to Western Tibet where he would find his disciples who would be his children and his grand children. [12] At Kyaru in Western Tibet he built his hermitage of Kyaru Gonpa (skya ru dgon-pa) and later he went to Western Lo (glo stod) in Mustang located in modern day Nepal. And hearing it said that the hermit Rong Togmed Zhigpo (Rong rtog-med zhig-po) never looks upon the sun and the moon because he never leaves his retreat, he made inquiries regarding this Lama and was told that he had attained realization through the Dzogchen practices of the Zhang-zhung Nyan-gyud. [13] The cave where Togmed Zhigpo resided was pointed out to him, and having heard all this, he developed great faith in this master who was the last in this line of the Upper System (stod lugs). He made preparations to go the next day and perform a Ganapuja at which he would request the transmissions. That night, Togmed Zhigpo had a dream where a Dakini appeared to him, telling him that an emanation of Pangla Namshen [14] himself was coming to him to seek instruction in the Zhang-zhung Nyan-gyud. Later that night, he had a second dream of a Bonpo attired as a Tantrika (bon-po sngags-pa) with long hair, but part of it tied up in a knot. The very next day Sherab Gyaltsan himself came to his hermitage, looking exactly like the Tantrika in the dream.

Sherab Gyaltsan told the master that he had already received teachings for the Zhang-zhung Nyan-gyud and the Mantras for Zhang-zhung Meri. But the master replied that what the former had received so far was only the Experiential Transmissions and the Mantras, which was fine in itself, but what he himself possessed was the entire *bKa'-rgyud bzhi skor* that had come down from Ponchen Tsanpo and Guge Sherab Lodan. However, the first cycle, the *lTa-ba spyi-gcod*, he had already taught to Lunggom Togmed (Lung-sgom rtog-med) and so Sherab Gyaltsan would have to obtain the transmission from him since it represented a single transmission to one disciple only (gcig-rgyud). Nevertheless, Togmed Zhigpo bestowed upon Sherab Gyaltsan the remaining three cycles of secret oral instructions of the Precepts Transmission.

Sherab Gyaltsan practiced wherever he went, transforming with his meditation every site were he stayed into a divine celestial palace of the Sugatas. He exhibited many signs of realization (grub rtags) and magical powers (mthu rtsal). In a vision that came to the Khandro Yeshesal, [15] he appeared as a Vidyadhara who removed all obstacles and gave guidance on the spiritual path. In his previous life, he had been the son of a king and so, in his present life, he came to meet with innumerable accomplished Lamas. Having received the instructions for the Experiential Transmission from his masters, at no place or time was he separated from that unchanging dimension that is the Natural State. [16]

It was largely due to Yangton Chenpo Sherab Gyaltsan that we have the texts of the Zhang-zhung Nyan -gyud in their present form. He taught the Experiential Transmission in its extensive version (nyams brgyud rgyas-pa) only to certain individuals among his disciples. To others he taught the intermediate version ('bring-po so-bzhag), and to yet others he taught the highly condensed version (chung-ba 'thor-bu). These three versions came to form three lines of transmission generally known as the Upper System (stod-lugs), the Lower System (smad-lugs), and the Intermediate System (bar-lugs). Then, in accordance with a previous prophecy, Yangton died at the age of sixty-three. .

The lineages that followed Yangton Chenpo were as follows: The Nine Masters of the Northern Lineage of Transmission: (byang rgyud kyi bla-ma dgu)

1. Lunggom Togmed (Lung-sgom rtog-med),
2. Nyelgom Trulmed Zhigpo (sNyel-sgom 'khrul-med zhig-po),
3. Nyaggom Riwa Shertsul (gNyag-sgom ri-ba sher-tshul),
4. Uri Sonam Gyaltsan (U-ri bsod-nams rgyal-mtshan),
5. Sonam Yeshe (bSod-nams ye-shes),

6. Gyaton Yeshe Rinchen (rGya-ston ye-shes rin-chen),
7. Jyatangwa Tsultrim Zangpo (Bya-btang-ba tshul-khrims bzang-po),
8. Saleod Tsultrim Gyaltsan (Sa-le-'od tshul-khrims rgyal-mtshan),
9. Langton Sonam Gyaltsan (gLan-ston bsod-nams rgyal-mtshan).

The Eleven Masters of the Southern Lineage of Transmission:
(lho rgyud kyi bla-ma bcu-gcig)

1. Dampa Bumje Od (Dam-pa 'bum-rje 'od),
2. Ludragpa Tashi Gyaltsan (kLu-brag-pa bkra-shis rgyal-mtshan),
3. Togdan Wonpo Yeshe Gyaltsan (rTogs-ldan dbon-po ye-shes rgyal-mtshan),
4. Yangton Gyaltsan Rinchen (Yang-ston rgyal-mtshan rin-chen),
5. Chigchod Dadpa Sherab (gCig-chod dad-pa shes-rab),
6. Druchen Gyalwa Yungdrung (Bru-chen rgyal-ba g.yung-drung),
7. Latod Riwa Sherab Lodro (La-stod ri-ba shes-rab blo-gros),
8. Rangdrol Lama Gyaltsan (Rang-grol bla-ma rgyal-mtshan),
9. Athok Yeshe Gyaltsan (A-thog ye-shes rgyal-mtshan),
10. Kartsa Sonam Lodro (Kar-tsa bsod-nams blo-gros),
11. Paton Tan-gyal Zangpo (sPa-ston bstan-rgyal seng-ge bzang-po).

The latter was the author of the large hagiography text (rnam-thar chen-mo), translated in part here, entitled the *rDzogs-pa chen-po zhang-zhung snyan-rgyud kyi brgyud-pa'i bla-ma'i rnam-thar*, "the Hagiographies of the Masters of the Lineages for the Oral Transmission from Zhang-zhung for the Great Perfection Teachings." The colophon to this text states that the work was composed by Patsun Tan-gyal Senge Zangpo in the year 1299 at Latod in Tsang province. The list of masters in the lineage of transmission ceases, of course, with the name of the author, but some further names have been supplied in a series of lists compliled by Lopon Tenzin Namdak. [17]

The Nine Masters of the Northern Lineage of Transmission:

1. Lunggom Togmed

Luggom Togmed (Lung-sgom rtog-med) came from Tsang province and belonged to the Lung clan. Having met with the great kindness of

54. Lunggom Togmed

his teacher, he requested the *gSang-ba'i snying gtam tshig gsum* from Yangton Chenpo Sherab Gyaltsan and in turn transmitted the Outer Cycle of the Precepts Transmission, the *lTa-ba spyi-gcod*, to him. From Lama Trulmed Zhigpo ('Khrul-med zhig-po), who was at the same time his disciple, he obtained the instructions for the *Nyams-rgyud*. He lived mainly in mountain hermitages (ri-khrod) in Tsang province. He was free of all grasping and partialities and he displayed innumerable signs of of realization and magical powers [18] Remaining in retreat in his hermitage, there arose within his mind-stream the bliss of full confidence and his discovery of intrinsic Awareness was definitive. [19]

2. Nyelgom Trulmed Zhigpo

Nyelgom Trulmed Zhigpo (sNyel-som 'Khrul-med zhig-po), came from Shar-ri in Eastern or Lower Lo and belonged to the Nyel (snyel) clan. [20] These three masters, Yangton Chenpo, Lunggom Togmed, and Trulmed Zhigpo all taught each other and received teachings from each other. Coming to understand the illusory nature of all phenomena, he was free of all worldly desires and exhibited the signs of realization. He spent most of his life in isolated places and hermitages at Shar-ri in the region of Lo (Mustang). [21] He

55. Nyelgom Trulmed Zhigpo

exhibited inconceivable signs of realization and remained unattired in any worldly taints. He came to understand that all appearances were illusory. He used to say that, "Just leaving everything in its original condition is the essence of the real meaning (of the Natural State). One should know how to practice in that way!" [22] A confident belief and a definitive realization having been produced in his mind, he remained in his hermitage and persevered in his practice. And after only one year he attained full confidence in his understanding of the Natural State. [23]

3. Nyaggom Riwa Shertsul

Nyaggom Riwa Shertsul (gNyag-sgom ri-ba sher-tshul) came from Dang-ra Chyangon in Northern Tibet. [24] His belonged to the Nyak (gnyag) clan and his tribe was Gya (rgya). When he met both Lunggom Togmed and Nyelgom Trulmed Zhigpo, he was accepted as a disciple and received from them the complete Upadeshas of the Four Cycles of the Precepts Transmission. Having practiced them extensively, he developed clairvoyant powers (thugs shes) and even the non-human spirits attended him as his servants. He received from these spirits a

56. Nyaggom Riwa Shertsul

prophecy that foretold the coming of his disciple Uri from the east. At that time he resided on the great glacial mountain of Targo (sta-rgo) and in particular at the entrance of the Zephuk cave at Chyangon hermitage in the Dang-ra lake region. [25] He displayed many signs of realization. There arose in his mind-stream a confident belief and from further practice, he ultimately gained full confidence in his understanding of the Natural State.

4. Uri Sonam Gyaltsan

Uri Sonam Gyaltsan (U-ri bsod-nams rgyal-mtshan) was born in the region of Beri in Eastern Tibet and belonged to the Dang clan. [26] His father was named Argyal (A-rgyal) and his mother Draza Dronne (Gra-za sgron-ne). His mother died when he was only five years old and at the age of thirteen, because his father had many sons, he was permitted to become a monk and he received the monastic name of Sonam Gyaltsan. He studied the *Gab-pa dgu skor*, the *bsGrags-pa skor gsum*, and the *Srid-pa mdzod-phug*, that is, the texts of Dzogchen and

57. Uri Sonam Gyaltsan

cosmology respectively, with Lopon Reton (slob-dpon Ras-ston) and Bonzhik Lode (Bon-zhig blo-bde). At the age of thirty he went on pilgrimage to Mount Kailas and the two lakes. [27]

When Lama Riwa Shertsul was in retreat at the Zephuk cave, he had a dream in which a Dakini appeared to him and told him that Uri was his spiritual son. When the Lama's servant went to fetch water in the morning at a spring, he met Uri and took him to the entrance to the cave where the master resided. Accepting Uri as his disciple, the master put the young man into a one month retreat and bestowed upon him the full transmission for the Zhang-zhung tradition. Thereafter Uri returned to his native country of Beri in the east. Having already received the *Gab-pa* from Bonzhik Lode and now the entire *bKa'-rgyud* from Riwa Shertsul, he came to understand the identity of Samsara and Nirvana. He lived to the age of eighty-one and left behind many relics at his cremation.

Uri was not only a great meditator (sgom-chen), but also a scholar famous for his learning, having writen the *Nyi 'od rgyan* and the *Khrid rim gsal-ba'i me-long* among other texts. Among his disciples were Kontsa Tashidar (Kon-tsha bkra-shis-dar), Sonam Yeshe (bSod-nams ye-shes), and Matang Yurtse (Ma-tang g.yu-rtse). After having heard the secret teachings of his own Lama in Northern Tibet, within five months, all discursive thoughts that arose in him as memories dissolved into the state of Tathata (the Ultimate Reality) and he became liberated like a snake uncoiling its knots. Within his mind-stream there arose the primal cognition of understanding and he attained the ultimate realization. [28]

5. Sonam Yeshe

Sonam Yeshe (bSod-nams ye-shes) was born in the region of Darding in Tsang Province and belonged to the Nyel (snyel) clan and the Nya (snya) tribe. [29] When still a student, Sonam Yeshe was sent by his teacher Shenchen Yeshe Lodro (gShen-chen ye-shes blo-gros) to Lama Uri in Beri in Eastern Tibet and from the later he obtained the entire *bKa'-rgyud bzhi skor*, as well as the Experiential Transmission. He returned home from Beri to Darding and taught the Precepts Transmission to his own Lama, Shenchen Yeshe Lodro. Among the disciples of Sonam Yeshe was Mutowa Yeshe Rinchen (Mu-lto-ba Ye-shes rin-chen). Sonam Yeshe spent the remainder of his life practicing meditation and came to exhibit many signs of realization. When his master Lama Uri told him, "Just leave your mind in its own original condition and intrinsic Awareness will become separated from its support (the

58. Sonam Yeshe

thought process)," [30] he immediately understood the meaning and a confident belief regarding the Natural State was produced in his mind-stream. Having practiced extensively, he attained stability in the real meaning of the Natural State. [31]

6. Gyaton Yeshe Rinchen
As for Gyaton Yeshe Rinchen (rGya-ston ye-shes rin-chen), his region was Mechak (smad chags) and he was born in the valley of Walrong (dbal rong). His father was named Gyabon Trogom (rGya-bon khro-sgom) and belonged to the Gya (rgya) clan, while his mother was Kyamo Palkyong (sKya-mo dpal-skyong). He was the youngest of four children and they called him Trogyal (Khro-rgyal). Later, in the presence of Lenton Yeshe Senge (gLen-ston ye-shes seng-ge) he was ordained as a monk. And at the monastery of Laphuk (la-phug

59. Gyaton Yeshe Rinchen

dgon-pa), which was the seat of the Pa (gdung-rus spa) clan, he was initiated into the Tantric cycles of Trowo, Walphur, and Zhang-zhung

Meri. [32] At the age of twenty-seven, he studied with Kunkhyen
Yeshe Lodro of Darding (Dar-lding gi kun-mkhyen Ye-shes-blo-gros)
and with Lopon Bodongpa Zhonnu Losal (slob-dpon Bo-dong-pa
gzhon-nu blo-gsal), and later with Dronya Sonam Yeshe (sGro-snya
bsod-nams ye-shes) from whom he received the *bKa'-rgyud skor gsum*
and the *Nyams-rgyud*. He had visions of the Tantric meditation deity
Tsochok, who had a white body, and also visions of many Vidyadharas
and Dakinis. He became very learned in the Secret Mantras, as well as
in all Nine Vehicles of Bon.

He practiced meditation in many different holy places and places
of realization where he had many visionary experiences and displayed
the signs of heat. [33] But when he traveled to Darding again, he found
that his master, the great Shen Yeshe Lodro, had already died.
Therefore, he gave away all his worldly possessions and went into
retreat. Later, when he travelled westward to Laphuk monastery, he
discovered that his other teacher Pa Gyalwa Lodro (spa rgyal-ba blo-
gros) had also passed away. So he went to Gedrak (dge-brag) where he
practiced Chudlen [34] throughout the winter months, whereupon the
non-human spirits even transformed the sand into tsampa or roasted
barley flour for him to eat. And during the summer months he
continued to practice Chudlen, eating only nettles, while he stayed at
the hermitage of Lhadzong in Kyagya (rkya-rgya'i lha-rdzongs dgon-
pa). At the hermitage of Chubar (chu-bar gyi dgon-pa), he again
practiced Chudlen, this time for forty days, taking no food whatsoever
and drinking only water. Then at Kyagya Dzongri (skya-rgya'i rdzong-
ri) he was requested to establish a monastery there, but in reply he gave
only a discourse on compassion and impermanence. At the hermitage
of Zarkha (zar-kha dgon-pa) he engaged himself in ascetic practices
(dka'-spyod) for three years and obtained a vision thereby of the
Bonpo meditation deity Kunzang Akor (Kun-bzang A-skor). He
owned nothing of his own except for a tattered robe and a small bowl
for drinking. At the monastery of Lemi (dgon-pa sle-mi) in Shiri, he
performed a Ganachakrapuja together with Lama Paldan Senge (dPal-
ldan seng-ge) at which he sang a song concerning his ascetic practices,
whereafter he became known as the great ascetic (mu-lto-ba chen-po).

He lived mostly in the region around Mount Kailas and the two
lakes, but he also resided in the Tiger Valley (stag-rong). He
understood the real meaning of the Natural State and thereby
comprehended the Primordial State of Buddhahood. [35] He displayed
many signs of realization. For example, his mere presence could
overcome both humans and the non-human spirits, while his glance

could remove obstructions both external and internal. In particular, it is said that at the age of sixty years his white hair turned black and at age sixty-three he grew five new teeth. While he was staying at Chorten Borpo in Puhrang (pu-hrang gi mchod-rten 'bor-po), in the middle of the rays of light that appeared in the sky in front of him, he saw the vision of a white man who was like a white crystal. He was clear and radiant without any inside or outside. He realized that this was the Lord Tapihritsa and the Lord spoke to him, granting him many Upadeshas. [36]

When he was staying at the hermitage of Zurkhang (dben gnas zur-khang), his meditation deity Kunzang Akor [37] delivered a prophecy to him, saying that he must teach Bon to others. For that reason, he first taught Bon to Gurib Tsankyab (Gu-rib btsan-skyabs) and after that he took on many disciples. When he was at Droshod (gro-shod) in the West, he knew it was time for him to die. At a Ganachakrapuja, he expounded the Dzogchen teachings, as well as the hagiographies of the previous masters in the lineage (zhal-gdams rnam-thar) and at the age of eighty-five, he passed away. At his cremation, rainbows appeared in the sky and the earth itself trembled. But before he died, he said, "Because of letting everything abide in its spontaneous perfection without any thoughts (or evaluations) and remaining free from the duality of subject and object, I continued (in contemplation) without being connected or separated from anything. Therefore, I encountered directly the Mother who is the Natural State." [38] And moreover, because of his unceasing diligent practice, he encountered face to face the Nirmanakaya Tapihritsa himself. Thus, it came about that he was liberated into a state of total inactivity with regard to ordinary appearances wherein Samsara and Nirvana were experienced as being inseparable. [39]

7. Jyatangwa Tsultrim Zangpo

As for Jyatangwa Tsultrim Zangpo (Bya-btang-ba tshul-khrims bzang-po), his father was named Gurbon Tsankyab (Gur-bon btsan-bskyab) and his mother was Chagmo Chogge. He was born in the region of Kyagya (rkya-rgya) and he belonged to the Gurib clan. He was the older brother; his younger brother being Saleod Tsultrim Gyaltsan (Sa-le-'od tshul-khrims rgyal-mtshan). When he met his master Namdrol Yeshe Rinchen, [40] he requested the teachings for Dzogchen. Thereafter he became thoroughly disgusted with Samsara and went to his wife, telling her that now the endless round of rebirths terrified him and that he would like to become an ascetic (bya-bral) in order to obtain a better rebirth. He resolved to leave his wife and family and

60. Jyatangwa Tsultrim Zangpo

departed, taking with him only a few clothes and a sack of tsampa or roasted barley flour.

He wandered from place to place visiting many hermitages, monasteries, and holy places. When he return to his master, the latter was pleased to see that he had become a homeless yogin. Mainly he lived in the region of Mount Kailas and the two lakes of Mapang and Lag-ngar [41] where he practiced, taught, listened to, and meditated on the Mahayana. Among his many disciples Ugom Sonam Gyaltrul ('U-sgom bsod-nams rgyal-mtshan) and Lanton Sonam Gyaltsan (gLan-ston bsod-nams rgyal-mtshan) were the most prominent. He died sitting upright in meditation position in front of a pillar in the great cave of the Tiger Valley (stag rong gi phug-mo-che). Thus, he determined the time of his own death. Before his death, he advised his disciples, saying, "Just keep whatever self-arises unmodified and unadulterated; definitively deciding (upon the nature of) thoughts, you should practice contemplation." [42] Understanding and liberation were produced in his mind simultaneously.

8. Saleod Tsultrim Gyaltsan

Saleod Tsultrim Gyaltsan (Sa-le-'od tshul-khrims rgyal-mtshan) was the younger brother of Jyangtangwa above. He is included among the nine masters of the Northern Lineage, but he does not have a separate hagiography in the text here.

9. Lanton Sonam Gyaltsan

As for Lanton Sonam Gyaltsan (gLan-ston bsod-nams rgyal-

61. Saleod Tsultrim Gyaltsan

mtshan), his father was Lama Tsultrim Gyaltsan (Tshul-khrims rgyal-mtshan) and his mother was Wonmo Dzese who belonged to the famous Pa clan (sPa tshang gi dBon-mo mdzes-se). His place of birth was Nyanang Ladrang and clan was Lan, which belonged to the Zangtsa tribe. [43] An only son, from childhood he displayed a great discriminating wisdom and sharpness of intellect.

At the age of five, he was taken by Pa Paldan Zangpo (sPa dpal-ldan bzang-po) to Laphuk (la-phug), the famous monastic establishment of the Pa clan, where

62. Langton Sonam Gyaltsan

the Shen Sogyal Pal (gShen bsod-rgyal dpal) gave him his ordination name. Then, in the presence of Pa Paldan Zangpo and Treton Gyaltsan (Tre-ston rgyal-mtshan) he was ordained there as a monk. But at the age of eleven, his father died and so he was forced to return to his home and take over the affairs of his family. However, at the age of twenty, he went to the sand cave at Kharthab in Puhrang in Western Tibet (pu-hrang bye phug gi mkhar thabs) where he requested the Zhang-zhung Nyan-gyud from Lama Jyatangwa. There he experienced many visions and magical apparitions, but he definitively decided that all of them were merely creations of his own mind. Through consistently practicing meditation, a discriminating wisdom [44] arose within him and he developed great ability to expound the Bon teachings. Whereupon he came to be greatly respected by both the Bonpo and the Buddhist Geshes living in Western Tibet, such as Aya Jowo (A-ya jo-bo) of Puhrang and all the people of Lo, Dolpo, and the nomad region.

At the age of forty, he received empowerments from Pa Paldan Zangpo for the *Khro-bo dbang-chen* cycle of Tantric practice and for the goddess Sidpa Gyalmo riding on a red mule (srid-rgyal dre'u dmar). [45] Mainly Lanton resided at Gekyi Jyiwakhar (gas kyi byi-ba mkhar) where he taught the cycles of the Nine Vehicles of Bon and Dzogchen to his disciples. When his teacher Pa Paldan Zangpo warned him that his family line would be cut and suggested that be become a Ngakpa and marry, he adamantly refused and remained a monk, totally abandoning the worldly life. Nevertheless, he remained closely connected with the Pa clan. He wrote many learned books.

When Lama Jyatangwa had said to him, "As all phenomena, whether good or bad, occur in their spontaneous perfection, they never go beyond the state of just that single meaning (which is the Natural State)," Lanton immediately understood. [46] Thereby he attained a total confidence that all the phenomena of both Samsara and Nirmana were the creations of his own mind, [47] and so he became liberated.

The Eleven Masters of the Southern Lineage of Transmission

Then, as for the Southern Lineage of Transmission (lho-rgyud), this line descends also from Yangton Sherab Gyaltsan through his sons and grandson (sras dbon).

1. Dampa Bumje Od

Dampa Bumje Od (Dam-pa 'bum-rje 'od) was the oldest among the three children of Yangton Sherab Gyaltsan who belonged to the famous Ya-ngal clan. Their mother was named Nyanmo Tashi Jocham (gNyan-mo bkra-shis jo-lcam). The younger son of this couple was called Ludragpa Tashi Gyaltsan (kLu-brag-pa bKra-shis rgyal-mtshan) and their daughter was known as Ya-ngal Jocham (Ya-ngal Jo-lcam). [48] Dampa Bumje would join his father's disciples when he gave them instructions. He studied the *bShad-rgyud kyi bka' gter* extensively in order to

63. Dampa Bumje Od

remove his own doubts as well as the doubts of others. Moreover, he went to the Lopon Druton Nyima Gyaltsan (slob-dpon Bru-ston nyima rgyal-mtshan) for teachings in the diverse sections of the Dzogchen tradition— the external, the internal, and the secret. [49] After the passing away of his father, he took instructions from his mother Tashi Jocham in both the Mantras and Dzogchen (sngags sems gnyis). He meditated and practiced according to these instructions and so he fell into a swoon where he experienced bliss without pollutions. But he awoke from this when his mother shouted at him, "My son, you now have much work to do to benefit other sentient beings!" [50]

Meeting with the kindness of his teachers, he followed faithfully their spiritual advice and, in consequence, he realized many virtuous qualities. He went to meet Lama Orgom Kundul and requested the transmission of the empowerments for the real meaning of Dzogchen. However, Lama Orgom only granted him some of the brief instructions that were merely gateways to the Precepts and when he requested the texts containing these instructions, [51] the master said that he did not have any such texts and that he could only give him the oral instructions for the practice. But the Lama prophesied that within six year's time he would come to realize the fruition of the precepts of Dzogchen in terms of his immediate experiences. Dampa Bumje began his practice in the autumn, but became distracted in the winter by worldly affairs at home. He began to feel depressed, but then he experienced an auspicious dream. And this led him to return in the spring to his master, the Lama Orgom.

This time Dampa Bumje dreamed that the hosts of deities of the Secret Mantras cycle of Zhang-zhung Meri, such as the three Gonpos or Protectors, actually showed him their faces. [52] Therefore, he requested the complete empowerments for the entire cycle of instructions from the Oral Transmission from Zhang-zhung (snyan-rgyud kyi gdams skor kyi dbang). The Lama told him that the mandala would not require the usual material characteristics. [53] The master and his disciple went into a strict retreat and at midnight they performed the meditation and the rites for Walphur and Meri (dbal-phur me-ri) and then at day break Lama Orgom, employing only words and meditation, conferred upon his disciple the empowerment for the real meaning of the Oral Transmission. [54] The master thereafter had several visions. He saw that his disciple would have much good fortune and this would become an obstacle for him. Nevertheless, he imparted the complete cycle of instructions and explanations for the *sNyan-rgyud* in their extensive, intermediate, and condensed versions. [55] The master granted his permission for Dampa to teach the precepts to others and finally he propitiated the guardian deities Nyipangse and Menmo. He also gave his permission for Dampa to show his notes to others who have poor memories. And he advised him to practice the *This kyi skor*, or action practices associated with the cult of Meri.

Dampa Bumje had extraordinary meditation experiences where his mind became as pure as the sky and he freed himself from all defilements. Therefore, Lama Orgom made Dampa Bumje his Dharma heir and encouraged him to transmit this heritage in the form of writing to his qualified disciples. Thereupon Dampa Bumje integrated his own instructions for the Experiential Trasmission with those of his father Sherab Gyaltsan and with those he had received from the master Orgom Kundul. In this way he created a grand compendium and communicated this to a number of disciples. Thus it was that with Yangton Chenpo and his son Dampa Bumje that the corpus of texts belonging to the Zhang-zhung Nyan-gyud largely came into their present form. [56]

Dampa Bumje lived at Zhalu Gongtra (Zha-lu gong khra), a place where the non-human spirits used to assemble, for some seventeen years. At the beginning of his practice he saw the faces of the Yidam deities of the Meri cycle, then there arose in his mind-stream experiences and understanding without partialities and he employed the guardian deities to overcome those enemies who would destroy the teachings of Bon. In this way he came to establish the teachings of Bon in Lo Mustang, in Dolpo, and among the nomads of Western Tibet. His liberation came simultaneously with his understanding and having developed full confidence in this, it is said that he eventually attained a Buddhahood that was omniscient (rnam-mkhyen gyi sangs-rgyas su gyur-pa).

2. Ludragpa Tashi Gyaltsan

Ludragpa Tashi Gyaltsan (kLu-brag-pa bKra-shis rgyal-mtshan) was the younger brother of Dampa Bumje. In his early years he learned the Secret Mantras belonging to the Tantric cycle of Meri from his father and his older brother. He became a powerful Tantrika and married a lady named Langtrugma from Chok (Chog gi gLang-phrug-ma). They had one son and when he was three years old, his mother died, but the Lama refused to take another wife.

At the age of thirty-three, he departed for Tsang province to the

64. Ludragpa Tashi Gyaltsan

north There he studied the Bonpo Tantras with Zhangton Sonampal of Bathang (Ba-thang gi zhang-ston bsod-nams dpal), with Sumton

Lhabum (Sum-ston lha-'bum), and with Mengongpa (sMan-gong-pa) at Nyimo Zangri (sNyi-mo bzang-ri) monastery. [57] In the presence of Shenchen Yeshe Lodro (gShen-chen Ye-shes blo-gros) he took ordination as a monk. In particular, he received the precepts of the Zhang-zhung Nyan-gyud from his older brother Dampa Bumje. He became a Yogin practicing great austerities, residing especially at Ludrak Nyen (kLu-brag gnyan), the mighty rock of the Nagas. Hence he received the epithet of Ludragpa (klu-brag-pa). This site in Northern Nepal was inhabited by the Nagas (klu) and other wild non-human spirits and it had previously been sanctified by the presence of Dranpa Namkha himself. [58] He lived until the age of eighty-five and realized many siddhis.

He displayed many miracles such as hanging his blue cloak on the rays of the sun and his phurpa dagger spontaneously produced flames. He was able to bring the rains to extinguish the fire on the mountain. He gathered the elements under his control and assembling the gods and demons under his power, he bade them do his bidding. The demons, who were rock Nagas, [59] used to help dig beneath the earth in his cave. He made the waters flow for irrigation. All the gods and demons attended his words and made prostrations to him. it is said that his older brother Dampa Bumje wore a rock cave as his hat, because he always stayed in the same place, but that the younger brother filled the mountains and the valleys with his footprints as he restlessly moved about. [60] He especially established the Bonpo doctrines in Latod (la-stod). There having arisen the bliss of a totally confident belief in his understanding (of the Natural State) within his mind-stream, he became non-dual with the Body of Kuntu Zangpo.

3. Togdan Wonpo Yeshe Gyaltsan

Togdan Wonpo Yeshe Gyaltsan (rTogs-ldan dBon-po ye-shes rgyal-mtshan) was the nephew of his teachers who were his two uncles and he was the grandson (dbon-po) of the great Yangton. He came from the region of Mustang (Mus kyi sta-mo). His father was named Ogye Rogpo ('O-rgyad rog-po) and his mother was Jocham (Ya-ngal Jo-lcam), the daughter of Yangton Chenpo Sherab Gyaltsan.

But when he was a young man he followed the profession of his father who was a bandit (ar-pa) and spent some years engaged in fighting and brigandage. Then one day he met a diviner (mo-ma) who said to him, "You will receive a blue horse with a red spot on his chest. When this happens, you should give this to me!" But Yeshe Gyaltsan was wounded in the fighting by a spear and his father and some of his men were killed. He was also struck down by a sword thrust, but he

65. Togdan Wonpo Yeshe Gyaltsan

was saved by his two servants as he lay wounded. They gathered up his intestines and sewed his abdomen back up so that he survived. After cremating his father's body, he sought revenge. But eventually he grew weary of the ceaseless fighting and went to his uncle Dampa Bumje in order to learn how to read religious texts. But when his uncle scolded him for his slow progress in this, he went to his other uncle Ludragpa, and announced, "I don't know how to read yet. But even though I don't know this, if you know the instructions for attaining Buddhhood, please give them to me! If not, I will continue my life as a bandit!"

His uncle, the Lama, told him that he possessed the Dzogchen Zhang-zhung Nyan-gyud that contained the instructions for the arising into visible manifestation of the Primordal State of Kuntu Zangpo [61] and for this one did not need to able to read books. He gave his nephew the empowerments and the transmissions. Afterwards he practiced in many different places. Thereupon he exhibited many signs of realization. Having received the transmission of the Zhang-zhung Nyan-gyud, he practiced at Ludrak Nyan (kLu-brag gnyan) and attained a realization equal to that of Dranpa Namkha himself. [62]

4. Yangton Gyaltsan Rinchen

As for Yangton Gyaltsan Rinchen (Yang-ston rgyal-mtshan rin-chen), his father was Ya-ngal Phurpa and his mother was Nyamo Kunkyid (Nya-mo kun-skyid). When Ya-ngal Basu (Ya-ngal 'ba'-su), the son of Lama Ngakpa (bLa-ma sngags-pa), died at the age of twenty-one, that left no living descenends of the Ya-ngal clan in Dolpo. When the disciples of Lama Ngakpa from Lo, Dolpo, and the nomad region [63] gathered together at Samling monastery in Dolpo, the Lama sadly told them that his family lineage had been cut off at the root. Therefore, he instructed them to take the teachings of Bon elsewhere and began to give away the family's ritual items. His senior disciples conferred together regarding the situation and sent four monks to Tagtse in Western Tsang province. [64] When they returned, they brought back with them the boy Gyaltsan Rinchen, who at the time was only eight

years old, because he was kin of
the Ya-ngal family. The boy was
greeted in Dolpo with much
ceremony and Lama Ngakpa
enthroned him as the future head
of the clan. All of the Bonpos in
Lo, Dolpo, and the nomad region
sent gifts to the boy.

From then until the age of
twenty-one, he wore his hair long
as a Tantrika. He studied
thoroughly the Tantras (rgyud-
sde) and practiced the recitations
and the sadhanas for the Secret
Mantras. [65] Then, when Lama
Togdan Wonpo (rTogs-ldan dbon-
po Ye-shes rgyal-mtshan)

66. Yangton Gyaltsan Rinchen

intended to consecrate an image at Bi-cher in the region of Dolpo, he
sent a letter to Geshe Khyunggod (dge-bshes Khyung-rgod) in Lo
(Mustang) requesting him to come there, together with Gyaltsan
Rinchen, in order to perform the divinations (mo) at the consecration
ceremony. When the two arrived at Bi-cher, Gyaltsan Rinchen
requested the precepts of the Zhang-zhung Nyan-gyud from his
kinsman. During the winter and the spring months the complete
instructions for the Oral Transmission of Dzogchen (rdzogs-chen
snyan-rgyud kyi gdams-pa) were bestowed upon him.

Generally this master resided at Sirik in Lo (glo-bo si-rig), as well
as other various hermitages in Dolpo. He had a palace constructed at
the monastery of Dedan Samling (bde-ldan bsam-gling) and he lived
there until the age of sixty-two. He manifested many ordinary siddhis
and signs of realization, but he was especially accomplished in the
practice of inserting the psychic winds and the experiences of bliss into
the interior of the central channel by way of wisdom and means. And
as an ultimate attainment, he realized the great bliss of equinimity. [66]

5. Chigchod Dadpa Sherab

As for Chigchod Sherab (gCig-chod dad-pa shes-rab), his father was
Sobon Trotan (Sro-bon khro-bstan) and his mother was Gonmogyan
(mGon-mo rgyan). Before his birth, his parents had received several
prophecies from the mountain god Tise Lhatsan (Ti-se'i lha-btsan) and
his consort Yidwongma (Yid-'ong-ma) that a son would come to them
in the future. However, his mother died when he was only six. Even

67. Chigchod Dadpa Sherab

from an early age he was very intelligent. [67] When he was thirteen years old, his father died. According to his father's last testament, the boy was to be entrusted to the care of Lama Ya-ngal (Gyaltsan Rinchen) in whose presence he was later ordained as a monk. He undertook the study of the Sutras and the Tantras with that Lama and by the age of nineteen he was able to attend his master and be of service. But when Druton Geshe (Bru-ston dge-bshes) and Ya-ngal Tongod (Ya-ngal ston-rgod) were killed in Bartsik in Lo (glo-bo'i bar-tshigs), he was sent there to collect the blood money from the killers. On the way, however, he fell seriously ill and only barely recovered with medical treatment. Thereupon he became disillusioned with life. Praying to his Lama, he had auspicious dreams and received many prophecies from the goddess Sidpa Gyalmo. [68]

Thereafter, abandoning his native country, he went and requested the Oral Transmission for Dzogchen from the master Yangton Gyaltsan Rinchen, as well as the four complete empowerments for the Peaceful and Wrathful Deities (zhi-khro dbang bzhi). But when he requested the Zhang-zhung Nyan-gyud specifically, the master hesitated. With some impatience, while he was staying at Samling in Dolpo, he began to study on his own the texts of the *Ma rgyud thugs-rje nyi-ma*, the Bonpo Mother Tantra, and went to practice in certain cremation grounds and other dangerous places. Nevertheless, he gained some experiences in meditation and received some prophecies. There arose immediately within him the knowledge that his own mind was this Primordial State of Buddhahood. [69] But up until that time, he had no direct introduction to the Natural State from a master and so doubts began to arise again within him.

He went to his master once more and the latter examined him. When opening the text of the Zhang-zhung Nyan-gyud, his finger happened to fall on the phrase *lTa sgom gyi bya bral rjes med*, "the view and the meditation, which are free of deliberate action, leave behind no traces!" His master took this as an auspicious sign. But he fell ill again and almost died and even thought of practicing Phowa, the transference of consciousness, at that time. However, he received a number of positive prophecies from the Dakinis and the Protectors of Bon, and performing a rite of expiation (bskang-ba), he recovered from his near fatal illness.

He went to his Lama and offered him a large turquoise for the Dzogchen teachings. Both the master and his disciple examined their dreams and found them to be auspicious. In one dream, Ponchen Tsanpo wearing his blue hermit's hat even appeared to him. So the teachings of the Zhang-zhung Nyan-gyud were bestowed upon him in their entirety. Thereafter he practiced meditation at Mount Kailas and the two lakes. But he also went to practice in the four quarters of Central Tibet, [70] as well as in the south in Mon-yul and Bumthang, in the north at the sky lake of Namtso (gnam-mtsho), and in the west at Guge, Ruthok, Jalandhara, Puhrang, Lemi, Omlo, and Dolpo. But he did not settle in his own place.

From an early age he received many prophecies from the Dakinis and later he displayed many signs of realization. Because there arose in his contemplation the states of space, vast expanse, and dimension, the fruit of the Trikaya became manifest for him and thereby he ultimately accomplished the benefit of living beings. [71] And in his visions, he was blessed especially by the presence of the great sage Tsewang Rigdzin and thereby became a master of the profound oral transmission. [72]

Having received the Upadeshas of the experiences of past masters, [73] he first practiced at Dedan Samling in Dolpo, the famous monastery of the Ya-ngal clan, where appearances liberated of themselves and his delusions self-destructed. Thereby his attachments to appearances were cut off and he came to understand that everything is without a cause, insubstantial, inherently pure, and without a root. Thus, he became non-dual with the Primordial State of the great ascetic Tsewang Rigdzin himself. [74]

6. Druchen Gyalwa Yungdrung

The career of this master, Druchen Gyalwa Yungdrung (Bru-chen rgyal-ba g.yung-drung), is dealt with elsewhere in this book. [75]

7. Latod Riwa Sherab Lodro

Latod Riwa Sherab Lodro (La-stod ri-ba Shes-rab blo-gros, var. Sher-blo) came from Dolpo and his clan was Sang. [76] Even when he was a small child, he had developed great faith in Bon and was much concerned with the effects of impermanence. Thereupon much

69. Latod Riwa Sherab Lodro

compassion and devotion arose within his mind-stream. He met both Chigchod Dadpa Sherab (gCig-chod Dad-pa shes-rab) and Dru Gyalwa Yungdrung (Bru rGyal-ba g.yung-drung) in person and requested from them the three cycles of the Zhang-zhung Nyan-gyud, together with the Upadeshas for both the *bKa'-rgyud* and the *Nyams-rgyud*. Thereafter he traveled to the various pilgrimage sites (gnas chen), hermitages (ri-khrod), monasteries (grwa-pa), and practice places (grub gnas) in the three regions of Western Tibet, Central Tibet, and Dokham in the east. His disciples included Pa Namkha Zangpo (sPa Nam-mkha' bzang-po), Khyungpo Rangdrol Lama Gyaltsan (Khyung-po rang-grol bla-ma rgyal-mthsan), and Segom Ural Samtan Gyaltsan (Se-sgom dbu-ral bSam-gtan rgyal-mtshan). Even until an advanced age, he studied and expounded upon the Zhang-zhung Nyan-gyud, practicing Clear Light, as well as Tsalung. [77] In terms of his practice, externally he purified unnecessary worldly activities into their own original condition, internally he liberated the powers of his intrinsic Awareness into their own original condition, and in between his Self-Awareness became manifest without any duality of subject and object. Thereupon he developed a total confidence with regard to the unchanging Natural State. [78]

8. Rangdrol Lama Gyaltsan

Rangdrol Lama Gyaltsan (Rang-grol bla-ma rgyal-mtshan) was born in the region of Tserlung and belonged to the Khyungpo clan. [79] His father was the patron Trowosung (yon-bdag Khro-bo bsrung) and his mother was Gyaltriza Tashikyid (rGyal-khri-za bkra-shis skyid). When he was fifteen years old, having come to experience impermanence for himself personally, he fled into the mountains. Everyone thought he had become mad and had been possessed by Gyalpo and Senmo (rgyal bsen) spirits. [80] They attached many protective amulets ('khor-lo) to his body and performed many religious rituals (rim-'gro) to bind these spirits and restore his sanity. When he was seventeen, he requested the Genyen ordination from Lhasum Jyadral (Lha-gsum bya-bral) and became the master's personal attendent. This Lama predicted that the boy would be of benefit to living beings and gave him a direct introduction to the Natural State. At the age of twenty-four, he visited various monasteries in Central Tibet and requested initiations and transmissions for the outer, inner, and secret cycles of Bon teachings from Sumton Dragpa Zangpo (Sum-ston gragspa bzang-po), Zhugye Yeshe Gyaltsan (Zhu-rgyas ye-shes rgyal-mtshan), and Pa Paldan Zangpo (sPa dpal-ldan bzang-po). Then while residing at the foot of

70. Rangdrol Lama Gyaltsan

Mount Kailas, he requested the *Bon gcod chen* from Tsura Odzer Gyltsan (Tsu-ra 'od-zer rgyal-mtshan). He was blessed by the marooncolored goddess Sidpa Gyalmo (sMug-mo srid-rgyal) in a vision and he came to be regarded as an emanation of the ancient sage Drungmu Hara. In particular, at Tul-khyu monastery in Droshod (Gru-shod) he came into the presence of Riwa Sherlo (Ri-ba sher-blo, Shes-rab blogros) and requested the Dzogchen Zhang-zhung Nyan-Gyud. At this time he received prophecies in visions from both Tapihritsa and Gyerpungpa. At the great glacial mountain of Targo, he requested the transmissions of the *bsGrags-pa skor gsum* and the *Yang-rtse klongchen*. [81] The signs arising from his experiences were excellent. Moreover, it was at this time that the exposition and the listening to the explanations regarding meditation practice in relation to Dzogchen became something more public.

From the time he was thirty onwards, he wandered about, but often resided at the hermitage near the mountain of Chari Tsugdan. [82] Moreover, he was connected with the monastic colleges of Zhu, Shen, Pa, and Meu. [83] He travelled to Central Tibet twice and even debated with the great Je Tsongkhapa for seven days. [84] On other occasions, he frequently debated with other Buddhist monks. He was especially remembered for his teaching of Dzogchen in the Bon tradition. The goddess Yeshe Walmo protected him like her only child. [85]

71. Athok Yeshe Gyaltsan

9. Athok Yeshe Rinchen

Athok Yeshe Gyaltsan (A-thog ye-shes rgyal-mtshan), came from the region of Wensakha (dben-sa-kha) and belonged to the Athok clan. [86] Even when he was a small child, his mind was very intelligent and skillful. [87] He mastered his studies and himself became a teacher, for which reason he was called Athok Tonpa Yeshe Rinchen (A-thog ston-pa Ye-shes rin-chen). He thereupon entered into the service of Dru Gyalwa Yungdrung as the latter's personal attendant.

During this time, the Togdan Chigchod Dadpa Sherab (rtogs-ldan gCig-chod Dad-pa shes-rab) came to visit Dru Gyalwa after having been on pilgrimage to the sky lake of Namtso (gnam-mtsho) in Northern Tibet. Dru Gyalwa requested from him the precepts for the Zhang-zhung Nyan-gyud. The master thereupon requested the others in the room to withdraw, including Athok, telling Dru Gyalwa that the Single Transmission should not be contaminated by its words being overheard by others. Dadpa Sherab gave him the complete transmissions after having examined their dreams for auspicious signs. Dru Gyalwa also asked the master to give the transmissions to his attendant Athok. The master agree to transmit the *bKa'-rgyud*, but told Dru Gyalwa that he himself should give him the Single Transmission.

Later Athok resided at Tsawa Gangtod (tsha-ba sgang-stod). Because of his practice of Kentse (Ken-tse la bsgrubs-pa), his discriminating wisdom (shes-rab) increased immeasurably and he became very learned. When his disciple Kartsa met him, Athok was already one hundred and ten years old. Kartsa attended him for five years and he bestowed the complete transmissions for the Zhang-zhung tradition upon this Lama. In this way the guardian deities (the king and the goddess) [88] attached themselves to him. Thereafter he exhibited many signs of realization, such as control over the elements, and he mastered the yoga of the channels and the winds through practice with a consort or Karmamudra and thereby gained the powers of experience and understanding. [89] As Lama Athok had received the Single Transmission from Dru Gyalwa, Samsara and Nirvana became merged for him like flour and water and he encountered the Mother who is the Ultimate Reality itself, transcending all the characteristics of conceptual elaborations. [90] In total, the master lived for some one hundred and twenty years.

10. Kartsa Sonam Lodro

Kartsa Sonam Lodro (Kar-tsa bsod-nams blo-gros) came from the region called Gyoddu (gyod-du) in Amdo and belonged to the Kartsa clan. [91] His father was Trowoyak (Khro-bo yag) and his mother was Phagmodar (Phag-mo-dar). He was the second among five children. When he was still young, he learned to read and write and became very learned in the procedures of the Causal Bon, especially in the practices of divination and medical diagnosis. [92] He married at an early age. Because he became involved in many disputes and unsuitable

72. Kartsa Sonam Lodro

activities (ma rung-ba'i spyod-pa) in his youth, he was called by the name Gyod-ru, "he who likes to quarrel." He recited the mantras for Walse and for the black Garuda [93] hundreds of thousands of times, so that he came to have the power to force the eight classes of spirits to do his bidding. It was said that his blessing could cure diseases and exorcise evil spirits (nad dang gdon sel-ba).

Then on one occasion in the autumn, he stole a yak from his neighbors and butchered it near a spring. He remained the entire night at that spot wearing the hide of this yak, whereupon the ancient sage Tsewang Rigdzin appeared to him and uttered a prophecy, proclaiming, "Because you are not leading sentient beings to liberation through guiding them by way of the Dharma of the Mahayana, what is the benefit of this?" [94] When two men came the next morning, searching for the stolen yak, he overheard them say that it must have been taken by Gyodru. He thereupon abandoned any notion of fighting with them and allowed them to take what remained of the yak.

Then he retired to the mountains in order to practice meditation. One night he had a visionary experience (nyams snang) in which he saw a white deity whom he took to be the compassionate Kunzang himself who is the source of the Dzogchen transmission. [95] Thereupon, what had previously not been clear to him, now became clear. In particular, at that time there arose such signs as sounds, lights, and rays in his vision practice. When the Lama directly introduced him to their significance, they became the support for his meditation practice.

Meeting with the kindness of his teachers, he met Asak Sonam Gyaltsan of Domed (mdo-smad gyi A-shag bsod-nams rgyal-mtshan) and he requested the teachings of the *Rdzogs-pa chen-po A-khrid*. He also received teachings from Togdan Kyangtse (rtogs-ldan sKyang-tshe) for the *Dri-med lhan-skyes*, from Tsultim Odzer (Tshul-khrims 'od-zer) for the *Shar-ba'i don 'grel*, and from Ragshi Yeshe Gyaltsan (Rag-shi Ye-shes rgyal-mtshan) for the *Drung-mu'i bon gcod*. [96] And in particular, he received the Zhang-zhung Nyan-gyud from Athok Yeshe Rinchen. Lama Kartsa attended the master for five years. When he was later ordained as a monk, he received the name Sonam Lodro (bSod-nams blo-gros). He practiced austerities at many different hermitages and holy places. He taught many disciples and it is said that he even taught the Dharma to the birds. Eventually he became the master of Pa Tangyal, transmitting to him the *bKa'-rgyud*, the *Nyams-rgyud*, and the *gCig-rgyud*. [97] Lama Kartsa realized many different siddhis and displayed his power over the elements. For example, he could walk on water and leave his footprints in solid rock. The guardian deities attended him. After receiving instructions from Lama Athok, within three days he became free of conceptual elaborations and severed the knot of grasping at the reality of things. He understood the real meaning of total selflessness. [98]

11. Paton Tan-gyal Senge Zangpo
As for Paton Tan-gyal Zangpo (sPa-ston bsTan-rgyal bzang-po), his father was Pa Nyipal Zangpo (sPa Nyi-dpal bzang-po) and his mother was Ponse Chammo Namkha Khyedren (dPon-gsas lcam-mo nam-mkha' khye-'dren). He was their youngest child and many auspicious sins and omens manifested at his birth.

During his lifetime he met with many teachers who showed him great kindness, but his principal master was Kartsa Sonam Lodro. From the later he received the instructions for the Experiential Transmission in their three versions, [99] together with the practice of Tsalung (rtsa rlung phyag-len). After he had practiced for year, his master told him that there did indeed exist a precious unique Single Transmission. [100] His master explained that Lama Dadpa Sherab had given this to Druchen Gyalwa Yungdrung, he to Athok Yeshe

Rinchen, and he to Lama Kartsa himself. Due to certain signs received from the goddess, [101] Pa Tan-gyal requested the transmission, and after some hestitation, the master agreed. The master told him that it was customary in the Zhang-zhung tradition to examine the signs and omens (mtshan ltas brtag-pa), especially those appearing in one's dreams in order to discover whether or not the transmission would be proper. They did this together and their dreams were auspicious. Therefore, Lama Kartsa gave him the Single Transmission.

73. Paton Tan-gyal Zangpo

Pa Tangyal also studied the Mantras for Meri, as well as the Zhang-zhung Nyan-gyud, with Gyagom Tanzang (rGya-sgom bstan-bzang), and in particular the *lTa-ba spyi-gcod*, together with the *Ma bu cha-lag*. [102] He also obtained the *Byang-rgyud* or Northern Lineage of Transmission according to the recension of Treton Gyaltsanpal (Tre-ston rgyal-mtshan-dpal). Because of this, all of his doubts dissolved.

He practiced at Rikhud Degang (ri-khud bde-sgang), at the cave of Jeribon (rje ri-bon phug), and at Mount Kailas and the two nearby lakes. [103] He died at Rikhud Degang, at home with his family.

Although he was a great meditator, Pa Tan-gyal was also a scholar who wrote many commentaries (bka' brten). He displayed many inconceivale signs of realization, such as transforming himself into the form of a vulture, the king of birds, and circumabulated Mount Kailas in that form. [104] At the bathing spot on the Mapang Lake, wherever his feet trod, lotus flowers sprang up and rainbows appeared. The Yidam deities showed him their faces. And in terms of his understanding becoming manifest, when Lama Kartsa gave him the direct introduction, it was said that he purified his own sense doors of whatever appearances arose to them by way of dissolving them into the Natural State. He recognized that their original nature meant that they did not really exist as external objects, but were projections of his own mind. And having dissolved his mental processes and his meditation into their original condition, which is emptiness, he visibly obtained thereby a state of total non-meditation. [105]

Although this final hagiography is included in the text, it was obviously not composed by the author himself, but probably by one of his disciples. This concludes the summaries of the hagiographies found in the text *rNam-thar chen-mo*.

The Dzogchen Master and Prince of Zhang-zhung, Dranpa Namkha.

PART TWO

THE LITERATURE OF THE ZHANG-ZHUNG NYAN-GYUD CYCLE

CHAPTER 10

The Texts in the Menri Edition of the Zhang-Zhung Nyan-Gyud

The Four Cycles of Precepts

According to the *Legs-bshad mdzod*, [1] the texts that elucidate the Dzogchen teachings are innumerable, but they may be condensed into the following three groups:

I. the Four Cycles of the Transmissions of Precepts (bka' brgyud skor bzhi):

1. *Phyi lta-ba spyi-gcod*,
2. *Nang man-ngag dmar-khrid*,
3. *gSang-ba rig-pa gcer mthong*,
4. *Yang-gsang gnas-lugs phugs-chod*;

II. the Three Cycles of Revelations (bsGrags-pa skor gsum) [2]

III. the Nine Cycles of the Lesser Mind Series (Sems smad sde dgu):

1. *Byang-sems gab-pa dgu skor*,
2. *Rig-pa'i khu-byug*,
3. *Sems phan sde bdun*. [3]

The four texts in the first group comprise the root texts of the *Zhang-zhung snyan-rgyud* which, according to tradition, were transmitted orally by Tapihritsa and subsequently written down by Gyerpungpa and his successors. These four collections, together with the *Nyams rgyud* cited below, "the Experiential Transmission," constitute the main corpus of the Zhang-zhung Nyan-gyud. According to Lopon Tenzin Namdak, [4] in general the *Zhang-zhung snyan-rgyud*, together with the *bsGrags-pa skor gsum* and the *Gab-pa dgu skor*, appear to derive from the same Zhang-zhung tradition of Dzogchen, although the former represents a continuous tradition (snyan-brgyud) from early times, whereas the latter two collections are Terma or rediscovered treasure texts. These two collections belong to the tradition of the Southern Treasures. However, our attention here is necessarily restricted to the first of these three transmissions of Dzogchen. [5]

As indicated, the Dzogchen teachings from the Zhang-zhung Nyan-gyud were classified into four categories, which are outer, inner, secret, and exceedingly secret respectively. These are collectively known as the Four Cycles of Transmission of the Precepts (bka' brgyud skor bzhi) and are as follows:

1. The Outer Cycle (phyi skor)— the Explanation of the General Exposition of the View represents the Outer Aspect of the Teachings (phyi lta-ba spyi-gcod du bshad-pa): The teachings presented here [6] introduce the Dzogchen view in general (lta-ba spyi-gcod), while distinguishing among the philosophical views of Sutra, Tantra, and Upadesha in order to establish the supremacy of the Dzogchen view.

2. The Inner Cycle (nang skor)— the Explanation of the Secret Oral Instructions that provide clear and vital guidance to practice represents the Inner Aspect of the Teachings (nang man-ngag dmar-khrid du bshad-pa): These teachings focus upon the practice of meditation (sgom-pa) in terms of entering into and remaining in the state of contemplation, that is, being in the Natural State, which is elsewhere known as Trekchod (khregs-chod).

3. The Secret Cycle (gsang skor)— the Explanation with regard to intrinsic Awareness seeing nakedly, which represents the Secret Aspect of the Teachings (gsang-ba rig-pa gcer mthong du bshad-pa): The teachings presented here especially focus upon the practice of vision or Clear Light ('od-gsal), which is otherwise known as Thodgal (thod-rgal). This practice of vision is here, properly speaking, considered to be the activity or the conduct (spyod-pa).

4. The Exceedingly Secret Cycle (yang gsang skor)— the Explanation regarding the Discovering of the Source which is the Natural State represents the Exceedingly Secret Aspect of the Teachings (yang gsang gnas-lugs phug chod du bshad-pa): The teachings found here focus on the removing of any doubts concerning the Natural State of the individual. The emphasis is on the Fruit or the final result ('bras-bu).

Fortunately, the most important group of these texts from the *Zhang-zhung snyan-rgyud* collection have been republished in India within recent decades. When he fled the Chinese occupation of his native country, one of the few texts that Lopon Tenzin Namdak brought with him was a xylograph edition of the *Zhang-zhung snyan-rgyud* made from blocks at Menri monastery, carved sometime in the 1950s. This was reprinted in New Delhi, India, by Dr. Lokesh Chandra and Lopon Tenzin Namdak as *History and Doctrine of Tibetan Nispanna Yoga*, Satapitaka Series v. 73, International Academy of Indian Culture, New Delhi 1968. [7] This published collection, however, is, in actuality, only an anthology of texts from the much larger Zhang-zhung Nyan-gyud cycle, and does not in itself represent a canon of scriptures. It includes a number of commentaries by later authors, as well as a collection of hagiographies. There is no indication in the colophons as to who was the final editor of this collection, which was probably prepared at Menri monastery. [8]

The Collections of the Experiential Transmissions

Subsequently two more volumes of Zhang-zhung texts were published through the efforts of the Lopon and these present the Zhang-zhung Nyan-gyud cycle in terms of three groupings of texts: the extensive (rgyas-pa), the intermediate ('bring-po), and the condensed (bsdus-pa) versions. These two manuscript collections originally belonged to Khyungtrul Rinpoche, formerly head of a Bonpo monastery in Western Tibet near Mount Kailas. [9] They were republished in India by the Tibetan Bonpo Monastic Centre in 1973 under the auspicies of the former abbot at Dolanji, Yongdzin Sangye Tenzin. These three collections, the extensive, the intermediate, and the condensed, contain not only the instructions imparted by Tapihritsa, but the precepts based on the personal meditation experiences (nyams) of many different masters, at first transmitted orally and later set down in writing.

These collections and their contents are as follows:

I. *Zhang-zhung snyan-rgyud kyi bla-ma'i nyams rgyud rgyas-pa skya smug gnyis*, Tibetan Bonpo Monastic Centre, New Delhi 1973: [10]

1. sNyan-rgyud rgyas-pa'i skor ma bu sa-bcad (ff. 1-4),
2. rDzogs-pa chen-po zhang-zhung snyan-rgyud kyi nyams rgyud skya-ru (ff. 5-231),
3. sNyan-rgyud smug-gu (ff. 233-432).

II. *Zhang-zhung snyan-rgyud kyi bla-ma'i nyams rgyud 'bring-po sor bzhag-pa dang bsdus-pa thor-bu*, Tibetan Bonpo Monastic Centre,

New Delhi 1973:

A. The Middle Length Collection of Precepts for the Experiential Transmission (Nyams-brgyud 'bring-po) (ff. 1-167):

1. sTong thun gyi 'grel-pa (ff. 1-13),
2. sNyan-rgyud thugs kyi nges don 'bring-po sor bzhag las klad kyi zhwa dang 'dra-ba'i gdams-pa (ff. 15-46),
3. Lus kyi gos dang 'dra-ba'i gdams-pa (ff. 47-81),
4. rKang gi lhwam dang 'dra-ba'i gdams-pa (ff. 83-102),
5. sGro 'dogs bcod-pa don gyi brgyud-pa zhes bya-ba rang gi lus dang 'dra-ba'i gdams-pa (ff. 103-132),
6. Nyams su blangs man-ngag gi brgyud-pa mi tshig gis lhad ma zhugs 'ching-ba'i sked rag dang 'dra-ba'i gdams-pa (ff. 133-144),
7. Yid-ches grub-pa bsnyems-pa'i brgyud-pa khog-pa'i snying dang 'dra-ba'i gdams-pa (ff. 145-158),
8. dPal-ba'i mig dang 'dra-ba'i gdams-pa (ff. 159-167).

B. The Condensed Collection of Precepts for the Experiential Transmission (Nyams-brgyud bsdus-pa) (ff. 169-648):

9. Rigs drug rang sbyong gi gdams-pa (ff. 169-189),
10. Rang sbyong gsol 'debs (ff. 191-193),
11. sNyan-rgyud 'od gsal sems kyi me-long (ff. 195-529),
12. Zhang-zhung snyan-rgyud kyi 'od-gsal mtshams-bcad kyi man-ngag dang rtsa rlung 'khrul-'khor 'od-gsal (ff. 531-546),
13. 'Khrul-'khor drug-pa (ff. 547-548),
14. Zhang-zhung snyan-rgyud rtsa rlung gags sel 'khrul-'khor gyi rim-pa (ff. 549-569),
15. sNyan-rgyud rtsa khrid mun sel shel phreng (by Rang-grol bla-ma rgyal-mtshan) (ff. 571-648).

These latter two collections deal with the personal meditation experiences (nyams) of many individual Dzogchen masters. 11] The term *nyams brgyud* indicates the transmission of personal experiences one has attained in meditation practice and, in this case, it means the Natural State. In the lineage lists given above, this Experiential Transmission (nyams brgyud) was contrasted with the Transmission of the Precepts (bka' brgyud) that represent the root texts of the tradition. [12] In the middle length collection, the instructions (gdams-pa) appear to be related on the basis of a metaphor:

1. the instructions that are like a hat on one's head (klad kyi zhwa dang 'dra-ba'i gdams-pa),

2. the instructions that are like the clothes on one's body (lus kyi gos dang 'dra-ba'i gdams-pa),
3. the instructions that are like the shoes on one's feet (rkang gi lhwam dang 'dra-ba'i gdams-pa),
4. the instructions that are like one's own body (rang gi lus dang 'dra-ba'i gdams-pa (ff. 103-132),
5. the instructions that are like a tie at the waist (sked rag dang 'dra-ba'i gdams-pa),
6. the instructions that are like the heart in one's chest (khog-pa'i snying dang 'dra-ba'i gdams-pa), and
7. the instructions that are like the eyes on the forehead (mig dpral-ba dang 'dran-ba'i gdams-pa).

The shorter or condensed collection appears to consist of miscellaneous instructions and to be unstructured as a whole. The colophons of the middle length collection and the shorter collection tell us that that the redactor Orgom Kundul ('Or-sgom kun-'dul) in the 11th century set down the precepts at the request of Yangton Sherab Gyaltsan (Yang-ston shes-rab rgyal-mtshan). [13]

The Contents of the Menri Edition

In the first of these collections, the New Delhi reprint of the xylograph edition from Menri monastery, there is included at the beginning a history of the lineage of masters for these teachings, entitled "The Hagiographies of the Masters of the Lineages for the Oral Transmission from Zhang-zhung for the Great Perfection Teachings," (*rDzogs-pa chen-po zhang-zhung snyan-rgyud kyi bla-ma'i brgyud-pa'i rnam-thar*, ff. 1-130). This is the first text in the New Delhi edition. Here we find a series of hagiographical accounts of various masters. [14]

Then follow two texts pertaining to the Inner Rushan exercises. In general, the Rushans, both outer and inner, are preliminary exercises in the Dzogchen tradition that prepare the practitioner for a direct introduction to the intrinsic Awareness that is the characteristic of the Natural State (rig-pa ngo-sprod). As with the Nyingmapa tradition, for example, in the *kLong-chen snying-thig* system of Jigmed Lingpa, [15] the Rushan exercises have the function of leading the practitioner to distinguish between the mind (sems) or thought process and the Nature of Mind (sems-nyid) that lies beyond the operations of mind. Thus, the full name for these exercises is *'khor 'das ru-shan dbye-ba*, "the distinguishing between Samsara and Nirvana," where Samsara indicates mind, or the ever cyclical thought-process, and Nirvana indicates the Nature of Mind. The inner Rushans found in the text by Jigmed Lingpa also serve to purify the six realms of rebirth, as do the Bonpo exercises presented here. The instructions for the Outer Rushans are not included in the text here and are normally only given orally.

The first text, *Rigs drug rang sbyong gi gdams-pa* (ff. 131-142), "The Instructions for the Self-Purification of the Six Realms", describe in detail these exercises, where one meditates on the six deities known as Dulshen ('dul gshen drug) who are the guides for beings in the six realms of rebirth. These six sages, who subdue and convert beings, are all regarded as emanations of Tonpa Shenrab projected into the six different realms or destinies of rebirth. They correspond to the six Munis in the Buddhist system of the Tibetan Book of the Dead. [16]

The second text, *sKu lnga rang-khrid* (ff. 143-144), "Self-Instruction on the Five Bodies," pertains to meditation on the Five Pure Deities and their Consorts. These deities correspond, more or less, to the five Dhyani Buddhas and their Consorts in the Buddhist system of the Tibetan Book of the Dead. They represent the purification of the five skandhas or aggregates of conscious experience in the form of the five Buddhas and the purification of the five material elements in the form of the five Consort Goddesses. Because they involve more elaborate visualizations, these Inner Rushan exercises appear to be more related to the Tantric system than Dzogchen. [17]

The main part of the edition compiled at Menri moastery, generally known as the *Zhang-zhung snyan-rgyud* as such, is divided into four sections: the outer, the inner, the secret, and the supremely secret (phyi nang gsang-ba yang-gsang bzhi). [18] In this first section, the outer or external cycle (phyi), we find nine texts, the root text being the first in the list, while the second is designated as a Tantra. Both consist of twelve brief Upadeshas transmitted by Tapihritsa to Gyerpungpa, but the original source was asserted to be the Primordial Buddha Kuntu Zangpo Himself. [19] All of these texts, both root and commentary, focus on the view (lta-ba) of Dzogchen:

1. *Phyi lta-ba spyi-gcod kyi man-ngag le'u bcu-gnyis-pa* (ff. 145-168). [Scripture: "The Twelve Chapters of the Upadesha concerning the General Exposition of the View." This is basic text for this section, consisting of the twelve Upadeshas that expound the view in general (lta-ba spyi-gcod) attributed to Tapihritsa.]

2. *rGyud bu-chung bcu-gnyis* (ff.169-179). [Scripture: "The Tantra of the Twelve Small Precepts," consisting of twelve Upadeshas attributed to Kunzang Tapihritsa.]
3. *rGyud bu-chung bcu-gnyis kyi don bstan-pa* (ff. 181-192). [Commentary: "Demonstration of the Meaning of the Tantra of the Twelve Small Precepts," a commentary on the meaning of the above text.]
4. *'Phrul-'khor lde-mig* (ff. 193-198). [Commentary: "The Key to the Circulation," a scholastic commentary on the above Tantra.]
5. *mDo 'grel gsal-ba'i sgron-me* (ff. 199-231). [Commentary: "The Lamp which clearly illuminates the Commentary to the Sutra."]
6. *lTa-ba spyi-gcod kyi mnyam-bzhag sgom-pa'i lag-len* (ff.233-244). [Commentary: "The Manual for the Meditation Practice of Even Contemplation in relation to the General Exposition of the View," presenting the instructions on the practice of contemplation in relation to the view, including the preliminaries.]
7. *dGongs rgyud dgu'i yig-chung* (ff. 245-246). [History: "The Small Text of the Ninefold Lineage of the Mind," giving a brief account of the Nine Buddhas in the Mind Transmission Lineage.]
8. *rJe Ta-pi-hri-tsa'i lung-bstan* (ff. 247-254). [Scripture: "The Prophetic Sayings of the Lord Tapihritsa," being the instructions orally transmitted by Tapihritsa to Gyerpungpa at their first meeting.]
9. *Zhe-sa dgu phrugs* (ff. 255-256). [Scripture: "The Nine Respectful Polite Expressions," that is, the questions addressed by Tapihritsa to Gyerpungpa regaring the latter's health and progress on the path.]

These texts constitute the Outer Cycle (phyi skor) generally known as the Outer Section concerning the General Exposition of the View: *Phyi lta-ba spyi-gcod*. The practice here is principally that of Trekchod (khregs-chod) or remaining in the state of contemplation, although this particular term is not found in the texts in the collection. [120]

The second section, the inner or internal cycle (nang skor), contains a number of texts which focus on the practice of meditation (sgom-pa):

10. *mJal thebs bar-ma* (f. 257). [Scripture: "The Intermediate Advent and Encounter," where the text gives an account of the second meeting of Gyerpungpa with Tapihritsa.]

11. *Bon ma nub-pa'i gtan-tshigs* (ff. 259-267). [History: "The Reasons why Bon did not Decline." The text gives an account of the assassination of Ligmigya, the last king of Zhang-zhung, and of Gyerpungpa's subduing of the Tibetan king Trisong Detsan by means of a golden magical missile . This narrative provides the reason (gtan-tshigs) why the Bon teaching of the *Zhang-zhung snyan-rgyud* did not decline and disappear due to the persecution of Bon.]

12. *sGron-ma drug gi gdams-pa* (ff. 269-292). [Scripture: "The Instructions concerning the Six Lamps," orally transmitted by Tapihritsa to Gyerpungpa at the hermitage at the deer-faced rock (brag sha-ba gdong gi dgon-pa). The text gives a detailed exposition of the Six Lamps (sgon-ma drug) according to Thodgal.]

13. *sGron-ma'i 'grel-pa nyi 'od rgyan* (ff. 293-354). [Commentary: "The Ornaments of Sunlight, being a commenatary on the *sGron-drug*," the root text of this cycle, composed by U-ri bSod-nams rgyal-mtshan (13 cen.).]

14. *sGron-ma drug gi dgongs don 'grel-pa* (ff.355-422). [Commentary: "A Commentary on the Meaning of the Intention of the Six Lamps," being a condensed commentary on the *sGron-drug* above, composed by Bru-chen rGyal-ba g.yung-drung (1242-1290).]

The principal text, dealing with the Six Lamps or Lights (sgron-ma drug) of the Thodgal practice for the development of vision, is the third in this group. [121] These texts constitute the Inner Cycle (nang skor) consisting of the Upadeshas providing Vital Explanations: *Nang man-ngag dmar-khrid.*

The third section, the secret or esoteric cycle (gsang skor), contains several texts chiefly relating to activity (spyod-pa), and here this means the actual practice of Thodgal:

15. *Kun-gzhi zhal-shes gsal-ba'i sgon-ma* (ff.423-431). [Commentary: "The Lamp that illuminates the Clear Explanation of the Basis of Everything," wherein is presented an explanation concerning the Kunzhi in order to remove doubts with regard to it.]

16. *Byang-chub sems kyi gnad drug ces bya-ba lag-len* (ff. 433-448). [Commentary: "The Practice Manual called the Six Essential Points of the Bodhichitta," wherein are given the instructions for the actual practice of Thodgal in terms of six essential points (gnas drug).]

17. *'Khor-lo bzhi sbrugs* (ff. 449-464). [Commentary: "The Setting Side by Side of the Four Wheels," wherein the text is divided into four chapters, each called a wheel, which deal with the Base, interdependent origination, the body and the psychic channels, and the Bardo experience.]

18. *Bya-bral rjes med* (ff.465-477). [Scripture: "Free of Activity and without Traces," orally transmitted by Tapihritsa to Gyerpungpa. It gives a concise exposition of the origin of the world.]

19. *Man-ngag le'u brgyad-pa* (ff. 479-501). [Scripture: "The Upadesha in Eight Chapters," orally transmitted by Tapihritsa to Gyerpungpa on an island of a lake in Draje (dra-bye) in Zhang-zhung. These eight chapters deal with the Natural State.]

Among the texts above, the *Le'u brgyad-pa* constitutes the root text or scripture, whereas the *gNas-drug* is the most important commentary and is said to have been composed by Yangton Sherab Gyaltsan. These texts constitute the Secret Cycle (gsang skor) where intrinsic Awareness sees everything in its nakedness: *gSang-ba rig-pa gcer-mthong*.

The fourth section, the supremely secret or exceedingly esoteric cycle (yang gsang skor), containing four texts, is concerned with the realization of the Fruit ('bras-bu) through the practice of Thodgal:

20. *gZer-bu nyi-shu rtsa gcig* (ff. 503-519). [Scripture: "The Twenty-One Little Nails," orally transmitted by Tapihritsa to Gyerpungpa and concerned with actualizing one's understanding of the Natural State.]

21. *gZer-bu nyer-gcig gi 'grel-pa* (ff. 521-581). [Commentary: "Commentary to the Twenty-One Little Nails," said to be composed by Gyerpungpa.]

22. *'Od-gsal sems kyi me-long* (ff. 583-598). [Scripture: "The Mirror of the Mind of the Clear Light," orally transmitted by Tapihritsa to Gyerpungpa and concerned with the evolution of the mind and body out of the primordial unity of the Natural State as experienced in the Bardo of the Clear Light.]

23. *rTags tshad gsal sgron* (ff. 566-611). [Scripture: "The Lamp which clearly illuminates the Full Measure of the Signs," orally transmitted by Tapihritsa to Gyerpungpa and deals with the signs (rtags) that may indicate success when they appear during the course of practice.]

24. *rTags sgron chung-ba* (ff. 613-617). [Commentary: "The Small Lamp of the Signs," being a condensed version of the above text.]

Among the above texts, the *gZer-bu* is the principal text in the cycle. These texts constitute the Exceedingly Secret Cycle (yang gsang skor), which Discovers the Source that is the Natural State: *Yang-gsang gnas-lugs phug-chod*.

Then follow five texts appended to the four cycles of the collection:

1. *rTsa rlung gi man-ngag* (ff. 619-629). ["The Upadesha concerning the Channels and the Energies," which provide instructions on the practices of the yoga of the channels and energies (rtsa rlung), chiefly pranayama.]

2. *'Phrul-'khor zhal-shes man-ngag* (ff. 631-643). ["The Upadesha giving a clear explanation of Yantra Yoga," the instructions for the physical exercises of yantra yoga, the yoga of movements ('phrul-'khor).]

3. *sNyan-rgyud bka'-srung srog-bdag rgyal-po nyi-pang-sad kyi bka'-bsgo* (ff. 645-646). ["The Propitiation Rite for Gyalpo Nyipangse, the Custodian of the Life-Force and the Guardian of the Precepts of the Oral Transmission," being an invocation of the guardian deity Nyipangse (nyi-pang-sad) who was personally subdued and coverted by Gyerpungpa and made the special protector of the Zhang-zhung Nyan-gyud teachings; composed at Tashi Menri (bkra-shis sman-ri) monastery by Sherab Gyaltsan (gShen gyi drang-srong mnyam-nyid Shes-rab rgyal-mtshan,1356-1405), the founder and first abbot of that monastery.]

4. *rGyal-po nyi-pang-sad dang sman-mo gnyis kyi bskul-ba* (ff. 647-648). ["The Entreaty to Gyalpo Nyipangse and the Goddess Menmo," being another invocation of the guardian deities Nyipangse and his consort Manmo (sman-mo gNam-phyi gung-rgyal) who are the special guardians of the teachings (bka'-srung) of the Zhang-zhung Nyan-gyud cycle.]

5. *Bon-bstan rgyas-pa'i smon-lam yid-bzhin kun 'grub* (ff. 649-652). ["The Wish-granting Gem that realizes Everything: A

Prayer of Aspiration for the continued spreading of the Teachings of Bon," a prayer composed at Yungdrungling (g.Yung-drung gling) monastery in Tsang province by Ponlob Tsultrim Gyaltsan (dPon-slob Tshul-khrims rgyal-mtshan, b.1893) at the request of Lopon Sangye Tenzin, formerly Lopon at Manri monastery and later Abbot at Dolanji.]

It is often difficult to separate theory, the view of Dzogchen (lta-ba), from the practice of Dzogchen in terms of meditation (sgom-pa) and conduct (spyod-pa) in these old texts. Nonetheless, the translations in this present volume are those of texts found in the collection cited above that deal primarily with the history of the lineage and with the philosophical view of the Dzogchen expounded in the Zhang-zhung tradition.

CHAPTER 11

The Practice Manual for the Zhang-Zhung Nyan-Gyud

The Life and Works of Druchen Gyalwa Yungdrung

Although the texts found in this Zhang-zhung Nyan-gyud collection are arranged into these four cycles of outer, inner, secret, and exceedingly secret corresponding to the view, the meditation, the conduct, and the fruit respectively, this arrangement is in fact not well suited to the actual practice of Dzogchen. This is because the texts in question deal with a variety of topics, more in terms of theoretical matters, rather than in terms of systematic practice. We must look elsewhere for that and fortunately there does exist a thirteenth century practice manual

68. Druchen Gyalwa Yungdrung

and commentary on the Dzogchen system of the Zhang-zhung Nyan-gyud. This latter collection is known as the *sNyan-rgyud rgyal-ba'i phyag-khrid* and was written by the illustrious Bonpo master belonging to the Dru family, Druchen Gyalwa Yungdrung. [1]

Druchen Gyalwa Yungdrung (Bru-chen rgyal-ba g.yung-drung) was born into the Dru clan at Yeru Wensakha (g.yas-ru'i dben-sa-kha) in Central Tibet in 1242. The Bonpo monastery bearing the same name, which was under the control and patronage of the Dru clan throughout its history, was founded by his ancestor, Druchen Yungdrung Lama (Bru-chen g.yung-drung bla-ma) in 1072. [2] It was destroyed in a devastating flood in the fourteenth century, whereafter it was rebuilt by Nyamnyid Sherab Gyaltsan (mNyam-nyid shes-rab rgyal-mtshan) and called Tashi Menri (bkra-shis sman-ri). Before its destruction, Yeru Wensakha became the greatest seat of Bonpo learning in Central Tibet, most of its abbots being drawn from the Dru family. According to family legend, the clan possessed this name because it originally came to Tsang province in Central Tibet from a country to the west known as Drusha (Bru-sha). Moreover, Yungdrung Lama's grandfather, Drusha Namkha Yungdrung (Bru-sha nam-mkha' g.yung-drung), [3] the patriarch of the clan, had been a disciple of the illustrious Shenchen Luga (gShen-chen klu-dga').

It was this Shenchen Luga who discovered in 1017 two large wooden boxes containing Bonpo texts, which had been buried near the ancestral seat of the Shen clan, of which he was a descendent. [4] It was principally this discovery that lead to the revival of Bon in Central Tibet in the eleventh century, this being similar in character to the revival of the Nyingmapas which occurred at the same time. In part, this renaissance was a reaction to the development of the Sarmapa or New Tantra schools of Buddhism that were inspired by the translation of Tantric texts recently brought out of India, many of them previously unknown in Tibet. [5]   Shenchen Luga commissioned Namkha Yungdrung, together with the latter's son, to copy and record the philosophical texts (mtshan-nyid) that he had recovered from this buried library of the Shen clan, which had reportedly been concealed in the eighth century at the time of the persecution of the Bonpos by the Central Tibetan government. This large collection of hidden treasure texts became widely known as the System of the Southern Treasures (lho gter lugs).

Prominant among these texts was that of the Bonpo cosmological work, the *Srid-pa'i mdzod-phug*, "the Source Treasury of Existence", which is extant as a root text in both Zhang-zhung and Tibetan versions. [6] The commentary to this root text, discovered at the same time, was by the eighth century Bonpo master Dranpa Namkha (Dranpa nam-mkha'), also known to the Nyingmapa tradition, where he is made into a disciple of Padmasambhava. [7] Contained in this collection of rediscovered texts were also the *Khams-chen*, the large collection of the Bonpo redaction of the Prajnaparamita Sutras in sixteen volumes, and the *Gab-pa dgu skor*, also known as the *Sems phran sde bdun*, an important collection of Dzogchen texts closely related to the Zhang-zhung Nyan-gyud. Thus, it was recorded in the Bonpo histories that the Dru lineage became pre-eminant in the transmission of the Bonpo philosophical tradition. [8] Druchen Namkha Yungdrung himself wrote a commentary on the *Srid-pa'i mdzod-phug* and his son, Khyunggi Gyaltsan (Khyung gi rgyal-mtshan), also wrote a commentary that established the philosophical and exegetical tradition of this lineage. Both father and son had listened to Shenchen expound the philosophy and cosmology of the *Srid-pa'i mdzod-phug*, which represents a kind of Bonpo Abhidharma text. [9]

Possessing a brilliant intellect, even at a young age Druchen Gyalwa Yungdrung was expounding the philosophical and cosmological system of the *mTshan-nyid srid-pa'i mdzod-phug* to his listeners. Thereafter he took the vows of a monk, eventually becoming a fully ordained Drangsong, corresponding to the fully ordained Buddhist monk, [10] and he was given the name of Gyalwa Yungdrung. He received many transmissions and initiations in terms of the Bonpo Tantras, but he is said to have especially exerted himself in *gNas-lugs theg-chen*, "the Great Vehicle of the Natural State," that is to say, Dzogchen. Being widely renowned for both his scholarship and his pure conduct of life, he eventually obtained the abbacy [11] of his family monastery of Yeru Wensakha and it is said that he ceaselessly instructed his many students and disciples in the teachings of Yungdrung Bon.

According to the hagiography found in the *rNam-thar chen-mo*, there are five principal considerations with regard to this history of Druchen Gyalwa Yungdrung:

1. the history of his parents and how he obtained a pure human body,
2. how he met with his benevolent teachers who showed him great kindness,
3. how he resided at certain special places that served as his support during his lifetime,
4. how his virtuous qualities and his signs of realization that were ordinary manifested immediately in his present life, and
5. how his extraordinary understanding ultimately became manifest. [12]

"As for this disciple of the foregoing master (Chigchod Dadpa Sherab), [13] within the life story of Druchen Gyalwa Yungdrung there are five topics to be considered. First, there is the history of how he obtained a pure human body from his parents to be considered. His native region was Yeru Wensakha and his clan was called Dru. His father was named Druzha Sonam Gyaltsan (Bru-sha bsod-nams rgyal-mtshan) and among four brothers, he was the third son. [14]

"Furthermore, because he was a Nirmanakaya (from the very beginning) who had come into this world in order to benefit beings, from his earliest childhood he possessed the various virtuous qualities of purification. At eight years of age he explained to his listeners the meaning of the text of the *Srid-pa'i mdzod-phug*. Later, in the presence of his uncle Dulwa Rinpoche, he took the vows of a pure monk and the name of Gyalwa Yungdrung was bestowed upon him as his ordination name. Thereupon, in terms of his training and discipline, he acted consistently in accordance with real meaning of his monastic vows. [15]

"Elsewhere, it is said that he requested the initiations and the scriptural authorizations, together with the blessings, for the three sections of Bon, namely, the outer, the inner, and the secret, and thereby he purified his mind-stream (by practicing these teachings). In particular, he performed the commitments of his daily practice with one-pointed concentration and without distraction. [16]

"Moreover, according to the statements made by the Lama himself, 'In the beginning, having requested the training in the monastic vows which are to be guarded well, I guarded them without secrecy and without ostentatious display. Then, in between, having considered the kindness bestowed upon me by my masters in terms of hearing and reflecting upon their teachings, I thoroughly cut off all my doubts. And finally, I came to recognize correctly the face of the Natural State, even though I will not fully comprehend it in this present life nor in my next one— still all this represents the threefold kindness of my masters.'

"Elsewhere, from Yilton Namkha Sonam (dByil-ston nam-mkha' bsod-nams), the nephew of Yilton Khyunggodtsal (dByil-ston khyung-rgod rtsal), [17] from Lunggom Tashi Gyaltsan (Lung-sgom bkra-shis rgyal-mtshan) of the lineage of Lungton Lhanyan (Lung-ston lha-gnyan), [18] from Maton Drangsong (rMa-ston drang-srong) of the lineage of Maton Siddzin (rMa-ston srid-'dzin), [19] and so on, he requested the initiations, the scriptural authorizations, and the instructions, together with the blessings. [20]

"Then, at the time when Lama Togdan Dadpa Sherab was fifty-five years old he made a pilgrimage to all the monasteries, places of realization, and great holy places of the Bonpos found in Central Tibet.

[21] And in particular, he went to meet the famous Dru Tsandan Dulwa (Bru tshan-ldan 'dul-ba), the uncle of Gyalwa Yungdrung, who was residing at Lhodrak (lho-brag). Coming into the presence of Tsandan Dulwa, the former requested such scriptural authorizations as the *rDzogs-pa chen-po A-khrid dmar byang*, the *Dri-med lhan-skyes dbang ye dbang chen-mo*, and so on. [22] Because there was some mention of the teachings on the *sZhang-zhung snyan-rgyud*, Tsandanpa himself said, "Indeed, you possess the complete scriptural authorizations for the *sNyan-rgyud*. [23] But now I am too old to ask for it. And if I should die soon, I would not have the opportunity to practice it. Therefore, please transmit this authorization (lung) to my nephew Gyalwa Yungdrung!"

"Second, because his karma had ripened and he possessed good fortune, he met with the kindness of his benevolent masters. Later, at the time when Lama Togdanpa (Dadpa Sherab) came from his pilgrimage journey to the Namtso lake and arrived at the monastery of Wensakha, Lama Gyalwa addressed him as follows: 'These instructions for the Oral Transmission from Zhang-zhung have never been concealed beneath the earth (as treasure texts). Their blessings have never declined nor disappeared. They are very special because they have been transmitted orally from one Mahasiddha to another without interruption. Just having heard the sound of their name and also seeing some words from some of the texts has produced great devotion within me. I made some inquiries regarding them to some Lopons who were said to have possessed these instructions. When I requested the scriptural authorization for these texts (dpe lung), I heard all of them speak of Yangalwa as the master holding the lineage for the descent of these teachings. [24] I sent a request with a messenger, together with some powerful medicine pills, to the monastic residence of Lama Yangalwa. Having considered the matter, he replied to me in a letter, writing, 'Now, there exists just a single essential explanation for the Experiential Transmission (nyams-rgyud dmar-khrid gcig). But we live in two distant places and so it is unlikely that we will meet personally. These instructions have not been previously set down in writing. And because they represent a singular transmission, there exist only the oral precepts from those previous Mahasiddhas. But even though that is the case, there is one of my disciples who has obtained the Experiential Transmission from me. You should try to meet him and look to him for this!' Also my uncle Tsandanpa had written to me and said, 'The Togdan is the one who has the scriptural transmission for the Oral Transmission (snyan-rgyud kyi lung). Therefore, you must request it from him! Now, let us discuss this question of the scriptural authority for the Oral Transmission.'

"There having occurred many such discussions regarding the Oral Transmission, finally the Togdan conferred the empowerment and the scriptural authority upon the three scholars, Lama Gyalwa and his two companions Lopon Mewon (sLob-dpon me-dbon) and Menyak Ringdrak (Me-nyag ring-grags). When the ceremony was completed, Lama Gyalwa said to the master, 'Now, there exists the question of the existence of the Experiential Transmission that has in no way been contaminated by being set down in written words. Have you considered that?' But the Togdan replied, 'This is all of it. There is not even as much as a grain of sesame remaining. The authorization I have already given will have to do!' And he remained adamant in this.

"However, Lama Gyalwa cited once more the history contained in the letter from Lama Dansapa [25] which clearly indicated that what the three scholars had received was not sufficient, and that there existed a further Experiential Transmission. He should consider transmitting that also. To this the Togdan replied, "Well then, if you have such a fervent desire, according to the system of these teachings, now we must make examinations of your name, your conduct, your body marks, as well as your dreams. Although there are many examinations to be made, for a man such as yourself, it will not be necessary to examine all of them. But let us at least propitiate the non-human spirits [26] and then tomorrow we will make an examination of our dreams.

'That night, among the experiences of the master, he dreamed that he saw a beautiful valley that resembled the mountain of Yartse Hauri (ya-rtse ha'u ri) and this valley appeared to be filled with various different flowers and fruit trees. Moreover, there were innumerable beautiful young girls, aged fifteen and sixteen, adorned with jewel ornaments, who came forward carrying fruits and kusha grass on their backs. And as they came, the entire region of Wensakha monastery became filled with fruits and kusha grass. Where there were no fruits, they freely scattered them about. In the direction south of Wensakha also, there were the trunks of many fruit trees that bore bright blossoms. In the middle of all that, there was a spring gushing forth that resembled that spring at Damkhari. At the head of that spring, three Bonpo priests had gathered. They had prepared many extensive offerings and they were engaged in invoking the gods (lha gsol). This was how he described his dream.

"Then again Lama Gyalwa dreamed that he found himself on the road. Then, in a valley filled with flowers and fruit trees, there was the facade of a high castle. At that site he blew a conch shell, raised a silken banner, and scattered many flowers into every direction. [27]

"Third, as for the special places of practice that served as his supports anywhere during his lifetime, he principally engaged in the practice of meditation at such places of realization (grub gnas) as the rock at Yeru Kharna (g.yas-ru mkhar-sna'i brag) and at Ragong Yonpo (Ra-gong yon-po), and elsewhere. Moreover, the Lama himself said, "Due to the compassion created by my fervent devotion to those earlier Mahasiddhas, there came forth within me a confident belief and definitive decision (regarding the Natural State), which cut off the extremes that are conceptual elaborations." [28]

"Furthermore, there arose from within the interior of his mind the bliss of pristine awareness without thoughts and he cut off the stream of distinguishing characteristics associated with subject and object. [29] And because of that, there arose for him without interruption the Clear Light, which is the spontaneously perfected Base (in terms of Thodgal visions). The distinctive characteristics of the three: the sounds, the lights, and the rays, were liberated into their own original condition on the Path. And as the Fruit, at the ultimate stage (in the development of vision) the Trikaya became visibly manifest to him. [30] Thereby the Great Bliss remained in its own original condition of the Dharmakaya and he came to behold the face of his own meditation deity, the Yidam Tsochok (gtso-mchog), whereupon the Generation Process and the Perfection Process, all emanating and reabsorbing, were liberated into their own original condition. In consequence, immeasurable numbers of liberations of experience and understanding were born in his mind. [31]

"Moreover, the treatises composed by him, born of the above understanding, and after having condensed them into the outer, the inner, and the secret classes, were as follows: [32]

1. *Lag-len pod chung* (outer, inner, and secret rituals),
2. *gZungs 'dus* (dharani-mantras),
3. *rDzogs-chen snyan-rgyud kyi lag-len dmar-khrid* (essential explanations regarding the practice manual for the Zhang-zhung Nyan-gyud),
4. *dBal-gsas khrig-ma lag khrid* (the practice manual for the deity Walse),
5. *rTsa rlung gi gdams-pa* (instructions on Tsalung practice),

6. *Drang-don snod bcud kyi yig-sna* (assorted texts on the universe and its inhabitants according to Relative Truth),
7. *Dong sprugs zlas lung* (mantra recitations for stirring up the depths of Samsara),
8. *Zhal gdams mgur 'bum* (songs of spiritual instruction),
9. *gSol-'debs* (various invocations and prayers),
    (And in particular)
10. *A-khrid kyi gzhung rgyab skor* (the cycle of the principal and ancillary texts of the A-khrid system of Dzogchen practice) [33] whereby he arranged innummmerable disciples on the Path of spiritual instruction and liberation.

"Fourth, his virtuous qualities and the signs of his realization that were ordinary manifested during his lifetime. According to the prophecy found in the *gNad byang drug-cu rtsa gcig-pa*: of Chyangphak: [34] 'There will come forth in the future one called Drusha Tsun (Bru-sha btsun) who will be an emanation of (the ancient sage) Nangwa Dogchan (sNang-ba mdog-can). There will be fourteen Bodhisattvas who are lineage-holders (in his lineage of transmission) and he will come to guide living beings. Gyalwa Yungdrung will come as the emanation of the Sugatas, those noble ones who are the makers of medicines, for the sake of benefiting living beings. Those who merely touch his lotus-like feet will become arrayed on the path to freedom from the five aggregates of rebirth and the doors to liberation for some three hundred-thousand beings will be opened.' [35]

"Fifth, his extraordinary understanding became manifest. All of his experiences and signs (nyams rtags) in meditation practice were very auspicious and even the non-human spirits could not bind him with their disturbances. Having requested his two companions to depart from the room first, Lama Gyalwa, in the presence of his own master (Chigchod Dadpa Sherab), requested to receive the oral instructions, together with the permissions for the practices (zha-gdams rjes-gnang). Moreover, Lama Gyalwa agreed to preserve the Single Transmission (gcig brgyud) and not to dispense the teachings either for wealth or for fame. There arose within him a confident belief and a definitive decision (yid-ches thag-chod) regarding the Natural State without reverting to either hopes or fears. All of his conceptual elaborations in the form of doubts, as well as his hopes and fears regarding the cycles of instructions (gdams skor) were removed for him like cutting through a spider's web. And he obtained all of the words and the meanings (tshig don) from the transmissions. Up until his own time, this teaching of the Zhang-zhung Nyan-gyud had not spread very much, but during the lifetime of Lama Gyalwa, it the teaching spread widely like the rays of the sun and became well known.

"Finally, as for the life-span of his physical body, having attained fourty-nine years, he displayed the method of passing beyond sorrow. He is said to have died at his monastery of Yeru Wensakha. His principal disciples were his younger brother Dru Namkha Odzer (Bru Nam-mkha' 'od-zer) and his nephew Druton Sonam Gyaltsan (Bruston bsod-nams rgyal-mtshan)." [36]

Contents of the Practice Manual: *rGyal-ba phyag-khrid*

Among his many literary works cited above is a noted commentary on the practice of the *A-khrid* system of Dzogchen, entitled the *Thun-mtshams bco-lnga-pa man-ngag khrid kyi rim-pa lag-len thun-mtshams dang bcas-pa.* [37] And in addition, he composed the practice manual and commentary on the *Zhang-zhung snyan-rgyud* that we have here, namely, the *sNyan-rgyud rgyal-ba'i phyag-khrid.* I am aware of two published versions of this text:

1. a litho edition in the *dbu-med* script published in India, no date; and
2. the reprint of a xylograph edition published in a volume entitled *sNyan rgyud nam-mkha' 'phrul mdzod drang nges skor* and *Zhang-zhung snyan-rgyud skor*, Tibetan Bonpo Monastic Centre, New Delhi 1972, ff. 539-726. Within this collection composed by Gyalwa Yungdrung, we find three classes of texts:
   (1) the preliminary practices (sngon-'gro),
   (2) the principle practices (dngos-gzhi), and
   (3) the ancilliary texts or branches (yan-lag). These latter texts are four in number and deal with the view (lta-ba), the meditation (sgom-pa), the conduct (spyod-pa), and the fruit ('bras-bu), respectively.

The texts included in the *rGyal-ba'i phyag-khrid* collection are as follows:

0. *Zhang-zhung snyan-rgyud kyi lo-rgyus rnam-thar dang bcas-pa*, "The History of the Oral Transmission from Zhang-zhung, together with the Hagioigraphies," (ff. 539-589). This history is found in the xylograph reprint but not in the *dbu-med*

manuscript. It is a different text than the one similarly titled found in the collection that is the basis for the present study.
1. *sNgon-'gro rim-pa rnams*, "the Stages of the Preliminary Practices" (ff.1-22), including an invocation of Tapihritsa, *sNgon-'gro gsol-'debs*, "the Invocation for the Preliminary Practices" (ff.23-28). In the xylograph reprint the text is called *Bon-spyod dgu-rim*, "the Nine Stages for the Conduct of Bon" (ff. 591-607). This text contains the explanations by Druchen for the preliminary practices (sngon-'gro) and it is divided into nine distinct practices:
   (1) the Conferring of Empowerments (dbang-bskur),
   (2) the Meditation on the Impermanence of Life (tshe mi rtag-pa),
   (3) the Confession of Sins (sdig-pa bshag-pa),
   (4) the Producing the Bodhichitta (sems bskyed),
   (5) the Going to Refuge (skyabs 'gro),
   (6) the Offering of the Mandala (mandal 'bul)
   (7) the Reciting of Mantras for Purification (sngags kyi bzlas-pa),
   (8) the Cutting off of Attachments (gcod), and
   (9) the Praying to receive the Guru's Blessings (gsol-'debs) which is the Guru Yoga (bla-ma'i rnal-'byor) proper.
2. *Zab-mo gnad kyi gdams-pa dngos-gzhi*, "The Instructions concerning the Profound Essential Points for the Principal Practices" (ff.29-76), and in the xylograph reprint *Khrid rim lag-len*, "The Manual for the Stages of the Explanation" (ff.609-638). This text represents the principle practice, including both Trekchod (khregs-chod) and Thodgal (thod-rgal), but with the emphasis on the latter. The Thodgal practice for the development of vision (snang-ba) is divided into dark retreat practice (mun-mtshams), space or sky practice (nam-mkha'), and sunlight practice (nyi 'od) which represents Thodgal as such. Complete instructions for these practices are provided by Druchen. [38]
3. *gZhi rang ngo-sprad-pa gcer-mthong lta-ba'i khrid*, "The Explanation of the View, being a Direct Introduction to one's own Base through Seeing Nakedly", abbreviated as *lTa-khrid* (ff. 77-100; ff. 639-655). Here begins the section consisting of four texts or commentaries known as auxiliaries or branches (yan-lag). They are also composed by Druchen. The first

provides the explanation of the view (lta-khrid) of Dzogchen.
[39]

4. *Lam nyams su len-pa'i 'od-gsal sgom-pa'i khrid*, "The
Explanation of the Meditation regarding the Clear Light
Practice on the Path,"abbreviated a *sGom-khrid* (ff.101-124;
657-673). The text provides the explanation of the meditation
practice (sgom-khrid) in relation to Dzogchen, focusing on
Clear Light vision practice or Thodgal.

5. *rKyen lam du slong-ba rtsal sbyong spyod-pa'i khrid*, "The
Explanation of the Activity concerning the Forceful
Purifications employed on the Path in accordance with
Secondary Conditions," abbreviated as *sPyod-khrid* (ff.125-
156; ff.675-697). The text provides explanations for the
activities that are practiced along the path (spyod-khrid) from
the standpoint of Dzogchen, including forceful purifications
(rtsal sbyong).

6. *'Bras-bu rang sa bzung-ba sku gsum dmar thag-bcad-pa'i
khrid*, "The Explanation that is Vitally Definitive regarding the
Trikaya apprehended as one's own Original Condition which
constitutes the Fruit," abbreviated as *Thag-bcad-pa'i khrid* or
Thag gcod-pa'i khrid (ff.157-176; ff.699-713). The
explanation for vitally and definitively deciding upon (dmar
thag-bcad-pa'i khrid) the Fruit which is the Trikaya as realized
through the practice of vision.

7. *'Od-gsal gyi dmigs-pa dang gags sel*, "Visualizations for the
Clear Light Practice and the Removing of Obstacles,"
abbreviated as *dmigs-rim*, "The Stages of Visualization" (ff.
177-204). A text dealing with the visualizations (dmigs-pa)
used in practice and various methods for removing obstacles to
practice (gags sel). This text is not found in the xylograph
reprint.

8. *'Od-gsal bdun skor* (ff. 295-222) or *gCig-rgyud 'od-gsal bdun
skor* (ff.715-726). This text, "the Seven-fold Cycle of the Clear
Light", gives intructions for making a forty-nine day retreat in
total darkness (mun-mtshams) according to the Zhang-zhung
Nyan-gyud tradition. Both this and the preceding text appear to
be later additions to the collection and not to have been written
by Druchen. [40] Then there follows some additional material
(mkhas-pa.... zhal gdams) in the manuscript (ff. 223-228).

The Guru Yoga for Tapihritsa

Introduction

According to the Bonpo tradition, originally Tapihritsa was an ordinary human being, a native of Zhang-zhung in Northern Tibet, but through the dedicated practice of Dzogchen, both in terms of the state of contemplation, that is, Trekchod, and the visions of the Clear Light, that is, Thodgal, he attained realization and full enlightenment. In general, Tapihritsa is said to be the most important master in the lineage of transmission for the Zhang-zhung Nyan-gyud. [1] He was the twenty-fifth individual master in the lineage for the transmission that came from Tonpa Shenrab and Sangwa Dupa to the divine Shen practitioner Yongsu Dagpa and which descended to his own teacher Tsepung Dawa Gyaltsan in the seventh century. All of these twenty-four masters became Jalupas or Rainbow Bodies of Light. [2] After practicing for nine years in a cave in the mountains in Northern Tibet, he attained enlightenment and liberation from Samsara, thus exemplifying the realization of the Rainbow Body of the Great Transfer [3] without leaving any material traces of his physical body behind.

With his clairvoyance, Tapihritsa perceived that the Tantric adept and Mahasiddha Gyerpung Nangzher Lodpo was a suitable vessel to receive the transmissions of the Dzogchen precepts. [4] But the latter first needed to be tested and his intellectual pride and emotional arrogance subdued. Therefore, after having attained enlightenment, Tapihritsa reappeared, resurrected and transfigured, as a Body of Light in the guise of a precocious young boy who took employment as a servant with a local nomad chief in Zhang-zhung. This was not because of any necessity on his part, but it represented only an exercise in the skillful means expressing his great compassion in order to awaken and open Gyerpungpa for the transmission of the Dzogchen precepts. Once he had prepared and matured the mind-stream of his disciple, Tapihritsa abandoned the disguise of the small ragged orphan boy and reappeared in the sky above in a more glorious and exalted form in order to proceed with the process of the transmission.

According to the Lopon, because he thus exemplified the realization of the Great Transfer, Tapihritsa has come to be taken in the Zhang-zhung tradition as the archetype of the Mahaguru who embodies within his visible form all of the masters of all of the lineages for the Dzogchen teachings. Tapihritsa manifested visibly to Gyerpungpa in the numinous form of the Nirmanakaya, that is to say, as a sixteen year old youth, translucent and radiant, white in color and clear like crystal, naked and unadorned, sitting in the center of a rainbow sphere of light suspended in the middle of the sky. Having previously attained enlightenment long before this revelation of the Nirmanakaya, the Awareness of Tapihritsa truly existed outside ordinary time and history, the linear causal sequence of human events, and outside the limited dimensions of the profane space of the world that is perceived with ordinary human understanding. Moreover, he now possessed the capacity to reappear and manifest at will as a Body of Light in any form and at whatever time and place in order to teach and transmit the knowledge of Dzogchen to receptive disciples. It is said that he still possesses that power, even in our own degenerate times, but this appearance or hierophany depends on the devotion, the receptivity, and the pure vision of the practitioner. Even though Tapihritsa may appear in any form whatsoever, within the dimension of human karmic vision he has generally appeared in the guise of a human being in order to communicate with other human beings.

Furthermore, it was in this archetypal form of the eternal youth and the wise child of light ('od kyi khye'u-chung), described below, that Tapihritsa manifested and bestowed the Dzogchen precepts upon Gyerpungpa. For this reason, the practitioner of the Zhang-zhung Nyan-gyud tradition performs the Guru Yoga meditation while visualizing Tapihritsa in precisely that same youthful form suspended in the sky in front of oneself. Thereupon one prays to him with fervent and intense devotion in order to receive the blessings of his knowledge and inspiration (byin rlabs). Although Tapihritsa appears here to be similar in terms of his iconography to the Primordial Buddha Kuntu Zangpo, with whom he is ultimately identical at the Dharmakaya level and is, therefore, called Kunzang Tapihritsa, still his manifestations to his disciple Gyerpungpa constituted hierophanies or revelations of the

Nirmanakaya. Hence, he is simply called "the Nirmanakaya (sprul-sku)"

From the Primordial Buddha Kuntu Zangpo Himself down to Tapihritsa in the seventh century, the precepts of Dzogchen have been transmitted as Upadeshas or secret oral instructions (man-ngag) to only a single disciple at a time (gcig brgyud). Therefore, these precepts were kept supremely secret. However, it is said that Tapihritsa possessed prescience, or foreknowledge of the future, and therefore knew that a persecution of the Bonpos would occur in the next century. For this reason, he allowed Gyerpungpa to set down the precepts in writing in the language of Zhang-zhung using the *sMar-yig* script. In this way, the Zhang-zhung teachings of Dzogchen would not be lost to the humanity of future generations in this degenerate age when understanding of spirituality is limited and the powers of memory are weak. Moreover, Tapihritsa gave permission for his disciple to teach these precepts to more than a single disciple of his own. Thus, in a real sense, with Tapihritsa and Gyerpungpa, the Dzogchen teachings entered into human history. Therefore, according to the Lopon, one visualizes Tapihritsa in the Guru Yoga practice not only because he exemplifies the Great Transfer, but because of his great kindness and benevolence in the revealing the Dzogchen precepts to his disciple and permitting him to set them down in writing.

The Guru Yoga (bla-ma'i rnal-'byor) for the Zhang-zhung Nyan-gyud is generally performed while the practitioner visualizes Tapihritsa in the sky in front of oneself, just as this master had originally appeared to Gyerpungpa when he revealed to the latter the transmissions for the Dzogchen precepts and the experiences in meditation of the previous masters in the lineage. By means of this visualization process, the practitioner creates a sacred space and a sacred time, repeating the archetypal actions of Gyerpungpa when he first requested and received the transmissions from his own enlightened master. Again, according to the Lopon, to become a lineage-holder for the Zhang-zhung Nyan-gyud, there is no question that one must practice this Guru Yoga for Tapihritsa. The Guru Yoga is considered to be the single most important preliminary practice in the Dzogchen tradition. This luminous figure of the Guru as the archetypal wise child or eternal youth in the space above and in front of oneself in the sky is imagined to embody and encompass within his radiant form the essences of all the masters of the Dzogchen teachings. The principle here is one of integration and unification (rnal-'byor, Skt.

yoga), that is to say, unification with the essence or the Nature of Mind of all these masters (bla-ma, Skt. guru).

The function of the Guru is to bestow the blessings (byin-brlabs) that represent a kind of spiritual energy of inspiration. Ultimately this spiritual energy emerged spontaneously out of the inexhaustible effulgence of the enlightened awareness and being of the Primordial Buddha Himself. It was then transmitted down through a lineage of realized adepts or Mahasiddhas to one's own master, much as electricity may be transmitted over power lines to the cities across the country side from its ultimate source at the generators high in the mountains. The master then communicates this spiritual energy to the practitioner, which in turn acts as a catalyst to awaken, open, and ripen the spiritual potential within the mind-stream of that individual (rgyud smin). In this way, the power of inspiration is infused into the very being of the practitioner and, indeed, this process is repeated every time one performs the Guru Yoga.

How to Practice the Guru Yoga

The Necessity of an Attitude of Devotion

How is one to do the practice? Finding a quiet place where one will not be disturbed, the practitioner should first cultivate intense faith and fervent devotion toward the Guru and his teachings. One should feel that one is actually sitting in the immediate physical presence of Tapihritsa, who in turn is identical with one's own personal Root Master or Tsawe Lama (rtsa-ba'i bla-ma). This is the master or spiritual teacher with whom one has close karmic links over many past lives and whom in this present life gives one the most important empowerments and explanations of the teachings (dbang khrid), including the direct introduction to one's own Mind (rig-pa ngo-sprod). Praying with great faith and fervent devotion, one asks for help and guidance by way of having revealed to oneself the short and quick path to enlightenment, which is Dzogchen. It is with this sense of faith, reverence, devotion, and intimacy, while reciting the invocation, that one fixates the mind on the clear visualization of Tapihritsa in the open sky in front of oneself. One feels his actual presence there. One opens one's heart unreservedly to him and surrenders totally in spirit of perfect trust. The blessings of the Guru Tapihritsa are like the light of the sun; they are shed impartially upon all. But in order to enjoy the delight of the warm sunshine, one must first step out of the dense cool darkness of the cave, which is one's own restricted selfish existence and ego consciousness. This attitude of total devotion, openness, and surrender (mos-gus) in the context of the Guru Yoga practice cannot be emphasized enough. For it is just this emotional intensity, rather than intellectual comprehension, which fires and actualizes the Guru Yoga practice, making its realization concrete and effective and alive. This is no mere intellectual exercise, for it embodies concretely an intimate personal relationship. And as the master Jigmed Lingpa has said, the Guru Yoga is only effective when one's skin tingles and one's hair stands on end.

The Five-Point Sitting Position

Taking a comfortable seat, one assumes the five-point meditation position, thereby aligning the psychic channels in order to ensure that the prana, or the vital winds of psychic energy (rlung, Skt. vayu), flow smoothly and harmoniously within the body, so that distracting thoughts tend not to arise. [5] Consequently, the mind may more easily be tamed and controlled. This position, which represents the essential point of the body (lus gnad), is as follows:

1. One sits in a cross-legged manner, which regulates and controls the activities of the vital winds in the lower part of the body, especially the Apana-vayu (thur-sel), the downward moving vital wind that is concerned with the activities of the lower digestive tract and the elimination of waste products such as urine and feces.

2. The spine is held straight like an arrow, which keeps the joints and the muscles in alignment, as well as harmonizing the functions of the winds and channels in their proper places throughout the body, especially the Vyana-vayu (khyab-'jug), or all-pervading vital wind, that enables the muscles to be moved. The four limbs of the body are held tight and firm, but not tense and never loose and flaccid

3. The hands are held in samadhi-mudra, the gesture of equipoise (mnyam-bzhag phyag-rgya), the left hand lying over the right hand. This gesture regulates and controls the activities of the internal organs of the body. It balances and harmonizes their functions, especially the Samana-vayu (me-mnyam), the heat-equalizing vital wind, concerned with bodily heat, metabolism, and digestion. In this gesture, the left hand rests on top of the right hand, the thumb of each hand pressing at the base of the ring fingers.

4. The neck is bent forward just a little like an iron hook. This regulates and controls the activities of speech and other functions involving the throat such as swallowing, and especially the Udana-vayu (gyen-rgyu), the upward-moving vital wind, that regulates these operations.
5. The shoulders are hunched a little like the wings of a vulture that can soar through the sky. This regulates and controls the activities of the vital winds in the torso or upper body, especially the Prana-vayu (srog-'dzin), which regulates respiration in the lungs and the circulation of blood from the heart.

Moreover, one's gaze is level and straight ahead, with the eyes open and focused on the space in front beyond the tip of the nose. The eyes are half closed and one avoids moving the eyes or blinking too much. This control of the gaze also serves to regulate the activities of the Prana-vayu and thus keep distracting thoughts from arising due to the unregulated and restless movements of this vital wind. Furthermore, the tongue floats and does not touch the palate. There is a space between the teeth in the mouth like one is softly sounding "aaaah...." [6]

By sitting in this five-point meditation posture, one balances the physical body and harmonizes the movements and flow of the vital winds or psychic energies, thereby inhibiting the arising of distracting thoughts. One can also employ a meditation belt (sgom-thag) for additional support of the body in order to hold the position for long periods of time.

Sitting in this cross-legged position with the hands resting on the lap and the palms turned upward, with the left hand resting over the right and the thumbs of each hand pressing against the point at the base of the ring finger, one closes and seals temporarily the Klesha-nadi or psychic channel through which negative provocations of energy (gdon) might gain access to one's body from the external environment. According to the tradition of Tibetan shamanism, it is through these two channels of the right and left hands, extending from the tips of the ring fingers to the heart, that spirits might enter the body and come to possess the individual. By closing these two channels, the practitioner protects oneself when meditating.

When practicing being in the state of contemplation or the Natural State, the practitioner should simply relax into a condition of inaction or immobility of one's body, speech, and mind. Otherwise, the activities of one's mind and energy cause imbalances in the psychic channels and the vital winds and this, in turn, gives rise to distracting thoughts and feelings that disturb one's state of contemplation. In the context of the Dzogchen teachings, contemplation or samadhi refers not just to a calm state of mind (shamatha) or intense concentration and withdrawal from the senses (dhyana), but to being in the Natural State (rig-pa). For this purpose there is a special body posture where the physical body is bound with the five mudras described above. Holding the body immobile limits physical activities that might disturb the vital winds and the psychic channels. Mind or consciousness is always associated with these subtle winds representing the movements of psychic energies. Mind (sems) and psychic energy (rlung) are linked together like a rider mounted on an unruly horse. If the vital winds are unbalanced, the mind or flow of thoughts becomes unbalanced and distractions arise into consciousness. Gentle deep breathing and maintaining silence renders these vital winds immobile. Without the movements of these winds, discursive thoughts do not arise. Concentration and fixation of awareness on some object of meditation bring about immobility of the mind. Therefore, these three immobilities (mi g.yo-ba gsum) of body, speech, and mind facilitate the practitioner remaining in the Natural State with a bright alert awareness. Therefore, it is said that this five-point position for meditation practice is very important.

The Nine Breathings for Purification
Then one performs the nine breathings for purification of one's vital winds and channels, which is generally known as taming or training the breath (rtsa 'dul), by breathing three times out each nostril while closing the opposite nostril with one's finger. This makes a total of six exhalations. For the last three exhalations, one breathes out both nostrils. Thus, the stale air (rlung ro) in the lungs, as well as all residual emotional defilements or impurities, are expelled from the body, so that one comes to feel cleansed and purified.

In the Buddhist system, the three principal channels are known as Rasana (ro-ma), which is on the right, Lalana (rkyang-ma), which is on the left, and Avadhuti (dbu-ma), which is in the center. In the Hindu system, they are called Pingala, Ida, and Sushumna respectively. The Avadhuti or central channel is visualized in the precise center of the body, not in the spinal column, but in front of it. These psychic channels (rtsa, Skt. nadi) represent potential pathways for the movements of psychic energy; they are subtle structures, not gross physical anatomy. Therefore, by visualizing or imagining them (dmigs-pa) one makes them actual and moves one's vital winds (rlung,

Skt. vayu) through them. Thus, there exist in the Tantras, both Buddhist and Bonpo, a number of different systems for visualizing the three principal psychic channels. What visualization system the practitioner employs depends on how and where one is moving these psychic energies or winds.

One visualizes the central channel as deep azure in color like the bright clear sky, being situated in the middle of the body, beginning at the secret center, some four finger-widths below the navel, and extending to the aperture or opening at the crown of the head. This channel is straight like the shaft of an arrow and is the size of a hollow bamboo cane. In general, this central channel is said to have the four characteristics of being straight, shiny, hollow, and blue in color. Parallel to it on both sides are two smaller channels, which are like fine silk threads. The right-hand channel is white in color like crystal, and the left channel is red in color like powdered coral. They symbolize the cool white lunar masculine energy, which is like the moon, and the fiery red solar feminine energy, which is like the sun, respectively. In the Tantra system, the moon symbolizes semen, the male element, because it is white and the sun symbolizes menstrual blood, the female element, because it is red. This is the reverse of the symbolism in Western astrology. These channels and colors are the reverse in women. The two side channels enter into the central channel at the Kunda or juncture of the three channels (rtsa gsum 'dus mdor) below the navel and this juncture resembles the Tibetan letter CHA. These three channels extend upward to the physical heart and then curve behind it and go to the spine and up through the neck. They join again at the *Ag-tse*, or joint of the spine and skull. Previously running in parallel to the central channel, they now go inside the skull case (klad phor) and arch over the membrane of the brain (klad sprin). These two side channels then turn down to the nostrils of the nose where they terminate. Inside the skull, the central channel widens a bit as its approaches the aperture at the top of the head, so that it comes to resemble a horn or a flower. Thus, it has been compared to the blue flower called *spangs-rgyan* (Gentiana stipitala Edjew.) which blooms in autumn. The mouth or upper extremity of the central channel extends out through the aperture at the crown of the skull. This is known as the aperture of Brahma (tshangs-pa'i bu-ga, Skt. brahmarandhra).

In particular, for men, using the left hand, one closes the right nostril with one's ring finger and inhales the fresh clean air through the left nostril and the left channel while visualizing that one is absorbing into oneself luminous light blue wisdom air (ye-shes kyi rlung). And one holds the breath a little. Then closing the left nostril with the thumb and opening the right nostril, one blows the stale polluted air (rlung-ro) out the right nostril and the right hand channel. One visualizes this stale air that is being expelled as light bluish-gray smoke, which represents the polluted residues of the negative emotion of anger. Thereupon one changes nostrils and does just the opposite. Closing the left nostril with the thumb of the left hand, one inhales the wisdom air through the right nostril and holds the breath a little. Then opening the left nostril and closing the right nostril with the ring finger, one exhales the stale air while visualizing it to be light red smoke in color representing the polluted residues of the negative emotion of desire. Thereby each side is purified in this way alternatively three times. Women should proceed in exactly the opposite fashion, first purifying the left side for anger and then the right side for desire.

Then one inhales the clean luminous wisdom air through both nostrils simultaneously and, in the same way, proceeds to expel the stale polluted air, visualizing it as smoke of a dirty brown color representing the polluted residues of the negative emotion of confusion. This negative emotion or klesha is actually a mixture of the two principal passions, anger and desire, and is characterized by ignorance, confusion, indecision, and bewilderment. One visualizes this stale air being expelled through the hole in the top of one's head.

In each case, the inhalation is done slowly and gently, whereas the blowing out of the disturbances is done a bit more forcefully. Men begin by cleansing the right channel, whereas women begin by cleansing the left channel, because these two side channels are the reverse in men and women due to Tantric polarity. The white lunar channel, where the residues of anger accumulate, is on the right side in men and on the left side in women, whereas the red solar channel, where the residues of desire accumulate, is on the left side in men and on the right side in women.

Thus, while three times alternately exhaling the stale air of the white lunar channel on the right side of men and the left side of women, one should think that each time one expels negative energy, it has four characteristics associated with it:

1. anger (zhe-sdang, Skt. dvesha), as well as obstacles linked with the past in general;
2. wind diseases, that is, diseases due to lack of vitality or imbalances in the Vayu or wind humor (rlung gi nad),

3. the color of light blue smoke, and
4. disturbances coming from male spirits (pho gdon).

Next, while three times alternately exhaling the stale air from the red solar channel on the left side of men and the right side of women, one should think that each time one expels negative energy, it also has four characteristics associated with it:

1. desire ('dod-chags, Skt. raga), as well as obstacles linked to the future;
2. diseases due to imbalance in the Pitta or bile humor (mkhris-pa'i nad),
3. the color of light red smoke, and
4. disturbances coming from female spirits (mo gdon).

Finally, one inhales and exhales three times through both nostrils. Here the fresh wisdom air goes into the central channel and the stale air is forcefully expelled from the top of one's head (actually both nostrils). The negative energy of confusion also has four characteristics:

1. confusion or bewilderment (gti-mug, Skt. moha), as well as obstacles linked to the present;
2. diseases due to an imbalance in Kapha or the phlegm humor (bad-kan gyi nad),
3. the color of dark brown smoke, and
4. disturbances due to the Nagas or subterranean spirits (klu gdon).

The Four Phases of the Guru Yoga Practice
This process of the nine breathings represents the preliminary purification. The principal practice of the Guru Yoga is described in terms of four phases:

1. the visualization of the presence of the Guru in the sky in front of oneself and the reciting of the invocation,
2. the receiving of purification from the Guru by way of the wisdom nectars,
3. the receiving of the blessings of the Guru by way of the empowerments with the three lights, and
4. the recitation of prayers and mantras.

Phase One: Visualization of the Guru
Then sounding the seed syllable A, the practitioner proceeds to visualize the Guru Tapihritsa in the sky in front of oneself above the

crown of one's head. [7] In this case, Tapihritsa is transparent or translucent, his body being clear and empty like the rainbow, because he represents the inseparability of clarity and emptiness (gsal stong dbyer-med). He is pure white like a quartz crystal because he has been thoroughly purified of all obscurations and defilements (sgrib-med). He is entirely naked and unadorned because he is completely free of all discursive thoughts (rtog-med) and operations of mind pertaining to the thought process. And he

Guru Tapihritsa

is visualized as sitting in peaceful contemplation in the center of a rainbow sphere of light (thig-le) suspended in the sky because he has already attained the Body of Light of the Great Transfer ('pho-ba chen-po'i 'od sku). This indicates that his nature is wisdom, primordial awareness, or gnosis (ye-shes). But one should not visualize him as being flat and two-dimensional in aspect like a painting on the wall, but rather as three-dimensional, translucent, and immaterial like the rainbow appearing in the sky. One should feel that he is alive and actually present before one in space and that he sees the practitioner sitting there below him and looks down upon one with compassion and loving kindness. Therefore, this is a very personal encounter.

Furthermore, one should think that this luminous figure of Tapihritsa embodies the unification of all the Gurus and masters and all the lineages of transmission for Dzogchen that one has received in this present life and in all one's previous lifetimes. One proceeds to pray fervently with heart-felt devotion to this master, as if he is actually present before one, presenting offerings to him, including a Ganachakra Puja, whether these offerings are actually present or merely visualized in imagination. Finally one requests the blessings of the empowerments of the Body, the Speech, and the Mind of the Guru. [8]

Having visualized the Guru clearly in this way and fixating one's mind on him, one recites the invocation many times, or at least three times. For this purpose, the Lopon suggests the following verse of supplication:

"In the palace of great bliss on the crown of my head,
Is my benevolent Root Guru to whom I pray;

The Buddha as my own Mind is the precious Teacher:
Please grant the blessing that I may recognize my own nature!" [9]
    The pronunciation and interlinear translation is as follows:
CHYI-TSUK DE-WA CHEN-PO PHO-DRANG DU,
In the palace of great bliss on the crown of my head,
DRIN-CHAN TSA-WE LA-MA LA SOL-WA DEB,
Is my benevolent Root Guru to whom I pray;
SANG-GYE SEM SU TON-PA RIN-PO-CHE,
The Buddha as my own Mind is the precious Teacher:
RANG NGO RANG GI SHE-PAR JYIN GYI LOB.
Please grant the blessing that I may recognize my own nature!

Phase Two: Purification with the Wisdom Nectars
In response to one's attitude of fervent devotion and opening oneself
unreservedly to him, from the heart center of Guru Tapihritsa, one
visualizes that there issues forth an effulgence of white light that
spontaneously transforms into streams of the luminous white nectars
of wisdom (ye-shes kyi bdud-rtsi). This flows and enters into the
aperture at the crown of one's head and descending through the central
channel, it comes to fill one's entire body. This luminous white nectar
represents the wisdom of the Guru (bla-ma'i ye-shes) and it washes
away and cleanses all of one's sins and obscurations, including all the
emotional defilements and karmic traces inherited from the
immemorial past. One's body becomes thereby totally cleansed and
purified, so that one's whole being is transformed into a suitable
vessel, like a pure crystal vase filled with light, prepared for the
receiving of the blessings and empowerments that the master will
bestow. [10]

Phase Three: Receiving the Empowerments
At the conclusion of this process of purification, the practitioner is now
well suited to receive the initiations and the transmission of the
Dzogchen precepts. One sounds the syllables A OM HUM, signifying
the dimensions of the body, speech, and mind of the individual. Again
in response to one's cultivating intense faith and devotion, these
syllables, in the form of luminous Tibetan letters, then appear
spontaneously on the surface of the body at the three secret places or
three secret doors (sgo gsum) of the Guru, that is to say, at his
forehead, at his throat, and at his heart. [11] Thereupon rays of lights
in their respective colors issue forth from these syllables and touch the
three corresponding places on the surface of one's own body where

these lights and their energies are absorbed. In this way one receives and unifies with the knowledge and the wisdom (ye-shes) of the Body, Speech, and Mind of the Guru. In particular, from the white syllable A at the forehead of the Guru comes a brilliant white ray of light, which enters one's own forehead center. Thus all one's sins and obscurations of body are purified and one receives the empowerment and the spiritual attainments (or siddhis) of the Body of the Guru. One is now empowered to do the Kyerim (bskyed-rim) or visualization transformation practice and this indicates that one will eventually come to realize the Nirmanakaya or the bodily manifestation of enlightenment. From the red syllable OM at the throat of the Guru comes a brilliant red ray of light, which enters one's own throat center. Thus all one's sins and obscurations of speech are purified and one receives the empowerment and the spiritual attainments of the Speech of the Guru. One is now empowered to do the Tsalung (rtsa-rlung) or mantra recitations and breathing practices (pranayama) and this indicates that one will eventually come to realize the Sambhogakaya or the energetic aspect of enlightenment. From the blue syllable HUM at the heart of the Guru comes a brilliant blue ray of light, which enters one's own heart center. Thus all one's sins and obscurations of mind are purified and one receives the empowerment and spiritual attainments of the Mind of the Guru. One is now empowered to do the Dzogrim (rdzogs-rim) or the internal yoga practices for the realizing of the inseparability of bliss and emptiness and this indicates that one will eventually come to realize the Dharmakaya or the ultimate mind aspect of enlightenment. Each of these lights dissolve and are absorbed into the locations or centers of one's own being, like pouring water into water, so that the Body, Speech, and Mind of the Guru merge with one's own body, speech, and mind. In this way the practitioner becomes both purified and empowered, accessing and assimilating into oneself the energies and capacities of the Body, Speech, and Mind of the Guru. This initiation and empowerment occurs at the culmination of the process of the visualization of the Guru. This connects the practitioner with all the masters in the lineages of the Dzogchen teachings and whenever the Guru Yoga exercise is repeated, it helps to maintain that connection or spiritual link.

Phase Four: Reciting Prayers
At this point, having received the empowerments and blessings of the Guru, one may recite "the Invocation to Tapihritsa," which is translated in the next section. One may recite this one time or as many

times as one likes, while maintaining an attitude of faith, devotion, and intense longing for liberation and enlightenment.

As we have said, in the presence of the master, the practitioner develops a personal relationship with him and deliberately cultivates intense feelings of faith, trust, and fervent devotion. It is to this perfect master that one surrenders unreservedly and opens oneself up totally, like a small child before a loving parent. One prays with intense faith and devotion to the figure of the Guru, who, at the same time, is identical in essence with one's own Root Guru, and requests to receive the blessings of the empowerments and transmissions, so that one may practice and come to a genuine understanding of the real meaning of Dzogchen. Indeed, according to the Lopon, Guru Yoga is regarded as the most effective means to maintain and enhance the transmissions that one has received previously. So, the Guru Yoga is not something that is done only once in the beginning like an initiation ceremony, but is a meditation practice that is performed repeatedly, at least once a day, or even at the beginning of each session of practice.

At the end of the recitations, the vision of the Guru in the sky dissolves into a mass of light. This light approaches the practitioner and merges into oneself. This moment of unification represents the real Guru Yoga, a true *unio mystica* or mystical union. Moreover, this visualization recapitulates and repeats the original mystical vision and ecstatic experience undergone by the Mahasiddha Gyerpungpa in Zhang-zhung so long ago. Thus, in this way, one enters into and remains in the lineage of the transmission, remaining in the condition of the sacred transcending profane space and time.

Conclusion: Dedication of Merit

At the conclusion of each session of practice, the Lopon has suggested that one should recite the following short verse of the dedication of merit and the commitment (bsngo smon):

"Whatever merit I have accumulated through the purity of my three gates,
I now dedicate to the benefit of all the sentient beings of the three realms;
Having purified all my negative karma and obscurations accumulated in all the three times,
May I quickly come to attain the perfect Buddhahood of the Trikaya!"
[12]
The pronunciation and interlinear translation is as follows::
GO SUM DAG-PE GE-WA GANG GYI-PA,

Whatever merit I have accumulated through the purity of my three gates,
KHAM SUM SEM-CHAN NAM KYI DON DU NGO,
I now dedicate to the benefit of all the sentient beings of the three realms;
DU SUM SAG-PE LE DRIB KUN JYANG NE,
Having purified all my negative karma and obscurations accumulated in all the three times,
KU SUM DZOG-PE SANG-GYE NYUR THOB SHOK.
May I quickly come to attain the perfect Buddhahood of the Trikaya!

When one is in a retreat situation, there would normally be four or even six meditation sessions each day, such as in the early morning, before midday, in the late afternoon toward sunset, and in the evening before retiring. In the Dzogchen tradition, it is always necessary to at least perform the Guru Yoga at the beginning of each session of meditation practice. This keeps the practitioner inseparably linked and connected to the master and to the transmission, as well as to the contemplation of the Natural State to which the master has introduced to one directly. If one does not maintain this spiritual connection, then there could arise troubles with the Guardians for both the master and the disciple. It is said that the Guardians have little patience with abuse or neglect of the lineage of the teachings and of the practice.

According to the Bonpo tradition, it usually takes a continuous retreat of three months to complete the practice of all these preliminaries, each being done one hundred-thousand times. [13] But in terms of daily practice, one could perform all nine sections in sequence during the early morning session. Sitting down in meditation in the five-fold posture, one might run through each exercise in sequence. If possible, each is repeated three times or five times. And at the conclusion one makes the dedication of merit and the commitment to attain Buddha-hood as soon as possible. During the midday session, the mantras from the Ngondro text are again recited. [14]

The Invocation to Tapihritsa

As said, the Lopon has indicated that, in addition to the short verse of supplication given above, one may also recite the following "Invocation to Tapihritsa" (Ta-pi-hri-tsa'i gsol-'debs) while visualizing the Guru in the sky in front of oneself as decribed above and before proceeding to receive the empowerments from the master. This invocation is contained in the manuscript version of the *rGyal-ba phyag-khrid* collection and it is said to have been composed by Gyerpungpa himself. [15] This text embodies the essential meaning of Dzogchen and thus it is well suited for meditation practice while visualizing the resplendent form of Tapihritsa inside a rainbow sphere of light suspended in the sky in front of oneself.

Translation of the "Invocation to Tapihritsa". *gSol-'debs*

The translation of the text is as follows:

EMAHO!
O Nirmanakaya emanated from the Mind of Kuntu Zangpo! Your body color is a luminous white like crystal,
Immaculate and of clear luster, and rays of light emanate from you into the ten directions.
You are totally naked and without ornaments, signifying that you are the essence of the Primordial State.
By virtue of your compassion and by means of the two knowledges, you continuously contemplate the benefit of all living beings.
The nectar from the Hearts of all the Sugatas is Dzogchen, the Great Perfection, which is supreme among all teachings,
The pinnacle among all the vehicles to enlightenment, and the essence of all Tantras, Agamas, and Upadeshas:
From the Natural State, which is the (Primordial) Base, originates both the liberation that is Nirvana and the delusion that is Samsara;
Whereupon, as sounds, lights, and rays, all the defects (of Samsara) and all the virtues (of Nirvana) become clearly visible (as visions).
But once having cleared away everywhere all the darkness obscuring the minds of living beings (everything becomes clear),
Then the Base, which is empty and without a source, is decisively understood to represent the Sole Path.
Experiences and understanding become manifest (on the Path) and both Samsara and Nirvana are liberated into the Nature of Mind.
And thus, the Trikaya of the Fruit becomes clearly visible (as visions), arrayed before one in the dimension of space.
To you, O Tapihritsa, the protector of beings,
I pray with single-minded devotion
To grant the blessing of conferring empowerment upon me and upon all other beings
For the pacifying all our obscurations outer, inner, and secret!
When I am liberated from ignorance and from all grasping at the reality of delusions,

My own inherent intrinsic Awareness will become manifest; and having finally realized the proper view and the conduct,
At that very moment, please bestow upon me (the realization of)
The actual meaning of the Primordial State that is empty, without a source, and totally transcending the intellect.
To you, O Tapihritsa, our Lord who is the protector of beings, I pray—
By virtue of your compassion, may you liberate my mind-stream from all entanglements within the six destinies of rebirth!
[Thus Gyerpung Nangzher Lodpo prayed to the Nirmanakaya Tapihritsa who is the visible embodiment (of all the Lineage Gurus).
Good fortune! Virtue!] [16]

Pronunciation and Interlinear Translation
EMAHO
KUN-ZANG THUG TRUL-KU DOG SHEL KAR OD/
O Nirmanakaya emanated from the Mind of Kuntu Zangpo! Your body color is a luminous white like crystal,
DRI-MED DANG SAL OD ZER CHYOG CHUR TRO/
Immaculate and of clear lustre, and rays of light emanate from you into the ten directions.
GYAN-MED CHER-BU YE-NYID NYING-PO DON/
You are totally naked and without ornaments, signifying that you are the essence of the Primordial State.
KHYEN NYI THUG-JE DRO-WE DON LA GONG/
By virtue of your compassion and by means of the two knowledges, you continuously contemplate the benefit of all living beings.
DE-SHEG THUG CHUD DZOG-CHEN KUN GYI CHOG/
The nectar from the Hearts of all the Sugatas is Dzogchen, the Great Perfection, which is supreme among all (teachings),
THEG-PE YANG TSE GYUD LUNG MAN-NGAG NYING/
The pinnacle among all the vehicles (to enlightenment), and the essence of all Tantras, Agamas, and Upadeshas:
ZHI YI NE-LUG KHOR DE DROL TRUL DANG/
From the Natural State, which is the (Primordial) Base, (originates both) the liberation that is Nirvana and the delusion that is Samsara;
DRA OD ZER SUM KYON YON RAB SAL ZHING/
Whereupon, as sounds, lights, and rays, all the defects (of Samsara) and all the virtues (of Nirvana) become clearly visible.
DRO-WA LO YI MUN-PA KUN SAL NE/
But once having cleared away all the darkness (obscuring) the minds of living beings,
ZHI TONG TSA DRAL-WA LAM CHIG CHOD TOG/

Then the Base, which is empty and without a source, is decisively understood to be the Sole Path.

NYAM TOG NGON-GYUR KHOR DE SEM SU DROL/
Experiences and understanding become manifest (on the Path) and both Samsara and Nirvana are liberated into the Nature of Mind.

DRE-BU KU SUM YING SU GOD DZAD-PA/
And thus the Trikaya of the Fruit becomes clearly visible, arrayed (before me) in the dimension of space.

DRO-WE GON-PO TA-PI-HRI-TSA LA/
To you, O Tapihritsa, the protector of beings,

DAG LO TSE-CHIG MO-PE SOL-WA DEB/
I pray with single-minded devotion

DAG SOG DRO LA WANG-KUR JYIN GYI LOB/
To grant the blessing of conferring empowerment upon me and upon all other beings

CHYI NANG SANG-WE BAR-CHAD ZHI-WA DANG/
For the pacifying all our obscurations outer, inner, and secret!

MA RIG TRUL-WE GAD-DZIN DROL-WE KYANG/
When I am liberated from ignorance and from all grasping at the reality of delusions,

RANG-RIG NGON-GYUR TA CHOD THAR-CHYIN NE/
My own inherent intrinsic Awareness will become manifest; and having finally realized the view and the conduct,

YE TONG TSA-DRAL LO-DE CHEN-PO DON/
As for the actual meaning of the Primordial State that is empty, without a source, and totally transcending the intellect,

DAN-TA NYID DU DAG LA TSAL DU SOL/
At that very moment, please bestow upon me (this realization)!

JE DRO-WE GON-PO TA-PI-HRI-TSA LA/
To you, O Tapihritsa, our Lord who is the protector of beings,

SOL-WA DEB-SO DRO DRUG THUG-JE ZUNG LA DAG GYUD TROL/
I pray— By virtue of your compassion, may you liberate my mind-stream from all entanglements within the six destinies of rebirth!

Commentary to the Translation of the Invocation

Preface

In this prayer or invocation (gsol-'debs), Tapihritsa is addressed as the Nirmanakaya (sprul-sku), that is to say, as an emanation (sprul-pa) of the enlightened awareness of the primordial Buddha Kuntu Zangpo.

This "hierophany," or eruption of the sacred into the mundane reality of humanity, appears as a pure vision to the master Gyerpungpa. A Nirmanakaya such as Tapihritsa appears in time and history to ordinary sentient beings whose minds are too clouded with obscurations to perceive directly the glorified form of the Sambhogakaya. On the contrary, Kuntu Zangpo, the Primordial Buddha, has been enlightened from the very beginning, primordially (ye nas), and so He has never experienced or undergone the delusions of Samsara. These experiences of this cyclical existence known as Samsara are the products of our existential ignorance as sentient beings, where we do not recognize our primordially enlightened Nature. Nevertheless, because of His infinite and total compassion (thugs-rje chen-po) for all sentient beings still caught up in Samsara, He, as the Sambhogakaya, emanates an infinite number of Nirmanakayas, much like the sun in the sky above our heads emanates countless numbers of rays of light that illuminate the surface of our world. These individual Nirmanakayas drive back the darkness of ignorance and reveal with their light the pathways to liberation to deluded and confused sentient beings. Again, these Nirmanakayas are hierophanies or revelations of the sacred, the higher spiritual order. They appear spontaneously throughout time and history in all worlds and dimensions inhabited by intelligent life-forms, where they function as spiritual guides who point the way to liberation and enlightenment.

Although Tapihritsa was indeed a historical figure who flourished in the seventh century in Zhang-zhung or Northern Tibet, it is said that he attained enlightenment by way of the practice of Dzogchen. In that case, he realized the Dharmakaya and this single Dharmakaya was simultaneously non-dual with Kuntu Zangpo, who, as we have said, did not need to attain enlightenment because He was enlightened from the very beginning. Through the practice of contemplation or Trekchod, Tapihritsa attained realization, the realization of the state of total primordial purity (ka-dag chen-po), wherein there was no longer any distinction between the individual stream of consciousness and the Dharmakaya. But the realization of the Dharmakaya is only one side of the story of enlightenment; the other is the transformation into the Form Body (Rupakaya) or Sambhogakaya. To give the traditional example, the Dharmakaya is like the vast open sky, without any borders or limits, whereas the Sambhogakaya is like the presence of the sun in the sky, and the countless multitudes of Nirmanakayas are like the rays of the sun. Because Tapihritsa, upon his enlightenment, became non-dual with Kuntuzangpo, in the text of this invocation he is addressed as the Nirmanakaya manifestation that has emanated from the enlightened state or Nature of Mind of the Primordial Buddha Kuntu Zangpo. Tapihritsa represents one ray of light from this central spiritual sun. It was through the practice of vision, known as Clear Light ('od-gsal) or Thodgal, that Tapihritsa transformed his Samsaric existence into the Body of Light of the Great Transfer ('pho-ba chen-po'i 'od lus), that is to say, into a specific form of enlightened awareness (in this case, a miraculous child) in order to communicate directly in a person-to-person manner with the consciousness of Gyerpungpa. The specific form or iconography of this pure vision is described briefly in the text.

Tapihritsa represents the visible symbol of the Primordial State (ye-nyid), which is, in individual terms, the Nature of Mind. Therefore, he appears similar to the iconic representation of Kuntu Zangpo. And because this pristine state is completely devoid and denuded of all discursive thoughts (rtog-med) and conceptual elaborations (spros-med), he is totally naked and without any ornaments or garments whatsoever, as we have said already. In this context, his nakedness represents the Essence of the Primordial State (ye-nyid snying-po'i don), by which is meant emptiness or the state of Shunyata. Moreover, he is luminous white in color and translucent like crystal and not sky blue like Kuntu Zangpo, because this white light symbolizes the dawning of the Clear Light of intrinsic Awareness, which represents the innate capacity of the Nature of Mind. This Clear Light is the embodiment of total compassion (thugs-rje chen-po) because it is active and dispels the darkness of ignorance. This enlightenment reflects the two knowledges (mkhyen-pa gnyis) of quantity and quality that represent the omniscience of the Buddha. His audible speech expounds only the supreme doctrine of Dzogchen, the Great Perfection, which in itself represents the nectar of the Hearts of all the Sugatas or Buddhas (bde-gshegs snying bcud), the highest teaching or pinnacle (yang rtse) found among the nine successive vehicles to enlightenment (theg-pa rim dgu), and the essence distilled from all the esoteric scriptures of the Tantras, the Agamas, and the Upadeshas (rgyud lung man-ngag gsum). The Tantras (rgyud) are extensive texts expounding upon and elucidating many aspects of the theory and practice of Dzogchen and Tantra. Agamas (lung) are shorter texts that focus upon a few salient points referred to a more lengthy Tantra text. Upadeshas (man-ngag) are brief secret oral instructions or "pith-instructions" communicated personally and in confidence from a master to a disciple regarding practice and personal experience.

The Six Verses
We now come to the six verses or lines of verse, consisting of nine syllables each. [17] These six verses recited in his invocation of his master Tapihritsa are as follows:

1. From the Natural State, which is the Primordial Base, originates both the liberation that is Nirvana and the deluded condition that is Samsara,
2. Whereupon, as the sounds, the lights, and the rays that manifest to the deceased consciousness in the Bardo, all the defects of Samsara and all the virtues of Nirvana became clearly visible as visions.
3. But, once having cleared away the darkness obscuring the minds of living beings, everything becomes clear,
4. And the Base, which is empty and without a source, is decisively understood to represent the Sole Path to the realization of liberation and enlightenment.
5. Experiences and understanding thereupon become manifest as the Path and both Samsara and Nirvana are liberated into the Nature of Mind, their original condition.
6. And thus the Trikaya of the Fruit becomes clearly visible, arrayed before oneself as visions in the dimension of space. [18]

This neatly summarizes the view of Thodgal. Or to rephrase the verses thus: There is a single Base, the Nature of Mind (sems-nyid), which is the source for both the liberation and the enlightenment experiences of Nirvana realized by an enlightened Buddha and the delusions experienced as Samsara by an ordinary sentient being. When after death, the visions arise in the Bardo experience, initially as the sounds, the lights, and the rays (sgra 'od zer gsum), which represent the manifest expression of the inherent energy of the Nature of Mind (rang-rtsal), the deceased consciousness either recognizes them and understands them to be the self-manifestations of one's own Mind or fails to recognize and understand them. One mistakenly thinks that they are autonomous external realities outside there in space due to extraneous causes. From this recognition and understanding or failure thereof, arise all the virtues of Nirvana and all the defects of Samsara respectively. But if one has cleared away the darkness of the obscurations of negative emotions and discursive thoughts by way of the practice of contemplation or Dzogchen during the course of one's previous life before one has died, then one will discover, both during one's lifetime and after death, that this Base, the Natural State of the Nature of Mind, represents the Sole Path to enlightenment and the realization of Buddhahood. And due to practicing contemplation, the experiences of bliss, clarity, and non-discursiveness, as well as understanding, will manifest within the practice of the Path and one will become familiar with the Natural State and recognize it after death. [19] Moreover, because of the practice of vision in contemplation, the visions that arise, whether of Samsara or Nirvana, will ultimately dissolve into the Natural State of the Nature of Mind. Then the Trikaya, the Bodies of the Buddha, will spontaneously manifest out of the Base and this represents the Fruit. Nirvana, as the visions of the Buddhas and the Mandalas, will be arrayed spontaneously in the dimension of space surrounding oneself.

The text in the first line of verse is speaking in general when it asserts that all the phenomena or appearances of Samsara and Nirvana ('khor 'das) originate from the Natural State of the Base (gzhi yi gnas-lugs), which is also known as the Bodhichitta (byang-chub sems) and the Nature of Mind (sems-nyid). This single Primordial Base (ye gzhi) is the source for both the system of delusion ('khrul lugs) that evolves as Samsara and the system of liberation (grol lugs) that evolves as Nirvana. There is this single Base, but two possible Paths, Samsara or Nirvana, and two possible fruits, a deluded ordinary sentient being or an enlightened Buddha. Here the text is speaking in general. But for the individual consciousness, one is either one or the other, either deluded or enlightened. Therefore, this single Base is the primordial source of both the darkness and the light. On the side of emptiness or pure potentiality, this Base, which is the Nature of Mind, is the source for the manifestation of all possible worlds. [20]

Although one cannot speak of an absolute beginning or creation of Samsara and Nirvana in time and history, for the individual stream of consciousness, which again and again becomes embodied as a sentient being during the course of beginningless cycles of rebirth, in the relative sense there is a beginning to Samsara each time that one dies. During the process of dying, one's elements, vital winds, and thought processes all dissolve back into the space from which they originated. Deprived of the definition and constraint of a material body, consciousness finds itself in a vast dark empty space without any borders or walls. If one is not a practitioner of Dzogchen and familiar with the practice of contemplation, one will experience this as a black-out or a mere state of unconsciousness. But this space is not just non-existence or a blank nothingness, a mere absence; it is the vast, open, infinite space of one's own Nature of Mind. This vast space or dimension is the Kunzhi, the basis of everything, the state of Shunyata. However, this represents only the spacious and empty side (stong cha) of the Nature of Mind. There is equally the awareness side (rig cha) or clear luminosity side (gsal cha) of this same Primordial Base. Because this open empty spaciousness and this aware luminosity have been inseparable from the very beginning (ye nas rig stong dbyer-med), the inherent luminosity of intrinsic Awareness (rig-pa'i rang gsal) spontaneously manifests in the dimension of space as the Clear Light ('od-gsal), just as night must inevitably recede with the approach of day. [21]

At the culmination of the process of dying and before the onset of the dream-like karmic visions of the Bardo in the intermediate state between death and rebirth, when the consciousness comes to separate from the body, there occurs the moment of the Boundary (so-mtshams). All of the activities of one's previous body, energy, and mind, belonging to one's previous life, fall into abeyance and all of the karmic traces or propensities inherited from past lives beyond counting remain latent and dormant before they awaken and germinate and give rise to the experiences of the Bardo. At that time one is suspended in the midst of infinite space without any boundaries, borders, definitions, or walls. There is no subject or object; there is simply empty space. But this vast dark space is not dead. It is the Kunzhi. And it is also totally aware as an objectless awareness. And it is just at this moment of the Boundary in the dead of the night, just before the beginning of daybreak, where the practitioner has the maximum opportunity to awaken into enlightenment, as did the Buddha Shakyamuni sitting in contemplation beneath the Bodhi Tree at the first break of day. He thereby realized liberation from cyclical existence; he no longer thought in the same way as does the ordinary sentient being. If at this time, the practitioner recognizes and understands (rtogs-pa) this Clear Light that is dawning to be one's own self-manifestation of the intrinsic Awareness of one's own Nature of Mind, like seeing the reflection of one's own face in front of oneself in the mirror of clear empty space, then one will realize enlightened awareness and Buddhahood. But if one does not recognize and understand the Clear Light and seeks to flee from the coming light, one will fall again and again into levels of unconsciousness. In the first case, that of enlightened awareness, the visions of Nirvana with their Buddhas and Mandalas begin to unfold naturally and spontaneously within the Clear Light. Whereas in the second case, the light becoming less intense due to not understanding, the constricted and distorted visions of Samsara begin to unfold naturally and spontaneously in the lesser duller lights that represent the deficiencies of awareness. This initial process of the dawning of the Clear Light and the recognizing or failing to recognize it occurs each time one dies, not only when the material body dies, but also when one dies again and again in the Bardo experience, or even when one falls asleep at night. [22]

However, even though one's original nature, as light and space, is like the clear open sky, it becomes obscured and clouded over by an ignorance that grasps at the reality (bdag 'dzin) these clouds that represent one's delusions or Samsaric visions. Becoming liberated from these clouds, one's own real nature as awareness or Rigpa comes into visible manifestation, just as when the clouds in the sky dissipate, the face of the sun becomes clearly visible. Thereby one's view and one's conduct and activity in the world become inseparably linked. One acts spontaneously in terms of the Natural State, without any deliberation or artifice. This Primordial State, the Nature of Mind, being Shunyata and being without any source or ground (gzhi-med rtsa-bral) in the causal processes of Samsara, totally transcends the intellect (blo 'das chenpo). Yet, at the same time, it may be directly discovered within one's own immediate experience in this present life by way of the practice of contemplation, a state that goes beyond the mind.

Gazing into the daybreak of the Clear Light, these initial primal manifestations, which arise before creation, which arise and proliferate before the onset of the Bardo visions, are known as the sounds, the lights, and the rays (sgra 'od zer gsum). The "sounds" are subtle vibrations in space, the "lights" are clear luminosity, and the "rays" are colors and images. These appearances are self-manifestations (rangsnang) because they arise naturally and spontaneously and without any extrinsic causes. They are not appearances due to some other outside cause (gzhan snang). They are pure sensations as distinguished from perceptions of visible objects (snang yul), which are created by the discursive or functional mind (yid) when one applies names and concepts to what one sees. These initial or primal events are visible manifestations of the inherent energy of awareness (rig-pa'i rang rtsal) of the Nature of Mind. If one recognizes them at the outset and understands that they represent self-manifestations of the inherent energy of awareness, then one will instantly become liberated from cyclical existence and will realize enlightenment. Thereupon these initial self-manifestations evolve naturally and spontaneously into the visions of Nirvana. [23]

However, if one does not recognize and understand the advent of the Clear Light due to a co-emergent ignorance (lhan-skyes ma rig-pa), which is a lessening of awareness, there opens up the possibility for the schism and duality of subject and object arising in mental consciousness. This consciousness then thinks that these visible phenomena of the sounds, the lights, and the rays really exist in the space outside of oneself, where they are thought to be caused by other extraneous causes, and one feels attraction or aversion with regard to these appearances. Thereafter the impure karmic visions of the destinies of rebirth within Samsara progressively and inevitably unfold like the floods coming in the spring when the snow melts in the mountains. The Boundary after death and before the Bardo is thus the moment for the separation (gyes tshul) between Samsara and Nirvana where the practitioner may choose one's future destiny. At this point, it is gnosis or understanding that makes the difference; it is the knowledge that liberates; it is the knowledge of true self-discovery.

Thus both Samsara and Nirvana are contained in all their potential within this single Base that is the Nature of Mind. This means that all of the virtuous qualities (yon-tan), which are the pure visions associated with Nirvana and Buddhahood, are contained in their full potentiality within the Nature of Mind. When one actually understands this, all these virtuous qualities naturally and spontaneously manifest out of the inexhaustible effulgence of the Nature of Mind. Therefore, there is no necessity to cultivate the ten perfections or Paramitas successively and individually throughout countless lifetimes as a Bodhisattva. But equally, all the faults and defects (nyes skyon), which are the impure karmic visions of Samsara, are contained in their full potentiality in the Natural State and with the unfolding of Samsaric visions, these naturally and spontaneously manifest and one comes to experience suffering again and again. Thus, with the advent of the Clear Light, all the faults and all the virtues of Samsara and Nirvana become clearly and intensely visible (skyon yon rab gsal).

One may ask why does a living being ('gro-ba) not recognize and understand the Clear Light when it manifests after death? It is for the same reason that one does not recognize it at this very moment. The Clear Light of Awareness is the very ground of consciousness, its base or background, so to speak. But normally one is unconscious of this ground, which is the very source and matrix of consciousness. Without the perpetual presence of this ground, which is Rigpa, there would not be any consciousness at all. But under normal conditions, consciousness is dualistic in its operations, separating reality into subject and object and it is distracted by thoughts and emotions. The normal condition of everyday life is like the sky filled with clouds. This situation obscures the face of the sun and the clear blue sky beyond. This represents the state of non-recognition and not understanding. It represents the two-fold ignorance of spontaneously born co-emergent ignorance (lhan-skyes ma rig-pa) and the ignorance that conceptualizes everything (kun-rtog ma rig-pa). It is principally the thought process (blo) that fills all of space with the thick clouds of obscurations. This is what fills the mind with darkness (mun-pa).

How does one remove these clouds that obscure the light of awareness, these clouds which represent both emotional and intellectual obscurations? This is accomplished by way of the practice of contemplation, which is the finding of oneself in a state of presence or intrinsic awareness (rig-pa) while one is yet alive. Therefore, one needs to become familiar with this state. This practice is the best preparation for dying, for the experience of death and after-death. The practice of contemplation is also known as Trekchod (khregs-chod), the relaxing or releasing of all the tensions and rigidities of one's body, energy, and mind. Trekchod is not the repressing of thoughts, but just a letting them be without interference and without pursuing them ot trying to do something about them. It is a profound process of radical and total relaxation (lhod-pa chen-po). [24] By way of the practice of contemplation, distractions and discursive thoughts become less in their numbers and their power, whereby the spaces between thoughts open up. For example, when there comes a break in the clouds covering the sky, we can then occasionally catch a glimpse of the face of the sun and the clear blue sky beyond. It is the same way here with the practice of contemplation. In terms of Dzogchen, one meditates with the eyes open because all of the senses are engaged and functioning. However, one has moved beyond thoughts, even though they may continue to arise. One moves beyond images and concepts, thereby everything becomes fresh and new and clear (kun gsal) without judgments or definitions. When the clouds dissipate, we discover the original state of the primordial purity (ka-dag) of the sky of the mind.

If during the course of one's lifetime, one has practiced Dzogchen assiduously, thereby one will clear away the clouds of both emotional and intellectual obscurations and come to recognize the Clear Light when it dawns in space before the onset of the Bardo and its dream-like karmic visions. Therefore, it is said in the text, "Having cleared away all the darkness obscuring the minds of living beings, then everything becomes clear ('gro-ba blo yi mun-pa kun gsal nas)." Then the Primordial Base that abides as the Nature of Mind, that is to say, one's own innate Buddha-nature, which is itself the state of emptiness, uncreated and unceasing, becomes recognized and understand. By this means alone one will attain enlightenment. Thus it says in the text "Then the Base, which is empty and without a source, is decisively understood to represent the Sole Path (gzhi stong bral-ba lam gcig chod rtogs)."

Because the practitioner has received from the master (bla-ma) the direct introduction to intrinsic Awareness (rig-pa ngo-sprod) and practices finding oneself in that state of contemplation or objectless awareness again and again, [25] one comes to a definitive understanding (chod rtogs) of just this being the Sole Path (lam gcig) to liberation and enlightenment. One does not have to search for any other method than the practice of contemplation. There is no higher or further method than this. One has discovered within oneself and within one's immediate everyday experience the Base or Natural State, which is empty and without a root or source (gzhi stong rtsa bral-ba). While practicing the path, that is to say, entering into contemplation or the state of Rigpa, while yet alive and before one dies, both experiences and understanding regarding the intrinsic Awareness of the Natural State will develop. These experiences in contemplation, like glimpses of the sun seen through openings in the clouds, represent what is called "the Son Clear Light." One becomes familiar with the face of the sun during one's lifetime. Then at the time death, when body and consciousness separate, one comes to recognize "the Mother Clear Light." [26] Therefore, the practice of contemplation represents the supreme preparation for dying and the experiences that come after death in the Bardo, where one will have the opportunity to recognize one's own original face that one has had before one was born. Therefore, it says in the text, "Experiences and understanding become manifest on the path (nyams rtogs mngon-gyur)." Here we are speaking of the practice of contemplation, also known as Trekchod. But then, linked with it is the practice of vision known as Thodgal. While in the state of contemplation, all of one's senses are open and engaged. With the support of the total darkness of the dark retreat, or of the empty space of the clear cloudless sky, or the rays of sunlight after sun rise, one allows the visions to manifest freely of themselves. What must be understood here is that one should be all the time during the practice in the state of awareness or contemplation. This practice is not like watching an entertaining cinema show with a distracted mind.

Whether the impure karmic visions of Samsara, such as the visions of our everyday life, arise or the pure visions of Nirvana of the Buddhas and the Mandalas arise, they will all progressively liberate and dissolve again into the Natural State of the Nature of Mind, out of which they initially arose. [27] According to Dzogchen, the Nature of Mind is the source for the arising of both the visions of Samsara and the visions of Nirvana. And coming to stand upon the threshold of enlightenment, all visions, whether pure or impure, are liberated and dissolve back into their original source.

At this point, the practitioner has purified and exhausted all one's past karmic traces inherited since time without beginning. All of them are absorbed back into the source; their causal efficacy is exhausted. Externally the material body begins to dissolve into pure radiant energy, a process known as the Rainbow Body ('ja'-lus), so-called because the elements of the physical body manifest as clear lights like the rainbow. During the course of three to seven days, the material body diminishes in size and gradually fades away, dissolving into space. One's vital energies and one's mind or thought process also dissolve back into the ultimate source, the Kunzhi. But just at the point of death, when the body, the energy, and the mind all dissolve, and there is only empty space, Rigpa manifests once more as the Clear Light. However, in the case here with the practice of Thodgal, because all karmic traces have been purified and dissolved, it is not a new embodiment in Samsara that re-manifests and gradually becomes visible, but rather the Trikaya , the fruitional Three Bodies of the Buddhas ('bras-bu sku-gsum), and this re-manifestation is the fruit or the result of the Thodgal practice. And these Trikaya become arrayed or manifest in the dimension of space (dbyings su 'god) as the visions of the Mandalas. The mind is now the Dharmakaya, the energy is now the Sambhogakaya, and the body is now the Nirmanakaya. But this coming into manifestation of the Trikaya is not a causal process; it is not the result of some cause or practice. Rather, Thodgal simply opens things up and provides the space for the Trikaya to manifest, which it does naturally and spontaneously. The Trikaya does not occur, as in the Sutra system, as the result of the two accumulations of wisdom and meritorious karma, or as with the Tantra system as the result of some process of transformation, but it arises out of the primordial purity of the Nature of Mind as something spontaneously self-perfected (lhun-grub).

Ultimate enlightenment and final liberation do not represent, according to Dzogchen, just a blank inert state where one is totally spacious and blissful, where no individuality remains, like dropping a crystal of salt into the ocean. Rather, the final result is not annihilation and oblivion, but the manifestation of the Trikaya, which has been there in potential in the Nature of Mind from the very beginning. It has been there all the time, like the sun present in the sky during the day. When the clouds dissipate, the presence of the sun comes into view. The practitioner, in terms of one's Samsaric or mundane existence, totally dissolves into the state of Shunyata and is no more, but then re-emerges or re-crystallizes or precipitates out of solution as an enlightened being. *Solve et coagula.* Thereby one simultaneously realizes the non-dual ultimate reality, the Dharmakaya, which is a state of being that is general and universal, but simultaneously realizes the Rupakaya or Form Body, which is individual and particular. These two, the Dharmakaya and the Rupakaya do not exclude each other. Here it is not a case or either/or. They represent two sides of the same coin, the inseparability of appearance and emptiness (snang stong dbyer-med). Therefore, it says in the text, "The Fruit, as the Trikaya, becomes arrayed in the dimension of space ('bras-bu sku-gsum dbyings su 'god mdzad-pa)." This becoming arrayed in space as the pure visions of the Buddhas and the Mandalas is also what occurs in Thodgal practice. Moreover, this visible display of the Trikaya in space, the Dharmakaya and the Rupakaya being inseparable, is what is known as the Body of Light. Thus, the visible appearance of Tapihritsa to Gyerpungpa is in itself the revelation. [28]

Indeed, by way of the practice of contemplation and of vision, one comes to realize enlightenment as the Trikaya. This is not something acquired or brought about by extraneous causes. The Trikaya has been primordially present in the Base from the very beginning (ye), but through the practice of the Path, it gradually comes into visible manifestation (mngon), and in terms of the Fruit or ultimate result, it comes into fulfillment or the total perfect and complete manifestation (rdzogs) of Buddhahood. Thus, the texts speak of Primordial Buddhahood (ye sangs-rgyas-pa) as the Base, Buddhahood coming into manifestation (mngon sangs rgyas pa) as the Path, and completely perfected Buddhahood (rdzogs sangs-rgyas-pa) as the Fruit or final result. The Fruit, therefore, refers to the culmination of the practice of vision or Thodgal, whereby the practitioner realizes this Body of Light. According to Dzogchen, through the practice of contemplation or Trekchod one comes to realize the Dharmakaya, but through the practice of vision or Thodgal one comes to realize the Rupakaya, which represents the manifestation of the enlightenment of the Buddha in visible form as the Sambhogakaya and the Nirmanakaya and thus one is able to communicate with ignorant sentient beings. Thus, the practice of Dzogchen is here elucidated in terms of the Base, the Path, and the Fruit.

The Conclusion

At the conclusion that follows upon this Upadesha, Gyerpungpa prays to Tapihritsa with single-minded devotion (rtse-gcig mos-pa), addressing him as the Protector of Beings ('gro-ba'i mgon-po). His own understanding now having become manifest as self-awareness (rang-rig mngon-gyur), he fervently requests the master to bestow upon him the realization of the actual meaning of the Primordial State that is empty and without a source and totally transcending the intellect (ye stong rtsa-bral blo 'das chen-po'i don). This is accomplished through the mystical union experienced in the Guru Yoga practice, where the state of contemplation of the master merges with the contemplation of the disciple, thereby becoming inseparable, like pouring water into water. Thereupon the mind-stream of Gyerpungpa became liberated (rgyud khrol) from all entanglements with the delusions of Samsara.

Guru Yoga and the Practice of Contemplation

As indicated above, the Guru Yoga is considered by the Tibetan Lamas, both Buddhist and Bonpo, to be the most important daily practice within the Dzogchen tradition. Although the Dzogchen teachings, which present the possibility of liberation and enlightenment within a single lifetime, originated with the Primordial Buddha Kuntu Zangpo, it is from one's own master in this present life that the practitioner receives both the transmission of the precepts (bka' brgyud) and the transmission of the experiences (nyams brgyud) of the accomplished masters of the past with regard to their understanding of the Natural State of the Nature of Mind. Through a repeated practice of the Guru Yoga, at least once a day, the practitioner maintains the vital link and connection with all of the transmissions one has received. The Guru Yoga is, therefore, the indispensable preliminary practice for the realization of Dzogchen.

However, it is the practice of contemplation, or resting in the Natural State of the Nature of Mind (sems-nyid gnas-lugs), a process also called Trekchod (khregs-chod), "the relaxing of rigidities," that constitutes the essential principal practice of Dzogchen (dngos-gzhi). When one speaks of "contemplation" (mnyam-bzhag, ting-nge 'dzin) in the context of Dzogchen, this does not mean a meditation that is coerced or constructed by way of the activities of the mind or thought process. Rather, it is simply a relaxing of all mental activities and processes, what is usually known as the activities of discursive thoughts (rnam-rtog), and a coming to rest in the Natural State of the Nature of Mind that lies beyond all operations of mind. It is a process of actually going beyond the mind and its operations. Contemplation (mnyam-bzhag) must then be clearly distinguished from meditation (sgom-pa), which still involves the operations of mind, no matter how subtle these may be. Even ascending to the highest among the four dhyanas (bsam-gtan bzhi) still requires the presence of a one-pointed concentration (rtse-gcig) and that represents an operation of mind. But contemplation is a state beyond the mind and beyond the sequences of cause and effect we know as time and causality, even though, as the Natural State, it remains the source, ground, and matrix of these very phenomena.

All this is very easy to say, "Just stop the mind! Just stop thinking!" But the mind is not simply a computer on one's desk that can be switched off at will. Its programs continue to run whether one desires it or not. It is the very nature of the mind to produce thoughts and to produce them almost incessantly during the waking state. When one deliberately tries to suppress these thoughts, they simply re-emerge later, infused with even more energy. So, with the practice of contemplation it is not a matter of trying to do something, whatever that may be, but a question of simply relaxing, relaxing the functions of one's body, speech, and mind in a very radical manner. But how does one come into this total relaxation? Usually the human being, involved in continuous social intercourse during the day, is all charged up with energy; the mind is running away like a wild horse out of control. Since the fluctuations of mind are related to the movements of the body, as well as to breathing, it is necessary for the beginning practitioner of contemplation to assume a relaxed, yet immobile position of the body and make one's breathing smooth, regular, and even. This reduces the disturbances of the prana or psychic energy (rlung). When the body and the breathing, which are more easily controlled, become immobile and quiescent, then the mind and its though processes will follow suit. To aid in this process of radical relaxation or total relaxation (lhod-pa chen-po), Dzogchen possesses many exercises that are known as Rushans (ru-shan dbye-ba) or "discriminations" and Semdzin (sems-'dzin) or "fixations of the mind."

However, the aim here is not just a suspension of thoughts. Contemplation in the context of Dzogchen does not just mean a state of non-discursiveness or no thoughts whatsoever (mi rtog-pa). This matter has been a crucial misunderstanding on the part of many critics of Dzogchen. A cow in the pasture, chewing on her cud, experiences a state of no thought, yet this is not contemplation, but simply a dull neutral state of mind (lung ma bstan). Rather, the state of contemplation in Dzogchen is characterized by an aliveness and alertness (lhug-pa) and a total openness to all manner of sense experience. One practices contemplation with the senses open and in full operation. This is why one practices meditation with the eyes open and in contact with external appearances, in contrast to the usual practice of visualization in Tantra where the eyes are closed. This Natural State, which one encounters in contemplation, is characterized by an intrinsic Awareness or Rigpa, whereas the condition of "no thoughts" (mi rtog-pa) is just an experience (nyams) and in the absence of Rigpa, it does not constitute contemplation as such. It is not just emptiness that characterizes the state of Dzogchen, but equally this luminous clarity or Awareness. In the state of contemplation, emptiness and awareness are inseparable (rig stong dbyer-med). It is this thoroughly relaxed condition of the Nature of Mind, pregnant with all possibilities for manifestation, which is characterized by Rigpa, and this is what is pointed out or indicated by the master when he gives a direct introduction. Once having been directly introduced to the Natural State, the practitioner will recognize it again and again when one encounters it in its nakedness (rig-pa gcer mthong). Basically, contemplation is a relaxing into the alert Natural State of the Nature of Mind, and this can in no way be coerced nor created by thoughts and mental exercises. Contemplation is a condition that is beyond the mind. For this reason, contemplation is called non-meditation (sgom-med). It is neither dull nor drowsy, but fully alert and aware, without being influenced or carried away by the arising of discursive thoughts. Entering into the Natural State and remaining in it once one has entered it is the aim of Dzogchen.

All of the visualizations done within the practice of the Guru Yoga belong to the domain of the operations of the mind; they are created by one's thoughts. These visualizations represent the work of the mind. Nevertheless, mind is the greatest of all things. Mind can create anything. It can even create this experience of linking up and connecting with all of the masters of the past, the present, and the future. But this visualization of the Tree of the Assembly that contains all of the past masters, as beautiful and elaborate and inspiring as it may be, still belongs to the conditioned dimension of time and causality. This Guru Yoga visualization is not something beyond the mind. But at the conclusion of the process of Guru Yoga, one dissolves the visualization of the Guru, whether of a single Guru figure such as Tapihritsa or of the entire Tree of the Wisdom of the Gurus, into a mass of light suspended in space. This dissolving of the visualization is done so that the practitioner does not become attached and cling to mere external appearances, but comes to understand experientially the inseparability of appearances and emptiness (snang stong dbyer-med). This mass of light, representing the collective knowledge and wisdom of all the spiritual masters, then merges into one's own body and being, like water being poured into water, so that one comes to understand experientially the inseparability of clarity and emptiness (gsal stong dbyer-med). One becomes that light of wisdom, which embodies the heart-essences of all the masters. This is the moment of the true Guru Yoga, the mystical union or unification with all of the masters, and so one comes to understand experientially the inseparability of intrinsic Awareness and emptiness (rig-stong dbyer-med).

One relaxes totally into this unification, releasing all tensions and rigidities of body, speech, and mind, relaxing into a state of even contemplation where awareness and emptiness remain inseparable, at least for a few moments. Then, as may be expected, discursive thoughts arise again into manifestation. At this point, after the process of the Guru Yoga proper, the practitioner may, for the remainder of the meditation session (thun), if one so chooses, practice fixation and continue to observe one's thoughts. One simply observes them without making judgments or attempting to interfere with them in any way. One simply allows them to arise and liberate of themselves. And in order to facilitate this, one may fixate on the white Tibetan letter A by way of visualizing it in the empty space in front where it is luminous and white. Or else, one gazes fixedly without blinking and with half closed eyes at a picture or drawing of the white letter A against a dark background on a card and set at a comfortable distance in front of oneself by being mounted on a stick thrust into the earth. While fixating on the white A, the practitioner may repeatedly sound "Aaaaah......" so that the visualization or vision, the energy of the sound, and the awareness of it all become integrated. When one focuses attention acutely on this white letter A, this allows no space for distracting thought to arise. This is like aiming an arrow at a target with much care and attention. Then one should relax this acute fixation somewhat. And when one relaxes the fixation of attention, from time to time thoughts will arise. But this is perfectly all right. It is only natural for thoughts to arise in the open dimension of space of the mind. If one does not grasp at them, or become attached to them, or try to do something about them, they will pass away again of themselves and dissolve once more into the empty space out of which they arose originally, like clouds dissipating in the sky. One should simply observe these thoughts without engaging or interfering with them in any way. One should just let them be as they are in themselves. If too many distracting thoughts arise, one fixates again more acutely on the white letter A in the space in front and continues for a time in this way..

During the course of this non-interventionist process of observation, one looks carefully and searches for the creator of these thoughts. Who is it who creates these thoughts? If it is the mind that creates these thoughts, where is it located? Is it in the head or in the body? Or is it outside? Has the mind a shape or a color? One looks for where thoughts originate. Where do they come from? Where do they stay? Where do they go? Even though one may search exhaustively for this "mind" over the course of many days, one will find nothing there. Yet it is this very "unfindability" (mi rnyed) that is the real discovery. One discovers experientially the real meaning of Shunyata or emptiness. One discovers the Nature of Mind that lies beyond mind. This Nature of Mind has always been with us since the very beginning, since before Samsara came into manifestation, and yet it has gone unrecognized until now. It is like the sun that is present in the sky, shedding its light everywhere, although unrecognized because its face is hidden from view by the thick layer of clouds. These clouds are all the karmic traces and obscurations accumulated over all of one's previous lifetimes in the cyclical existence of Samsara. The Dzogchen teachings introduce the individual to the Natural State where there is no watcher and nothing that is watched. This transcends the primary dichotomy of subject and object— this is the timeless time before creation. Having found oneself in the Natural State in terms of contemplation, it is not necessary to do anything else about this. It just is what it is and should be kept just as it is. That is the secret.

The practice of fixation on the white letter A represents meditation with an object (dmigs-bcas), but one may also practice fixation without an object (dmigs-med) by way of the fixating of attention on a specific location in empty space with no visualization present, or one may simply gaze into the depths of the open expanse of the clear empty sky (nam-mkha' ar-gtad) while remaining alertly relaxed. In either case, the essential point is to remain alert and aware in the state of Rigpa, whether or not thoughts arise. And for this sort of practice, it is better to engage in a number of shorter sessions of contemplation, rather than trying to force oneself, which would only cause obstacles. At the end of the session one should recite the dedication. This is how to combine the practice of contemplation with the Guru Yoga, which is normally given as oral instructions only. [29]

Lopon Tenzin Namdak at Triten Norbutse Monastery inKathmandu, Nepal, together with the translator, working on these translations from the Tibetan.

APPENDIX TWO

The Preliminary Practices

Introduction

The Preliminary Practices in General

Before one can enter into a retreat to engage in the principal practices of either Tantra or Dzogchen, there are certain preliminary practices to be observed which serve to purify the mind and prepare the practitioner to receive the blessings of the masters in the lineage of transmission. Thus, at the inception of this probationary period, the disciple receives the empowerments from the master and thereafter, by way of practice, one prepares oneself in terms of the purification of one's obscurations (sgrib sbyong) and the accumulation of meritorious karma (tshogs bsags). These represent the two principal functions of the preliminaries or Ngondro (sngon-'gro), literally, that which goes ('gro-ba) before (sngon du). These preliminaries culminate in the practice of the Guru Yoga (bla-ma'i rnal-'byor), that is to say, the unification of one's own individual stream of consciousness with that of the enlightened masters in terms of the functions of body, speech, and mind. [1]

However, there exist a number of necessary prerequisite conditions for this. First, the practitioner must find a qualified master or teacher who has received the transmission of the lineage, in this case, that of the Zhang-zhung Nyan-gyud, which has come down to him in an unbroken line. Moreover, this teacher must understand the meaning of the words of the texts in a clear and precise manner, unmixed with the teachings from the other vehicles. And this is not a matter of just repeating the words of the text, for it is not a matter of intellectual knowledge alone. Rather, the teacher himself must have engaged in the practice of contemplation and thereby come to an immediate experience and understanding of the Natural State, at least to a certain degree of realization. Such an individual possesses the lineage of transmission, as well as the understanding (rtogs-pa) and the direct personal experience (nyams) of the Natural State. Only such a master can point out and directly introduce the practitioner to his Natural State and its intrinsic Awareness. Then on his part, the disciple should possess both faith and devotion toward the master and the teachings. On the other hand, it is not a matter of this teacher being a fully enlightened being at present, although, while listening to the transmission of the teachings, one should think of him as such, as if it were the Buddha himself who was speaking. But rather, the presence of this teacher and his communicating of the precepts of Dzogchen serve as a channel or conduit for the transference of the blessings of the past masters, who have attained the realization of the Rainbow Body, to the receptive disciple who has become a pure vessel for their reception.

Second, it is, therefore, absolutely necessary that the disciple possess a pure faith in the teacher and in the transmission, unmixed with doubts and reservations, particularly at the time when the transmission is occurring, for otherwise, the transmission may be blocked or dissipated. This does not mean, however, that the disciple must then become a mindless servant of the individual who serves as the Guru on that occasion, or that one must accept everything that individual says apart from the event of that transmission. Even so, one must continue to respect that individual as a source for the transmission that one has received in this lifetime, despite whatever idiosyncrasies or inadequacies of character and behavior that individual may manifest subsequently. The relationship here between master and disciple is a functional one in terms of the transmission. It is not a relationship of total intimacy and dependency as might exist, albeit temporary, between lovers. So, Guru devotion must be put in its proper perspective in terms of maintaining the transmission.

And third, one must exercise diligence and perseverance with regard to engaging in the practices. Having found a qualified teacher and having developed faith in that teacher and the teachings are not enough by themselves. One must also make these teachings concrete and real in one's own personal experience by actually practicing them. Generally, the samaya (dam-tshig) or commitment taken at the time of initiation is the solemn promise made to do the practice. Without such practice, no realization will occur in one's stream of consciousness. It is not a question of merely comprehending intellectually some teaching and then being able to expound it verbally, but one of arriving at an understanding born of immediate experience. Moreover, one should not speak loosely of one's personal experiences and understanding, especially to those who would not understand because of their own limitations and obscurations of mind. However, compassion lies at the base of all practice, and so when it is skillful and useful to do so, one may speak of such matters to a fellow disciple or to those who are sincerely interested because it will be helpful and beneficial to share this with them.

Both the teacher and the disciple, therefore, must be qualified, each in his own terms, for the transmission to be fruitful and successful. And then, it is necessary to find a suitable place for teaching and practice, one where there will be few disturbances or distractions, and whatever is needed in terms of food and supplies are available. Ideally, such a place of practice is rather isolated, so that one may avoid casual entertainments and gossip at all cost because they distract the mind from its higher purposes in terms of practice. [2]

Generally speaking, the Ngondro or preliminary practices are divided into the ordinary preliminaries and the extraordinary preliminaries. The ordinary preliminaries chiefly consist of the four meditations that bring about a total change in one's attitude toward life. [3] These are as follows:

1. The unique opportunity (dal-'byor) of having obtained a precious human rebirth (mi lus rin-po-che). Among the various destines of rebirth, it is said that a human rebirth offers the maximum opportunity for attaining realization and liberation.

2. Life is impermanent (tshe mi rtag-pa) and, although it is certain that death will come to all, it is uncertain when the hour of death will occur. Therefore, one should not waste this unique opportunity.

3. All of the happiness and sorrow that one experiences in this present life time, as well as in past lives and in future lives, is the result of one's karma, the consequences of one's actions. But, even though one's present existence is the aggregate result of past karmic causes, yet at the present moment, one is free in one's moral choices and it is these choices that create one's future karma. So, it is not a matter of fatalism or predestination, for it is the individual's free will actions in the present that determine one's future lifetimes. And the results of this karma follow one as inevitably as the shadow follows the body.

4. Throughout all the destinies of rebirth within Samsara, one will experience suffering as the result of negative karma. Therefore, there is no safe or permanent refuge to be found anywhere within Samsara. Coming once to understand this in the most radical manner, that suffering is the existential predicament of all sentient beings, one then develops a total disillusionment or disgust with Samsara (nyes-dmigs) in terms of one's own fate and a deep abiding compassion (snying-rje) in terms of the fate of others still caught up in the suffering of Samsara.

These four considerations, when fully meditated upon so that an understanding arises in each case, bring about a reversal or a radical and total change in one's whole attitude, where one turns away from the things of the world toward a higher spiritual dimension of existence. [4] Dissatisfied with the worldly life and its inevitable fate, one seeks freedom from bondage to ignorance and suffering and enters on to the spiritual path of liberation. Thus, the ordinary preliminaries are principally concerned with one's motivation for entering into the spiritual life.

Having fully cultivated this motivation by means of these four meditations, one proceeds to develop the thought of aspiration (smon sems) to benefit others and to help alleviate their suffering. But aspiration alone is not enough; one must next enter into the thought of actually engaging ('jug sems) in the practice of the Dharma or the spiritual path by way of the accumulations of merit and wisdom realized through the ten perfections.

This leads the novice practitioner to the extraordinary preliminaries. Among the Buddhists of the Nyingmapa and the Kagyudpa schools generally, there exist five such practices:

1. the Going to Refuge (skabs-'gro) in the Three Jewels of the Buddha, the Dharma, and the Sangha;
2. Cultivating the Bodhichitta (sems-bskyed) where one considers that all sentient beings, in some lifetime or another, were one's loving parents, and so now one desires to alleviate their suffering experienced in Samsara through becoming an enlightened Buddha who has the power to do so;
3. the Confession of Sins (sdig bshags) and purification of one's obscurations (sgrib sbyong) by way of the Meditation and Mantra Recitation of Vajrasattva (rdor-sems bsgom bzlas);

4. Offering the Mandala (mandal 'bul) to the Three Jewels, this mandala symbolically representing all the wealth of the world, where acts of generosity represent the best means to accumulate merit (tshogs bsags); and

5. the Guru Yoga or Unification with the Master (bla-ma'i rnal-'byor), which maintains one's links with the transmission and with the blessings of all the realized masters in the lineage. [5]

In general, the Ngondro represents a preparation designed to purify one's mind stream (rgyud sbyong) so that it becomes a suitable clean vessel to receive the full transmission from the master of the Dzogchen teachings. This full transmission, as explained, does not occur until the completion of the Ngondro practices and the appearance of the requisite signs of success (grub rtags). The initial transmission includes a pointing out or direct introduction (ngo-sprod) to the Natural State of the Nature of Mind (sems-nyid gnas-lugs) and its intrinsic Awareness (rig-pa) in its nakedness, free of discursive thoughts and the normal conventional operations of mind or the thought process.

For the tradition of the Zhang-zhung Nyan-gyud, we are fortunate to have a Ngondro text composed by the great master Druchen Gyalwa Yungdrung (1242-1290) and included in his *Phyag-khrid* collection of texts that represents a type of practice manual and instruction book for the Zhang-zhung Nyan-gyud. [6] This text is entitled *rDzogs-pa chen-po zhang-zhung snyan-rgyud las bon spyod dgu rim*, "The Nine Stages of the (Preliminary) Practices of Bon, according to the Oral Transmission from Zhang-zhung for the Great Perfection Teachings." The translation of this text is given below, together with some brief notes and commentary based on the Lopon's oral instructions. In this text, the preliminary practices are listed as nine, rather than as five, but they cover the same general material found in the Ngondro texts of the other traditions, in the case of Dzogchen among the Nyingmapas and for Mahamudra among the Kagyudpas. And so, there is nothing lacking here. These preliminary practices are as follows:

1. The Receiving of Empowerments and Blessings (dbang-bskur byin-rlabs).
2. The Meditations on Impermanence (tshe mi rtag-pa),
3. The Confession of Sins (sdig-pa bshags-pa),
4. The Producing of the Bodhichitta (sems-bskyed),
5. The Going to Refuge (skyabs su 'gro-ba),
6. The Offering of the Mandala (man-tal 'bul-ba),

7. The Ritual Service of the Mantra Recitation (bzlas lung bsnyen-pa),
8. The Offering of one's own Body (gcod), and
9. Praying to Receive the Blessings (mos-gus gsol-'debs).

Thus, there are in total nine preliminary practices, divided into three groups of three each.

Instructions for Practicing the Preliminaries

By way of elucidation, let us here quote in part and briefly from another text in the Zhang-zhung Nyan-gyud collection entitled, "A Manual for the Meditation Practice of Contemplation in terms of the General View according to the Oral Tradition from Zhang-zhung for the Great Perfection Teachings." [7]

"Homage to Kuntu Zangpo who is that inherent Self-Awareness that abides equally everywhere!

"Considering the two aspects which are the view in general (lta-ba spyi-gcod) and the state of contemplation (mnyam-bzhag), in order to lead fortunate disciples along the path to the Base (which is the Natural State), this nectar from the hearts of the Nine Victorious Ones of the Mind Lineage and the condensed essences of the Twenty-Four August Persons (of the Oral Transmission) is revealed here in this manual for the meditation practice of contemplation. A master who possesses the Four Transmissions (of the Dzogchen Precepts) should teach in their completeness this heart's nectar to any disciple who is a suitable vessel. Such a disciple is one who possesses faith, diligence, wisdom, and compassion, who carries one's meditation deity and one's master upon the crown of one's head, who is fearless like a lion's cub, and whose mind is stable and unchanging, and who is open-minded, but who keeps silent and is capable of remembering the teachings.

"Having received the instructions from the master, one should retire to an isolated place where the conditions for meditation practice are agreeable and abundant, and where heat and cold can be regulated with food and with the proper proportions of the elements for one's health. One reduces moving about, whether inside or outside the hermitage, and one does not neglect the times for concentration in meditation practice. Thereupon, both external objects and internal consciousness are appropriately purified by means of the outer and the inner preliminaries. [9]

(A. The Outer or Ordinary Preliminaries)

"First, one should engage in purifications with respect to the objects that represent external appearances. [10] One does this by reflecting upon the real significance of the difficulty of obtaining a precious human rebirth. One enters systematically into reflecting upon the significance of having obtained (this human rebirth and the unique opportunity it affords), and that it has not yet been exhausted (by terminal illness and death). One continues to reflect systematically on this unique opportunity, as well as its impermanence and the certainty of the inevitable coming of death. In this way, one cuts through all entanglements with worldly attachments by means of the certainty that worldly delusions and illusory appearances are truly deceptive. One casts aside all worldly activities and avoids all attachments to the concerns of Samsara.

"Furthermore, because of the sufferings that will be experienced in Samsara within the six destinies of rebirth are sure and certain for oneself, one should reflect upon what is the mind that experiences them and produce a certain knowledge (nges-shes) with regard to that. In this way, one will vanquish laziness and indolence that are the enemies (of all spiritual development) and, like the warrior, one mounts upon the swift horse of vigorous diligence. And producing in one's heart a fervent faith in the teachings, one enters on to the path to liberation.

(*B. The Inner or Extraordinary Preliminaries*)

"Second, in terms of the purifying of one's internal awareness, at the outset one should produce the thought of supreme enlightenment, which is the Bodhichitta, and meditate systematically on the unlimited states of compassion, friendliness, sympathetic joy, and even-mindedness toward all sentient beings, who being ignorant and deluded, (remaining entrapped within Samsara).

"Following that, one goes to Refuge in the Sources of Refuge which are outer, inner, secret, and exceedingly secret, and so on. [11] One should do so one-pointedly and with intense feeling.

"Then, in order to purify one's emotional defilements, as well as one's sins and obscurations, [12] one should set about to amass a vast accumulation of meritorious karma (by way of deeds of generosity). The superior practitioner proceeds to purify oneself by way of renouncing the three cycles (of the giver, the gift, and the recipient). [13] The intermediate practitioner does so by way of an extensive ceremony of the Ganapuja, wherein one makes offerings to the Sugatas, to the Deities, to the Dakinis, and to the Protectors of Bon. [14] One fervently prays for the purification of all one's hindrances (and one's generosity and purity of intention) will most surely delight the Masters and the Gurus. The inferior practitioner should simply offer the Mandala possessing the four aspects throughout the four seasons and the four times of day. [15] This action represents the process for the accumulating of merit.

"Then, in terms of the successive stages in the purifying of one's obscurations, [16] by way of making puja offerings and of presenting sacrificial cakes to offset retribution, [17] one proceeds to purify all one's sins and obscurations, as well as make payments for karmic debts entailing retribution to all the beings of the six realms of rebirth. This is accomplished in general by making miniature figures (of barley flour) as offerings, by making water offerings, as well as by making prostrations and circumambulations. In this way, one purifies the obscurations of one's body. [18] Then by going to refuge and by reciting the heart mantras, one comes to purify the obscurations of one's speech. [19] Then, by means of the rays of the light of compassion emanating from Kuntu Zangpo (visualized in the sky above), one vanquishes the seed syllables that represent the five poisons (within one's physical body) that are the sources or germs for the future growth of the six realms and destinies of rebirth. [20] And finally, by way of emanating and reabsorbing of the rays of light from the white syllable A (visualized in one's heart center), one purifies the obscurations of one's mind, such as the five poisons. [21] Thus, in this way, one completes the preliminary practices."

The text of the manual goes on to describe the process of fixating the mind (sems-'dzin) on an object of meditation, such as the white Tibetan letter A, as a means for entering into the state of contemplation. However, this material belongs to the principal practice, rather than to the preliminaries and so, it is not presented here. [22]

OUTLINE OF THE CONTENTS OF THE NGONDRO TEXT
"The Nine Stages of the Practice of Bon," according to "The Oral Transmission from Zhang-zhung for the Great Perfection." (rDzogs-pa chen-po zhang-zhung snyan-rgyud las bon spyod dgu rim bzhungs)

CONTENTS OF THE COLLECTION OF TEXTS
I. The Outer Aspect which is the General View (phyi lta-ba spyi-gcod).
II. The Inner Aspect which is the vitally clear Expanation of the Upadesha (nang man-ngag dmar khrid).
III. The Secret Aspect which is seeing Awareness in its Nakedness (gsang-ba rig-pa gcer-mthong).
IV. The Exceeding Secret Aspect which is the Explanation of the Definitive Realization of the Natural State (yang-gsang gnas-lugs phugs chod du bshad-pa).

CONTENTS OF THE PRELIMINARY PRACTICES
I. The Preliminary Practices **(sngon-'gro)**
At the beginning there is the performing of the Preliminary Practices
that bring about a cleansing and complete purification of one's own
individual mind-stream (dang-po rgyud yongs su dag cing sbyong-bar
byed-pa sngon-'gro'i bya-ba).
Then, within the first part concering the practice of the
preliminaries, there exist three sections, namely,

IA. the individual practices in detail (bye-brag so-so ru nyams su
len-pa),

IB. the ordinary practices in general (thun-mong spyi dril tu nyams
su len-pa), and

IC. the signs of "heat" resulting from having practiced them
(nyams su blangs-pa'i drod rtags).

IA. The Individual Practices in Detail
(bye-brag so-so ru nyams su len-pa)
The author has divided the preliminary practices into three main
sections or methodologies which are designated

1. discipling the mind-stream (rgyud 'dul-ba),
2. cleansing the mind-stream (rgyud sbyong-ba), and
3. purifying the mind-stream (rgyud dag-par bya-ba).

IA.1. The Practices that are Valuable in General:
Disciplining one's mind-stream by means of the three preliminary
practices that are valuable in general (spyir gces-pa'i sngon-'gro gsum
gyis rgyud 'dul-ba).
IA.1.1. Conferring Empowerments: (dbang-bskur byin-rlabs)
This represents the explanation regarding the blessings received from
the conferring of the empowerment (dbang bskur byin rlabs kyi khrid);
the explanation of the confering of the empowerment that blesses the
mind-stream of the individual receiving it (rgyud byin gyis rlob-pa
dbang bskur gyi khrid).
IA.1.2. Meditation on Impermancncc: (tshc mi rtag-pa)
This represents the explanation that motivates one by way of entreaties
according to the conventional meaning (drang don bskul 'debs kyi
khrid); the explanation for the meditation on impermanence that
completely disciplines the mind-stream of the individual (rgyud yongs
su 'dul-ba mi rtag-pa'i khrid).

IA.1.3. Confession of Sins: (sdig-pa bshags-pa)
This represents the explanation concerning the practice of confession that cleanses and purifies all sins and obscurations (dag tshangs bshags-pa'i khrid); the explanation of the confessing of sins that brings about a purifying of the mind-stream (rgyud tshangs-par byed-pa sdig bshags kyi khrid).

IA.2. The Practices that are in Agreement with Everything:
Cleansing one's mind-stream by means of the three preliminary practices that are in agreement with everything else (in terms of the Sutra and the Tantra systems) (kun dang mthun-pa'i sngon-'gro gsum gyis rgyud sbyong-ba).

IA.2.1. Producing the Bodhichitta: (sems-bskyed)
This represents the explanation for the producing of the thought to benefit others (gzhan don sems bskyed kyi khrid); grasping the base with compassion and the four unlimited states, one produces the Bodhichitta or thought of enlightenment (snying-rje tshad-med kyi gzhi bzung ste sems bskyed-pa)

IA.2.2. Going to Refuge: (skyabs su 'gro-ba)
This represents the explanation of the going to Refuge with faith and longing (dad 'dun skyabs 'gro'i khrid); grasping the base with faith and devotion, one goes to Refuge (dad mos gus-pas gzhi bzung ste skyabs su 'gro-ba)

IA.2.3. Offering the Mandala: (man-tal 'bul-ba)
This represents the explanation concerning the Mandala that signifies the clouds of offerings (mchod sprin man-tal gyi khrid); grasping the base as a purified self-manifestation, one offers the Mandala (rang snang dag-pas gzhi bzung ste man-tal 'bul-ba).

IA.3. The Especially Exalted Practices:
Purifying one's mind-stream by means of the three preliminary practices that are especially exalted (khyad-par 'phags-pa'i sngon-'gro gsum gyis rgyud dag-par bya-ba).

IA.3.1. Ritual Service of the Mantra Recitation:
(bzlas lung bsnyen-pa)
This represents the explanation for the recitation of the mantra and the text that purifies the obscurations (sgrib sbyang bzlas lung gi khrid); the stages of the ritual practice (seva) of the text and mantra recitations that purifies the karmic traces and the obscurations (bag sgrib sbyong-ba bzlas lung bsnyen-pa'i rim-pa).

IA.3.2. The Offering of one's own Body: (gcod)
This represents the explanation for the accumulating of the collection of merit by the generous giving of offerings (tshogs sogs mchod sbyin

gyi khrid); the stages of transforming the aggregates of the body and mind in order to accumulate merit (bsod-nams bsags-pa lus sems tshogs bsgyur gyi rim-pa)

IA.3.3. Praying to Receive the Blessings: (mos-gus gsol-'debs) This represents the explanation regarding the practice of praying with fervent devotion (to the Gurus) (mos-gus gsol-'debs kyi khrid); the stages of praying with devotion in order to access the blessings (of the Gurus) (byin rlabs 'jag-pa mos-gus gsol-'debs kyi rim-pa).

(Thus, there are in total nine preliminary practices, divided into three groups of three each.)

IB. The Ordinary Practices in General
The common ordinary practices in general for the stages of the nine (preliminary) practices of Bon (bon spyod dgu rim thun-mong spyi dril tu nyams su len-pa)

IC. The Signs of Heat
The signs of "heat" resulting from having practiced them (nyams su blangs-pa'i drod rtags)

II. The Principal Practices (dngos-gzhi)
In the middle there are the successive stages of the Principal Practices that ripen the mind-stream and brings about liberation (bar du rgyud smin cing grol-bar byed-pa dngos-gzhi'i rim-pa).

III. The Conclusion (rjes mjug)
Finally there are the auxiliary practices of the Conclusion that cause understanding to become manifest in the mind-stream (tha-ma rgyud rtogs shing mngon du gyur-par byed-pa rjes mjug gi yan-lag).

These represent the three major divisions of the practice of Dzogchen according to the tradition of the Zhang-zhung Nyan-gyud. The Principal Practices and the Four Auxiliary Texts of the Concluding Section are found as separate texts in the *Phyag-khrid* collection.

Translation of "the Preliminary Practices Text": *sNgon-'gro*

Here is contained "The Nine Stages of the Practice of Bon," according to "The Oral Transmission from Zhang-zhung for the Great Perfection" (rDzogs-pa chen-po zhang-zhung snyan-rgyud las bon spyod dgu rim bzhugs).

Homage to Kuntu Zangpo, the all-pervading and all-encompassing guide of living beings, who becomes manifest as Self-Awareness!

Preface
I pray to the Vidyadharas, to the Masters, to the Dakinis, and to the hosts of Protectors of the Precepts who effulgently emit the light of

compassion everywhere into the ten directions so that they may release the seals on the Precepts that elucidate the essential points of the propound path of Dzogchen. Even though there exists no traditional system for arranging in writing this oral transmission, it being the special Upadesha of the Experiential Mind Transmission (descending from the Primordial Buddha), nevertheless, thinking with much affection to purify the forgetfulness of my confused disciples, I have composed these verses which are in harmony with the authentic meaning (for the practice of Dzogchen); and I pray to the hosts of Dakinis and Guardians of the Precepts for their forbearance.

Herein (this set of instructions regarding the practice of Dzogchen represents) the elixir of the enlightened Mind of Kuntu Zangpo, the precepts and scriptures of the Sugatas and Jinas, the oral instructions of the exalted Vidyadharas, the innermost nectar of all teachings, the ultimate source of all oral transmissions, the ultimate realization of all enlightened Minds, the highest peak of all views and states of contemplation, the root Sutra of all definitive meanings, the condensed essential points of all Tantras and Agamas, the distilled essence of all Upadeshas, the spiritual attainment of Gyerpung Nangzher Lodpo, and the experiences and realizations of previous Mahasiddhas, as well as the guide to the Path for subsequent disciples possessing meritorious karma. It is the ultimate statement of all the essential points of the profound meaning of the Great Perfection. It definitively discloses the source of delusion and brings forth gnosis (or genuine knowledge) from its concealment. [1] It reveals intrinsic Awareness in its nakedness and thereby the mind and the visions meet together as Mother and Son.

Thereupon, having accepted that cause and effect are indeed false, one comes to realize Buddhahood by way of these powerful methods. [2] Having brought regular practice into one's mind-stream, one immediately exhibits a confident belief (in the efficacy of the teachings of Dzogchen and their methods). Internally having decided definitively with great intensity (on the essential point of the Natural State), thereupon, externally, the signs of realization come to be displayed. [3]

Contents of the Text

With respect to the instructions regarding the Oral Transmission from Zhang-zhung for the Great Perfection, they are expounded in four sections, namely,

1. The Outer Aspect consists of the Explanation of the General View (of Dzogchen),

2. The Inner Aspect consists of the Upadeshas that provide vitally clear Guidance,
3. the Secret Aspect consists of Explanation of Awareness Seeing Nakedly, and
4. the Exceedingly Secret Aspect consists of the Explanation concerning the Definitive Realization of the Natural State.

Herewith, having extracted the essences of all the teachings, condensing their essential points, distilling enlightened realization, and bringing forth the pristine knowledge from concealment, [4] one takes them in hand in terms of the three phases:

1. at the beginning there is the performing of the Preliminary Practices that bring about a cleansing and complete purification of one's own mind-stream,
2. in the middle there are the stages of the Principal Practices that ripen the mind-stream and brings about liberation,
3. and finally there are the auxiliary practices of the Conclusion that cause understanding to become manifest in the mind-stream. (These represent the three major divisions for the practice of Dzogchen.)

The Preliminary Practices
Then, within the first part, known as the practice of the preliminaries, there exist three sections to be considered in turn, namely,

I. the individual practices in detail,
II. the ordinary practices in general, and
III. the signs of "heat" resulting from having done the practices.

I. The Individual Preliminary Practices in Detail
Next, within the first section (in terms of the individual practices in detail), there are three subsections:

A. Disciplining one's mind-stream by means of the three preliminary practices that are valuable in general;
B. Cleansing one's mind-stream by means of the three preliminary practices that are in agreement with everything else; and
C. Purifying one's mind-stream by means of the three preliminary practices that are especially exalted. (Thus, there are in total nine preliminary practices, divided into three groups of three each.)

A. The Practices that are Valuable in General

Within the first subsection, there are three further sections, namely:

(1) the explanation of the conferring of the empowerments that bestow blessings upon the mind-stream,

(2) the explanation of the meditation on impermanence in order to completely discipline the mind-stream, and

(3) the explanation regarding the confessing of sins in order to bring about a purifying of the mind-stream.

1. The Receiving of Empowerments and Blessings

Retiring to a location that is isolated and where virtues are increased thereby, and which is free of distractions caused by deluded thoughts of worldly entertainments, a disciple who has faith in and devotion to an excellent master possessing all the requisite marks, such as the proper view of Dzogchen and the realization of the Natural State, should turn the wheel of the Ganachakra Puja, requesting the empowerments and the scriptural authorizations for the instructions, as well as perform extensive religious rites for amassing the two accumulations of merit and wisdom. And as for the benefits of doing this, one will purify both the external and the internal hindrances, one will realize whatever benefits one considers, and one will be gathered under the protection of the Supreme Objects (of Refuge, namely, the Three Jewels and the Three Roots).

This concludes the explanation regarding the blessings received from the conferring of the empowerments. U-YA SMAR-RO!

2. Meditation on Impermanence

Adopting the essential point of the body, either the five-fold sitting position or else crouching (like a Rishi), one focuses the eyes on the space between the eyebrows.

Then, with respect to the mind, one should think that everything that is conditioned is impermanent, everything changes constantly, everything that is created will be destroyed, everything that comes together will be separated again, everything that is accumulated will be dissipated again, and everything that has been born will eventually die. [5] When one thinks about everything everywhere and analyzes matters in this way, one finds that all of them are without any essence, even though one has repeated apprehended them as being certain, real, and permanent. Therefore, one should think, "How sad!" [6]

Previously, one has circulated in Samsara from beginningless time, and even though one still wanders again and again (throughout the destinies of rebirth in Samsara), one feels no regret at one's actions, and one is satisfied with one's lot of suffering in this world. Nevertheless, it is certain that suffering will come (again and again in the future). And when that time does come, there is nothing that can forestall it. Yet one grasps at things as being permanent. Therefore, one should think regarding this, "How sad!"

a. Meditation on the Loss of Wealth and Power

Then (for example, one should meditate that) one is seated like a king on a beautiful throne inside a mighty castle in the midst of many cities. On all sides there is spread out a great abundance of attendant retinues, enjoyments, foods, wealth, games, and power. Then one imagines that all of one's entourage suddenly rebel. They carry off with them all of one's food and wealth, as well as killing off all of one's loyal subjects and kinsmen. All of one's cities are overthrown and demolished, and one finds oneself utterly alone and destitute, with empty hands and an empty mouth. Thinking thus, one meditates on impermanence for one session.

b. Meditation on Illness and the Decay of the Body

Again one imagines that one is suddenly struck down with an exceedingly painful and unendurable disease where the upper part of one's body withers and the lower part rots away. All the people of the country side, including one's friends and relatives gather around. They try casting divinations, performing religious rituals, and making medical diagnoses. [7] However, despite whatever they do, whether from knowledge or from memory, one's health continues to decline and death approaches. Thinking thus, one meditates on impermanence for one session.

c. Meditation on the Time of one's Death

Then, just as the moon will disappear in the heavens (at the end of the month) and the sun will disappear into the earth (sinking below the horizon at sunset), so the time of one's death will inevitably come. One knows for certain that one will die and that there exists no means to avert it. Many such thoughts may arise or do not arise in one's awareness. Thinking thus, one meditates on impermanence for one session.

d. Meditation on Dying and the Bardo Experience

Then one imagines that one looses the respective strengths of the four elements of the physical body [8] and even though one desires to continue living, one is without the power to remain. The external sense faculties cease to function and the consciousness is expelled from the body, whereupon the visions of the Bardo arise and the illusory body (here meaning the physical body) remains behind as a mere trace of one's former existence. Thereafter one's food and one's wealth are appropriated by others. The Lama calls out (when performing the Bardo rites and one's relatives and friends) utter lamentations. Thinking thus, one meditates on impermanence for one session.

e. Meditation on Wandering in a Desolate Land

Then one imagines that one is abandoned, naked and with empty hands. One wanders about alone without friends or companions in a country that is alien and unfamiliar. There is no place to stay and no place to go. Even though memories persist in the mind, one does not find any reason for doing anything. Thinking thus, one meditates on impermanence for a single session.

f. Meditation on the Deaths of Others

Furthermore, one thinks about the deaths of those who have died previously, which one has seen for oneself or just heard about. Each of those individuals were similar to oneself in terms of being able to speak, to think, and to understand the meaning (of what has happened to them). Thinking thus, one meditates on impermanence.

g. Meditation on Inevitable Change

Furthermore, thinking about the vicissitudes and reversals of this world, such as happiness and sorrow, wealth and poverty, enemies and friends, good and evil, strengths and weaknesses, and so on, one meditates on impermanence.

h. Meditation on the Ceaseless Flow of Time

Furthermore, thinking about the aeons of time, the enumerations of the years and the months and the days, and the modes of change in even shorter periods of time, one meditates on impermanence.

i. Meditation on the Inevitability of Death

Furthermore, even though the place, time, condition, and manner of one's death is uncertain, it is certain that one will surely die. One never knows when one will die, but on that occasion, there will come no help from anyone. Thinking thus, one meditates on impermanence.

Moreover, one reflects that there was no one in the past who did not die and that it is not possible that there is someone who exists at present who will not die. Whether in the past or in the future, without exception there is no one who escapes death and lives forever. Thinking thus, one meditates on impermanence.

In that way, these meditations on impermanence are enumerated and one divides one's practice into sessions accordingly. Because one meditates thus, integrating the three gates (of one's body, speech, and mind), one's attitude toward Samsara is reversed by the inherent power of that (meditation) and one produces in the mind (a feeling of all-pervasive and total) impermanence. Thereupon all external appearances arise to oneself as illusions and one cuts off all entanglements with attachments to them being real. [9] These worldly appearances will arise according to whatever is familiar and habitual. As it says in the *Lung drug*, "However, one attaches names to them and they will appear like that." And again, "Since one produces in the mind-stream a strong awareness of the impermanence of everything, when one becomes mindful of death, all such practitioners belonging to future generations will take the opportunity presented at present for entering into the practice."

Therefore, one should meditate in this nine-fold manner on impermanence and the inevitability of death. This has been expounded by Lachen (Dranpa Namkha). [10]

This concludes the explanation that motivates one by way of exhortations according to the conventional meaning. U-YA SMAR-RO!

3. Confession of Sins

Third, one engages in the Generation Process (by way of visualizing the images of) the Gurus and the Sugatas in the atmosphere in front of oneself and then integrates (the Wisdom Beings invoked into these visualizations).

Whereupon one should think as follows: "All sentient beings such as myself, from past incarnations until the present, have wandered in Samsara, have suffered the full measure of karmic purifications, have been fettered by the grasping at a self, and have been repeatedly purged of sins without any opportunity for happiness. This beginningless process of karmic purification through suffering originates from our past conduct consisting of countless numbers of sinful deeds. Therefore, sentient beings such as myself have committed sinful actions from lifetime after lifetime, such as, most importantly, the five immeasurably heinous crimes, the four lesser crimes, the four heavy transgressions, the eight wrong actions, the nine deluded actions, the ten non-virtuous actions, and so on. These masses of sins and non-virtuous actions where either committed by myself alone or else I urged others to do so, and thereafter rejoiced in them. These deeds committed by sentient beings such as myself, because we all were lacking in awareness and an understanding of the consequences of past actions. Thus, these deeds all possessed the nature of ignorance (because we did not recognize their character). However, all of these deeds, united into a single mass, are vividly present to the Minds of the Omniscient Ones (the Buddhas). Therefore, I shall offer my confession, accompanied by remorse and regret, in the field of their vision." [11]

Having produced an intense regret, like goose-flesh separating the skin from the bones, one offers one's confession. Henceforth one's own immaculate mind becoming established as one's witness, and having entered into the gateway of the Mahayana, one should renounce and abandon all of the masses of sins and non-virtuous actions to which one is prone. And correspondingly one should cultivate the roots of virtue to the subtlest degree. For truly, everywhere in all the worldly realms, those holy persons who cultivate the virtues, both the conditioned and the unconditioned, are exceedingly marvelous! One should always hold the thought of rejoicing (at their presence in the world) and make offerings of confession accordingly to them.

As it is said in the Outer Tantras, "One should confess one's sinful deeds and non-virtuous actions individually, and then pursue each corresponding virtuous action." [12]

Therefore, having purified all the sins and obscurations committed previously, one will become suitable as a vessel for the Mahayana. However, if that is not the case, one should understand that, just as an oily paper does not retain the letters written upon it, so one will not become a suitable vessel for the Mahayana.

This concludes the explanation concerning the practice of confession that cleanses and purifies (all sins and obscurations). U-YA SMAR-RO!

B. The Practices according to the General System:

Second, with respect to cleansing the mind-stream by means of the three preliminary practices that are in agreement with everything (in the general system of the Sutras and the Tantras), there exist three sections:

1. adhering to the base with compassion and the four unlimited states, one produces the Bodhichitta or thought of enlightenment,
2. adhering to the base with faith and devotion, one goes to Refuge, and
3. adhering to the base as a purified self-manifestation, one offers the Mandala.

4. Producing the Bodhichitta

In the field of vision of those Sources of Refuge who are generated (by visualization) in the sky in front of oneself, as was done above, one should think as follows: "Since among all the sentient beings that exist, there is not one of them who has not been (in some lifetime or another) my very own father or mother or child or kinsman, how sad it is that they continue to wander in Samsara and endlessly experience suffering!" And thinking in this way, one produces an uncontrived yearning to help them and an intense compassion for them.

(In consequence, one cultivates the intention as follows:) "Therefore, because I lack at present the capacity to bring about their benefit by means of my own actions, for that reason I shall strive to attain the enlightened state of a Buddha. Within this seal, my present physical body, and with patience and forbearance, in order to secure the benefit of beings whose numbers are equal in extent to the sky, I will lead them to liberation until Samsara itself is emptied of beings. Because there exists the urgency of both past and present with regard to the benefiting of sentient beings, at this present time I shall strive to obtain the fruit of Buddhahood for the sake of rescuing all sentient beings (from the sufferings of Samsara!)" Thinking in this way, one should recite the words above.

This concludes the explanation for the producing of the thought to benefit others. U-YA SMAR-RO!

5. Going to Refuge

Second, in the sky in front of oneself, one visualizes that one's own Root Guru in the guise of Kunzang Shenlha is seated on a lion throne and a seat that is a lotus, a sun, and a moon. One should think that, in all directions in front of him, there sit the hosts of Deities who are the Yidams, both external and internal, as well as the Buddhas of the ten directions, the Vidyadharas, the hosts of Bodhisattvas, the Gurus of the Lineages of Transmission, together with the hosts of Dakinis and Protectors of Bon, gathering like clouds. Everywhere at his back there are arrayed all of the pure realms of the ten directions. Moreover, the supreme supports of the Body, Speech, and Mind (namely, images, scriptures, and stupas) are set about with their surfaces clear and bright, like massive rock mountains.

Then, one's own body becomes multiplied hundreds, even millions or billions of times. Moreover, each of them is leading multitudes of sentient beings (in going to Refuge in the above Sources of Refuge) and all of them focus on this one-pointedly their three gates (of body, speech, and mind) with great faith and devotion. In this way, thinking to go to Refuge in them with a fervent intensity, one recites the words.

This concludes the explanation regarding the going to Refuge with faith and intense longing. U-YA SMAR-RO!

6. The Mandala Offering

Third, the best materials for constructing the Mandala are gold and silver, the next best or intermediate material is bell metal (an alloy of gold, silver, zinc, and iron), and the inferior materials are wood and clay. The various parts are constructed so that they have the proper proportions, shape, and material and on that are arranged the decorations and ornaments.

Initially, at the time when one wipes clean (the surface of the Mandala with the palm of one's right hand), one should think that one is purifying all the karmic traces and obscurations of oneself and others. While cleaning it well, one recites the mantra OM NA-MA A-DKAR GSHA' YA NI SHAG SA-LE SANG-NGE SWAHA. [13] Then, still holding it in the (left) hand while reciting the mantra BRUM RI TI GAR MA LA HO, one arranges in the center (using the right hand a heap of grains of rice, which signifies the Meru mountain). Next, starting from the front (representing the eastern direction) and proceeding to the right (counterclockwise), one arranges in the four cardinal directions and in the eight intermediate directions (the twelve smaller heaps of rice signifying the twelve continents) while reciting the mantra A YAM RAM MAM KHAM BRUM SHAG SA-LE SANG-NGE SWAHA. Again, while reciting the mantra OM PHYOD PHUR SA-LE HA-LO SENG, one arranges (the rice grains as the offering substances) in the four directions about the center. Similarly, these seventeen heaps (representing the Meru mountain, the twelve continents, and the four elements) should be made in an attractive and appropriate manner, while thinking of their respective qualities, without crowding them together, or scattering them, or separating them too much, or cutting them off as incomplete.

Then, one thinks that, in the sky in front of oneself, the entire atmosphere is filled with the Objects of Refuge as above, like clouds gathering or like the scattered hosts of stars. And with respect to this Mandala, the superior procedure is to visualize it as being equal to (the infinity of all) space, the intermediate procedure as its being equal to the three thousand-fold universe, and the inferior procedure as its being equal only to the Brahmaloka. Furthermore, below, on the immaculate golden foundation of the earth, there is found the Meru mountain, the seven (golden) mountains, the four great continents, the (eight) lesser continents, together with the encircling ring of iron mountains. Inside of that, in terms of the clouds of offerings, it is filled to the brim with such inconceivable clouds of offerings that grant enjoyment to both gods and humans, much like wish-granting gems, such as the eight auspicious emblems and the seven precious jewels, and all delightful sensual qualities adorned with sights, sounds, smells, tastes, and touches.

One's own body becomes multiplied hundreds, even millions of times. And moreover, each of them guides animate sentient beings who are transformed into gods and goddesses. Then conjuring up and dispersing whatever offerings may be desired anywhere, thinking to accomplish deeds of offering, one offers all of these things by relinquishing them without any desire or attachment. Whereupon one prays that there will be produced in one's mind-stream a special experience and understanding of the Natural State and of the Mahayana. One makes the supplications while thinking in this way. Reciting the words, one makes the offerings and the commitments.

Then, at the time of gathering up (the grains of rice from the Mandala), without being haphazard or careless, one gathers them up until the last one. Thereafter one makes the dedication of merit.

Then at the time of the early morning and at sunset, one thinks of one's own physical body as being the Mandala itself as described above. Whereupon, one's own consciousness becomes innumerable offering goddesses and one thinks that they accomplish deeds of offering, just as one had made the offerings as described above.

This concludes the explanation concerning the Mandala that signifies the clouds of offerings. U-YA SMAR-RO!

C. The Especially Exalted Preliminary Practices

Third, with respect to the activity of purifying the mind-stream by means of the three preliminary practices that are especially exalted (in terms of the practice of the Higher Tantras), there are three sections, namely,

1. the stages of the ritual service for the scripture and the mantra recitations that purifies the karmic traces and the obscurations,
2. the stages of transforming the aggregates of the body and mind in order to accumulate merit, and
3. the stages of praying with fervent devotion in order to access the blessings (of the Gurus).

7. Ritual Service of the Mantra Recitation

With respect to the first practice, in the sky in front of oneself there is seated one's Root Guru in the guise of Kunzang Shanlha, surrounded by the external and the internal Yidams, the Buddhas of the ten directions, the Vidyadharas, the Bodhisattvas, and the Gurus of the Lineages of Transmission, together with the Dakinis and the Protectors of the Precepts. One clearly visualizes them as filling all the atmosphere, whereupon one invokes (the Jnansattvas or Wisdom Beings) from out of the dimension of space and they are absorbed (into the visualizations of the Samayasattvas or Symbolic Beings).

Then, one repeatedly sounds the long HUM, and from these figures emanate countless rays of light that come to pervade the full extent of the sky. Because of that, the physical bodies of all sentient beings are transformed into rainbow lights (that is, their physical forms dissolve into pure radiant energy). Then one thinks that from everywhere in the eight cardinal and intermediate directions, as well as from above and below, these lights are swept up and absorbed into the essence of one's own consciousness. Next the entire external universe dissolves into rainbow light and similarly one thinks that everything from all ten directions is swept up and absorbed into one's own illusion body.

Then, because on utters "PHAT!", one's physical body, together with one's consciousness, becomes larger and larger, until the full extent pervaded by space is filled with one's own body. Similarly, everything is pervaded by one's own consciousness. Thereupon one's physical body becomes transformed into the realms of countless world-systems. And inside of these realms, due to the magical potency of Rigpa or intrinsic Awareness, innumerable sentient beings belonging to the three realms are produced. Thinking of the full measure of purification they experience therein due to their individual karma, one meditates on their condition with fervent longing and compassion.

Then, from the hearts of the Sugatas in the atmosphere (who are situated in the visualized Tree of the Assembly), there emanate countless masses of the flames of wisdom, sounding like thunder and appearing like lightening flashes. Thus, instantly, all of the karmic traces and obscurations of these sentient beings are suddenly burnt up and consumed by these fires. Again, the winds of wisdom, making a roaring sound and appearing like shooting stars, emanate along all the pathways (coming from the hearts of the Sugatas), whereupon all of the karmic traces and obscurations of all sentient beings swirl upward and are blown away as purple vapors. Again, the waters of wisdom, make a rushing sound and appear like shooting arrows (coming from the hearts of the Sugatas), whereupon all the karmic traces and obscurations of all sentient beings are purified and washed away as black gritty fluids.

Then, once more, from their hearts emanate an infinite series of A syllables, both subtle and gross in aspect, and they come to fill the entire atmosphere. Since these syllables are absorbed into the crowns of the heads of each individual sentient being, all sentient beings are transformed into the nature of Kuntu Zangpo. Lights emanate from the Sugatas and all realms are transformed thereby into great celestial palaces of the gods. Moreover, one should think that all of these sentient beings, in their activities and in their conduct, have divine bodies wherein they practice the Mahamudra, their minds have come under the influence of the Primordial State (of contemplation) that is profound and free of all conceptual elaborations, and their speech and voices resound with the murmuring of the inherent sounds of TRI SHU!

Thinking thus, and cutting off ordinary speech and talking, one performs the ritual service of reciting the mantra some one hundred or one thousand or ten thousand or one hundred thousand times, as the case may be. Afterwards, one affixes the seal with non-conceptuality (that is, enters into the state of even contemplation, free of all discursive thoughts) and dedicates the merit to the enlightenment of all sentient beings.

Because of this practice, it is not possible for one's karma and obscurations from former lifetimes to remain behind; they pass away like the chaff dispersed by the wind or the frost struck by the morning sun. Therefore, one should always exert oneself in the practice.

This concludes the explanation concerned with the recitation of mantra and scripture that purifies the obscurations. U-YA SMAR-RO!

8. The Practice of Chod: the Offering of one's own Body

With respect to the second practice, in the sky in front of oneself, one generates by means of visualization the Gurus, the hosts of Meditation Deities, the Jinaputras and Bodhisattvas, the Dakinis and the Protectors of Bon, together with the Palgon, or the glorious Protectors, the eight classes of spirits, and all the beings belonging to the six realms of rebirth, all of whom fill the atmosphere in numbers inconceivable to the mind.

Then adventitiously, when a great cavity of wisdom suddenly bursts open directly in one's own breast, wherein one's own consciousness becomes visible as a tiny sphere of light, this consciousness is expelled and comes out like sparks scattered from the heart of the fire. By means of its dissolving into light, it becomes transformed into a Jnana Krodha, or wrathful deity of gnosis, light blue in color, having a single face and two hands. In his right hand he holds a sword and with this sword he cuts off the four limbs of one's corpse and erects them as a make-shift hearth. Cutting off the top of the skull, he places it directly on them (the four posts that are one's limbs, so that everything here) becomes vast and extensive. Inside of that (skull cauldron), having cut them into little pieces, he puts all the flesh, bones, fat, connective tissue, intestines, skin, and all the internal organs and guts. These immediately increase in extent to being an immeasurable multitude.

Thereupon that Krodha or wrathful deity becomes transformed into innumerable beautiful young goddesses who present the puja offerings (which they extract from the cauldron). And they offer clouds of pure puja offerings to the Wisdom Deities. Because the fluids of the body become transformed into an ocean of amrita nectar, this propitiates the pure races of the Palgon or glorious Protectors. Because the thick sediments that remain become transformed into various kinds of delightful sensual qualities, the eight classes and all the beings belonging to the six realms become satisfied. Thereby the Victorious Ones are delighted and the Oath-bound Ones are propitiated. Moreover, even the malicious minds of the gods and demons are pacified and the desires of all beings belonging to the six destines of rebirth are satisfied. Thinking that one's illusory body has literally become these masses of gifts and offerings, one makes the offerings by reciting the words as indicated.

By way of this practice, one repays in one's own condition the karmic debts (that are owed to others) with the offering to them of one's own physical body and mind. This represents the instruction for receiving all attainments simultaneously, such as the purifying of all obscurations and the uniting of the two accumulations, and so on.

This concludes the explanation regarding the accumulating of a collection of merit by means of the giving away of offerings. U-YA SMAR-RO!

9. Praying to receive the Guru's Blessings

With respect to the third (practice among the nine preliminaries), one clearly visualizes one's Root Guru in the Sambhogakaya form on a seat that is a sun, a moon, and a lotus blossom, located above the crown of one's head. Then above him, extending upward, the Lineage Gurus are seated in a vertical array. Beyond him, in rows, there are visualized the external and the internal hosts of Deities, the Buddhas of the ten directions, the Vidyadharas, the Bodhisattvas, together with the Dakinis, both mothers and daughters. Feeling great devotion towards all of them, a devotion that is sincere, intense, and one-pointed, and without being irregular or defective in the practice, one holds fast to the essential points of the practice from the depths of one's heart.

And because of that, the Buddhas and the rest emanate from their own heart centers the lights of primordial awareness. Because these lights become transformed into streams of pure lustral waters that are absorbed into the crowns of the heads of all sentient beings such as oneself, they cleanse and wash away in actuality the karmic traces and obscurations accumulated from lifetimes without beginning until the present. Thereupon, rays of light in the colors of white, red, and blue (are emitted from their three places of Body, Speech, and Mind) and because they are absorbed into one's own three places (of body, speech, and mind) respectively, one comes to obtain all the siddhis of the Body, Speech, and Mind of the Gurus. Because of receiving the blessings of these three empowerments, one thinks that one comes to obtain whatever virtuous qualities are associated with the Gurus, such as knowledge, activity, conduct, experience, view, and realization. Producing an intensity of intrinsic Awareness, one prays to the Gurus with longing and with fervent devotion.

Since one practices diligently with regard to that, the blessings of the Gurus come to enter into oneself and all one's hindrance and obstacles are removed. One obtains all virtuous qualities and quickly realizes all siddhis that represent psychic and spiritual attainments. Experiences and understanding increase and the Gurus will apprehend one with their compassion.

This concludes the explanation regarding the practice of praying with fervent devotion to the Gurus. U-YA SMAR-RO!

II. The Ordinary Practices in General

Second, on the occasions of practicing in general the ordinary preliminaries contained in "The Nine Stages of the Practice of Bon," on each day while in retreat, beginning at daybreak and continuing throughout the early morning, one arranges oneself well in the essential points of the body (that is to say, one assumes the five point position) and meditates with a fierce intensity for a time on impermanence again and again. Then, either three times or five times, one performs (in sequence) the confessing of sins, the producing of the Bodhichitta, the going to Refuge, the offering of the Mandala, the reciting of the mantras, the transforming of the aggregates (of body and mind into offerings), and the engaging in prayer (which represents the Guru Yoga). Thereafter, when one is finished, one dedicates all of the merit accumulated from these preliminary practices to the attaining of enlightenment for the sake of benefiting all living beings. Furthermore, one should practice everything in the proper sequence without making any mistakes or mixing anything up.

Then, at the time of midday, one may practice any other suitable activities of whatever kind, such as prostrations and circumambulations, and so on.

At the time of performing all of these practices, one's body remains inside the confines of the retreat, one's speech does not mix with ordinary worldly talk, and one's mind is not separated from samadhi (mindful awareness and concentration on the practice). Again, one should not create shame for oneself by spinning one's head around in circles (of distraction and self-deception). [14]

Rather, as it says in the Sutra, "The Precepts of the Teacher (the Buddha) should be adhered to with out distractions and these true words should be retained without ever forgetting them." [15] Or as it is explained from the conventional meaning, "The deceiving of oneself by oneself, and then feeling heartfelt satisfaction in this, is a sin against oneself." [16]

III. The Signs of Heat

Third, with respect to the signs of "heat", at the time when one practices these branches of the preliminaries in that way, one focuses the three gates (of the body, speech, and mind) one pointedly, without being irregular or defective in practice or merely saying that one has done them. One takes the body and the mind in the grip of the carpenter's vice. And because one practices regularly, there will arise the signs of realization, either actually or in terms of experiences, visions, or dreams, [17] such as the rising sun, bathing, flying, climbing upwards, coming into a valley full of flowers, washing, sounds being made, seeing the faces of the Meditation Deities, eating foods of delicious taste, washing off blood and insects, prophecies being revealed, one's body and mind becoming pure, and so on. There exist signs for superior, intermediate, and inferior capacities in this regard, and one should hold fast to the essential points of the practice until a fervent belief and confidence is produced.

Conclusion

Similarly, this most quintessential Upadesha represents the very nectar of the Primordial State of Dzogchen. [18] The merit accrued from diligently practicing this manual for the preliminaries of the path, where one enters into the instructions of the profoundly condensed meaning of the Oral Transmission, I dedicate to the attaining of the Indestructible State for the sake of benefiting all other living beings.

May those individuals who are suitable vessels (for receiving the Dzogchen teachings) attain experience, understanding, and liberation. [19]

The stages of the preliminaries that serve to bring about the cleansing and purifying of the mind-stream by way of the Oral Transmission of Dzogchen is hereby completed. [20]

Commentary to the Translation of the Ngondro Text

Title

The instruction manual for the Zhang-zhung Nyan-gyud cycle is known as the *sNyan-rgyud rgyal-ba phyag-khrid*, where *phyag-khrid* means an explanation regarding practice and *rgyal-ba* refers to the name of the author of the text, the illustrious Bonpo master belonging to the Dru clan, Druchen Gyalwa Yungdrung (Bru-chen rGyal-ba g.yung-drung, 1242-1290) of Yeru Wensakha (g.Yas ru dben-sa-kha) monastery. *sNyan-rgyud* refers to the oral transmission from Zhang-zhung.

The first text found in the xylograph reprint of the *sNyang-rgyud rgyal-ba'i phyag-khrid* collection is "The Nine Stages of the Practice of Bon," according to "The Oral Transmission from Zhang-zhung for the Great Perfection" (rDzogs-pa chen-po zhang-zhung snyan-rgyud las bon spyod dgu rim bzhugs, ff. 591-607). In the manuscript version, this first chapter is entitled "The Stages of the Preliminaries," (sngon-'gro rim-pa rnams, ff.1-22), and here it is immediately followed by an invocation to Tapihritsa (sngon-'gro gsol-'debs, ff.23-28). [1]

Homage

Following the title (mtshan) comes the homage (phyag-'tshal-ba) addressed to the Primordial Buddha who is identical with the Nature of one's own Mind: "Homage to Kuntu Zangpo, the all-pervading and all-encompassing guide of living beings, who becomes manifest as Self-Awareness!" (Kun tu bzang-po khyab bdal 'gro-ba'i 'dren/ rang-rig mngon du gyur la phyag 'tshal-lo). Self-Awareness (rang-rig) is the characteristic capacity of the Nature of Mind (sems-nyid). The Primordial Buddha Kuntu Zangpo, who becomes manifest as Self-Awareness (rig-pa mngon du gyur) resides in the heart of every single sentient being. And thereby He is the all-pervading and all-encompassing (khyab bdal) as the spiritual guide for the spiritual evolution of each living being ('gro-ba'i 'dren). As the spiritual principle or enlightened Buddha-nature inherent within sentient life, He has been present from the very beginning. The purpose of the spiritual path is to bring the practitioner to the realization of this, thereby attaining enlightenment and liberation from the delusions of Samsara. Hence the invocation of Buddhahood at the outset of the path that is at the same time, the goal of the path. [2]

Preface
This homage is followed by the promise (dam-bca') of the author to his readers. The author prays to the Vidyadharas or knowledge-holders (rig-'dzin), the masters (dpon-gsas), the Dakinis (mkha'-'gro), and the hosts of Protectors of the Precepts (bka'-skyong) who are the custodians of these teachings, the precepts of Dzogchen. He asks that the light of their compassion for the suffering of sentient beings in Samsara may release the seals of secrecy placed upon these precepts (bka'), so that he may now elucidate the essential points (gnad) of the practice of the profound path (zab lam) of Dzogchen. Previously, there had existed no system in writing regarding the actual scheme of practice for this special Upadesha of the Experiential Mind Transmission [3] that descended from the Primordial Buddha. But now the author will set down in a clear and systematic fashion these practices in the proper order and begs the permission and the indulgence for this from the hosts of Dakinis and Guardians.

According to Lopon Tenzin Namdak, a master must first ask the permission of the hosts of Dakinis and Guardians of the Precepts regarding the question of whether or not a particular disciple is a suitable vessel to receive the Dzogchen teachings. The permission of the Guardians is always required in these matters. For this reason, both the master and the disciple must observe and check their dreams very carefully. If the indications in dreams are inauspicious, more purification practices must be performed and the signs examined once more. The master observes and checks the conduct and manner of the disciple externally and makes inqueries regarding his internal realization and understanding. A master must keep close watch over and check the spiritual progress of the disciple in terms of signs outer, inner, and secret. Traditionally, this process of examination takes three years in order to determine whether or not the candidate is now a suitable vessel for the full transmission of the precepts. Initially, the Bodhichitta and some portions of the outer, inner, and secret sections of the teachings are revealed to the student, but other sections are taught to him only after the signs of realization appear in response to the requisite practices. [4]

The author then proceeds to characterize the exalted nature of these Dzogchen teachings that represent the ultimate spiritual attainment (dngos-grub) of Gyerpung Nangzher Lodpo. What is revealed here by way of a direct introduction (ngo-sprod) is the intrinsic Awareness (rig-pa) of the individual in its nakedness (gcer-bu), an awareness that is denuded of all activities of the mind and the thought process. Thereupon the walls are dissolved. The internal awareness and the external appearances or visions, which are actually manifestations of mind (sems kyi snang-ba), come to meet together as Mother and Son. [5] The Mother is the Natural State and she gives rise to all appearances, whether good or bad, beautiful or ugly, all of which are her progeny. What appears in the space outside the individual is actually a manifestation or projection of what is inside that individual. Dzogchen employs certain very powerful methods (btsan thabs), such as the practice of vision (thod-rgal), also known as the Clear Light ('od-gsal), and thereby Dzogchen becomes the short path (nye-lam) to the realization of Buddhahood.

Contents of the Text
The various instructions (gdams-pa) from the Zhang-zhung Nyan-gyud are arranged into these four sections cited previously, namely,

1. The Outer Aspect which is the General View (phyi lta-ba spyi-gcod),
2. The Inner Aspect that is the intensely clear Explanation in terms of the Upadeshas (nang man-ngag dmar khrid),
3. the Secret Aspect which is intrinsic Awareness seeing nakedly (gsang-ba rig-pa gcer mthong), and
4. the Exceedingly Secret Aspect which is the Explanation concerning the Definitive Realization of the Natural State (yang gsang gnas-lugs phugs chod du bshad-pa). [6]

In terms of the practice, there are three phases, each with its own purpose and function:

1. At the beginning there is the performing of the Preliminary Practices that bring about a cleansing and complete purification of one's own mind-stream (dang-po rgyud yangs su dag cing sbyong-bar byed-pa sngon-'gro'i bya-ba). These preliminary practices (sngon-'gro), nine in number, purify the mind-stream (rgyud sbyong) of the practitioner. The preliminaries are dealt with in the present text and prepare the individual for the receiving of the Dzogchen teachings in terms of view and practice in their entirety.

2. In the middle there are the stages of the Principal Practices that ripen the mind-stream and brings about liberation (bar du rgyud smin cing grol-bar byed-pa dngos-gzhi'i rim-pa). The principal practices (dngos-gzhi), consist of contemplation (khregs-chod) and vision practice (thod-rgal), the latter in terms of total darkness, empty space, or sunlight, where these three serve as supports for the manifestation of the visions. These practices function to ripen and mature the mind-stream (rgyud smin) of the individual in order to bring about its liberation (grol byed).

3. And finally there are the auxiliary practices of the Conclusion that cause understanding to become manifest in the mind-stream (tha-ma rgyud rtogs shing mngon du gyur-par byed-pa rjes mjug gi yan-lag). The four auxiliary sections that represent the conclusion (rjes mjug), and which develop the view, the meditation, the conduct, and the fruit, serve to make understanding become manifest with the mind-stream (rgyud rtogs mngon du gyur) of the individual. These represent the three major divisions of the practice of Dzogchen.

The Preliminary Practices

Then, within the first part concerning the practice of the preliminaries, there exist three sections in the text to be considered in turn, namely,

I. the individual practices in detail (bye-brag so-so ru nyams su len-pa),
II. the ordinary practices in general (thun-mong spyi dril tu nyams su len-pa), and
III. the signs of "heat" resulting from having practiced them (nyams su blangs-pa'i drod rtags). These are more commonly known as the signs of success (grub rtags).

I. The Individual Preliminary Practices in Detail

The author has divided the preliminary practices that prepare the practitioner for the principal practices of Dzogchen into three main sections or methodologies that are designated

1. discipling the mind-stream (rgyud 'dul-ba),
2. cleansing the mind-stream (rgyud sbyong-ba), and
3. purifying the mind-stream (rgyud dag-par bya-ba).

Thus, within the first section of the text, in terms of the individual practices in detail, these three subsections are described as follows:

A. Disciplining one's mind-stream by means of the three preliminary practices that are valuable in general (spyir gces-pa'i sngon-'gro gsum gyis rgyud 'dul-ba). "In general" means these methods are exoteric in nature and belong properly to the the Sutra system.

B. Cleansing one's mind-stream by means of the three preliminary practices that are in agreement with everything else (kun dang mthun-pa'i sngon-'gro gsum gyis rgyud sbyong-ba). "In agreement with everything else" means in harmony with the general system of the Sutras and the Tantras. These methods are, therefore, only partly esoteric in nature.

C. Purifying one's mind-stream by means of the three preliminary practices that are especially exalted (khyad-par 'phags-pa'i sngon-'gro gsum gyis rgyud dag-par bya-ba). Here the emphasis is on the fully esoteric methods of the Higher Tantras.

Each of these groups in turn are divided into three sections, making a total of nine preliminary practices in all. And each of these nine successive practices (dgu rim) is traditionally performed one hundred-thousand times in retreat, for which reason they are known as the *sngon-'gro 'bum dgu,* "the nine preliminary practices that are done a hundred-thousand times each." These nine preliminaries may be listed as follows:

A. The first group consists of the Practices that are Valuable in General. One disciplines one's mind-stream by means of the three preliminary practices that are valuable in general (spyir gces-pa'i sngon-'gro gsum gyis rgyud 'dul-ba):

1. The Receiving of Empowerments and Blessings (dbang-bskur byin-rlabs):
This represents the explanation regarding the blessings received from the conferring of the empowerments (dbang bskur byin rlabs kyi khrid); also known as the explanation of the conferring of the empowerments that bless the mind-stream of the individual receiving it (rgyud byin gyis rlob-pa dbang bskur gyi khrid)

2. The Meditation on Impermanence (tshe mi rtag-pa):
This represents the explanation that motivates one by way of entreaties according to the conventional meaning (drang don bskul 'debs kyi khrid); also known as the explanation of the meditation on impermanence that completely

disciplines the mind-stream of the individual (rgyud yongs su 'dul-ba mi rtag-pa'i khrid)

3. The Confession of Sins (sdig-pa bshags-pa):
This represents the explanation concerning the practice of confession that cleanses and purifies all sins and obscurations (dag tshangs bshags-pa'i khrid); also known as the explanation of the confessing of sins that brings about a purifying of the mind-stream (rgyud tshangs-par byed-pa sdig bshags kyi khrid)

B. The second group consists of the Practices that are in Agreement with Everything. One cleanses one's mind-stream by means of the three preliminary practices that are in agreement with everything (in terms of the general Sutra and Tantra systems) (kun dang mthun-pa'i sngon-'gro gsum gyis rgyud sbyong-ba):

4. The Producing of the Bodhichitta (sems-bskyed):
This represents the explanation for the producing of the thought to benefit others (gzhan don sems bskyed kyi khrid); that is, grasping the base with compassion and the four unlimited states, one produces the Bodhichitta or thought of enlightenment (snying-rje tshad-med kyi gzhi bzung ste sems bskyed-pa)

5. The Going to Refuge (skyabs su 'gro-ba):
This represents the explanation of the going to Refuge with faith and longing (dad 'dun skyabs 'gro'i khrid); that is, grasping the base with faith and devotion, one goes to refuge (dad mos gus-pas gzhi bzung ste skyabs su 'gro-ba)

6. The Offering of the Mandala (man-dal 'bul-ba):
This represents the explanation concerning the Mandala that signifies the clouds of offerings (mchod sprin man-tal gyi khrid); that is, grasping the base as a purified self-manifestation, one offers the Mandala (rang snang dag-pas gzhi bzung ste man-dal 'bul-ba)

C. The third group consists of the Especially Exalted Practices. One purifies one's mind-stream by means of the three preliminary practices that are especially exalted (khyad-par 'phags-pa'i sngon-'gro gsum gyis rgyud dag-par bya-ba):

7. The Ritual Service of the Mantra Recitation (bzlas lung bsnyen-pa):
This represents the explanation for the recitation of the mantra and the text that purifies the obscurations (sgrib

sbyang bzlas lung gi khrid); that is, the stages of the Seva or ritual practice of text recitation and mantra recitation that purifies the karmic traces and the obscurations (bag sgrib sbyong-ba bzlas lung bsnyen-pa'i rim-pa)

8. The Offering of one's own Body (gcod)
   This represents the explanation for the accumulating of the collection of merit by the giving of offerings (tshogs sogs mchod sbyin gyi khrid); that is, the stages of transforming the aggregates of the body and mind in order to accumulate merit (bsod-nams bsags-pa lus sems tshogs bsgyur gyi rim-pa)

9. The Praying to Receive the Blessings (mos-gus gsol-'debs):
   This represents the explanation regarding the practice of praying with fervent devotion (to the Gurus) (mos-gus gsol-'debs kyi khrid); that is, the stages of praying with devotion in order to access the blessings (of the Gurus) (byin rlabs 'jag-pa mos-gus gsol-'debs kyi rim-pa).

II. The Ordinary Practices in General
The common ordinary practices in general for the stages of the nine (preliminary) practices of Bon (bon spyod dgu rim thun-mong spyi dril tu nyams su len-pa)

III. The Signs of Heat
The signs of "heat" resulting from having practiced them (nyams su blangs-pa'i drod rtags), that is, the signs of success or realization (grub rtags) from doing the practices.

The Principal Practices (dngos-gzhi)
In the middle there are the successive stages of the Principal Practices that ripen the mind-stream and brings about liberation (bar du rgyud smin cing grol-bar byed-pa dngos-gzhi'i rim-pa).

The Conclusion (rjes mjug)
Finally there are the auxiliary practices of the Conclusion that cause understanding to become manifest in the mind-stream (tha-ma rgyud rtogs shing mngon du gyur-par byed-pa rjes mjug gi yan-lag).

These represent the three major divisions of the practice of Dzogchen according to the tradition of the Zhang-zhung Nyan-gyud. The Principal Practices and the Four Auxiliary Texts of the Concluding Section are found as separate texts in the *Phyag-khrid* collection. [7] These nine preliminaries may be elucidated as follows:

1. The Practice of Receiving Empowerments and Blessings (Guru Yoga, first version)

Properly speaking, in order to practice the preliminaries, one makes a retreat for a period of time in an isolated place free of distractions and worldly entertainments. One makes such a retreat (mtshams) after having come into contact with a Lama or master possessing all the requisite marks of a spiritual teacher; he is one who possesses the view and understanding of Dzogchen. [8] Entering into a retreat situation, or at least a session of meditation practice, one makes offerings, such as a Ganachakra Puja or Tantric feast, and requests from the master the empowerments (dbang), the scriptual authorizations (lung), and the explanations of the teachings (khrid). One also performs other extensive religious rites for the amassing of the two accumulations of merit and wisdom. [9] The ritual actions performed in order to accumulate merit include presenting puja offerings, making prostrations, reciting religious texts, and so on, whereas the activities performed to accumulate wisdom include the meditation practices of shamatha and vipashyana. Through these latter one comes to an understanding of emptiness and the absence of any inherent existence in phenomena. Then the benefits (phan-yon) of doing this are decribed in the text. [10]

The first of these nine preliminaries is also known as "the explanation regarding the blessings received from the conferring of the empowerments" (dbang-bskur byin-rlabs kyi khrid). In the Zhang-zhung language, U-YA SMAR-RO means "May everything be auspicious!"

According to Lopon Tenzin Namdak, this first section among the nine preliminaries represents a kind of Guru Yoga or unification with the master. It is called "the conferring of empowerments which bestows blessings upon the mind-stream of the practitioner" (rgyud byin gyis rlob-pa dbang-bskur). These empowerments are for the Body, Speech, and Mind of the Guru (sku gsung thugs), which become integrated with one's own body, speech, and mind (lus ngag yid). The moment of this unification at the conclusion of the practice session represents the actual Guru Yoga. In most ways the practice here is quite similar to the ninth and final section called "praying with fervent devotion to access the blessings of the masters (byin-rlabs 'jag-pa mos-gus gsol-'debs). This last practice also represents a kind of Guru Yoga. However, the first practice emphasizes the requesting and receiving from the master the transmission by way of the conferring of empowerments (dbang-bskur). In this way the blessings of spiritual energies of inspiration of the Body, Speech, and Mind of the Guru becomes merged and integrated into one's own ordinary and profane body, speech, and mind while sitting in the presence of the master. The final practice emphasizes praying to the Guru with faith and fervent devotion (dad-pa dang mos-gus) for the continuing bestowal of his blessings upon the practitioner. Here one also concludes the practice session by integrating with and unifying with the master, which is the Guru Yoga proper.

In this way, through these repeated meditations, one maintains the links and the spiritual connections, not only with one's personal Guru in this present life, but with all of the other enlightened masters of the past belonging to the different lineages of transmission for Dzogchen. The repeated meditative process of this unification brings about the integration within one's individual mind-stream with the higher principle of enlightenment at the core of one's being. In the context of one's meditation practice, by repeating the Guru Yoga at the beginning of each session, the practitioner enters into the sacred time and the sacred space where the Dzogchen precepts were first revealed within human history. One repeats the archetypal actions of Gyerpungpa requesting the teachings and taking initiation, thereby receiving the blessings and the transmission from his own master. One should think when practicing that Guru Tapihritsa is actually present in front of oneself in the sky and that one actually receives the blessings of wisdom and inspiration from him.

How one actually performs the Guru Yoga practice, in terms of the invocation, visualization, and making the request, receiving purification of one's negativities by way of the elixirs of wisdom, and the receiving of the empowerments of the Body, Speech, and Mind of the Guru, have been described previously. [11] During a single session of meditation practice (thun), one may focus on just a single practice or run through each of the nine preliminaries in sequence, beginning with the Guru Yoga and concluding with the Guru Yoga. Thereby one unifies one's own state with that of the master Tapihritsa and with the other masters of the Lineage.

When entering into a retreat or even into just a session of meditation practice, one should think that one has prepared a sumptuous Tantric feast or Ganachakra Puja (tshogs 'khor) and while offering this to the Guru, one should pray to him, making requests for the empowerments (dbang), the scriptural authorizations (lung), and the explanations (khrid) of the teachings and the practices. For a transmission to be complete, all three of these should be present, otherwise one is only receiving the blessings (byin-rlabs). Although this request and the receiving of empowerments was done in actuality at the commencement of the retreat, the process is repeatedly performed in one's meditation practice, so that the initial opening of one's mind-stream to spiritual progress and evolution is maintained. It is suggested by the Lopon that at the beginning the novice should perform the Guru Yoga for four sessions (thun bzhi) each day whenever that is possible. Even relatively short sessions of practice are feasible for this, such as five or ten minutes.

In the text, it is suggested that one practice the Guru Yoga while visualizing the Sambhogakaya Buddha Shenlha Odkar (gShen-lha 'od-dkar), together with the entire Tree of the Assembly (tshogs shing), which include the Three Jewels and the Three Roots, as well as all the Gurus of the lineages. This visualization is described a bit more in detail below in the Bodhichitta section. But such elaborate visualizations may be difficult for non-Tibetans. Therefore, the Lopon maintains that is sufficient for the practitioner just to visualize Guru Tapihritsa sitting in the center of a sphere of rainbow light in the sky above and in front of oneself. However, this visualization is not merely a flat two-dimensional picture, but should be seen as three-dimensional, translucent, and alive. The invocation should be repeated many times, or at least three times, and the visualization should be held clearly in mind with the eyes open or closed.

The invocation or verse of supplication suggested by the Lopon is as follows:

"In the palace of great bliss on the crown of my head,
Is my benevolent Root Guru to whom I pray;
The Buddha is (my own) Mind: O precious Teacher,
Please grant the blessing that I may recognize my own nature!"
[12]

Moreover there are additional prayers of invocation that may be used for this purpose. [13]

2. The Practice of Meditation on Impermanence

Second, there is the meditation on the impermanence of life (tshe mi rtag-pa). This section is also called the explanation that motivates the practitioner by way of exhortations according to the conventional meaning (drang-don bskul debs kyi khrid). The conventional meaning (drang don) accepts phenomena as they appear in conventional reality, as apparently real and abiding entities. This is in contrast to the certain meaning (nges don) where phenomena are understood as being empty, lacking any inherent existence, and without actual origination. The purpose here is not to bring on a feeling of deep depression and hopelessness with regard to one's life, but to make one keenly aware of the fact of the impermanence of all things, including one's own physical body. And if the human body is impermanent, how much more so is the mind or thought process that is changing from moment to moment. Becoming aware of and meditating upon the impermanence of all things and the inevitability of one's own death serves to produce in the practitioner an intense feeling of disillusionment and disgust (nges 'byung) with pursuing the worldly life with its inevitable frustrations, disappointments, and fleeting goals that pass through one's fingers like sand. Because of this disgust, one develops and cultivates an intrense motivation to practice the Dzogchen teachings in order to obtain liberation from the frustrations and suffering attending cyclical existence, where one is under the sway of time, change, and inevitable decay.

Again one adopts the fivefold meditation position of the body. Then, according to Lopon Tenzin Namdak, one should reflect upon one's existential situation of being in the world. One should reflect upon the fact that all conditioned things are impermanent. Whatever one makes or creates will eventually disintegrate. Whatever one saves, one will eventually loose. Nothing is eternal because all things are conditioned by causes. Making an examination of everything, one will discover that all things are impermanent, including one's own physical body. It is a delusion to think that one can live on and on without dying. Although one does not know the hour of one's death, it is certain that one will eventually die. Therefore, one should not put off practice until tomorrow because the Lord of Death may intervene at any time. One must decide right now what is truly important and useful and what is merely distracting and wasteful. One will not be able to take one's possessions with one into the Bardo when one dies. Before this present life, one has wandered without purpose in Samsara over the course of countless deaths and rebirths. But one has found neither happiness nor satisfaction. Sickness, suffering, frustration, and anxiety have been experienced throughout all of these previous lifetimes. In each of them one has been born, grown old, sickened, and died. What then? One will only be reborn in order to die once more. So how can one think that this present life will last forever?

One should consider how many others have died before one's own time and are no longer visible. They were once just like one is now, vibrant and full of life, yet now they are gone. One should reflect upon this fact very carefully. One has become attracted to the worldly life as if it were something permanent. Moreover, one should consider all those others who have fallen into poverty and destitution, after once having enjoyed great wealth and power. One should look at how friends have become enemies and how enemies have become friends. Everything changes from moment to moment; nothing remains the same. Therefore, there is nothing in this world that can be wholly trusted and relied upon for refuge. Therefore, one should not be attached to and rely upon the things of the worldly life. Only consider how the seasons are constantly changing. Even one's own life has changed from infancy to childhood to adolescence and now to adulthood. This will soon be followed by middle age, old age, sickness, and eventually death. Although one does not know how or when one will die, one's death is certain. One can use medicines and hospital technologies to postpone death, but there is no escaping from it. All the living beings that have been born in the past have eventually died. From the very beginning until now there has existed no living being who has not died. Even the Buddhas and the great saints have passed away. One should think well upon this. And next time it is not even certain that one will be reborn as a human being, for one might be reborn as an animal or as a restless spirit. But a human existence is much better than the other possibilities of rebirth because it provides the maximum opportunity for the practice of the spiritual teachings. Therefore, one should not waste this unique opportunity, putting off practice until tomorrow or until one's next life.

This precious human body or human existence (mi lus rin-po-che) represents a unique opportunity (dal-'byor) for entering on to the spiritual path in order to ultimately attain liberation and enlightenment. Possessing certain unique qualities, a human existence is, therefore, more advantageous and conducive to this process of enlightenment than other types of existence, even among the Devas and the Asuras. This attitude is clearly reflected in a verse cited by the Lopon known as "the teaching on the unique opportunity provided by a human existence that serves as the support for virtuous conduct" (dge-sbyor gyi rten dal-'byor bstan-pa). This is as follows:

"The eight opportunities and the ten assets possess eighteen virtuous qualities;

By way of numerous examples, one should examine intensely the difficulties of obtaining this ;

Now, in terms of the usefulness of this precious support which is the human body,

One should produce diligence with regard to deeds of perfect virtue!" [14]

In the practice manual, three phases are indicated in general for the meditations on the impermanence of life:

I.   The exercises where one visualizes one's environment in the process of decaying. Thus, one reflects upon the impermanence of all conditioned things.

II. The exercises where one visualizes oneself at first attaining all manner of wealth and worldly success, and then loosing it all when one is informed that one is about to die, and so on. Thus, one reflects on the futility of all worldly status and success.

III. The exercises where one visualizes one's own death and the decay of the elements of one's body. Thus, one reflects upon one's own physical mortality.

Specifically, there are nine exercises where one visualizes and reflects upon the meaning of impermanence in concrete experiential terms:

1. meditation on the inevitable loss of wealth, power, and success;
2. meditation on illness and the inevitable decay of the human body;
3. meditation on the occasion of one's death;
4. meditation on the process of dying and entering into the Bardo;
5. meditation on wandering lost in a desolate land;
6. meditation on the deaths of others in the past;
7. meditation on how conditions inevitably change with time;
8. meditation on the ceaseless flow of time; and
9. meditation on the inevitability of one's death.

In terms of the after-death experience, the visions that arise in the Bardo are similar to the visions experienced every night in the dream state, as well as to the profane hallucinations that appear in the sensory deprivation experience of the dark retreat. [14] These visions are impure, that is to say, they are conditioned by one's karma from the past, as well as by recent circumstances. Both dream practice and the dark retreat serve as preparations for the after-death experiences of the Bardo.

In terms of meditating on wandering in a barren desolate land, even though memories persist everywhere in the mind (yid la ci yang dran) of one's past life, yet one does not find any reason for doing anything. This is a visionary description of a state of deep depression and total destitution, where one wanders aimlessly without meaning or purpose through a barren and unknown land, naked and without companions. For some individuals, this may come to be experienced in the Bardo. But it also resembles the condition of the landscapes found in the Pretaloka, the dimension of existence of the hungry ghosts. In any case, all external appearances arise to oneself as illusions and so one must cut off all entanglements with attachments to them as being real. [16] These worldly appearances will arise to one's consciousness in the Bardo according to whatever was familiar and habitual to oneself in one's previous life, just as dreams at night often reflect the experiences of the previous day.

The author quotes in support of his argument another text, the *Lung drug*, "However, one attaches names to them and they will appear like that." "Since one produces in the mind-stream (a strong awareness of) the impermanence (of everything), when one becomes mindful of death, all such practitioners belonging to future generations will take the opportunity (presented at present) for entering into the practice." [17] Thus it was expounded by the Great Guru. [18] This is a reference to Dranpa Namkha, the Mahasiddha and the prince of Zhang-zhung who was a famous practitioner of Dzogchen.

3. The Practice of Confession

After developing a disillusionment and disgust with the world and the worldly life with all its vain pursuits, one comes to the practice of making confession for one's sins (sdig-pa bshag-pa). In the broader sense, this practice represnts a powerful and effective means to purify both one's sins and one's obscurations (sdig sgrib sbyong-ba). In the context of Dharma, whether Buddhist or Bon, the term we translate as "sin" (sdig-pa, Skt. papa) has no connotation of rebellion against the will of the Creator God or some divine parent figure. Rather, the term refers to all those negative actions of body, speech, and mind that one may commit that cause pain, injury, and suffering to other living beings. Obscurations (sgrib-pa) cloud one's vision and darken one's mind-stream, distorting how one perceives the world. There are principally of two types of obscurations (sgrib-pa gnyis): emotional obscurations consisting of all one's negative emotions or defilements (kleshas) and intellectual obscurations consisting the wrong views and distorted ideas that pervert one's clear view of reality. Just as the oil that has seeped into a sheet of paper prevents anything from being written upon it, so one's negative karma, in terms of these sins and obscurations, prevents one from developing spiritually and coming to realize the fruits of one's practice. As a practitioner, one should conscientiously endeavor not to become like the pot exhibiting any of the three defects (skyon gsum). A pot that is turned upside down cannot hold or receive anything. This is like the individual who turns away and does not listen when the Dharma is being taught. A pot that has a hole in its bottom cannot hold anything. This is like the individual who hears the teachings, but soon loses and forgets them. A pot that has become contaminated by poison will spoil whatever is pu into it. This is like the individual who, although he has heard the teachings and retains them in memory, distorts their meaning because of his negative emotions and wrong views. This will prevent him from cultivating a spiritual or Dharma-oriented life-style.

The practice invoked here is more or less identical with the meditation and mantra recitation for Vajrasattva (rDor-sems bsgom bzlas) in the Buddhist tradition, where the function is similarly the purification of obscurations (sgrib sbyong). Like Vajrasattva (rDo-rje sems-dpa'), Shenlha Odkar represents the visible manifestation of the Sambhogakaya as he appears in purified vision. In both cases, the spiritual exercise is founded on the four powers (stobs bzhi):

1. the support, which is the visualization of the Guru and the Refuge Tree, represents the need for a witness to whom one makes confession,
2. the cultivating of feelings of remorse and deep regret at one's past negative actions,
3. the promising and making the commitment not to engage in these negative actions again in the future, and
4. the recitation of the hundred syllable mantra by means of which one effects the purification.

Again one assumes the fivefold position for meditation and produces the visualization of the Refuge Tree in the sky in front of oneself. First one engages in the Generation Process (bskyed-rim) by way of visualizing the luminous forms the Gurus and the Sugatas in the atmosphere in front of oneself and then one absorbs (bstim-pa) the Wisdom Beings invoked into these visualizations that constitute the Symbolic Beings. [19] The visualized Symbolic Beings (dam-tshig-pa) are created by one's own mind and the Wisdom Beings (ye-shes-pa) represent the blessings or spiritual energies of the enlightened Buddhas that are invoked, descend, and are absorbed into these visualized forms, like pouring water into a vessel. Thus these symbolic forms become ensouled and alive. The largest figure in the center of the Tree is the Sambhogakaya Shenlha Odkar, here called Kunzang

Shenlha. He is surrounded by the Tree Jewels and the Three Roots, as well as the lineages of the Gurus, as described previously. Furthermore, he is surrounded by the vast multitude of sentient beings who have once been, in some lifetime or another, one's own mother. One considers and thinks about one's past actions with regard to them, examining how they have helped or harmed others, and one rejoices at the good actions of other beings. Having considered all of this, one makes a declaration of confession and then atones for all one's ill deeds by reciting the hundred syllable mantra (yig-brgya-pa). And again the Lopon suggests that if this visualization of the entire Tree of the Assembly (tshogs shing) is too complex and difficult to create with one's mind, one may simply visualize the Guru Tapihritsa suspended in the sky in front as described previously. But what is important here is to be consistent and do not keep changing the visualization. If the practitioner remains consistant with the visualization, it will become more and more clear.

The practice of the confessing of sins (sdig-pa bshag-pa) as described here is performed according to the teachings of the great master Dranpa Namkha of Zhang-zhung who was a famous exponent of the Dzogchen teachings. This section is also known as the explanation of the practice of confession, which cleanses and purifies all sins and obscurations (dag tshangs bshag-pa'i khrid). The quotation from Dranpa Namkha found above in the translation of the text may be meditated upon or even recited while engaging in the visualization as part of the meditation. In addition, the Lopon elaborated on this reflection as follows: Throughout our countless lifetimes in Samsara, we have accumulated a vast amount of negative karmic traces. So now, in front of our Guru Tapihritsa, the Buddha whose knowledge is pure and all-wise so that he can perceive all that we have done in the past, we feel contrite and confess our sins and obscurations. This is like coming before a wise and all-knowing judge, one whom combines mercy equally with justice. In our past lives since beginningless time, we were ignorant and did everything without knowledge or awareness. But now we regret that and promise not to behave in this ignorant and heedless fashion again. Through the practice of confession it is possible for us to purify our obscurations and our karmic traces, so that our wisdom and our awareness increases and grows stronger. Our Dzogchen view will become more and more stable. In the practice here we invoke the four powers, namely, the Guru to whom we confess, our feelings of remorse and regret over past wrong deeds, our promise and commitment not to do them again, and the reciting of the one hundred syllable mantra for purification.

We will surely be reborn in hell without any intervening experience of the Bardo for committing the five heinous crimes such as murdering our parents, killing our Root Guru, murdering innocent children, and so on. Torturing and killing human beings is the heaviest of crimes. But also such actions as harming practitioners of the Dharma, destroying temples, religious images, and holy books, as well as burning down forests, polluting lakes and rivers, and so on, are very heavy crimes. Telling lies, spreading slanders, stealing from others, and so on, are also serious. These willful actions all create negative karmic traces that will result in suffering to be experienced in future lives. It is also a bad thing if we agree with and praise the bad actions of others. We might then acquire a similar karmic trace. But if we praise the generosity and virtuous conduct of others and seek to emulate them, then we will acquire a similar merit. In the past, ignorance obscured our minds, so that we did not know the difference between virtue and wrong deeds. So now we make confession in the presence of our Guru and promise to cease henceforth from all such activities. We feel regret at these past vices and now assume responsibility for our actions. From now on we shall walk in the path of the Mahayana. This is our commitment. We promise to practice virtuous actions and to praise the meritorious deeds of others. If we do not do this, it will create an obstacle for ourselves regarding the Dzogchen teachings in our next life. It will become like trying to write on paper that was soaked in oil. But this practice of confession before the Guru is the means whereby we can purify and wash away our negative karmic traces.

One has committed sinful actions from lifetime after lifetime. Among them the most important are the five immeasurably heinous crimes, the four lesser crimes, the four heavy transgressions, the eight wrong actions, the nine deluded actions, the ten non-virtuous actions, and so on. [20] These five heinous crimes, considered the worst of all, are the killing of one's father, the killing of one's mother, the killing of a saint or holy man, causing injury to the body of a Buddha, and causing schism within the spiritual community or Sangha. These sins are said to be inexpiable and entail immediate rebirth in hell following one's death without any sojourn in the Bardo. The other crimes and sins are not identified in the text. However, the ten non-virtuous actions are well known: killing, stealing, raping, lying, slandering, harsh speech, gossiping, covetous thoughts, malicious thoughts, and wrong views. These represent the sins of the body, the speech, and the mind respectively.

All of one's sins committed previously due to ignorance and to not understand what is right and wrong are united into a single mass that are vividly present to the Minds of the Omniscient Ones, the Buddhas. Thus, one should offer confession, accompanied by remorse and regret, in the field of their vision. One's own immaculate mind becomes established as one's witness. One should cultivate the roots of virtue to the most subtle degree. [21]

Having confessed all one's past sins and obscurations of body, speech, and mind, committed over countless lifetimes due to ignorance, as well as all one's broken promises, vows, and samayas, in the presence of the Guru, one then intensely cultivates feelings of regret and remorse with regard to them and promises solemnly and sincerely to the Guru not to commit these negative actions again in the future. One should recall that one's present situation in life is the aggregate result of one's karma, the actions that one has committed in past lives and that one's future existence in this life and the next will be determined by what one does now. One's fate and future destiny depends entirely upon what one does in the present. Recalling and being mindful of all this, it is seen that this practice of confession in the presence of one's Guru is a powerful method to eliminate the secondary causes for the germination and activation of the seeds of one's past negative karma accumulated since beginningless time. Now one makes the solemn commitment to follow henceforth the path of the Mahayana in order to help alleviate the suffering of others and liberate them from the prison of Samsara.

For the purpose of confession, the Lopon suggests reciting the following verse known as 'the exposition of the words for the confession of the sins that one has accumulated" (sdig tshogs bshags-pa'i tshig-bshad):

"I and all other living sentient beings,
From our lifetimes without measure from the very beginning,
Up until now when we have obtained this present human body,
Whatever sins and non-virtuous actions we may have committed,
We confess to you, O Sugatas, without concealing anything whatsoever and we seek to atone for them;
Whatever non-virtuous action we committed were due to our obscurations;
Because of your compassion for us, please bring about the purification of all of them,

And thereafter we shall come to rejoice at all of these virtues!" [22] This purification by way of the confession is authenticated by the recitation of the one hundred syllable mantra (yig brgya-pa), which may simply be recited or sung aloud to the melody. It is as follows:

bswo dmu-ra ta han wer ni brum hrun/
mu-tre mu-tre dmu-ra mu-tre/
mu-ye mu-ye ha-ra mu-ye/
mu-spros mu-spros we-ro mu-spros/
mu ni gyer to ye khyab khar-ro/
spros bdal hri hro wer ni wer-ro/
shud la wer-ro na hu ta ka/
shud-dho shud-dho du shud-dho-ya/
sa-le sa -le tri sa-le-ya/
sang-nge sang-nge su sang-nge-ya/
dmu-ra ta han khri tse drung mu ha-ha brum brum ho-ho lam lam/
hum hum phat phat//

This mantra is largely in the language of Zhang-zhung, so its precise meaning is obscure. [23]

In addition, for the same purpose of purification, the Lopon suggests that one may recite the Great Mantra in eight syllables, namely, OM MA-TRI MU-YE SA-LE 'DU. Each syllable of this mantra corresponds to a manifestation of enlightened awareness. [24]

The ten virtuous actions (dge-ba bcu) are the opposite of the ten non-virtuous actions (mi dge-ba bcu), that is to say, not killing, not stealing, and so on. Having purified all the sins and obscurations committed previously, one will become suitable as a vessel for the Mahayana. [25] (sngar byas kyi sdig sgrib thans-cad byang nas/ theg-pa chen-po'i snod du rung-par byed).

When pursuing the preliminaries, it is important, according to the Lopon, to keep up a regular practice. For this, in the beginning, one may do the Guru Yoga, the meditation on impermanence, and the confessing of sins and obscurations, practicing them one after the other, engaging in each spiritual exercise clearly and carefully. In this way, the practitioner comes to tame the wild nature of the mind-stream (rgyud 'dul-ba), purify the mind (blo sbyong), and bring about a radical change in one's whole attitude toward life (blo ldog), orienting it toward spiritual concerns rather than worldly pursuits.

4. The Practice of Producing the Bodhichitta

Here we come to cleansing the mind-stream by means of the three preliminary practices that are in agreement with everything in the general system of the Sutras and the Tantras (kun dang mthun-pa'i sngon-'gros rgyud sbyong-ba). In terms of the first of these preliminary practices, this section is called the explanation regarding the producing the thought to benefit others (gzhan don sems bskyed kyi khrid) This resolute intention to strive ceaselessly to attain the enlightenment of a Buddha for the sake of helping to alleviate the sufferings of others and liberate them from Samsara is called the Bodhichitta (byang-chub kyi sems). It represents the very foundation of the spiritual path, the generation of compassion toward the sufferings of others. According to the Sutra system, it is the very seed out of which grows the great tree of Buddhahood.

Although most human beings naturally have feelings of compassion and empathy toward other living creatures, especially when they see others suffer, this is not always the case, even when one considers oneself to be religious and "spiritual." Therefore, it is necessary to make some effort to cultivate feelings of compassion in order to develop the intention that is called Bodhichitta or the thought of enlightenment. There are a number of stages in this process:

1. First, one should think that all sentient beings have at one time or another been one's own mother (mar shes-pa) in some lifetime,
2. And one should recall the kindness that one's mother showed (drin dran-pa) to her child at that time.
3. Therefore, one ardently desires to repay and reciprocate for these kindnesses (drin gzo-ba) that have been shown to one by others.
4. One naturally comes to generate feelings of loving kindness and friendliness (byams-pa) toward these other beings,
5. And develops empathy and compassion (snying-rje) for their sufferings experienced in this present lifetime.
6. Consequently, one thinks (lhag bsam) to liberate all these suffering beings and develops the aspiration (smon sems) to attain Buddhahood in order that one might accomplish this.
7. This aspiration develops into a concrete intention in terms of action ('jug sems) to benefit other living beings and this is known as the Bodhichitta (byang-chub sems).

Here there exist three phases in this practice of producing the Bodhichitta (sems bskyed):

1. Visualizing the Tree of the Assembly,

2. Cultivating feelings of compassion through reflecting that all sentient beings have once been one's loving parents, as well as by exchanging oneself for another, and
3. Reciting the verses for generating the Bodhichitta.

As before, one assumes the fivefold posture for meditation and performs the nine breathings for purification. Then one visualizes the Tree of the Assembly (tshogs shing) or Field for the Accumulating of Merit (tshogs zhing) in the sky in front of oneself. This visualization is also called the Sources of Refuge (skyabs gnas) and is described briefly in the text: In the field of vision of these Sources of Refuge who are generated by way of visualization in the sky in front of oneself as was done above. [26] For a further description of this visualization, see the Refuge section which follows.

Here a brief meditation is suggested in the text where one considers that all sentient beings, in some lifetime or another, were once one's own loving parents. Considering their present suffering in Samsara, one feels how sad and aweful this is (snying re rje). Reflecting in this way, one produces an uncontrived and spontaneous yearning to help them and an intense compassion for them. [27]

Lopon Tenzin Namdak briefly elaborated on this practice: How do we produce and develop the Bodhichitta? It is the very basis of the Mahayana. We should think that all other sentient beings were once been our very own loving mother in some past lifetime or another. In the infinite series of our past lives since time without beginning, all other beings, at some time or another, have been our very own parents. For example, if we put a single black pea into a vase filled with rice grains and shake up the vase, this pea will eventually touch all of the other grains of rice many times. It is the same with all the beings in Samsara. As we transmigrate through Samsara, we come into direct contact with all other sentient beings in all possible combinations and relationships. In each lifetime we have had different parents and our past lives have been infinite in number. It may be true that we were connected with them a long time ago in some other world system, but nevertheless at that time they were kind to us, showing us love and affection as our parents. Even the fierce lioness is a good mother to her cubs. It is the same way with all of these other beings. They once cared for us like a loving mother cares for her only child. They loved us and did not complain. They were kind and patient with us. Just consider that. For example, when we do a good turn for some other person and they do not recognize that kindness, but rather they ignore us, or worse, abuse us— how do we feel? So, we must remember our mother's great kindness to us. What can we do now to repay the kindness shown to us by our parents? At the present moment, our mother (all of these other beings) is suffering and lost in the delusions of Samsara— what can we do? We want to free her from this misery, but how can we do this? Nothing at the present. For all of us are equally powerless in our delusion and suffering. But if we recognize the wisdom and the power of the Buddha, for only the Buddha can remove the suffering of our mother, this thought will then motivate us to practice the teachings so that we too will eventually come to realize Buddhahood. Having ourselves become a Buddha, we will then possess the wisdom and the capacity to lead others out of the sufferings experienced in Samsara. That is our motive for practicing the spiritual path.

One makes the promise and commitment that "I too shall strive to attain the enlightened state of a Buddha," (sangs-rgyas kyi dgongs-pa thob-par byas). Here the Tibetan term *dgongs-pa*, which in the ordinary sense means "intention," means the primordial state of the individual. In terms of one's spiritual conduct, one may practice the Bodhichitta like a shepherd, that is, a shepherd tends and watches over his flock of sheep, protecting them from wolves and other dangers. Or one may practice the Bodhichitta like a guide, that is, a guide finds the right path and leads others along it to safety. Or one may practice the Bodhichitta like a boatman, that is, he takes others in his boat to the safety of the farther shore. How one actualizes the Bodhichitta in one's conduct toward others depends on one's level of capacity, but the intention (dgongs-pa) remains the same in each case.

To generate the Bodhichitta, the Lopon suggests that the following verse known as "the exposition of the words for producing the thought (of enlightenment)" (sems bskyed-pa'i tshig-bshad) may be recited:

"Just as did (all the previous) Victorious Ones and Exalted Ones
Belonging to the three times, by means of the abundant powers of their merits,
Do so in order to bring all sentient beings to the realization of Buddhahood,
So also shall we similarly produce the thought of supreme enlightenment!" [28]

In this formula, the Victorious Ones (rgyal-ba, Skt. Jina) are the Buddhas and the Exalted Ones ('phags-pa, Skt. Arya) are the great Bodhisattvas.

5. The Practice of Going to Refuge

Now the practice of going to Refuge (skyabs 'gro) is presented. This section is also called the explanation regarding the going to Refuge with faith and intense longing (dad 'dun skyabs 'gro'i khrid). In terms of the Sutra system, the practitioner goes to Refuge in the Three Jewels that are the Buddha, his teachings, and his spiritual community, whereas in terms of the Tantra system, one also goes to Refuge in the Guru (bla-ma), the Meditation Deity (yi-dam) and the Dakini or female energy manifestation (mkha'-'gro-ma). These are known as the Three Roots (rtsa-ba gsum). However, according to the Dzogchen view, the most important Object of Refuge is the Guru or realized master. It is this master who directly introduces the practitioner to the Natural State in the context of an intimate personal encounter and dialogue. This is the Refuge in the absolute sense, the direct introduction to the Nature of Mind, but there also exists Refuge in the relative sense in terms of Sutra and Tantra, which are also useful in practice.

According to Lopon Tenzin Namdak, the practice of going to Refuge may either come before, as is always the case in Buddhist liturgies, or it may come after the practice of producing the Bodhichitta. Here in the Bon tradition, the Bodhichitta is done first because, as the intention to attain enlightenment, it represents the very foundation of the spiritual path of the Mahayana and the basic motivation for pursuing it. But the going to Refuge is not just the repeating aloud of some formula or reading some well-intended pious words. "Refuge" means having an absolute trust in and making a total surrender to the Buddhas, to their spiritual teachings, and to the spiritual community. This going to Refuge depends on one's faith and devotion. If the practitioner has a genuine and fervent devotion, then the refuge will be very strong, effective, and powerful. Again all this depends on the decision of the individual practitioner, on one's trust and devotion. The Ultimate Refuge is present there all of the time within the individual mind-stream as the principle of enlightenment, but in the concrete sense, the practitioner creates the Refuge by opening oneself unreservedly and surrendering to it. It is the same with the sun in the sky. It is there all the time, but the individual most come out of the shadows of the cave in order to receive and enjoy its light. For this reason, the Bodhichitta and the Refuge should be practiced every day.

What is most important here is to have perfect trust in the Buddha. For that reason, one no longer puts one's trust in the worldly gods or nature spirits, nor goes for refuge to them. For these worldly gods and spirits, no matter how powerful or long-lived or wise they may be, are not enlightened and still belong to the conditioned order of existence that is Samsara. Whereas the Buddha, on the other hand, is an omniscient and enlightened being; there is nothing higher than the Buddha who totally transcends Samsara. Therefore, one should not rely on the worldly gods who speak through fortune telling and divination over the word and power of the Buddha. This is the conduct that flows from the going to Refuge in the Buddha. And since one has gone to Refuge in the Teachings of the Buddha (the Dharma or Bon), one should show respect to the holy scriptures and spiritual books generally, as well as to images and pictures of the Buddhas, to stupas and temples, and so on. And finally, one goes to Refuge in the spiritual community of the Bodhisattvas, which ceaselessly continues to benefit living beings and lead them into liberation from Samsara. Why does one go to Refuge to this community of Bodhisattvas? At the commencement of their spiritual careers, they made vows to help all sentient beings and guide them to liberation from the prison of Samsara. And because of the innumerable lifetimes they have spent in the unceasing practice of the teachings, they have developed the knowledge and the capacity to do just this. They are no longer just ordinary beings that are deluded and powerless in Samsara, but form a spiritual community whose purpose is to inspire and guide the spiritual evolution of this planet toward the realization of Buddhahood, which is the ultimate goal of all evolution. The practitioner comes to participate in this collective effort. Therefore, one does not speak ill of one's spiritual brothers and sisters and does not sew dissention and schism within their spiritual communities. These are the vows of Refuge.

According to the Sutra system, it takes countless lifetimes over the course of three immeasurable kalpas in order to attain Buddhahood and there exist many obstacles to this process that are met with along the way, both visible and invisible ones. What can the ordinary practitioner do? It is for this reason that one goes to Refuge in the Buddha, the teachings, and the spiritual community of the Great Bodhisattvas, as well as to the Guru. These represent the Four Precious Jewels. But among them the Guru or Lama is the most important. This is because the Buddha lived a long time ago and now is only a memory, whereas the Guru or master is present in this life here and now. He is able to transmit to the practitioner those empowerments that ripen the mind-stream and those secret oral instructions that liberate the understanding. The various Nirmanakaya Buddhas propagated the teachings of the Dharma during their respective earthly careers long ago and these teachings remain in the world even now as one's guide. The Guru or master is the representative of the Buddha here and now in this present situation, precisely and concretely. He directly introduces one to the Nature of one's own Mind. He does this is the same way that Tonpa Shenrab, or Shakyamuni, or any other Buddha for that matter, did originally. However, it is not necessary to make an examination to see if one's Guru has precisely the same qualities as the various historical Buddhas. Rather, it is sufficient to be aware when he is transmitting the teachings in the correct way, in the same way as did the previous Buddhas. This is the reason why the practitioner takes Refuge in the Guru.

According to the Lopon, the Tree of the Assembly (tshogs shing) to be visualized here that is suggested in the text is that of the tradition of his own monastery of Menri (bkra-shis sman-ri) in Tsang province, founded in 1405 by Nyammed Sherab Gyaltsan. [29] This foundation replaced the much older establishment of Yeru Wensakha, of which Druchen Gyalwa Yungdrung had once been the Abbot. In the center of the Tree is the figure of the Sambhogakaya Buddha Shenlha Odkar (gShen-lha 'od-dkar), also known as Kunzang Shenlha (Kun-bzang gshen-lha), attired in the crown, the rich silks, and the jewel ornaments appropriate to the Sambhogakaya aspect. He is sitting cross-legged and his hands are held in samadhi-mudra, cradling a precious jewel. Above him flies the Garuda (khyung), the king of birds and symbol of the Dzogchen teachings. Then extending into the sky above him are three clusters of figures, like billowing cumulous clouds, representing the Gurus of the various lineages of the Bon teachings. The central group immediately above the Sambhogakaya consists of the various Abbots for Menri monastery, the largest figure among them being Nyammed Sherab Gyaltsan himself in their midst. In the sky above the head of the Abbot Sherab Gyaltsan, the three lineages for the Bonpo Dzogchen teachings, with that of the Zhang-zhung Nyan-gyud in the center, extend upward to the zenith of heaven where their ultimate transcendent source, the Primordial Buddha Kuntu Zangpo, sits in serene contemplation. The other two lineages of Gurus are to the right and left of this central column of figures. Collectively, these three Dzogchen lineages within the Bon tradition are known as *A rdzogs snyan gsum,* "the three: *A-khrid, rDzogs-chen,* and *sNyan-rgyud.*" To the left of the three Dzogchen lineages in the center, there is the lineage for the Vinaya ('dul-ba), or monastic disciple, descending from the figure of Tonpa Shenrab and to the right is the Lineage for the Secret Mantras (gsang sngags) or Tantras descending from the figure of Shenlha Odkar. In the sky to the far right is the cluster of the nine enlightened Teachers or Buddhas (ston-pa rab dgu) who represent the nine-fold Transmission of the Mind (dgongs brgyud dgu) and, opposite on the left, there are a group of figures representing the tradition of the Five Paths (lam lnga), namely, the paths of accumulation, application, vision, meditation development, and ultimate realization. To the immediate left of the central Shenlha Odkar there is a large cluster of Yidams or Meditation Deities, including above the group of more wrathful inner Yidams belonging to the Higher or Inner Tantras (nang rgyud) and below the group of more mixed Outer Yidams belonging to the Lower or Outer Tantras. Then to the right, that being the left side of the Buddha, there is a cluster of wildly dancing naked Dakinis, with Yeshe Walmo (Ye-shes dbal-mo), the two-armed form of Sidpa Gyalmo (Srid-pa rgyal-mo) at their center. Below the Buddha and these clusters of Yidams and Dakinis representing the Three Roots (rtsa-ba gsum), there are the hosts of the various Guardians (srung-ma) and Protectors of Bon (bon skyong). Collectively, this entire Tree of the Assembly (tshogs shing) or Field of Merit (tshogs zhing) is known as the Object of Refuge (skyabs yul) or as the Source of Refuge (skyabs gnas).

Here there exist two phases in the practice:

1. the visualization of the Tree of the Assembly and
2. the offering of prostrations while reciting the Refuge formula.

The prostrations and the recitations are performed one hundred-thousand times during the course of the retreat.

One visualizes the Tree of the Assembly in the sky before and above oneself as described. At the center of the Tree is one's Root Guru in the form of the Sambhogakaya Buddha Shenlha Odkar, surrounded by thousands of miniature figures of the Three Jewels and the Tree Roots. Thus the sky before the practitioner becomes everywhere filled with the glorious and luminous manifestations of the Sambhogakaya and the Nirmanakaya as living presences. They come to fill all the heavens and one prays to them with fervent devotion using the verse given below. But the practitioner may use the many different invocations and formulae of Refuge found various practice manuals. One should think that the Buddhas in the sky in front of oneself actually see who it is that is praying to them. Rays of light come out from their hearts and ascending into the heavens, these rays invoke the blessings or spiritual energies (byin-brlabs) of enlightenment in the form of Wisdom Beings or Yeshepas which descend as miniature images of light, like so many snow-flakes, and these are absorbed into the visualization of the Tree of the Assembly in front. This visualization actually represents something created by the finite discursive mind of the practitioner and is, therefore, known as the Symbolic Being. However, these two, the Wisdom or Gnostic Beings and the Symbolic Beings, merge into each other and unite, becoming one and inseparable, like pouring water into water. In this way, the visualization becomes ensouled and infused with a life and an intelligence of its own, and is no longer something merely created by one's own mind and imagination.

In the visualization, one multiplies one's body and leads all other beings in going to refuge and in performing the prostrations. The prostration may be done either in the short form where one simply kneels and touches the floor with the palms of the hands and the forehead or the long form where one extends one's body fully prostrate on the floor and joins one's hands above the head. In either case, having generated the visualization, one stands upright and facing it, one feels, with faith and a firm conviction, that one is actually present before the Objects of Refuge, that they can actually see one, hear one, and know what one is doing. One joins the palms of one hands before one's chest, cupping them a bit as if one is holding a large precious jewel which one is now offering to the Objects of Refuge, especially to Kunzang Shenlha from whom one is requesting empowerment and initiation. In turn one raises one's joined palms before one's forehead, then one's throat, and finally one's heart, thinking that one is receiving the empowerments of Body, Speech, and Mind from Kunzang Shenlha. Bringing one's hands down, one thinks that one has thereby become purified of all past negative karmic traces and obscurations. Then one goes down on the floor on all fours, with one's limbs, the two knees and the two palms, and one's forehead all touching the ground. One thinks that thereby the five poisons that are the emotional defilements are purified. Then, rising to one's feet once more, one feels that one now stands in the pure dimension of enlightenment, the sacred space of the Objects of Refuge. As one exhales, one realizes the primordial purity of that dimension.

Before making each prostration, the Lopon suggests one recite the following verse known as "the exposition of the words for the going to Refuge" (skyabs 'gro'i tshig-bshad):

"To the master Shenrab, the most abundant source of the Trikaya,
To all the Sugatas of the three times, the protectors of all living beings,
To the images which are their representations, to the holy scriptures,
and to the stupas, all of which are their supports,
And to all the Shenrabpas of the ten directions, who are the lamps upon
the pathway to liberation—-
    To these four Sources (of Refuge), while making our prostrations,
we and other all beings go to them for Refuge." [30]

6. The Practice of Offering the Mandala

    The next practice is that of offering the mandala (mandal 'bul).
This section is also called the explanation concerning the mandala that
signifies the clouds of offerings (mchod sprin man-dal gyi khrid).
Whereas the practice of the confession aimed at purifying one's sins or
negative karma (sdig sbyong), the purpose of the practice of offering
the mandala is to accumulate merit or positive karma (dge bsag). Here
there exist two considerations, namely, to whom one offers the
mandala and what it is that is offered. The mandala, which is a
representation of the entire world, together with all its wealth and
abundance, is offered to all the enlightened beings. This is not done for
their benefit because they are lacking nothing, but for one's own
benefit because one is deficient in the accumulation of merit and acts
of generosity are the best means to generate meritorious karma. First,
there is the mandala that is like the celestial palace of the gods and this
is what the practitioner visualizes in the sky in front, just as one has
done previously with the Tree of the Assembly. The presence of this
celestial palace is invoked with the sounding of the seed syllable
BRUM that stands upon the foundation of the five successive elements
beginning with space at the bottom and proceeding upward to earth.
This mandala of the enlightened beings is the pure dimension that is a
field of merit. A fuller description of the Tree has been given above.
Second, there is the mandala that is offered to the Buddhas and the
assembly of Bodhisattvas, who are the Objects of Refuge (skyabs yul).
This mandala has four different levels of meaning:

1. the External Mandala: this mandala is a symbolic
   representation of the external world and all the riches it
   contains. See below.
2. the Internal Mandala: this is the symbolic offering of one's
   own physical body (lus sbyin) as a Ganachakra Puja or Tantric
   feast, as in the Chod practice that follows below.
3. the Secret Mandala: this is the offering of one's thoughts and
   emotions, including the 84,000 upakleshas, or lesser emotional

defilements, based on ignorance, into the unlimited state of the Nature of Mind, whereby they are transformed into 84,000 kinds of knowledge or primary cognitions (ye-shes).

4. the Exceedingly Secret Mandala: this is the self-originated Mandala of Dzogchen. This means the actualizing and remaining in the Natural State without being distracted, so that no disturbances from discursive thoughts or the emotions arise. In this way, everything becomes part of the total offering to one's own Natural State.

In terms of the External Mandala, there are two principal methods to make the offering. First one makes the mandala-mudra with one's two hands and recites the mantras. In this mudra, the two ring fingers are pressed back to back and they represent the Meru mountain at the center of the world. The tips of the other fingers grasp each other and these signify the four continents, whereas the circles made by the thumbs represent the sun and the moon. The cups formed by the palms are the oceans, and so on.

The other more elaborate method, which is proper to the Ngondro, one uses a silver plate and three silver rings which are progressively filled with rice and other precious items. These rings are piled one on top of the other. The parts of the mandala are constructed so that they have the proper proportions, shape, and material and upon that are arranged the decorations and ornaments. [31] The foundation of the world is represented by this round metal plate and the three rings that are set on top of it. These rings are progressively filled with rice and stacked one on top of the other. They signify the three thousand-fold universe, that is, a universe having 1000 x 1000 x 1000 world systems inhabited by intelligent beings to whom Buddhas may manifest. The first ring represents the first one thousand worlds, the second ring the second thousand, and so on. Each of these worlds is filled with all the wealth and precious things belonging to Devas, Nagas, and humans— all this is offered to the Gurus and the other Objects of Refuge visualized in the sky.

One assumes the fivefold posture of meditation and performs the nine breathings as usual. In terms of the actual practice, there exist two phases:

1. the visualization of the Tree of the Assembly and
2. purifying and offering the mandala while reciting the mantras and actualizing the visualization.

At first one's hands are held in the samadhi mudra that signifies the nonduality of space and awareness. Then, holding the mandala with the left hand, when one rubs and wipes clean the surface of the silver plate with the palm of one's right hand, one should think that one is purifying all the negative karmic traces and obscurations of oneself and others. [32] One does this at first three times counterclockwise and then three times clockwise, and finally three times straight across. One should think that this counterclockwise motion cleanses all one's past negative karma, the clockwise motion cleanses all one's future negative karma, and the forward and back motion cleanses all one's negative karma of the present. While cleaning the surface well, one recites the mantra OM NAMA A-DKAR GSHA' YA NI SHAG SA-LE SANG-NGE-YE SWAHA. [33] The function of this mantra is to cleanse and purify the surface of the mandala offering. The mantra is recited each time, that is, for a total of nine times. Then, still holding the plate in the left hand while reciting the mantra BRUM RI TI GAR MA LA HO, [34] one arranges in the center, using the right hand, a large heap of grains of rice. The function of this mantra is to establish the center. This heap in the center signifies the Meru mountain (ri-rab). Next, starting from the front, representing the eastern direction, and proceeding to the left (counterclockwise), one arranges in the four cardinal directions and in the eight intermediate directions the twelve smaller heaps of rice signifying the twelve continents while reciting the mantra A YAM RAM MAM KHAM BRUM SHAG SA-LE SANG-NGE-YE SWAHA. [35] The function of this mantra is to establish the four great continents and the eight lesser continents of this world-system. The preceding syllables are for the five elements of space, air, fire, water, and earth respectively. These five successive elements form the foundation for the material world. While reciting the mantra OM PHYOD PHUR SA-LE HA-LO SENG, [36] one arranges the rice grains as the offering substances in the four directions about the center like the petals of a flower. The function of this mantra is to establish the sun and moon, as well as the eight auspicious emblems, and so on. In summery, the seventeen heaps of rice (tshom-bu bcu-bdun) represent the Meru mountain, the twelve continents, and the four elements. One adds the rice inside each ring, placing one upon the other as each ring becomes filled. All the time that one is doing this, one should be aware that this mandala represents the entire world with all its wealth and riches of Devas, Nagas, and humans, as well as the eight auspicious symbols (bkra-shis rtags brgyad) and the seven emblems of royalty (rgyal-srid rin-chen sna bdun). The first group consists of the parasol, the golden fish, the treasure vase, the lotus, the conch shell, the endless knot, the victory banner, and the wheel; the second group consists of the wheel, the jewel, the queen, the minister, the elephant, the horse, and the general. Then, when actually offering the mandala as a silver plate and rings, one holds the Mandala a bit upward with the left hand, and snaps the fingers of the right hand at the end of each recitation. This is the symbol of actualizing the offering.

According to the Lopon, not only oneself, but all other sentient beings as well, are simultaneously offering mandalas to the Gurus and the Three Jewels. All of these figures are emanations like oneself. Everyone together as a single group, the collectivity of all living beings, is making offerings to the Buddhas and the Bodhisattvas. The purpose of offering the mandala is to accumulate meritorious karma. One offers to them everything in the world that is precious and valuable. Although one may not possess the capacity to do this in actuality, nevertheless this intention is present in the mind of the practitioner. The practice of generosity is the best method for the accumulating of merit. Moreover, the practice of offering overcomes one's attachments to possessions. Normally when one offers something from one's property, one expects something in return as payment. This is an impure offering because the intension is impure. It is like offering old and rancid butter for lamps on the altar at the temple because the butter is no longer edible. Does one think that if humans cannot eat it, then one can always offer it to the Buddhas? But the Buddhas cannot be tricked nor hoodwinked so easily. Therefore, one's mandala offering must be made with a pure intention. One offers everything found in this world that is clean and of best quality. But one should give it away freely, holding nothing back, being in no way attached to whatever is offered. The practice of confession is necessary for the purification of obscurations and the mandala is offered for the purpose of accumulating meritorious karma. This preparation consisting of confession and offerings transforms the practitioner into a suitable vessel for the receiving of the pure wisdom of the teachings. Before putting the nectar into it, the vase must be cleansed and purified, for otherwise the impurities therein would contaminate and spoil the nectar. The offerings may be made actually or just visualized in the mind, whichever is appropriate, because what really matters here is one's intention. Thus, one should offer everything one has in the world without attachment.

The visualization of the Objects of Refuge (skyabs yul rnams) has been described above.

With respect to this mandala offering, the superior procedure is to visualize it and to think of it as being equal to the infinity of all the universes filling the vastness of space, the intermediate procedure is to visualize it and to think of it as its being equal to the three thousand-fold universe, and the inferior procedure is to visualize it and to think of it as being equal to only the Brahmaloka. [37] The Brahmaloka is the higher mental plane inhabited by the Brahmas or Creator Gods.

The Lopon suggests that the following verse known as "the exposition of the words for offering the Mandala" (mandal 'bul-ba'i tshig-bshad) may be used for this purpose, serving as the offering prayer:

"OM NA-MA A DKAR GSHA' YA NI SHAG SA-LE SANG-NGE-YE SWAHA!
BRUM RI TI GAR MA LA HO!
A YAM RAM MAM KHAM BRUM SHAG SA-LE SANG-NGE SWAHA!
PHYOD PHUR SA-LE HA-LO SENG!
Ema!
On top (of the foundation built) of the five elements is the Meru mountain and the seven (golden) mountains,
The four (great) continents and the (eight) lesser continents, together with all the outer and inner delightful sense qualities they contain,
And adorned with the sun and moon: these hundreds of millions (of world systems),
Presented by our minds, we offer to you; please accept them!
OM A DA-DA DE-DE PHYOD PHUR SA-LE HA-LO SENG!
BSWO MU-YE SPROS KHYUNG YE LAM KRI KHRI TAR DAR!
gsal 'bar 'od dpag RAM SWAHA!" [38]
The function of this final mantra is for the destroying or dissolving of the mandala.

Having conjured up an infinitude of offerings, whatever is desired or needed by sentient beings, one then prays that there will be produced in one's mind-stream a special experience and understanding of the Natural State and of the Mahayana. Reciting the words, one makes the offerings and the commitments. [39] This practice of offering one's own physical body as a mandala is similar to the Chod practice described below.

7. The Practice of Mantra Recitations

The three final practices are according to the special system of the Higher Tantras (nang rgyud), whereas the previous triad of practices are according to the general system of the Sutras and the Lower

Tantras. However, all the practices found in the Ngondro belong the methods of purification and accumulation of merit according to the methods of the Sutras and the Tantras, while the principal method of Dzogchen is not this, but the practice of contemplation as such, the coming to rest in the Natural State of the Nature of Mind. All these practices are only preparations for the real thing, the entering into and continuing in the Natural State. But this does not mean that these preliminaries are not exceedingly useful, or even necessary, for purification and for preparation. They remove the negative karma and obstacles that obstruct one's entering into the Natural State. The exercises presented below are said to be the three preliminary practices that are especially exalted with respect to bringing about a purification of the mind-stream of the practitioner. [40] First there is the recitation of mantras in order to purify one's karmic traces and obscurations, next the offering of one's own body (lus sbyin) in order to overcome fears and attachments, and finally the prayers to the Guru in order to invoke his blessings of inspiration continuously.

Here in this section the practice is that of the reciting of mantras (sngags kyi bzlas-pa) and again the principal function is the purifying of negative karmic traces (bag-chags), obscurations (sgrib-pa), and the rendering positive of various conjunctions of events (rten-'brel) through the power of mantra. This section is also called the explanation concerning the recitations of mantra (sngags) and scripture (lung) for the purpose of the purification of obscurations (sgrib sbyang bzlas lung gi khrid). In the Tantra system, the practice of mantra recitation is also called Seva or ritual service (bsnyen-pa). As before, the practitioner assumes the fivefold posture of meditation and performs the nine breathings of purification. Then one visualizes the Tree of the Assembly, with Shenlha Odkar at its center as described previously, and invokes the descent of the Wisdom Beings (ye-shes-pa) into the visualization. There are seven stages in the practice:

1. Sounding a long HUM, one visualizes white rays of light emanating from the figure of Shenlha and these dissolve all sentient beings into masses of light like rainbows which thereupon merge into oneself;
2. Then sounding PHAT, one sees one's body grow to an infinite size so that it comes to fill all of space and encompasses all sentient beings and world-systems within itself;
3. Thereupon the fires of wisdom emanate from the heart of Shenlha and these flames come to purify all sentient beings by burning up and consuming all their sins and obscurations;

4. Thereafter the winds of wisdom emanate from him and come to purify them as well by scattering the ashes;
5. And finally, the waters of wisdom emanate from him and purify all beings by washing away whatever may remain;
6. Streams of white A syllables emanate from the heart of Shenlha and enters the crowns of the heads of all sentient beings, whereupon they are transformed in to divine beings; and
7. One recites the mantras to authenticate this transformation.

Then in more detail: The practitioner visualizes that in the sky in front of oneself is seated one's Root Guru in the guise of Kunzang Shenlha. [41] This is just another name for the Sambhogakaya aspect Shenlha Odkar. He is surrounded by the external Yidams of the Lower or Outer Tantras (phyi rgyud) and the internal Yidams of the Higher or Inner Tantras (nang rgyud), the Buddhas of the ten directions, the Vidyadharas, the Bodhisattvas, and the Gurus of the Lineages of Transmission, together with the Dakinis and the Protectors of the Precepts. Then one invokes the Jnanasattvas or Wisdom Beings (ye-shes-pa) from out of the dimension of space, which is the vast expanse of the enlightened Mind, and these miniature figures, descending as rays of light from the sky, are absorbed into the visualizations of the Samayasattvas or Symbolic Beings (dam-tsig-pa) that have been created by the practitioner's finite discursive mind. The Symbolic Beings are embodied in the visualization of the Tree of the Assembly (tshogs shing).

Then, one repeatedly sounds the long HUM (HUM ring bgrang) very slowly. From the central figure of Kunzang Shenlha especially there emanate countless rays of brilliant pure white light like sun beams, which have the quality of compassion. They emanate into all directions and come to pervade the full extent of the sky. These white lights have the quality of purifying, pacifying, and healing. Then these white lights touch all the sentient beings of the six realms of rebirth, especially those beings with whom the practitioner has conflicts and problems, whereupon their physical bodies are transformed into masses of rainbow light, [42] that is, their physical forms dissolve into pure radiant energy. Their physical bodies having dissolved into formless light, it is only their Namshe (rnam-shes) or streams of consciousness that remain. Then one thinks that from everywhere in all ten directions, these lights are swept up and absorbed into the essence of one's own consciousness, [43] that is to say, these lights dissolve into one's heart center. Thus, these disincarnate consciousnesses are absorbed into one's own body. Then the entire external universe also dissolves into rainbow light and similarly one thinks that everything from all the ten directions is swept up and absorbed into one's own illusory body. [44] Thus, the entire external universe is absorbed into one's body.

Then one utters a strong PHAT! and visualizes that one's own physical body, together with one's consciousness, becomes larger and larger until the full extent pervaded by the space of the universe is filled with one's own body and everything is pervaded by one's own consciousness. One has expanded oneself until the entire external dimension of physical existence becomes one's own body. Similarly, everything becomes equally pervaded by one's own consciousness, so that one's mind is inseparable from the consciousnesses of all living beings. Whereupon one's physical body multiplies and increases and becomes transformed into the realms of countless world-systems. [45] Each of these forms has transformed into a universe with its own sun, moon, and stars. And inside each of these worlds, due to the power of the magical potency of Rigpa (rig-pa'i cho-'phrul las), there exist countless living sentient beings belonging to the three realms (khams gsum). One thinks that they are all reciting the mantras and the invocations together with oneself. One should also think of the suffering that these beings have experienced in their different lifetimes within the cycles of Samsara. And having thus expanded infinitely the physical dimension of one's body, one expands and develops one's internal space and influences everything in the environment through this white light of gnosis that has the quality of compassion.

Then, from the heart of Kunzang Shenlha especially, as well as from the hearts of the Sugatas in the atmosphere, who are situated in the visualized Tree of the Assembly, which is still outside oneself, there emanate countless masses of the flames of wisdom (ye-shes kyi me), which are great fire storms, sounding like thunder and appearing like lightning flashes, or like the fires from a terrifying volcano. These fires touch all living beings. Instantly, all of the negative karmic traces and obscurations of oneself and of all these sentient beings are suddenly burnt up and consumed utterly by these fires of wisdom, which are like the fires that consume the universe at the end of the kalpa. Then the winds of wisdom (ye-shes kyi rlung), like wind storms or hurricanes making a roaring sound, issue forth from the hearts of the Sugatas. Thereby all of the ashes and remnants of the karmic traces and obscurations of all sentient beings swirl upward into the sky and are blown away as purple vapors. Finally the waters of wisdom (ye-shes kyi chu), as great floods making a rushing sound, issue forth from the hearts of the Sugatas. Thereby all traces of these ashes of the karmic traces and obscurations of all sentient beings that were scattered by the winds are totally washed away as black gritty fluids, so that no impurities whatsoever remain left behind. Thus, in this way, all beings have become entirely purified.

Then one sounds a long A syllable three times. From the heart of Kunzang Shenlha and the hearts of the other Sugatas emanate an infinite series of white A syllables, both subtle and gross in aspect, which signify the wisdoms of the Buddhas, and they come to fill the entire atmosphere. These streams of luminous white A syllables rain down over all lands and places wherever living beings dwell. They then touch, enter, and are absorbed into the crowns of the heads of each individual sentient being, coming to fill each being completely, illuminating their bodies and minds, and thereby these beings are transformed into the glorious aspect of Kunzang Shenlha himself, [46] because all sentient beings have potentially the nature of Kunzang Shenlha. Again rays of lights emanate and thereby all realms are transformed into great divine celestial palaces in the center of mandalas. In this way, all forms become deities and mandalas, all sounds become mantras, and all thoughts and memories become contemplation. Thus, all living beings and all places in the environment become purified and transformed and all beings come to realize the Body, Speech, and Mind of the Buddhas. The Natural State of each sentient being is realized to be the Primordial State of Kuntu Zangpo. This process represents the essence of the Tantric method, the path of purification and transformation. What is transformed here is energy and the way in which energy manifests. This is part of the dimension of Speech (gsung). Energy also manifests as vision and here impure karmic vision is transformed into pure vision.

One should think that all of these sentient beings, in their activities and conduct, have divine bodies wherein they practice the Mahamudra (mdzad spyod lha'i sku/ phyag-rgya chen-po la spyod-pa). [47] In the Tantric system of transformation, Mahamudra (phyag-rgya chen-po) means that the practitioner experiences oneself as an enlightened being, not only in terms of visualization, but as well in the actuality of all the senses, external and internal. The minds of all these beings have come under the influence of the Primordial State, that is, the Natural State of the Nature of Mind, which is profound and free of all conceptual elaborations (thugs nyid spros-bral zab-mo'i dgongs-pa la dbang sgyur-ba). [48]

One then recites aloud, or even sings the mantras in a melodious voice, in order to authenticate the experience. This is the Seva as such or ritual service of reciting the mantra (bsnyen-pa). There exist three mantras that are very widely spread in Bonpo practice and the Lopon suggests that they may be used here for the purposes of purification and transformation. These mantras should be recited as much as possible, or at least one hundred-thousand times over the course of the full retreat. One should neither eat nor talk while engaged in a session of mantra recitation. These mantras, which are known as the three essential heart mantras (snying-po rnam gsum), are as follows:

1. A A DKAR SA LE 'OD A YAM OM 'DU
   This is the mantra especially associated with the Dharmakaya aspect Kuntu Zangpo and is also employed for developing the Dzogchen view in relation to contemplation and vision. [49]

2. OM MA TRI MU YE SA LE 'DU
   This is the Great Mantra is especially associated with Tonpa Shenrab and it serves the purpose of purifying the six realms or destinies of rebirth. As explained above, the first two syllables signify the Buddha and the Great Mother, the Perfection of Wisdom, while the remaining six syllables signify the Dulshen or six emanations of Tonpa Shenrab into these six destinies of rebirth. [50]

3. A DKAR A RMAD DU TRI SU NAG-PO ZHI ZHI MAL MAL SWAHA
   This is another mantra for purifying the six realms, for the confession of negative actions, and for purification generally. It is associated with the Sambhogakaya aspect Shenlha Odkar. [51]

Afterwards, one affixes the seal of non-conceptuality, that is to say, enters into a state of even contemplation free of all discursive thoughts. And rousing oneself from that, one dedicates the merit to the enlightenment of all sentient beings. [52]

8. The Practice of Offering One's Own Body (Chod)

The next practice among the preliminaries is the offering up of one's own physical body, this representing the Internal Mandala, a practice which is known as *lus sbyin*, "the offering of the body". More commonly this procedure is known as Chod (gcod). This Tibetan word *gcod* means "cutting off" and what is severed or cut off here is the attachment to one's ego, symbolized by one's physical body. All living beings are very attached to their bodies, but this practice of Chod serves to eliminate such attachment. Chod has a twofold function: not only does it eliminate attachment to the ego and to the body, but it serves as a means to cultivate generosity. One gives away to others what one values most, namely, one's own life and material body. This serves as a means to repay one's karmic debts accumulated from past lifetimes in different dimensions of existence with regard to different classes of beings. Moreover, it is of much benefit as a preparation for death when consciousness and physical vehicle finally separate, because then, having practiced, one will experience neither fear of death nor attachment to the body one is loosing. Chod brings the individual face to face with what a living being fears most, the primal fear of death where one is killed and devoured as food by another, such as a fierce predatory animal. Life and death, eating and being eaten, are inevitably part of Samsara. One's sense of ego and identity and personal worth are very much tied up with one's physical body, its health and its pleasing and attractive appearance. Feeling that "I" and "my body" are one and the same, the individual becomes inordinately attached to it. But the experience of Chod will teach one otherwise. The practice of Chod is widely popular in Tibet in both Buddhist and Bonpo traditions, but here it is not just a matter of subjugating the spirits in the wilderness, although Chod practitioners are well known for their ability to exorcise the evil spirits that cause plagues and infectious diseases. Chod is even more important as a spiritual exercise. This section here in the text is also known as the explanation regarding the accumulating of a collection of merit by means of giving away offerings (tshogs sogs mchod sbyin gyi khrid).

Again one assumes the fivefold position of meditation and performs the nine breathings for purification. Then there is described a simplified version of the more elaborate practice of Chod. The practice is in five phases:

1. the visualization of the Tree of the Assembly;
2. the invitation to the Four Guests to attend the feast;
3. one's consciousness emerging from a hole in the chest of one's corpse and its assuming of the form of a Krodha or wrathful deity;
4. the butchering of one's corpse by him and the making of a cauldron from one's skull in which one's flesh is cooked; and
5. transforming this deity into the offering goddesses who distribute the food to the Four Guests.

In the sky in front of oneself, one generates by means of visualization the Objects of Refuge consisting of the Three Jewels and the Three Roots as described above as the Tree of the Assembly with Shenlha Odkar at its center, as well as the glorious protectors or Palgon (dpal mgon) who are the guardian spirits of the teachings, specifically the seventy-two Palgon who come from the the sun, moon, and stars, together with the eight classes of spirits (sde brgyad), and all the beings belonging to the six realms of rebirth (rigs drug), all of whom fill the atmosphere in numbers inconceivable to the mind. [53] These constitute the Four Guests (mgron-po bzhi) who are invited to the feast that one prepares as described. These Four Guests are conventionally listed as follows:

1. the Three Jewels and the Three Roots who are the Objects of Refuge;
2. the Guardians who protect the Teachings;
3. the eight classes of worldly spirits; and
4. all the beings of the six destinies of rebirth, especially those to whom one owes karmic debts from past lives.

These guests are fully in attendance at the feast and are seen as present in the space in front of oneself.

One visualizes one's corpse lying dead, spread out on its back on the ground. One is looking at it as if watching a cinema show. Then suddenly a great hole of wisdom bursts open in its chest, whereupon one's own consciousness (rnam-shes) becomes visible inside this cavity as a tiny sphere of light. [54] With the sudden sounding of the syllable PHAT!, this consciousness principle is expelled as a tiny sphere of light (thig-le), coming out like a brilliant spark scattered from the heart of the fire. This spark dissolves into light, becoming instantly transformed into a Jnana Krodha or wrathful deity of wisdom or gnosis (ye-shes kyi khro-bo), whether male or female, as described in the text. With his sword in hand, he cuts off the four limbs of one's corpse and planting them in the earth, erects them as a make-shift hearth for the cooking fire. Then cutting off the top of one's skull, he places it on these four posts that are one's limbs. This skull cauldron or cooking pot now becomes as vast and extensive as the universe itself. Butchering the corpse, the wrathful deity methodically throws all the pieces of one's body into the cauldron, so that it is filled to overflowing. These pieces of one's flesh immediately increase in extent to become a vast multitude of food offerings. All of this flesh and the blood is cooked over the fire until this mass is turned into amrita or wisdom nectars (ye-shes kti bdud-rtsi), possessing a delightful aroma.

Thereupon the wrathful deity becomes transformed into innumerable beautiful young goddesses or Puja Devis who present the puja offerings (mchod 'bul gyi lha-mo) to all the guests, extracting the nectar from the cauldron by using the skull cups they hold as offering bowls. This delightful nectar of wisdom they offer first as cumulous clouds of pure puja offerings to the Wisdom Deities (ye-shes kyi lha), that is, to the Three Jewels and the Three Roots who fill the sky and who constitute the first group of guests invited to the feast. They are all delighted and thoroughly satisfied with these offerings. Due to this act of impartial generosity, one accumulates a vast stock of meritorious karma. And having delighted one's guests, one will then receive the blessings of all the Buddhas and the Gurus of the lineages.

Because the fluids of one's body become transformed into an ocean of amrita nectar, this propitiates and satisfies the pure races of the Palgon or glorious protectors (dpal mgon), who are the Guardians of the Teachings and who constitute the second group of invited guests. Since the thick sediments that remain become transformed into various kinds of delightful sensual qualities, [55] the eight classes, who are the third group of invited guests, and all the beings belonging to the six realms, who are the fourth group, also become satisfied. [56] By offering what one values most, that is, one's own physical body, to the Buddhas and to the other enlightened beings, as well as to the Guardians, one accumulates a great deal of meritorious karma by this act of supreme generosity and self-sacrifice. This is in terms of the higher guests who are invited to the feast.

But even the capricious and malicious minds of the worldly gods and demons are pacified. [57] The desires of the beings belonging to the six destines of rebirth are equally satisfied. In this way, both the higher guests and the lower guests become entirely satisfied and delighted. Furthermore, one has purified the causes for illness and suffering arising from negative provocations of these eight classes of worldly spirits (sde brgyad). By offering one's material body as food to the eight classes, one averts their negative provocations of energy (gdon) and so they no longer come to disturb one's meditation practice or to disrupt one's life and fortune. Rather, these spirits become friendly and supportive, acting even as friends.

There are various different lists of these none-human worldly spirits (mi ma yin) who haunt the wild and mountainous landscapes of Tibet, but generally they include the Lha or gods, white in color and corresponding to the Indian Devas, the Lu (klu), green or blue in color and corresponding to the Indian Nagas, the Dud (bdud), black in color and corresponding to the Indian Maras, the Tsen (btsan), warrior spirits red in color, the Mamo (ma-mo), violent female spirits who are black in color and who correspond to the Indian Matrikas, Gyalpo (rgyal-po), troublesome spirits of dead warriors and monks who are white in color, Za (gza'), varicolored spirits connected with electricity, and so on.

And in terms of offering one's material body to the sentient beings of the six realms, thereby one repays all one's karmic debts (lan-chags bu-lon) that are owed to others, as for example, when one has killed another sentient being in a previous lifetime in the course of a war or in hunting for food. Thus, one has repaid in full all of one's karmic debts accumulated up until the present time. In addition, by their partaking of one's flesh, one has established in all of these worldly beings the cause for their eventually attaining Buddhahood. One now has irreparable karmic links with them and when one attains liberation and enlightenment, one will be able to help them do likewise within one's spiritual field of activity..

Thinking that one's illusory body, that is, one's material body, which is the aggregate result in this present life of one's past karma and which is here offered in sacrifice, becomes this great mass of gifts and offerings, [58] one makes the offering by reciting the liturgy. The Lopon has suggested the following verses for this purpose known as "the exposition of the words for the offering of one's own illusion body as a Ganachakra Puja" (sgyu-lus tshogs 'bul gyi tshig-bshad):

"Kye-ho!
I offer to all of you my own body as a Ganachakra Puja:
I pray that (this offering) may be acceptable to you!
The forms of my limbs are planted (into the ground)
Forming a hearth that is stable and blazing brilliantly (with the cooking fire).
Having thrown into this vast cauldron, which is my own precious skull,
All of my flesh, blood, heat, breath, skin, fat, water, sinews, and bone marrow,
All of my elements and my sense-fields, both root and branch,
Together with my sense organs and the supports of my senses,
As well as my guts, my internal organs and my interior cavities which are containers,

My skeleton, teeth, finger-nails, head hair, and the masses of my body hairs,
As well as my bodily fluids, both pure and impure,
And having increased all of them to the size of the entire three thousand-fold universe,
I offer all of this inferior and polluted physical body as repayments (for my past karmic debts).
(And in exchange I request) the view and the contemplation, as well as the special experiences and understanding;
I pray that they may be bestowed upon me at this present moment!
Then having purified myself with this offering for repaying all my karmic debts and obligations,
May all those (spirits) who cause harm now come to realize the thought of supreme enlightenment!
And because of the merit which is hereby dedicated without conceptions,
May I come to liberate those same beings from their bondage by just my mere glance!" [59]

9. The Practice of Praying for Blessings (Guru Yoga, second version)

The final section is called "the explanation regarding praying with fervent devotion (to the Gurus) (mos-gus gsol-'debs kyi khrid). As noted above, this final practice is almost identical with the first, but it is done with a different attitude. Whereas with the first, it was a matter of requesting and receiving empowerments, here it is more a matter of praying to receive the blessings of the masters continuously. And this also constitutes a kind of Guru Yoga. Again, there are four stages in the practice:

1. the visualization of Shenlha and the Tree of the Assembly above one's head in the sky and the recitation of the initial invocation;
2. the receiving of purification by way of the wisdom nectars of fire, wind, and water from the heart of the Guru;
3. the receiving of the blessings of the empowerments from the heart of the Guru with the three lights that are white, red, and blue; and
4. thinking that one has received the ewmpowerments, the reciting of further prayers and mantras.

After assuming the five point position of the body and performing the nine breathings for purification, one sounds the seed syllable A and visualizes the Guru in front of oneself. According to the text, one should visualize in the sky in front one's own Root Guru in the Sambhogakaya guise of Shenlha Odkar, seated on a red sun disc, a white moon disc, and a lotus blossom above the crown of one's head. Shenlha is the central and largest figure, located at the center of the Tree of the Assembly (tshogs shing). White in color, with a single face and two arms, his two hands in samadhi-mudra holding a flaming jewel, he is adorned with the precious jewels and exquisite silks that express the richness and effulgence of the Sambhogakaya. He is surrounded by the Three Jewels, that is, the Buddhas of the three times, the holy scriptures of Bon, and the exalted community of great Bodhisattvas. Here also are gathered all the Siddhas and Vidyadharas, all the practitioners of Yungdrung Bon from Zhang-zhung and Tibet. And he is also surrounded by the Three Roots: the Gurus of all the lineages extending upward into the sky above his head, while below the meditation deities or Yidams fill all the branches of the great tree. Below them are the hosts of Dakinis, both mothers and daughters (ma srin mkha'-'go dang bcas-pa), and the hosts of Guardians (srung-ma) or Protectors of the Teachings (bon skyong). Or again, according to the Lopon, one may simply visualize Tapihritsa as described previously, sitting in the sky above one's head. [60]

When this visualization is complete, one can recite the verse of supplication used previously that represents "the exposition of the words for the prayer," (gsol-'debs kyi tshig-bshad):

"In the palace of great bliss on the crown of my head,
Is my benevolent Root Guru to whom I pray;
     The Buddha as my own Mind is the precious Teacher:
Please grant the blessing that I may recognize my own nature!" [61]
This is repeated many times, or at least three times.

Gazing up at the luminous and resplendent form of one's beloved master, the practitioner deliberately cultivates feelings of intense and one-pointed love and devotion toward him, which is in no way irregular or defective. [62] How does one pray? One should think that one is sitting in the actual presence of all the masters of the lineages. They are gazing down at one with eyes filled with love and compassion. One feels intensely that they actually see oneself sitting there before them and one prays to them with great faith and fervent devotion. One recalls that one has promised them to strive ceaselessly to attain Buddhahood for the sake of benefiting and liberating all sentient beings from the sufferings they experience in the rounds of Samsara. Now one prays for their help in revealing the short path to enlightenment and liberation within a single life time which is

Dzogchen. One fervently requests the blessings of their wisdom, knowledge, and inspiration. One thinks that one is making offerings to them when one makes this request. This is not just a reciting of mere words, for one has the firm and unshakeable conviction that all of these august beings are actually present in the sky above. One has a total trust in them and surrenders to them unreservedly. Thus they will now continuously look after the practitioner like a loving mother looks after her only child.

One proceeds with the essential points (gnad) of the practice as described previously for the Guru Yoga. [63] One cultivates faith and devotion from the depths of one's heart. One can develop this strong and pure devotion toward the Guru by way of chanting the invocation and fixating the mind on the clear visualization. And in response to this heart-felt devotion, like the sun rising in the eastern sky, from the heart center of the Guru, whether visualized as Shenlha Odkar or as Tapihritsa, there emanate and flow forth abundantly the lights of gnosis or wisdom (ye-shes kyi 'od 'phros). These white rays of light transform into streams of pure lustral waters or wisdom nectars (ye-shes kyi bdud-rtsi) that enter into the aperture at the crown of one's head, descend through the central channel, and come to fill one's entire body. In this way, all one's negativities, all one's karmic traces (bag-chags) and obscurations (sgrib-pa) of body, speech, and mind are purified and washed away. One's entire being becomes thoroughly cleansed and purified; one's body becomes filled with light and is translucent like a pure crystal vase. Now one is a suitable vessel to receive the blessings of the masters of the lineages. [64] In this way, one's own being, the vase for receiving the empowerments, is cleansed and purified, then the three lights from the three doors of the Guru actually transmit the empowerments. One may also envision this same process happening simultaneously to all the sentient beings inhabiting the six destinies of rebirth who are also sitting in the presence of the masters.

Again, because of cultivating intense faith and devotion on the part of the practitioner, the three mystic syllables appear spontaneously at the three secret places or three doors (sgo gsum) on the resplendent form of the Guru. From these three syllables in the three secret places of the Guru, or alternatively from all the Gurus simultaneously, come the brilliant rays of light which are white, red, and blue, respectively. These lights dissolve into one's own three centers and thus one receives the blessings and siddhis of the Body, Speech, and Mind of all the Gurus of all the lineages of the Dzogchen teachings. Now one is inseparably linked to these lineages of transmissions and will receive all their blessings continuously. One has a personal relationship with these masters and will experience directly their wisdom and their compassion. This process awakens and quickens the spiritual ripening of one's own mind-stream (rgyud smin). Thus, because of receiving the blessings of these three empowerments, one thinks that one has come to realize all the virtuous qualities (yon-tan) of these enlightened masters, such as knowledge, activity, conduct, experience, view, and realization. With great intensity of one's intrinsic Awareness, one prays to them with longing and with fervent devotion. [65] At the conclusion, the visualization of the Guru dissolves into a mass of light and is absorbed into one's own being. This section concludes the explanation regarding the practice of praying with fervent devotion to the Gurus (mos-gus gsol-'debs kyi khrid).

II. The Ordinary Practices in General

In this section, the text speaks about of how to practice the nine preliminaries in a unified and integrated manner in a retreat situation, which in Tibet traditionally lasted for three months. In the Bon tradition, it usually took that long to complete all of the preliminaries, performing each fully one hundred-thousand times ('bum dgu). According to the Lopon, however, one may do all nine sections in sequence during the early morning session of practice. Sitting down in the five-fold posture of meditation and performing the nine breathings for purification, one runs through each spiritual exercise in turn. Each may be repeated three times or five times, as one finds convenient. At the conclusion of the session, one recites the dedication of merit and the commitment to attain Buddhahood as soon as possible, as given below. During the afternoon session, just the mantras may be recited. In a retreat situation, usually four sessions are observed, but six sessions are also possible..

On the occasions of practicing in general the ordinary preliminaries contained in "The Nine Stages of the Practice of Bon," on each day while in retreat, beginning at daybreak and continuing throughout the early morning, one arranges oneself in the essential points of the body, that is to say, one assumes the five-fold position of the body. After completing the Guru Yoga, one meditates with a fierce intensity for a time on the impermanence of life again and again [66] as described above. Then, one performs in sequence the confessing of sins, the producing of the Bodhichitta, the going to Refuge, the offering of the Mandala, the reciting of the mantras, the transforming of the aggregates (of body and mind into offerings), and the engaging in prayer which represents the Guru Yoga proper. [67]

At the conclusion of each session of practice, one dedicates all of the merit accumulated from performing these preliminary practices to the attaining of enlightenment for the sake of benefiting all living beings. The Lopon has suggested that one could recite the following short verse for the dedication of merit and the commitment (bsngo smon):

"Whatever merit we have accumulated through the purity of our three gates,
We dedicate to the benefit of all the sentient beings of the three worlds;
Having purified all our negative karma and obscurations accumulated in all the three times,
May we quickly come to obtain the Perfect Buddhahood of the Trikaya!" [68]

At the time of midday, one may practice any other suitable activities that accumulate merit, such as prostrations and circumambulations, and so on. In general, midday is considered a poor time for meditation practice because the heat of the day and also the taking of a meal tends to make the mind become dull and drowsy.

III. The Signs of Heat

The signs of "heat" result from having performed the practices successfully (nyams su blangs-pa'i drod rtags). These signs of realization (sgrub rtags) occur either actually or in terms of experiences, visions, or dreams, such as seeing the faces of the Meditation Deities. [69] For example, in terms of dreams, the eating of foods of delicious taste indicates the taking into oneself of positive energy, while vomiting up vile things or diarrhea or washing off blood and insects indicates the expelling and getting rid of negative energy. Other auspicious signs in dreams are dreaming of sunrise, snow mountains, putting on new clothes, taking a bath, flying upward, being in a garden with many flowers, hearing beautiful sounds, seeing the face of one's meditation deity, receiving the teachings, and so on, or in general, the body feeling light or the mind becoming clear.

The signs of realization form practice may reflect superior, intermediate, and inferior capacities. One should hold fast to the essential points of the practice until a fervent belief and confidence is produced. [70]

Conclusion

Attaining of the Indestructible State or Svastika-bhumi [71] indicates the attaining of Buddhahood. The Bonpo term swastika (g.yung-drung) has the same meaning as the Buddhist term vajra (rdo-rje). Both terms mean "indestructible". This concludes the commentary and notes to the translation.

MU-TSUG SMAR-RO!

Translation of "The Exposition of the Words Text": *Tshig-bshad*

Here is contained the Exposition of the Words for the Prayers from the Preliminary Practices of the Oral Tradition from Zhang-zhung for the Great Perfection (rDzogs-pa chen-po zhang-zhung snyan-rgyud kyi sngon-'gro gsol-'debs tshig-bshad rnams bzhugs-so).

Homage to Kuntu Zangpo who realized the two benefits of oneself and others! [1]

[Note that in this text there are found no words to be recited (tshig-bshad) in the first section for the requesting and receiving of empowerments and blessings (dbang-bskur byin-rlabs)]

2. The Practice of Meditating on Impermanence

[As for the exposition of the words for (the meditation on) impermanence (mi rtag-pa'i tshig-bshad):]

Kye-ma! (Oh, alas!)

(1) Accordingly, even though all the phenomena of Samsara are without any essences,

Yet I continue to grasp at them as objectively real— Oh, compassion!

May there come forth in my mind-stream the blessing of producing the realization of impermanence!

(2) Even though this happiness lasts barely for a moment or an instant,

Yet I hope that it will continue always— Oh, compassion!

May there come forth in my mind-stream the blessing of producing the realization of impermanence!

(3) Even though I continue to wander continually (in Samsara), still I am not weary of all this;

I am so foolish and without courage— Oh, compassion!

May there come forth in my mind-stream the blessing of producing the realization of impermanence!

(4) Even though my actions within Samsara are without happiness,

Still I feel dejected and am without awareness—- Oh, compassion!

May there come forth in my mind-stream the blessing of producing the realization of impermanence!

(5) Even though I postpone everything in my present life without adding anything,

Yet I always hope (that this life) will continue always—- Oh, compassion!

May there come forth in my mind-stream the blessing of producing the realization of impermanence!

(6) Even though there will occur the time (of my death) when I will not be accompanied by anyone,

Yet I always hope that this will not occur—- Oh, compassion!

May there come forth in my mind-stream the blessing of producing the realization of impermanence!

(7) Even though death is certain to come, in addition to time passing (generally) in whatever ways,

Yet I expect to live on and on without death—- Oh, compassion!

May there come forth in my mind-stream the blessing of producing the realization of impermanence!

(8) Accordingly, everyone of us also see, hear, and know (of the coming) of death,

Yet I always expect that this self will be eternal—- Oh, compassion!

May there come forth in my mind-stream the blessing of producing the realization of impermanence!

(9) Accordingly, I know that all phenomena are constantly changing,

Yet I always hope that they are one (and self-identical)—- Oh, compassion!

May there come forth in my mind-stream the blessing of producing the realization of impermanence!

(10) When I think about (death and impermanence), at that instant I am without distractions,

Yet I become lazy and afterwards I postpone everything—- Oh, compassion!

May there come forth in my mind-stream the blessing of producing the realization of impermanence!

(11) Even though it is not at all certain when I shall die and find myself in the condition of a corpse,

Yet I heedlessly leave everything and do as I like—- Oh, compassion!
May there come forth in my mind-stream the blessing of producing the realization of impermanence!
(12) Even though everyone has only one sure way to go,
Yet I hope to be free from this (inevitable destiny)—- Oh, compassion!

May there come forth in my mind-stream the blessing of producing the realization of impermanence!
May I be granted the blessing to remain mindful of death!
May I be granted the blessing to turn away from the depths of attachment!
May I be granted the blessing to produce in my mind-stream the want of nothing!
May I be granted the blessing to understand that everything is an illusion!

3. The Practice of the Confessing of Sins
[As for the exposition of the words for the confessing of one's sins or harmful deeds (sdig-pa bshags-pa'i tshig-bshad):]
All sentient beings, such as myself, throughout our previous lifetimes
Have committed non-virtuous and sinful deeds in whatever way,
Whether these were actually done by us or encouraged by us or requested by us or merely rejoiced at by us,
Or have thought of or have spoken about doing, or have actually committed,
Whether small things or coarse things or merely related to negative actions,
Accordingly, whatever we have done or will come to do,
Even though just a little, we should remain mindful of them without forgetting.
And having condensed all of them in our minds, (presenting as a single mass) all of our sins and obscurations,
In the presence of these Holy Supreme Objects,
We confess fervently with thoughts of shame, regret, and dismay,
And having continually renounced our non-virtuous deeds and obscurations,
We shall henceforth pursue only virtuous actions!

4. The Practice of Producing the Bodhichitta
[As for the exposition of the words for producing the thought (of enlightenment) (sems-bskyed-pa'i tshig-bshad):]
Just as did (all the previous) Victorious Ones and Exalted Ones, [2]

Belonging to the three times, by means of the abundant powers of their merits,
Did so in order to bring all sentient beings to the realization of Buddhahood,
So also shall we similarly produce the thought of supreme enlightenment!

5. The Practice of Going to Refuge

[As for the exposition of the words for going to refuge (skyabs su 'gro-ba'i tshig-bshad):]

To the Master Shenrab, the most abundant source of the Trikaya,
To all the Sugatas of the three times, who are the protectors of all living beings,
To the images which are their representations, to the holy scriptures, and to the stupas, all of which are their supports,
And to all the Shenrabpas [3] of the ten directions, who are the lamps upon the path to liberation—-
To these four Sources (of Refuge), while making our prostrations, we and all other beings go to them for refuge!

6. The Practice of Offering the Mandala

[As for the exposition of the words of the mandala offering (mandal gyi tshig-bshad):]

(OM NAMA) A-DKAR GSHA' YA NI SHUG SA-LE SANG-NGE-(YE) SWAHA!
BRUM RI-TI GAR MA LA HO!
A YAM RAM MAM KHAM BRUM SHAG SA-LE SANG-NGE-(YE) SWAHA!
(OM) PHYOD PHYOD PHAR SA-LE HA-LO SENG!
[Pronunciation: Om A-kar sha-ya-ni shuk sa-le sang-nge-ye swaha! Drum ri-ti gar ma la ho! A yam ram mam kham drum shak sa-le sang-nge-ye swaha! Om chyod chyod phar sa-le ha-lo seng!]
[So saying, this represents the arranging (of the mandala).] [4]
Emaho! (How marvellous!)
Within this infinitely vast realm that is wondrous and marvellous,
There are found copious heaps of jewels that are beautiful, attractive, shining, and luminous,
Such as Meru, the seven (golden) mountains, the (seven) dancing seas, and the (twelve) continents,
The wish-granting tree, the sun and moon, the jewel that increases whatever is desired,
As well as the (eight) auspicious substances and the seven precious jewels (of royalty), [5]

Together with lamps, flowers, libations, incense, delicious cakes for the gods,
Gold, silver, turquoise, copper, iron, crystal glass, pearls,
The white and the sweet things, costly offerings, abundant harvests, grains, nectars,
Excessive ornaments, silken hangings, pleasant and agreeable puja substances,
Beautiful forms and pleasant sounds and aromatic scents,
Delicious tastes, soft bolts of cloth, all agreeable substances—-
Indeed, all of our wealth (whatever there may be), whether actually seen and heard,
(Or whatever may be) emanated from the mind (and visualized) or gathered by the mind,
Including life-force, body ornaments, enjoyments, psychic powers, and so on, are here prepared (as our offerings).
All of these puja substances of the world, which come to pervade all of the sky,
We offer to the Guru, to the Buddhas, together with their spiritual sons,
[6] as well as to the Dharma,
And having accepted these (offerings), for the benefit of living beings, as well as ourselves,
Please gaze upon us and heed us at this time!
May experiences and understanding, as well as belief, realization, and confidence arise within us!
Please cause the primal cognitions of self-awareness to arise within us!
To the Victorious Ones and their spiritual sons, as well as to the roots and the branches of the Teachings,
We pray that they may abide here continuously for a long time!
May we realize the accumulation of merit, produce entreaties and intense longings,
And may we rejoice at all accumulations of merit (by others)!
The Teachings of the Teacher represent precious magical speech;
May it come to spread and increase in all the ten directions!
In all of our lifetimes, may we possess the methods of the conduct of the Bodhisattvas!
May we become great captains (of the ship of) merit
And ultimately become the source of protection and refuge for all!
May we quickly come to obtain the great Nature of Refuge!
By way of knowledge and love, means and compassion,
May there be brought about the benefit of beings without reluctance or fatigue!

Whatever accumulations of merit may exist, which come forth from that,
We dedicate all of them for the sake of obtaining the Body of Reality.
May we all come to obtain quickly the Supreme Fruit that is certain and without conceptions!
[Then, when this (intention) is condensed, one recites:]
OM A DA-DA DE-DE PHYOD PHYOD SA-LE HA-LO SENG!
[Pronunciation: Om A da-da de-de chyod chyod sa-le ha-lo seng!] [7]

7. The Practice of the Mantra Recitation
[Then, one should engage in emanating and re-absorbing (the visualization, combined with) reciting the Mantra and the Agama (or explanation of the mantra):] [8]
Homage to the Supreme Teacher Shenrab, who abundantly guides to liberation
All of the sentient beings of Samsara due to his (great) compassion!
A-DKAR A-RMAD DU TRI SU NAG-PO ZHI ZHI MAL MAL SWAHA!
[Pronunciation: A-kar A-med DU TRI SU nag-po zhi zhi mal mal swaha!]
A-DKAR means the Nature of Mind is completely pure.
A-RMAD means primordial awareness is clearly visible as light.
With DU TRI SU the evil destinies (of rebirth in Samsara) are purified respectively.
NAG-PO means the sins and obscurations of one's karma are purified.
ZHI ZHI indicates that the sufferings of Samsara are pacified.
MAL MAL means one comes to possess thoughts of happiness.
SWAHA indicates that one vanquishes Rudra, (the demon) of wrong views.
By means of this heart-mantra that brings about the pacification of all suffering,
Once having stirred up the depths of the evil destinies of Samsara,
May all living beings come to attain Buddhahood in the Dimension of Reality!

8. The Practice of Offering One's Own Body
[Then, as for the exposition of the words for the offering of one's own illusory body as a Ganapuja (the Four Guests) (sgyu-lus tshogs 'bul gyi tshig-bshad):] [9]
Kye-ho!
I offer to all of you my own physical body as a Ganachakra Puja.
I pray that (this offering) may be acceptable to you!
The forms of my limbs are firmly planted (into the ground),

Forming a hearth that is stable and blazing brilliantly (with the cooking fire).

Then, having thrown into this vast cauldron, which is my own precious skull,

All of my flesh, blood, heat, breath, skin, fat, water, sinews, and bone marrow,

All of my elements and my sense fields, both root and branch,

Together with my sense organs and the supports of my senses,

As well as my guts, my internal organs, and my interior cavities,

My skeleton, teeth, finger nails, head hair, and masses of body hairs,

And having increased all of them to the size of the entire three thousand-fold universe,

I offer all of this inferior and polluted physical body as repayment (for my past karmic debts).

(And in exchange I request) the view and the contemplation, as well as the special experiences and understanding;

I pray that they will be bestowed upon me at this present moment!

Then, having purified myself with this offering for repaying all my karmic debts and obligations,

May all of those (spirits) who would cause harm now come to realize the thought of supreme enlightenment!

And because of the merit that is hereby dedicated without conceptions,

May I come to liberate those same beings from their bondage by my mere glance!

9. The Practice of Praying for Blessings

[Then, as for the exposition of the words of the prayer (gsol-'debs kyi tshig-bshad):]

Emaho!

As for those mind-streams from which come forth all the Buddhas of the Trikaya,

We pray to these Holy Gurus.

As the culmination of your compassion, please bestow the empowerments, the explanations, and the practices upon us!

We pray that these kindly and benevolent Gurus

May establish for us the path and the stairway to liberation through the narrow passage-ways of Samsara.

Holding the transmissions coming from above, please lead us along the pathways below!

We pray to the Gurus of the Lineages,

Who destroy the inherent currents of Samsara with the light of their wisdom.

We pray to these Gurus who liberate the mind-streams (of sentient beings)
That we may definitively decide upon the source of delusion by means of their profound instructions!
We pray to those Gurus who represent the root,
Who protect living beings with their wisdom and love like their own sons.
We pray to the Buddhas of the ten directions,
Who emanate everywhere their diverse forms by way of skillful means and compassion,
We pray to the hosts of Deities, both outer and inner,
Who increase the primal cognitions of understanding along the paths and stages,
We pray to the hosts of Bodhisattvas who are Vidyadharas,
Who bestow magical powers, blessings, capacities, and siddhis,
We pray to the hosts of Dakinis, both mothers and sisters,
Who cleanse and purify extremes and obscurations, both external and internal,
And we pray to the hosts of the oath-bound Guardians,
That having liberated us from the subjects and objects of Samsara (that represent) not understanding,
Please grant us the blessing that the primal cognitions of Self-Awareness will arise within us!
[Then, as for the Lineage Prayer in particular:]
[I. The Direct Mind-to-Mind Transmission of the Buddhas]
I. As for the Gurus who became manifest as the Trikaya, [10] namely,

(1) Kuntu Zangpo (Kun tu bzang-po) who was the Dharmakaya (from the very beginning and who abided perpetually) in the state of supreme bliss,
(2) Shenlha Odkar (gShen-lha 'od-dkar) who was the Sambhogakaya possessing all the marks and characteristics,
(3) Gyalwa Shenrab (rGyal-ba gshen-rab) who was the Shen (Nirmanakaya) possessing the four-fold great compassion,
(4) Tsadmed Oddan (Tshad-med 'od-ldan), the Shen who guided all living beings,
(5) Trulshen Nangdan ('Phrul-gshen snang-ldan), the Shen who was the self-arising Self-Awareness,
(6) Barnang Khujyuk (Bar-snang khu-byug), the father who was the visible manifestation of Means and Wisdom,
(7) Zangza Ringtsun (bZang-bza' ring-btsun), the mother who produced both Samsara and Nirvana,

(8) Chimed Tsugphud ('Chi-med gtsug-phud), the chief among
those who taught the subduing of the demons, and
(9) Sangwa Dupa (gSang-ba 'dus-pa), the owner of the profound
Mantras,

We pray to these nine who represent the Mind Transmission of the
Victorious Ones
That, having been liberated from the subjects and the objects of
Samsara (arising from) not understanding,
May the blessings arise (in our mind-streams) for the primal cognition
of Self-Awareness! [11]
[II. The Oral Transmission of the Siddhas]
IIA. As for the Gurus who have totally transcended conceptions of the
Natural State, 12] namely,

(1) Yongsu Dagpa (Yongs su dag-pa) who was without partiality
or one-sidedness like the sky,
(2) Lubon Banam (kLu-bon ba-nam) who was without moving
like the dimension of space,
(3) Tride Zambu (Khri-sde zam-bu) who was in the state that is
free of all elaborations,
(4) Banam Kyolpo (Ba-nam skyol-po) who abided within a vast
expanse of space without thoughts, and
(5) Trishod Gyalwa (Khri-shod rgyal-ba) who had definitively
decided upon what should be known,

We pray to these five Shenpos who subdued (and disciplined) all living
beings
That, having been liberated from the subjects and the objects of
Samsara (arising from) not understanding,
May the blessings arise (in our mind-streams) for the primal cognition
of Self-Awareness!
IIB. As for the Gurus who penetrated directly into the essential points
of the six meanings, [13] namely,

(6) Rasang Samdrub (Ra-sangs bsam-'grub) who was
primordially pure like the sky,
(7) Darma Sherab (Dar-ma shes-rab) who was like the vast
expanse of space,
(8) Darma Bodde (Dar-ma 'bod-de) for who the Trikaya was
spontaneously perfected,
(9) Zhang-zhung Triphen (Zhang-zhung khri-'phen) who holds
(the Natural State) without loosing it,

(10) Muye Lhagyung (Mu-ye lha-rgyung) who abided in the state devoid of a root, and

(11) Mashen Legzang (rMa-gshen legs-bzang) whose pure body was without defects,

We pray to these six Bodhisattvas who were without equal (mnyam-med sems-dpa' drug)

That, having been liberated from the subjects and the objects of Samsara (arising from) not understanding,

May the blessings arise (in our mind-streams) for the primal cognition of Self-Awareness!

IIC. As for the Gurus who taught abundantly the nine instructions, [14] namely,

(12) Gyershen Taklha (Gyer-gshen stag-lha) for whom arose the Primordial State that is without birth,

(13) Rasang Yungdrung (Ra-sangs g.yung-drung gsas) in whom the Bodhichitta became manifest,

(14) Sechen Yungphen (gSas-chen Ra-sangs g.yung-'phen), for whom non-duality was present in his Mind,

(15) Gephar Dondrub (dGe-'phar don-grub) for whom manifest Buddhahood was supremely attained.

(16) Gyerpung Gephen (Gyer-spungs dge-'phen) who abided in the State single-pointedly,

(17) His son Gegyal (dGe-rgyal) who found within himself the Ultimate Truth,

(18) Zhang-zhung Namgyal (Zhang-zhung rnam-rgyal) within whom Self-Awareness became manifest,

(19) Mugyung Karpo (dMu-rgyung dkar-po) who destroyed the delusions of subject and object, and

(20) Horti Chenpo (Hor-ti chen-po), the Shen who could be very proud of his learning and realization,

We pray to these nine Siddhas who were Vidyadharas (grub-thob rig-'dzin dgu)

That, having been liberated from the subjects and the objects of Samsara (arising from) not understanding,

May the blessings arise (in our mind-streams) for the primal cognition of Self-Awareness!

IID. As for the Gurus who were the four head-ornaments of the Upadeshas (man-ngag dbu-rgyan bzhi yi bla-ma), [15] namely,

(21) Donkun Drubpa (Don-kun grub-pa) who displayed a view devoid of any root,

(22) Rasang Phengyal (Ra-sangs 'phen-rgyal) who practiced both clarity and bliss,

(23) Gurub Sega (Gu-rub gsas-dga') who continued in the conduct of equal tastes, and

(24) Dawa Gyaltsan (Tshe-spungs zla-ba rgyal-mtshan) who remained in the original condition of Reality,

We pray to these four Mahasiddas who were translators and scholars
That, having been liberated from the subjects and the objects of Samsara (arising from) not understanding,
May the blessings arise (in our mind-streams) for the primal cognition of Self-Awareness!

III. As for the Gurus who are the sources of the oral instructions and the precepts, [16] namely,

(1) Tapihritsa (Ta-pi-hri-tsa), the Nirmanakaya who was all-knowing, and

(2) Nangzher Lodpo (Gyer-spungs snang-bzher lod-po) who obtained both siddhis and prophecies,

We pray to these two kind Nirmanakayas (sprul-sku drin-can gnyis)
That, having been liberated from the subjects and the objects of Samsara (arising from) not understanding,
May the blessings arise (in our mind-streams) for the primal cognition of Self-Awareness!

IV. As for the Gurus who possessed the signs of realization, [17] namely,

(1) Gyalzik Sechung (Pha-ba rgyal-gzigs gsas-chung), who liberated both material appearances and the configurations of his physical body,

(2) Mushen Tsoge (dMu-gshen tso-ge) who remained without interruption in the Clear Light,

(3) Gyershen Tsotang (Gyer-gshen tso-stangs, v. dzo-btang) who displayed magical apparitions and signs of realization,

(4) Shodtram Chenpo (dMu Shod-khram chen-po) for whom whatever he saw, it appeared as an illusion,

(5) Mu Gyalwa Lodro (dMu rgyal-ba blo-gros) who definitively decided upon Samsara and Nirvana, and

(6) Pongyal Tsanpo (dPon-rgyal btsan-po, v. dpon-chen) who went forth in order to subdue the noxious Rakshasa spirits,

We pray to the six (masters) who were holy and worthy
That, having been liberated from the subjects and the objects of
Samsara (arising from) not understanding,
May the blessings arise (in our mind-streams) for the primal cognition
of Self-Awareness!
V. As for the Gurus who possessed experiences in meditation, [18]
namely,

(1) Guge Lodan (Gu-ge shes-rab blo-ldan) for whom great bliss
arose in his mind-stream,
(2) Puhrang Kunga (Pu-hrang kun-dga') who obtained liberation
by the strength of his purifications,
(3) Naljor Sechok (rNal-'byor gsas-mchog) who continued
naturally in the source of power,
(4) Khyungjyid Muthur (Khyung-byid mu-thur) who possessed
power, energy, and strength,
(5) Dewa Ringmo (rTsi bde-ba ring-mo) who obtained the siddhi
of being decided upon one thing (the Natural State),
(6) Togmed Zhigpo (Rong rtog-med zhig-po) for whom arose the
sun of Self-Awareness,

We pray to these six Ascetics possessing understanding
That, having been liberated from the subjects and the objects of
Samsara (arising from) not understanding,
May the blessings arise (in our mind-streams) for the primal cognition
of Self-Awareness!
VI. As for the Gurus who possess virtuous qualities without
partialities, [19] namely,

(1) Lhundrub Muthur (Lhun-grub mu-thur) who liberated his
contemplation from the Generation Process and the Perfection
Process,
(2) Shengyal Lhatse (gShen-rgyal lha-rtse) who abides in the state
of the Great Perfection (alone),
(3) Lhagom Karpo (Lom-thing lha-sgom dkar-po) in whom the
secret conduct became manifest,
(4) Ngodrub Gyaltsan (dNgos-grub rgyal-mtshan ring-mo) for
whom arose understanding and pride in his realization,
(5) Orgom Kundul ('Or-sgom kun-'dul) who possessed the
dharani (mantras) whithout forgetting,

We pray to these five Mahasiddhas
That, having been liberated from the subjects and the objects of Samsara (arising from) not understanding,
May the blessings arise (in our mind-streams) for the primal cognition of Self-Awareness!

VII. As for the Gurus who possessed the sources of the oral transmission, [20] namely,

(1) Pangla Namshen (sPang-la nam-gshen), the Shen who was the guide of living beings,

(2) Lung-gom Togmed (Lung-sgom rtog-med) the Shen in whom Self-Awareness was self-arisen,

(3) Nyelgom Trulmed (sNyel-bsgom 'khrul-med) who definitively decided upon the source of delusion,

(4) Nyag-gom Shertsul (Nyag-sgom sher-tshul) who became clear and removed the darkness of obscurations and coverings,

(5) Uri Sodgyal (U-ri bsod-rgyal) who increased the teaching that possessed worth,

(6) Gonya Sodye (sGo-snya bsod-ye, v. bsod-nams ye-shes) for whom actions were spontaneously perfected,

(7) Gyagom Yerin (rGya-bsgom ye-rin, v. ye-shes rin-chen) for whom arose the Primordial State of Kuntu Zangpo,

(8) Jyatang Chednyi (Bya-btang mched-gnyis) who became systematically established in the Natural State, and

(9) Lenton Sonam (glen-ston bsod-nams rgyal-mtshan) (the two brothers) who possessed the real meaning of learning and righteousness, [21]

We pray to these nine Gurus who possessed the source
That, having been liberated from the subjects and the objects of Samsara (arising from) not understanding,
May the blessings arise (in our mind-streams) for the primal cognition of Self-Awareness!

VIII. As for the Gurus who teach the Mantras and the Mind of the Oral Transmissions, [22] namely,

(1) Kangtsa Tradar (rKang-rtsa bkra-dar), the Shen in whom Self-Awareness was self-arisen,

(2) Monlam Lodro (sMon-lam blo-gros) who obtained liberation through purification and understanding,

(3) Khetsun Treton (mKhas-btsun tre-ston) who uttered the roar of Bon without partialities,

(4) Paton Nyipal (sPa-ston nyi-dpal) who accomplished the Nature of the Mantras and the Mind, and
(5) Gyagom Tanzang (rGya-bsgom bstan-bzang), the Shen of the mantras of Meri,

We pray to these five Gurus of the Mantras and the Mind
That, having been liberated from the subjects and the objects of Samsara (arising from) not understanding,
May the blessings arise (in our mind-streams) for the primal cognition of Self-Awareness!
IX. As for the Gurus who accomplished the benefit of living beings without any partialities ('gro don phyogs-med mdzad-pa'i bla-ma), [23] namely,

(1) Yangton Chenpo (Yang-ston chen-po Shes-rab rgyal-mtshan), the Nirmanakaya who was all-knowing,
(2) Dampa Bumje (Dam-pa 'bum-rje 'od) who possessed completely the nectar of the Pitakas,
(3) Tashi Gyaltsan (kLu-brag-pa bkra-shis rgyal-mtshan) who commanded the Maras and the Rakshasas demons as his servants,
(4) Togdan Wonpo (rTogs-ldan dbon-po ye-shes rgyal-mtshan) who liberated everyone without partialities,
(5) Gyaltsan Rinchen (Yang-ston rgyal-mtshan rin-chen) who loved living beings like they were his sons,
(6) Chigchod Dadshe (gCig-chod dad-shes, v. dad-pa shes-rab) who liberated the grasping at a self into its original condition,
(7) Khetsun Druchen Gyalwa (mkhas-btsun Bru-chen rgyal-ba g.yung-drung) who became the sovereign of the teachings, [24]
(8) Ripa Sherlo (La-stod ri-pa sher-blo, v. shes-rab blo-gros), the Shen who taught the Tantras and the Agamas, and
(9) Yeshe Rinchen (Ye-shes rin-chen), the Shen who could be proud of his learning and realization,

We pray to these nine Vidyadharas of the Precepts Transmission (bka' brgyud rig-'dzin dgu)
That, having been liberated from the subjects and the objects of Samsara (arising from) not understanding,
May the blessings arise (in our mind-streams) for the primal cognition of Self-Awareness!
X. As for the Gurus who liberate into the Primordial State that is like space, [25] namely,

(1) Lama Gyaltsan (Rang-grol bla-ma rgyal-mtshan), the Shen who guided living beings,
(2) Sonam Lodro (Kar-tsa bsod-nams blo-gros) for whom Self-Awareness became manifest,
(3) Tan-gyal Zangpo (sPa-ston bstan-rgyal bzang-po) who knew the three times without any obscurations,
(4) Tsultrim Gyaltsan (Tshul-khrims rgyal-mtshan) who became systematically established in the Natural State,
(5) Ngari Sogyal (mNga'-ri bsod-rgyal) who possessed the nectar of the Upadeshas,
(6) Tashi Gyaltsan (bKra-shis rgyal-mtshan) who understood Samsara and Nirvana as having a single taste,
(7) Paljyor Lhundrub, the Shen of the profound path of Meri, and
(8) Kunga Gyaltsan (Kun-dga' rgyal-mtshan) who was the guide of living beings for the four initiations,

We pray to these eight who are the sovereigns of the profound path
That, having been liberated from the subjects and the objects of Samsara (arising from) not understanding,
May the blessings arise (in our mind-streams) for the primal cognition of Self-Awareness!
XI. As for the Gurus who have love in their hearts and benefit others, [26] namely,

(1) Tsandan Ripa (mTshan-ldan ri-pa) who possessed the profound nectar and
(2) Namgyal Kara (rNam-rgyal ka-ra) who increased his wisdom and love without any self,

We pray to these two protectors of living beings
That, having been liberated from the subjects and the objects of Samsara (arising from) not understanding,
May the blessings arise (in our mind-streams) for the primal cognition of Self-Awareness!
XII. As for the Gurus who hold the transmissions of the Precepts and the Upadeshas, [27] namely,

(1) Togdan Sherpal (rTogs-ldan sher-dpal) who taught abundantly and was free of extremes,
(2) Namkha Odzer (Nam-mkha' 'od-zer) in whom the Mother and Son encountered each other in the vast expanse of space, and
(3) Yungdrung Yeshe (g.Yung-drung ye-shes) who instantly understood inseparability,

We pray to these three Gurus possessing the Lineages of Transmission
That, having been liberated from the subjects and the objects of
Samsara (arising from) not understanding,
May the blessings arise (in our mind-streams) for the primal cognition
of Self-Awareness!

XIII. As for the Gurus who demonstrated manifestly the profound
meaning, [28] namely,

(1) Rinchen Lodro who increased virtuous qualities impartially,
(2) Sherab Gyaltsan (mNyam-med Shes-rab rgyal-mtshan) who
possessed empowerments and the samaya commitments, [29]
(3) Rinchen Gyaltsan whose view and conduct was completely
pure,
(4) Namkha Yeshe (Nam-mkha' ye-shes), the Shen who was the
source of the supreme and the ordinary (siddhis),
(5) Kunzang Gyaltshan (Kun-bzang rgyal-mtshan) who increased
wisdom and love and spread the scriptures and reasoning,
(6) Rinchen Gyaltsan (Rin-chen rgyal-mtshan) who possessed a
style of behaviour that was inexhaustible,
(7) Tsultrim Gyaltsan (Tshul-khrims rgyal-mtshan) who saw his
own face as the Nature of Mind, and
(8) Sonam Yeshe (bSod-nams ye-shes) who accomplished the
illumination of the teachings,

We pray to these eight who are the unequalled life-force of the
teachings
That, having been liberated from the subjects and the objects of
Samsara (arising from) not understanding,
May the blessings arise (in our mind-streams) for the primal cognition
of Self-Awareness!

XIV. As for the Gurus who hold the teachings of the Three Trainings,
[30] namely,

(1) Sonam Yungdrung (bSod-nams g.yung-drung) who attained
excellence in the Three Trainings,
(2) Shetsu Drungmu (She-tsu drung-mu) who delivered enemies
and obstacles into the teachings,
(3) Sherab Odzer (Shes-rab 'od-zer) who possessed the real
meaning of learning and righteousness,
(4) Yungdrung Gyaltsan (g.Yung-drung rgyal-mtshan) increased
the teaching of the Three Vows,
(5) Sherab Lodro (Shes-rab blo-gros) grasped the life-force of the
teachings of the Three Trainings,

(6) Sherab Odzer (Shes-rab 'od-zer) for whom Self-Awareness
became manifest, and

(7) Tsugphud Odzer (gTsug-phud 'od-zer) with whom the Three
Trainings were completely pure,

We pray to these seven who are the Lords of the Three Trainings
That, having been liberated from the subjects and the objects of
Samsara (arising from) not understanding,
May the blessings arise (in our mind-streams) for the primal cognition
of Self-Awareness!

XV. As for the Gurus who hold the Treasury of the Nine Vehicles, [31]
namely,

(1) Yungdrung Tsultrim (g.Yung-drung tshul-khrims) who
increased his wisdom and love without an ego,

(2) Rinchen Odzer (Rin-chen 'od-zer) in whom the profound
meaning became manifest,

(3) Rinchen Lhundrub (Rin-chen lhun-grub) whose many desires
were spontaneously perfected,

(4) Sherab Tenzin (Shes-rab bstan-'dzin) in whom arose the
Primordial State of Kuntu Zangpo,

(5) Sherab Wangyal (shes-rab dbang-rgyal) who definitively
decided upon the source of delusion,

(6) Yungdrung Wanggyal (g.Yung-drung dbang-rgyal) who
systematically established himself in the Natural State,

(7) Phuntsok Namgyal (Phun-tshogs rnam-rgyal) within who
arose Self-Awareness, and

(8) Sherab Gonggyal (Shes-rab dgongs-rgyal) who knew all the
three times without any obscurations,

We pray to these eight who possessed confidence without equal
That, having been liberated from the subjects and the objects of
Samsara (arising from) not understanding,
May the blessings arise (in our mind-streams) for the primal cognition
of Self-Awareness!

XVI. As for the Gurus who exhibited nakedly the Natural State, [32]
namely,

(1) Nyima Tenzin (Nyi-ma bstan-'dzin) who taught the
inseparability of Dimension and Primordial Awareness, [33]

(2) Chyoglay Namgyal (Phyogs-las rnam-rgyal) who liberated
both Samsara and Nirvana into their own original condition,

(3) Sherab Yungdrung (Shes-rab g.yung-drung) with whom there
arose abundantly the teaching of living beings,
(4) Sangye Tenzin (Sangs-rgyas bstan-'dzin) who was liberated
instantly into the Natural State,
(5) Tenzin Tsultrim (bsTan-'dzin tshul-khrims) who understood
the Nature that is free of any root,
(6) Phuntsok Lodro (Phun-tshogs blo-gros) for whom visions
arose (continuously as ornaments (of the mind), and
(7) Gyalwa Lodro (rGyal-ba blo-gros) who liberated both Samsara
and Nirvana into the Mind,

We pray to these seven who liberated everything without partialities
That, having been liberated from the subjects and the objects of
Samsara (arising from) not understanding,
May the blessings arise (in our mind-streams) for the primal cognition
of Self-Awareness!

XVII. As for the Gurus who had pride in their realization of the Secrets
and the Mind, [34] namely,

(1) Tanpa Lodro (bsTan-pa blo-gros) who was the treasury of the
Primordial State of the great vast expanse of space,
(2) Nyima Wanggyal (Nyi-ma dbang-rgyal) who liberated his
skandhas and his elements into the Deity,
(3) Shes-rab blo-gros in whom Primordial Awareness became
manifest, and
(4) Our Root Guru Sangye Tenzin (rtsa-ba'i bla-ma Sangs-rgyas
bstan-'dzin), the Nirmanakaya who subdued living beings,
[35]

We pray to these four supreme individuals who are most worthy
That, having been liberated from the subjects and the objects of
Samsara (arising from) not understanding,
May the blessings arise (in our mind-streams) for the primal cognition
of Self-Awareness!

XVII. As for the Gurus for whom there arise in their mind-streams a
sure and certain knowledge [36]
That the Kunzhi is completely pure from the very beginning and free
of any root,
That Rigpa is inherently clear free of all obscurations, coverings, and
defects,
And that the sounds, the lights, and the rays are indeed self-
manifestations of the energy of Mind,
We pray to these three: the Mother, the Son, and the Energy,

That, having been liberated from the subjects and the objects of Samsara (arising from) not understanding,
May the blessings arise (in our mind-streams) for the primal cognition of Self-Awareness!

[As an auxiliary for producing pure visions on the part of future generations, these prayers to the successive (masters) of the Special Experiential Transmission, was composed by me, the Shenpo of Dru, Gyalwa Yungdrung. May well-being increase everywhere!] [37]

The Guardian Goddess Yeshe Walmo, a form of the Great Goddess Sidpa Gyalmo, the special protector of the Dzogchen Teachings.

The Invocations to the Guardian Deity Nyipangse and to the Goddess Menmo

Introduction

The Dharma Protectors

Just as is the case with the Buddhist tradition of Tibet, the Bonpo tradition possesses its own guardian deities who defend and protect its teachings and its practitioners. They are variously known as Guardians (srung-ma), Guardians of the Precepts (bka'-srung), Protectors of the Precepts (bka'-skyong), Protectors of the Teachings (bstan-skyong), Protectors of Bon (bon-skyong), and so on. This latter term, *bon-skyong*, corresponds to the Tibetan Buddhist term *chos-skyong* (Skt. Dharmapala). [1]

These guardian deities are traditionally divided into those who are supra-mundane, being of a transcendent and a spiritual nature ('jig-rten las 'das-pa'i srung-ma), and those who are worldly guardians ('jig-rten-pa'i srung-ma). The former represent emanations in the form of fierce guardian deities that derive from some enlightened spiritual being, such as, for example, the Bonpo guardian goddess Sidpa Gyalmo (srid-pa rgyal-mo). She, in fact, is said to be a direct emanation of the Great Goddess of Wisdom, the Prajnaparamita, Sherab Jyamma (shes-rab byams-ma). However, in her function, Sidpa Gyalmo is clearly a Guardian rather than a Meditation Deity or Yidam (yi-dam lha). Moreover, in many ways, Sidpa Gyalmo corresponds in her two-armed form to the guardian goddess Ekajati in the Nyingmapa system and in her four-armed form riding upon a mule to Paldan

Lhamo (dpal-ldan lha-mo) among the New Tantra Schools. In this latter form, she and her mule may be black or red in color. [2]

On the other hand, those guardian deities, who are not emanations of some enlightened spiritual being, but rather represent worldly gods and spirits still caught up in Samsara, the beginningless cycle of death and rebirth, were at some point in time subdued or otherwise converted to the Dharma, whether termed in Tibetan *Chos* or *Bon*, by the Buddha or some other spiritually realized master like Guru Padmasambhava or the Mahasiddha Gyerpungpa. These gods and spirits were not then and are not now enlightened beings beyond karma and Samsara, no matter how great their knowledge, their life spans, or their powers. They are still Samsaric beings and, in the ultimate sense, they are still ignorant and will come to experience the results of their karma at a future time. But due to the influence of some enlightened being in the past, usually in the form of a magical contest, the god or the spirit in question was defeated by superior magical power and thereby subdued, tamed, and converted ('dul-ba) to the higher spiritual and ethical principles of the Dharma. This was necessary because of the great pride that usually characterizes such entities. Thus, the defeated god or demon, in fear for its life, was bound by fierce oaths to henceforth protect the spiritual teachings of the Dharma and its practitioners. Therefore, such spirit entities become known as "oath-bound" (dam-can) and during the course of the ritual invocations of the Guardians, they are reminded of the vows that they once made long ago in the presence of the Buddha or some other great spiritual being. The teachings imparted to the gods and spirits by these powerful enlightened beings were called "spiritual" or Dharma (chos, bon) because the goal was transcendent, that is to say, the ultimate goal of liberation from Samsara. The aim was not merely obtaining some worldly power or benefit, such as prosperity or wealth or sensual pleasure, and so on. However, the truth of the Dharma was not always self-evident and so it must, on occasion, be demonstrated forcefully to these gods and spirits by way of an impressive display of magical power because otherwise they might continue to wreak their capricious wills and their vengeance upon a hapless humanity.

In this way, most of the old pagan gods and shamanic spirits of Tibet have now been incorporated into the pantheon, or spiritual hierarchy, of the higher religion as Dharmapalas, the Guardians of the Teachings. Such guardian deities are invoked and propitiated with elaborate puja offerings, characteristically at an evening service held at nearly every Tibetan temple and monastery, whether Buddhist or

Bonpo. It is felt that the powers of the spirits increase with the setting of the sun and the onset of night, because these spirits belong to the twilight world of the collective unconscious psyche of humanity. During these nocturnal rites of the Guardians, often conducted in a special chapel called a "protector house" (mgon-khang), the presence of the chief Guardians and their respective entourages of attendant spirits are invoked with the sounding of the large shamanic drum known as a ngachen (rnga-chen) and the deep-voiced sonorous chanting of the congregation of Lamas. Before invoking the presence of these hosts of spirits from out of the twilight spaces, the chief officiating Lama at the ceremony is careful in his meditation and visualization to transform his visible appearance into that of a powerful spiritual being commanding the respect of the spirits, such as Mahakala or Hayagriva in the Buddhist tradition or, perhaps in the case of Bon, into Namjom (rNam-'joms) or Nampar Gyalwa (rNampar rgyal-ba). These latter figures represent wrathful emanations of Tonpa Shenrab who subdued countless hosts of dangerous spirits in prehistoric times. Moreover, the officiating Lama and the congregation must also be careful to provide on an altar the appropriate puja offerings for the Guardians, who otherwise they might take offense at being treated disrespectfully and cause disturbances. Included among the offerings there must be present meat and wine. It should be remembered that when one invites powerful and influential guests into one's home, it is only proper to offer them hospitality.

Also present on the altar are elaborately sculptured figures known as tormas or sacrificial cakes (gtor-ma, Skt. bali). Due to the influence of both Yungdrung Bon and Indian Buddhism upon the Tibetans in general, the practice of blood sacrifice or "the red offering" (dmar-mchod), has largely been abandoned centuries ago in most Tibetan communities. Nevertheless, such practices continue among various tribal peoples related to the Tibetans, such as the Gurungs, the Tamangs, and so on, living in the Himalayas of Nepal. [3] In both Buddhist and Bonpo practice, the blood offering of a living victim has been replaced by the substitute offering of sacrificial cakes usually made from roasted barley flour (rtsam-pa) and often painted bright red with vegetable dye. These red tormas clearly represent the flesh and blood sacrifices once offered to these same gods and spirits in ancient times. In contrast, the non-blood offerings made to peaceful deities are generally white in color, as for example, the tormas offered to the Nagas. These tormas, whether peaceful or wrathful in nature, may frequently be very elaborate sculptures, decorated with butter and other items. They may also be made of other materials such as wood, metal, or clay, and yet they will continue to represent offerings of flesh and blood.

In ancient times and even occasionally today, those spirits that belong to the lower astral and etheric planes of existence, the dimensions of existence known in Buddhist terms as the Kamadhatu or Desire World, often draw their sustenance and nourishment from the prana or life-force (srog) liberated into the immediate atmosphere from the warm blood of a living sacrificial victim. Many of these lower spirits or astral entities, from most ancient times, had become addicted to blood and could be seen, it is said, by the clairvoyant eye as gathering about the altar like a flock of vultures and feeding upon the sacrifices like a type of etheric vampire. And so, one must be careful to propitiate them in the proper manner, at least symbolically.

Both the Buddhist and the Bonpo traditions are rich in stories where an enlightened spiritual being, by virtue of his or her superior spiritual knowledge and magical power, subdues in fierce magical combat some local god or spirit who had been oppressing human beings or otherwise causing mischief and harm in the world. In the Buddhist tradition, such stories are usually told about Shakyamuni Buddha, Vajrapani, and Padmasambhava. In the Bonpo tradition, it is usually Tonpa Shenrab who fulfills this function. For example, in the Sutra of the *gZi-brjid*, the story is told of how Tonpa Shenrab transformed himself in to the wrathful aspect of Nampar Gyalwa, who resembles the Buddhist Vajrapani in both form and function, in order to subdue and tame the dangerous gods and demons that have oppressed humanity and the world. [4] In this way, Tonpa Shenrab brought the old pagan religion of Central Asia, with its requisite practice of blood sacrifice, under the guidance of the higher spiritual reality represented by the Dharma of the Buddhas. [5]

Consequently, in the East the teachings and activities of these enlightened spiritual masters did not lead to suppressing entirely the old pagan religious cults. These cults continued to thrive side by side with the practice of the higher religion, as may be seen in Buddhist countries even today. Rather, these worldly indigenous cults of the old pagan gods and local nature spirits were transformed, moved up an octave or two so to speak, and harmonized with the more universal ethical perspectives and higher spiritual reality revealed by the Dharma. In this way, the cults of the old gods and the local spirits were brought into the service of the Dharma, rather than being persecuted out of existence.

Furthermore, the Dharma was not revealed to humanity by way of contact with the pagan gods and the non-human spirits because these latter were not enlightened beings beyond Samsara. In the ultimate sense, they were still ignorant and dominated by their sensual desires and passions. They still belong to Samsara and for this reason the practitioner does not go for refuge to them. They belonged to the Kamadhatu, or at best to the lower levels of the Rupadhatu in terms of Buddhist cosmology. And although Mahabrahma, the chief Creator God, and his retinues of fellow Brahmas, did not demand a cult of blood sacrifices, being too refined and too exalted in their station as Creator Gods and Old High Gods, nevertheless, even they were never enlightened beings nor were they liberated from the delusions of Samsara. But it was principally the lesser gods and the nature spirits, dwelling close to the earth and to humanity and its this-worldly concerns, who demanded such blood sacrifices from mankind in order to be propitiated and to satiate themselves on an occasional diet of blood and vital energy.

This represented a contractual arrangement between the human community in question and the Otherworld of the old gods and spirits. Blood sacrifice was the principal individual and collective religious practice for invoking and communing with these gods and spirits. This actually represented an exchange of energy between two dimensions of existence. In exchange for regularly providing these sacrifices and offerings, the gods and spirits guaranteed the timely rains, the fecundity of cattle, and the fertility of the earth with abundant harvests, as well as the good health and the prosperity generally of the human community, whether the family, the clan, or the tribe. But where these gods and spirits became irritated and angry with the human community, the very opposite occurred. But in all this ritual activity, there was no thought or concern with individual karma or with individual salvation from a future rebirth in Samsara, which is the perspective proper to the Dharma. It was the collective, not the individual that was the paramount concern. [6]

In contrast to this worldly activity, the higher spiritual reality, the Dharma, was first revealed to humanity, not by the pagan gods who are still deluded Samsaric beings, but by certain enlightened beings who transcend the world and belong to a dimension of being beyond Samsara. These Buddhas and Bodhisattvas periodically descended to earth and incarnated among humanity from these higher dimensions of existence in order to bring the knowledge of salvation, the gnosis that liberates the individual from the sorrows of bondage to Samsara. This higher spiritual perspective was precisely what was introduced among humankind in prehistoric times by Tonpa Shenrab. According to the Bon tradition, it was Tonpa Shenrab, who fulfilled this role as a Buddha in Olmo Lung-ring, or Shambhala, in ancient Central Asia, some eighteen thousand years ago. But Shenrab was only one Buddha in a long line of Buddhas who have appeared in the past and who will appear again in the future among humanity in order to stimulate and guide its spiritual evolution.

But in his own day, when Tonpa Shenrab briefly visited Kongpo in Ancient Tibet, the Tibetan people were still too primitive and too addicted to animistic practices to comprehend human conduct in terms of the higher ethical principles of the Dharma. Consequently, they were not yet ready to understand the higher spiritual teachings of the Dharma of the Buddhas. So instead of Yungdrung Bon, Tonpa Shenrab largely taught the shamanic practices of the invocations of the gods (lha gsol-ba) and the exorcism of the baleful influences of the demons and evil spirits (sel-ba). [7] It was much later that the Dharma in the form of Yungdrung Bon coming from Central Asia to the west and in the form of Buddhism coming from India to the south was introduced into Tibet. Until the advent of the Buddha Dharma, the aboriginal peoples of the Tibetan plateau were still largely animists, thoroughly under the influence of the non-human spirits (mi ma yin) and addicted to the cult of blood sacrifice originally introduced among them in Palaeolithic times by the Sinpo spirits (srin-po). An account of this situation is given in the traditional Bonpo histories. [8]

The Three Zones of the Traditional Cosmos
The gods and the spirits of the old pagan pantheon of Tibet were arrayed in three cosmic zones:

1. the upper region (steng) of the atmosphere and the heavens, which was the home of the Lha (lha) or heavenly gods,
2. the middle region (bar) above and on the surface of the earth, which was the home of the Nyen (gnyan) and the Tsen (btsan), that is, the tree and the earth spirits, and
3. the lower region ('og) or underworld beneath the earth and within the bodies of water, which were the home of the Lu (klu), the serpentine water spirits.

When this old pagan religious culture came into contact with Indian Buddhism and its rich cosmological and mythological heritage, the above three types of spirits (lha gnyan klu gsum) were seen to correspond to the Devas, Yakshas, and Nagas of Indian myth and folklore. The upper regions of the sky are inhabited by several races of celestial deities and spirits, headed the Lha, who are now more or less completely identified with the Indian Devas. They have the god Indra as their king who dwells in his sumptuous celestial palace atop the cosmic mountain Meru at the center of the world. Their characteristic color is white and they may also be seen as mounted upon thoroughbred horses and they are attired in armor as warriors carrying lances and banners. This is especially the case with the Dralha. [9] These Lha or gods the principal representatives of the White Side (dkar-phyogs) who embody the forces of light and order, the principle known as *Ye*, are engaged in a perpetual warfare against the Dud (bdud) or demons of the Dark Side (nag-phyogs) who represent the forces of darkness and chaos, the principle known as *Ngam*. [10] These black demons, the Dud, have invaded the order of the universe from outside and seek, in their animosity and perverse desires, to overthrow and destroy whatever is good, just, and orderly. They are irrevocably opposed to the Dharma. However, because they are sentient beings, within them lies the spark of enlightenment, and so they are also capable of redemption by the efforts and teachings of the Buddhas. Such was the case with the demon-sorcerer Khyabpa Lagring (bDud-rgyal khyab-pa lag-rings) who eventually became a disciple of Tonpa Shenrab. [11]

In terms of the middle region, the Nyen (gnyan) are generally considered to be tree spirits, but they can also be associated with certain rock formations in the landscape. However, chief among the races of spirits inhabiting the surface of the earth, dwelling in its rocks, cliffs, outcrops, and mountains, are the Tsen (btsan), "the mighty ones." In temperament, they are fierce, war-like, and aggressive. Normally they are seen as mounted on fine horses, clad in the helmets and armor of warriors, and hold in their hands spears and other weapons of war. Their wild rides through deserted and remote landscapes at night can be terrifying. The characteristic color of themselves and their horses is red, so that they are often associated with red rocks, cliffs, soils, and mountains. When they are disturbed by the careless and polluting actions of human beings in the wilderness and in the mountains, they also can cause many diseases, especially cancers.

Finally there are the Nagas or Lu (klu) who dwell in subterranean and sub-aqueous abodes. In particular, they are shape-shifters and most frequently appear to human eyes in serpent form or as half-serpent half-human. But they can appear in many other fabulous guises, having, for example, different animal heads. Their characteristic color is green or sometimes blue. Although generally well disposed toward humanity, and even, it is said, capable, on occasion, of interbreeding with humans, they can become disturbed and offended, even themselves injured, by humanity's polluting the lakes and rivers and destroying the wilderness lands and forests. When their natural habitats are disturbed or destroyed, in retaliation they can cause many kinds of illness to appear among humanity, especially diseases of the skin, such as boils, rashes, cancers, and leprosy. Much of Tibetan shamanic healing deals with propitiating the Lu since they control the wealth and fertility of nature, as well as bringing the rains, and equally with healing the Lu themselves in relation to the damage done to the natural environment due to pollution caused by the careless activities of humanity.

However, it is not only the Buddhas who can subdue these fierce gods and demons and other restless spirits who permeate the natural environment, but also certain realized masters known as great adepts or Mahasiddhas. Gyerpungpa was such a Mahasiddha and it was he who subdued the powerful god Nyipangse and converted him into a guardian and protector of Bon. [12]

Meaning of the Name Nyipangse

The guardian deity Nyipangse (nyi-pang-sad) should be reckoned among the Lha or celestial gods, as indicated by his white color and his residence upon the southwest corner of the Meru mountain at the center of the world. In the invocation translated below, he is given many names and titles, reflecting his multiplicity of forms and functions. But when he is called *btsan gyi rgyal-po*, which could in Tibetan be understood as "king of the Tsen," it appears likely that *btsan gyi* should be understood as an adjective meaning "mighty," that is, "the mighty king." Moreover, he is white, not red in color and he wears no armor as do the Tsen spirits. In addition, his solar, celestial, and atmospheric associations are suggested by his other titles. So his manifestation is not that of a Tsen spirit.

The name Nyipangse (nyi-pang-sad) itself appears to come from the Zhang-zhung language, which is in some ways related to the Tibetan language, but which is much more closely related to the Kinauri language spoken in the Western Himalayas. According to the glossary of the Zhang-zhung language published some years ago by Lopon Tenzin Namdak, [13] *sad* means "god" (Tib. lha) and *nyi* is from *nyi-ri*, "sun" (Tib. nyi-ma). The syllable *pang* is uncertain in its meaning. The significance of the name suggests that Nyipangse might have been some sort of solar deity, perhaps related to the Iranian Mithra. However, his other two principal names, Dapangse (zla-pangsad), "the moon god" (Tib. zla-ba, moon), and Zhapangse (gzha'-pangsad), "the rainbow god" (Tib. gzha', rainbow), also suggest his general celestial and radiant character, which need not be exclusively solar.

The Guardian Deity Tsangpa Karpo

It appears that Nyipangse came to be incorporated into the pantheon of Tibetan Buddhism as the guardian deity Tsangpa Karpo (Tshangs-pa dkar-po), "the white Brahma." In the Rite of Invocation composed by the great Nyammed Sherab Gyaltsan (1356-1415), Nyipangse and Tsangpa Karpo are specifically identified. [14] The traditional iconography in the Hindu tradition depicts Brahma as a bearded Brahman priest, with two arms, having four faces with which he recites the Four Vedas, and as riding on a hamsa or white swan. However, in the Buddhist context, Brahma is not a single Creator God, but a generic term for a whole series of deities of a higher spiritual status. In general, the Devas inhabit the sensual paradises of the Desire World or Kamadhatu, which are somewhat physical or etheric in nature, whereas the Brahmas inhabit the various attenuated mental planes of the Form World or Rupadhatu. They are, therefore, beyond the domain of the sensual desires and are in that sense "pure". But despite the Tibetan name Tsangpa (tshangs-pa), used to translate the Sanskrit name Brahma, "the pure one," in Tibet there exist no Hindu characteristics in the cult of this guardian deity that would indicate an Indian origin. On the contrary, he shows all the marks of an old Tibetan deity of the oath-bound class (dam-can).

According to Nebetsky-Wojkowitz, [15] who presents several versions of his iconography and sadhana, in his Sogdak (srog-bdag) form he is called Tsangpa Karpo, "the white Brahma," and as a Lha, he is called Tsangpa Dunggi Thortsugchan (Tshangs-pa dung gi thor-tshug-can), "the Brahma having plaited hair with a white conch shell in it." [16] Riding upon a white horse, he carries a crystal sword and a white battle lance. Tsangpa Karpo Dunggi Thortsugchan represents the peaceful form of Tsangpa, but as Setrabchan (bse'i khrab-can), wearing a cuirass of leather, he represents the fierce aspect of the deity. [17] Elsewhere it is said that Setrabchan was emanated from a ray of light issuing from the heart of Tsangpa Karpo. Called a Yaksha, this great wild Tsen Setrabchan is red in color, wears a helmet and cuirass, and carries the weapons of war. Furthermore, the founder of Menri monastery, Sherab Gyaltsan, invited the Gyalpo Setrabchan to be one of the six patron guardian deities of his new monastery. [18] Other deities like Lijyin Hara (Li byin ha-ra) are also said to be emanations of Tsangpa Karpo.

Tsangpa Karpo is important, as well, in the Gesar Epic where he is called Gyalpo Tsangpa (rGyal-po tshangs-pa) and functions there as a god of healing. Also, according to the Hindu tradition, the origin of medical science is attributed to Brahma. There exist as well many sadhanas for Tsangpa Karpo where he is called Lhai Gingchen Tsangpa Karpo (Lha'i ging-chen tshangs-pa dkar-po). [19] But despite Tsangpa and Nyipangse frequently being called a king, this does not mean that either deity is thought of as a member of the class of spirits known as Gyalpo (rgyal-po). These latter, according to Tibetan tradition, are usually said to be the souls of Lamas and warriors, possessing a great deal of capacity, who have died a violent death and return to wreck havoc upon humanity in the spirit of vengeance for the wrongs done to them in their previous lifetimes.

There exist several versions of the myth of origin of Lhachen Tsangpa Karpo, who is now ranked as one of the main protectors of the Gandan Phodrang Government of Tibet. [20] Some versions assert that he became oath-bound (dam-can) during the reign of the first Buddhist king of Tibet Songtsan Gampo (627-649). But even before that event, he had been an attendant at the court of the king of the gods Indra Shatakratu who lived in his celestial palace of Vijayanti on the summit of the cosmic mountain Meru. Later he was subdued and oath-bound to protect the Buddhist teachings by the mighty wrathful Bodhisattva Vajrapani, who is also known as Guhyapati (gsang-bdag), the Master of Secrets. And still later he was subdued again and transformed into a Protector of the Dharma by Hayagriva, a wrathful emanation of Avalokiteshvara, who embodies the Speech function of the Buddha. [21] And at an even later date, the Tibetan king Songtsan Gampo, who is also regarded as an emanation of Avalokiteshvara, when he had completed the erecting of the temple of Tradruk Lhakhang, [22] charged Tsangpa Karpo to become the guardian of the external and internal repositories of Body, Speech, and Mind to be found in the temple, that is to say, the Buddha images, the holy scriptures, and the stupas. Thereupon Tsangpa Karpo became known as the personal protector of this king. [23] And during his war in 632 against the emperor T'ai Tsung of the T'ang dynasty of China, the Tibetan king appointed Tsangpa Karpo as chief over the war gods of Tibet in order to take on in battle the gods of the enemy Chinese.

Later, when Padmasambhava had come to Tibet, while the king Trisong Detsan was reigning over that country (754-797), the precious

Lotus-born Guru again subdued and oath-bound the god, obtaining his solemn oath to protect the Dharma for as long as the present kalpa endures. Padmasambhava placed the deity in the Mandala of the playful blood-drinking Herukas. [24] According to the *sBa-bzhed*, with the help and advice of Padmasambhava, the king of Tibet thereupon entrusted to Tsangpa Karpo the protection of the Namdak Trimkhang Ling temple at Samye monastery. [25]

Then in the time of the great Fifth Dalai Lama, [26] Lhachen Tsangpa Karpo was entrusted with the protection of the newly installed Gandan Phodrang Government of Tibet. And since that time, this guardian deity has been consulted through his oracles whenever decisions on matters of state of critical importance need to be made. The principal oracle for Tsangpa Karpo in Tibet is at Lamo monastery, near the village of Lamochok, about sixty kilometers east of Lhasa on the road to Kham. For this reason Tsangpa is also called Lamo Jyangchub Choggi Chokyong after the residence of his chief oracle. [27] This oracle was held in high esteem and, in the same way as Nechung, he has been frequently consulted by the Tibetan government in the past. Several other oracles were also possessed by wrathful forms of Tsangpa Karpo— one at Nyethang, southwest of Lhasa, and another at Nyima Thang. [28]

Similarity to the Buddhist Guardian Pehar

According to Nebesky-Wojkowitz, [29] in several texts this two-armed Tsangpa Karpo is clearly identified with Pehar. And true enough, Nyipangse has a number of traits in common with this important Buddhist guardian deity known as Pehar. Both of them are addressed as Shelgying Karpo (shel 'gying dkar-po), "the mighty white crystal," both are white in color, and both are called Sogdak (srog-bdag), "owner of the life-force." The precise meaning of the name Pehar, which is not Tibetan, is uncertain, but because he has been called in some texts by the epithet *Bi-har rgyal-po*, the name might have originally been Sanskrit. [30] The Bonpos sometimes also address Pehar as a Guardian of Zhang-zhung (Zhang-zhung gi srung-ma) and assert that among the gods or Lha he is known as Tsangpa Dunggi Thortsugchan (Tshangs-pa dung gi thor-tshugs-can).

There exist a number of stories that explain how Pehar came to Tibet. Some sources say that he originated in Zahor in Northern India, [31] but that he subsequently transferred himself to the meditation school at Bhata Hor in the country of the Uighur Turks in Central Asia. While residing at Bhata Hor, he exercised his powers on behalf of the Uighurs and their kingdom as their tutelary deity, whom they also knew as Pholha Namtheb Karpo and as Namlha Karpo. [132] Again, according to the history of Tibet by the Fifth Dalai Lama, there were five royal demons ('dre rgyal) who existed in ancient times in the Uighur country: one that was white, another that was black, and a third one that was yellow. Only the white deity was brought to Tibet, where he became known as *Pe-dkar*. [33]

According to other sources cited by Nebesky-Wojkowitz, in the first kalpa or cycle of time, Pehar resided in the heights of the blue sky. At that time he ruled over the Thirty-Three Gods and was known as Tsangpa Gunggi Thortsugchan. [34] In the middle kalpa, he came to dwell in the country of Hor, that is, among the Uighur Turks, where he became well known as Shelgying Karpo (Shel-'gying dkar-po) and resided at the meditation school of Bhata Hor where he was venerated as a divine figure wearing a leather helmet. In the most recent kalpa, he descended upon Tibet and came to reside at Samye monastery where eventually he came to rule over all of the spirits for the whole of Tibet. In yet another source, he is said to have been the son of the deities Namgyi Karpo and Shugdan Gyalmo and was originally called Gyajyin Karpo. Then later he went to the eastern country of Hor where he became known as Namlha Karpo. And when residing at the temple of Bhata Hor, he received the name of Sogdak Karpo. [35] In the most recent kalpa, when numerous stupas had been erected at Samye monastery by the king Trisong Detsan, on the advice of Padmasambhava, the deity was invited to become the guardian of the monastery's treasures and scriptures and his residence was set up in the northeastern shrine of Pekar Ling (Pe-dkar gling).

According to the Nyingmapa tradition, after the erecting of Samye monastery by the king of Tibet, Padmasambhava decided to appoint a deity as the guardian of the treasures housed in the shrines of the monastery. At first the great Guru invited the Naga king Zurphud Ngapa, but the latter refused. [36] Then the Guru suggested that the mighty king of Tibet send his armies into the country of the Uighurs in order to bring the image of the deity Pehar back with them to Central Tibet. By means of his magic, the Guru compelled the deity to leave his abode in the north and come to settle at Samye in Tibet. Pehar mounted on to a wooden bird studded with jewels and flew south to Tibet, together with his entire retinue. Thus, the Uighurs were deprived of the power of their god and he came thereafter to reside with the Tibetans. Padmasambhava placed his vajra on the crown of Pehar's head and transformed him into a Dharma Protector, installing the image in a shrine at Samye.

Pehar remained at Samye for many centuries. But later, in the time of the great Fifth Dalai Lama (1617-1682), Pehar left Samye and took up his residence in a small Nyingmapa monastery by the name of Nechung near the great Gelugpa monastic university of Drepung. Once settled there, Pehar regularly possessed a monk from this small monastery and issued prophesies using him as a medium. Consequently, this monk became the official State Oracle of the Gendan Phodrang Government of Tibet. Nechung monastery and the State Oracle have now been relocated to Dharamsala in India, home of the Tibetan Government in exile. Nevertheless, the Lamas of the Gelugpa school generally regard Pehar as the chief of the Dharma Protectors. Some would take him to be an emanation of Amitabha Buddha and the leader of some three hundred and sixty Gyalpo spirits. [37]

The Mahasiddha Gyerpungpa

But as a guardian deity, Nyipangse is especially associated with the Dzogchen tradition of Zhang-zhung. During the times of the twenty-four Jalupas who preceded Gyerpungpa, the Zhang-zhung Nyan-gyud remained an oral tradition, having no texts whatsoever. Only with the advent of the master Tapihritsa was permission given for his disciple Gyerpungpa to set down the Dzogchen precepts in the writing system of Zhang-zhung (zhang-zhung smar-yig). While doing so, Gyerpungpa decided that he needed a special protector or guardian deity for this enterprise. Because he was a great Tantric practitioner of the meditation deity Zhang-zhung Meri, he had acquired mastery of the magical missile (btswo) by which means he could subdue the various gods and spirits of the countryside and compel them to do his will. He went to a high cliff in Northern Tibet where he performed the practice of the magical missile. These golden missiles having caused terror among the gods and demons of both heaven and earth, he brought under his power all the various races of the male spirits of existence. [38] At that time, the king of great power Nyipangse, who dwelt on the southwest corner of the summit of the Meru mountain, offered the prana or life-force of his heart to the Mahasiddha [39] and promised that henceforth he would accomplish all those deeds not yet realized by the master. In particular, he promised to be the special guardian and protector of the teachings of the Zhang-zhung Nyan-gyud. Here Nyipangse is addressed as *dBang chen gyi rgyal-po* (Skt. Mahendraraja), "the great king Indra," thus equating his power and status with that of Indra, the king of the gods himself.

In this way, Nyipangse came to be invoked as the principal Guardian of the Dzogchen Precepts, although he was subordinate to and owed allegiance to a higher spiritual power, Walchen Gekhod, the patron deity of the Zhang-zhung kingdom. The Mahasiddha Gyerpungpa, in his meditation practice, had assumed the form of Zhang-zhung Meri, a special aspect of this deity Gekhod, in order to dispatch these magical missiles that tamed and subdued the gods and demons. But whereas Nyipangse represents the particular guardian deity practice associated with the Zhang-zhung Nyan-gyud, Meri is the Yidam practice, or practice of Tantric transformation, specifically associated with the same tradition. Meri represents a specialized wrathful warrior form of Gekhod and is especially linked to the Zhang-zhung Nyan-gyud since he was the personal meditation deity and Tantric practice of the Mahasiddha Gyerpungpa himself. Among the meditation deities of the Father Tantras known as the Five Supreme Ones of the Divine Citadel, it is Gekhod who represents the Quality Aspect of enlightened awareness. [40] However, according to Lopon Tenzin Namdak, the practices of Gekhod and Meri are little performed these days among the Bonpos, having been eclipsed in popularity by Walse (dbal-gsas), Tsochok (gtso-mchog), and Phurpa as the principal practices for the Father Tantras.

The practice of dispatching magical missiles (btswo'i sgrub-pa) was the specific magical action practice associated with the sadhana of this fierce warrior god who is clad in shining golden armor. This practice formed part of the *Me-ri this-las* rites and granted realization of magical powers (mthu) and telekinetic abilities (rdzu-'phrul) to the practitioner. In turn, this method was transmitted to the leading disciples who were the successors of Gyerpungpa in both Zhang-zhung and Tibet, but precise knowledge of this magical practice was later lost to subsequent generations and its rites are no longer performed. [41]

The Iconography of Nyipangse

According to the text translated below, cited in Nebesky-Wojkowitz as the *bsTan-srung nyi-pang-sad kyi bstod bskul bka' bsgo*, [42] Nyipangse is depicted in the guise of a mighty king, mounted on a white horse marked with red spots. His skin color is white like a conch shell and he is dressed in long white robes of the finest silk. Bound up in his plaited hair is a white conch shell (dung gi thor-tshug-can), and on his head is a white turban like those worn in ancient Central Asia. A bow case and quiver hang from his belt. He brandishes a lance of white crystal to which is attached a banner of white silk. He is accompanied by a great multitude of gods and spirits. However, Nyipangse does not display any fierce (drag-po) or wrathful (khro-bo) characteristics; there appear to be no demonic attributes at all about him. Yet he has the ability to appear in innumerable forms and guises. Thus it says in the text that his emanations as gods and spirits can appear anywhere. [43]

There is here also the suggestion of a mandala pattern in his activities and manifestations, citing different forms of the deity in different countries in the five directions. [44] In the second text translated below, Nyipangse is described as having five aspects, namely, the five classes of great kings (rgyal-po chen-po sde lnga), who are powerful sovereigns with dominion over the five directions of the world. [45]

The Goddess Menmo

In the Zhang-zhung tradition, Nyipangse is associated with a goddess. According to the text translated below, after Gyerpungpa had subdued Nyipangse and converted him into a Guardian, he then similarly brought under his power all the races of the female spirits of existence. Thereupon the goddess Menmo Kumaradza (sMan-mo ku-ma-ra-dza) offered the prana of her heart to the Mahasiddha. [46] And then together, these two deities promised to accomplish all those deeds not yet realized by Gyerpungpa.

The term *sman-mo* refers to a class of ancient pre-Buddhist goddesses. They appear in the Gesar Epic as the female companions and counterparts of the Dralha warrior gods (dgra-lha, sgra-bla). The Dralha are a class of gods or spirits of the lower atmosphere, depicted as riding horses and clad in armor as warriors. They serve as the retainers of the hero Gesar. The Menmo are attired as noble ladies in silk robes.

This particular goddess, called Menmo Kumaradza in the ritual invocation translated below, is also identified as the sky goddess Namchyi Gunggyal (gnam-phyi gung-rgyal), "the Grandmother of the Sky, the Queen of Heaven." [47] As her entourage, she is accompanied by glacial mountain goddesses, slate mountain goddesses, rock cliff goddesses, alpine pasture goddesses, forest goddesses, river goddesses, lake goddesses, and island goddesses, that is, by all the feminine energies of the earth. This refers to her universal character as the Great Goddess of heaven and earth. In her role as Namchyi Gunggyal, the Queen of Heaven, she appears as the source of all medicines, bestowing these healing nectars upon the earth. [48]

Menmo is depicted in peaceful form, dressed as a Tibetan princess in white silk robes and riding upon a white female yak or dri ('bri).

The Texts and the Rituals

At the end of the Menri edition of the Zhang-zhung Nyan-gyud printed in New Delhi, there are found two short texts concerned with the cult of the two guardian deities Nyipangse and Menmo:

1. *sNyan-rgyud bka'-srung srog-bdag rgyal-po nyi-pang-sad bka'-bsgo*, [645ff], "The Invocation Rite of the King of the Owners of the Life-Force, Nyipangse, who is the (principal) Guardian of the Precepts of the Oral Transmission," and

2. *rGyal-po nyi-pang-sad dang sMan-mo gnyis kyi bskul-ba* [647ff], "The Entreaties to both the king Nyipangse and to the goddess Menmo."

The first text here presents an invocation rite (bka' bsgo) for calling the deity into one's presence and an exhortation to come to the aid of the client. At the opening of the text, homage is paid to Walchen Gekhod, the basic form of the meditation deity associated with this tradition who is, as well, the patron deity of Mount Kailas and the Zhang-zhung kingdom. [49] His principal function is the subduing of all evil spirits and demons that cause harm to living beings. Zhang-zhung Meri is a special aspect of this deity. The mystic syllable BSWO (pronounced "swo!") is an ancient invocatory interjection calling on the gods and spirits to come and be present at the rites. In the liturgical text itself, the various epithets and praises of the deity are recited first, then the deity is charged with protecting the teachings and its practitioners, averting evils, increasing abundance, and so on. The concluding long mantra actuates the presence and activity of the guardian deity. The colophon states that this text was composed at Tashi Menri monastery by the monk-practitioner Sherab Gyaltsan (1356-1415), the great Bonpo scholar and monastic reformer who founded Tashi Menri in the year 1405. [50]

The second liturgical text, also presumably by Sherab Gyaltsan, provides the text of the entreaties (bskul-ba) or prayers to the guardian deity and his consort that are meant to accompany the puja offerings. The descriptions of the tormas offered to the deities are presented in the instructions. The torma for Nyipangse has a square base and sits on a square stand also made of tsampa or roasted barley flour. On top of this is a generalized representation of his castle that is painted red in color. This is surrounded by four smaller tormas in the four directions that represent his retinue of four deities. The central torma is ornamented with flames sculptured from butter. The torma of Menmo is roughly shaped like a human breast, surmounted by a miniature torma (shog-bu), and surrounded by eight smaller tormas that represent her retinue of eight attendant goddesses. Chang (wine or beer) and incense are offered during the puja ceremony for the Guardians and at the conclusion of the recitation of the liturgy, the chang is poured onto the earth as a libation. The ritual invocation and liturgy for the puja offerings are translated below.

Translation of the Texts

1. The Rite of Propitiation for Nyipangse

Homage to the great flaming Walchen Gekhod who subdues all those spirit entities that cause harm!

[This utterance represents the Invocation Rite of Sogdak Gyalpo Nyipangse, "the King of the Owners of the Life-Force," who is the principal Guardian of the Precepts for the Oral Transmission Teachings from Zhang-zhung.]

BSWO!

Never forgetful and never negligent, may you never forget your previous vows of commitment!

Never neglecting them and never going beyond them, may you never forsake your vows and the teachings!

You are the loyal attendant of Walchen Gekhod!

O Werro Nyipangse, Guardian of the Precepts that have been revealed,

O King of the Dralha warrior gods, most powerful among the Sogdak owners of life,

You are the man in white, white like the conch shell, and bearing the lance.

Your body is attired in a cloak of white silk, lhubs-se-lhub!

At your waist is a tiger-sword in a leopard-skin scabbard, tra-la-la!

On your head, your hair is plaited with a conch shell, dems-se-dem!

And with your hand, you hoist aloft a banner of white silk, cha-ra-ra!

As your mount, you ride a white stallion marked with spots of red, drings-se-dring!

And within your retinue, there are one thousand troops of lesser kings, ubs-se-ub!

You are well known by name to the Bonpos of Zhang-zhung,

Where you are called the mighty white crystal sun god, Shelgying Karpo Nyipangse.

You are well known by name to the kings of Trom,

Where you are called the king of the world, Sogdak Sidpe Gyalpo.

You are well known by name to the followers of Yungdrung Bon in Tazik,
Where you are also called the mighty white crystal, Shelgying Karpo.
You are well known by name to the Dharma practitioners of India,
Where you are called the Brahma with a white conch shell in his plaited hair, Dungi Thortsugchan.
You are well known by name to the kings of China,
Where you are called the king Dapangse.
And you are well known by name to the Pugyal kings of Tibet,
Where you are called the great Kyahrang Chenpo.
Your many emanations as gods and demons emanate everywhere;
Your many companions, who are the eight classes of spirits, accompany you everywhere;
Your many magics diffuse everywhere as many different kinds of magical displays.
And in terms of your dwelling, you dwell on the summit of the Meru mountain.
In your movements, you move everywhere above and below, in all the cardinal and the intermediate directions.
In your actions, you accomplish the guarding of the Precepts of the Bon teachings.
In your accomplishments, you realize various different activities on behalf of the excellent Shen practitioners.
By way of your emanations, together with your retinues who are also your emanations,
Without neglecting your previous vows.
We pray that you may come here like lightening with your magical feet.
We pray that you may come here to us like a mother with thoughts of loving kindness.
We pray that you may come here like a friend with thoughts of longing.
Please enjoy— enjoy this abundance adorned with all delightful sense qualities!
Please accept— accept this powerful torma representing the command! Please protect— protect the teachings of the Yungdrung Bon!
Please realize— realize the thoughts of us excellent Shen practitioners!
Please praise— praise the exalted status of the Bon in the entire three thousand-fold universe!

Please avert— avert all hindrances and disharmonious conditions for us!

Please accomplish— accomplish friendship and companionship for us with all the attendant white virtues!

Please increase—increase the capacity and the felicity of our retinues and of our possessions!

Please bestow—bestow followers and long life and wealth and prosperity and success upon us!

Please summon—summon in haste all enemies who defile the teachings!

Please liberate—liberate quickly those enemies who have transgressed their vows!

O most powerful king among the Guardians of the Teachings, you who are never forgetful,

Do not neglect the commands and vows of Walchen Gekhod!

Without neglecting or forsaking previous fervent vows and past teachings,

May you accomplish the realization of those deeds with which you have been charged!

TRI TRI RATSA SA MA RA YO DZAH/

BSWO OM A THUN NYE LO YO THUN SPUNGS-SO THAD-DO/

A MA MA HA LA RAM DZA HRIG NAN/

E TRI NRI SROG LA THUM RIL KHA-THUN THAD-DO THUN BHYO! /

[This is the Rite of Invocation for the Protector of the Precepts Nyipangse. Having relied upon the incantations found in many scriptures of the Secret Mantras, it was composed in the hermitage of Tashi Menri by the monk Shen-gyi Drangsong Sherab Gyaltsan. Virtue!]

2. The Puja Offerings for Nyipangse and the Goddess

Here is contained the Entreaties to the King Nyipangse and to the Goddess Menmo.

[As for the puja offering for the Guardians of the Precepts, one should offer the Ganapuja and the tormas in the general way done for the Protectors of Bon according to the practice found in the scriptures. The torma for Nyipangse, the king of the Guardians of the Precepts of the Oral Transmission Lineage, is consecrated in the usual way. With respect to making the torma for the king Nyipangse, in its lower part it is square and the top is square with ornaments. And it is surrounded by four smaller square tormas in the four directions. Then, on top of the second torma in the shape of a woman's breast, which is offered to the

Goddess, is a single round shobu or small torma. And this is surrounded by eight horns, or else, by eight white tormas. Having presenting the puja offering to the Protectors of Bon, one recites the following invocation:]

Kyai!

Among the powerful loyal attendants of the Sugatas and the Shenrabs,
Those who have promised to act as Guardians of the Oral Transmission Lineage,
Is the mighty king Werro Nyipangse:
You are the king of all the eight classes of gods and demons.
The appearance of your body displays various different magical apparitions.
To the magically powerful sovereigns holding dominion over the world,
The five classes of great kings,
Nyipangse and Dapangse,
Zhapangse and Werro Gyalpo,
Namkha Gyalpo and Yacho Gyalpo,
And Gyalpo Chenpo Tsugphudchan,
Together with the retinues of Gyachen Nyipangse,
By the blessings of the Sugatas and of the Gurus,
And the contemplation done by us Shen practitioners,
By the blessings of the powers of Truth,
We present this torma of delightful sensual qualities.
Please accept this torma that is commanded!
Guard well the teachings of the Yungdrung Bon
And be the friends and helpers of us Shen practitioners!
Tong-gyung Thuchen of Zhangzhung,
Lachen Dranpa Namkha, both father and son,
As well as Gurub Nangzher Lodpo,
And the other Gurus of the Vidyadhara Lineage,
And in the presence of our Root Guru:
In accordance with whatever pledges and promises have been made,
By way of guarding the Precepts of the Oral Transmission Bon,
Become the friends and helpers of us Shen practitioners!
Guard well the teachings of the Yungdrung Bon!
And do not cause troubles, arguments, or obstacles!
Without neglecting the commands or your promises,
Please accept this torma possessing delightful sensual qualities!
Having thus propitiated your desires,
May you have thoughts of loving kindness towards us,

And in accordance with your previous promises,
May you zealously accomplish the task of guarding the teachings!
A OM HUM/
WER-RO RATSA SAD MIN BHALINGTA LA KHAHI KHAHI/
SAD MIN SPUNGS-SO THIM THEM YE SWAHA! /

3. Puja Offerings for the Goddess

[Then one should present the Goddess Menmo with offerings of the three white things and the three sweet things, as well as nectars and medicines, and then chant this invocation:]
Kyai!
O Goddess of the Sky, the Mother Namchyi Gunggyal,
Your retinues consist the glacier mountain goddesses, the slate mountain goddesses,
The cliff goddesses, the alpine pasture goddesses, the forest goddesses,
The river goddesses, the lake goddesses, and the island goddesses.
To you, O Queen of the Dralha, Mother and Sky Goddess,
Our Goddess who guards the Precepts of the Zhang-zhung Bon,
And to the hosts of goddesses who accomplish the guarding of the Precepts of the Oral Transmission Lineage,
This white torma and shobu, as well as the consecrated foods,
Yogurt and butter, the white things and the sweet things— we offer as fresh samples;
And we make burnt offerings with incense.
Having propitiated all your desires,
In accordance with your previous promises,
Guard well the teachings of the Yungdrung Bon!
By way of guarding the Precepts of the Oral Transmission Bon,
Become the friends and helpers of us Shen practitioners!
Do not neglect the commands and your promises
And accomplish the realization of those deeds with which you have been charged!
BSWO MA MA SANG SANG/
SING SING BHALINGTA KHAKHA KHAHI! /
[These prayers and offerings to Nyipangse, the King of the Guardians of the Precepts, should be retained in one's mind.]

The Biography of Lopon Tenzin Namdak

Birth and Tengchen Monastery in Khyungpo District

The Venerable Yongdzin Lopon Tenzin Namdak Rinpoche [1] is an accomplished scholar and practitioner of the Bon tradition, and in particular Dzogchen and the Ma Gyud or Mother Tantra, and the most learned and foremost expert on Bon outside of Tibet. He has also been in the forefront of the reviving of Bonpo religious culture among the Tibetans living in exile from their homeland in India and Nepal since the 1960s, where he  has established Bonpo communities and monastic educational institutions.

Lopon Rinpoche was born in 1926 in Khyungpo Karru (khyung-po dkar-ru) in Khyungpo district of Kham province in Eastern Tibet. His father was a farmer with his farm in Chamdo district, where he possessed many yaks, sheep, horses, goats , dogs, and other animals. At the age of seven in 1933, [2] he entered Tengchen monastery (steng-chen dgon-pa), which was the local monastic establishment in the same district, [3] where his uncle Kalzang Tsultrim (bsKal-bzang tshul-khrims) was the Umdze (om-mdzad) or chant leader among the monks. Tengchen monastery belonged to the tradition of Old Bon (bon rnying-ma), otherwise known as Yungdrung Bon (g.yung-drung bon) in contrast to New Bon (bon gsar-ma), [4] and had close affiliations with Menri monastery and Yungdrung Ling monastery in Central Tibet. This monastery had the only school in the district at the time and here young Lopon Rinpoche was taught to read and write, thus beginning his extensive education. Here also he took his novice monk vows at the age of fourteen.

Yungdrung Ling Monastery

In 1941 when he was fifteen years old, Lopon Rinpoche traveled with his uncle to Yungdrung Ling (g.yung-drung gling), one of the two leading Bonpo monasteries in Central Tibet. [5] Coming from a family famous for its many artists, he was largely engaged here from 1941 to 1943 in helping to execute a series of wall paintings or frescos in the new temple at this monastery. The Lopon had been trained as an artist and painter since the age of eleven and this training in drawing and painting has served him throughout his entire life. [6]

Pilgrimage to Nepal

In 1944 at the age of seventeen, he went on pilgrimage with two other monks to Nepal, first visiting Solu-Khumbu and then Kathmandu, where he meditated at the holy hill of Swayambhunath at the western end of the valley, which had once been graced and blessed by the presence of the Buddha Tonpa Shenrab himself. [7] Lopon Rinpoche returned to Tibet by way of Pokhara and Mustang, the later also being an area in Nepal of Bonpo settlement. From there he went on pilgrimage to the Mt. Kailas region of West Tibet, which lies at the heart of the old Zhang-zhung kingdom.

Studies with Gang-ru Rinpoche

In 1945, Lopon Rinpoche returned to Yungdrung Ling to begin his studies in philosophy (mtshan-nyid). From 1945 to 1950, he lived more or less a hermit's existence with his tutor and master Gang-ru Tsultrim Gyaltsan Rinpoche (sGang-ru Tshul-khrims rgyal-mtshan). This master was an exceedingly learned Lama in the Bonpo tradition and for some eighteen years he had been the Lopon at Yungdrung Ling monastery. After retirement from this monastery, Gang-ru Rinpoche lived in a meditation cave at the Namtso (gnam-mtsho) lake in Northern Tibet. The young Lopon Rinpoche lived with this master for four years in this cave. With him, he studied the same subjects as taught at Yungdrung Ling, namely, grammar (sgra), poetics (snyan-ngag), monastic discipline ('dul-ba), cosmology (mdzod-phug), and the stages of the path to enlightenment (sa-lam).

Geshe Studies at Menri Monastery

Following his master's advice, in 1950 he went to Menri monastery [8] in Tsang province, near Sakya monastery in Central Tibet, in order to complete his studies in preparation for the Geshe (dge-bshes) degree examination, the Tibetan equivalent of a Doctor of Philosophy. Here he underwent a full course of scholastic studies. At this time, his principal teacher was Lopon Sangye Tenzin (slob-dpon lJong-ldong Sangs-rgyas bstan-'dzin). At Menri, he studied Tibetan and Sanskrit grammar, poetics, astrology and medicine, as well as chanting and ritual practices. His advanced studies included Prajnaparamita, Madhyamaka philosophy, Abhidharma, Vinaya, Tantra, and Dzogchen. In 1953 at the relative young age of twenty-seven, he passed his oral examinations and was awarded the Geshe degree from Menri monastery. In the same year, due to his outstanding learning and scholarship, he was elected to serve in the position of Lopon or head teacher for the academic course of studies at the college of the monastery, succeeding his own master Lopon Sangye Tenzin. From 1953 until 1957, he remained in this position only to retire in that year as the conflict between the native Tibetans and the encroaching Chinese Communists increased in Central Tibet.

Escape from Tibet

Until 1960, he remained at Se-zhig monastery on the Dang-ra lake in Northern Tibet. March 10, 1959, saw the Lhasa uprising against the Communist Chinese tyrannical rule over Tibet. Many of the most famous living Lamas of Tibet, including H.H. the Dalai Lama and H.H. the Gyalwa Karmapa, were forced to flee from their homeland and a flood of Tibetan refugees entered India and Nepal. In 1960 after his long retreat, Lopon Rinpoche also sought to flee, seeking refuge in India, but on the way south he was shot by Chinese soldiers and incarcerated in a Chinese military prison for nearly ten months, enduring great hardships. Finally, he was able to make an escape, leading a small party of monks. They traveled by night and hid during the day for some twenty-two days until and finding their way to safety in Nepal by way of the small principality of Lo Mustang.

Three Year Residence in England

Coming finally to Kathmandu, Lopon Rinpoche stayed for some months at Najyin (gna'-sbyin) monastery. In 1961, while residing in Kathmandu, Lopon Rinpoche met and was befriended by the celebrated English Tibetologist, Dr. David Snellgrove of London University, who invited him to come to London, along with Lopon Sangye Tenzin and Geshe Samten Karmay. Thus, receiving a Rockefeller Foundation Grant in the Visiting Scholar Program, the Lopon came first to the University of London and then he resided for a time at Cambridge University. Toward the end of his stay in England, he made a retreat at a Benedictine monastery on the Isle of Wight.

During this time, his collaboration with Professor Snellgrove resulted in the publication of *The Nine Ways of Bon* (Oxford University Press, London 1967), which contains translated extracts from the famous *gZi-brjid*, the most extensive hagiography of the Buddha Tonpa Shenrab. This was the first scholarly study of the Bonpo tradition from original sources to be made in a Western language. [9] Lopon Rinpoche remained in England for some three years from 1961 to 1964.

Return to India and Publishing Bonpo Texts in New Delhi

In 1964, the Lopon returned to India from England and subsequently was employed as a Tibetan expert by the American Library of Congress in New Delhi, where, under the PL 480 Program, the American Government purchased all the different books published in India in some fourteen different languages including Tibetan. The project of purchasing Tibetan texts was under the supervision of the celebrated Tibetologist E. Eugene Smith, from the University of Washington, a famous center for Tibetan studies in the United States. It was Mr. Smith who was initially responsible for encouraging Tibetan Lamas, including the Lopon, to republish Tibetan texts by way of photo offset in India. This program insured that these precious texts would not be lost to Tibet or the world.

While in New Delhi, the Lopon was also befriended by Dr. Lokesh Chandra of the International Academy of Indian Culture and their collaboration led to the publication by way of photo offset of a text made from a block-print at Menri, being an anthology or collection of texts from the Zhang-zhung snyan-rgyud. [10] Published in New Delhi in 1968, the book was entitled *History and Doctrine of Bon-po Nispanna-Yoga*. [11]

Establishing the Bonpo Settlement at Dolanji

Among the nearly one hundred thousand Tibetan refugees who had fled the Chinese Communist occupation of Tibet, a small number belonged to the Bonpo tradition. [12] Escaping from Tsang province, the monks of Menri monastery, which had been totally destroyed by the Red Guards during the Cultural Revolution inspired by Chairman Mao Tse Tung, these Bonpo refugees found themselves in the Kulu-Manali distrinct of Himachal Pradesh state in northwestern India. Impoverished, they were forced to secure a livelihood as road workers. Among their number was Sherab Lodro (Shes-rab blo-gros), the thirty-second Abbot of Menri monastery (1935-1963). Finding the road work tiring and exhausting in an alien climate, many of the monks died or suffered from serious illness, as did the Abbot himself.

Thus, Lopon Tenzin Namdak, when he returned to India in 1964, undertook the task of raising funds and finding land in order to establish a Bonpo settlement in Northern India. From 1964 to 1967, the Lopon worked desperately to keep the Bonpo people and their culture alive in exile. In 1967, with the financial help of the Catholic Relief Service he purchased a piece of undeveloped forest land at Dolanji, near Solan in Himachal Pradesh, and began to establish a settlement there. The first Bonpo families who settled there initially lived in tents on the cleared land. Later the new monastery developed nearby.

In 1967 the settlement was formally registered with the Indian Government under the name of the Tibetan Bonpo Foundation. About seventy families transferred there from Manali and each received a house and a small piece of land, the size depending on the number of people in the family in question. The Tibetan Bonpo Foundation possessed its own constitution and administration, with the Abbot of Menri acting as president. The new settlement at Dolanji was given the name Thobgyal Sarpa (thob-rgyal gsar-pa) after the village of Thobgyal in Tsang province, which was located near the original site of Menri monastery. However, most of the Tibetans in the new settlement came from the Mt. Kailas region and from Upper Tsang in the west and from Hor, Kongpo, Derge, Amdo, and Gyarong in the east.

After the death of Sherab Lodro, the thirty-second Abbot of Menri (1935-1963), in 1963, the Abbot of Yungdrung Ling, the second most important monastery for the Bonpos in Central Tibet, became the spiritual head of the Bonpo community in exile in India. He came to Dolanji in 1967, together with a group of monks, and founded a new monastic community, overseeing the erection of small houses and a small prayer chapel for religious services. In 1969, the Abbot of Yungdrung Ling arranged the ceremony to find a successor to the deceased Abbot of Menri to be chosen by lot. The names were put into a vase and while prayers to the Bonpo deities were being chanted, the vase was churned until a name fell out. The selection of the office fell to Jongdong Sangye Tendzin (lJong-ldong Sangs-rgyas bstan-'dzin, 1928-1977), who thus became the thirty-third Abbot of Tashi Menri monastery. At that time, Sangye Tenzin was working at the University of Oslo, Norway, in collaboration with the celebrated Tibetologist Per Kvaerne. For the rest of the year, he and the Abbot of Yungdrung Ling worked together on the monastery project. Following the death of the Abbot, Sangye Tendzin assumed the spiritual leadership of the Bonpos in exile. More houses were erected, as well as a library, and an Abbot's residence (bla-brang) was constructed. Monastic life was organizes around the ordinances of the Vinaya ('dul-ba). The foundation for a main temple was laid in 1969 and completed in 1978. This temple was given the name Pal Shenten Menri Ling (dpal gshen bstan sman-ri gling). The whole complex was designated as the Bonpo Monastic Centre and it formed part of the Tibetan Bonpo Foundation. At the time, this was the only Bonpo monastery in India. [13]

Visit to Munich

The Lopon made a second visit to Europe in 1969, when at the invitation of Professor Helmut Hoffmann of the University of Munich, he was a visiting scholar at the University of Munich, contributing to the monumental Tibetan-German-English dictionary being compiled there, and yet to be published. The Lopon resided for seven months in Munich.

Establishing a Lama's College at Dolanji

From 1970 to 1979 Lopon Rinpoche continued teaching and writing while residing at the Bonpo Monastic Centre, and in addition, he was much engaged in the publishing in New Delhi of a large number of important Bonpo texts. From 1967, when the first monks came to Dolanji, the teaching was largely done by Lopon Sangye Tenzin, the former teaching master at Menri in Tibet, assisted by his successor, Lopon Tenzin Namdak, the founder of the settlement at Dolanji. Due to various difficulties, especially the lack of the basic canonical books, the teaching was only partial and consisted mainly of training the young monks in the practices of the Dzogchen tradition, especially the *Zhang-zhung-snyan-rgyud*, which was considered by both Lopons to be of prime importance. One year later, after a protracted illness, when

Sangye Tenzin died in 1977, Lopon Tenzin Namdak was assigned the full responsibility for the education of the younger generation of monks. By 1978, a sufficient number of important Bonpo texts had been published, many having been borrowed from the collection housed at Samling monastery in Dolpo, Nepal, and reprinted in New Delhi, so that classes could be organized around them as a curriculum. Moreover, the premises for use as classrooms were now available. Thus, a Lama's College or Shedra (bshad-grwa) was established in 1978, organized under the guidance of Lopon Rinpoche, who served as one of the two professors at the college. The official name of this institution was Yungdrung Bon Shedrub Lobnyer Dude (g.yung-drung bon bshad-sgrub slob gnyer 'dus-sde). In that year the full training in Bonpo academic studies began and the first class of monks graduated in 1986. [14]

The Abbot of Menri becomes Head of the Bonpo School

In 1978, Lopon Rinpoche visited H.H. the Dalai Lama, head of the Tibetan Government in exile at Dharamsla in order to inform him of the purpose of establishing the Bonpo settlement at Dolanji and its Lama's College or Dialectics School, with its nine year program of Geshe studies. Moreover, he requested the official recognition by the Tibetan Government in exile in Dharamsala of Menri Trizin Rinpoche, the Abbot of Menri monastery, as the head of the Bonpo school among Tibetans. In that same year, he conducted funerary and post-mortem rites following the death of his own teacher Sangye Tenzin. The present throne-holder or thirty-fourth Abbot of Menri is H.H. Lungtog Tenpai Nyima (sKyabs-rje lung-rtogs bstan-pa'i nyi-ma dpal bzang-po), who resides at Dolanji, but who has visited the West on a number of occasions.

Namkhai Norbu Rinpoche Visit to Dolanji

In 1978, Namkhai Norbu Rinpoche, together with a group of his Italian students came to visit Dolanji and, because of his wide non-sectarian interest in Dzogchen, he requested from the Lopon the initiation for Zhang-zhung Meri, the Yidam or meditation deity practice closely associated with the *Zhang-zhung snyan-rgyud* and which had been the personal Tantric practice of Gyerpungpa himself. It is traditional to receive this empowerment before enter into the practice of Dzogchen according to the Zhang-zhung tradition. [15] Years later, when the

Lopon visited Merigar, the retreat center of Norbu Rinpoche in the hills of Tuscany north of Rome, he gave the complete Lung or scriptural authorization to Norbu Rinpoche and the latter's students in the Dzogchen Community.

The Dialectics School and Academic Teaching at Dolanji

From 1976 to 1986, Lopon Rinpoche educated the young monks at Dolanji and himself wrote several texts, including some that are used in the Dialectics School. In 1986 Geshe degrees were awarded to the first six young monks to complete the nine year training at Dolanji. For three years Lopon Sangye Tenzin to to a group of about fifteen monks the Dzogchen teachings oif the Zhang-zhung snyan-rgyud and when he had completed this first cycle of teaching, he was requested to teach it again to the same group. But in the middle of this second cycle he became seriously ill and Lopon Tenzin Namdak took over the burden of teaching. Lopon Sangye Tenzin died in 1977 and had requested that the money left over from his estate after his death be spent on the dialectics school. With his departure this left as teachers Lopon Tenzin Namdak and Geshe Yungdrung Langyal. Lopon Rinpoche continued to teach Dzogchen. Geshe Yungdrung Langyal was a Gesge Lharampa in both the Bonpo and the Gelugpa traditions, having studied at Drepung, and he was the principal teacher for the philosophical studies, focusing on Madhyamaka and logic, required for the Geshe degree, teaching some twelve students.

The purpose of this new Lama's College at Dolanji was to preserve the tradition of education in philosophy (mtshan-nyid) first established and developed at Yeru Wensakha, where philosophical analysis and logic were applied to the understanding of the *mDo sngags sems gsum*, that is to say, the teachings of Sutra, Tantra, and Dzogchen. At Tashi Menri in Tibet, the monks studied the five scriptural systems (mdo gzhung lnga) in the philosophy college, but all of the instruction in Tantra and Dzogchen was done is a more private context with individual masters. The five scriptures, actually five collections of texts, are:

1. tshad-ma – pramana or logic and epistemology;
2. phar-phyin – Prajnaparamita or the Perfection of Wisdom Sutras;
3. dbu-ma – Madhyamaka philosophy;
4. mdzod-phug – Abhidharma or cosmology; and

5. 'dul-ba – Vinaya or monastic discipline.

However, at the revived Menri monastery at Dolanji, students also study Tantra and Dzogchen in the college, as well as the five above-mentioned scriptural systems that pertain to the Sutra level of teaching. Also included in the course of studies are the secular sciences (rig-gnas), such as grammar, poetics, astrology, medicine, and so on. [16] The college has a nine-year program of studies that prepare the student for the Geshe degree examination. The first group of young monks completed the course in 1986.

First Return Visit to Tibet

In the same year of 1968, Lopon Rinpoche made a return visit to Tibet to visit the site of Menri monastery and other important Bonpo monasteries, seeking to inspire the few remaining monks who were living under the Chinese occupation. He also traveled to Eastern Tibet and visit Luphug (klu-phug) in Hor district where he met Ragshi Togdan Rinpoche with who he exchanged important empowerments and where he ordained about seventy monks. Then he proceeded to Patsang (spa-tshang) monastery where he met Khabo Togdan Rinpoche from who he received the scriptural authorization (lung) of the *Mi nub mtshan mdo*.

In his native district of Khyungpo, he visited Karleg (dkar-legs) monastery where he conferred the Matri initiation [17] on the local people. At Ritsedruk (ri rtse drug) monastery, he inaugurated a dialetics school, teaching for sixteen days on Bon and the Vinaya and ordained about one hundred monks. He was at Yungdrung Palri monastery for a few days, where upon request he performed *Byang-bu* (a kind of Phowa or transference of consciousness) for people who had died previously and also ordained about forty monks. Then he went to Kodgon monastery and taught the text of the *Theg-rim* (the successive vehicles to enlightenment according to the Central Treasures System) for about twenty days. He also gave long life empowerments and ordained about twenty monks. He then went to Ritro (ri-khrod) monastery for sixteen days where he gave the scriptural authorization for the *Zhang-zhung snyan-rgyud*, as well as teaching on Bon and the Vinaya. Here he also conferred vows upon about eighty monks and gave the *rNam-dag padma klong-yangs* initiation to the local people. He enthroned Sherab Gelek (Shes-rab dge-legs) as the new Abbot of Tengchen monastery and offered donations for the restoration of the monastery, which was at that time in a sorry state of disrepair. These repairs and restorations continue today under the direction of the Abbot.

Subsequently, he was reunited with his mother for the first time after forty-five years. He then returned to Lhasa and flew to Changdu in China in order to visit temples and the holy mountain of Langchen Gyingri. Then he proceeded to Amdo Shar-khog where he visited many monasteries, giving initiations and teachings and also visited Sertso or the Golden Lake. At Amdo Ngawa (nga-ba), he made offerings and prayers before the stupa (gdung-'bum) of his deceased disciple Tanpa Rabgye, lineage holder and former head of Nangzhik (snang-zhig), the largest Bonpo monastery in Tibet, which at that time had over five hundred monks in residence. [18] He offered tea and money to all of them, as well as advice and encouragement to the older monks on running the monastery. By way of Lhasa, he returned by air to Kathmandu.

Land for a Monastery in Nepal: Triten Norbutse

Once in Nepal, he donated all the remaining money he had collected in Tibet and elsewhere to acquiring a small piece of land at the foot of Nagarjun hill to the west of the famous hill of Swayambhu at the far end of the Kathmandu valley, in order to build the future monastery of Triten Norbutse (khri-brten nor-bu-rtse). The monastery was formally founded in 1987 and one of his former students from Dolanji, Geshe Nyima Wangyal, was put in charge of the project. Later the Geshe became the first Khenpo or Abbot of the new monastery. In 1988 Lopon Rinpoche contracted jaundice, but continued his regular teaching schedule after first moving into the small building erected on the land. [19]

The Visit of H.H. the Dalai Lama to Dolanji

Unique to the Bonpo monastic tradition and the education with which its provides its monks is the debating of the view of Dzogchen in relati0on to Madhyamaka and other Buddhist philosophies. Unlike the Nyingmapa tradition, which generally transmitted Dzogchen in the context of secret meditation instructions conferred in private between master and disciple, the Bonpos developed a system of logic and debate specifically related to the Dzogchen teachings and thereby, in a certain sense, brought Dzogchen out of the closet into the philosophical market place of the discussion of ideas. This has elicited some criticism from Lamas belonging to other Tibetan schools.

However, in 1988, H.H. the Dalai Lama, himself also well versed in Dzogchen and a practitioner of it, visited the Dialectics School at Dolanji and was quite pleased with the fact that the Bonpo monks use debate and logic as a method of studying Dzogchen, especially in relation to other philosophical systems. With much delight and enthusiasm, His Holiness observed the monks debating various philosophical points of the Dzogchen view. [20]

Visits to the West

In 1989, Lopon Tenzin Namdak Rinpoche, made his third visit to the West, this time to England, America, and Italy, at the invitation of the Dzogchen Communities of Namkhai Norbu Rinpoche in those countries. During the course of several months, March through August, at Conway, Massachusetts, at Santa Rosa and at San Francisco in California, and at Coos Bay, Oregon, Lopon Rinpoche presented to interested Western students the Dzogchen teachings according to the Bonpo tradition of the *A-khrid* and the *Zhang-zhung snyan-rgyud*. While in Los Angeles, the Healing Light Center generously paid the hospital costs for a badly needed operation to extract six gall-stones. Thereafter Lopon Rinpoche recovered completely and was subsequently able to visit Italy, both Rome and Merigar, the retreat center of Namkhai Norbu Rinpoche in Tuscany, before returning to Nepal.

Again the Lopon was invited to the West in March and April by students of the Dzogchen Community, first to Bischofshofen in Austria and then to Rome and Merigar in Italy and to South Devon in England. Thereafter the Lopon taught for the first time in Amsterdam in the Netherlands. At this time, he was accompanied by Geshe Nyima Wangyal. After his return to Nepal, in August a small group of English students met with the Lopon at Triten Norbutse where every morning for two hours he presented an exegetical commentary on a Dzogchen text composed by the famous Shardza Rinpoche (1859-1933) [21] known as the *Kun-bzang snying-thig*. The edited transcripts of this teaching resulted in the publication in 1993 of *Heart Drops of Dharmakaya*. [22] In October he came to New York City at the invitation of H.H. the Dalai Lama to attend the Kalachakra initiation and to give a lecture on the Nature of Mind as the representative of the Bonpo tradition of Tibet. For this lecture, the Lopon had previously composed a paper while teaching in South Devon entitled "The Condensed Meaning of an Explanation of the Teachings of Yungdrung Bon," which was published in time for the presentation before the actual Kalachakra initiation. [23] He taught briefly in New York City and Amherst, Massachusetts. After a tour of the American Southwest and various American Indian reservations, he taught on Dzogchen at Coos Bay, Oregon in November. The transcripts of these teachings were later in 1992 published and privately circulated by the Bonpo Translation Project as *Bonpo Dzogchen Teachings*. [24]

Visits to Dolanji and Tibet

In 1992, he returned from Nepal to Dolanji to attend the Geshe examinations and give the initiation for the Ma Gyud, or Bonpo Mother Tantra, the most extensive of all Bonpo Tantric initiations, requiring seven days to complete the cycle. At this time, the Lopon, also enthroned the first Abbot of Triten Norbutse in the presence of H.H.Menri Trizin, the current Abbot of Menri at Dolanji.

That summer, Lopon Rinpoche again visited Tibet, going on pilgrimage of the Lhasa area, and then proceeding to the Nag-chu region of Kham or Eastern Tibet where he gave many teachings and initiations. At Lungkar (lung-dkar) monastery in Hor district he gave the Mawe Senge (smra-ba'i seng-ge) initiation, the Bonpo form of Manjushri, together with monastic vows to about seventy monks. He made a return visit to Tengchen monastery in his native district of Khyungpo, which had been rebuilt since his previous visit in 1986. He remained at the monastery for a time, giving the Mawe Senge initiation and teaching the Vinaya to the monks. He visited adjacent regions and then his mother once again. At Yungdrung Palri monastery he did the *Byang-bu* ritual for the deceased and conferred higher vows on eight ordained monks. At Ako Gonpa (a-ko dgon) monastery he taught the text of the *Theg-rim*, as well as Tantra and Zhine meditation for several days. He also visited other sites in the Khyungpo region. At Tromtsang (khrom-tshang) monastery he gave lay-vows (dge-gnyen) and initiations to a large group of people. Therafter he returned to Lhasa, where he purchased a small piece of land in order to build a reception house for the Bonpos living in the city where they could meet and assemble for religious practices. [25]

Inauguration the Dialectics School at Triten Norbutse

In 1994, Lopon Rinpoche traveled again to Lhasa and Nag-chu, but conditions had changed in China and he was not able to give any teachings or initiations. When he returned to Triten Norbutse monastery in Kathmandu, he performed the consecration (rab-gnas) of the new Lhakhang or temple at the monastery. The event was also attended by H.H. Menri Trizin from Dolanji and the latter officially inaugurated the Dialectics School and Meditation Group at the monastery.

At the Dialectics School, each week one monk was subjected to an exhaustive and thorough examination by Lopon Rinpoche and all the other monks enrolled in the Geshe degree program. Each monk in turn posed questions to the examinee, even the youngest monks take their turns at asking questions. It is not usual for such an oral examination to last five to six hours. In the course of one year each monk in the program is tested two or three times in this manner. Upon successful completion of the nine-year Geshe program, the monks are awarded the distinguished Geshe degree by the representative of H.H. the Dalai Lama during the course of the graduation ceremony.

In addition to the Geshe Degree Program, Lopon Rinpoche provided personal guidance and daily meditation instruction to a small group of advanced practitioners who focus their study and practice on Dzogchen. Lopon Rinpoche also oversaw the monastic education of a small group of orphaned boys who receive pre-Geshe training and instruction, which also includes training in debating.

In the fall of 1994, Lopon Rinpoche inaugurated the nine year program of Geshe studies at Triten Norbutse, inclucing six years of the study of Sutra, with the focus on Madhyamaka philosophy, two years study of Tantra, and one year study of Dzogchen. Also included are debating, astrology, medicine, Tibetan grammar, calligraphy, drawing of mandalas and stupas, rituals and liturgies, and so on. [26]

In early 1994, there were only twenty monks in residence at Triten Norbutse, but since the inception of the Dialectic School, the monastic population had increased dramatically in a matter of months. Currently there are over one hundred monks in residence and new monks arrive at Triten Norbutse at times on a daily basis. Most come directly from Tibet, but some also from Dolanji in India and some from the border regions of Nepal, including Dolpo and Mustang. Also in recent years, a number of Bonpo nuns have fled Tibet and come to the monastery in hope of receiving teachings from the Lopon and other senior monks.

Since the Cultural Revolution in China and Tibet in the 1960s, the availability of Bonpo teachings in Tibet has become quite limited. Currently, monks can only receive teachings at the Sutra level because in general there are no qualified teachers available to give the higher level teachings of Tantra and Dzogchen. The Bonpo education currently available in Tibet focuses upon the preliminary practices, zhine meditation, and the one hundred day Tummo (or psychic heat) retreat. As a result, in order to receive a complete education in the Bonpo tradition, monks and nuns must leave Tibet in order to obtain these teachings from Lopon Rinpoche. The primary purpose in the Lopon's establishing of the Dialectics School is to train Bonpo monks in exile so that they can eventually bring the the Bonpo teachings back to Tibet. [27]

Further Visits to the West

In 1995, Lopon Rinpoche toured the Netherlands, Austria, and Germany in Europe in order to teach Dzogchen from the Bonpo tradition, and then traveled to the United States where he taught the Dzogchen text of *The Twenty-Ones Nails* (gzer-bu nyer-gcig) at the Ligmincha Institute established by his former student from Dolanji, Geshe Tenzin Wangyal Rinpoche. [28] He also taught in several other American cities. In 1997 he traveled to Italy and France in order to teach Dzogchen. In 1998 he again traveled to Austria, Germany, France, the Netherlands, Denmark, and the USA again at the invitation of Tenzin Wangyal Rinpoche. Since this time the Lopon has been regularly teaching retreats in France each spring or summer where the Association Yungdrung Bon was set up by his students to facilitate his work in the West and in particular Europe. In 2001 this process led to plans to establish a permanent Bonpo teaching, research, and retreat center in France to be known as Shenten Dargye Ling (gshen bstan dar-rgyas gling), meaning "the place for the spreading of the teachings of the Buddha Tonpa Shenrab."

For further information regarding the monastery, its programs and future plans, contact:

Khenpo Tenpa Yungdrung
Triten Norbutse Bonpo Monastery
Ichangu, G.B.S. Ward No. 6,
G.P.O. Box 4640
Kathmandu, Nepal
E-mail: triten@wlink.com.np

And for general information and the Lopon's schedule of teaching in the West, contact the Association Yungdrung Bon:
www.yungdrung-bon.org

Notes

Chapter 1: The Bonpo and Nyingmapa Traditions of Dzogchen

1. See John Myrdhin Reynolds, *The Golden Letters*, Snow Lion, Ithaca 1996, pp. 199-286.

2. For example, see the *Deb-ther sngon-po* of Go Lotsawa ('Gos lo-tswa-ba gZhon-nu dpal, 1392-1481), translated in *The Blue Annals* by George Roerich, Part I, Book I, Motilal Banarsidass, New Delhi reprint 1979; pp. 35-37. See also Tarthang Tulku, *Ancient Tibet*, Dharma Publishing, Berkeley 1986; pp.102-106, 140-148.

3. See Geza Uray, "The Old Tibetan Verb Bon," in *Acta Orientalia Academiae Scientarium Hungaricae*, 1964, vol. 17, no. 3, pp. 323-34.

4. Shamanism, now recognized to be a world-wide religious and cultural activity of great antiquity, has been extensively described by Russian and other anthropologists, as well as by scholars of the History of Religions such as Mircea Eliade and others. See especially Mircea Eliade, *Shamanism: Archaic Techniques of Ecstasy*, Pantheon Books, New York 1964.

5. On Tibetan shamanism generally, see Rene de Nebesky-Wojkowitz, *Oracles and Demons of Tibet*, Mouton, The Hague 1956, pp. 538-553, as well as Per-Arne Berglie, "Preliminary Remarks on Some Tibetan Spirit Mediums in Nepal," in *Kailash* 4 (1), Kathmandu 1976, pp. 85-108. For an account of a contemporary Tibetan shaman from Ladakh and practicing in Kathmandu, see Larry G. Peters, "The Tibetan Healing Rituals of Dorje Yudronma: A Fierce Manifestation of the Feminine Cosmic Force," in *Shaman's Drum* 45, Ashland OR 1997, pp. 36-47.

6. See Joseph Rock, "Contributions to the Shamanism of the Tibetan Chinese Borderland," *Anthropos* LIV (1959), pp. 796-818.

7. See Larry Peters, *Ecstasy and Healing in Nepal*, Udena Publications, Malibu 1981. See also Stan Royal Mumford, *Himalayan Dialogue*, University of Wisconsin Press, Madison 1989.

8. On the relations of the old Tibetan kingdom with Central Asia generally, see Christopher Beckwith, *The Tibetan Empire in Central Asia*, Princeton University Press, Princeton NJ 1987. In view of this connection, as

suggested by Beckwith, the term *bon* might possibly be a borrowing from the Central Asian Iranian language of Sogdian, where the word *bwn* means "dharma." This word also occurs as the first element in the title of the Zoroastrian book dealing with the process of creation, the *Bundahishn*. Beckwith has also pointed to a possible Indo-Iranian substratum in the Zhang-zhung language. See Beckwith, *The Tibetan Empire in Central Asia*, op. cit., pp. 3-36. The Sogdians were a major trading people along the Silk Route to the northwest of Tibet and many Buddhist texts in the Sogdian language have been recovered from Central Asia. On Zhang-zhung in particular, see Tsering Thar, "The Ancient Zhang Zhung Civilization," in *Tibet Studies*, Lhasa 1989, pp. 90-104.

9. According to the *bsTan-rtsis* of Nyima Tenzin, translated by Per Kvaerne in "A Chronological Table of the Bon-po: The *bsTan rcsis of Nyi-ma bstan-'jin*," in *Acta Orientalia* XXXIII, Copenhagen 1971, pp. 205-282.

10. There exist three principal biographies or hagiographies of Tonpa Shenrab in the Bon tradition:

    1. *mDo 'dus* or *Dus gsum sangs-rgyas byung-khungs kyi mdo*, 2. *gZer-myig* or *'Dus-pa rin-po-che'i rgyud gzer-myig*, and 3. *gZi-brjid* or *'Dus-pa rin-po-che dri-ma med-pa gzi-brjid rab tu 'bar-ba'i mdo*.

    A summery of the hagiography of Tonpa Shenrab, drawn from the *gZer-myig*, will be found in Helmut Hoffmann, *The Religions of Tibet*, George Allen and Unwin, London 1961, pp. 84-98. A brief version of the hagiography may be found in Richard Gard and Sangye Tandar, *The Twelve Deeds: A Brief Life Story of Tonpa Shenrab, the Founder of the Bon Religion*, LTWA, New Delhi 1995. Although the monastic career of Tonpa Shenrab in his later life bears many resemblances to the account of Shakyamuni Buddha's Great Renunciation and subsequent teaching activities, as found, for example, in the *Lalitavistara*, his life story is otherwise of an origin quite independent of anything remotely Indian Buddhist. Indeed, the noted Russian scholar Kuznetsov sees Tonpa Shenrab as being of Central Asian or Iranian origin. See B.I. Kuznetsov, "Who was the Founder of the Bon Religion," in *Tibet Journal*, Vol. I, No. 1, Dharamsala 1975. Certain contemporary Tibetan scholars see Tonpa Shenrab as being a native-born Tibetan, rather than a prince or priest coming from a Central Asian origin. See Namkhai Norbu, *The Necklace of gZi: A Cultural History of Tibet*, LTWA, Dharamsala 1981. Karmay also appears to suggest this. See Samten G. Karmay, "A General Introduction to the History and Doctrines of Bon," in *The Memoirs of the Research Department of the Toyo Bunko*, No. 33, Tokyo 1975, pp. 171-218. Lopon Tenzin Namdak, following Bonpo tradition, is adamant in asserting that Tonpa Shenrab was not a Tibetan, but originated in *'Ol-mo lung-ring*, which he identifies with Shambhala. In that case, *'Ol-mo lung-ring* was a mystical domain and not a precise geographical location somewhere northwest of Tibet in historical times. On the significance of *'Ol-mo lung-ring* and Shambhala, see Edwin Birnbaum, *The Way to Shambhala: A Search for the Mythical Kingdom beyond the Himalayas*,

Anchor Press/ Doubleday, New York 1980, pp. 12-13, 44, 79-81, 102; and especially see Daniel Martin, *Mandala Cosmology. Human Body Good Thought and the Revelation of the Secret Mother Tantras of Bon*, Asiatische Forschungen Band 124, Harrassowitz Verlag, Wiesbaden 1994. On the signicance of mystical geography in general, see Mircea Eliade, *The Sacred and the Profane: The Nature of Religion*, Harcourt Brice & World, New York 1957, and also Henry Corbin, *Spiritual Body and Celestial Earth*, Princeton University Press, Princeton 1977.

11. On the bard and the epic generally in the Tibetan tradition, see R.A. Stein, *Tibetan Civilization*, Faber and Faber, London 1972, pp. 272-281. Also see his more detailed study, *Recherches sur l'epopee et le barde au Tibet*, Annales du Musee Guimet, Paris 1959.

12. This does not mean that the Dalai Lama considers the Bonpos to be Buddhists. According to most Tibetan Lamas, the Buddhists follow *chos* and the Bonpos follow *bon*. Nevertheless, both Buddhists (chos-pa) and Bonpos are considered "Insiders" (nang-pa), as opposed to "Outsiders" or Non-Buddhists (phyi-pa), such as Hindus, Jains, Muslims, and Christians.

13. For example, see the *Grub-mtha' legs bshad shel kyi me-long* by Chos kyi nyi-ma dpal bzang-po (1674-1740). The section of this text dealing with Bon has been translated by Sarit Chandra Das in *Contributions on the Religion and History of Tibet*, Manjusri Publishing House, New Delhi 1970, pp. 1-19; reprinted from *Journal of the Asiatic Society of Bengal*, 1881. The author, a Gelugpa scholar, distinguished three phases in the historical development of Bon: '*jol bon, 'khyar bon,* and *bsgyur bon*. Although this is not how the Bonpos see their own history, the text is useful in indicating how the other Buddhist schools saw them. The account found here may be summarized as follows:

1) Revealed Bon ('jol bon): During the reign of the sixth king of Tibet, Tride Tsanpo (Khri-lde btsan-po), a demon or evil spirit ('dre) kidnapped a boy of thirteen who belonged to the Shen (gshen) clan and took him to different wild places in the mountains of Tibet and Kham. Other accounts add the detail that this thirteen year old boy was discovered to have had the ears of a donkey, apparently from birth, whereupon the evil spirits absconded with him. For thirteen more years thereafter, this boy wandered in the wilderness and came to be fully instructed in the magical arts of the non-human spirits (mi ma yin). At the age of twenty-six he was permitted to return to his native village. Because of his Otherworld journeys and the knowledge he acquired thereby, he knew the names and the haunts of all the spirits and demons. He knew which spirits caused troubles among mankind and which spirits brought good luck and prosperity. And he knew how to appease hostile spirits with rituals and offerings. Thus this young man was the first to introduce Bon among the Tibetans and from his time onward, the kings of Tibet followed Bon and no other religion. It is said, moreover, that when he returned to his village from the wilderness, he hid his donkey's ears by wearing a white woolen turban,

for which reason the white turban became the distinctive head-gear of the ancient Bonpos. It was said of these early Bonpos that below ('og) they tamed the evil spirits, above (steng) they invoked the gods of their ancestors, and in the middle (bar) they purified the hearth when it became polluted which would thereby offend the hearth god (thab lha) and other household spirits. This account is an obvious scenario of shamanic initiation and, therefore, it would appear to account for the origin of shamanism in Tibet.

2) Deviant Bon ('khyar bon): This represented innovations made due to foreign influences coming into Tibet from the outside. When the king of Tibet, Drigum Tsanpo (Gri-gum btsan-po), was killed because of his persecution of the Bonpos, it became necessary to prevent the restless spirit of the murdered king, which had become a *gshin* or ghost, from doing mischief among the people. Therefore, three Bonpo practitioners were invited from Kashmir (Kha-che), Gilgit (Bru-sha), and Zhang-zhung, respectively, in order to perform the appropriate funeral rites to set the spirit to rest. This was because the local priests did not know how to do this. Such rites are known as *'Dur*. All three of these Bonpos were foreigners from countries that lay to the west of Tibet. One of these Bonpos, presumably the one from Zhang-zhung, propitiated the deities Ge-khod (the patron deity of Zhang-zhung), Khyung (Garuda), and Me-lha (the god of fire). Thereby he was able to fly through the sky on his drum and divine mineral and metal deposits hidden beneath the earth. The second Bonpo, presumably the one from Gilgit, was skilled in divination and could foretell the future by means of the knots and threads, a practice known as *ju-thig*, and the use of scapula (sog dmar). Moreover, he made inspired oracular utterances (lha bka'). This would appear to locate the origin of this method of divination in Gilgit. The third Bonpo from Kashmir, a land famous for its Sanskrit learning among both Buddhists and Shaivites, was an expert in conducting the funeral ceremonies. Previously there had existed no philosophy of Bon in Tibet, but now Bon became mixed up with the Shaivite doctrines of the Tirthikas, that is, the Hindus of Kashmir, and therefore this became known as Deviant Bon (mu-stegs dbang-phyug-pa'i grub-mtha' 'khyar-ba bon).

3) Transformed Bon (bsgyur bon): This occurred in three phases. First, an Indian Pandita, having slandered a famous Buddhist teacher and being charged with immoral acts, was expelled from the Sangha or monastic community. He went to the north of Kashmir and dressing himself in blue robes (sham-thabs sngon-po-can), he proclaimed himself a great teacher. There he wrote several heretical books and hid them underground. After a few years, he invited the public to witness the discovery of these texts that he had hidden previously. He proclaimed them to be the sacred scriptures of Bon and thereby he brought about a transformation in the Bon religion.

Second, during the reign of the great Buddhist king of Tibet, Trisong Detsan, an edict was issued requiring all Bonpos to renounce Bon and to embrace the Buddhist faith of India. A Bonpo named Rinchenchok (Rin-chen mchog) refused to do so and was punished by the king for his obstinacy. He became very angry at this and thereupon he and some other Bonpo priests composed Bonpo scriptures by way of the wholesale plagiarizing of the Buddhist ones. When the king heard of this activity, he was outraged and had these priests beheaded. However, some conspirators survived and hid copies of these plagiarized texts under rocks in various places. Later these priests rediscovered these texts and they became the Bonpo Termas.

Third, after the overthrow and death of the Tibetan king Langdarma in the ninth century, some Bonpo priests continued to alter other Buddhist texts using different orthography and terminology. In Upper Tsang, two of them, Shengur Luga (gSen rgur klu-dga', i.e., gShen-chen klu-dga') and Daryul Drolag (Dar-yul sgro-lag), composed more texts and hid them under rocks. Thereby they converted many Buddhist scriptures into Bon texts, such as transforming the extensive Prajnaparamita (Yum rgyas) into the *Khams-chen*, the Bonpo version of the Prajnaparamita. Later, they brought them out as apparently accidental discoveries. These caches of texts were known as "the White Water" (Chab dkar) and the Fruitional Bon ('bras-bu'i bon).

The tone of the account here is rather anti-Bon and this may be contrasted with the Bonpos' own account of the origin and development of their tradition such as found in the *Legs-bshad mdzod* of Shardza Rinpoche, for example. See the translation of this work in Samten G. Karmay, *The Treasury of Good Sayings: A Tibetan History of Bon*, Oxford University Press, London 1972.

14. Oral communication from Lopon Tenzin Namdak. See also his history of Bon, *g.Yung-drung bon gyi bstan-pa'i 'byung khungs nyung bsdus*, Kalimpong 1962.

15. According to the traditional accounts found in the *gZer-myig* and the *gZi-brjid*, the demon prince and sorcerer Khyabpa Lagring (bDud-rgyal Khyab-pa lag-ring) stole the seven horses of Tonpa from their stable in *'Ol-mo lung-ring*, and after spiriting them away, he concealed them in Kongpo, a country in Southeastern Tibet. Tonpa Shenrab took this as an opportunity to travel to Tibet in order to subdue the fierce demons (srin-po) who at that time dwelt in the country and oppressed primitive humanity. See H. Hoffmann, *The Religions of Tibet*, op. cit. Also see Tarthang Tulku, *Ancient Tibet*, op. cit., pp. 107-108.

16. See David Snellgrove, *The Nine Ways of Bon*, Oxford University Press, London 1967. Also see Namkhai Norbu, *Drung, Dreu and Bon: Narrations, Symbolic Languages, and the Bon Tradition in Ancient Tibet*, Library of Tibetan Works and Archives, Dharamsala 1995,

17. See Snellgrove, *The Nine Ways of Bon*, op. cit. Also on Bonpo ritual, see John Myrdhin Reynolds, *The Cult and Practice of Zhang-zhung Meri*, Bonpo Translation Project (privately printed), San Diego 1996.
18. Oral communication from Lopon Tenzin Namdak. On the conflict between Buddhist Lamas and indigenous shamans regarding the question of blood sacrifice, see Mumford, *Himalayan Dialogue*, op. cit. On a parallel situation in seventeenth century Mongolia, see Walther Heissig, *The Religions of Mongolia*, University of California Press, Berkeley 1980 and Walther Heissig, "A Mongolian Source to the Lamaist Suppression of Shamanism in the 17th Century," in *Anthropos* 48, pp. 493-533.
19. On 'Chi-med gtsug-phud and the lineages for the Bonpo Dzogchen teachings, see Chapter Three below and also the translations of the *Yig-chung* and the *rNam-thar*.
20. On the Zhang-zhung language, see Erik Haarh, "The Zhang-zhung Language: A Grammar and Dictionary of the Unexplored Language of the Tibetan Bonpos," in *Acta Jutlandica* XL: 1, Copenhagen 1968, pp. 7-43. On the relationship of Kinnauri to the Zhang-zhung language, see D.D. Sharma, *A Discriptive Grammar of Kinnauri*, Studies in Tibeto-Himalayan Languages 1, Mittal Publications, Delhi 1988.
21. Samten G. Karmay, *The Treasury of Good Sayings*, op.cit.
22. On the *sMar-yig* script of Zhang-zhung, see Tshering Thar, "The Ancient Zhang Zhung Civilization," op. cit. Also see Namkhai Norbu, *The Necklace of gZi*, op. cit..
23. On the Bonpo Terma tradition, see Samten Karmay, *The Treasury of Good Sayings*, op. cit. All of the early Terma discoveries of the Bonpos were *sa-gter*, that is, the actual physical texts written in previous times and concealed in various places of Tibet and Bhutan. Most of the actual discoverers of these collections of Terma texts were not learned Lamas, but simple farmers and hunters, who could not have possibly forged or otherwise plagiarized these texts. Among the most famous of these early "Tertons" were three Nepali thieves known as the three Atsaras, who in the year 961 CE stole a heavy locked chest from the *Cha-ti dmar-po* temple at Samye monastery. Escaping into the mountains with their loot and thinking that it contained gold, they broke into the chest. But when they opened it, they found only some old texts. Greatly disappointed, they sold these old books to some local village Bonpo Lamas for some gold and a horse.
24. According to Lopon Tenzin Namdak, *sTang-chen dMu-tsha gyer-med* was a disciple of Dranpa Namkha, the prince of Zhang-zhung and not the later Tibetan Dranpa Namkha who lived in the 8th cen., as is believed by Karmay, *The Treasury of Good Sayings*, ibid., pp.xxxvii, xxxvx. This sage appeared to Lodan Nyingpo in a series of visions, dictating a number of texts, which the latter wrote down. At this time, it is said that Lodan Nyingpo was 23 and 24 years old, and these visions came to him spontaneously and without his conscious control. Even though this

process would be designated a Mind Treasure (dgongs-gter) or a pure vision (dag-snang) by the Nyingmapas, the Bonpos classify such vision revelations as *snyan-brgyud* or oral transmissions, even though they do not represent a continuous oral transmission from the earliest time. In all, Lodan Nyingpo received four cycles of oral transmissions in visions from the Vidyadharas and the Dakinis. See Karmay, ibid., p 183, 340.

25. On the Nyingmapa Terma tradition, see Eva Dargyay, *The Rise of Esoteric Buddhism in Tibet*, Motilal Banarsidass, Delhi 1977. Also see Tulku Thondup, *Hidden Teachings of Tibet: An Explanation of the Terma Tradition of the Nyingmapa School of Buddhism*, Wisdom Publications, London 1986, and Tulku Thondup, *The Tantric Tradition of the Nyingmapas*, Buddhayana, Marion MA 1984.

26. The Nine Ways of Bon, or rather, the nine successive vehicles of Bon (bon theg-pa rim dgu), as classified in the System of the Southern Treasures (lho gter lugs), is expounded in as many chapters in the *gZi-brjid*, the most extensive hagiography of Tonpa Shenrab. These chapters have been translated by Snellgrove in consultation with Lopon Tenzin Namdak. See David Snellgrove, *The Nine Ways of Bon*, Oxford University Press, London 1967. Here the Nine Ways are listed as follows:

1) The Way of the Practice of Prediction (phywa gshen theg-pa): Literally *theg-pa* means a vehicle or conveyance, rather than a road or a way. *gShen*, a word of obscure origin and meaning, can here be translated as "practice" or "practitioner" according to the Lopon. And the term *phywa* means prediction or prognostication. This way, or vehicle, is principally concerned with divination (mo), astrological and geomantic calculations (rtsis), medical diagnosis (dpyad), and the performing of healing rituals (gto).

2) The Way of the Practice of Visible Manifestations (snang gshen theg-pa): This way is principally concerned with visible manifestations (snang-ba) perceived as positive manifestations of the activities of the gods (lha) who come to the aid of humanity. Therefore, the emphasis is placed on invoking the gods (lha gsol-ba) for their aid. This includes such classes of deities as the *Thugs-dkar*, the *sGra-bla*, the *Wer-ma*, and so on.

3) The Way of the Practice of Magical Power ('phrul gshen theg-pa): This way is principally concerned with magical rituals to ensure prosperity and control over the spirits evoked, especially the rites of exorcism (sel-ba) to eliminate negative energy and the negative provocations of evil spirits (gdon) who come to disturb human existence. The practitioner works with these energies in terms of evocation, conjuration, and application (bsnyen sgrub las gsum).

4) The Way of the Practice of Existence (srid gshen theg-pa): Here the term "existence" or "becoming" (srid-pa) properly refers the processes of death and rebirth. This way is also known as *'Dur gshen*, the practice of ceremonies for exorcising ('dur) the spirits of the dead who are disturbing the living. It is, therefore, principally concerned with the

three hundred and sixty kinds of rites for accomplishing this, as well as methods for ensuring the good fortune and the long life of the living. These four represent the Four Causal Ways of Bon (bon rgyu'i theg-pa bzhi). These are followed by the higher ways of a more spiritual nature, whose goal is liberation and enlightenment, which are collectively known as the Fruitional Ways ('bras-bu'i theg-pa):

5) The Way of the Virtuous Lay Practitioners (dge-bsnyen theg-pa): This way is principally concerned with morality and ethics, such as the ten virtuous deeds (dge-ba bcu), the ten Perfections or Paramitas, and so on, as well as pious activities such as erecting stupas, and so on, especially on the part of lay practitioners (dge-bsnyen, Skt. upasika).

6) The Way of the Ascetic Sages (drang-srong theg-pa): The term *drang-srong* (Skt. rishi), meaning a sage, has here the technical significance of a fully ordained monk who has taken the full complement of vows, corresponding to the Buddhist bhikshu (dge-slong). The principal concern is with the vows of the monk and the rules of the monastic discipline ('dul-ba).

7) The Way of the White A (A-dkar theg-pa): This way is principally concerned with the Tantric practice of transformation by way of visualizing oneself as the meditation deity and the practices associated with the mandala. Here are included both the Lower Tantras and the Higher Tantras.

8) The Way of the Primordial Shen (ye gshen theg-pa): This way is concerned with certain secret Tantric practices includung the proper relationship with the Guru and with the Tantric consort, as well as with the methodologies of the Generation Process (bskyed-rim) and the Perfection Process (rdzogs-rim) and the conduct connected with them.

9) The Ultimate Way (bla-med theg-pa): This ultimate and unsurpassed (bla na med-pa) way is comprised of the teachings and practices of Dzogchen, the Great Perfection, which describes the process of enlightenment in terms of the Base, the Path, and the Fruit, as well as the practice of contemplation in terms of view, meditation, and conduct.

27. The Nine Ways according to the System of the Central Treasures (dbus gter lugs) are also divided into the Causal Vehicles (rgyu'i theg-pa) and the Fruitional Vehicles ('bras-bu'i theg-pa). These are as follows:

1) The Vehicle of Gods and Men where one relies upon another (lha mi gzhan rten gyi theg-pa): that is to say, this is the vehicle of those disciples who must first hear the teachings from another. This vehicle corresponds to the Shravakayana in the Buddhist system and the philosophical view is that of the Vaibhashikas.

2) The Vehicle of the Shenrabpas who understand by themselves alone (rang-rtogs gshen-rab kyi theg-pa): These practitioners do not need to hear the teachings first from another, but they discover the meaning of the teachings for themselves in their meditation practice. This vehicle

corresponds to the Pratyekabuddhayana of the Buddhists and the philosophical view is that of the Sautrantikas.

3) The Vehicle of the Compassionate Bodhisattvas (thugs-rje sems-pa'i theg-pa): This vehicle corresponds to the Mahayana Sutra system or Bodhisattvayana vehicle in the Buddhist system. In particular, the reference is to the Bodhisattvas who practice the ten Paramitas of generosity, morality, patience, vigor, meditation, strength, compassion, commitment, skillful means, and wisdom. The philosophical view is that of the Yogacharins or Chittamatrins (sems-tsam-pa) who discern the absence of any inherent existence in terms of the internal self, as well as external phenomena.

4) The Vehicle of the Bodhisattvas that are without conceptual elaborations (g.yung-drung sems-pa'i spros med-pa'i theg-pa): This vehicle also corresponds to the Bodhisattvayana in the Buddhist system. The Bonpo term *g.yung-drung sems-dpa'*, literally Svastikasattva or "Swastika being," has the same significance as the Buddhist term Bodhisattva (byang-chub sems-dpa'). Here one finds the same practice of the ten Paramitas. However, the philosophical view of emptiness and the absence of any inherent existence in the internal self and the external phenomena is understood by way the Madhyamaka (dbu-ma-pa), rather than the Chittamatra (sems-tsam-pa).

These four lower ways represent the Causal Vehicles (rgyu'i theg-pa), while those which follow are known as the Fruitional Vehicles:

5) The Vehicle of the Primordial Bon of Pure Conduct and Ritual Activity (bya-ba gtsang-spyod ye bon gyi theg-pa): Focusing on ritual activity (bya-ba, Skt. kriya) and purity of conduct, this vehicle corresponds to the Kriyatantrayana in the Nyingmapa system. In terms of method, the Wisdom Being (ye-shes-pa) is invoked into one's range of vision and treated as a great lord being petitioned by a humble servant and thereby the practitioner receives the knowledge (ye-shes) and the blessings (byin-rlabs) of the deity.

6) The Vehicle of the Clairvoyant Knowledge that possesses all of the aspects (rnam-par kun-ldan mngon-shes kyi theg-pa): The focus is equally on external ritual action and internal yoga practice. This vehicle corresponds to the Charyatantrayana in the Nyingmapa system. Together with the practice of the ten Paramitas and the four Recollections, the presence of the Wisdom Being is invoked, but this time the deity is regarded as an intimate friend rather than as a superior lord. These two vehicles represent the Outer or Lower Tantras (phyi rgyud), while the vehicles that follow represent the Inner or Higher Tantras (nang rgyud).

7) The Vehicle of Visibly Manifestating Compassion in terms of the Actual Generation Process (dngos bskyed thugs-rje rol-pa'i theg-pa): This vehicle corresponds to the Yoga Tantra and to a certain extent to the Mahayoga Tantra and the Anuttara Tantra in the Buddhist system

of classification for both the Nyingmapas and the Newer Schools. Establishing oneself in the higher view of the Ultimate Truth and remaining in the original condition of the Natural State, one engages in the Generation Process (bskyed-rim) and transforms oneself into the meditation deity, thereby realizing the qualities attributed to that manifestation of enlightened awareness.

8) The Vehicle wherein Everything is Completely Perfect and Exceedingly Meaningful (shin tu don-ldan kun rdzogs kyi theg-pa): Becoming established in the Ultimate Truth and the original condition of the Natural State as was the case above, here one places the emphasis on the Perfection Process (rdzogs-rim) rather than the Generation Process (bskyed-rim), so that Space and Awareness are realized to be inseparable (dbyings rig dbyer-med). And particularly in terms of the meditation deity, the practitioner comes to realize the gnosis, or pristine awareness, of the inseparability of bliss and emptiness (bde stong ye-shes). This vehicle corresponds to the Mahayoga Tantra and especially the Anuyoga Tantra classifications of the Nyingmapas.

9) The Unsurpassed Vehicle of the Highest Peak of the Primordial Great Perfection (ye nas rdzogs-chen yang-rtse bla-med kyi theg-pa): This vehicle comprises the Dzogchen teachings in terms of the Mind Series (sems-sde) which emphasize the awareness side of the Natural State and the Space Series (klong-sde) which emphasize the emptiness side, as well as the Secret Instruction Series (man-ngag sde) which emphasize their inseparability.

On the Central Treasures, see John Myrdhin Reynolds, *Yungdrung Bon: The Eternal Tradition*, Tibetan Translation Project (privately printed), New York 1994, and also Lopon Tenzin Namdak and John Reynolds (tr), *The Condensed Meaning of an Explanation of the Teachings of Yungdrung Bon*, Bonpo Foundation, Kathmandu n.d. Also see Tenzin Wangyal, *Wonders of the Natural Mind*, Station Hill Press, Barrytown NY 1993, pp. 35-37, 203-208.

28. Oral Communication.

29. According to Lopon Tenzin Namdak, the translations of these technical terms *chab dkar* as "white water" and *chab nag* as "black water" are problematic. Indeed, *chab* does mean "water" in Tibetan, but the word may originally have been a Zhang-zhung term and had a different and now forgotten meaning. In the old Bonpo usage, the terms "white" (dkar) and "black" (nag) did not have the moral connotations that they have in English, such as "white magic" done for good purposes and "black magic" done for evil purposes. In this context, "white" refers to invoking the aid of the gods and spirits, drawing positive energy to oneself, while "black" refers to the exorcizing and expelling of negative energies, perceived as a process of purification. The exorcised negative energies are felt to appear black in color, but the intention here is positive, namely, that of purification.

30. According to Karmay, the name '*Phan-yul* designates the district of '*Phan-yul* to the north of Lhasa. This may have been the location where the Bonpo translation of the Prajnaparamita was made in the early period, then later concealed in a different region and rediscovered at a later time by *gShen-chen klu-dga'* in the 11th century. However, the Lopon disputes this theory and holds that '*phan-yul* was probably a Zhang-zhung word whose meaning has been forgotten. The Tibetan term '*bum*, literally meaning "one hundred thousand," is the usual designation in the Buddhist tradition for the entire collection of the Prajnaparamita Sutras, the largest of which consists of one hundred-thousand verses.

31. See Snellgrove, *The Nine Ways of Bon*, ibid.

32. The Termas revealed to *bLo-ldan snying-po* (b. 1360), *Mi-zhig rDo-rje*, otherwise known as *rDo-rje gling-pa* (1346-1405), *Kun-grol grags-pa* (b. 1700), *bDe-chen gling-pa* (b.1833), *gSang-sngags gling-pa* (b. 1864), *mKha'-'gro bDe-chen dbang-mo* (b.1868), etc., are considered recent treasure text discoveries (gter gsar). Among those listed here, Dorje Lingpa is also well known as a Nyingmapa Terton. On him, see Eva Dargyay, *The Rise of Esoteric Buddhism in Tibet*, Motilal Banarsidass, Delhi 1977, pp. 139-143. On the New Bon Termas in general, see Karmay, *Treasury*, ibid., pp.182-190.

33. On the Tibetan translator Vairochana as a Bonpo, see Samten G. Karmay, *The Great Perfection: A Philosophical and Meditative Teaching of Tibetan Buddhism*, Brill, Leiden 1988, pp. 17-37, 216-223.

34. See Samten G. Karmay, *The Great Perfection*, op. cit. Also see Eva Dargyay, *The Rise of Esoteric Buddhism in Tibet*, op. cit.

35. See the discussion in Reynolds, *The Golden Letters*, op. cit., pp. 199-286.

36. See Eva Dargyay, *The Rise of Esoteric Buddhism in Tibet*, ibid. The Nyingmapa class of the Mahayoga Tantras is divided into the Tantra Section (rgyud-sde), consisting of eighteen Tantras, headed by the *Guhyagarbha Tantra* (rgyud gsang-ba snying-po), and the Sadhana Section (grub-sde) consisting of the texts for the practices of these eight Herukas.

37. See the translation of the *Man-ngag lta-ba'i phreng-ba* in Samten Karmay, *The Great Perfection*, op. cit., pp. 137-174.

38. The state of even contemplation (mnyam-bzhag, Skt. samahita) represents the culmination of the Tantric process of transformation known as sadhana (grub-thabs). Just as the visualization process begins from the state of emptiness, or Shunyata, generating the pure forms of the deity and the mandala out of this primordial condition of pure potentiality, so at the conclusion of the practice of the transformation, the visualization of the deity and its sacred space is dissolved once more back into its source, the state of Shunyata. The dissolving of all the pure forms generated in the creation process (bskyed-rim) of the sadhana back into emptiness does not, however, represent a true destruction or annihilation in any absolute sense. To assert that this is the case would represent the erroneous philosophical position of nihilism (chad-lta). Rather, it represents a

dissolving or re-enfolding of manifest forms back into their source, where they remain in their full potentiality. Having dissolved the visualization once more, the meditator rests for a period of time in Shunyata, or pure unmanifest potentiality, in what is called a condition of even contemplation (mnyam-bzhag), out of which, subsequently, the sights and sounds of normal everyday life re-emerge as the post-meditation condition (rjes-thob). The Sanskrit term samahita is cognate with the more familiar term samadhi, both of which I translate into English as "contemplation," in order to distinguish them from "meditation" (sgom-pa, Skt. bhavana). In terms of Dzogchen, this remaining in the state of contemplation is equated with being in the Natural State (gnas-lugs). However, within the practice of Tantra, it is necessary to first go through this elaborate process of visualization and transformation in order to find oneself in the condition of contemplation once the visualization is dissolved back again into Shunyata. This visualization process recapitulates the creation, the evolution, and the dissolution of the entire manifest universe. But in the context of Dzogchen practice, it is not necessary to first transform something into something else in order to find oneself in the condition of contemplation. Rather, one simply relaxes and just finds oneself in contemplation at the very beginning of practice and remains thereafter in it, by whatever means. This represents the principal practice of Dzogchen, in relation to which all Tantric transformation practices are considered secondary.

39. There has been much discussion among scholars about the location of Uddiyana (o-rgyan). Tucci located it in the Swat valley in Pakistan on the basis of two medieval Tibetan texts. See Giuseppe Tucci, *Travels of Tibetan Pilgrimes in the Swat Valley*, The Greater India Society, Calcutta 1940. However, there is much evidence to indicate that Uddiyana was a far larger region embracing much of Eastern Afghanistan. See C.S. Upasak, *History of Buddhism in Afghanistan*, Central Institute of Higher Tibetan Studies, Varanasi 1990.

40. On *Gyer-spungs sNang-bzher Lod-po* and his disciples and successors, see Chapters Five through Eight below.

41. On the origin of the Mahayana in the Northwest of India, see Etienne Lamotte, *History of Indian Buddhism*, Louvain 1988. And on the origin of Dzogchen in the same region, see Samten G. Karmay, "A Discussion of the Doctrinal Position of the rDzogs-chen from the 10th to the 11th Centuries, in *Journal Asiatique* 1-2, Paris 1975, pp. 147-155; as well as his *The Great Perfection: A Philosophical and Meditative Teaching of Tibetan Buddhism*, ibid.

42. On the *Guyasamaja Tantra*, see Alex Wayman, *The Buddhist Tantras: Light on Indo-Tibetan Esotericism*, Samual Weiser, New York 1973, and also his *The Yoga of the Guhyasamajatantra*, Motilal Banarsidass, New Delhi 1977.

43. On the origin of the *Kalachakra Tantra* and of Shambhala, see Edwin Bernbaum, *The Way to Shambhala*, ibid.

44. Lopon Tenzin Namdak and other Bonpo Lamas I have spoken to have identified '*Ol-mo lung-ring* with Shambhala. For a discussion of Shambhala in the Tibetan tradition in general, both Buddhist and Bonpo, see Bernbaum, *The Way to Shambhala*, ibid.
45. This has already been suggested by Snellgrove in *Indo-Tibetan Buddhism*, ibid.
46. See C. Beckwith, *The Tibetan Empire in Central Asia*, ibid.
47. Oral communication from Lopon Tenzin Namdak. The Lopon spent two years in that region hiding from the Chinese Communists.

In terms of Tibetan history, the tendency is for scholars, both Western and native Tibetan, to begin by focusing on the Indian Buddhist heritage that first came to Central Tibet in the time of king Songtsan Gampo in the 7th century CE. However, Tibet's ancient history was not purely Buddhistic. As was pointed out in Namkhai Norbu's *The Necklace of gZi*, LTWA, Dharamsala 1981, the civilization of Tibet originated at a much earlier time than the 7th century and this occurred in association with the ancient kingdom of Zhang-zhung located in the lake district of Northern Tibet, just south of the vast barren Changtang (byang-thang) plateau, and in the Mt. Kailas region of Western Tibet. Although certain prehistoric monuments were noticed in Western Tibet by G. Tucci when he visited that region, the proto-history of Tibet has otherwise largely been ignored. But it was John Vincent Bellezza, relying upon Bonpo texts, who has been able recently to survey more systematically this region, the lake country in Northern Tibet. He also noted the similarity of certain of these megalithic monuments and foundations to Iron Age Celtic hill forts.

Both the lakes of Darok (da-rog sman mtsho) and Dang-ra (dang-ra g.yu mtsho) have oral histories speaking of a time of much denser population and more advanced civilization in ancient times. At the Darok (da-rog) and Namtso (gnam-mtsho) lakes, the majority of archaeological sites are located on headlands along the northern shore, thereby giving them a southern exposure. Again, the ruins at Dang-ra and Namtso show a relatively advanced material culture as early as the Neolithic. But it is hard to tell, according to Bellezza, if a particular structure is Neolithic, Bronze Age, Iron Age, or the historical period. According to Lopon Tenzin Namdak, these sites predate the annexation of the Zhang-zhung kingdom by the Yanrlung dynasty to the south into their growing Tibetan empire. The sheer numbers of of ruins suggest that at one time the material culture of the northern lake country was more highly developed than in the later feudal period. Until the 1950's, permanent structures at Namtso consisted of five monasteries, some small hermitages, and some small houses belonging to nomad chieftains. But the settlements at the Dang-ra lake were much more extensive, with four monasteries in full operation, several hermitages, and eight agricultural villages. Nevertheless, this lake country was sparsely settled. The amount of abandoned agricultural land around the shores of the Dang-ra lake indicates that in the time of the Zhang-zhung kingdom, this lake could boast of a more expanded population and sophisticated infrastructure. On the southern shore of the lake is found the ruins of *Khyung-rdzong*, "the garuda castle," at times the residence of the Zhang-zhung kings of the *Lig-mi-rgya* dynasty. See John Vincent Bellezza, "A Preliminary Archaeological Survey of of gNam mtsho and Dang ra g.yu mtsho," in *The Tibet Journal*, vol. 21, Dharamsala 1996, pp. 58-84.

However, the nomads who now inhabit what was once the Zhang-zhung kingdom and who are descendents of the ancient Zhang-zhung-pas, some groups even baring the old clan names, as was also noted by Lopon Tenzin Namdak, have, consequent to their conversion to Kagyudpa Buddhism centuries ago, completely forgotten their Bonpo heritage. They now associate these megalithic structures with the epic hero Gesar of Ling and his lady Lhamo Drugmo (Lha-mo 'brug-mo), who, it is said, had struggled for years in that country in order to defeat the demon king Dudlutsan (bdud klu btsan) with the help from the local mountain god Nyenchen Thanglha (gnyan-chen thang-lha).

On this region and its archeaological remains, see John Vincent Bellezza, "High Country Culture: A Civilization Flourished in the Himalayas before Buddhism Reached Tibet," *Discovering Archaeology* v.1 n.3, May-June 1999, pp. 78-83; as well as Bellezza, "Pre-history of Tibet," *Himal*, December 1999, Kathmandu, pp.42-43.

48. Snellgrove and Richardson, *A Cultural History of Tibet*, ibid. Lopon Tenzin Namdak asserts that this monk Bodhisattva was not the famous Indian Buddhist scholar Shantirakshita who later became the first abbot of Samye monastery. But see the translation of the *Bon ma nub-pa'i gtan-tshigs* in Chapter Seven below.

49. On the *A-khrid* system and *rMe'u-ston dGongs-mdzod ri-khrod chen-po*, see Per Kvaerne, "Bonpo Studies: The A-khrid System of Meditation," Part One: "The Transmission of the A-khrid System," in *Kailash* v. I, n. 1, pp. 19-50, Kathmandu 1973.

50. *A-za bLo-gros rgyal-mtshan*, 1198-1263.

51. *Bru-chen rGyal-ba g.yung-drung*, 1242-1209, composed the practice manual entitled the *A-khrid thun mtshams bco-lnga-pa*, "the Fifteen Sessions of Practice for A-khrid." For the translation of most of this text, see Per Kvaerne and Thubten Rikey, *The Stages of A-khrid Meditation: Dzogchen Practice of the Bon Tradition*, Library of Tibetan Works and Archives, Dharamsala 1996. And on the *A-khrid* system generally, see Per Kvaerne, "Bonpo Studies: The A-khrid System of Meditation," Part One: "The Transmission of the A-khrid System," in *Kailash* v. I, n. 1, pp. 19-50, Part Two: "The Essential Teachings of the A-khrid System, in Kailash v. I, n. 4, pp. 248-332, Kathmandu 1973. For a translation of the hagiography of this master, see Chapter Eleven below.

53. *Shar-rdza bKra-shis rgyal-mtshan*, 1859-1934. Shardza Rinpoche was a realized practitioner of Dzogchen who, at the end of his life, manifested the Rainbow Body. On the dark retreat according to Shardza Rinpoche, see the monograph, John Myrdhin Reynolds, *The Instructions of Shardza*

Rinpoche for the Practice of Vision and the Dark Retreat, Bonpo Translation Project (privately printed), New York 1992.

53. On the *rDzogs-chen sems-sde*, see Reynolds, *The Golden Letters*, ibid. and also Namkhai Norbu, *The Crystal and the Way of Light: Sutra, Tantra, and Dzogchen*, Arkana Penguin Books, London 1993.

54. *sNya-chen Li-shu stag-rings* was said to be a contemporary of the Tibetan king Trisong Detsan and was actively involved in the concealing of Terma texts. See Karmay, *Treasury*, ibid. On Li-shu stag-rings, see also Chapter Four below. The text of the *rDzogs-chen yang-rtse'i klong-chen* was reprinted in India in 1973.

Chapter 2: The Primordial Buddha Kuntu Zangpo

1. Both Yungdrung Bon and the Nyingmapa school originated in the early period of the Tibetan monarchy, the 7th through the 9th centuries CE. Therefore, they may be called "old" or "ancient" (rnying-ma) in relation to the religious movements that arose later. These Newer Schools (gsar-ma-pa) originated with the revival and "reform" of monastic Buddhism accompanying the inauguration of the New Translation system of Rinchen Zangpo in Guge in Western Tibet in the 11th century. See David Snellgrove and Hugh Richardson, *A Cultural History of Tibet*, Geo Weidenfeld & Nicolson, London 1968. The first school to come into existence on the basis of the New Translations and to set itself apart consciously from the older styles of non-monastic practice was the Kadampa. This school was later followed by the Sakyapa, the Kagyudpa, and the Gelugpa. The latter eventually came to absorb the Kadampas, so that it no longer exists as a distinct school. The Nyingmapas did not distinguish themselves as a separate school until the rise of these Newer Schools put them on the defensive. The Bonpos were always regarded as foreign to the body of Buddhism, although not necessarily hostile to it. The Kadampa and these other schools can be said to be "reformed" in the sense that their respective Tantric systems are based on the New Translations of the Tantras which had been brought from India to Tibet. Many of the Old Translation Tantras were regarded as suspect by Buton Rinpoche, the principal editor of the Kangyur, and by other scholars as well, because no Sanskrit originals were said to exist for them. This included all of the Dzogchen Tantras. However, the notion of an Adibuddha, or Primordial Buddha, whether called Samantabhadra or Vajradhara, is found in all schools, both old and new.

2. In both Buddhism and Bon, the enlightenment of a Buddha has three aspects, or levels of manifestation. These aspects of Buddhahood are called "Bodies" (sku, Skt. kaya). These are not bodies in a literal sense, but rather dimensions of manifestation where the figure in the foreground and the field in the background are one and inseparable. Although the Dharmakaya is called a "Body" or "dimension of existence" in the texts, it is, in itself, formless and all-pervading like the infinity of space (nam-

mkha' ltar). It transcends conception by the finite intellect and expression in words. It is given an iconographic form as Samantabhadra or Vajradhara merely as concession to limited human understanding. In particular, the Dharmakaya represents the wisdom and the emptiness side (stong-cha) of Buddhahood or enlightened awareness, which is generally felt to be feminine in character. But this is only a matter of emphasis because wisdom and compassion are considered equally to be the coefficients of the enlightenment of a Buddha. When the Dharmakaya is compared to the sky, it is the daytime sky that is suffused with sunlight to which the comparison is made. Therefore, the Dharmakaya need not be exclusively represented by a male figure.

Again, in terms of Dzogchen, the clear luminosity or manifestation side (gsal-cha) is represented by the Rupakaya, or "Form Body," of the Buddha, which is twofold: the Sambhogakaya and the Nirmanakaya. This Sambhogakaya manifests only in eternity at the summit of existence, which is, at the same time, the center of all existence. This Body, or manifestation of clear luminosity, is said to be visible only to the great Bodhisattvas and the saints who have sufficiently purified their perceptions by attaining the higher successive spiritual levels known as the ten Bhumis (sa bcu). This Sambhogakaya, the Body of Perfect Enjoyment (rdzogs-par long-spyod gyi sku), is a glorified Body of Light manifesting outside time, history, and conditioned existence generally. This dimension is full, complete, and perfect, where nothing is lacking or inferior, and iconographically its inexhaustible richness and abundance is symbolized by the precious jewels and exquisite silks in which this form of the Buddha is attired. A single Sambhogakaya has the potentiality to emanate an infinite number of Nirmankayas into all world-systems within its field of enlightened activity in order to teach and carry out the great work of liberating all sentient beings from ignorance. Therefore, a Nirmanakaya manifests within time and history, within conditioned existence itself, the world below, so to speak, as an emanation or incarnation, visibly appearing to mortal sentient beings whose spiritual faculties have not been sufficiently purified and ripened to perceive the splendor and glory of the Sambhogakaya directly. This Nirmanakaya appears, as an expression of the infinite compassion of the Buddha, like the rays of light from the sun, in order to teach the Dharma, the true facts of existence, as well as the path to liberation, to ignorant and deluded sentient beings still caught up in the illusions of Samsara. Ordinary sentient beings perceive this Nirmanakaya, or Body of Emanation (sprul-pa'i sku), as an epiphany or a hierophany, an eruption of a higher sacred order of being into mundane time and history, which thereby reveals and makes possible a path to salvation, that is to say, the realization of Buddhahood which is potential and latent within every single sentient being. Since a Nirmanakaya may manifest literally at any time and place, as the case may be, the circumstances of its manifestation is said to be uncertain (nges-med).

Thus, the mind-stream of an enlightened being or Buddha may manifest a multiplicity of Nirmanakayas in order to teach the Dharma to deluded sentient beings. These emanations, or Nirmanakayas, manifest throughout the inhabited world-systems of a universe, which, therefore, represent the Buddhakshetra or field for the enlightened compassionate activities of that Buddha. However, a Buddha is said to manifest only a single Sambhogakaya which never departs from the center of existence known as Akanishtha. Therefore, the Buddha is compared to a central spiritual sun that simultaneously illuminates all world-systems in the ten directions of space.

3. It is important to understand that this principle of Buddhahood is both transcendent and immanent. Moreover, there appears to be a certain convergence between the understanding of the Trikaya of the Buddha in Mahayana Buddhism and the understanding of God and the Incarnation in Christianity. The question of the possible historical connections and cross-cultural influences is much too complex to go into here.

4. On the significance of this awakening into understanding (rtogs-pa), see the discussion in Part Three in the subsequent book in this series, *Space, Awareness, and Energy*, Snow Lion, forthcoming.

5. Indeed, Kuntu Zangpo is not a person at all, not in the conventional sense, but a state of being. This is because personhood as such (gang-zag, Skt. pudgala) is not a monadic, self-existing entity, but a stream of consciousness in continuous flux where the contents of consciousness are ever-changing like the waters of a river. And this process called "a person" belongs to the dimension and sphere of operation of the five skandhas which are conditioned and, therefore, impermanent. When the Buddha Shakyamuni attained enlightenment beneath the Bodhi Tree, he realized a vision of reality that contrasted with not only with the naive, commonsense view of the world, but with the conventional metaphysical orientation of the bulk of humanity. This unconventional view formed part of the core of the kerygma, or original message, of the Buddha and is generally known as the doctrine of Anatman or Anatmavada, which can be translated as the teaching of "no self" (bdag-med, Skt. anatman). Probably this term could better be translated in this context as "non-substantiality." On this question in general, see Edward Conze, *Buddhist Thought in India*, George Allen & Unwin, London 1962. On the question of traditional substantialist metaphysics as against the non-substantialist or process philosophy of the Buddha, see T.R.V. Murti, *The Central Philosophy of Buddhism: A Study of the Madhyamika System*, George Allen & Unwin, London 1955.

6. See the discussion of Samsara and Nirvana in terms of vision and image in the subsequent volume in this series, *The Path of the Clear Light*.

7. These layers of obscurations (sgrib-pa) consist principally of the obscurations that are the kleshas or emotional defilements (nyon-mongs-pa'i sgrib-pa), including all one's negative emotions and neurotic impulses and obsessions, and the obscurations to knowledge (shes-bya'i

sgrib-pa) that consist of all one's wrong views and conceptual elaborations about things.

8. In the Dzogchen texts from Zhang-zhung, these two sides, the Essence and the Nature, are frequently called Kunzhi and Rigpa, that is, Space and Awareness. This is interesting in view of the fact that Descartes distinguishes two substances, or orders, of reality, namely, consciousness and extension. However, here in the context of Dzogchen, Space and Awareness represent two sides of the same coin. Especially with regard to the relationship between Kunzhi and Rigpa, see the discussion in Part One in the subsequent volume in this series, *Space, Awareness, and Energy.*

9. In the Buddhist perspective, discursive consciousness (rnam-shes), left to its own devices, evolves or unfolds according to the law of karma, which is cyclical in the broadest sense. To break out of this cycle of habit, metaphorically called "sleep," requires conscious effort on the part of the individual, a "waking up," that is to say, one must consciously enter into the spiritual path and practice it. This spiritual path entails a different mode of consciousness than cyclical worldly consciousness (Skt. laukika-chitta), namely, a consciousness that is directed toward a transcendent goal (Skt. lokottara-chitta). It is this spiritual path that progressively leads to the state of liberation and enlightenment, and not nature on its own unaided. And in itself, progress on this path, over the course of many lifetimes, is not something that is automatic or predetermined. It requires conscious effort.

10. How then is Dzogchen to be approached? It represents a discovery or rediscovery of what has been there all the time, from the very beginning. The means for entering into the practice of the Sutra system is the taking of vows (sdom len), and the means for entering into the practice of the Tantra system is the taking of initiations or empowerments (dbang-bskur), whereas the means for entering into the practice of Upadesha or Dzogchen is by way of receiving a direct introduction (ngo-sprod). The practitioner is directly introduced by the master to this Natural State, this innate, primordially present Buddha-nature or enlightenment, called the Bodhichitta, discovered at the core of the individual's personal experience. The Lama or master is qualified to give this direct introduction because he has experienced the Natural State in contemplation for himself— he has entered into a primordial state that lies beyond the mind, beyond the incessant functioning of time and karmic causality. Time and causality are like the reflections in the mirror, whereas the Natural State is like the mirror itself; it is immaculate and perpetually untainted by Samsara or the conditioned thought process. This Natural State of the Nature of Mind has been present there all the time, although it has gone unrecognized since time without beginning because it has been covered over by obscurations, just as the face of the sun high in the sky may go unrecognized because it is obscured by clouds. By removing or purifying these layers of accidental obscurations, the inner

sun, concealed at the core of our being, unfolds into view. The persistent presence of solar imagery in Dzogchen texts is striking.

11. The iconography of the Primordial Buddha Vajradhara (rDo-rje 'chang) in the system of the New Tantras is quite distinct from that of Samantabhadra or Kuntu Zangpo (Kun tu bzang-po) in the Old Tantra system of the Nyingmapas and the Bonpos. Vajradhara may also be sky blue in color, but like the Sambhogakaya, He is depicted as sitting on a lotus and a throne and as attired in the crown, the precious jewels, and the rich silks of an Indian prince of the time before the Christian era, whereas Kuntu Zangpo appears as a sky-blue nude ascetic suspended in the middle of the infinity of space. One may compare this iconography of the Sambhogakaya with the Western icon of God enthroned as the King of Heaven, surrounded by the choirs of angels. However, the existence of certain similarities in symbolism within these two traditions should not be construed as identity in terms of function and interpretation.

12. This luminous female figure would appear to correspond to the Eternal Consort of God found in Gnosticism and the Western Mystical tradition where She is called Sophia. The similarity of the Buddhist Prajnaparamita and the Gnostic Sophia, the eternal wisdom of God, was first pointed out to me by Conze. See Edward Conze, *Thirty Years of Buddhist Studies: Selected Essays*, University of South Carolina Press, Columbia 1968, pp. 207-209.

13. On *Shes-rab byams-ma*, the Bonpo equivalent of the Prajnaparamita as the Eternal Wisdom and the Great Goddess, see Per Kvaerne, *The Bon Religion of Tibet: The Iconography of a Living Tradition*, Serindia Publications, London 1995, p. 28.

14. On *Sa-trig Er-sangs*, the name for the Great Goddess in the Zhang-zhung language, see Per Kvaerne, *The Bon Religion of Tibet*, op. cit., p. 25.

15. This symbolism has been reversed, however, in the *Ma rgyud thugs-rje nyi-ma*. The *Ma rgyud* or Bonpo Mother Tantra represents a major Tantric system within the Bon tradition, consisting of three Tantras relating to the Base, the Path, and the Fruit of Buddhahood. It was a Terma text discovered by *Gu-ru rNon-rtse* (b. 1136). See Karmay, Treasury, ibid. pp. 50-51, 166-167, and see Per Kvaerne, *The Bon Religion of Tibet*, op. cit., pp. 74, 86-87. Also see my forthcoming study of this cycle entitled *The Mandala of the Sun*. Dan Martin has also studied a commentary to this text. See Daniel Martin, *Mandala Cosmology. Human Body Good Thought and the Revelation of the Secret Mother Tantras of Bon*, Asiatische Forschungen Band 124, Harrassowitz Verlag, Wiesbaden 1994.

16. *rNying-ma'i rgyud 'bum*. Many Tibetan scholars belonging to the New Tantra schools regard the the Old Tantras of the Nyingmapas as having a questionable authenticity because they are lacking any extant Sanskrit originals for these Tibetan translations done in the early days. For example, see Buton Rinpoche quoted in Reynolds, *The Golden Letters*, Snow Lion, Ithaca 1996, pp. 275-276.

17. In the usual system found in the Buddhist Yoga Tantras and Anuttara Tantras, Vajrasattva is often considered apart from and superior to the other five Dhyani Buddhas, each of whom are allotted a specific direction, a specific color, and other correspondences. See Alex Wayman, "Analogical Thinking in the Buddhist Tantras", in *The Buddhist Tantras*, Samual Weiser, New York 1973, pp. 30-35.

18. Dargyay insists that this language represents an evolution of Mahayana Buddhism tending toward Western style monotheism. See her articles: Eva Dargyay, "The Concept of a Creator God in Tantric Buddhism," in *Journal of the International Association of Buddhism*, vol. 8, no,. 1, Madison 1985, pp. 31-47; and "A Nyingmapa Text : The *Kun-byed rgyal-po'i mdo*," in *Soundings in Tibetan Civilization*, Barbara Aziz and Matthew Kapstein (eds), Manohar Manushiram, New Delhi 1985, pp. 282-293. She gives this so-called Buddhist theism a feminist twist in her book: E. K. Neumaier-Dargyay, *The Sovereign All-Creating Mind, the Motherly Buddha*, SUNY, Albany NY 1992. I have dealt with this question in relation to the *Kun-byed rgyal-po* Tantra in Reynolds, *The Golden Letters*, ibid., pp. 236-248. Moreover, Dudjom Rinpoche makes it quite clear that the Teacher, the Adibuddha Samantabhadra, and His audiance, the Sambhogakaya Vajrasattva, such as appear in the dialogue in the *Kun-byed rgyal-po*, do not really represent two distinct persons, but are two manifestations of the same underlying Ultimate Reality which, although they are distinguished iconographically, are identical in essence. See the opening of Part Two in Dudjom Rinpoche, *The Nyingma School of Tibetan Buddhism*, vols. I & II, Gyurme Dorje and Matthew Kapstein (eds), Wisdom Publications, Boston 1991, pp. 447ff.

19. On *gShen-lha 'od-dkar*, see Per Kvaerne, *The Bon Religion of Tibet*, ibid., pp. 24-26. Among the four principal Peaceful Deities (zhi-ba'i lha bzhi) in the Bonpo system, he represents the Sambhogakaya (rdzogs-sku), but he is also described as "the God of Wisdom" (ye-shes kyi lha), a title parallel to the Zoroastrian designation of God, Ahura Mazda, "the Wise Lord." In general, there exist some interesting parallels and suggestive correspondences in old Bonpo literature to Iranian and Zoroastrian concepts and figures. Although present evidence is inconclusive, there may be a possible correspondence among, in this case, *Kun tu bzang-po* and Zurvan, on the one hand, and *gShen-lha 'od-dkar* and Ormazd or Ahura Mazda, on the other hand. See Samten G. Karmay, "A General Introduction to the History and Doctrines of Bon," in *The Memoirs of the Research Department of the Toyo Bunko*, No. 33, Tokyo 1975, pp. 171-218. On Zurvanism, see R.C. Zaehner, *The Dawn and Twilight of Zoroastrianism*, G.P. Putnam, New York 1961, pp. 193-247.

20. The five certainties (nges-pa lnga) or five supreme aspects (phun-tshogs lnga) of the Sambhogakaya are often referred to in Tibetan scholastic literature. See for example, Part Two in Dudjom Rinpoche, *The Nyingma School of Tibetan Buddhism*, vol. I, op. cit.

21. *g.Yung-drung gi tshig-rkang bcu-gnyis.* For the full translation of the Tantra in which they are contained, the *Bu-chung bcu-gnyis,* see Part Two in the subsequent volume in this series, *Space, Awareness, and Energy.*

22. See Samten G. Karmay, "A General Introduction to the History and Doctrines of Bon," op. cit., pp. 171-218.

23. *Srid-pa'i mdzod-phug,* "the Source Treasury of Existence," published as *sNang srid mdzod-phug gi rtsa-ba dang spyi-don bcas,* or in English, *mDzod-phug: Basic Verses and Commentary by Dran-pa Nam-mkha',* lithography edition by Lopon Tenzin Namdak, New Delhi 1966. This cosmological treatise is preserved with its root text (rtsa-ba) in the Zhang-zhung language, as well as a Tibetan translation of it, together with a commentary (spyi-don). This text has been called the Bonpo version of the Abhidharma. According to the preface written by the Lopon to the above publication, the root text was composed by Tonpa Shenrab himself and taught to his eight disciples in *'Ol-mo lung-ring.* It was then taught widely in Tazik and Zhang-zhung and thereafter translated into Tibetan by Zhang-zhung *sTong-rgyung mthu-chen* and *Bod Sha-ri dbu-chen* during the reign of the Tibetan king *Gri-gum btsan-po.* The text was concealed during the persecutions at *Dang-ra khyung-rdzong,* the capital in Northern Tibet of the later Zhang-zhung kings. This root text, in both the Zhang-zhung and the Tibetan languages, was rediscovered in the year 1108 by *Gyer-mi nyi-'od* and therefore it is classified as Terma. The commentary written in Tibetan was attributed to *Dran-pa nam-mkha'* and was concealed by *gNyan-'thing Shes-rab rdo-rje.* Note that there exist some confusions in Bonpo histories between the earlier and later persecutions under the Tibetan kings *Gri-gum btsan-po* and *Khri-srong lde'u-btsan,* respectively, and the personalities involved in both cases. The *Bon ma nub-pa'i gtan-tshigs,* translated below in Chapter Seven, makes *sTang-rgyung mthu-chen* a contemporary of the latter rather than the former king of Tibet. See also Samten G. Karmay, "A General Introduction to the History and Doctrines of Bon," ibid, pp. 171-218.

Chapter 3: The Mind-to-Mind Transmission of the Jinas

1. For the translations regarding the Lineage of the Nine-fold Mind Transmission of the Sugatas and the Lineage of the Oral Transmission of the Siddhas in the *brGyud-pa'i bla-ma'i rnam-thar,* see below. A shorter account of the Mind Transmission is given in the *Yig-chung* translated below.

2. In his account of the history of Bon, written in 1922 and entitled the *Legs-bshad rin-po-che'i mdzod dpyod-ldan dga'-ba'i char,* "A Rainfall of Delights for those possessing Discrimination, being a Precious Treasury of Good Sayings," or more briefly the *Legs-bshad mdzod,* "The Treasury of Good Sayings," Shardza Rinpoche (Shar-rdza bkra-shis rgyal-mtshan, 1859-1935) divides this early period into

1) how the transmission originated (brgyud-pa byung tshul),
2) how the teachings first spread (snga dar byung tshul),
3) how they declined the first time (snga nub tshul),
4) how the teachings spread a second time (bar du dar tshul),
5) the process by which they declined again (nub lugs tshul),
6) how retribution came forth (dbu-yog byung tshul),
7) how the treasure texts were conceled (gter du sbas tshul), and
8) how the teachings spread a third time (phyis su dar tshul).
The bulk of this text on the history of Bon has been translated into English by Samten G. Karmay, in *The Treasury of Good Sayings: A Tibetan History of Bon*, Oxford University Press, London 1972. This volume also included a critical edition of the Shardza text (ff. 115b-265b), which I have used for my translations here. This is a xylograph edition in 274 folia. A more recent edition has been published in China. On the history of the transmission of the Tantras and Dzogchen, see Karmay, op. cit., pp. 39-58, covering ff. 135a-149b in the Shardza text.

3. Karmay, *Treasury*, ibid., p. xxi

4. Oral communication.

5. Suggestively, the Tibetan name *gSang-ba 'dus-pa*, "the secert assembly," translates the Sanskrit term Guhyasamaja, which is the title for the chief Father Tantra in circulation among the Buddhists, the *Guhyasamaja Tantra*, and is also the name for the Yidam, or wrathful meditation deity, of this Tantric cycle. See Note 59 below.

6. This accounts for the origin of the Father Tantras (pha rgyud), wherein, in terms of meditation practice, the practitioner transforms harmful negative energy into positive enlightened awareness in the form of a wrathful deity. The *sPyi-spungs skor*, consisting of the wrathful deities *dBal-gsas*, *Lha-rgod*, and *gTso-mchog*, represents the most important cycle of Father Tantras preserved among the Bonpos. These Tantras are said to have been brought to Tibet at the time of the second king of that country, Mutri Tsanpo (Mu-khri btsan-po), who was an ardent practitioner of them. As for their origin, see Karmay, *The Treasury of Good Sayings*, ibid., pp. xxv, 44-46. On Sangwa Dupa, also see Karmay, *Treasury*, ibid., p. xxi.

7. *History and Doctrine of Bonpo Nispanna Yoga*, Lokesh Chandra and Tenzin Namdak (eds.), Satapitaka Series v. 73, International Academy of Indian Culture, New Delhi 1968. For the titles of the various texts found in this collection, see Chapter Ten below.

8. Usually the designation Sugata (bde-bar gshegs-pa), "one who has gone into the bliss (of Nirvana)," is employed for these enlightened beings rather than the term Buddha (sangs-rgyas). However, these terms are synonymous.

9. On this Oral Transmission (snyan-brgyud) and on the later masters in the lineage of transmission (brgyud-pa'i bla-ma), see below. Patsun Tangyal Senge Zangpo (sPa-btsun bstan-rgyal seng-nge bzang-po), the author of this large hagiography text, lived in the 13th century.

10. *Bru-chen rGyal-ba g.yung-drung*, 1245-1290. For this hagiographical text, see the *sNyan-rgyud rgyal-ba'i phyag-khrid*, in *sNyan rgyud nam-mkha' 'phrul mdzod drang nges skor* and *Zhang-zhung snyan-rgyud skor*, Tibetan Bonpo Monastic Centre, New Delhi 1972.

11. *Kun tu bzang-po thugs-rje rgyun-chad med la phyag 'tshal-lo*. It is customary to open these texts in the Zhang-zhung Nyan-gyud with a homage (phyag-'tshal-ba) to the Primordial Buddha Kuntu Zangpo because He is the ultimate source for all of the Dzogchen teachings.

12. Each of the nine enlightened beings, or Sugatas (bder-gshegs dgu), are conceived as residing in a higher dimension of spiritual existence called Akanishtha ('og-min), literally "it does not exist (min) below ('og) anything else." The term, therefore, refers to the highest plane of existence, one that totally transcends matter and contingent worldly existence. Generally, in the Tantric tradition of Tibetan Buddhism, there are three Akanishthas that differ in their respective natures:

1) First, there is the Akanishtha of the Shuddhavasa Devas, "the Gods of the Pure Abodes," which is located, according to the Abhidharma system of cosmology, as the topmost of the seventeen intellectual or mental planes of the Rupadhatu, or Form World (gzugs khams). This dimension, therefore, represents the summit of existence in Samsaric terms, there being nothing visible higher than it, even though the invisible infinite dimensions of formless cosmic consciousness, known as the Arupadhatu, or Formless World (gzugs-med khams), might be thought to surpass it in a certain sense. This highest dimension of existence, just as is the case with the other mental planes, is attained by the mastery of the highest intensities of concentration in trance known as the dhyanas (bsam-gtan). Ascending progressively by way of the four successive levels of dhyana grants the meditation practitioner access to these subtle mental planes of the Rupadhatu. However, all of these dimensions of existence that are realized thereby are produced by antecedent causes and so, no matter how exalted or attenuated they may be, they still represent conditioned existence and, therefore, belong to Samsara. They do not represent Nirvana.

2) Second, there is the Akanishtha which is the dimension of existence of the Sambhogakaya. This transcendent dimension, being the true summit of existence beyond the limits of Samsara because it transcends conditioned existence and the cyclical manifestations of time and history, is, at the same time, the center of all existence. It is, therefore, even more exalted than the highest of the Brahmalokas of the Rupadhatu. This conception might be compared to the Ogdoad in the Gnostic cosmology, the imperishable pure realm of light that lies beyond the stars and the domains of the planetary powers known as the Hebdomad. See the discussion below and in Part Three of the subsequent volume in this series, *Space, Awareness, and Energy*.

3) Finally, there is the Akanishtha of the Dharmakaya. Although this represents the mode of being of pure enlightened awareness, which has

ever been so from the very beginning and remains untainted by
Samsara in a state of total primordial purity (ka-dag chen-po), in
actuality, the Dharmakaya does not have any particular location in
space, neither at the center nor at the periphery (dbu mtha' med-pa).
Like the limitless extent of infinite space itself, it is all-pervasive
(khyab) and all-encompassing (bdal). Indeed, in this Akanishtha,
which is the all-pervading and all-encompassing Dimension of the
Ultimate Reality (bon-nyid khyab bdal dbyings kyi 'og-min na), Kuntu
Zangpo, who is the Dharmakaya that is inexpressible in words, has
resided from the very beginning, that is, as the Primordial Teacher or
the Teacher in Eternity (ye-nyid ston-pa). Indeed, He resides entirely
outside of time and the temporal process. This mode of being,
metaphorically a place of residence (gnas), is known as the
Dharmadhatu, the Dimension of All Existence (bon dbyings, chos-
dbyings). As the inexpressible and inconceivable Dharmakaya, who is
the Teacher in Eternity, from the uncreated state of the self-originated
primordial purity, He revealed the ultimate Dzogchen teachings in the
center of the heart or Mind (thugs) of the Second Teacher, His own
emanation, who is the ultimate expression of compassion and love (ye-
nyid ston-pa brjod-med bon-sku yis/ rang-'byung ka-dag skye-med
ngang nyid nas/ thugs-rje'i ston-pa'i thugs kyi dkyil du bshad). That is
to say, this revelation occurred primordially (ye nas), outside of time
and history, a communication in the mode of a direct mind-to-mind
transmission (dgongs brgyud) of the understanding (rtogs-pa) of the
Dzogchen teachings regarding the Natural State of the Nature of Mind,
without any words whatsoever intervening (brjod-med). This
telepathic communication of understanding was instantaneous. It
occurred outside time, even before creation came into existence.
In actual fact, there was no difference, in essence, between the
Dharmakaya, the Teacher (ston-pa), metaphorically called "the Father,"
and His audience ('khor), metaphorically called "the Son," the latter
being an emanation of the former. Although one in their essence, these
two distinct persons (or hypostases) only appear to be so for the sake of
understanding by way of human discourse. As the expression of
compassion (thugs-rje) and the exercise of skillful means (thabs), they
appear as two persons in order that the dialogue may occur and thus
render the Dzogchen teachings comprehensible to human understanding.
This Supreme Audience for the Dzogchen teachings, the Teacher who is
Compassion, is none other than the Sambhogakaya. In the Buddhist
Tantras, this emanation is called Vajrasattva (rDo-rje sems-dpa'). The
term vajra (rdo-rje) or diamond-like has the connotation not only of purity
and indestructibility, but of incorruptible spirituality. It refers to a higher
order of being, one that is spiritual, indestructible, and eternal. In Bon,
this same principle is represented by the symbol of the Swastika (g.yung-
drung). In the Bonpo tradition, this same emanation, who is the manifest
embodiment of compassion, is known as Shenlha Odkar (gShen-lha 'od-

dkar). In this dialogue occurring in eternity, the real understanding of Dzogchen is transmitted from the Ultimate Reality, itself without form, to the highest conceivable form (to human beings at least), the Sambhogakaya, who is untainted by the corruptions of matter and consists only of pure light and is the celestial prototype of the human.

Indeed, whereas the Dharmakaya is beyond all conception by the finite mind and beyond all expression in words or language (blo 'das brjod-med), the Sambhogakaya, a pure vision of Clear Light, can come into view when the faculties and the intellect of the human being have been sufficiently purified and developed. Therefore, the Sambhogakaya has the capacity to communicate and disclose the meaning of Dzogchen on the level of human understanding by way of emanating countless numbers of Nirmanakayas, just as the sun emanates countless rays of light in order to illuminate the surface of the earth.

This Sambhogakaya is the eternal Logos, the Word of the Buddha, which is outside time and history, yet ever-present and active in it, where it can erupt into human consciousness at any moment as revelation within the depths of the human soul. This revelation is not restricted to some particular time in the distant past and now only recorded in scripture and dispensed by an established priesthood; rather, it is something that is on-going, continuous, and ever-present, even now. It is present in the sky like the sun, but there is only one sun present in the sky above the earth. Does this mean that, as the emanation of the Dharmakaya and as the eternal Logos, there is only one Sambhogakaya? This depends on whether a text is speaking soteriologically or cosmologically. Every individual stream of consciousness that awakens, realizing enlightenment and liberation from the dream-like delusions of Samsara, not only discovers the Dharmakaya, which has been present all along, but also manifests the Rupakaya. Whereas the Dharmakaya, as the state of Shunyata that is like the infinity of space, represents the universal aspect of enlightenement, the Rupakaya embodies its individual and particular aspect, reflecting, according to the Sutra system, the salvation-history of that individual stream of consciousness since beginningless time in Samsara. This is because, according to the Sutra system, whereas the Dharmakaya is realized through the accumulation of wisdom, the Rupakaya is realized through the accumulation of merit that has been accrued by the individual Bodhisattva over the course of three immeasurable kalpas due to various virtuous actions. Therefore, each Buddha or enlightened being manifests as an individual Sambhogakaya, but this single Sambhogakaya may emanate and project, in turn, an infinite number of Nirmanakaya manifestations. Collectively, the Sambhogakaya and these Nirmanakayas comprise the Rupakaya of a Buddha. Whereas the Sambhogakaya may be compared to the sun in the sky, these Nirmanakayas may be compared to the rays of the sun that illuminate all the dimensions of existence. This is the usual metaphor employed in Dzogchen texts. On this question, see the discussion in the Appendix of John Myrdhin Reynolds, *Self-Liberation*

through Naked Awareness, Snow Lion Publications, Ithaca 2000.
Each individual Buddha, or enlightened being, is a sun or Sambhogakaya
in the sky of existence, spiritually illuminating its Buddha Field or field
of compassionate activity with the light of the teachings of the Dharma.
In this sense, each individual Buddha represents a single Sambhogakaya,
but, as said above, such a Buddha may project a multiplicity of
Nirmanakaya emanations in order to teach the Dharma, or path to
liberation and enlightenment, to deluded sentient beings in the various
dimesions of existence. Therefore, each Buddha possesses not only the
Rupakaya, but its specific field of activity or Buddhakshetra (zhing-
khams). This may be a pure dimension such as Sukhavati (bde-ba-can),
the Buddha Field of Amitabha Buddha, or an impure field of a mixed
character such as our own universe of the Sahalokadhatu, the world of
travail. Such a field is mixed or impure because the living beings dwelling
therein are still afflicted with delusions and with impure karmic vision.
Nevertheless, a field such as our own universe is the field for the
compassionate activity, in cosmological terms, of a single Sambhogakaya.
This luminous figure is known in the Bon tradition as Shenlha Odkar
(gShen-lha 'od-dkar) and in the Buddhist tradition variously as
Vajrasattva, Vairochana, or Amitabha. This position of the Sambhogakaya
is said, in some texts, to be an office held for a single world-cycle or kalpa
by a single enlightened individual and, upon the completion of this world-
cycle, a new individual assumes this exalted office. Thus, according to
certain Bonpo scriptures, such as the *gZer-myig*, the present
Sambhogakaya or Wisdom Deity (ye-shes lha) is Shenlha Odkar, and his
emanation, or representative on earth as the Buddha and the World-
Teacher (ston-pa), is Shenrab Miwoche (gSen-rab mi-bo-che) who
appeared in Olmo Lung-ring ('Ol-mo lung-ring) some 18,000 years ago.
According to certain Buddhist Tantras, the present Sambhogakaya is
Amitabha, who is assisted by the great Bodhisattva Avalokiteshvara,
otherwise known as Padmapani, whereas the great Nirmanakaya, or
Incarnation for the present age of the Kali Yuga, is Shakyamuni. In the
future world-age, the Sambhogakaya will be Amoghasiddhi and the
Nirmanakaya, or Incarnation, will be Maitreya. According to certain
scriptures, such as the *Karuna-pundarika Sutra*, the specific Buddha Field
of Maitreya is already coming into manifestation because the majority of
human beings incarnate at the present time are karmically linked with this
future Buddha, rather than his predecessor, Shakyamuni, and therefore
belong to his specific sphere of enlightened activity. In this way, the future
is already impinging upon the present. Thus, in cosmological terms, the
Buddhist texts speak of a single Sambhogakaya, sometimes called a
Dhyani Buddha in the terminology of the Vajracharyas of Nepal, and a
single great Nirmanakaya or Uttama-Nirvanakaya, both of whom
manifest within a single world-age (yuga) of a particular Buddha Field or
world-system. This system of the Buddhist Tantras, with the figures who
succeed each other in turn, may be tabulated as follows:

1) The Dhyani Buddhas, or Sambhogakaya manifestations:
   Vairochana, Akshobhya, Ratnasambhava, Amitabha, and Amoghasiddhi.
2) The corresponding Buddhakula or Buddha Family:
   Tathagatakula, Vajrakula, Ratnakula, Padmakula, and Karmakula.
3) The Dhyani Bodhisattvas, or associated Great Bodhisattvas:
   Chakrapani, Vajrapani, Ratnapani, Padmapani, and Vishvapani.
4) The Maha-Nirmanakayas, or Great Incarnations:
   Krukuchanda, Kanakamuni, Kashyapa, Shakyamuni, and Maitreya.

On this system of symbols and corrspondences, see Alex Wayman, "Analogical Thinking in the Buddhist Tantras", in *The Buddhist Tantras*, Samual Weiser, New York 1973.

The similarities to Christology and certain Biblical metaphors as "The Ancient of Days" are suggestive. Although not necessarily due to historical contact, though this should not be ruled out, there do appear to be certain similar ways of thinking found in Buddhism, especially the Mahayana, that are also found in Christian Gnosticism. Nevertheless, the conception here in terms of the Buddhist context is different from the more familiar theism prevalent in the West. Kuntu Zangpo is not some king enthroned in heaven, commanding his minions of angels and intervening in human history. This image of the great king, the God of all creation, enthroned in the highest heaven, is more appropriately applied to the Sambhogakaya. Rather, Kuntu Zangpo transcends the activities of Samsara and is in no way touched by the corruption of the world. He does not Himself manifest in time and history, which is the creation of an ignorant, profane consciousness. Although the principal manifestation and enlightened activity of Kuntu Zangpo, as the Primordial Buddha, is indeed compassion and love (thugs-rje), which is furthermore understood as creative energy (rtsal), it primarily manifests as the teaching of the Dharma, that is, the revelation of the knowledge or gnosis of the nature of our true being. At the same time, this is the knowledge that liberates us. Thus, this Buddha activity is not the creation of the profane world of Samsara, nor is it a divine providence that intervenes periodically and capriciously in the political and military events of history. That is the task of lesser intermediaries, the gods and spirits who are less-than-enlightened beings. Kuntu Zangpo does not have any politics. He does not favor one human group above another. Rather, His infinite compassion and love is totally impartial toward all (phyogs ris med-pa) and is expressed as the bestowing of the understanding of reality upon all those sentient beings who are ready and open to receive this light of the central spiritual sun. One has only to step out of the shadows of the cave in order to experience the light of the sun on one's face. The Sambhogakaya, whose nature is luminous clarity, may be compared to the sun in the sky. The sun does not withhold its light from anyone, no matter how ignorant or denegrated they may be. But still, the individual must make the initial effort and step out of the shadows in order to receive it. It is not forced upon them. The Primordial State of Kuntu Zangpo is present there all of the time, even at this very moment; it is only ignorant and deluded sentient beings like ourselves, still caught up in our distractions, who do not recognize Him. This Primordial Buddhahood (ye sangs-rgyas) is ever present from the very beginning. Enlightenment is ever-present, but it goes unrecognized throughout the world as though a stranger in exile. Akanishtha is here and now. According to Dzogchen, the clear luminosity of the sun of Rigpa, which is the Sambhogakaya, resides in the hollow space of the heart in each sentient being, even at this very moment.

By way of comparison, in the Q Document and the Gospel of Thomas, Jesus of Nazareth spoke in much the same way about the Kingdom of God, which in Buddhist terms would be Akanishtha. This teaching on the Kingdom of God, which has its parallel in the Buddhist notion of a pure Buddha Field, appears to have been part of the original kerygma or message of Jesus of Nazareth. See Burton Mack, *The Lost Gospel: The Book of Q and Christian Origins*, Harper Collins, San Francisco 1993.

13. Having received the Dzogchen teachings in a direct mind-to-mind transmission from the ultimate source, which is the Dharmakaya, the Sambhogakaya thereupon contemplated their real meaning which, indeed, was inexpressible in words even from the very beginning (ye nas brjod du med-pa'i don du dgongs). In the Dzogchen context, contemplation (dgongs-pa), as opposed to meditation (sgom-pa) where the discursive mind is still functioning, means entering into and remaining in the Natural State of the Nature of Mind (sems-nyid gnas-lugs). Nevertheless, this process of revelation only represents a visible display for the benefit of sentient beings because the source, the Dharmakaya, and the recipient of the transmission, the Sambhogakaya, being the emanation of the former, represent one and the same state of primordial enlightened awareness.

14. Then the Sambhogakaya, having instantaneously understood the transmission of the Dzogchen teachings regarding the Natural State of the Nature of Mind, abides continuously in his own original condition in the Akanishtha of the all-pervading and all-encompassing Dimension that is unmoving (mi g.yo khyab bdal dbyings kyi 'og-min na). The term "unmoving" (mi g.yo, g.yo-ba med-pa) indicates that the Sambhogakaya has never, even for a moment, departed from this primordial state of Akanishtha, where he remains eternally in samadhi, or contemplation. This is ever the case, even though he unceasingly and uninterruptedly (ma 'gags-pa) projects and emanates out of the inexhaustible effulgence and richness of his being countless numbers of Nirmanakayas into all the myriads of world-systems and dimensions of existence. These projections, or emanations (sprul-pa), are like magical apparitions (cho-'phrul), but they possess all the marks and characteristics of an enlightened being or Buddha. They may appear spontaneously and creatively at any point in space and at any moment of time and history in order to teach the Dharma and reveal it to those sentient beings who have purified their senses and their minds, so that they become receptive to the

transmissions. This unceasing Buddha activity, which is the visible expression of infinite compassion (thugs-rje chen-po), may be compared to the light of the sun that illuminates the dark surface of the earth. In the text, the Sambhogakaya is called the Teacher of Compassion Kuntu Zangpo (thugs-rje'i ston-pa kun tu bzang-po), here meaning not the Primordial Buddha, but the Sambhogakaya properly known as Shenlha Odkar (rdzogs-sku gshen-lha 'od-dkar). He is, nevertheless, an emanation, or projection,of the Primordial Buddha Kuntu Zangpo. The longer hagiographical text that follows below makes this matter clearer. This luminous figure represents and embodies the infinite compassion or energy of compassion (thugs-rje) of the Primordial Buddha, visibly manifesting as the Clear Light of Awareness. Thereupon, from the state of his unmoving Mind, that is, the Natural State, he expounded telepathically the Dzogchen teachings in the center of the Mind of the Teacher who is an Emanation (thugs nyid g'yo-ba med-pa'i ngang nyid nas/ sprul-pa'i ston-pa'i thugs kyi dkyil du bshad). This third Teacher is the Supreme Nirmanakaya Shenrab Chenpo, the celestial prototype in human form of all the Nirmanakayas that appear in human experience throughout time and history. Again, there appears to exist a clear parallel to the Gnostic and Hermetic sequence of emanations: Nous, Logos, and Anthropos. Having received the revelation of Dzogchen in Akanishtha, thereupon, this Nirmanakaya entered into and remained in the state of primordial contemplation (dgongs-pa) wherein he contemplated the real meaning of the Natural State as being like the all-pervading sky, that is to say, like the infinity of space (kun khyab nam-mkha' lta-bu'i don du dgongs). Again, "unmoving" (mi g.yo-ba) means never departing from this condition of contemplation that is the Natural State of the Nature of Mind. On the activity of this celestial prototype of the Nirmanakaya, see the translation of the hagiographical text which follows below.

The Sambhogakaya (rdzogs-par longs-spyod-pa'i sku) is the dimension (dbyings) and the visible form (sku) of enlightened awareness, manifesting as pure light devoid of materiality. Even though the Sambhogakaya never departs from the Akanishtha of the contemplation of total primordial purity (ka-dag chen-po), like the orb of the sun in the sky, its light rays are projected as emanations throughout all the dimensions of existence. Because the Sambhogakaya eternally remains unmoving and beyond time and corruption while abiding in the state of contemplation, its nature is said to represent perfect (rdzogs-par) enjoyment (longs-spyod). Apart from this ceaseless process of transcendent illumination, the Sambhogakaya never actually enters into the process of Samsara, just as the sun remains in the sky without ever falling to the surface of the earth, which it illuminates from above. Rather, it is the Nirmanakayas that are projected, descend, and enter into all the worlds, dimensions, and diverse levels of Samsaric existence. So it is here that the Supreme Nirmanakaya, the celestial prototype, or Anthropos, to use the Gnostic term, first appears at the beginning of time in that

Akanishtha that represents the highest plane of Samsaric existence. This soteriological process may be compared to the Gnostic myth of the descent of the Logos and Savior into the Hebdomad, the seven planetary spheres, which is known as the Heimarmene, the domain of fate. On this Gnostic myth of the Descent of the Savior, which appers to have pre-existed Christianity, see Hans Jonas, *The Gnostic Religion: The Message of the Alien God and the Beginnings of Christianity*, Beacon Press, Boston 1963.

15. The Supreme Teacher, the Sambhogakaya, abides in the Akanishtha of the all-pervading and all-encompassing Dimension that is spontaneous perfection (lhun-grub khyab bdal dbyings kyi 'og-min na). The term "spontaneous perfection" (lhun-grub) means that forms emerge spontaneously out of the state of Shunyata, or Kunzhi, being complete and perfect just as they are, without any need for correction or modification by the discursive mind. According to the text: *lhun-grub khyab bdal dbyings kyi 'og-min na/ ma g.yos ngang las g.yo-ba'i cho-'phrul gyis/ bon kyi sku la mtshan dpe yongs su rdzogs/ gang la gang 'dul gang mos sku ru bstan/ sprul-pa'i ston-pa gshen-lha 'od-dkar gyis/ thugs-rje chen-po'i byin-rlabs ngang nyid nas/ cir yang sprul-pa'i sku'i thugs kyi dkyil du bshad/ mtha' dbus med-pa 'od kyi snying-po-can/ mkha' la nyi shar lta-ba'i don du dgongs.* This Supreme Teacher Shenlha Odkar, the Sambhogakaya, from a state that does not move from Akanishtha, emanates out of the inexhaustible effulgence of his being an infinite number of magical apparitions (cho-'phrul) that move about everywhere throughout the universe in terms of time and space. Each of these emanations, being complete and perfect in terms of the marks and characteristics of enlightenement, serve to teach the Dharma to sentient beings everywhere. The heart-essence (snying-po) refers to the Bodhichitta, or spark of light, corresponding to the Gnostic sperma pneumatikos, inherent within every sentient being.

16. One of the Nirmanakayas emanated by the Sambhogakaya into the Samsaric realms of existence was known as the Teacher of Awareness Tsadmed Oddan (rig-pa'i ston-pa tshad-med 'od-ldan) This figure, whose name means "he who possesses light without measure," bears comparison with the Buddha Amitabha ('Od dpag-med) whose name also means "light without measure." As the Buddha especially associated with the west, with his celestial paradise of Sukhavati (bde-ba-can) also located in the western direction, the cult of Amitabha became very popular in ancient Central Asia around the time of Christ. The method for obtaining rebirth in his pure land or Buddha Field, known as Sukhavati, is the principal subject of several Mahayana Sutras. From Central Asia, his cult was brought to China and then to Japan where it came to form the basis for Pure Land Buddhism or Jodo Shinshu. This Teacher, Tsadmed Oddan, manifested as a Nirmanakaya in the Akanishtha of the Abhasvara Devas, "the Gods of Clear Light," which is an intermediate Devaloka, or pure realm (bar lha 'od-gsal lha'i 'og-min na). Among the seventeen mental

planes of the Rupadhatu, or Form World of traditional Buddhist cosmology, this heaven is the sixth when ascending from below. Once having received the transmission of the Dzogchen teachings as described above, then from a state of total self-arisen primordial awareness, he revealed them in turn in the center of the Mind or heart of the Deva Trulshen Nangdan, who thereupon contemplated that the real meaning (don du dgongs) of this gnosis is like the light and rays of the sun (rig-pa'i ston-pa tshad-med 'od-ldan gyis/ ye-shes rang-shar chen-po'i ngang nyid nas/ 'phrul-gshen snang-ldan thugs kyi dkyil du bshad/ nyi 'od nyi zer lta-bu'i don du dgongs). Similarly, Rigpa, or primordial Awareness, is compared to the orb of the sun in the sky, and its primal cognitions or gnoses (ye-shes), are like the rays of light of this sun.

17. In response to my querries, Lopon Tenzin Namdak replied that both Tsadmed Oddan and Trulshen Nangdan may be regarded as emanations of Tonpa Shenrab. However, according to the Bonpo myth, the latter was a Deva or god belonging to the race of the Chya Gods (phya) dwelling on the summit of the Sumeru mountain. Called the Teacher of the Great Means (thabs chen ston-pa), he is regarded as the spiritual father of Chimed Tsugphud, the celestial pre-existence of Tonpa Shenrab. See below. The Great Means, or the most skillful among all means (thabs chen), refers to the process for manifesting the Nirmanakaya. According to the text: *mgon btsun phya yul gser steng 'og-min na/ thabs chen ston-pa 'phrul-gshen snang-ldan gyis/ rang-rig rang gsal sgrib-med ngang nyid nas/ bar-snang ston-pa'i thugs kyi dkyil du bshad/ chu dang chu zla lta-bu'i don du dgongs*. On the metaphor of being like the image of the moon reflected on the water (chu dang chu zla lta-bu), see the translation of the *Kun-gzhi zhal-shes* in Part Two of the subsequent volume in this series, *Space, Awareness, and Energy*.

18. The cuckoo (khu-byug), with its sky-blue color and its traditional role in Tibet as the herald of spring, is the sacred bird of the Bonpos. From his original heavenly abode, Tonpa Shenrab assumed the form of a cuckoo in order to descend to earth where he might be reborn and proclaim the Dzogchen teachings. This Teacher, the cuckoo who appeared in the atmosphere (bar snang khu-byug), the emanation of Tonpa Shenrab, manifested in the Akanishtha of the Thirty-Three Gods (sum-cu rtsa gsum lha'i 'og-min na), the divine plane of existence on the summit of the Sumeru mountain at the center of the world. From a state where discriminating wisdom and skillful means were inseparable in their manifestation, he revealed the Dzogchen teachings in the center of the Mind of the Secret Consort Zangza Ringtsun (gsang-ba'i yum bZang-za ring-btsun). See below. Whereupon, she contemplated that the real meaning was that all appearances lack any inherent existence. As the text says: *bar-snang khu-byug sprul-pa'i ston-pa yis/ thabs shes dbyer-med rol-pa'i ngang nyid nas/ gsang-ba'i yum thugs kyi dkyil du bshad/ snang la rang-bzhin med-pa'i don du dgongs*. As the mother of the future Buddha, this figure is regarded as the embodiment of the Prajnaparamita,

the Perfection of Wisdom. The Prajnaparamita is known as the Great Mother (yum chen) because she is the Mother of all the Buddhas of the three times. A Buddha only becomes a Buddha by virtue of this Perfection of Wisdom. At the same time, she is the Holy Virgin who miraculously gives birth to the future Buddha following an immaculate conception. The meaning that "all phenomena lack any inherent existence" represents the understanding proper to the Prajnaparamita or the Perfection of Wisdom. This goddess is a manifestation of the Prajnaparamita and, as such, she is the mother of the Logos, or Nirmanakaya. This may be compared with the Christian notion of the Theotokos, the Mother of God.

This scenario is parallel to the usual North Asian mythological motif of a messenger of the gods descending to earth in the form of a bird, often an eagle, in order to impregnate miraculously a virgin and subsequently be reborn as the first human shaman. Some scholars such as Helmut Hoffmann, speculate that the archaic Tibetan term *gshen* originally meant a shaman. See his *The Religions of Tibet*, ibid., pp. 13-27, 84-110. On the myths of the celestial origin of the shaman, see Mircea Eliade, *Shamanism: Archaic Techniques of Ecstasy*, Pantheon Books, New York 1964. This mythological shamanic motif of the descent to earth of a divine messenger from heaven who brings a saving knowledge to humanity is also found, in other contexts, with the birth stories of the Buddha and of Jesus Christ. Often this descent from heaven is to a mountain or to a tree that symbolizes the center of the world, the *axis mundi*. It is at this symbolic center that free communication and travel is possible between the heaven worlds above and the earth, and even into the netherworlds below the earth. The shaman has access to this center and line of communication by way of an altered state of consciousness. Generally, in the case of North Asian shamanism, the myth states that in ancient times the harmony and intimacy between heaven and earth was broken, God ceased to walk among mankind on familiar terms, and so the primitive human race fell prey to hostile demons and evil spirits who inflicted diseases of the body and other afflictions upon hapless humanity. The gods, looking down from heaven above, took compassion upon humanity's suffering and decided to teach human beings the art of shamanizing, which has the capacity to exorcise these afflictions. They, therefore, dispatched one of their number as a messenger in the guise of a bird in order to incarnate among humans as the first shaman and teach them the arts of healing.

19. At that time, Zangza Ringtsun, who is the Mother of Wisdom (bZang-za ring-btsun shes-rab yum), dwelt on the Sumeru mountain in the center of the world, in the paradise which was the Akanishtha consisting of the heavenly evergreen forest of jewels and turquoise (rin-chen g.yu steng tshal gyi 'og-min na). From the state of Shunyata where Dimension and Gnosis, or Primordial Awareness, are inseparable (dbyings shes dbyer-med), she revealed the Dzogchen teachings in the center of the heart, or Mind, of her miraculously born son, Chimed Tsugphud. He contemplated

that the real meaning here was that clarity and emptiness are inseparable (bzang-za ring-btsun shes-rab yum nyid kyis/ dbyings shes dbyer-med stong 'chi-med tsug-phud thugs kyi dkyil du bshad/ gsal stong dbyer med-pa'i don du dgongs). As the manifestation of Primordial Wisdom, the Prajnaparamita, the goddess Zangza Ringtsun embodies the state of Shunyata itself. This state is what wisdom (shes-rab) brings into view as the essence of all phenomena. All phenomena, or appearences, are understood to be in themselves empty (stong-pa) and lacking in any inherent existence (rang-bzhin med-pa). The Primordial State manifests both of these sides, namely, space or dimension and pristine awareness or gnosis, and they are inseparable from the very beginning (ye nas dbyings dang ye-shes dbyer-med). Coming to understand this, one realizes the inseparability of clarity and emptiness (gsal-stong dbyer-med). This inseparability is a recurrent theme in Dzogchen texts.

20. In the Akanishtha which is the secret crystal cave in the turquoise valley of evergreen trees (g.yu lung shel phug gsang-ba'i 'og-min na), the son of this goddess was born as Chimed Tsugphud ('Chi-med gtsug-phud). The etymology of this name is given in the translation of the following text. This luminous figure represented the heavenly pre-existence of Tonpa Shenrab before he was reborn on earth. It was in this guise that he revealed the Bonpo Tantras and the Upadeshas of Dzogchen to his disciple Sangwa Dupa. See below. This event occurred on the slopes of the Sumeru mountain. According to the text: *sprul-pa'i ston-pa 'chi-med gtsug-phud kyis/ dgongs-pa'i nyin-khu phul du phyin-pa 'di/ rgyud lung man-ngag tshig don 'brel-pa tu/ rgyud khung ston-pa'i thugs kyi dkyil du bshad/ gsang-ba'i man-ngag don du 'dus-par dgongs.* Note that the Western savior figures Mithras and Jesus Christ were also the result of an immaculate conception and birth in a cave from a virgin mother. This is the traditional divine scenario, or archetype, of the birth of the savior god among humanity.

21. Sangwa Dupa (gSang-ba 'dus-pa), the chief disciple of Chimed Tsugphud, received from the latter the transmissions for the Tantras and the Upadeshas of Dzogchen in a heaven world. According to the Bonpo tradition, he is considered to have been the previous incarnation of Shakyamuni Buddha. According to the text: *lha yul bar-ba gsal-ba'i 'og-min na/ man-ngag don 'dus gsang-ba 'dus-pa yis/ theg-pa'i yang-rtse rgyud lung rtsa-ba 'di/ lha klu mi gsum las sogs nyi-shu rtsa bzhi la/ thugs nas lung du rig-pa thabs kyis brgyud.*

22. *rDzogs-pa chen-po zhang-zhung snyan-rgyud kyi rnam-bshad gsal-ba'i me-long zhes bya-ba*: "The Clear Mirror" or the mirror which elucidates, illuminates, or clarifies (gsal-ba'i me-long), that is to say, it presents a complete explanation (rnam-bshad). This second title appears to be the name given to the present text by its author, whereas the first appears to be a title given by the editor of the collection, which describes the contents of the text.

23. The text translated here, in part, contains only Part One, providing an introduction to Bon, albeit briefly, and an account of the origin and history of the Dzogchen teachings of the *Zhang-zhung snyan rgyud*. Presumably, Parts Two and Three are represented by the other texts. The present text was written by Paton Tan-gyal (sPa-ston bstan-rgyal), whose name concludes the list of the masters in the lineage. According to the colophon, Paton Tan-gyal Senge Palzang concluded writing the text on the tenth day of the tenth month in the earth-pig year of 1299 in the white palace of Dechengang at the hermitage of Palri Khudyang at Latod in Tsang province (sa-mo-phag gi lo/ zla-ba bcu-pa'i tshe bcu/ skar-ma bya-ba bzhug la/ dpal ri khud yang bden bde-chen sgang gi pho-brang dkar-po ru/ spa btsun bstan-rgyal seng-ge dpal-bzang bdag gis ni). Some further names in the later lineages have been provided by Lopon Tenzin Namdak.

24. One enters the gateways or the Portals of Bon (bon sgo) by way of taking initiations or empowerments (dbang-bskur). Properly speaking, "initiation" is the entranceway into Tantra, the path of transformation, rather than into Dzogchen as such, just as the taking of vows (sdom-pa) is the means for entering into the Sutra, the path of renunciation. The direct introduction to intrinsic Awareness (rig-pa'i ngo-sprod) represents the entranceway, as such, into the practice of Dzogchen. Here, in this context of the Zhang-zhung Nyan-gyud, one first takes initiation externally (phyi) and enters into the visible mandala possessing characteristics (phyi mtshan-bcas kyi dkyil-'khor la 'jug-pa) for the Tantric deity Zhang-zhung Meri. Literally, this name means fire (me) mountain (ri) or volcano. Meri was a special armor-clad terrifying form of Gekhod, the tutelary mountain god of Mount Kailas, the sacred mountain or soul-mountain (bla-ri) of the Zhang-zhung kingdom. Moreover, Meri was the personal meditation deity (yi-dam lha) of the Mahasiddha Gyerpungpa and is known as the one who guards the scriptures for the practice of the Rites of the Peaceful and Wrathful Deities (me-ri zhi-khro'i cho-ga'i gzhung bsgrub). According to Shardza Rinpoche in his *Legs-bshad mdzod* (Karmay, *Treasury*, ibid.), the lineages for the Zhang-zhung Nyan-gyud and for the practice of Zhang-zhung Meri are more or less the same. Thus, taking initiation for this meditation deity represents the external means for entering into the practice of the former. According to Lopon Tenzin Namdak, the principal function of the diety Meri is the protection of the Zhang-zhung teachings and their practitioners. I have separately prepared a study on the practice and symbolism of this deity entitled *The Cult and Practice of Zhang-zhung Meri*, Bonpo Translation Project (privately printed), Berkeley 1989. Some of this material will be included in an appendix in a subsequent volume of this series. On the iconography of Meri, see Per Kvaerne, *The Bon Religion of Tibet*, Serindia Publications, London 1995, pp. 84-86, 100-103. On the Tibetan cult of sacred mountains and mountain gods, see John Vincent Bellezza, *Divine Dyads: Ancient Civilization in Tibet*, Library of Tibetan Works and Archives, Dharamsala 1997.

Internally (nang), the candidate receives the blessings of spiritual inspiration (byin gyis brlabs-pa) from the masters in the lineage of transmission of the Twenty-Four August Persons (gang-zag nyer-gcig), the twenty-four Jalupas who attained the Rainbow Body of Light, at the various stages in the process of initiation (nang dbang gi rim-pas gang-zag gi rgyud byin gyis brlab). Generally, this takes the form of showing the candidate a series of pictures or initiation cards (tsa-ka-li) depicting each master during the course of the initiation. This represents the internal entrance into the practice. Secretly (gsang-ba), the candidate receives a direct introduction (ngo-sprod), or "pointing out," of the Natural State and its capacity for intrinsic Awareness (rig-pa). This is accomplished by way of examples that illustrate or exemplify it (gsang-ba dbang gcig brda thabs mthon-pa'i dpe la ngo-sprad-pa), usually by displaying to the candidate such symbolic objects as the mirror, the crystal, the peacock feather, and so on. This process represents the symbolic method of the single initiation lineage (dbang gcig brda thabs) and constitutes the secret entrance into the Zhang-zhung tradition of Dzogchen. Moreover, this will also usually include a verbal introduction to Dzogchen at the conclusion of the initiation ceremony. This direct introduction, or pointing out, brings about an immediate face-to-face encounter of the candidate with one's own Nature of Mind. Originally, this was given by a master privately and secretly to only a single disciple (gcig brgyud).

25. *Shes-bya snang-srid thams-cad bon yin/ bon gyis snang-srid thams-cad la ma khyab-pa med..... des khyab tshad ni nam-mkhas khyab ste.* Here, the technical usage of the term *bon* precisely corresponds to the usage in Buddhist texts of the term dharma (chos). In this present context, basically "bon" and "dharma" mean the nature of existence and, therefore, also the teachings of the enlightened Buddhas that reveal the nature of existence. In the plural form, dharmas, the word means the phenomena that appear to consciousness. See the discussion of the use and meanings of the technical term "dharma" in the Buddhist tradition in Edward Conze, *Buddhist Thought in India*, George Allen & Unwin, London 1962.

The *kLu-'bum,* or "One Hundred Thousand Nagas," is an ancient Bonpo ritual text containing innumerable healing rituals (gto) for propitiating the Nagas (klu), the serpentine water spirits who control the powers of fertility and the wealth of the earth. These rituals are usually prefaced by a myth of origin (smrang), which describes the occasions and reasons why this ritual was first performed. Within the *kLu-'bum* there are three collections of texts known as the white, the black, and the mixed (dkar nag khra gsum). An abridged version of the *kLu-'bum* was later adapted for Buddhist use. On the *kLu-'bum* in general, see R.A. Stein, *Tibetan Civilization*, Faber & Faber, London 1972, pp. 243-245.

26. In the traditional cosmology of Buddhism and Bon, the external physical world, or universe, is compared to a vessel, or container (snod), whereas the living beings that the world contains, its inhabitants, is compared to

the nectar (bcud) found within the vessel. The text refers to the worlds comprising this universe (snod kyi 'jig-rten).

27. *Ye-shes kyi spyan*, "the eye of gnosis," often called the wisdom eye or third eye in Western literature.

28. This scholastic methodology referred to in the text is not elucidated here.

29. The *dBal-mo las thig* is a Tantric text containing rituals and practices associated with the cycle of the Tantric deity Walse (dBal-gsas).

30. *Bon ni mi g.yo skyob-pa'i sgra zhes dang/ g.yung zhes bya don la mi yengs-pa/ drang zhes bya-ba rtags la mi 'gyur-pa/ bon zhes bya-ba sems-nyid bdal-ba'i klong zhes dang.* The Bonpo technical term *g.yung-drung* (Skt. svastika, literally "auspicious") corresponds in usage to the Buddhist term *rdo-rje* (Skt. vajra, "diamond"). Both of these terms indicate indestructibility. The Sutra (mdo) probably refers to one of the hagiographies of Tonpa Shenrab, such as the *gZi-brjid.* The *bsDus-pa* is probably the *mDo bsdus*, the shorter hagiography of Tonpa Shenrab.

31. This is a text associated with the Tantric *sPyi-spungs* cycle.

32. *gZer-bu* refers to the *gZer-bu nyer-gcig*, "The Twenty-One Little Nails;" each little nail (gzer-bu) represents an essential point (gnad) of the Dzogchen teachings. This text is found in the exceedingly secret section (yang gsang skor) of the Zhang-zhung Nyan-gyud.

33. The terms *tsi-ta* and *snying-po* both mean "essence," but *tsi-ta* from Skt. chitta, "mind, thought," employed in these Dzogchen texts, usually means the physical heart. The second term, *snying-po,* also means "heart" (Skt. hridaya) and "embryo" (Skt. garbha), as well as "essence" (Skt. sara).

34. *sTon-pa'i byon tshul.*

35. *dGongs-pa'i thugs rgyud.* On the Nine Sugatas, or enlightened beings, in the Mind Transmission Lineage, see also the preceding translation of "The Small Text."

36. For the *Yig-chung*, see the preceding translation.

37. The ultimate source of the Dzogchen teachings is discussed in terms of these two considerations: the Supreme Place (gnas) of its manifestation, where the primordial revelation of Dzogchen occurred, and the Supreme Teacher (ston-pa) who first revealed the Dzogchen teachings. This supreme location, or place, of the revelation is called the Akanishtha that is the Dimension of the all-pervading and all-encompassing Ultimate Reality (bon-nyid khyab bdal dbyings kyi 'og-min). This dimension is not something created by any primary causes or secondary conditions (rgyud rkyen las ma bskyed), nor does it originate in the world or among its inhabitants (snod bcud du ma chags), and it is not created having any color or shape (mdog dbyibs su ma grub). It does not abide at the center or at the periphery, nor in any cardinal or intermediate direction (mtha' dbus phyogs mtshams su mi gnas-pa). This supreme location, which is all-pervading and all-encompassing (khyab bdal), has, in fact, no specific location in space at all, because it is co-extensive with space, or dimension as such (dbyings-nyid). It is, therefore, the Dimension of all Reality, the Dharmadhatu (bon-dbyings).

This Teacher in Eternity (ye-nyid ston-pa) is Kuntu Zangpo, the Primordial Buddha, yet He is totally devoid of a self or any substantial existence (bdag-med kyi kun tu bzang-po). He is untouched by any limitations whatsoever that pertain to Samsara or Nirvana ('khor 'das gang gis kyang mthas ma reg). He is spontaneously perfected Buddhahood from the very beginning, but is inexpressible (in words and indefinable) because He is completely free of the eight extremes that necessarily delimit conceptual elaborations (ye gdod-ma nas lhun gyis grub-pa'i sangs-rgyas te/ spros-pa'i mtha' brgyad dang bral-bas 'di zhes brjod du med). In terms of His outer aspect, He is just existence, or being, as such (phyi ltar du yin kyang). However, in terms of His inner aspect, having already perpetually abided as the Kunzhi, the basis of everything, that represents the state of total primordial purity (nang ltar du kun-gzhi ka-dag chen-po'i gnas), the Primordial Buddha as Rigpa, or intrinsic Awareness, becomes manifest in the guise of the self-arisen Teacher, whereupon He confers the blessings (or energies) of compassion upon the retinues of the mind, that is to say, upon the thought processes and the functional mind (rig-pa rang shar gyi ston-pas/ sems dang blo yid kyi 'khor la/ thugs-rje byin-rlabs kyi skyob-par byed-pa). In other words, out of the Mind itself, or rather the Nature of Mind (sems-nyid), there arise the spontaneous manifestations of its inherent energy (rang rtsal) in the form of the operations of mind (sems) in the more limited sense, together with the thought processes (blo) that produce conceptual elaborations and the functional mind (yid) that coordinates sense perceptions with those thoughts and memories. These three functions (sems blo yid gsum) constellate in space as the retinue of the Primordial Buddha, metaphorically speaking. This entourage appears to naked Awareness in the Bardo of the Clear Light as the unfolding of the Peaceful and Wrathful Deities (zhi khro lha tshogs). They represent a process of emanation, or of projection, out into space of what is already latent and potential within the Natural State, but is, for the moment, implicit and unmanifest. For a further discussion, see the subsequent volume in this series, *The Path of the Clear Light.*

Or to put it another way, as the Primordial Teacher, which is to say, as Mind, He delimits and transforms what was originally and fundamentally inconceivable and inexpressible into something that is conceivable and comprehensible to the finite intellect and into something that is expressible in language, thereby the unmanifest is made manifest to human understanding. Thereupon, He confers this primordial revelation upon the Logos who is the Sambhogakaya. But it should not be thought that this revelation was an event that occurred in time and history, even at the very beginning of history. This process of revelation was primordial and, therefore, ever-present and ever-occurring, now and forever, because it lies outside time and yet pervades and encompasses all of time and history. It is what makes possible time and history.

As we have pointed out above, there exists some interesting parallels here between the emanation of the Trikaya as the Dharmakaya, the Sambhogakaya, and the Nirmanakaya in the Buddhist and Bonpo systems of India, Central Asia, and Tibet with the emanation of the hypostases in the Hermetic and Gnostic systems of Egypt before and after the time of Christ. For example, there is the Hermetic Trinity of Nous, Logos, and Anthropos elucidated in the *Corpus Hermeticum*. There also exist some parallels with the Kabalah of Jewish mysticism. This process of emanation (sprul-pa), whether Gnostic or Buddhist, where manifest existence proceeds out of an inconceivable and inexpressible non-dual Ultimate Reality, represents not only the Theogenesis, or divine economy, but the Psychogenesis, the origin of the mind and evolution of consciousness of the individual sentient being. The Trikaya are latent and invisible within the stream of consciousness of the ordinary deluded sentient being, and yet the Trikaya represent the very basis for conscious existence itself. Without the full presence of the Trikaya, like the presence of the sun in the sky although concealed by the clouds, there would be no life nor consciousness in the universe at all. Usually the Buddhist texts speak of the Ultimate Reality in negative terms, by way of the *Via Negativa*, as non-duality (gnyis-med) and as inseparability (dbyer-med). But at times, the texts employ more positive terms such as the Primordial Base (ye gzhi), the state of total primordial purity (ka-dag chen-po), the Unique Sphere or singularity (thig-le nyag-gcig), and so on. However, one should not fall into the trap of the extreme of thinking of this non-duality as a single entity or substance, out of which everything emerges and evolves, except metaphorically. Dzogchen is not simply a re-statement of a monistic Absolutism, asserting "Only the One exists; all the multiplicity of the world is simply an illusion," such as it may be asserted,at times, in Neo-Platonism and Advaita Vedanta. Buddhism and Bon both follow the Middle Way (madhyama-marga) advocated by the Buddhas, seeking to avoid all assertions regarding the existence or non-existence of an Ultimate Reality, singular or plural. Indeed, mere language, as marvelous and multifarious as it may be, cannot encompass this Ultimate Reality that transcends the thought process itself. Therefore, when one speaks of non-duality (gnyis-med, Skt. advaya), it is not at all the same as asserting the existence of a single substance. Furthermore, Mahayana in both Buddhism and Bon, does not teach that Nirvana means the ultimate extinction of the individuality of the stream of consciousness in the oceanic One, following upon the attaining of enlightenment. On this question of the One as against the many, see the discussion in the Appendix of Reynolds, *Self-Liberation through Seeing with Naked Awareness*, ibid., as well as the discussion in Part Three in the subsequent volume in this series, *Space, Awareness, and Energy*. On the question of the Primordial Buddha, see Chapter Two above. On Hermeticism and Gnosticism in general, see Hans Jonas, *The Gnostic Religion: The*

Message of the Alien God and the Beginnings of Christianity, Beacon Press, Boston 1963.

38. *Kun-gzhi byang-chub kyi sems/ khyab bdal phyogs ris med 'di ni bon-nyid kyi dbyings yin la/ gnas de na rang-rig ka-dag chen-por bzhugs-pa ni/ bon kyi sku la shar-ba yin.* This text, the *Byang-chub sems kyi gnad drug,* "The Six Essential Points of the Bodhichitta," is found in the Zhang-zhung Nyan-gyud collection. The translation of the text will be presented in the succeeeding volume.

As pointed out previously, Kuntu Zangpo refers not only to the Primordial Buddha who has never actually entered into Samsara, but also to the Bodhichitta, or Buddha-nature, inherent in every single sentient being still caught up in Samsara and its manifold delusions. The Kunzhi refers to the spaciousness, or emptiness side, of this primordial Buddha-nature. The indication (rtags) here is that the Buddha-nature, or Nature of Mind, which is the *don,* or "the real meaning," is untouched and uncorrupted by the processes of Samsara, even though the stream of consciousness of the individual is caught up in the labyrinthine delusions of the six destinies of rebith that constitute Samsara. These delusory reincarnations or existences are like magical apparitions or holograms (cho-'phrul) projected by the mind enmeshed in the processes of time and karma. The example (dpe) here is the mirror which has the capacity to reflect whatever is set before it, whether light or dark, beautiful or ugly, good or evil, and so on, and yet is in no way changed, modified, or corrupted by these reflections. In the same way, the Nature of Mind (sems-nyid) has the capacity to reflect or to be aware (rig-pa) of whatever phenomena manifest before it, but it is in no way changed or modified in its essence by this. This is so because the Nature of Mind transcends or lies outside the causal processes of the mind. For this reason also, it represents a total primordial purity (ka-dag chen-po).

This Nature of Mind, or Bodhichitta, is identified as Kuntu Zangpo, "the ultimate good," that is to say, the good that transcends all relativities and dualities. But is this Kuntu Zangpo one or many? Is there only one Dharmakaya pervading all of existence or an individual Dharmakaya in each individual stream of consciousness? The answer depends on one's perspective or frame of reference. The example (dpe) here is space (nam-mkha' ltar), meaning not just the blue sky of the atmosphere of the planet earth, but all of the infinity of space that contains all universes. This great or total space (dbyings-chen) is the universal principle that pervades and encompasses all phenomena and all minds. In this sense, space may be said to be universal and general in character, indeed, co-extensive with all of existence. Therefore, one may speak of the Nature of Mind as being the Universal Base (spyi gzhi), as being the Primordial Base (ye gzhi), and as being totally all-pervading and all-encompassing (khyab bdal chen-po). Under this aspect, it may be referred to as the dimension of all existence (bon-nyid dbyings, Skt. dharmadhatu).

Does this mean that there exists only one single Nature of Mind in which all individual minds participate, like a series of radios receiving a single broadcast? No, it does not. The Nature of Mind is individual (sems-nyid gcig-pu); but this does not mean there is only the One Mind. Mind (sems) is a causal process that occurs in time as a sequence of events and is always individual. This mind-stream has coherence and meaning; it is not just the simultaneous reception of static on all wave-lenths from the general background noise of the universe. But, just as one may speak of the total dimensionality of infinite space (dbyings-chen) that is all-pervading and all-encompassing, on the one hand, so, on the other hand, one may speak of the individual spaces found in a series of clay vessels. The space inside each vessel is individual, and yet, in a sense, they are not different one from the other in essence, apart from the shape of the individual vessel. Break any of these clay vessels and the space inside and the space outside will no longer be separate. However, in this case, there has been no merging or blending of different substances together, like pouring a cup of milk into the ocean. When the clay vessel of the human physical body and the human mind-stream of the five skandhas is broken at death, there is no longer any difference between the dimension of space inside (nang dbying) and the dimension of space outside (phyi dbying). This is not the same as saying that there occurs a total extinction, or loss, of individuality with the merging of the individual mind-stream into the great oceanic One. When the individuality of the stream of consciousness dissolves into the state of Shunyata following death, this is only a temporary experience, because the continuity of individual consciousness is conserved by way of the process of karma and re-emerges, reconstituted in the Bardo experience as an individual. This is not only true with death, but with enlightenment itself. The individuality of the mind-stream re-emerges, although transformed, with the experience of the Clear Light. The Rigpa, which knows the Clear Light, is always individual. Both the universal and the individual are potential in Shunyata. This spacious aspect (dbyings-cha), or emptiness aspect (stong-cha), which, in a sense, is the universal, is only one side of the Dharmakaya. The clarity aspect (gsal-cha), or awareness aspect (rig-cha), of the Nature of Mind is always particular and individual. So, in this sense, Dzogchen does not speak of "the One Mind." See the further discussion in Part Three in the subsequent volume of this series, *Space, Awareness, and Energy*. On the question of "the One Mind" in particular as a misunderstanding of the Dzogchen teachings, see the Appendix in Reynolds, *Self-Liberation through Seeing with Naked Awareness*, ibid. H.H. the Dalai Lama also addresses this question from the Buddhist perspective. See the Dalai Lama, *The Buddha Nature: Death and Eternal Soul in Buddhism*, Bluestar Communications, Woodside CA 1997.
The Dharmadhatu is the Dimension of the Ultimate Reality (bon-nyid kyi dbyings). Self-Awareness (rang-rig) refers to Rigpa and should not be confused with the similar Yogacharin term *rang-rig* (Skt. svasamvedana),

which refers to a reflexive consciousness that is still dualistic in operation. In the Natural State, Rigpa, or Self-Awareness, remains in its original condition of total primordial purity (ka-dag chen-po) and, therefore, the Dharmakaya is simply present in its nakedness, naturally and spontaneously. This is like the clear luminous sky being free of all clouds. For a discussion regarding the *Kun-gzhi*, see Chapter Five of Part Two in the subsequent volume of this series, *Space, Awareness, and Energy*.

39. *De ngang ngam shugs las..... snod la snga-ba nam-mkha' dang/ bcud la snga-ba rig-pa zung du 'brel-bas/ 'byung-ba lnga las phyi'i snod dang rigs drug gi bcud du srid.* The five elements ('byung-po lnga, Skt. pancha mahabhutas) are not actually substances, but represent processes, that is, five modes of manifestation for the creative energy of the Natural State. On the process of the evolution of the external world and its living inhabitants, see Part Four in the subsequent volume of this series.

40. In terms of the Teacher of Compassion, there exist three considerations rather than two: 1. the Supreme Place (gnas), 2. the Supreme Teacher (ston-pa), and 3. the method of the Mind-to-Mind Transmission (dgongs-pa'i rgyud tshul). According to the *Yig-chung*, the location for the revelation is the Akanishtha of the all-pervading and all-encompassing Dimension of the unmoving state (mi g.yo khyab bdal dbyings kyi 'og-min na). Even though it may be called the celestial palace that does not pass beyond Akanishtha ('og-min 'da'-ba med-pa'i pho-brang zhes bya-ba), it is not something that is earthly or material. This immeasurable celestial palace of light is a magical apparition, or hologram (cho-'phrul); it was created from the self-manifestations of gnosis, or primordial awareness (cho-'phrul 'od kyi gzhal-yas khang/ ye-shes kyi rang-snang las grub-pa der).

41. Citing the text called the *Khu-byug rang-'grel*, it is stated that the Teacher is *gShen-lha 'od-dkar*, the Sovereign of Compassion who possesses the eyes of gnosis. The rays of light of his compassion pervade everywhere (stong-pa gshen-lha 'od-dkar ni/ thugs-rje'i mnga'-bdag ye-shes spyan-can/ thugs-rje'i 'od zer gyis yongs la khyab-pa). Here, the confusion in the Small Text above is clarified and the Teacher of Compassion is unquestionably identified with Shenlha Odkar (gShen-lha 'od-dkar), "the Shen deity of white light," that is to say, the visible manifestation of infinite compassion as such. He is the personification of the Clear Light that is in itself colorless, but which refracts into the lights of the five primary colors, personified by the five Dhyani Buddhas (rgyal-ba rigs lnga). The latter form the retinue and the audience of the Sambhogakaya. This is experienced directly in the Bardo of the Clear Light. See Part Three in the subsequent volume in this series, *Space, Awareness, and Energy*.

Similarly, in the Manichean system, these five lights are called the Five Sons of Light. As a High God, or celestial deity, Shenlha would appear to derive from ancient Indo-Iranian mythology. His connection with the sky, with light, and with the eyes of wisdom, or gnosis (ye-shes kyi spyan), all point to the Vedic figure of Varuna, the guardian of Rta (or Dharma), that is, the natural and the moral orders of the universe. With the religious reform of Iranian paganism by the prophet Zarathushtra, or Zoroaster as he was known to the Ancient Greeks, probably in the 7th century BC, Varuna became known in the Avestan language by the title of Ahura Mazda, "the God of Wisdom." Precisely the same title is born by gShen-lha in the Bon tradition, namely, *Ye-shes kyi lha*, "the God of Wisdom." Whereas Varuna remains remote and distant from humanity, enthroned in heaven as an emperor, or great king, his junior colleague, or "son," Mithra is active in propagating truth and justice (Skt. rta, Av. arta, asha) among humankind upon earth. As pointed out elsewhere, in terms of Indo-European linguistics, most scholars would derive the name Maitreya, the designation for the future Buddha, from the Indo-Iranian name Mitra/Mithra. Dispite Varuna's remoteness from the earth in the heights of heaven, he is all-seeing and all-knowing of the events that occur among humanity by virtue of his eyes of wisdom. He is very much concerned with propagating righteousness and moral conduct among mankind, being "the god that binds" men with the cords of their own karma. Thus, the archetype of the High God in heaven, Varuna, who guards and ensures the natural order of things, and the younger god, his junior colleague or son, Mithra, who guards and ensures the moral order among humanity, appear to prefigure the Buddhological concepts of the Sambhogakaya and the Nirmanakaya. These luminous figures already existed in ancient Indo-Iranian religion and myth in the second millennium BC, as testified to by the treaty between Mitanni and the Hittites, long before the historical rise of Buddhism. Not without reason does the Lopon adamantly insist on the origin of Yungdrung Bon in Tazik or Iranian speaking Central Asia and its "Bonpo-Buddhistic" culture that existed well before the 7th century of our era. On Varuna and Mithra, see Georges Dumezil, *Mitra-Varuna*, Zone Books, New York 1988.

The whole question of the possible relationship of Buddhism and Bon to ancient Indo-European religion and mythology needs further research. Is there a genetic relationship, or do both go back to shared ancestral belief and myth? In terms of comparison, a "family" relation does not necessarily equal a direct relationship, and there are Indo-Europeanists who question Dumezil's thesis. However, these questions are too complex to go into here.

From the inexhaustible rays of light emanating from that Supreme Deity originate multitudes of enlightened Buddhas, such as *Kun-snang khyab-pa*, both chief and retinue. This figure is the chief of the Five Dhyani Buddhas (rgyal-ba rigs lnga) in the Bonpo system. Because Shen-lha is the root deity and the source of all the Shenrabpa deities, his three aspects comprise the Supreme Place, the Supreme Teacher, and the Supreme Retinue (lha de'i thugs-rje'i 'od zer las/ kun-snang gtso 'khor las sogs mang du byung zhing/ gshen-rab thams-cad kyi rtsa-ba'i lha yin-pas/ gnas dang ston-pa 'khor phun-sum tshogs-pa). In particular, *Kun-snang* is the chief of all the Peaceful Deities, and therefore would correspond, in this case, to Vairochana in the Buddhist system.

42. *Phyi ltar na de ltar yin yang/ nang ltar na/ sgron-ma las/ snying mchong gur smug-po shel gyi kha-bad-can/ snang gsal 'od kyi gzhal-yas khang 'di ni/ 'og-min bde-ba chen-po'i gnas yin la/ gnas der rang-rig ye-shes la sgra 'od zer gsum lhun gyis grub cing/ 'khor 'das thams-cad lhun-grub tu rdzogs-pa ni/ rdzogs-sku rang la shar-ba yin.....* The translation of this text, the Six Lamps or the *sGron-ma drug*, will be found in a future volume of this series. The passage quoted above gives a description of the physical heart, or Tsita, which is likened to a tent, or pavilion, of maroon-colored cornelian material, having projections of white crystal or fatty material. The interior hollow space of the heart is filled with the light of Awareness (rig-pa), and this space represents the supreme place of Mahasukha Akanishtha ('og-min bde-ba chen-po'i gnas). Thus, the Pure Land, like the Kingdom of God, lies within and not in some distant heaven world beyond the present universe. On the connection of this with the initial Bardo experience, see Part Three in the subsequent volume of this series, *Space, Awareness, and Energy.*

43. *gSum-pa dgongs-pa'i rgyud tshul ni/ de dus thugs-rje'i ston-pa gshen-lha 'od-dkar nyid kyis/ ye-nyid ston-pa kun tu bzang-po la/ ting-nge-'dzin gyis mchod-pa bsam du med-pa phul/ thugs-dam gyi rgyud bskul-bas/ ye-nyid ston-pa brjod-med bon sku/ bka' rgyud rin-chen rnam-pa bzhi-po ni/ rang-'byung skye-ba med-pa'i ngang nyid las/ thugs-rje'i ston-pa'i thugs kyi dkyil du bshad/ ye nas brjod du med-pa'i don du dgongs......* This represents the dialogue in eternity between the Father, the Dharmakaya, and the Son, His emanation, the Sambhogakaya. The four aspects of the precious transmission referred to are the Four Cycles for the Transmission of the Precepts of the Zhang-zhung Nyan-gyud (bka' rgyud bzhi skor). These cycles of teaching, therefore, have a transcendental origin, one that is beyond the mind.

44. Here the Small Text (dGongs rgyud yig-chung) is cited again: "In the Akanishtha of the world of the Gods of the Pure Abodes," ('jig-rten gtsang-ma lha'i 'og-min na). It is indicated that this is the first and highest among the five Pure Abodes (gtsang-ma rigs lnga thog-ma), the topmost of the seventeen levels, or mental planes, of the Rupadhatu, the Form World. These Gods of the Pure Abodes, the Shuddhavasa Devas, despite their exalted status at the summit of existence, are not enlightened beings, but worldly gods ('jig-rten-pa'i lha rnams) still caught up in the cyclical existence of Samsara.

In this realm of the Pure Abodes at the summit of existence, the Supreme Nirmanakaya manifested as the Supreme Teacher, the Great Shenrab who is the guide of all living beings ('gro-ba'i 'dren-pa'i gshen-rab chen-po), whereupon he descended from the Rupadhatu, or mental planes, into the lower desire realms of the Kamadhatu. Thereupon, he subsequently descended from the realm of the Tushita Gods to the summit of the Sumeru mountain in order to teach eventually within the human dimension of this universe (dga'-ldan lha'i yul nas 'jig-rten mi'i yul du ston-pa la gshegs te). In the traditional Buddhist cosmology, Tushita (dga'-ldan) is the realm of the Tushita Devas, "the Satisfied Gods", as well as the dimension of existence where the future Buddha resides until he takes up his last incarnation on earth. Having emanated himself in order to accomplish this mission in the divine form of the king of birds, the turquoise-colored cuckoo ('dab chags kyi rgyal-po g.yu bya khu-byug tu skur sprul nas/ 'gro-ba rab 'dren 'od kyi mchod-rten la yid kyis babs), he descended by his willpower onto a stupa of light in order to become reborn as the supreme guide for living beings, both gods and humans. This location came to be called the stupa where the Teacher had descended from the realm of the Gods (ston-pa lha las babs-pa'i mchod-rten). The stupa of light was located on the Sumeru mountain in the realm of the Thirty-Three Gods, the Trayatrinsha Devaloka. Subsequently, Shenrab was incarned on earth in the country of 'Ol-mo lung-ring as the World-Teacher (ston-pa), some 18,000 years ago according to the traditional Bonpo chronology.

45. *'Gro-ba 'dren-pa'i gshen-rab chen-po des/ dga'-ldan lha'i yul nas/ 'jig-rten mi'i yul du ston-pa la gshegs te/ 'dab chags kyi rgyal-po g.yu bya khu-byug tu skur sprul nas/ 'gro-ba rab 'dzin 'od kyi mchod-rten la yid kyis babs/ ston-pa lha las babs-pa'i mchod-rten zhes de la bya'o/ de nas yum bzang-za btsun mchod-rten la bskor-ba mdzad-pa la/ yi-ge OM mthing nag gcig tu sprul nas lhums su zhugs/ zla dgu'am bcu nas gsal-ba 'od kyi gling/ me-tog mdzes-pa'i tshal/ shing skye-ba mong tsam gyi drung du/ dpyid zla ra-ba'i tshes brgyad/ skar-ma smin-drug/ gza' nyi-ma/ dus-tshod kyi dang-po nam-langs-pa la skye-ba bzhes te/ 'od kyi lha ri spo mthon gyi rtse-mo ru/ khams brgyad gtan la phab-pa'i 'bum gsungs shing/ lo zla gza' skar dus-tshod kyi mgo de nas mdzad-pa de'o.* [ff 7-8] In this way, the Logos of the Dzogchen teachings, Tonpa Shenrab, became flesh and was born upon the earth. This miraculous child, who was perfect in every way, ultimately realized the benefit of living beings by way of sixty deeds of a Buddha (de ltar rdzogs-pa'i gshen-rab des/ mdzad-pa drug-cus 'gro don mthar phyin). Subsequently, he demonstrated the means for attaining enlightenment, that is to say, the realizing of Buddhahood. At that time, when he ascended into the dimension of the sky, in the evening he subdued the demons, at midnight he entered into a state of even contemplation, and at daybreak he attained Buddhahood in the dimension of Reality (tha-ma dbyings su gshegs tshe yang/ srod la bdud btul gung la mnyam-par bzhag/ tho-rangs dbyings su sangs-rgyas-pa'o). These three watches of the night parallel the account of the enlightenment experience of Shakyamuni Buddha. One may also compare this account to the birth stories of Jesus Christ and of Garab Dorje. See Reynolds, *The Golden Letters*, ibid., pp. 177-213.

46. This manifestation or incarnation of the principle of enlightenment in the world below as the Nirmanakaya is called the outer aspect (phyi ltar). This is the appearance in time and history of a human-like figure in order to

reveal the teachings of the Dharma to the gods and to humanity. However, in terms of his inner aspect (nang ltar), according to the *sGron-ma drug*, it is stated: *gnas rtsa gsum 'khor-lo drug/ sdong-po yan-lag nying-lag dang bcas-pa 'di/ yi-ge 'khor-lo rdzogs-pa'i zhing-khams yin la/ sgo gsum gyi bya-ba sna-tshogs byed-pa ni/ sprul-sku rang la shar-ba yin.* That is to say, the Nirmanakaya is incarnated in every sentient being as the mystical anatomy of the psychic channels, centers, and energies. This represents the mystical prototype or morphogenic field of the human being. In Gnostic terms, the Logos descends into the world and incarnates as the Anthropos or Archetypal Man, the archetypal pattern of the human being, here conceived of as the psychic channels and charkas found within the human body. The translation of this text will be found in the subsequent volume of this series.

47. As for the method of the Transmission of the Mind (dgongs-pa'i rgyud tshul), again the Small Text is quoted: *thugs nyid g.yo-ba med-pa'i ngang nyid las/ sprul-pa'i ston-pa'i thugs kyi dkyil du bshad/ kun khyab nam-mkha' lta-bu'i don du dgongs.*

48. Again quoting the Small Text, it is said: *bar lha 'od-gsal lha yul 'og-min na.* Among the Sudarshana Devas of the seventeen levels of the Rupadhatu, there exists one place called the Realm of the Clear Light of the Intermediate Gods (gzugs-khams bcu bdun gyi shin tu mthong-ba'i lha/ bar lha 'od-gsal zhes bya der). This level represents the sixth mental plane from the bottom among the seventeen mental planes of the Rupadhatu.

49. *Nam-mkha' g.yu 'od sprul-pa las/ tsha grang gnyis kyi rab 'khrugs-pa/ 'od sgra rlung sprin 'khrugs-pa las/ sems kyi mi la yid kyi rta/ brtse sems thugs-rje'i bdag-nyid-can/ de la ming 'dogs mi med nas/ nam-mkha'i dbyings nas ming btags-pa/ nam-mkha' dbyings kyi mi-bo che/ tshad-med thugs-rje phyogs ris med/ 'od las sprul-pa'i mir gyur-pa/ tshad-med 'od-ldan g.yung-drung sku.*

According to the text known as the *Rig-'dzin thugs rgyud*, as the result of certain celestial processes, there arose the Man who is the Mind (sems kyi mi) which is intrinsic Awareness, and the horse that represents the functional mind (yid kyi rta), which is his mount. This Archetypal Man possessed the nature of compassion and love. This is "the First Adam", the Adam Kadmon, the celestial prototype of humanity (Gr. Anthropos). One may also compare this archetypal figure with the Kabalistic Tree of Life, the Etz Chayyim. This celestial figure appears reminiscent of the Anthropos in Gnostic myth. And in view of his name meaning "he who possesses light without measure" (tshad-med 'od-ldan), he may be compared with the Buddha Amitabha whose name means "boundless light" ('od dpag-med). The cult of this Buddha was exceedingly popular in Central Asia before the Muslim period. *Tshad-med 'od-ldan*, in the intermediate realm of the Gods of the Clear Light (bar lha 'od-gsal du), brought those Bodhisattvas (g.yung-drung sems-dpa') who were established in the higher stages of the spiritual path and who had purified their obscurations, to the knowledge of the realization of the ultimate stage of transcending all suffering which is Nirvana itself (shes-bya'i sgrib-pa sbyong zhing mya-ngan las 'das-pa'i sa thob-par mdzad).

50. *De nas ston-pa de la/ bla na med-pa'i mchod-pa ting-nge 'dzin gyis sprul te phul-bas/ sprul-pa'i ston-pa gshen-rab mi-bo yis/ thugs-rje chen-po'i byin-rlabs ngang nyid nas/ cir yang skal sku'i thugs kyi dkyil du bshad/ mtha' dbus med-pa 'od kyi snying-po-can/ mkha' la nyi shar lta-bu'i don du dgongs.*

51. Regarding *'Phrul-gshen snang-ldan*, according to the Small Text: *mGon btsun phya yul gser steng 'og-min na.* This is said to be a city of the Gontsun Chya gods who are counted among the Sudrisha Devas inhabiting the Five Pure Abodes (gtsang-ma rigs lnga'i gya-nom snang-ba'i lha). This luminous figure, who belonged to the race of the Chya gods (phya lha rigs) was regarded as a direct emanation of the Mind of Kuntu Zangpo (thugs kyi sprul-pa). The text says here: "From the rays of light (emanated from) the Dharmakaya Kuntu Zangpo, there came forth effulgently a deity who possessed the nature of compassion without any discursive thoughts. From this emanation of His Mind, there emanated a divine form from these unchanging rays of light (of compassion) and this was the Shen of Realization who possessed the appearance of a magical Shen," (kun bzang bon-sku'i 'od zer las/ mi rtog thugs-rje'i bdag-nyid-can gyi lha zhig phyung ste/ de'i thugs kyi sprul-pa las/ 'gyur-med zer las skur sprul-pa/ 'phrul gshen snang-ldan grub-pa'i gshen). He purified all the obscurations to knowledge afflicting the Intermediate Gods belonging to the Realm of the Clear Light (bar lha 'od-gsal-ba rnams). The text makes it clear that, like the Gnostic syzygies in the Pleroma and like the Sefiroth in the Kabalistic Tree of Life, these Sugatas or enlightened beings are really just successive emanations due to the unceasing and ever-active energy of compassion of the Primordial Buddha. It is just this energy of compassion (thugs-rje) that brings mind and forms into manifestation. Although they appear as distinct figures, each with its individual iconography, they are all of the same essence as Kuntu Zangpo. This progressive emanation or drama of revelation merely unfolds, effortlessly and spontaneously, for the benefit of the sentient beings of Samsara in order to bring about their salvation, that is, their liberation and enlightenement.

52. *Ye-shes 'od-gsal chen-po'i ngang nyid las.*

53. According to the Small Text, this manifestation occurred in the Akanishtha of Light in Trayatrimsha, the divine realm of the Thirty-Three Gods (sum-cu rtsa gsum). Among the six Devalokas belonging to the Kamadhatu, there exists the place of the thirty-two Upendras (nye dbang), together with Shatakratu (brgya byin), otherwise known as Indra, as the thirty-third (sum-cu rtsa gsum 'od kyi 'og-min na/ zhes-pas/ 'dod lha drug gi nang-tshan/ nye-dbang sum-cu rtsa gnyis/ brgya-byin dang rtsa gsum gyi gnas de'o). This divine realm is conventionally located on the summit of the Sumeru mountain. It is called the Heaven of the Thirty-Three or

Trayatrimsha because, reflecting the mythology of the ancient Vedas and Puranas of India, Indra and his thirty-two brother deities reside there.

54. With respect to *Bar-snang khu-byug*, according to the *Khu-byug rang- 'grel*, "From the Speech Emanation of the Teachers Kunzang and Shenlha, there came forth the Turquoise Cuckoo, the king of birds, who possessed a color similar to green turquoise (ston-pa kun-bzang gshen-lha'i gsung gi sprul-pa las/ 'dab-chags kyi rgyal-po g.yu bya khu-byug g.yu-ga ljang gi mdog 'dra-ba zhig). Coming originally from the status of the Ultimate Reality, he appeared in various places of the world among the sentient beings of the nine stages in the Samsara of the three worlds and abided in the great bliss of the Dharmadhatu (bon-nyid kyi sa nas 'jig-rten gyi gnas su/ khams gsum 'khor-ba'i sa dgu'i sems-can rnams/ bon dbyings bde-chen gnas su drung phyir byon). Therefore, he was called the Teacher in the Intermediate Spaces (bar klong gi ston-pa).

55. According to the Small Text, it says: *Rin-chen g.yu steng tshal gyi 'og-min na*. That is to say, the Mother (yum) bZang-za ring-btsun resided within a crystal cave in the turquoise valley where there existed a forest of jewel-like evergreen trees. This site is said to have existed on the summit of the Meru mountain. And according to another text, the *bSen-thub*, it is said: *klong dgu 'byung-ba'i snying-po las/ dran byed bsam-pa'i srid-pa byung/ de la shes dang rig tu srid/ bsam-pa dang ni dran-pa gnyis/ rgya-mtsho klong dgur sprul-pa las/ de la dbyal-mo gcig srid-pa*. Here, this luminous figure, described as the coming forth of thinking and memory (dran byed bsam-pa'i srid-pa 'byung), may be compared to the Gnostic Epinoia, also feminine, who emanates out of the Infinite. The nine vast expanses of space (klong dgu) are not elucidated here, but they relate to the manifestation of the Goddess, who, in turn, is considered to be the embodiment of the Primordial Wisdom and the incarnation of the Prajnaparamita known in the Bonpo tradition as *Shes-rab Byams-ma*. On the iconography of *bZang-za ring-btsun*, see Per Kvaerne, *The Bon Religion of Tibet*, ibid., pp. 118-119.

56. *Bar-snang khu-byug*, the Teacher who is an Emanation in the form of a turquoise cuckoo descending from the heavens above, from the state of contemplation that manifests the inseparability of Means and Wisdom (thabs shes dbyer-med rol-pa'i ngang nyid nas), revealed the Dzogchen teachings in the center of the heart (or mind) of the Secret Mother. Thereupon the Mother (yum) contemplated the real meaning (don dgongs-pa), namely, that all appearances are without any inherent existence (snang-ba thams-cad rang-bzhin med-pa), this being the essence of discriminating wisdom (shes-rab, Skt. prajna). Wisdom or Prajna, like Sphia and Hochmah in the West, is regarded as feminine and is personified as the Great Goddess.

57. As for the place where *'Chi-med gtsug-phud* resided, it is called "the Akanishtha of the crystal cave in the turquoise valley" (g.yu lung shel phug 'og-min na), according to the *Small Text*. This luminous savior figure experienced a miraculous virgin birth in accordance with the usual

archetype, as was also the case with Mithra, Christ, Garab Dorje, Padmasambhava, and so on. See Reynolds, *The Golden Letters*, ibid., pp. 177-213. The text here also provides an etymology of the name of this savior figure: His mother realized that he was indeed a Nirmanakaya or the incarnate Logos. Because he did not die after abiding there for nine days, she realized that he was immortal ('chi-med). Because a top-knot of crystal existed upon his head (dbu la shel gyi thor-tshugs yod-pas), that head-crest (gtsug-phud de) led to his being called "the immortal head-crest," or *'Chi-med gtsug-phud*. The Tibetan term *gtsug-phud* (Skt. chuda, shikha, chudala) means "a hair-tuft" or "a head-crest"; *gtsug-phud 'dzin*, "holding the head-crest" means a peacock, and *gtug-phud lnga-pa* (Skt. Panchashikha), "the five-fold head-crest" is a title of Manjushri and also suggests a connection with the savior god Mithra.

58. *mKha' dbyings sprul-pa'i ston-pa/ 'chi-med gtsug-phud kyis/ rgyud lung man-ngag tshig don 'brel-pa ru/ rgyud khung ston-pa'i thugs kyi dkyil du bshad*. Chimed Tsugphud ('Chi-med gtsug-phud) revealed these Dzogchen teachings in the middle of the heart or mind (thugs) of the Teacher of the Oral Transmission Lineage. The latter, condensing ('dus-pa) these extensive teachings of the Secrets or Mysteries (gsang-ba) found in the Upadeshas, became known as Sangwa Dupa (gSang-ba 'dus-pa, Skt. Guhyasamaja). In the Bonpo tradition, he is regarded as the previous incarnation of Shakyamuni Buddha, who in this former guise was principally responsible for revealing the Mysteries or the Secret Mantras to humanity.

Thus there exist two separate accounts of the incarnation of Tonpa Shenrab on earth, that is to say, (1) as Shenrab Miwo in Olmo Lung-ring of Tazik in Central Asia, where he principally, although not exclusively, taught the Sutra system; and (2) as Chimed Tsugphud on the Meru mountain at the center of the world where he principally revealed the teachings of the Tantras and of Dzogchen. These teachings, in turn, were subsequently revealed to humanity by Sangwa Dupa.

59. Descending from the place that is called the Devaloka of the Akanishtha of the Intermediate Gods of the Clear Light (lha yul bar lha 'od-gsal 'og-min nas), *gSang-ba 'dus-pa* was born in the country of *Shod ma gser steng* in a castle located on the peak of *Lang ling bang*. According to Lopon Tenzin Namdak, this country was said to be located in Tazik (stag-gzig) northwest of Tibet. The realm of the Abhasvara Devas, the Gods of the Clear Light, is located on the sixth level or mental plane of the Rupadhatu according to traditional Buddhist cosmology in the *Abhidharmakosha* and elsewhere. This Central Asian prince was born the son of the king *Zhi-ba ldan* and the queen *Lha byin mdzes*. Because he had obtained all the Dharani-mantras belonging to the Secret Mantra system, the name of *gSang-ba 'dus-pa* (Skt. Guhyasamaja) was bestowed upon him, meaning "he who condenses the secrets."

Sangwa Dupa represents the source of the Oral Transmission of the Siddhas (grub-thob snyan-brgyud) where the Dzogchen teachings were communicated in words and language rather than by telepathic communication directly from mind-to-mind. Sangwa Dupa thus represents the bridge or interface between the transcendent realm of enlightenment existing in eternity, which is beyond words and language, and the more limited realm of historical time where the Primordial Wisdom must be expressed in words and language. At first, these teachings of the Primordial Wisdom came to be expressed in words orally and later they were written down in texts known as Tantras (rgyud), Agamas (lung), and Upadeshas (man-ngag). In general, a Tantra, in the form of a dialogue between a Buddha or enlightened being and one or more spiritually advanced disciples, presents a lengthy exposition of the teachings concerning transformation and liberation, whereas an Agama focuses on a particular point or a few such points from the more lengthy Tantra. An Upadesha presents brief instructions concerning the understanding of the view and the practice of meditation. After having attained realization through the practice of contemplation, Sangwa Dupa transmitted the Dzogchen teachings to three wise Bodhisattvas belonging to three races— a Deva, a Naga, and a human being (lha klu mi gsum), that is, to Yongsu Dagpa (Yongs su dag-pa), the Deva Vidyadhara, to Banam, the Naga Vidyadhara, and to prince Tride Zambu (Khri-lde zam-bu) the human Vidyadhara, respectively. See below. These three represent the three zones of the world in traditional ancient Tibetan cosmolology: the heavens, the underworld, and the surface of the earth. On Sangwa Dupa, see Per Kvaerne, *The Bon Religion of Tibet*, op. cit., p. 118. And also Samten G. Karmay, *The Treasury of Good Sayings*, Oxford University Press, London 1972, pp. xxi, xxiv-xxv.

The folk etymology above explains why the prince received this name. However, the Sanskrit original, Guhyasamaja, "the Secret Assembly", as pointd out previously, is also the name of an important Buddhist meditation deity who is the chief among the deities of the Father Tantras belonging in the Anuttara Tantra class of the Buddhist canon. Some Western scholars believe that the *Guhyasamaja Tantra* is probably the oldest among the Higher Tantras, likely being composed in the third century of our era, and it served as the literary prototype for the later genre of Anuttara Tantras. On this question, see Alex Wayman, *The Yoga of the Guhyasamajatantra*, Motilal Banarsidass, New Delhi 1977.

According to the traditional Tibetan histories of the Vajrayana, this Tantra was not revealed in India by the historical Buddha. Rather, the Buddha Shakyamuni was invited to the Central Asian country of Uddiyana by its king, Indrabhuti or Indrabodhi, where the former revealed the Higher Tantras as the appropriate spiritual method of transformation for the king and his court. This was because the king could not follow the normal path of renunciation proper to the monk, since the welfare of his queen, his children, his court, and indeed his whole kingdom depended upon him in his role as king. Through the practice of this Tantra, the king and his court attained realization and passed over into enlightenment, so that part of the country itself became depopulated of its human inhabitants. In Tibetan sources also, Uddiyana, probably meaning Eastern Afghanistan, is indicated as the source for the higher or Anuttara Tantras. This is the same region from which the Dzogchen teachings derive. It appears likely that the Dzogchen teachings at first represented an Upadesha or secret oral instruction concerning a state that lay beyond the Tantric processes of transformation as represented by the Generation Process (bskyed-rim) and the Perfection Process (rdzogs-rim) as delineated in the Higher or Mahayoga Tantras. The *Guhyasamaja Tantra* is included among the eighteen root Tantras in the Mahayoga Tantra class in the Nyingmapa canon (rNying-ma'i rgyud 'bum). It appears that Zhang-zhung was connected in ancient times with that region to the west and this suggests the possibility that the Bonpo myth is employing this Tantric epithet of the Buddha. As indicated above, this Sangwa Dupa or Guhyasamaja, is regarded in the Bonpo tradition as the principal source for the revelation of the Tantras and the Upadeshas of Dzogchen. One may also note that in the hagiographies of Tonpa Shenrab as well, the Chinese sage Kong-tse (Confucius) is made into a disciple of Tonpa Shenrab. So there exists a parallel here.

60. *Thugs nas lung dang rig-pa thabs kyis rgyud*. In scholastic tradition, scripture (lung) and reason (rig-pa) represent the two valid sources of knowledge.

61. *Rig-pa thabs dang rdzu-'phrul gyis rgyal-ba dgongs-pa'i rgyud-pa*.

Chapter 4: The Oral Transmission of the Siddhas

1. See the translation of the hagiographical text below.

2. *Legs-bshad mdzod*, ff. 144b-147a. See Karmay, *Treasury*, ibid., pp. 50-56. Here Shardza Rinpoche brackets the Perfection Process (rdzogs-rim), as exemplified by the *Ma rgyud*, together with Dzogchen or the Great Perfection (rdzogs-pa chen-po): *gnyis-pa rdzogs-rim la gnyis/ ma rgyud dang rdzogs-chen snyan-brgyud dar tshul-lo*. The Perfection Process as such represents the culmination of Tantric transformation practice. Whereas transformation by way of visualization, known as the Generation Process (bskyed-rim), is emphasized in the Father Tantras (pha rgyud), transformation by way of the internal yogas is emphasized in the Mother Tantras (ma rgyud). The Bonpo Mother Tantra, the *Ma rgyud thugs-rje nyi-ma*, represents a major Tantric system among the Bonpos, although it is not practiced as much or as popular as the Father Tantras. The internal yogas of the Mother Tantra, including psychic heat or Tummo, sleep and dream practices, Chod, Bardo, and so on, bare comparison to the Buddhist system of the *Na-ro chos drug* among the Kagyudpas and the *rDzogs-rim chos drug* among the Nyingmapas. Elsewhere I have prepared a study of this material from the Mother Tantra, entitled "Philosophical Systems and the Debate over Ideas in the Bonpo Mother Tantra," delivered at the IATS conference in Leiden in 2000, to be published in the future in a more

extensive version entitled, "The Mandala of the Sun.". Properly speaking, Dzogchen represents the teachings regarding a state that lies beyond the processes of Tantric transformation, both the Generation Process and the Perfection Process, for which reason it is rightfully known as the state of total or great perfection. In the *Ma rgyud*, as with the Nyingmapa system of Anuyoga Tantra, the culminating stage of the process of transformation is also known as Dzogchen.

3. The Four Cycles of the Transmission of Precepts (bka' brgyud skor bzhi) refer to the Zhang-zhung Nyan-gyud as such and its division into four cycles of texts, the outer (phyi), the inner (nang), the secret (gsang-ba), and the exceedingly secret (yang gsang). See Chapter Ten below. The Three Cycles of Revelation (bsGrags-pa skor gsum) refer to three cycles of Dzogchen teachings originally revealed to the Devas (lha) in the upper world, the humans (mi) in the intermediate world, and the Nagas (klu) in the underworld. These precepts were mainly propagated in Tibet in the eighth century by Nyachen Lishu Tagring (sNya-chen Li-shu stag-ring). This is a Terma cycle of Dzogchen teachings. The Nine Lower Sections concerning the Mind (sems smad sde dgu) refers to what is more usually known as the *Gab-pa dgu skor*, the Nine Cycles of the Secrets, consisting of the *Byang-sems gab-pa*, the *Khu-byug*, and the *Sems phran sde bdun*. As with the above, these precepts were originally taught by Chimed Tsugphud and Sangwa Dupa. The *Gab-pa* is also a Terma cycle, being discovered in the early 11th century by Shenchen Luga (gShen-chen klu-dga'). According to Lopon Tenzin Namdak, these three collections of Dzogchen teachings are quite similar in character and all originate from the Zhang-zhung tradition.

4. These four cycles of texts represent the four sections into which the teachings of the Zhang-zhung Nyan-gyud are divided. See Chapter Ten below.

5. The longer lineages (ring brgyud) are so-called because their source in time is relatively remote in time from the present, whereas, in contrast, the shorter lineages (nye brgyud) decend from the time of Tapihritsa and Gyerpungpa in the seventh and eighth centuries of our era. See the translation of the hagiography text below. On Gyerpungpa, see Chapter Five below.

6. Oral Communication.

7. Usually these three Shenpos (gshen-po gsum) are included in the list of the Twenty-Four August Persons (gang-zag nyer-bzhi) who were the recipients of the oral transmission. In the list found in the *bLa-ma'i brgyud-pa'i rnam-thar* of Paton Tangyal (sPa bsTan-rgyal dpal-bzang), they are Lhabon Yongsu Dagpa (Lha-bon Yangs su dag-pa), the Bonpo among the Devas, Lubon Banam (kLu-bon Ba-nam), the Bonpo among the Nagas, and Mibon Tride Zambu (Mi-bon Khri-lde zam-bu), the Bonpo among the humans. Elsewhere, including the Dzogchen cycle of the *bsGrags-pa skor gsum* and the Tantric cycle of the *Ma rgyud thugs-rje nyi-ma*, these three are given as Lhashen Yongsu Dagpa (Lha-gshen

Yongs su dag-pa) for the Devas, Lushen Yeshe Nyingpo (kLu-gshen Ye-shes snying-po) for the Nagas, and Milu Samlek (Mi-lus bsam-legs) for the humans. For the list of the twenty-four sages, see below. The *bLa-ma'i brgyud-pa'i rnam-thar* gives first place to Tonpa Shenrab rather than Sangwa Dupa at the head of the lineage of twenty-four.

8. The divine Shen (lha-gshen) or divine Bonpo (lha-bon) Yongsu Dagpa belonged to the race of the Thirty-Three Gods who inhabited the summit of the cosmic mountain Meru or Sumeru (ri-rab lhun-po), a class of deities derived from the Vedic cosmology of India and headed by Indra and his thirty-two brothers.

9. Oral communication from Lopon Tenzin Namdak.

10. On these three Shenpos (gshen-po gsum) or practitioners among the Devas (lha), the Nagas (klu), and the humans (mi) who were the disciples of Sangwa Dupa, see above, Note 7.

11. From Chimed Tsugphud ('Chi-med gtsug-phud), the Teacher who is the Ultimate Source of the Transmission (brgyud khungs kyi ston-pa), the precepts were transmitted to Ponchen Horti (dPon-chen Hor-ti), otherwise known as Horti chenpo. The title *dpon-chen* means great master. His disciple was Kunkhyen Dondrub (Kun-mkhyen don-grub), otherwise known as Donkun Drubpa (Don-kun grub-pa). See the list of twenty-four above.

12. *'Jag-gsas*, that is, the above Jarong Sekhar ('Ja-rong gsas-mkhar).

13. The brief hagiographical notices in this lineage of transmission, extending originally from Chimed Tsugphud, usually give little more than the site where the Mahasiddha practiced his retreat and the siddhis (dngos-grub) or spiritual attainments he realized. Nevertheless, all of them attained Jalu, the passing away into the Rainbow Body ('ja'-lus su gshegs-par byung). A more graphic description of these masters is found in the text called the *Rig-'dzin 'dus-pa*. There also exist a series of tsakali or initiation cards depicting these masters and used in the initiation ceremony for the Tantric deity Zhang-zhung Meri. Some of these are included as illustrations in the present volume. For the lineage lists according to the hagiography text, see below. Also on the iconography of the masters in this lineage of transmission, see Samten G. Karmay, *The Little Luminous Boy: The Oral Tradition from the Land of Zhangzhung depicted on two Tibetan Paintings*, Orchid Press, Bangkok 1998.

Note that *thag-bcad* in the context of Dzogchen is a technical term meaning that one "definitively decides" something because one has directly experienced it for oneself. This is the opposite of just hearing or reading about something second hand and then coming to a conclusion or forming an opinion based on reasoning. Namkhai Norbu Rinpoche has indicated that the term means to discover something for oneself in immediate experience, so that no doubt remains. This represents the second statement of Garab Dorje. Oral communication. See Reynolds, *The Golden Letters*, ibid. In the context here, the reference is to the visions experienced in Thodgal practice. Also in the context, "belief" (yid-ches), the term that occurs in the Tibetan text, refers not to intellectual belief, but to immediate experience which gives rise to confidence (gdeng), the actual meaning of the term here.

14. Karmay, *Treasury*, ibid., p. 56.
15. Karmay, *Treasury*, ibid., pp. 21-23.
16. See Reynolds, *The Golden Letters*, ibid., pp. 205-213.
17. The *gZer-bu* or *gZer-bu nyer-gcig*, "The Twenty-One Little Nails," is the principal text in the fourth section (yang gsang skor) of the Zhang-zhung Nyan-gyud. The translation of the root text and its commentary will be found in a subsequent volume in this series.
18. The text does not explain why the celestial pre-existence and incarnation of Shenrab as Chimed Tsugphud ('Chi-med gtsug-phud) (see above) is said to be "heat born" (drod skyes) nor why Yeshen Tsugphud (Ye-gshen gtsug-phud), said by Lopon Tenzin Namdak to be another emanation of Shenrab, is said to be "egg born" (sgong skyes). Accordingly, Sangwa Dupa (gSang-ba 'dus-pa) is said to be "apparitionally born" as are the Devas or gods (lha), the newly born suddenly appearing in a miraculous manner in the middle of a lotus blossom.

The translation of this first section presents a series of short replies to questions addressed to miscellaneous teachers. The hagiographical material is minimal, the names of the teachers being listed without much in terms of biographical details.
19. This statement could be interpreted that it was Horti Chenpo who organized the Bon teachings into Nine Successive Vehicles (bon theg-pa rim dgu) in about the 7th century CE.
20. The great Shen practitioner, Shen Horti Chenpo (gShen Hor-ti chen-po), was renowned as a great scholar and lived a generation or two before Gyerpungpa in Zhang-zhung, according to Lopon Tenzin Namdak. Although a Dzogchen practitioner, he was also famed as a learned scholar of all the Nine Vehicles of Bon (theg-pa rim dgu), including the Bon of the Causes and Characteristics (rgyu mthsn gyi bon), and also of the Secret Mantras (gsang sngag) or Bonpo Tantras. His disciple was the all-knowing Dondrub (Kun-mkhyen don-grub).
21. Here Horti is refering to the Sutra system or Path of Renunciation (spong lam), to the Tantra system or Path of Transformation (bsgyur-lam), and to Dzogchen known as the Path of Self-Liberation (grol-lam). The Sutra system is also known as the Bon of Characteristics (mtshan-nyid kyi bon), that is to say, philosophy or the investigation of the essential characteristis of things (mthsan-nyid, Skt. lakshana). The Tantra system is also known as the Bon of the Mantras (sngags kyi bon) and Dzogchen is called the unsurpassed teaching (bla na med-pa'i bon).
22. *Thun-mong dang mchog gi dngos-grub*, that is, ordinary in the sense of psychic magical powers that bring worldly results and supreme in the sense of meaning liberation from Samsara.
23. He was both the father and a teacher of Tapihritsa. See Chapter Five below.

24. *rGyu 'bras kyi bon rnams*, that is, both the lower and the higher vehicles of Bon, known as Causal Bon (rgyu yi bon) and Fruitional Bon ('bras-bu'i bon) respectively.
25. *Phung-po lhag-med du sangs-rgyas-pa lags-so.*
26. *Ra-sangs* was the clan name (gdung-rus ra-sangs) of both Tapihritsa (var. Ta-pi-ra-tsa) and his father Rasang Lugyal (Ra-sangs klu-rgyal). Here in the text, Kumaratsa is called the son (sras) of Tapihritsa.
27. *sNod ngan gyis mi thub gyi/ gar thod thod du ma ston cig.*
28. The Garuda chick, hatching full grown from its egg, and the lion cub strutting about the jungle fearlessly, are both traditional metaphors for the non-gradual path and for instantaneous enlightenement. See David Jackson, "Birds in the Egg and New-Born Lion Cubs: Metaphors for the Potentialities and Limitations of 'All-at-once" Enlightenment," IATS, Narita Conference, Japan 1990, pp. 1-23. Also see David Jackson, *Enlightenment by a Single Means: The Tibetan Controversies on the "Self-Sufficient White Remedy" (dkar po chig thub)*, Der Ostereichischen Akademie der Wissenschaften, Vienna 1994.
29. *sMon-lam btab.*
30. *mKhas-par blo sbyong btsun-par khrims mnos bya-ba yin gsungs.* This has reference to the three qualities of being learned, sanctified, and good (mkhas btsun bzang gsum) appropriate to a Lama.
31. *Lho gcen 'phrong rong gi ri la stag mi zan chibs nas 'byon-pa.... (32) Sum-pa'i bon-po a-ba-ldong..... rgya'i bon-po gsal-ba 'od-chen..... sum-pa dang rgya'i yul du brgyud-do.*
33. That is to say, first there are the instructions orally transmitted from the master to the disciple, which the master has received from his own teachers. Next, there are the instructions which the master has himself practiced and from which he gained experiences in meditation. Finally, there are the instructions which the master had not himself practiced, but in which one may have full trust and faith.
34. *bLa-ma jag-rong gi zhal nas/ rnal-'byor-pa la 'dug tshul gsum yin te/ seng-ge lta-bu'i rnal-'byor-pa/ snag-ba la zhen-pa log-pa/ ma-mo bu mi 'dod-pa lta-bu dang/ rgyal-po lta-bu'i rnal-'byor-pa/ snag-ba la spyod la ma chags-pa/ khyung nam-mkha' la lding-ba lta-bu dang dun-tse dung-rna lta-bu'i rnal-'byor-pa/ snang-ba la rmi-lam lta-bur 'dzin chags dang bral-ba'o/ de gsum-par 'thad gyis shig gsungs.* The ancient sage Dun-tse dung-rna is at present unidentified.
35. *bLa-ma'i zhal nas/ rig-pa gtan la phebs-pas mi 'gyur g.yung-drung sku/ shes-pa ma bcos rin-chen gser dang 'dra/ gang nas ma byung nam-mkha' me-tog 'dra/ gang na mi gnas bar-snang gzha'-tshon 'dra/ mtha' dbus bral-ba nam-mkha' 'dra/ bon rnams de ltar ma rtogs na/ nor-bu rin-chen rnyed nas stor-ba yin gsungs-so.*
36. This name suggests that he was not a native Zhang-zhung-pa but came from the country of Tazik (stag-gzig) in Central Asia.
37. *bLa-ma'i zhal nas/ phyi snang-ba dang nang rig-pa gnyis su ma mchis kyi/ gcig chod du chod gcig/ yang na 'bral med yin gyi rgya chod/ yang*

na dngos-med yin gyi gang dgar zhog/ yang na nges-med yin gyi cog-ge zhog.

38. *gDams-pa la rgyud khungs med na.* Here the author, Pa Tan-gyal (sPa bsTan-rgyal), briefly discusses the authenticity of this transmission of instructions (gdams-pa) for Dzogchen. He meets the objection that, if we do not know the original source of the transmission (rgyud khungs), how do we know the transmission is authentically Bon? First the objection is raised and then the author replies below.

39. *sGong skyes rgyud khungs kyi ston-pa ye-gshen gtsug-phud nas rgyud-pa.* By calling him egg-born (sgong skyes), the suggestion is that Yeshen Tsugphud (Ye-gshen gtsug-phud) is a Naga and a disciple of Tonpa Shenrab like Sangwa Dupa. His relationship to Ludrub Yeshe Nyingpo (kLu-grub ye-shes snying-po), the Naga disciple of Tonpa Shenrab and previous incarnation of Nagarjuna, is not clear.

40. *rDzus skyes cir yang sprul-pa'i ston-pa gsang-ba 'dus-pa nas rgyud-pa.* On Sangwa Dupa, whom Bonpo tradition identifies as a previous incarnation of Shakyamuni, see above. The epithet *Lha-bon* meaning the Bonpo among the Devas (lha yi bon-po) would make it appear that Thodkar was a Deva or Lha, while his name, *Thod-dkar*, is the title for the celestial gods in the *sNang-gshen theg-pa* section of the *gZi-brjid*. See Snellgrove, *The Nine Ways of Bon*, ibid. Furthermore, the three sourses of tradition (rgyud khungs) sited here, namely, Chimed Tsugphud, Yeshen Tsugphud, and Sangwa Dupa, appear to correspond to the three zones of traditional Bonpo cosmology and to the three races to whom Tonpa Shenrab imparted the Dharma, namely, the Devas in heaven, the Nagas in the underworld, and the humans on the surface of the earth.

41. Lopon Tenzin Namdak, as well as Namkhai Norbu Rinpoche, believe that this figure, for whom no biographical material is given, represents the Garab Dorje (dGa'-rab rdo-rje) from the country of Uddiyana (o-rgyan) who is regarded by the Nyingmapa tradition as the first human teacher of Dzogchen. See Reynolds, *The Golden Letters*, ibid.

42. The lineage of the twenty-Four August Persons in this text gives Tonpa Shenrab rather than Sangwa Dupa as the teacher of Yongsu Dagpa. This would appear to refer not to the celestial pre-existence of Shenrab as Chimed Tsugphud, but to his manifestation as a Nirmanakaya in Olmo Lungring. Therefore, he is called the Teacher who is an emanation born from the human womb (mngal skyes sprul-pa'i ston-pa gshen-rab). Nevertheless, according to Lopon Tenzin Namdak, even where Sangwa Dupa heads the lineage list, he is considered to be an emanation of Tonpa Shenrab. Yongsu Dagpa belonged to the Deva race (lha rigs), therefore he was called a Deva Bonpo (lha bon) and was the son of a Deva called Lharab-od (lha-rab 'od kyi sras lha-bon yongs su dag-pa). Furthermore, the Deva Yongsu Dagpa possessed "a hook-shaped tongue" that could be extended a great distance from his mouth. Wherever this tongue touched the earth, flowers sprang forth. Because his contemplation in the Natural State was pure like the sky (dgongs-pa mkha' ltar du dag-pas), he came to

realize both ordinary siddhis, or psychic powers, and the supreme siddhi of liberation from Samsara. All of these twenty-four in the lineage similarly realized the Rainbow Body of Light ('ja'-lus-pa). Because all of these masters realized Jalu or the Rainbow Body of Light, they all became independent of the cycle of death and rebirth, and, at their discretion, they could re-manifest and become visible in the world as Nirmanakayas in order to transmit the teachings of the Dharma to sentient beings.

43. Banam belonged to the Naga race (klu rigs), therefore he was called a Naga Bonpo (klu-bon). He was the son of the Naga Brahmana Lhajyindze (bram-ze lha-byin-mdzes kyi sras klu-bon ba-nam). Like the peoples of India, the Nagas are divided into five social castes, the Brahmanas or priestly caste being the highest. Because his contemplation was completely unmoving like the dimension of space (dgongs-pa dbyings ltar g.yo-ba med-pas), he came to realize siddhis both ordinary and supreme.

44. The first two masters in the lineage, representing the celestial and the chthonic powers respectively, were non-human (mi-ma-yin), whereas Tride Zambu, belonging to the human race (mi rigs) represents the first human Bonpo (mi-bon). This prince was the son of the king Tride-od (rgyal-po khri-lde 'od gyi sras mi-bon khri-lde zam-bu). The location of this kingdom is not stated, but was probably situated in Tazik, according to the Lopon. Thereafter, the teachings of Dzogchen came to be propagated in the principal dimensions of this world, both human and non-human.

45. It is said of the next master in the lineage, Banam Kyolpo (Ba-nam skyol-po) that, in terms of the supreme siddhi, he realized non-duality with the God of Wisdom (ye-shes lha dang gnyis su med-do). This title, "the God of Wisdom", usually refers to the Sambhogakaya Shenlha Odkar, but in this case it might simply refer to the Meditation Deity (yi-dam lha) of this master, that is, Zhang-zhung Meri.

46. *Thun-mong gi dngos-grub ting-'dzin zas su gsol zhing/ khams kyi zas mi dgos..... mchog gi dngos-grub snang stong gnyis su med-par sangs-rgyas-so.*

47. *dGongs-pa klong ltar g.yo-ba med-pas/ thun-mong gi dngos-grub sa-bdag klu gnyan bran du 'khol-ba dang.....* The Sadak (sa-bdag) are the spirits of the soil and the earth, the Nagas or Lu (klu) are the spirits of the waters and the underworld, and the Nyan (gnyan) are the spirits of the rocks and the trees.

48. *dGongs-pa sku-gsum lhun-grub kyi rang sa zin-pas/ thun-mong gi dngos-grub gser btso 'phen-pa dang dug sman du bsgyur-bar nus/ mchog gi dngos-grub zhu lus 'od du yal-ba nas sangs-rgyas-so.* The dispatching of magical missiles (btso, btswo) is a siddhi or magical power specifically associated with the practice of the Bonpo Tantric deity Zhang-zhung Meri. The name *Dar-ma 'bod-de* appears to be a transliteration of the Sanskrit name Dharmabodhi. We cannot say whether or not this figure has any relation to the Bodhidharma who appeared in China and established

there the lineage for Ch'an Buddhism. The Zhang-zhung language appears to contain many Sanskrit loan words.

49. *Zhang-zhung khri-'phan* is the first master in the lineage who is spefically called a Zhang-zhung-pa. Because his contemplation possessed the Dharani-mantras without them being perceived (dgongs-pa 'tshor-med gzungs dang ldan-pas) by reading them in some text, he came to realize the ordinary siddhis. The Dharanis (gzungs) are long mantras, generally employed for magical purposes rather than for the spiritual transformation into a meditation deity.

50. The Theurong spirits (the'u-rong), who were among the early non-human inhabitants of Tibet and still occasionally incarnate among human beings, are not necessarily evil, but are certainly dangerous to humanity. However, in some traditional Tibetan clan histories, Theurong spirits are included among their original ancestors. Oral communication.

51. At the time of their passing into Nirvana, these masters attained Buddhahood as the nature of light without abandoning the condition of a physical body (mya-ngan 'das dus su/ sku lus sa la ma bor 'od kyi rang-bzhin du sangs-rgyas-so), that is to say, they dissolved their physical forms into Rainbow Bodies ('ja'-lus).

52. *dGongs-pa skye 'gag gnyis-med du rtogs-pas/ thun-mong gi dngos-grub sku lus du-mar sprul-pa dang/ nyi zer la zhon nas gling bzhir bgrod nus/ mchog gi dngos-grub skye 'chi med-pa'i rang sa zin-no.*

53. *mChog gi dngos-grub bon-nyid g.yo-ba med-pa'i ngang la gnas-so.*

54. The son of the preceding master (de sras), Rasang Yungphen (Ra-sangs g.yung-'phen), because his contemplation understood the totality of non-meditation (dgongs-pa sgom-med chen-por rtogs nas), came to realize the ordinary siddhis. Non-meditation (sgom-med) means the state of contemplation that lays beyond the mind.

55. *Thun-mong gi dngos-grub mngon-shes rtsal rnams rdzogs nas/ pha-rol gyi sems shes-pa dang/ lkog 'gyur sna-tshogs dgongs.*

56. *dGongs-pa mnyam-nyid rtogs-pas...... mchog gi dngos-grub dmigs-med kyi ngang la sangs-rgyas-so.*

57. *Rang-rig mngon du gyur-pas.... thun-mong gi dngos-grub rtsa-rlung la mnga' bsnyems shing/ thig-le la rang-dbang thob.* Tsalung (rtsa-rlung) is the yoga of physical postures and breath control that grants mastery over the psychic channels (rtsa, Skt. nadi), the winds or psychic energies (rlung, Skt. vayu), and the drop-like quanta of energy (thig-le, Skt. bindu) found in the sexual fluids.

58. The great scholar Horti Chenpo, who was renowned for his great learning, not only in the Sutras, but especially in the Dharani-mantras found in the Tantras. These are long mantras (gzungs) used for various magical purposes, rather than for the generation of the Yidam.

59. Again the reference is to attaining the Rainbow Body.

60. Elsewhere he is known as Kunkhyen Dondrub (Kun-mkhyen don-grub).

61. *Ro-snyoms spyod-pa skyobs.* In this practice where all experiences become a single taste (ro-snyams, Skt. samarasa), every phenomenon is

experienced as being the same in terms of being empty and lacking any inherent existence. All judgment is thereby suspended with regard to phenomena and one is totally detached. Even divine nectar and cow dung have the same taste for the practitioner.

62. Tsepung Dawa Gyaltsan (Tshe-spungs zla-ba rgyal-mtshan) was the master who remained in the original condition of the Ultimate Reality (bla-ma ni bon-nyid rang sa zin). He was a teacher of both Tapihritsa and Gyerpungpa.

63. *mChog gi dngos-grub rtog-med chen-po mngon du gyur nas sangs-rgyas-so.* Their attaining of these ordinary or worldly siddhis indicated that they had realized mastery over the elements.

64. *Kun-brtags kyi sgrib-pa'i sa-bon dang bcas-pa byang/ shes-rab kyis bden-pa mngon-sum du gzigs.*

65. The stages of the Svastikayana (g.yung-drung theg-pa'i sa) refer to the ten bhumis or stages (sa bcu) of the Bodhisattva path.

66. All of these realized masters did not die in the ordinary sense, but dissolved their physical bodies into space and light in the process of attaining the Rainbow Body ('ja'-lus). Thereafter they accomplished the benefit of countless numbers of sentient beings in the different fields and dimensions of existence by means of their Nirmitas or emanated forms. Such a Nirmita (sprul-pa) is a true resurrection because the form is not only visible to other sentient beings, but appearently physical since it may be touched and otherwise perceived with all five senses. In the case of the Zhang-zhung lineage, Tapihritsa is taken as the prime exemplar of such a resurrection in the Body of Light. However, one prime difference between the normative Christian view of Christology and the view here expressed in the Buddhist and the Bonpo traditions is that for the latter the "Christ event" or advent of the Nirmanakaya (sprul-sku) is not unique to any one moment in history or to any one geographical location or to any one nation or people. The infinite compassion (thugs-rje) of the Sambhogakaya has been unobstructed and unceasing from the very beginning and ever-present, having both creation and salvation aspects, and this compassionate enlightened activity, like the light of the sun itself, comes impartially to all sentient beings everywhere, so that the opportunity for liberation and enlightenemnt is open to all.

Chapter 5: The Masters Tapihritsa and Gyerpungpa

1. The dates for the Tibetan king Trisong Detsan (Khri-srong lde'u-btsan) are 724-797 CE. For these dates of the Yarlung dynasty of kings of the Early Tibetan Kingdom, I rely on those established in David Snellgrove and Hugh Richardson, *A Cultural History of Tibet*, George Weidenfeld and Nicolson, London 1968. Western scholars of Tibetology, as well as native Tibetan scholars often do not agree on the dates for the early kings for various reasons, but I have found Hugh Richardson's metholodology for establishing these dates using monument inscriptions (rdo-ring), as well

as old texts such as the Tun Huang Chronicles and Annals and historical texts such as the *sBa-bzhad* and the history (chos-'byung) by Pawo Tsuglak Trengwa (dPa'-bo gtsug-lag 'phreng-ba), to be most convincing. But there also exists evidence to connect Gyerpungpa with the next century. His chief disciple Phawa Gyalzik Sechung florished in the time of the Tibetan king Ralpachan (Ral-pa-can, 815-836 CE) and he met Gyerpungpa and received teachings from him when he was already an old man. See Chapter Eight below.

2. On Ponchen Tsanpo (dPon-chen btsan-po, var. dPon-rgyal btsan-po), see Chapter Eight below. Together with Tapihtritsa and Gyerpungpa, he is one of the most important masters in the lineage and most likely a historical figure in the 9th and 10th centuries. However, this translation of a tradition from the Zhang-zhung language into Tibetan may have been an oral process, because the bulk of the texts, at least of the Experiential Transmission (nyams rgyud), were put down in writing a century or so later by Orgom Kundul and Yangton Chenpo. It is probably those masters who created the canon. See Chapters Eight and Nine below.

3. The Lopon suggests that only brief Upadeshas or secret oral instructions (man-ngag) from his master Tapihritsa, such as the *rGyud bu-chung bcu-gnyis*, were actually written down by Gyerpungpa in the Zhang-zhung language, perhaps inscribed on wooden palettes or on yak horn. Only later was the tradition elaborated into the form we have now.

4. See David Snellgrove and Hugh Richardson, *A Cultural History of Tibet*, op. cit., p. 103.

5. Snellgrove and Richarson, *A Cultural History of Tibet*, op. cit., p. 103.

6. Snellgrove and Richarson, *A Cultural History of Tibet*, op. cit. See also David Snellgrove, *Indo-Tibetan Buddhism: Indian Buddhists and Their Tibetan Successors*, Serindia Publications, London 1987.

7. Oral Comunication.

8. For the hagiographies of Tilopa and Naropa, and an account of their famous encounter, see Herbert V. Guenter, *The Life and Teachings of Naropa*, Oxford University Press, Oxford 1963.

9. Tapihritsa is said to have realized the Rainbow Body ('ja'-lus), as did the other twenty-four preceding masters in the Zhang-zhung lineage. Specifically, he is said to have realized the Rainbow Body of the Great Transfer ('ja'-lus 'pho-ba chen-po). On this process and attainment, see Note 14 below. Also on Tapihritsa and Gyerpungpa, as well as the succeeding masters in the lineages of the Zhang-zhung Nyan-gyud, see Samten G. Karmay, *The Little Luminous Boy: The Oral Tradition from the Land of Zhangzhung depicted on two Tibetan Paintings*, Orchid Press, Bangkok 1998. Karmay draws on the same hagiographical text by sPa-ston in the course of identifying a series of figures of Bonpo Lamas in a thangka from Tibet.

10. On the Tibetan conquest of Zhang-zhung and the expansion of the Tibetan Empire in the 7th and 8th centuries into Central Asia, see Christopher

Beckwith, *The Tibetan Empire in Central Asia*, Princeton University Press, Princeton 1987.

11. Tsepung Dawa Gyaltsan (Tshe-spungs Zla-ba rgyal-mtshan), whose personal name means "victory banner of the moon," was the last of the Twenty-four August Persons (gang-zag nyer-gcig), all of whom became Jalupas or Rainbow Bodies ('ja'-lus-pa). See Chapter Four above. Tapihritsa's uncle Ponchen (dPon-chen Ra-sangs) also appears in some of the lineages.

12. On the Experiential Transmission (nyams brgyud) and the Precepts Transmission (bka' brgyud), see Chapter Eight below. According to the Lopon, it was Tsepung Dawa Gyaltsan who organized the precepts (bka') into the four cycles which are outer (phyi skor), inner (nang skor), secret (gsang skor), and exceedingly secret (yang gsang skor). This may be, but it appears that in the 8th century the Transmission of the Precepts consisted only of brief Upadeshas (man-ngag) only, whereas many of the texts in the collection were certainly composed in Tibetan after the time of Gyerpungpa.

13. The valley region of Drajye (dra-bye, var. drwa-bye, gra-bye) lies along the northern shore of the fresh water lake of Darok (da-rog sman mtsho) and is bounded on the north by the salt lake of Drajye (dra-bye tshwa-kha). The northern lake shore possesses a number of archaeological sites of interest for Zhang-zhung history investigated by Bellezza in 1997, such as *rDzong dkar-po, Lha-khang dmar-chag, Do yi phug, Sha-ba gdong lha-khang, mTsho do*, and so on. See John Vincent Bellezza, "A Preliminary Archaeological Survey of Da Rog mTsho," in *The Tibet Journal*, vol. 24, No. 1, Dharamsala, Spring 1999, pp. 55-90.

Coming to the Darok lake from the west, Bellezza first visited a small semi-permanent settlement of fourteen households on the northwest side of the lake. The area is sparsely settled largely because of the arid climate and the scarcity of pasturage for animals nowadays. But the archaeological evidence indicates a much denser settlement in ancient times, especially on the eastern side of headlands and islands along the western half of the north shore. This is the region known as Drajye. The northern side of the basin is only a few kilometers wide. Buildings were mainly erected close to the lake-shore, probably because the lake itself was the only permanent source of fresh water on the northern shore. Oral accounts speak of *'om-bu* trees (tamarisk) once growing in the region, including in Gyerpungpa's day, whereas now one only finds woody shrubs (bra-ma).

On the northwest shore, east of the settlement *Na-gnas* (two households) there is a multicolored escarpment overlooking the lake called *rDzong dkar-po*, "the white castle," which has several meditation caves (sgrub phug). Beyond the headland of *Do yi phug* further east, there lie more ruins. Then eastward beyond the nomad settlement of Gond-do, one finds the ruins of the Bonpo hermitage of *Lha-khang dmar-chag*, "the red chapel," which once functioned as a meditation center (bsan-khang). Here on the rocks are found Bonpo mantras written in headless *dbu-med* script in red ochre, such as OM MA-TRI MU-YE SA-LE 'DU. Also on the rock there is depicted the figure of Tapihritsa sitting in meditation, white in color in a rainbow aureole and a background of red ochre. Bellezza dates this hermitage provisionally at c. 950-1200. This would make it contemporary with the Guge kingdom and the revival of monastic Buddhism. But the Darok region is now exclusively Kagyudpa Buddhist and has been so for centuries. At the hermitage, there is no sign of current habitation.

According to the Lopon, who spent two years in Northern Tibet in hiding from the Chinese Communists, the historical traditions of the Zhang-zhung masters have all been lost among the Tibetan nomads who inhabit the lake-district and who are the direct descendents of the ancient Zhang-zhung-pas. Only the place names now remain, which are known also from Bonpo literature. Indeed, there exist many lakes in this nomad region, such as the fresh water lake of Darok and the salt lake of Drajye. Rock meditation caves (sgrub phug) abound in the whole region. The lion rock mountain where Tapihritsa practiced lies to the west of Drajye in the Mamik region. Nowadays, the Lopon reports, the Tibetan nomads are afraid of these caves, believing that they are inhabited by ghosts (gshin). The Tibetan nomads have entirely forgotten that these caves were once Bonpo holy sites and places of spiritual power. On the lifestyle of these nomads ('brog-po) of Northern Tibet, who are the direct descendents of the ancient Zhang-zhung-pas, see Melvyn Goldstein and Cynthia Beall, *Nomads of Western Tibet: The Survival of a Way of Life*, University of California Press, Berkeley 1990.

14. The Rainbow Body ('ja'-lus) is the name of the process where, at the time of death, the practitioner, who has become adept at the practice of Thodgal, dissolves the gross material elements of the physical body into their corresponding subtle forms of pure radiant energy, these being visible as the colored lights corresponding to each element, and hence the reference to the rainbow. The physical body is said to dissolve gradually into space and to disappear entirely, like the rainbow fading into the empty sky. This entire process is said to take about seven days and at its completion, only the clothes, the hair of the head, and the nails of the fingers and the toes remain behind. The hair and the nails remain and do not dissolve into radiant energy because they are not pervaded by consciousness as is the rest of the body. A number of Rainbow Bodies have been reported in Tibet in recent decades, some of these events even being witnessed by the sceptical Chinese Communists. For example, see Chogyam Trungpa, *Born in Tibet*, George Allen & Unwin, London 1966, who records one such incident during his youth. Usually the process occurs in a closed retreat or hermitage, so that only such phenomena as rainbow lights are witnessed by outside observers. At the end of seven days, the hermitage is opened and all that is found remaining is the clothing, the hair, and the nails, the body itself having disappeared. But if

this process is prematurely interrupted, which has happened on a number of occasions in Eastern Tibet under the Chinese Communist regime, it is reported that the corpse of the Lama was found to have shrunken to a miniature size, about half a meter. This miniaturized corpse may then be burned by the Communists, as was the case with Changchub Dorje Rinpoche of Khandrogar near Derge, or else at times preserved in a reliquery in a monastery, such as at Gyarong near the Chinese border. Oral communication from Tenzin Wangyal Rinpoche.

The Body of Light of the Great Transfer ('pho-ba chen-po'i 'od lus) differs from the Rainbow Body discribed above, although it also is realized by way of the Thodgal practice. The Great Transfer means that the practitioner realizes Buddhahood in one's present life time without the necessity of undergoing the death process or the Bardo experience. Unlike the case with the Rainbow Body, one does not need to enter into the process of dying known as the Chikhai Bardo ('chi-kha'i bar-do). Rather, one's physical body simply fades away and dissolves into space, in the same way as does as the rainbow in the sky. However, whenever there exists the need for benefiting others, the enlightened being is said to possess the capacity to remanifest or reappear in a Body of Light ('od lus), in whatever form is appropriate to the circumstances, in order to teach disciples with whom there exists a karmic connection. Tapihritsa is regarded as an example of this Body of Light of the Great Transfer, as are Padmasambhava and Vimalamitra in the Nyingmapa tradition. Having previously obtained enlightenment and liberation by way of Dzogchen practice and having manifested the Great Transfer, Tapihritsa subsequently reappeared in the guise of a wise child (khye'u chung) in order to teach the arrogant scholar and priest Gyerpungpa. In general, in the context of Dzogchen, by means of the practice of contemplation or Trekchod, one comes to realize the Dharmakaya. This is Buddhahood as such and there is nothing more to do. But this Dharmakaya is infinite and without limitations; it is invisible, having no form of its own. Its representation as the Adibuddha figure is only a convention and a concession to the finite human intellect. So, in order to communicate with and benefit other sentient beings still caught up in Samsara, an enlightened being manifests a specific visible form that will be perceptible and comprehensible to the sentient being with whom he would communicate the teachings of the Dharma.

One should also note that Thodgal, called in this Zhang-zhung tradition the practice of the Clear Light ('od-gsal), should not be confused with the Tantric practice of the same name deriving from the tradition of the *Guhyasamaja Tantra* and included among the Six Yogas of Naropa (na-ro'i chos drug). Nor should the Rainbow Body in Dzogchen be confused with the Tantric practice of the Illusion Body (sgyu-lus), also included among the same Six Yogas. The practices are quite different because the former two belong to Tantra, the method of transformation that employs visualization, mental constructions, and so on, whereas the latter two practices belong to Dzogchen whose proper method is not that of transformation, but of self-liberation. The former practices represent the Perfection Process (rdzogs-rim) of Tantra and not Dzogchen as such. The Nyingmapas also know these famous Six Yogas and call them the *rDzogs-rim chos drug*, indicating that they are not the exclusive property of Naropa.

Tapihritsa is called an Incarnation or Nirmanakaya (sprul-pa'i sku) in the texts. The Dharmakaya having no form in itself, being only purity and awareness, it is the Rupakaya that becomes visible to disciples and other sentient beings. The Sambhogakaya, being only a pure body of light and lacking in all gross materiality, does not actually manifest within the distorted and constricted spaces of Samsara, but remains in eternity, ever-present in the pure unconditioned state called Akanishtha ('og-min). This Body becomes revealed and visible only to certain advanced disciples whose mind and vision are entirely purified, for which reason they are known as Aryas or exalted ones ('phags-pa). Such a vision is a very private affair. But in public, to the ordinary run of sentient beings within the confines of Samsara, an enlightened being reveals himself as a Nirmanakaya. Thus, the Trikaya is not three different persons, but only one. Such a Body, the Nirmanakaya, although a pure emanation of light, appears to sentient beings to be perfectly material. It impinges fully on all the five senses; it is not only seen and heard, but touched, tasted and smelled. Nonetheless, it is still a Nirmita or emanation (sprul-pa). Tapihritsa appeared to his disciple Gyerpungpa as such a Nirmanakaya, first as a small boy and then as a naked youth suspended in the sky in a transparent sphere of rainbow light. This was because his disciple's mind and vision was still obscured by the defilement of pride. All disciples, linked to their master by their past lives and previous karmic causes, will come to perceive that master as a Nirmanakaya upon the latter's attaining enlightenment and such Nirmanakayas can manifest anywhere within the six destinies of rebirth. But what the disciple sees, how one perceives an enlightened master such as Tapihritsa, depends on the purified mind and pure vision of the disciple.

15. *Nye rgyud thog babs ni/ rnam-sprul 'gro don gyi rgyud-pa.* These shorter lineages of the transmission (nye brgyud) that directly occur in history (thog babs) have benefited living beings ('gro don) by way of emanations (rnam-sprul), that is to say, each of these masters was considered an emanation or Tulku (sprul-sku).

16. Tapihritsa was the disciple of the master Tsepung Dawa Gyaltsan (bla-ma'i de'i slob-ma tshe-spungs zla-ba rgyal-mtshan), who was the twenty-fourth in the lineage of the Oral Transmission. The history of the great master Tapihritsa (dpon-chen ta-pi-hri-tsa'i lo-rgyus), like each of the hagiographies (rnam-thar) that follows, has five elements or considerations:

1) the history of how he obtained a pure human body from his parents (gtsang-ma mi lus thob-pa yab dang yum gyi lo-rgyus),

2) how he met his masters who showed great kindness toward him (bka'-drin-can gyi bla-ma dang ji-ltar mjal),

3) how he dwelt during his lifetime while relying upon special places for practice (sa gnas khyad-par-can gang du rten-pa tshe du bzhugs-pa),

4) how the signs of realization and other virtuous qualities which were ordinary and realized in his present life appeared (thun-mong dang gnas-skabs kyi yon-tan grub rtags), and

5) how the extraordinary understanding ultimately became manifest within him (rtogs-pa mngon-gyur thun-mong ma yin-pa).

17. According to Lopon Tenzin Namdak, the name *Ta-pi-hri-tsa*, var. *Ta-pi-ra-dza*, is Zhang-zhung language and means "the son (tapi) of a king (ra-dza)." The Lopon Tenzin Namdak suggests that the word *ra-dza* was borrowed into the Zhang-zhung language from the Sanskrit raja. *Wer* is the usual Zhang-zhung word meaning "king". His clan name was *Ra-sangs* (gdung-rus ra-sangs), and according to the Lopon, this still survives as a clan name in Northern Tibet. His father was *Ra-sangs klu-rgyal*, this personal name meaning "Naga king", and his mother was *Shes-rig gsal* (-ma), which means "bright knowledge lady."

18. Each of the masters in the Zhang-zhung lineage resided at a special place (sa gnas khyad-par-can) where he practiced contemplation and attained realization. Most of these were located in the vicinity of Mount Kailas and in the lake region stretching eastward from that mountain. For nine years Tapihritsa practiced ascetic conduct (dka'-spyod) at the lion rock of Tagthab (stag-thabs seng-ge'i brag la dka'-ba spyod de).

19. *mChog dang thun-mong gi dngos-grub ma lus-par bsnyems nas/ phung-po lhag-med du sangs-rgyas-so.* There exist a number of methods and processes leading to the attainment of the Body of Light. One may enter into the process at the time of death, so that the practitioner does not come to experience undergoing the Bardo. But by far the most superior method (yang rab) is known as Jalu Phowa Chenpo ('ja'-lus 'pho-ba chen-po), the Rainbow Body of the Great Transfer, where the practitioner does not even have to undergo the death experience, but dissolves one's physical body directly into the dimension of space. In the tradition, Tapihritsa is held to be a primary example of this method, which he realized through the practice of Thodgal.

20. *rTogs-pa mngon-gyur thun-mon ma yin-pa..... bdag don du bon-sku mgon-gyur nas/ gzhan don du sprul-pa'i sku/ zhang skad kyi ta-pi-ra-dza zer-bar sprul/ byis-par sprul nas/ rnam-mkhyen gyi ye-shes thob/ sku ma nges-pa du mar sprul/ skal-ldan gyi rgyud gcig-char du grol-ba lags-so.* "Uncertain" (nges-pa) means one cannot predict in advance in what form he will appear.

21. Tswo (btswo) is the practice of magical missiles, of which there are several kinds, associated with the practice of the Tantric meditation deity Zhang-zhung Meri. The origin of the practice is explained by the myth of the god Gekhod, the tutelary deity of Mount Kailas, hurling golden boulders into the distant sea to destroy the demons. Meri, whose name

means "fire mountain" or volcano, is a special warrior form of the old pagan deity of Zhang-zhung, Ge-khod, whose name means in the Zhang-zhung language, "the subduer of demons" (or in Tibetan, bdud 'dul). See the monograph by John Myrdhin Reynolds, *The Cult and Practice of Zhang-zhung Meri: The Meditation Deity for the Zhang-zhung Nyan-gyud Tradition of Bonpo Dzogchen Teachings*, Bonpo Translation Project (privately printed), San Diego 1996. However, the transmission and instructions of how to practice Tswo were lost with the death of the Tibetan Tantrika and magician Lhun-grub mu-thur. See Chapter Eight below.

22. *bLa'i mchod-gnas*. That is, he performed rituals to ensure the happiness and prosperity of the kingdom and the health and longevity of its king.

23. His wealthy patron (yon-bdag) was named *sMrer phyug-po g.Yung-drung rgyal-mtshan*. He, as a nomad chief, was wealthy because he possessed large herds of sheep and yaks which grazed in the Drajye valley. The word *phyug-po* means "rich, wealthy." Along the northern shore of the Darok lake there exist many caves and one of them was known as *Brag sha-ba dgong gi dgon-pa*. Originally the word *dgon-pa* meant a solitary shelter or hermitage; only later did it come to mean a monastery, in the sense of a number of buildings where a group of monks live. According to the *Bon ma nub-pa'i gtan-tshigs* (ff. 277) on the west side of the Drajye valley, Gyerpungpa went to a place called *Brag sha-ba gdong*, "the rock like the face of a deer." He made a retreat there where he first met his master Tapihritsa and five years later he returned to the island in the lake (mtsho do) where he had another encounter with Tapihritsa.

According to Bellezza, the site of *Sha-ba gdong lha-khang* lies on the north shore of the Darok lake, but to the west of the retreat island of *mTsho-do*. Heading eastward from *Lha-khang dmar-chag*, one encounters more meditation caves (sgrub-phug). And proceeding along the narrow path ('phrang lam), one eventually reaches the site of *Sha-ba gdong lha-khang*, which is suspended some five meters in the escarpment and at present there exists no means for non-assisted access. The surrounding cliff is said by the nomads to look like the head of a deer (sha-ba gdong) facing toward the lake. With the help of local nomads, Yungdrung Gyaltsan was able to visit the site in the 1950's. In an interview with Bellezza he reported that the *lha-khang* consists of a large cave that is partitioned into several rooms. There are more retreat caves nearby, especially to the east.

Yungdrung Gyaltsan (g.Yung-drung rgyal-mtshan) is a Bonpo Lama who, for a time, was a practicing physician in the Changtang region. He visited the lakes of *gNam-mtsho* and *Dang-ra mtsho* while he was on his way for pilgrimage to *Da-rog mtsho* in 1954 or 1955. He soon became aware of the extensive ruins in the area, but the local nomads told him that these ruins were dangerous to visit alone and were haunted by demons and evil spirits ('dre gdon). He succeeded, however, in visiting *Sha-ba gdong* where Gyerpungpa had meditated, but failed to reach the big island of *mTsho do*, where Gyerpungpa had made his three year retreat, because it was the summer season and he had no means to cross the waters of the lake to the island. McNeil's deer (sha-ba) is said to be still found in the country, but none north of the Trans-Himalaya. This deer was a sacred animal connected with shamanic practices in the Changtang region and elsewhere, and has given its name to many topological features in Northern Tibet. According to Lopon Tenzin Namdak in his *'Bel gtam lung gi snying-po*, Gyerpungpa meditated at *Sha-ba brag* in *sGo-mang ru-ba*, as well as at the Darok lake. Bellezza suggests that this latter site may be the same as *Sha-ba brag*, a small Karma Kagyudpa monastery located on the north side of *Ring-mtsho gung-ma*. This monastery is associated with Milarepa and his sheltering a deer pursued by a hunter.

24. *Khye'u rnyed-legs.*
25. The young boy uttered the Nine Respectful Polite Expressions (zhe-sa gdu phrug), each one accompanied by a prostration, but not without some irony. These expressions are contained in a separate short text, *Zhe-sa dgu phrugs*, ff. 255-256.
26. Gyerpungpa interrogated the young boy. This dialogue represents an ancient style of teaching method called *lde'u*, where one speaks in symbols and riddles. On this, see Namkhai Norbu, *Drung, Dreu and Bon: Narrations, Symbolic Languages, and the Bon Tradition in Ancient Tibet*, Library of Tibetan Works and Archives, Dharamsala 1995, pp. 21-34. This dialogue is contained in the text entitled "The Prophetic Sayings of the Lord Tapihritsa" (rJe Ta-pi-hri-tsa'i lung-bstan), translated in Chapter Six below.
27. In Bonpo iconography, Tapihritsa is usually represented in this guise, being almost identical in form with the Primordial Buddha Kuntu Zangpo, but whereas the latter is sky blue in color, Tapihritsa is pure white like crystal. On the symbolism involved here, see Appendix One below.
28. *Bya bral rjes-med.* This is the title of another text in the collection. The translation will be found in a subsequent volume in this series.
29. *Legs-pa bzhi'i gdams-ngag.* The Upadeshas found here, embedded in the narrative, are known as the four good things (legs-pa bzhi), the four things that should be conjoined to one's mind-stream (rgyud la sbyor-ba bzhi), the five practices (nyams su len-pa lnga), the four trainings directly related to the natural disposition (gshis thog tu bkal-ba bzhi), and the three kinds of confidence (gdeng rnam-pa gsum). On these teachings and for the full story of this first encounter with the master, see the translation in Chapter Six below
30. *mJal thebs bar-ma.* For the translation of this text, see in Chapter Six below.
31. *sGrom-ma drug gi gdams-pa*, "The Teachings on the Six Lamps." The text is found in the Zhang-zhung Nyan-gyud collection (ff. 269) and the translation of this text will be found in a subsequent volume in this series. These teachings, which outline the technology of the practice of the Clear

Light, otherwise known as Thodgal, belong to the inner cycle of the Precepts, which pertain to meditation practice..

32. Tapihritsa is addressed as *Kun-bzang*, "the all-good," which is the epithet often used to designate the Dharmakaya. But the Dharmakaya in itself has no form. It is pristine awareness or gnosis alone, not some form in manifestation, whether human or divine. Technically this manifestation of Tapihritsa as a white, translucent, naked Body of Light is a Nirmanakaya. Nevertheless, it is a manifestation occurring in time and history of the invisible and ineffable Dharmakaya. Here I am following the oral account of the Lopon rather than a strictly literal translation of the text.

33. Both of these texts occur in the collection and their translations will be found in a subsequent volume of this series. "The Upadesha in Eight Chapters" (Man-ngag le'u brgyad-pa, 476ff) concerns the realization of the Natural State and belongs to the secret cycle of the Precepts. "The Twenty-One Little Nails" (Zer-bu nyi-shu rtsa gcig, 503ff) concerns the realization of the Fruit of Buddhahood and the removal of all doubts with regard to the Natural State. It belongs to the exceedingly secret cycle of the Precepts. The root text (rtsa-ba) was revealed by Tapihritsa and said to have been written down in the Zhang-zhung language by Gyerpungpa, whereas, according to the Lopon, the commentary ('grel-pa) is said traditionally to have been composed by Gyerpungpa himself in the same language. This seems uncertain because paper was very rare in those days, texts were usually written down only in brief form on birch bark or on yak horn according to the Lopon.

34. One may compare the similar manifestation of Garab Dorje who, resurrected in the Body of Light, confers his postumous teachings (zhal-'chams), known as "the Three Statements that strike the Essential Points" (Tshig gsum gnad brdeg), upon his disciple Manjushrimitra. On this, see Reynolds, *The Golden Letters*, ibid. There exists striking parallels with regard to the posthumous teachings of the master Tapihritsa here to the Gnostic teachings of the resurrected Christ, such as are found in the *Pistis Sophia* and other texts. See Hans Jonas, *The Gnostic Religion: The Message of the Alien God and the Beginnings of Christianity*, Beacon Press, Boston 1963. It appears, however, that we are dealing here, not with historical influences filtering in from the West via the Nestorian Christians, but with an independent manifestation of the same archetype of enlightenment that depicts the human potential in its fruition. Also see the discussion of these questions in the subsequent volume, *The Path of the Clear Light*.

35. Gyerpungpa belonged to the Gurib clan (gdung-rus gu-rib) which, according to the Lopon, is still a clan name found among many nomads in Northern Tibet. The district of Darok was his birth place and is the site of a famous large fresh water lake (da-rog sman mtsho). Nowadays, according to the Lopon, when he visited Darok, he found that the Buddhist Drikhung Kagyudpas had established a monastery there. There exist many rock caves in the region, especially at the western end of the

lake and, as mentioned above, the nomads fear and avoid these caves, saying that there were some Bonpos there in the early days and now they are inhabited only by ghosts. Much of this fear of the caves appears due to Buddhist propaganda. The intensive missionary activity by the Drikhungpas among the nomads of Zhang-zhung, both in the Kailas region and in the lake district, was certainly a contributory factor in the eclipse of the Bon traditions among these people. The legend of the magical contest between the great Kagyudpa yogi and ascetic Milarepa with the Bonpo Lama Naro Bonchung in a race to the summit of Mount Kailas and, therefore, the right to claim the mountain, is one legendary expression of this historical process. In the Kagyudpa tradition, Mount Kailas has become the sacred mountain of the chief meditation deity (yi-dam) of that school, namely, Chakrashamvara ('Khor-lo bde-mchog).

36. Dwelling in between the ravines of white rocks in the direction west of Mamik, (ma-mig gi nub phyogs brag 'phrong dkar-po'i gseb tu), his master Dawa Gyaltsan expounded the instructions for the five direct introductions to the Natural State (ngo-sprod lnga'i gdams-pa). According to the Lopon, this site, which is located in the Drajye region north of the Darok lake, is still well known to the local nomads, but it has a bad reputation for being inhabited by ghosts (gshin). This place of white rocks is located near the salt lake of *Dra-bye tshwa-kha*, var. *Dra-bye tshwa-dkar*, to the north of the fresh water lake of *Da-rog mtsho*. Then Gyerpungpa came to the Darok lake itself and proceeded to make a one year retreat on the island of *mTsho do*, which was extended for two more years when he and his attendent found themselves trapped there. Also, according to the *rNam-thar chen-mo*, Tapihritsa practiced Dzogchen meditation for nine years at *sTag-thabs seng-be'i brag* in this same Mamik region.

   Darok Mentso (da-rog sman-mtsho), as a large fresh water lake, in ancient times supported a larger population than now by way of agriculture. This lake was so-called because of the purity and the fine quality of its fresh water. The large valley of Drajye (dra-bye) to the north also has a salt lake called *Dra-bye tshwa-dkar* where the Chinese now mine sulfur. Most of the masters in the Zhang-zhung lineage made their personal retreats in the caves between Darok district and Mount Kailas. The Lopon was able to identify a number of these sites. Indeed, he asserted that these sites became power spots precisely because of the various Zhang-zhung masters who attained Jalu or the Rainbow Body there. However, the psychic residues of these long-past events at the cave sites are now interpreted by the present day nomads to be the activities of ghosts.

37. His special place for practice (sa gnas khyad-par-can) was in the district of Darok (da-rog) in Northern Tibet where there was a famous medicine lake (mtsho sman) of the same name. The Darok lake (da-rog mtsho, var.drwa-rog, da-rogs) is one of the few fresh water lakes in the Changtang (byang-thang) or the northern planes. At an elevation of 4566 meters, the lake is about 40 kilometers long. To the west of the lake is the

Lungkar (lung-dkar) mountain range. The principal river feeding the lake is the Butod Tsangpo (sbu-stod gtsang-po) flowing into it from the south. This is one of the largest rivers in the whole arid Changtang (byang-thang) region.

According to the extent Bonpo sources, such as the *Bon ma nub-pa'i gtan-tshigs* (see below in Chapter Seven), even in the 8th century CE when Gyerpungpa resided here, the Darok region had already declined in terms of population and civilization due to earlier climatic changes that made the area considerably more arid and desert-like. Thus, in Gyerpungpa's day, many of the ruins along the northern shore of the lake were already deserted and only occasionally visited by nomad sheep-herders. Thus, the northern shore of Darok, with its many meditation caves (sgrub phug), was eminently suited for retreats and ascetic practices, such as those engaged in by Gyerpungpa.

Having heard from Lopon Tenzin Namdak about the importance of this region of the protohistorical kingdom of Zhang-zhung, Bellezza made a preliminary archaeological survey of Darok, especially its northern shores, in November of 1997. See John Vincent Bellezza, "A Preliminary Archaeological Survey of Da Rog mTsho,"ibid., pp. 55-90.

The local goddess associated with this lake belongs to the *sMan-mo* or *klu-mo* class of indigenous female deities. Bellezza secured the text of a modern invocation to this goddess, entitled *Da-rogs g.yu mtsho gsol-ba*, from the Karma Kagyudpa monastery of *Lung-dkar bsam-gtan byang-chub gling*. The goddess *sMan-chung g.yu yi za-ma-tog* is said to have been the queen ruling over the nature spirits of the whole Darok region. Moreover, she is mated with a number of local mountain gods. In the text she is depicted as wearing a mantle of white silk, holding a golden flat-bell (gshang) in one hand, and as riding upon a female antelope with a gray muzzle. She is known as the goddess with the melodious voice. On the aboriginal Tibetan pagan cults of the mountain gods and the lake goddesses, see John Vincent Bellezza, *Divine Dyads*, LTWA, Dharamsala 1997.

According to Bellezza, nowadays, the local nomads connect the extensive ruins along the north shore of the lake with events in the cycle of the Gesar epic. It is said that an ally of Gesar who was an emanation of the Buddhist goddess *dMag-zor rgyal-mo* (the queen of the weapons of war) named *A-thog klu-mo*, is said to have stored her weapons in a cave she created at the lake called *Lha-mo mdung shubs* (the spear sheath of the goddess). As a reward for slaying her enemy, the black yak demon who had murdered her father, she gave a necklance of zi (gzi) stones to Gesar. However, some old nomads, and in particular a local shaman interviewed by Bellezza, remember that these ruins were once associated with the Bonpos.

According to Bellezza, proceeding eastward from *Sha-ba gdong* along the lake shore, one comes to a large peninsula with extensive ruins. The densest collection of these ruins is on the eastern side of the peninsula and, according to Bellezza's estimate, these ruins could have once housed hundreds of people and probably belonged to the protohistoric Zhang-zhung Iron Age period. Opposite this peninsula is a large island in the lake known as *mTsho do* and this is no doubt the site where Gyerpung made his three year retreat. In the *rNam-thar chen-mo* (ff. 28-29), this island is called *mTsho gling gi do*. Gyerpungpa came to this island after having received the Dzogchen teachings from his master Tsepung Dawa Gyaltsan at the white rocks of Mamik near the salt lake of Drajye (dra-bye tshwa-kha) to the north. See the translation below.

Together with a disciple-attendent, Gyerpungpa retired to this large island in the lake. The Darok region was inhabited at that time only by a few nomads ('brog-po) and the non-human spirits (mi-ma-yin). He practiced there the methods of ascetic conduct (dka'-ba spyod-pa'i tshul). Tibetan nomads generally do not know how to swim and Gyerpungpa lacked a boat which were not common in this desert country largely devoid of trees. Therefore, he and his attendant walked across the ice to the island in the middle of winter when the lake was frozen. But during the following two winters the lake did not freeze over and so they found themselves trapped on the small island facing stravation.

He made another retreat on this island after the assassination of king Ligmigya, when he exercised his magical powers against the Tibetan king. See the translation in Chapter Seven. When the horsemen dispatched by the king arrived at the north shore of the lake, the local nomads pointed across the water to the foot of a white cliff on the island where Gyerpungpa had erected his white silken tent marked with the emblems of prancing deer. The Tibetan soldiers killed a horse in order to make a boat out of its hide so that the ministers could proceed to the island. On the eastern side of the island, one can see a group of ruins--through his binoculars Bellezza saw visible ruins forming an aggregate of structures on a shelf above the east shore of the island. In the Bonpo texts, Gyerpungpa is said to have had dealings with the local nomad shepherds, but there is no mention of buildings or settlements in this account. According to the Lopon, Gyerpungpa lived a purely ascetic life, practicing largely in caves. So, when he came to this island in the second half of the eighth century, the island was already deserted and in a state of ruin. Therefore, the ruins probably belong to the Iron Age period in the Changtang. See Bellezza, "A Preliminary Archaeological Survey of Da Rog mTsho," ibid.

38. According to the Lopon, usually the lakes in Northern Tibet such as Darok, are covered with a thick layer of ice in the season from January to April, and so it would be easy to walk across them to any island. But when, in this case, the lake did not freeze over, the master and his disciple found themselves stranded.

39. The master explained that this was not allowed for them because it would be a breach of the samaya vow they had made when receiving the initiation of their meditation deity Zhang-zhung Meri. Even though

initiates were forbidden to eat the flesh of the horse or the wild ass, they were allowed to eat the meat of yaks, sheep, goats, and so on. A few days later when the attendant found the corpse of a nomad woman who had died of goiter, which had also washed up on the shore of the island, again the master said no, because, according to their samaya, they are not even allowed to touch a human corpse.

40. This motif is frequently found in ancient and medieval Celtic literature. Crossing over water symbolizes the transition from one reality to another. In the Otherworld, very often an island, time is different than in our ordinary reality in the human world, and when the traveler to the Otherworld returns, he will often find that centuries have passed and people vaguely remember his name as someone who lived long ago. This was the case with the Irish hero Brandan who journeyed to the otherworld islands in the western ocean. A number of similar legends circulate among the Tibetans regarding hidden lands or *sBas-yul*. On them, see Edwin Bernbaum, *The Way to Shambhala: A Search for the Mythical Kingdom beyond the Himalayas*, Anchor Press/ Doubleday, New York 1980.

41. At first they were given only ashes to eat by the nomads because they had been fasting for so long that solid food would kill them. Then they were given the milk of a white female yak ('bri dkar) mixed with the milk of a white female goat (ra dkar). In the Tibetan language, a yak (g.yag) refers to only the male animal, the female is called a dri ('bri).

42. This story is repeated in more detail in the text translated below in Chapter Seven. Lopon Tenzin Namdak suggests that these three terms (spu, khyung, rngub) represent the names of measures of gold in the Zhang-zhung language, although they appear also be the names of the rites of the magical missiles (btswo) in question here.

43. The Tibetan king promised that henceforward he would not persecute the teachings of the Dzogchen Zhang-zhung Nyan-gyud, as well as the Rites of Gekhod and Meri. Gekhod is the special tutelary deity of Mount Kailas and Meri is considered to be a special warrior aspect of this deity. As reparation, the Tibetan king was required to erect a representative image (sku-tshab) of the deceased Zhang-zhung king Ligmigya (Lig-mi-rgya), together with a golden stupa as a memorial at the neck of the soul-mountain of Gang Tise (bla-ri gangs ti-se'i mgul tu), that is, at Mount Kailas, which was the soul-mountain (bla-ri) of the Zhang-zhung kings.

44. *bTso'i bsgrub-pa mdzad de.* Gyerpungpa gathered under his power all the races of the male spirits of existence (srid-pa'i pho rigs thams-cad dbang du bsdus). At that time, a deity living on the summit of the Sumeru mountain, a king of great power named Nyipangse (Nyi-pang-sad) offered his heart's prana (dbang chen gyi rgyal-po nyi-pang-sad kyis srog snying phul te) and promised that he would accomplish all those deeds not yet realized by Gyerpungpa. Then Gyerpungpa brought under his power all the female spirits of existence (srid-pa'i mo rigs thams-cad dbang du bsdus), whereupon the beautiful goddess Menmo Kumaradza (sMan-mo ku-ma-ra-dza) offered her heart's prana to him. These two deities became

the Guardians (srung-ma, bon-skyong) of the Zhang-zhung teachings. Nyipangse is the source for the Buddhist guardian deity Tsangpo Karpo (Tshang-po dkar-po). On the iconography of Nyipangse and Menmo, see Per Kvaerne, *The Bon Religion of Tibet*, ibid., pp. 109-111. On their cult, also see Appendix Three in the present volume, as well as Reynolds, *The Invocations to the Guardian Deity Nyipangse and to the Goddess Menmo*, Vidyadhara Publications, Los Angeles 1999.

45. Gyerpungpa emanated everywhere in various unpredictable or uncertain forms, such as emanating lights while in the guise of an antelope horn of crystal (sku ma nges-pa shel gyi rna ru 'od 'phro-ba las sogs cir yang sprul-lo). The antelope horn is especially associated with the cult of his tutelary meditation deity Zhang-zhung Meri. The account of this event is also told below in Chapter Seven.

46. By practicing the *Me-ri this-las* rites, the practical magical rituals associated with the meditation deity Zhang-zhung Meri, Gyerpungpa came to possess magical powers (mthu) and telekinetic abilities (rdzu-'phrul). Becoming famous as a Tantric sorcerer, he was finally appointed as chief sacrifical priest (bla'i mchod-gnas) by the king of Zhang-zhung.

47. But all of these siddhis attained by Gyerpungpa due to his Tantric practices only represented worldly powers and achievements and certainly not the supreme attainment (mchog gi dngos-grub), which is the realization of Buddhahood and liberation from Samsara. Thereupon the Nirmanakaya Tapihritsa, in the guise of the wise child, subdued the fierce pride of those two, the fortunate priest and his patron (skal-ldan gyi yon mchod gnyis-po) and revealed to them the Natural State which is intrinsic Awareness: *rig-pa'i gnas-lugs bstan/ bcings tshad kyi sgrog las bkrol nas/ mnyam-pa'i thang la phyung te/ rig-pa rang sa sin-par byas-so.*

48. The Tokharians (Tho-gar) were a red-haired Indo-European speaking people, having a language that is not Iranian, but in some ways resembling Celtic and Old Irish. They ruled parts of Central Asia northwest of Tibet at the time. *Phrom* probably refers to Rome, or more precisely, to the Byzantine Empire. *Phrom* was also given as the name of the kingdom of the epic hero Gesar.

49. Drigum Tsanpo (Gri-gum btsan-po, var. Dri-gum btsan-po), was the seventh in the traditional list of the kings of Central Tibet, which, in the early days, included little more than the Yarlung valley. It is clearly stated that his reason for expelling the Bonpos was political, rather than doctrinal. Fearing the growing influence and political power of the Bonpo priests at his court, he expelled them from his kingdom. Later he was lured into a duel by Lo-ngam, one of his noble vassals. It is said that Lo-ngam tricked the king into polluting himself and thereby losing the protection of his guardian spirits, so that his *dmu-thag*, or the celestial cord that connected him to heaven, would be cut by his own sword. Thus Drigum was the first Tibetan king to leave a corpse behind at his death; the previous kings all dissolved their material bodies into the rainbow-like *dmu-thag* at the conclusion of their career on earth, thereby ascending to

heaven. Therefore, Drigum was the first king for which it was necessary
to build a tomb. The persecution of the Bonpos was lifted by the
assassinated king's son and successor, Pude Gunggyal (sPu-lde gung-
rgyal) when the latter ascended the throne. Thus, Bon was restored to its
former position in Central Tibet. See Snellgrove and Richardson, *A
Cultural History of Tibet*, ibid., pp. 23-26. According to the *bsTan-rtsis* of
Nyima Tanzin (Nyi-ma bstan-'dzin), Drigum died in 680 BC, but Western
scholars generally reject such an early date for this legendary king. See
Per Kvaerne, "A Chronological Table of the Bon-po: The *bsTan rcis* of
Nyi-ma bstan-'jin," in *Acta Orientalia*, vol. 33, Copenhagen 1971, pp.
205-282.

50. These dates for Trisong Detsan were suggested by Hugh Richardson after
his exhaustive study of monument inscriptions from the early period. See
Snellgrove and Richardson, *A Cultural History of Tibet*, ibid.

51. On this legend, see the translation in Keith Dowman, *The Legend of the
Great Stupa*, Dharma Press, Berkeley CA 1973.

52. *Legs-bshad mdzod*, ff. 169b-171a. Also see Karmay, *The Treasury of
Good Sayings*, ibid., pp.81-82.

53. The *rNam-'byed* is the *rNam-'byed 'phrul lde* attributed to Dranpa
Namkha.

54. The text referred to here in the Zhang-zhung Nyan-gyud collection is the
Bon ma nub-pa'i gtan-tshigs, "The Reasons why Bon did not Decline," ff.
259-267, which elaborates the legend of the Mahasiddha Gyerpungpa
subduing the mighty Tibetan king. See the translation of this text in
Chapter Seven below.

55. Lachen Dranpa Namkha (bLa-chen Dran-pa nam-mkha') and Nya Lishu
Tagring (sNya Li-shu stag-rings) where both famous masters of
Dzogchen. According to Lopon Tenzin Namdak, this Dranpa Namkha
was a Tibetan and should not be confused with the earlier Dranpa Namkha
who was a prince of Zhang-zhung. See Note 84 below. The *Yang-rtse'i
klong-chen* is a cycle of Dzogchen teachings belonging to the Central
Treasures (dbus-lugs) tradition. This tradition of Dzogchen is especially
associated with the name of Nyachen Lishu Tagring who, it would appear,
lived in the 8th century in Tibet.

56. Here the quotation is taken from the *Bon ma nub-pa'i gtan-tshigs*. Among
the many adepts or Siddhas (grub-thob) of Zhang-zhung there were *Tso-
mi gyer-chen*, and in Tibet there lived the four learned men (mkhas-pa mi
bzhi), such as *sPa Ji-phrom dkar po, sTong-rgyung mthu-chen,* and *bLa-
chen Dran-pa nam-mkha'*, etc. Thus, according to the traditions cited by
Shardza Rinpoche, the Bonpo sages (gshen-po) *Li-shu stag-rings, bLa-
chen Dran-pa Nam-mkha', Tso-mi gyer-chen, sPa Ji-phrom dkar-po,
sTong-rgyung mthu-chen, Tshe-spungs Zla-ba rgyal-mtshan,* and so on,
were all contemporaries of Gyerpungpa who lived in the 8th century
during the reign of the Tibetan king Trisong Detsan, 754-797. *bTsan-po*
was the title for the king of Tibet. *Lig-mi-rgya*, according to the Lopon,
was the dynastic title born by the kings of Zhang-zhung, being the

eqivalent of "maharaja" and meaning in the Zhang-zhung language "the king of men." Panta-li-kha (var. Pan-ra-ling) was the king of Mon or Mon-yul, which lay to the south of Tibet, probably in Northern Nepal or else Bhutan.

57. See Karmay, *Treasury*, ibid., pp. 82-84. For the Buddhist version of this story, see Keith Dowman, *The Legend of the Great Stupa*, op. cit. The Tibetan name for the great stupa of Baudhnath, some four kilometers east of Kathmandu city in the valley of Nepal is *Bya-rong kha-shor*. Lopon Tenzin Namdak indicates that he believes that this individual Bodhisattva was not Shantirakshita, but another Buddhist monk who was not an Indian, but a native-born Central Tibetan.

58. Many Bonpo priests of the time were considered to be experts in the practice of divination (mo). A portion of the first among the Nine Ways of Bon, namely, the *Phywa-gshen theg-pa*, "the way of the practice of prediction," is devoted to divination. See Snellgrove, *The Nine Ways of Bon*, ibid.

59. *gNyis-pa nub lugs la gnyis/ nub lugs dngos dang gter du sbas tshul-lo. Legs-bshad mdzod*, ff. 169. See Karmay, *Treasury*, ibid., pp. 81-82.

60. There were two historical processes relating to the decline of the teachings of Bon, one in Zhang-zhung and one in Tibet (Zhang-zhung du nub lugs dang bod du nub lugs-so). Again the source cited here is the *Bon ma nub-pa'i gtan-tshigs*. See Chapter Seven below. The citations here from Shardza Rinpoche are not always direct quotations, but rather paraphrases. Anyway, the wording in the two texts differ.

61. *Phrom ge-sar rgyal-po*. This is the hero of the famous Gesar Epic of Tibet. As said above, some scholars speculate that the name *Ge-sar* comes from Kaisar or Caesar and that the name *Phrom* or *Khrom* comes from the Middle Persian (Pahlavi) form "From," meaning Rome. Thus, *Ge-sar* and *Phrom* would represent a distant echo of the Byzantine empire, which at that time was at the height of its power and which to the Tibetans would have been entirely fabulous. On the Gesar epic, see R.A. Stein, *L'epopee tibetaine de Gesar dans a version Lamaique de Ling*, Annales du Musee Guimet, Bill. d'Et. LXI, Paris 1956. And for a brief retelling of the epic, see Alexandra David-Neel, *The Superhuman Life of Gesar of Ling*, Clude Kendall, New York 1934.

62. Patron and priest (yon-mchod) is a type of old Central Asian diplomatic relationship between two rulers, where one ruler acts, at least in theory, as a religious adviser and as a priest to a second more powerful ruler. In this case, the Dharmaraja of India acted as the priest or pujari (mchod-gnas) for the more powerful ruler, the king of Tibet, who was, therefore, the patron (yon-bdag). In general, the patron takes no concrete political or military action to actually control the country of his priest. The relationship is actually a personal one between two rulers, not one between governments in the modern sense. Moreover, this diplomatic relationship does not involve the modern idea of sovereignty. In the past, the Grand Lamas of Sakya established such a relationship with the

Mongol Emperors of China (the Yuan dynasty) and the later Gelugpa
Dalai Lamas had the same relationship with the Manchu Emperors of
China (the Ching dynasty). Both of these dynasties were of a foreign
origin, as far as China goes, and both the Sakyapas and the Gelugpas
entered into this personal relationship of patron and priest with the
respective emperors before the latter had completed their conquests of
China. The agreement was with the emperor personally and not with the
Chinese government. Therefore, this arrangement never implied that
Tibet was a part of China. The situation changed, of course, after the
Chinese Communist conquest of Tibet in 1952. On this relationship, see
Snellgrove and Richardson, *A Cultural History of Tibet*, ibid., pp. 148-
149, 184, 195, 218.

63. In view of the nomad character of the population of Zhang-zhung, such a
large army seems quite an exaggeration. On the character of this country
of Northern Tibet, see Goldstein and Beall, *Nomads of Western Tibet*, ibid.
Also see John Vincent Bellezza, "High-Country Culture," ibid.

64. The youngest queen was called *sNang-bza' sgron-legs*, *sNang* being her
clan name and *bza'* or *za*, a title meaning princess. The Tibetan minister
for intelligence gathering, named *sNan-nam legs-grub*, came to the young
queen while she was residing in the Garuda castle of *Khyung-rdzong*
located on the southern shores of the Dang-ra lake. The Lopon reports that
there was once a large agricultural settlement there as can be seen by the
extensive ruins and evidence of terrace agriculture, now all fallen in to
disrepair. See the translation of this story in Chapter Seven below.

65. At the site of *Brag-dmar 'gring-bzang* where the magical contest was
held, *Dran-pa Nam-mkha'* represented the Bonpos arrayed on one side
and Bodhisattva represented the Buddhists arrayed on the other side. The
Bonpo magicians were as follows: *sTong-rgyung mthu-chen, Dran-pa
nam-mkha', Se Sha-ri dbu-chen, lChe-tsha mkhar-po, lDe Gyim-tsha rma-
ching, sKu Gyim-thang rma-lo, Khyung-po sTag-sgra don-gtsug, sNya Li-
shu stag-ring, sPe Ne-gu, rMa-bon thugs-dkar*, and *Co-za bon-mo*. This
last figure on the Bonpo side was a woman. The Buddhist magicians were
as follows: *Padmasambhava, Bodhisattva, gNubs Nam-mkha'i snying-po,
rLang dPal gyi rdo-rje, 'Bre dPal gyi blo-gros, rLang gTsug-tor rin-chen,
rMa A-tsa-ra rin-chen, sKa-ba dPal-brtsegs, Ba-gor Vairochana, gNyan-
pa dPal-sbyin*, and *Lang-gro Kon-mchog 'byung-gnas*.

66. It may be noted here that a number of scholars among the Newer Schools
have accused the Nyingmapas of adopting a number of their early texts,
especially those of Dzogchen, from Bonpo originals, as for example the
Kun-byed rgyal-po'i rgyud. The Nyingmapa scholar Soglogpa (Sog-zlog-
pa) replied to these attacks and criticisms. See the discussion in Reynolds,
The Golden Letters, ibid., p.246-247, 263-286.
However, Lopon Tenzin Namdak cites the incident in the 10th century
when the great Nyingmapa Buddhist scholar *Zur-po-che Shakya 'byung-
gnas* received the transmission of the Experiential Transmission (nyams
brgyud) of the Zhang-zhung Nyan-gyud from the Bonpo master *gShen-*

rgyal g.yung-drung lha-rtse at the latter's hermitage near the Dang-ra lake in Northern Tibet. Zurpoche changed some of the names with his master's permission in order to give the transmission a fictitious Indian background to make it more acceptable to the Buddhists. This transmission coming from Ponchen Tsanpo, the teacher of Shengyal, has been incorporated, according to the Lopon, into the Nyingmapa tradition as the *rDzogs-chen sems-sde* known by the name of the *Rig-pa'i khu-byug*.

67. The wrathful goddess Madud Sidpe Gyalmo (Ma bdud Srid-pa'i rgyal-mo) is a principal guardian deity of the Bon tradition and especially of Dzogchen, in which role, according to the Lopon, she corresponds to the Buddhist goddess Ma Ekadzati. This would be her two-armed form known as Yeshe Walmo (Ye-shes dbal-mo), "the flaming wisdom." However, her more usual form is four armed and depicted as riding upon a mule, in which case she corresponds to the popular Buddhist guardian goddess Paldan Lhamo (dPal-ldan lha-mo). The Bonpo goddess may be depicted as black in color and riding upon a black mule (Srid-rgyal dre'u nag) or on red mule (Srid-rgyal dre'u dmar). It is said that the cult of this goddess as a protector of Bon (bon-skyong) was introduced by the great Terton Shenchen Luga (gShen-chen kLu-dga', 996-1035). See Per Kvaerne, *The Bon Religion of Tibet*, Serindia Publications, London 1995, pp. 107-108. See also a monograph on this deity, John Myrdhin Reynolds, *The Healing Practice for Sidpa Gyalmo*, Bonpo Translation Project (privately printed), San Diego 1996.

68. "The Four Portals of Bon and the Treasury as the fifth" (sgo bzhi mdzod lnga) represent a more archaic manner of classifying the extant Bonpo texts than the more familiar "Nine Ways of Bon" (Bon gyi theg-pa rim dgu). See Chapter One above.

69. This would account for the existence of Bon, even in the twentieth century, among the Na-khi people of Yunan. See Joseph Rock, "Contributions to the Shamanism of the Tibetan-Chinese Borderland", in *Anthropos* LIV (1959), pp. 796-818.

70. This was repeated by Shardza Rinpoche on the basis of the *Srid-pa rgyud kyi kha-byang* and the *bsGrags byang*. See Karmay, ibid., p. 92-93.

71. According to the *Srid-pa'i rgyud*, the concelment of the Bon texts occured in the earth-ox year or 749 CE. See Karmay's discussion of the date in ibid., p.94, n. 2. Examining the text of the *bsGrags byang*, Karmay would place this event in the wood-ox year or 785 CE, making this the year in which the concealment began. The magical contest that preceded the concealment occurred in the pig year, probably the water-pig year or 783 CE. Moreover, it was the king's edict proclaiming the abolition of Bon that prompted Dranpa Namkha to convert to Buddhism and take ordination as a Buddhist monk. The *Srid-rgyud* says that Dranpa Namkha was thirty-one when the abolition of Bon led him to take these steps. This would make the year of his conversion 784 CE.

Elsewhere, according to Lopon Tenzin Namdak, it is said that the Tibetan king Trisong Detsan himself actively helped with the concealing of the Bonpo texts at Samye and even in his own palace. The Bonpo texts that he kept in the palace he placed in a large copper box. At this time, his son and heir to the throne, Senakek (Sad-na-legs), had fled Tibet with a companion who was the son of a minister. The prince had been accused of killing some boys, including the son of a powerful minister. He spent three years in exile in Bhutan to the south and while there he explored some caves near Paro (spa-gro). When he finally returned to Tibet, he found that both of his parents were absent. Nevertheless, he wanted to preserve Yungdrung Bon and opposed the importation of a foreign culture into Tibet from India. So, together with the help of a Bonpo priest, he took the Bonpo books in the copper box that had been preserved by the king to Bhutan where he hid the copper box inside one of the caves at Paro. Having conceled these texts, he left instructions regarding where to find them again. This collection of Termas, which included the practices for *dBal-phur* and the *Zhi-khro* (the Bonpo versions of Phurpa and of the Peaceful and Wrathful Deities of the Tibetan Book of the Dead cycle, respectively), were recovered centuries later. See Karmay, *Treasury*, ibid.

72. *Bon ma nub-pa'i gtan-tshigs*, ff. 259-267. For the translation of the text, see Chapter Seven below.

73. This Bonpo account of the defeat and murder of Ligmigya has also been translated from this same text by Snellgrove and Richarson. See Snellgrove and Richardson, *A Cultural History of Tibet*, ibid., pp. 99-100.

74. *Phying-ba'i stag-rtse*, the ancient royal castle in Yarlung.

75. *gSum-pa dbu-yog byung tshul la gnyis/ zhang-zhung snyan-brgyud las bshad-pa/ byang gter las bshad-pa'o. Legs-bshad mdzod*, ff. 179a-180b. See Karmay, *Treasury*, ibid., pp. 97-99.

76. The senior queen of Ligmigya, the king of Zhang-zhung, was named Khyungza Tsogyal (Khyung-za mtsho-rgyal). This queen, bitter in her heart over the death of her husband, invited Gyerpungpa into her private chambers in the castle of Khyungdzong (Khyung-rdzong), first preparing for him a seat of many silken cushions, and then offering him a bowl of chang (wine or beer) into which she had put a small nugget of gold as a sign of great respect. Such an offering was known as *ser-skyem*, "golden liquor". She spoke in flattering language to Gyerpungpa, telling him that he had become a famous Tantrika and now he must display his powers because Ligmigya, the protector of Bon, had been killed, the kingdom of Zhang-zhung was falling into pieces, and the Bon religion was declining. This was because the Buddhist monks from India were hardening the heart of the king of Tibet and turning him against Bon.

77. According to Lopon Tenzin Namdak, these three terms *spu*, *khyung*, and *rngub* are not Tibetan, but represent Zhang-zhung names.

78. This folk etymology explains how the mountain of *Sog-kha'i phung-po ri* came to obtain its alternative name of *Yar-lung sha-ba rengs*. Note that Shardza Rinpoche reverses the order of these events that are recorded in

the *Bon ma nub-pa'i gtan-tshigs* text. See the translation in Chapter Seven.

79. *Drwa-bye'i lung.* This valley of Drajye (drwa-bye) lay in the vicinty of the Darok lake (mtsho da-rog) in Northern Tibet. This region was the birthplace and the frequent residence of Gyerpungpa himself. The one hundred horsemen, together with the delegation of ministers, dispatched by the king of Tibet arrived at the lake, but could not find the sage Gyerpungpa anywhere. So they asked the local Zhang-zhung-pa shepherds who told the Tibetans that Gyerpungpa was a Mahasiddha and that he could appear as anything anywhere, such as emanating himself as various wild animals, or as fire, or even as the wind. But, in particular, he frequented the island in the middle of the lake. The Tibetan soldiers killed a horse and made a boat out of its skin and bones. Crossing the lake to the island, they found there the white silken tent with the deer designs on it.

80. Within this tent, on top of a pile of silken cushions, there was a crystal antelope horn, a ritual object particularly associated with the cult of the Tantric deity Zhang-zhung Meri. Realizing that this radiant object must be Gyerpungpa himself, the ministers offered to it the horn of a wild yak ('brong) filled with gold dust (gser phye 'brong ru gang) and made their prostrations. Instantly, Gyerpungpa reverted to his human form.

81. *gSang this kyi sngags.* The effect of this rite of exorcism counteracted the adverse effects of the magical missile attack by the *btswo* or *dzwa*.

82. The first Buddhist monastery in Tibet, Samye (bSam-yas), was probably founded in 779 CE. This is the date established by Hugh Richardson after comparing all the Tibetan historical sources and all the extent monument inscriptions (rdo ring) in Central Tibet. See Snellgrove and Richardson, *A Cultural History of Tibet*, ibid.

83. In the Bonpo account of these events, the scholar-monk from India is called Bodhisattva. However, here he is represented as being a Tibetan by birth. Later he came to study in India with various Buddhist masters. He was hostile to the Bonpos remaining behind in Tibet because of certain events occuring in his early life which caused him to be exiled to India. For this reason, Lopon Tenzin Namdak maintains that "Bodhisattva" should not be identified with the Indian scholar-monk Shantirakshita from Zahor, even though, in the Buddhist accounts, he is sometimes called Bodhisattva. In the Nyingmapa tradition, Shantirakshita (zhi-ba 'tsho) becomes one of the triad of spiritual heroes of the early period who, along with Guru Padmasambhava and the Tibetan king Trisong Detsan, introduced the Indian style of Mahayana Buddhism into Tibet and founded the first Buddhist monastery in Central Tibet at Samye (bSam-yas). Whereas Padmasambhava propagated the Tantric form of Buddhism known as Vajrayana among the Tibetans, it was Shantirakshita, as the first Abbot of Samye monastery, who introduced the Sutra system into Tibet and especially the Svatantrika-Yogachara-Madhyamika school of philosophy. In addition, he introduced the Vinaya ('dul-ba) of the Mula-Sarvastivadin school and ordained the first seven native-born Tibetan

monks, known as the *Sad-mi mi bdun*. His opposition to native Bonpo practitioners was well known, presumably because of their practice of blood sacrifice. His opposition appears to have been more in terms of their shamanic sacrificial practices, rather than anything doctrinal. Nevertheless, he did not recognize these Bonpos as being some kind of Buddhists

84. In the Bonpo tradition, there were three sages known by the name of Dranpa Namkha (Dran-pa nam-mkha'). The first Dranpa Namkha (sTag-gzigs dran-pa nam-mkha') lived in very early prehistoric times in Tazik or Central Asia. Not much is known about him. The second Dranpa Namkha (Zhang-zhung dran-pa nam-mkha') was a prince of Zhang-zhung, living at Khyunglung Ngulkhar (Khyung-lung dngul-mkhar), the capital of Zhang-zhung, west of Mount Kailas on the Sutlej river. He is reputed to have been both a great scholar and a great Siddha. He lived some time before the 8th century, but the *bsTan-rtsis* (see the translation by Per Kvaerne, ibid.) gives his birth date as 914 BC. Many texts and cycles of teaching, including Dzogchen, are connected with his name and he also became very important in the New Bon as the source of a number of Terma texts. Moreover, he is said to have been principally responsible for the concealing of Terma texts in the time of the earlier persecution under the seventh king of Tibet Drigun Tsanpo in 683 BC. He is said to have received his name, "the sky (nam-mkha') of memory (dran-pa)," because he could remember his five hundred previous incarnations. This master was the father of another great Siddha Tsewang Rigdzin (Tshe-dbang rig-'dzin) and his younger brother Pema Thongdrol (Padma mthong-grol). According to the Bonpos, the latter became known as Padmasambhava when he went to Uddiyana to the west of Zhang-zhung. Considered to be an emanation of Sangwa Dupa, he is said to have born in 888 BC. Having left home as a child of eight years of age, he was thereafter discovered by the king Indrabodhi in the center of a lotus blossom on an island in the lake of Sindhu in 876 BC.

The third Dranpa Namkha was a native-born Tibetan (Bod-pa dran-pa nam-mkha') who lived in Central Tibet in the eighth century. Originally a Bonpo Lama, in the time of the persecutions of Bon under king Trisong Detsan, he became a disciple of Guru Padmasambhava and appeared outwardly in the garb of a Buddhist monk. But in his heart he secretly remained a Bonpo. He is now reckoned among the latter's twenty-five disciples (rje 'bangs nyer-lnga). In general, according to Bonpo tradition, Padmasambhava was well disposed toward the native Bonpos and displayed none of the hostility shown toward them by the Indian monk Shantirakshita.

85. There were two major persecutions launched against the Bonpos in Central Tibet. The first was inaugurated by the seventh king of Tibet, Drigun btsan-po, in 683 BC, according to the *bsTan-rtsis*. The motive for this first persecution was clearly political and not doctrinal.

The second persecution of Bon was launched by the great Buddhist king of Tibet, Trisong Detsan, in the 8th century, in the year 749 CE according to the *bsTan-rtsis*. According to the Bonpo account, the ultimate cause of this persecution was the perverse prayer of a demon and the proximate cause was the arising of the five poisons, including hatred and jealousy, in the hearts of certain fundamentalist Buddhist monks from India, so that a negative spirit entered into the heart of the Tibetan king. Inspired by the influence of these monks, he commanded that either the Bonpos convert to Buddhism and become Buddhist monks, or else be expelled beyond the borders of his kingdom. Some like the Tibetan Dranpa Namkha outwardly converted to Indian Buddhism. Others like Lishu Tagring, after interceding with the king, departed for a celestial realm. Nevertheless, the Vidyadharas and the hosts of Dakinis concealed countless numbers of Terma texts to be rediscovered for the benefit of future generations. However, the actual motive here appears to have been political. Certain noble families at court were opposed to the increasing political influence of the Indian monks and their Tibetan followers. It is clearly anachronistic to speak of the Bonpos of that time as being organized into any kind of sect, church, or school. Indeed, there were many different kinds of practitioners in Tibet, whether priests, magicians, or shamans, all of whom indiscriminately bore the designation Bonpo in the early days.
The source of the real opposition of the Indian Buddhist monks to Bon was not a question of opposing doctrines, but their horror at the shamanic practice of blood sacrifice (dmar-mchod). The same was the case centuries later in Mongolia. Both Buddhism and shamanism accepts the actual existence of the gods and the nature spirits, as well as the practice of making offerings in order to propitiate them. But the Buddhists opposed the shedding of blood and the sacrifice of living animals to the spirits because of the cruelty and the suffering it engendered. In the Buddhist practice of puja (mchod-pa), a substitute or sacrificial cake known as a Torma (gtor-ma, Skt. bali) is offered to them instead. This appears in the Tibetan context to work just as well. It must also be noted that Yungdrung Bon equally opposed blood sacrifice. Although in those early days, not all practitioners called Bonpo in the historical records were necessarily followers of the Yungdrung Bon from Zhang-zhung. On this question of the conflict of Buddhism with indigenous shamanism over the practice of blood sacrifice, see Stan Royal Mumford, *Himalayan Dialogue*, University of Wisconsin Press, Madison WI 1989. And on the same question in Mongolia, see Walter Heissig, *The Religion of Mongolia*, University of California, Berkeley CA 1980, and also Walter Heissig, "A Mongolian Source to the Lamaist Suppression of Shamanism in the 17th Century," in *Anthropos* 48, pp. 493-533.

86. Indeed, as a parallel to the suppression and concealing of Bonpo texts, one is reminded of the persecution of the Gnostic sectarians by the triumphant Christian Church, the newly designated official religion of the Roman empire in the third and fourth centuries, and of the concealing of the

proscribed Gnostic texts in such places as the caves at Nag Hammadi in Upper Egypt. See Hans Jonas, *The Gnostic Religion*, Beacon Press, Boston 1958 and Jean Doresse, *The Secret Books of the Egyptian Gnostics*, The Viking Press, New York 1960.

87. Many Tibetan scholars belonging to the New Tantra schools regard the Old Tantras of the Nyingmapas to be of questionable authenticity because they lack any extant Sanskrit originals for the Tibetan translations done in the early period. For example, see Buton Rinpoche as quoted in Reynolds, *The Golden Letters*, ibid., pp. 275-276. See also the discussion of the authenticity of the *Kun-byed rgyal-po* as a Buddhist Tantra, in the same volume, pp. 236-248. Also on this question, see E.K. Neumaier-Dargyay, *The Sovereign All-Creating Mind, the Motherly Buddha*, SUNY, Albany NY 1992.

88. One is reminded how, following instructions of Pope Gregory (c. 600 CE), much the same policy was pursued in Western and Northern Europe, where pagan shrines were converted into Christian churches and pagan holidays were co-opted as Christian ones. For example, see Tony van Renterghem, *When Santa was a Shaman*, Llewellyn, St. Paul MN 1995.

89. This is the Tibetan Dranpa Namkha who became a Buddhist monk and a disciple of Guru Padmasambhava, although he remained a crypto-Bonpo. On the concealing of these Terma texts, see Karmay, *The Treasury of Good Sayings*, ibid. pp. 99-104.

90. Translated in Snellgrove and Richardson, *A Cultural History of Tibet*, ibid., pp. 106-107.

91. On Nubchen Sangye Yeshe (gNubs-chen Sangs-ryas ye-shes), see Reynolds, *The Golden Letters*, ibid, pp. 248-253.

92. On the revival of Buddhism in the 11th century and the formation of the Newer Schools (gsar-ma-pa), see Snellgrove and Richardson, *A Cultural History of Tibet*, ibid., pp. 111-143, and also Helmut Hoffman, *The Religions of Tibet*, ibid., pp. 111-130.

93. Also see Chapters Eight and Nine that follow below.

94. On the Tun Huang library, see Snellgrove and Richardson, *A Cultural History of Tibet*, ibid., pp. 111-112.

95. Oral communication. This fact would also appear to be behind Karmay's assertion that Dzogchen, unknown in earlier centuries because of the absence of extant texts that establish its existence, was something fabricated in the 10th and 11th centuries by certain Bonpo and Nyingmapa Lamas, that is to say, by Ponchen Tsanpo and by Zurpoche, who anachronistically attributed the Dzogchen teachings to earlier illustrious figures like Tapihritsa and Padmasambhava, who belonged to the 8th century, in order to gain their acceptence among the Bonpos and Buddhists of their time. This assertion that Dzogchen is not authentic, but merely an innovation and a fabrication lacking any authentic lineage, is very much in line with the strategies of certain Lama-scholars belonging to the Newer Schools (gsar-ma-pa) to denegrate Dzogchen as something heretical and not in line with the official Prasangika Madhyamaka

doctrines of the Tibetan monastic establishmnet. See Samten G. Karmay, *The Great Perfection: A Philosophical and Meditative Teaching of Tibetan Buddhism*, Brill, Leiden 1988. Of course, at this point, we cannot prove that Ponchen Tsanpo actually inherited any texts written by Gyerpungpa in the Zhang-zhung language, but it now appears quite likely that the *sMar-yig* script of Zhang-zhung was known in Gyerpungpa's time in the 8th century and before. Even so, the Zhang-zhung Nyan-gyud in the early days was fundamentally an oral tradition (snyan-brgyud) and Zurpoche Shakya Jyungne had gone into various remote parts of Tibet specifically in order to collect such oral traditions pertaining to the practice of Dzogchen. The importance of and persistence of oral tradition is not always obvious to philologists who tend to believe that something cannot exist unless it is found recorded in some text or another. The mysterious figures of Gyerpungpa in the 8th century and Ponchen Tsanpo in the 9th century, like their illustrious Buddhist contemporary Padmasambhava, are certainly historical. And, as I have concluded in *The Golden Letters*, I see no good reason not to attribute the original propagation of the Dzogchen teachings to these great masters.

Chapter 6: The Prophetic Sayings of Lord Tapihritsa

1. All of these texts, both root and commentary, focus on the view (lta-ba) of Dzogchen:
    1) *Phyi lta-ba spyi-gcod kyi man-ngag le'u bcu-gnyis-pa* (ff. 145-168).
    2) *rGyud bu-chung bcu-gnyis* (ff.169-179).
    3) *rGyud bu-chung bcu-gnyis kyi don bstan-pa* (ff. 181-192).
    4) *'Phrul-'khor lde-mig* (ff. 193-198).
    5) *mDo 'grel gsal-ba'i sgron-me* (ff. 199-231).
    6) *lTa-ba spyi-gcod kyi mnyam-bzhag sgom-pa'i lag-len* (ff.233-244).
    Then follow a number of texts devoted to the hagiographies in the lineage:
    1) *dGongs rgyud dgu'i yig-chung* (ff. 245-246).
    2) *rJe Ta-pi-hri-tsa'i lung-bstan* (ff. 247-254).
    3) *Zhe-sa dgu phrugs* (ff. 255-256).
    4) *mJal thebs bar-ma* (f. 257).
    5) *Bon ma nub-pa'i gtan-tshigs* (ff. 259-267).
2. *Dra-bye dung-lung*. This valley lay to the north of the Darok lake in Northern Tibet. It was the home region of Gyerpung Nangzher Lodpo.
3. The archetype of the wise child who confounds his elders, the learned priests, is also a motif in the hagiographies of Garab Dorje and Jesus Christ. See Reynolds, *The Golden Letters*, ibid., pp. 177-189.
4. These hagiograpchial texts such as the *rJe Ta-pi-hri-tsa'i lung-bstan* and the *mJal-thebs bar-ma*, were composed long after the time Tapihritsa appeared to his disciple Gyerpungpa in a luminous Body of Resurrection. Here there appear to exist parallels to the way in which the original oral teachings of Jesus of Nazareth as wise sayings and parables in spoken

Aramaic were collected and elaborated by the later authors known as
Mark, Matthew, Luke, and John and embedded in the narrative texts of
their Four Gospels. Jesus, a Jewish teacher of Wisdom, apparently wrote
nothing himself and his wisdom sayings and parables (Gr. logoi sophon)
were remembered by his disciples and within a decade of his death they
were most likely written down in Aramaic. Not long afterwards, these
sayings collections were translated into colloquial Greek, which survive
today in the form of the Q Document and the Gospel of Thomas. Several
decades later, these sayings, though not in the same order, were inserted
into the narratives of the earthly career of Jesus composed by the above
authors of the Four Gospels found in the New Testament. On this whole
process of literary composition of the Gospels, see Burton Mack, *The Lost
Gospel: The Book of* Q *and Christian Origins,* Harper Collins, San
Francisco 1993. Also see Richard Valantasis, *The Gospel of Thomas*,
Routledge, London 1997, as well as Robert Grant, *The Gnostic Gospel of
Thomas*, Doubleday, Garden City NY 1960. The parallels are indeed
suggestive.

However, just as the wise sayings or *logia sophon* of the master Jesus
circulated in oral tradition before being collected together and inserted
into written narratives or Gospels, so the wise sayings (lung-bstan, man-
ngag) of Tapihritsa circulated orally and out of context until being
embedded in a literary narrative recounting Gyerpungpa's successive
encounters with his wise master. Most likely these Upadeshas do indeed
go back to the historical Tapihritsa, but their narrative context here is a
later literary composition by an author living after the time of
Gyerpungpa. However, this author certainly drew on the body of oral
material in circulation. This sayings collection preceded the narrative
Gospel in terms of composition. It would appear that the original sayings
collection for Tapihritsa probably resembled the Gospel of Thomas and
the Q Document containing the *logia sophon* of the master Jesus of
Nazareth. Lopon Tenzin Namdak would attribute all of this literary
activity to Gyerpungpa himself. But these works appear to have been
composed later with the Bonpo revival in the 11th century with Orgom
Kundul and Yangton Chenpo, the latter and his son Dampa Bumje being
the final redactors for the collection. See Chapter Nine below.

5. *Zhe-sa* designates a polite and respectful form of address. However,
according to the Lopon, Tapihritsa is being ironic about the Yogi's practice.

6. The hermitage of the deer-faced rock (brag sha-ba gdong gi dgon-pa) was
located near the fresh-water Darok lake (da-rog mtsho) in Northern Tibet.
Here he remained continuously in the state of contemplation (dgongs la
bzhugs), whereupon the Nirmanakaya appeared to him once more in a
resurrected Body of Light, here called the Body of Self-Originated
Awareness (rang-'byung rig-pa'i sku).

7. *rJe sprul-pa'i sku la phyag-'tshal-lo.*

8. Gyerpungpa purified his mind with learning (mkhas-par blo sbyangs) and
guarded his morality with noble and honorable conduct (btsun-par khrims

bsrung). Impressing on his mind all of the essential characteristics of things without confusion (mtshan-nyid thams-cad ma rmongs-par thugs su chud) means he mastered all aspects of philosophy and phenomenology. This would appear to indicate that, before his meeting with his master Tapihritsa, he had been a learned scholar in the various doctrines and methods of Bon and was the chief priest of the country of Zhang-zhung, even serving as the Purohita or personal chaplain of its king.

9. As contemporaries of Gyerpungpa, there lived the Siddhas or adepts (grub-thob) *sPa Ji-phrom dkar-po* and *Tso-men gyer-chen* (var. Tso-mi) in Tibet and Zhang-zhung respectively. *Tshe-spungs zla-ba rgyal-mtshan*, the master of Tapihritsa, was still alive in Zhang-zhung, as well as that great magician who exercised his magical powers on behalf of Yungdrung Bon, *sTong-rgyung mthu-chen*. The latter lived beside the sky lake of Namtso (gnam-mtsho) in Northern Tibet. Living then also were the four translators (lo-tsa-ba bzhi) *Se-sha dbu-chen, lDe-gyim tsa-rma chung, bLa Dran-pa nam-mkha'*, and *Me-nyag ltse-tsha mkhar-bu chung*, who assembled together for the task of translating the Zhang-zhung texts into Tibetan. This *bLa-chen Dran-pa nam-mkha'* appears to refer to the prince of Zhang-zhung, rather than to the Tibetan Bonpo priest who later became a disciple of Padmasambhava. On this figure, see Note 84 in Chapter Five above.

10. According to the Medieval Tibetan histories, the country of Zhang-zhung and its king Ligmigya were subdued by the great Tibetan king Songtsan Gampo in the previous century. But it would appear that in the eighth century that Zhang-zhung still maintained its individual identity and a certain degree of independence. The name Ligmigya (li-mi-rgya), meaning "the king of men," was, according to Lopon Tenzin Namdak, a dynastic title born by all the monarchs of that line. And in terms of actual historical circumstances, it appears that Ligmigya was in some way the vassel or otherwise subservient to the mighty king of Central Tibet, Trison Detsan (rgyal-po Khri-srong lde-btsan). The fortunes of Bon appeared to decline greatly in the mid eighth century with the final conquest of Zhang-zhung by the Central Tibetans and the death of the last native-born king of Zhang-zhung who was an avid patron of the Bon religion. This process of decline (nub lugs) is described more in detail in the last text translated in this section. In the following paragraph, the author of the text cites other historical accounts or summaries (kha-byang). This fact would appear to clearly indicate that the narrative here was written long after the time of Gyerpungpa and that the wise sayings of Tapihritsa, which had previously circulated orally, were inserted into this narrative in order to form a kind of "Gospel" text.

Although Tapihritsa wrote down nothing of his own teachings on Dzogchen, it is said that he permitted Gyerpungpa to set them down in the Zhang-zhung language as an aid to memory. These teachings consisted of extremely brief and pithy Upadeshas, such as those found in "the Tantra called the Twelve Small Precepts" (rgyud bu-chung bcu-gnyis), the translation of which will be found in a subsequent volume in this series, *Space, Awareness, and Energy.* Some of these brief sayings or Upadeshas also came to be inserted into a frame story, such as is the case with the *Tapihritsa'i lung-bstan* text here. It appears certain that this text was not written by Gyerpungpa himself, but it surely does reflect the oral tradition coming down from this master. In any event, in the 11th century, Orgom Kundul and Yangton Chenpo were especially associated with these literary developments. See Chapter Nine below.

11. Because of the accomplishments of his great learning, Gyerpungpa developed an overwhelming pride. This may be compared to the intellectual pride of another great Buddhist master Naropa when, as a famous professor at Nalanda monastic university, he was confronted by a Dakini in the guise of an old crone who mocked his great intellectual learning. See Herbert V. Guenther, *The Life and Teachings of Naropa*, ibid. But in this case the arrogant scholar is confronted by the wise child archetype. This motif is also found in Garab Dorje's confronting the five hundred Panditas in Uddiyana and Jesus of Nazareth confronting the Elders in the temple at Jersusalem. See Reynolds, *The Golden Letters*, ibid., pp. 177-189. The various enumerations of all essential characteristics (mtshan-nyid, Skt. lakshana) refers to philosophical investigations in a systematic sense, a process which defines and classifies the characteristics of all phenomena. This is a philosophy in the classical Indian sense, such as, for example, the Vaishashika philosophy or the Buddhist Abhidharma. This philosophical exercise of defining and classifying causes and characteristices, the Hetu-lakshana-yana, properly belongs to the Sutra system in terms of both Buddhism and Bon. Here, in general, four philosophical systems of tenets or siddhantha (grub-mtha') are distiguished in both traditions: 1. Vaibhashika, 2. Sautrantika, 3. Madhyamaka, and 4. Chittamatra. This is true at least for the Bonpo system of the Central Treasures (dbu gter lugs), whereas a different system of classification of the Nine Vehicles is presented in the system of the Southern Treasures (lho gter lugs). See Chapter One in Part One above.

12. *bLa' i mchod-gnas.*

13. The patron (yon-bdag) of Gyerpungpa during his retreat at this time was a wealthy man owning large herds of cattle, sheep, and yaks, named Merchyugpo Yungdrung Gyaltsan (sMrer phyug-po g.yung-drung rgyal-mtshan), who was camped with his family and retainers in tents in the river valley of Drajye Dunglung (dra-bye dung-lung) at the site of Drong Drajye (grong dra-bye). Here the term *grong* means an inhabited place, but not necessarily a town or village. *Dra-bye* or *Drwa-bye* is a district near the Darok lake in Northern Tibet where Gyerpungpa made a retreat after receiving the Dzogchen instructions from Tapihritsa. Here at this rock cave (brag-phug) in Drajye Dunglung, Tapihritsa manifested himself in the form of a young boy who was an emanation (sprul-pa'i khye'u).

14. The young boy tells the rich man that he is able to work, but that he is without a taskmaster or boss (las nus te bcol-mkhan med), that is to say, he is an orphan without a family. Finding that the boy was a hard worker and very useful to him as a servant, the rich man gave him the nick name of "the well-found young boy (Khye'u rnyed legs).

15. These nine polite expressions represent nine kinds of praises (zhe-sa dgu phrugs), after each of which the boy made a prostration to the master: *Zhe-sa dgu phrugs*, ff. 255-256.

16. Gyerpungpa is astonished at the young boy's precocious knowledge and says "Your thoughts seem to be informed with philosophical tenets" (grub-mthas blo bsgyur zhig), that is to say, he is very learned. He therefore asked the young boy these five questions: Who is your teacher? What is your practice? On what meditation do you meditate? What is your burden? And why are your doing this strange activity? (slob-dpon ni su yin/ nyams su ci len/ sgom-pa ci sgom/ khur ru na ci yod/ spyod-pa 'di 'dra byed cir yin.) This exchange represented a kind of traditional question and answer game or riddle (lde'u). On this practice of riddles, see Namkhai Norbu, *Drung, Dreu and Bon: Narrations, Symbolic Languages, and the Bon Tradition in Ancient Tibet*, ibid.

17. Gyerpungpa's querry is apparently literal and straightforward, but the wise child replied to him in terms of the understanding of Dzogchen practice: *sLob-dpon 'di ltar snang-ba yin/ nyams su rnam-par mi rtog len/ sgom-pa khams gsum snang tshad yin/ khur ru rnam-par rtog-pa yin/ spyod-pa 'gro-ba'i khol-po yin.*

18. Here the reference is to the practice of Thodgal. This indicates that to comprehend and understand the Natural State, there is no need for a teacher to explain and conceptualize matters, because normal vision is the spontaneous expression of the inherent energy (rang rtsal) of the Natural State. Rather, the teacher or master (bla-ma, Skt. guru) merely points out and directly introduces the practitioner to what is already present within oneself from the very beginning. There is nothing to acquire that is outside of oneself. This experience is one's own innate wisdom; it is not some extraneous knowledge that comes from outside. Hence, there exists the traditional folk etymology of the word Lama (bla-ma), as meaning the mother (ma) of the soul (bla).

19. "Normal vision" (snang-ba) here again refers to the practice of Thodgal through which Tapihritsa had attained liberation and enlightenment. Kuntu Zangpo had no Guru or teacher; He was enlightened from the very beginning because He understood that these visions were empty and lacking any inherent existence and that they represented only manifestations of mind (sems kyi snang-ba). Being without distraction by discursive thoughts refers to the practice of Trekchod or contemplation. The real meaning of the Ultimate Reality (bon-nyid) is without partialities (phyogs-med), that is, it cannot be judged or evaluated and transcends conception by the finite intellect. Having realized this Ultimate Reality, which is not just Shunyata or emptiness, but the inseparability of

emptiness and appearances (snang stong dbyer-med), all phenomena now have the same taste or flavor (ro-snyoms) for the practitioner. In some texts, *ro-snyams* refers to the process in meditation practice and *ro-gcig*, having a single taste, to the realization.

20. That is to say, those who practice Tantra or the Secret Mantras (gsang-sngags) are only busy creating things with their minds, as visualizations and as virtual realities (dmigs-pa), and do not leave things as they are in the Natural State. The wise child offers criticism of the Tantric practitioners and of the learned scholarly intellectuals, both of whom fall short of Dzogchen in terms of their immediate experience.

21. The essential characteristics of things (mtshan-nyid): this refers to the mental processes of defining and conceptualizing phenomena. But this is no more than the result of the use of language and words; it is not reality in itself. The map is not the territory. This confusion is the error of common sense and naive realism. One takes what is imputed by the use of language to be real, whereas it is not. The practitioners of the Secret Mantras or Tantras, however, understand that mind, the thought process, is the creator or manufacturer of the thoughts (sems la bzo byed) that we mistakenly take for reality. They come to this understanding by virtue of practicing the Generation Process (bskyed-rim) where, in meditation, the mind is employed to construct temporarily a virtual reality or pure vision (dag snang) and the practitioner enters into this totally while in a condition of sensory deprivation. Finally, the visualization is again dissolved into the state of Shunyata, so that one comes to an experiential understanding of the insubstantiality of all things, comprehending that life is like a dream. However, as for the learned scholars, they only possess a purely theoretical or conceptual knowledge of this that is without purpose (mkhas-pa rnams ni shes la don med yin). This knowledge is circular and tautological and does not serve the purpose of liberation. So, those who follow the naive realism of common sense, those who practice Tantric meditations by way of transformations, and those learned scholars engaged in philosophical speculations and debates do not understand the real meaning of the Natural State, which cannot be grasped or fabricated by discursive thoughts. Rather, the practice of contemplation is the natural path where there exists no necessity for the purification of anything whatsoever (gnyug-ma'i lam sbyong du med).

22. When Gyerpungpa regained his senses, he saw that the young ragged orphan boy had transformed into a beautiful sixteen year old youth who had ascended into the sky and was sitting suspended in space inside a sphere of rainbow light (thig-le). This youth was pure white like crystal, translucent like the rainbow, and completely naked, lacking any clothes or ornaments whatsoever.

23. *Da dngos la gdams-ngag cig zhu.*

24. The instructions concerning "the Four Good Things" (legs-pa bzhi'i gdams-ngag) are briefly as follows:

1) In terms of the view or way of looking at things, when external appearances or visions (snang-ba) are not grasped at by the mind or the intellect, they will self-liberate of themselves. Just that letting them go without judging or conceptualizing them in any way is the first good thing (btang-ba de-ka legs-pa yin).

2) In terms of the meditation practice, meditating without concepts represents remaining in a condition of mindful awareness and that represents inherent clarity (dmigs med kyi sgom-pa rang gsal). Just that guarding oneself against the distractions of judgment and conceptual elaboration is the second good thing (skyong-ba de-ka legs-pa yin).

3) In terms of the conduct, one's conduct should be without any attachments or expectations, yet it is alertly relaxed (chags-med kyi spyod-pa lhug-pa). Just that cutting off of attachments and conceptual elaborations is the third good thing (bcad-pa de-ka legs-pa yin).

4) In terms of the fruit or the goal, when one does not seek to obtain anything, everything will arise spontaneously by itself (thob med kyi 'bras-bu rang shar), and thereby all expectations and anxieties regarding the future are self-liberated into their original condition of emptiness. Just that process of liberation is the fourth good thing (grol-ba de-ka legs-pa yin).

One should note that these four good things: letting go (btang-ba), protecting or guarding (skyong-ba), cutting off (bcad-pa), and liberating (grol-ba) refer to the view or way of seeing (lta-ba), the meditation (sgom-pa), the conduct (spyod-pa), and the fruit ('bras-bu) respectively, in terms of the practice of Thodgal. See the final note in this section.

According to the procedures of the Zhang-zhung Nyan-gyud, one does not practice Trekchod and Thodgal sequentially, but one links them together in practice because they mutually reinforce each other. Of course, the practitioner must first be directly introduced to the Natural State and then develop a certain degree of stability in contemplation or Trekchod before one can profit from the practice of vision. Indeed, one must be in a state of contemplation while engaging in vision practice, otherwise it would be no better than watching a cinema show according to the Lopon. These four good things represence the essential points of Thodgal practice.

25. The second instruction is entitled "the Four Applications to the Mind" (rgyud la sbyor-ba bzhi), where four realizations are applied or linked (sbyor-ba) to the mind (rgyud). These are as follows:

1) No external or internal activity can diminish or exhaust the Ultimate Reality (bon-nyid, Skt. dharmata) because it is non-material (dngos med). One should apply this to the mind also.

2) One cannot conventionally know the Dharmakaya because it is beyond causes and conditions. One should apply this to the mind also.

3) One cannot find the mind anywhere by simply searching for it because it lacks any inherent existence. One should apply this to understanding the mind also.

4) One cannot change the Natural State by way of any modifications. One should apply this to the mind also.

That is to say, the Mind, or rather the Nature of Mind, is non-material, beyond causes and conditions, lacking in any inherent existence, and unchanging.

26. The third instruction consists of "the Five Practices" (nyams su len-pa lnga), namely,

1) One should practice without any partiality or one-sidedness (phyogs-med ris-med cig nyams su longs);

2) One should practice without either binding or liberating appearances (bcings grol med-par nyams su longs);

3) One should practice without either decreasing or increasing anything (bri gang med-par nyams su longs);

4) One should practice without either augmenting or obscuring anything (phel 'grib med-par nyams su longs); and

5) One should practice without either separating or linking anything ('bral-med dang 'brel-med du nyams su longs).

Here the question is how does one practice Thodgal with regard to external appearances that are really just visions (snang-ba)? There exists no partiality or one-sidedness in the Natural State itself in terms of judgments or conceptual elaborations and thus visions arise without any partiality in themselves. Therefore, one should practice without any partiality with regard to visions or appearances, that is, without any judgments, expectations, preconceptions, or subsequent conceptual elaborations. Just leave them exactly as they are and they will self-liberate of themselves. Whatever arises to vision is fine just as it is and should be accepted without any attempts at modification or correction. Therefore, one practices without trying to change or modify anything, but just leaves things be as they are. There does not exist any desire in the Natural State to grasp and apprehend external objects and thus external objects are allowed to simply liberate once more into the state of emptiness out of which they originally arose. They liberate of themselves because the mind does not attempt to process or interfere with them in any way. In the state of contemplation, the normal everyday activities of the mind and the thought process are suspended. All that remains is a clear pristine awareness, like the clean surface of the mirror. And therefore one should practice without attempting to bind appearances with judgments or conceptual elaborations, on the one hand, or trying to liberate them, on the other hand. One just lets them be and appearances will liberate of themselves. Within the Natural State there does not exist any birth or death, that is to say, any originating or ceasing, and so these visions or appearances exist in a condition that is not produced by anything else outside of themselves. They just manifest spontaneously and are perfect and complete just as they are. And therefore, one should practice without trying to increase them or decrease them in any way. These appearances are inconceivable and inexpressible in words; they just abide of themselves in the vast expanse of space without any need for expression in language. But once verbalized and conceptualized, they are elaborated and thereby falsified. Therefore, one should practice without trying to emphasize or obscure anything whatsoever. This awareness experienced while in the state of contemplation has never been separate from the Natural State from the very beginning, nor has it been contingent upon external appearances manifesting. Therefore, one should practice without trying to isolate awareness from appearances or by trying to link it to any specific appearance.

27. The fourth instruction concerns "the Four Direct Trainings in terms of the Natural Disposition" (gshis thog tu bkal-ba bzhi), that is to say, one should bind oneself directly in the training of remaining and continuing in that natural disposition (gshis de-ka'i thog tu khol la zhog) which is the state of contemplation. These are as follows:

1) One should not limit oneself in terms of time. One should rely upon short sessions of practice rather than long ones that might cause obstacles and disturbances.

2) One should not become distracted by experiences in meditation, such as experiences of bliss and pleasurable sensation (bde-ba'i nyams) or of luminous clarity and light (gsal-ba'i nyams), or of emptiness and no thought (mi rtog-pa'i nyams).

3) In terms of a session of practice, one should remain in the state of contemplation without interruption. The Natural State is unconditioned; nevertheless, its energy is expressed as the inseparability of appearances and emptiness, indeed, beyond Samsara itself.

4) By remaining in the Natural State, one has thereby entered into a state that is beyond birth and death, beyond origination or cessation.
These four trainings pertain to remaining in the state of contemplation which is Trekchod.

28. Here Tapihritsa speaks of "the Three Kinds of Confidence" (gdeng rnam-pa gsum). Only when one possesses these three can one justly call oneself a yogin (rnal-'byor-pa) or practitioner of Dzogchen. These are as follows:

1) Because one understands that all appearances or visions lack any real material existence (dngos-med), one will have the confidence to decide definitively on just that one single thing (gcig chad kyi gdeng), which is the singular understanding of the Natural State.

2) Because one understands that appearance and emptiness are inseparable (dbyer-med) in the Natural State, one will have the confidence that everything has but a single taste (ro gcig gi gdeng).

3) Because one understands that the Natural State is without partialities (phyogs-med) in terms of judgments and evaluations, one will have a confidence that is free of all limitations (mtha' bral gyi gdeng). The text reads: *dngos-med du rtogs-pas gcig chod gyi gdeng/ dbyer-med du rtogs-pas ro gcig gi gdeng/ phyogs-med du rtogs-pas mtha' 'bral gyi gdeng/ gdeng de gsum dang ldan na rnal-'byor zhes bya'o.* Compare these three with the Three Statements of Garab Dorje in the Nyingmapa tradition. See Reynolds, *The Golden Letters*, ibid.

29. *dGongs nyams.*

30. This is the key to the dialogue with one's own higher self or enlightened Awareness, one's innate Buddha nature. Therefore, Guru Yoga (bla-ma'i rnal-'byor), where one recollects and remains mindfully aware always (rjes su dran-pa) of the presence of the master, continually renewing one's contact with the master, receiving his blessings of inspiration, and maintaining the vital link with the transmissions one has received, is an essential practice in Dzogchen, as well as in Tantra. On the practice of the Guru Yoga in terms of the Zhang-zhung Nyan-gyud, see Appendix One below.

31. With these four good things (legs-pa bzhi), the four applications to the mind (rgyud la sbyor-ba bzhi), the five practices (nyams su len-pa lnga), the four trainings directly related to the natural disposition (gshis thog tu bkal-ba bzhi), and the three kinds of confidence (gdeng rnam-pa gsum), the exposition of this instruction by the Guru is completed. One should note that these five Upadeshas from Tapihritsa correspond to the five queries of Gyerpungpa initially addressed to the miraculous wise child who was an emanation (sprul-pa'i khye'u):

    1) "Who is your teacher?" corresponds to the four good things (legs-pa bzhi);
    2) "What is your practice?" corresponds to the four applications to the mind (rgyud la sbyor-ba bzhi);
    3) "What is your meditation?" corresponds to the five practices (nyams su len-pa lnga);
    4) "What is your burden?" corresponds to the four trainings relating to the natural disposition (gshis thog tu bkal-ba bzhi); and
    5) "What is your activity?" correspond to the three kinds of confidence (gdeng rnam-pa gsum).

32. *Brag sha-ba gdong gi dgon-pa.*

33. In terms of the physiology of Thodgal practice, the inner light of Rigpa resides inside the hollow space of the physical heart (tsi-ta), metaphorically spoken of as a miniature-sized human figure of light. This Awareness (rig-pa) and, in this case, the image of this Awareness is projected by way of a subtle hollow translucent channel out through the lenses of the eyes where it manifests in the empty space before the practitioner, as if this were an image projected on to a screen. Thus, what is actually inside oneself comes into visible manifestation in the space outside oneself. In this way, the enlightened Awareness of the practitioner

comes to appear in the external dimension of the sky as the luminous Guru figure and the dialogue ensues. Tapihritsa is this "Man of Light" and this is what occurred to Gyerpungpa. At daybreak, the master Gyerpungpa was engaged in Thodgal practice, when the Lord Tapihritsa appeared to him in a pure vision inside a rainbow sphere of light. Note that the narrative is speaking more of the practice of Guru Yoga by the individual practitioner than it is of supposed historical events.

34. *dGongs la bzhugs.*

35. *Rang-'byung rig-pa'i sku.* That is to say, Tapihritsa appeared to him as a Thodgal vision.

36. The Son of a Noble Family, or Kulaputra (skal-ldan rigs kyi bu), is a polite form of address, but technically it means an individual whose good karma has ripened and so one has met with the Dharma and the teacher of the Dharma.

37. The certain meaning (nges-pa'i don) or true meaning of the teaching, in this case Thodgal, is esoteric and restricted to the few, as opposed to the more popular, conventional, and public meaning. Whereas philosophy may be understood by way of public discourse, Dzogchen and especially Thodgal may only be understood by way of a direct introduction.

38. The ordinary Sutric meaning of this term *dgongs-pa* is "intention." But in the context of Dzogchen it means "the Mind" or "the Primordial State of the Buddha." It can also be translated as "contemplation", that is, remaining in the Natural State of the Nature of Mind, when it is a noun and when it is a verb as "to contemplate."

39. This Nature (bdag-nyid), which is the Unique Sphere of the Bodhichitta, refers to the Natural State. The aspect that is exceedingly secret (yang gsang) refers to the Fruit or the realization of Buddhahood.

40. *rGyal-ba dgongs rgyud dgu'i thugs bcud.....gang-zag nyi-shu rtsa bzhi'i snyan-rgyud.* This brief text represents the preface, more or less, to the Dzogchen teachings of Tapihritsa on the occasion of their second meeting. The principal teaching in this section concerns meditation practice rather than the philosophical view, that is to say, the Six Lamps (sgron-ma drug) that pertain to vision or Thodgal practice. The translation of this text will be found in the succeeding volumes in this series.

Chapter 7: The Reason why Bon did not Decline

1. See S. Karmay, *Treasury*, ibid.

2. Contemporary with the great *Gyer-spungs chen-po sNang-bzher lod-po* in the eighth century, there lived three other Mahasiddhas or great adepts (grub-thob chen -po) possessing extraordinary powers: in Zhang-zhung there was the Siddha *Tso-men gyer-chen* (var. Tso-mi, Tso-min) and in Tibet there were the Siddhas *sPa Ji-phrom dkar-po* and *sTong-rgyung mthu-chen*, the latter residing at the sky lake of *gNam-mtsho* in Northern Tibet. Among the learned scholars, the Zhang-zhung prince *Dran-pa nam-mkha'* is mentioned in the text, who was now in the latter part of his

exceedingly long life since he is also made a contemporary of the seventh Tibetan king, *Gri-gum btsan-po*. Generally the Lopon identifies this *Dran-pa nam-mkha'* with the prince of Zhang-zhung and not with the later Tibetan disciple of the same name. The four Nirmanakayas (sprul-sku bzhi) were *Zhang-zhung bkra-shis rgyal-mtshan, Gu-rub sTag-wer shing-slag, Ma-hor stag-gzig,* and *Tshe-spungs zla-ba rgyal-mtshan.* It was from the latter that the great Gyerpungpa received the ordinary teachings for the Sutras and the Tantras, whereas he received the supreme instructions for Dzogchen from Tapihritsa at a later time. See the translations in Chapter Five above.

3. But because of the power of the Wheel of Time, it came about that Yungdrung Bon declined (dus kyi 'khor-lo'i shugs kyis g.yung-drung bon nub-pa). Here the reference is not to the *Kalachakra Tantra,* but to the power of time and decay that brings about the inevitable decline of the Dharma, or spirituality generally, during the downward course of the yuga (dus) or cycle of time.

4. The king of Zhang-zhung (Zhang-zhung gi rgyal-po) named *Lig-mi-rgya* was the contemporary of the king of Mon (Mon gyi rgyal-po) named *Pan-ra-ling* (var. Panta-li-kha), and the king of Tibet (Bod gyi rgyal-po) *Khri-srong lde'u-btsan.* Mon or Mon-yul lay just south of Tibet in Nepal and Bhutan. At this time, Tibet (Bod) consisted only of the Yarlung valley in Central Tibet and certain adjacent areas. This Ligmigya became the last king of independent Zhang-zhung, but there is also a reference to king Ligmigya in the Royal Chronicles, discovered at Tun Huang, as living during the time of *Srong-btsan sgam-po* (609-649 CE), the first Buddhist king of Tibet. It appears that this Tibetan king defeated the former in a war and made the country of Zhang-zhung subservient to Tibet. However, this did not eliminate Zhang-zhung as an independent entity, but only reduced it to vassalage. Lopon Tenzin Namdak suggests that the name *Lig-mi-rgya,* which means "the king of men" in the Zhang-zhung language, was actually a dynastic title born by all the kings of that royal lineage who succeeded the kings of the earlier Jyaruchan (Bya-ru-can) dynasty of Zhang-zhung. This latter title means "he who possesses the horns of the bird," that is, the horns of the Garuda (khyung-po).

5. Originally the king of Tibet, like his neighbors, had only three ministers (blon-po gsum), that is, one minister for external affairs, one minister for internal affairs, and one minister acting as a liaison (phyi blon gcig nang blon gcig phrin blon gcig dang gsum). The latter minister was in charge of intelligence gathering and espionage. The Tibetan king's increasing the number of ministers from three to thirty was a sign of his overwhelming pride, as well as his political and military ambitions.

6. Tazik (stag-gzigs, var. stag-gzig), literally, "tigers and leopards," was a transliteration of the name for Iranian-speaking Central Asia, Tajik, which is reflected in the name of the modern day Central Asian republic of Tajikistan. In this case, the reference is, no doubt, to Sogdiana (Sog-yul), for a time invaded and conquered by the Tibetans until the coming of the

Arab armies. See Christopher Beckwith, *The Tibetan Empire in Central Asia*, Princeton University Press, Princeton 1987.

7. The Zhang-zhung kingdom, which appears to have been largely nomad in character in terms of its population, seems to have embraced all of Western and Northern Tibet in ancient times. Most of the people of Zhang-zhung were nomads ('brog-po) and lived in tents in encampments which changed locations with the seasons, as is the practice of their descendents even today in Northern Tibet. On the descendents of these Zhang-zhung-pa nomads, see Melvyn Goldstein and Cynthis Beall, *Nomads of Western Tibet: The Survival of a Way of Life*, University nof California Press, Berkeley 1990.

There were, however, in Zhang-zhung some extensive agricultural settlements at Khyung-lung along the Sutlej river to the west of Mount Kailas and along the shores of the Dang-ra lake to the east in Northern Tibet. The western region around Mount Kailas, being of a higher elevation, was known as Upper Zhang-zhung, whereas the eastern lake region of Northern Tibet, being of a lower elevation, was known as Lower Zhang-zhung. Lopon Tenzin Namdak, who spent almost two years in the Dang-ra region, saw evidence of the extensive practice of irrigation and terrace agriculture now long abandoned, as well as some ruins. The ruins of the Garuda Castle of *Khyung-rdzong*, the former residence of *Lig-mi-rgya*, the last king of Zhang-zhung, was nearby. According to the Lopon, the local nomads, forgetting their ancient Zhang-zhung heritage and descent, attributed these ruins to the *Sog-po* people. Nowadays this is one name given to the Mongols, but it ancient times it was applied to the Iranian speaking Sogdians (sog-po) who lived in Sogdiana (sog-yul) along the famous Silk Route to the northwest of Tibet. On the archaeology of Northern Tibet, see John Vincent Bellezza, *Divine Dyads: Ancent Civilization in Tibet*, Library of Tibetan Works and Archives, Dharamsala 1997. Also see his recent article, "High-Country Culture: A Civilization Flourished in the Himalayas before Buddhism Reached Tibet," *Discovering Archaeology* v.1 n.3, May-June 1999, pp. 78-83.

Namkhai Norbu Rinpoche, who personally visited the Garuda valley of Khyung-lung along the Sutlej river to the west of Mount Kailas, also reported seeing evidence of the extensive practice of irrigation and terrace agriculture from the distant past, as well as a vast network of cliff dwellings, quite reminiscent of those seen in the American Southwest. Also visible were the ruins of the silver castle of *Khyung-lung dngul-mkhar*, the former residence of the Zhang-zhung kings, on top of the cliff face. Presumably water had been drawn from the Sutlej river and regularly used for irrigation in the valley. In that case, the valley could have supported a much larger population than the few scattered nomads who roam the region today. Oral communication.

In the 8th century, the small country of Sumpa, which included present day Khyungpo in Upper Kham, and which is the home region of the Lopon, was a vassal of the larger and more powerful Zhang-zhung kingdom lying to the west. It also had a largely nomad population. And in view of the largely nomadic and pastoral character of both Zhang-zhung and Sum-pa, it is obvious that the text exaggerates both the military strength and the size of the population of the Zhang-zhung kingdom in relation to its Tibetan adversary to the south. There exists some confusion over the Tibetan word *stong*, "thousand" in this context, whether it refers to soldiers in regiments of one thousand, which seems unlikely, or simply to households or to holdings, such as nomad encampments, as the Lopon suggests. On the Zhang-zhung-pas being impressed into the victorious Tibetan armies as porters and attendants, see Christopher Beckwith, *The Tibetan Empire in Central Asia*, Princeton University Press, Princeton 1987.

8. The youngest of the three queens of the Zhang-zhung king was *Gu-rub-za snang-sgron legs-ma*, that is, the princess (za) belonging to the Gurub clan. The chief minister for intelligence gathering (phrin blon) was familiar with her precarious situation, her resentment over her position, and her vengeful character. The agent of this minister was the operative *sNam-nam legs-grub* (var. sNam-lam).

9. *Dwang-ri'i gser phug.*

10. *sPe ne-gu bya-ba'i mo-ma zhig la mo btab-pas.* This Bonpo Lama was a professional practitioner of divination (mo).

11. *Sel chen zhig gyis la.* A rite of exorcism (sel-ba) is performed in order to expel and banish any kind of negative energy. In this case, the performance was a kind of scape-goat ceremony and the boy, together with his burden of sin and pollution, was expelled from the community, which was thereby cleansed and purified.

12. The Vaibhashikas (Bye-brag smra-ba) were Hinayana Buddhists otherwise known as the Sarvastivadins. They were historically the first Buddhists to translate their scriptures, the Word of the Buddha, into the Sanskrit language from the original popular Prakrit dialect and for several centuries around the time of Christ, they were the predominant Buddhist school in Kashmir and elsewhere in Northwestern India. They received the name Vaibhashika because this school compiled and followed the *Mahavibhasha*, a large encyclopedic commentary on the Abhidharma. Shantirakshita, although a Mahayanist in his philosophical orientation, nevertheless, introduced the Vinaya of the Sarvastivadins into Tibet when he ordained the first seven native-born Tibetan monks at Samye monastery.

13. There was born in Tibet a young boy possessing ripened karma (khye'u yang las 'phro-can zhig 'byung), that is, because of his past karma, his spiritual qualities and spiritual opportunities manifested in his present life. Later in India, becoming a scholar and translator, he was given the name "Bodhisattva" (bho-te-sa-twa). Lopon Tenzin Namdak maintains that this individual was not the famous Buddhist scholar Shantirakshita (zhi-ba 'tsho), who also had the title Bodhisattva, because the latter was Indian by birth and not Tibetan. But Shantirakshita, who became the first abbot of

Samye monastery, was known for his opposition to the indigenous Bonpo priests and he did not recognize them as fellow Buddhists. According to the story presented in Bonpo histories, Bodhisattva was a native Tibetan by birth. Angered because the Bonpos had him expelled from Tibet, he went to India where he became a famous Buddhist scholar. Invited back to Tibet, it was he who persuaded the king Trisong Detsan to persecute the Bonpos due to his old animosities.

14. The chief queen of *Lig-mi-rgya*, the king of Zhang-zhung, was named *Khyung-za mtsho-rgyal*. She was the princess (za) belonging to the Khyung-po clan. This queen, bitter in her heart over the assassination of her husband, invited the master Gyerpungpa into her chambers in the castle of *Khyung-rdzong*, first preparing for him a seat of many silken cushions, and then offering him a bowl of chang (wine or beer) into which she had put a small nugget of gold as a sign of great respect. Such an offering is known as *ser-skyems*, "golden liquor". This Serkyem or libation is still a rite widely practiced in both Bon and Buddhism as a means of making offerings to the Guardians, consisting of consecrated alcoholic beverage (chang), but without actually placing a gold nugget in the liquid. The Lopon also explains the etymology of the term in this way. She spoke in flattering language to Gyerpungpa, telling him that he had become a famous Tantrika and now he must display his powers before it was too late because Ligmigya, the protector of Bon had been killed, the kingdom of Zhang-zhung was falling into pieces, and the Bon religion was declining. This occurred because the Buddhist monks from India were hardening the heart of the king of Tibet and turning him against Bon. After his meeting with the queen, Gyerpungpa returned to his island in the lake, erected the white silken tent with the deer designs that she had given him, and performed at her request the practices for *btswo* or the golden magical missile.

15. There are said to be ten *zho* in one *srang*, the usual Tibetan measure of weight for gold and silver. One *zho* represents a small weight of gold, in modern times a little more than half a talah or rupee (according to S.C. Das, *A Tibetan-English Dictionary*, Calcutta 1902). Here three types of magical missiles (btswo) prepared with gold dust are distinguished:
    1) Practicing mantras for three full years over a gram (srang) of gold dust would produce a magical missile according to the rite known as *Ral-spu*, "torn hair"; such a magical missile would destroy the entire country of Tibet with terrifying winds.
    2) Practicing mantras for only three months over half a gram (srang phyed) of gold dust would produce a magical missile according to the rite known as *Khyung*, "garuda", which could destroy the entire the Yarlung valley.
    3) Practicing mantras for only seven days over one small measure (zho) of gold dust would produce a magical missile according to the rite known as *rNgub*, "inhalation", which would only destroy the king by

way of a fatal illness. But the Lopon suggests that these three terms may actually be Zhang-zhung words and not Tibetan.

16. Here are presented several folk etymologies. The first magical missile dispatched toward Tibet at sunset dried up the lake located at the foot of the holy mountain of Yarlha Shampo. They respectively represented the soul-lake (bla-mtsho) and the soul-mountain (bla-ri) of the king of Tibet, as well as his clan and his dynasty. Furthermore, it drove off the Nagas (klu), or the serpentine water spirits, living in that lake who controlled the wealth, the prosperity, and the fertility of the adjacent countryside. Therefore, this lake became known as the dry lake of Yarlung (yar-lung mtsho skam). The Yarlha Shampo (yar-lha sham-po) mountain was the soul-mountain (bla-ri) and the special protecting local deity (yul-lha) of the Yarlung region and therefore also of the ruling dynasty. On sacred mountains and sacred lakes and their significance in Tibet, see John Vincent Bellezza, *Divine Dyads: Ancient Civilization in Tibet*, ibid. The second magical missile dispatched at midnight struck seven sleeping deer on the slopes of the mountain Ri kha-spun-po (var. Sog-kha spun-mo), paralyzing them, so that subsequently this site became known as "the mountain of the paralyzed deer" (sha-ba rengs kyi ri). The third magical missile dispatched at daybreak struck the ancient royal castle (mkhar) of the king which was located on "the Tiger Peak of Chyingwa" (phying-ba'i stag rtse), whereupon the king was stricken with a terminal illness.

17. *Tho-rang tshwo 'ong lugs kyis.*

18. *Drwa-bye'i lung.* This valley of Drajye (drwa-bye) lay north of the Darok lake (mtsho da-rog) in Northern Tibet. This region was the birth place and the frequent site of residence of Gyerpungpa himself. The one hundred horsemen dispatched by the king of Tibet arrived at the lake, but could not find the sage Gyerpungpa anywhere. So they asked the local Zhang-zhung-pa shepherds of his whereabouts and they told the Tibetans that Gyerpungpa was a Mahasiddha who could appear as anything anywhere-- emanating as wild animals, or as fire, or even as the wind. But, in particular, he frequented the small island in the middle of the lake. The Tibetan soldiers killed a horse and made a boat out of its skin and bones. Crossing the lake to the island, the ministers found there the white silken tent with the deer designs, which had been given him by the Zhang-zhung queen, and inside of it, on a stack of silken cushions, they saw a crystal antelope horn, a ritual object particularly associated with the cult of the Tantric deity Zhang-zhung Meri. Realizing that this radiant object must be Gyerpungpa himself, the ministers prostrated and offered to it the horn of a wild yak ('brong) filled with gold dust (gser phye 'brong ru gang).

19. *Bho-ti-sa-ta*, var. *Bho-ti-sa-twa*, for Skt. Bodhisattva. See note 13 above.

20. As for the demands imposed by Gyerpungpa: The three hundred and sixty sections of Bon (zhang-zhung bon sde) refer to the personal practice and teachings of the master Gyerpungpa, namely, the Dzogchen precepts from Zhang-zhung and the practice of the Tantric deity Zhang-zhung Meri. Because of the king's promise, the teachings and texts of the Bon of the

Zhang-zhung Nyan-gyud never declined (bon ma nub-pa) nor disappeared in Tibet and, therefore, they have remained a continuous oral tradition (snyan-brgyud). Gyerpungpa belonged to the Gurub clan (Gurub rus-gdung) and thus he sought to secure their freedom from tribute and taxes to the king of Tibet. Moreover, a golden stupa was to be erected to the memory of the Zhang-zhung king and financial restitution for her loss was to be paid to the former queen, the payment in gold being weighed against the thirteen parts of the body of the dead king.

21. In order to cure the Tibetan king of his fatal affliction caused by the *btswo* or magical missile of gold dust, Gyerpungpa performed the nine-fold cycle of *gSang-this 'phar-ma* which was a rite for afterwards reversing a magical attack (phyir ldog gi cho-ga gsang-this 'phar-ma dgu bskor mdzad).

22. *sKu-tshab*, literally a representative or deputy. Here this means an image the size of the body of the dead king and erected as a memorial monument.

23. The Portals of Bon (bon sgo) mean the Bonpo teachings. From Gyerpungpa, the great Bonpo Siddha *sTong-rgyung mthu-chen* requested these portals of Bon, which are generally listed as four: *Chab-dkar, Chab-nag, 'Phan-yul,* and *dPon-gsas*. The first two classes represent Tantra and magic respectively, the third the Prajnaparamita, and the last the Dzogchen teachings. See Chapter One above. The present text is called just an outline (zur tsam). A more extensive version of events is said to be found in the *Kha-byang rgyas-pa* or "the extensive catalogue." Portions of the above text were also translated in Snellgrove and Richardson, *A Cultural History of Tibet*, ibid., pp. 99-103.

Chapter 8: The Experiential Transmission and the Precepts Transmission

1. On the Nyingmapa Terma Tradition, see Eva Dargyay, *The Rise of Esoteric Buddhism in Tibet*, Motilal Banarsidass, Delhi 1977. And especially also see Tulku Thondup, *Hidden Teachings of Tibet*, Wisdom Publications, London 1986.

2. On the Bonpo Terma tradition, see Karmay, *The Treasury of Good Sayings*, ibid., pp. 105-192.

3. These masters are called the Six Mahasiddhas of Zhang-zhung Mar (zhang-zhung smar gyi grub-chen drug) because they were all native Zhang-zhung-pas and spoke the Zhang-zhung language (zhang-zhung smar). The last in the list, *dPon-chen btsan-po*, was bi-lingual, speaking Tibetan also, and it is said that he was the first Zhang-zhung master in his lineage to have Tibetan disciples.

   The term *smar* in the Zang-zhung language means "good, excellent" (Tib. bzang-po). The written language was called *Zhang-zhung smar* and the letters *smar-yig*. According to both Lopon Tenzin Namdak and Namkhai Norbu Rinpoche, this *smar-yig* was the source and the prototype for the headless script (dbu-med) of Tibetan. According to the traditional Tibetan histories composed by medieval Buddhist Lama-scholars, the letters used in printed books, known as "the script with heads" (dbu-can), was based on the Gupta script of ancient Kashmir and adapted for the Tibetan language by Thonmi Sambhota in the seventh century of our era, who was sent to Kashmir just for that purpose by the first Buddhist king of Tibet, Songtsan Gampo (Srong-btsan sgam-po, 627-649 CE). Probably this is true to a certain extent, however, the Bonpo histories consistently insist that Bonpo texts were written in the Zhang-zhung language from at least the time of the second king of Tibet, Mutri Tsanpo (Mu-khri btsan-po). It is said that he became a convert to the Bonpo Tantric system of *sPyi-spungs skor* and imported a number of Bonpo texts from Zhang-zhung. When the seventh king of Tibet, Drigum Tsanpo (Gri-gum btsan-po), inaugurated his persecution of Bon, the Bonpo priests are said to have concealed many of their books. See Samten G. Karmay, *The Treasury of Good Sayings*, ibid., xxvii-xl.

Western scholars, following the Buddhist tradition of Tibet, have generally regarded all these Bonpo claims of cultural priority in Tibet as pure fantasy, preferring to derive all higher culture in the Tibetan context from India and China and as principally due to the influence of Indian Buddhism. But indeed, this was also the ideological and propagandistic aim of these medieval histories written by Tibetan Lamas, that is to say, they sought to derive all of Tibet's higher culture and civilization from India to the greater glory of the Buddhist religion, itself of Indian origin. This conventional view was challenged by Namkhai Norbu Rinpoche in his *The Necklace of gZi: A Cultural History of Tibet*, Library of Tibetan Works and Archives, Dharamsala 1981, and by Lopon Tenzin Namdak in his *g.Yung-drung bon gyi bstan-pa'i 'byung khungs nyung bsdus*, Kalimpong 1962. And now it has been reported in Lhasa, in both Tibetan and Chinese publications, that Chinese archeologists in Western Tibet have found inscriptions in *sMar-yig* that pre-date the Central Tibetan kingdom of the 7th and 8th centuries. Oral communication from Lopon Tenzin Namdak.

4. *Legs-bshad mdzod*, ff. 147a-147b. See Samten Karmay, *The Treasury of Good Sayings*, ibid., pp. 55-56. Note that there are differences in the spelling of some of the proper names.

5. According to the *Legs bshad mdzod*, Tapihritsa became a Jalupa ('ja'-lus-pa) or Rainbow Body after he had meditated for nine years at the mountain site of *sTag-thabs seng-ge'i brag* in Northern Tibet. This event represents an example of the Rainbow Body of the Great Transfer ('ja'-lus 'pho-ba chen-po) because the master Tapihritsa attained enlightenment while still alive in his material body without the necessity of dying.

6. It was in a vision Gyerpungpa received the instructions from Tapihritsa for the *Man-ngag le'u brgyad-pa*, "the Upadesha in Eight Chapters," which belong to the secret cycle of the precepts. This occurred during

their third encounter. The translation of this text will be found in the subsequent volume of this series.

The attribution of such fabulously long lives to these ancient sages is quite in keeping with the Mahasiddha tradition generally. Such long lives are also reminiscent of the Patriarchs of the Biblical tradition. In general, in the Indian tradition, including Buddhism, it is believed the the average human life span has grown shorter over the centuries due to universal decline of Dharma or spirituality among humanity.

Thereafter Gyerpungpa realized the Body of the Great Transfer ('pho-ba chen-po'i sku), thereby transcending the necessity of dying and passing into the Bardo state in order to obtain liberation. And having thereafter accomplished infinite benefits for living beings, he entered into the equanimity of the Dimension of the Base ('pho-chen gyi sku bzung ste 'gro don mtha'-yas-par mdzad nas gzhi dbyings su snyoms-par zhugs-so), that is to say, he dissolved his visible external form into the Natural State. However, the Rainbow Body as such differs from the Great Transfer in that it is a process that occurs at the point of physical death, that is, during the Chikhai Bardo ('chi-kha'i bar-do). With the Great Transfer, the transition occurs during one's lifetime without the necessity of entering into and experiencing the death process. By means of the practice of Thodgal, here called the practice of the Clear Light ('od-gsal), it is believed that the Siddha may come to realize the Rainbow Body of Light (ja'-lus), where, at the end of his or her life, one dissolves the elements of the physical body, over the course of several days, into pure radiant energy. All of Tapihritsa's predecessors in the lineage of the Twenty-Four August Persons (gang-zag nyer-bzhi), attained this Rainbow Body. Simultaneously with realizing such a body, the Siddha passes immediately into full enlightenment and liberation from Samsara, without the necessity of passing through the Bardo or intermediate state experience following physical death. And having obtained a Body of Light, the Siddha can remanifest oneself, at any time or place and in any form one chooses, to one's disciples or other sentient beings in order to teach and instruct them and help guide them to liberation and enlightenment.

This notion of the Body of Light ('od-lus) is rather reminiscent of the Christian belief in the resurrection of the Christ where, after the death of Jesus by crucifixtion and the mysterious disappearence of his physical body from the tomb, he reappeared after three days to his leading disciples in a glorified body in order to teach them certain esoteric doctrines over the course of forty days before his ascension to heaven. Many of these esoteric teachings of Jesus found in the Gnostic texts, such as the *Pistis Sophia*, were given out by this Resurrection Body of the Christ. In Buddhist terms, it would appear that Jesus realized the Body of Light and such a body, despite its name, is not something ethereal or ghostly, but is sensed as being fully material by those who perceive it. This all suggests that the function of the Christ, like the corresponding figures of the Bodhisattva and the Nirmanakaya, is not unique to one historical individual or to one moment in history, but is a much more widespread religious phenomena among humanity. It would appear that the same archetype was at work in both Christianity and Mahayana Buddhism. And again, this suggests not so much the borrowing of ideas across cultural barriers as the phenomenon of conversion in the evolution of human consciousness. On the comparison of the Christ and the Bodhisattva figures, see Donald S. Lopez and Steven C. Rockefeller, *The Christ and the Bodhisattva*, SUNY, Albany NY 1987.

7. Shardza Rinpoche in his account (see Karmay, *Treasury*, ibid. p. 55) gives this master's name as *rGya-tig gsas-chung*, whereas the hagiography text in our collection has *Pha-ba rGyal-gzigs gsas-chung*. Also the years of his lifespan differ in the two accounts. He is said to have attained the Primordial State of the Dharmakaya (bon-sku'i dgongs-pa brnyes) in terms of his mind, and in terms of his body he passed away into the dimension of space (dbyings su gshegs-so), that is, he dissolved his visible physical body into space. This indicates his attaining the Rainbow Body.

8. Mu Tsogge (dMu Tso-ge) purified the impurities of his gross physical body (phung-po'i snyigs-ma dag), that is, he transformed the gross physical elements of his visible body into their essential form of radiant colored lights. And he passed away like a bird flying up into the sky (bya nam-mkha' la 'phur-ba ltar gshegs-so).

9. Shardza Rinpoche gives the name as *dMu Tso-stong* (Karmay, *Treasury*, p. 55), whereas the hagiography text gives the form *dMu Tso-stangs* (f.33.6). He practiced meditation so that the elements of his gross physical body were purified into their original condition ('byung-ba rang sar dag), that is to say, into the clear radiant lights of the characteristic colors. And he passed away like a Garuda soaring into the sky (khyung nam-mkha' la lding-ba ltar gshegs-so).

10. Mu Shodtram Chenpo (dMu Shod-khram chen-po) attained the Body of Perfect Gnosis (ye-shes rdzogs-pa'i sku brnyes). Finally he passed away like a lion leaping into the sky (seng-ge gnam la mchongs-pa ltar gshegs-so). These three examples, "like a bird flying up into the sky," "like a Garuda soaring in the sky," and "like a lion leaping into the sky," also refer to purifying one's gross physical elements and dissolving them into pure radiant energy and dissolving into space, thereby attaining the Body of Light. The visible aspect of this process is called the Rainbow Body ('ja'-lus). And the state thereby attained, which is one of pure gnosis or primordial awareness (ye-shes), is called the Body of Perfected Gnosis (ye-shes rdzogs-pa'i sku).

11. Mu Gyalwa Lodro (dMu rGyal-ba blo-gros) arrived at the full measure of the four stages of vision (snang bzhi tshad du phyin nas). In the practice of Thodgal or the Clear Light there are four stages of the development of visions (snang-ba bzhi). With the attaining of the final stage of vision (snang-ba mthar-thugs), which is also known as the exhaustion or

culmination of Reality (bon-nyid zad-pa), the practitioner is on the
threshold of realizing the Rainbow Body and dissolving the elements of
one's gross physical body into pure radiant energy, that is to say, into the
five clear lights which represent the elements in their subtle and most
essential form. And having extensively accomplished the benefit of
infinite numbers of sentient beings, he attained Buddhahood like the wind
becoming calm in the atmosphere (sems-can mtha'-yas-pa'i don rgya-
cher mdzad nas bar-snang gi rlung zhi-ba ltar sangs-rgyas-so).

12. Ponchen Tsanpo dPon-chen btsang-po, var. dpon-rgyal) attained the
Primordial State of the Victorious One (rgyal-ba'i dgongs-pa brnyes),
which is another way of designating the realization of Buddhahood, and
after one thousand and six hundred years, he transformed himself into a
turquoise cuckoo bird and flew away to the southwest in order to subdue
the cannibalistic Rakshasa demons (slar lho nub srin-po'i kha gnon du
g.yu bya khu-byug tu sprul nas gshegs-so). This feat at the end of his
career in Tibet and Zhang-zhung is reminiscent of that of
Padmasambhava when he finally departed from Tibet, proceeding in a
southwestward direction to the great island of Chamaradvipa (rnga-yab
gling) in order to subdue the Rakshasas (srin-po). This great island in the
Indian ocean probably represented Madagascar.

13. For the translation of the hagiographies of these six Mahasiddhas from
Zhang-zhung, see below. The texts are located in the collection as
follows:
A. sPrul-sku drin gnyis:
   1) dPon-chen Tapihritsa (Tapiratsa) [26.5ff.]
   2) Gyer-spungs chen-po snang-bzher lod-po [27.4ff.]
B. Zhang-zhung smar gyi grub-chen drug:
   1) Pha-ba rGyal-gzigs gsas-chung [31.5ff.]
   2) dMu Tsog-ge [33.2ff.]
   3) dMu Tso-stangs [33.6ff.
   4) dMu Shod-tram chen-po [34.4ff.]
   5) dMu rGyal-ba blo-gros [35.3ff.]
   6) dPon-chen bTsan-po [36.3ff.]

14. The master's name is given in the text as Pha-ba rGyal-gzigs gsas-chung.
Pha-ba is an additional title, meaning "the elder". However, Shardza
Rinpoche gives the name of this master as rGya-tig gsas-chung (Karmay,
Treasury, ibid., p. 55). His father was Ya-ngal gsas-rgyal who belonged to
the famous Ya-ngal clan much associated with the Bonpo tradition. See
the hagiographies of Yangton Chenpo and Dampa Bumje in Chapter Nine
below. His father was both a minister (blon-po) and a priest, or literally "a
body-guard" (sku-srung), to the Tibetan king Ralpachan (Khri Ral-pa-
can, 815-836 CE), which would place him and his son in the early nineth
century of our era. By this time, Zhang-zhung had ceased to be an
independent kingdom and had been incorporated as a district into the
Central Tibetan Empire. Gyerpungpa selected the elderly Gyalzik and the
young child Mu Tsogge to be his disciples for the reception of the

transmission of the Dzogchen precepts. Gyalzik was already a priest learned in religious rituals and in philosophy before he met Gyerpungpa. If this connection is historical, it calls into question the traditional eight century date for Gyerpengpa, but this is explained by the Bonpos by way of his fabulously long life span.

15. *mTshan-nyid thams-cad ma rmongs-par mkhyen-pas. mTshan-nyid* (Skt. lakshana), "essential characteristic", is the usual Tibetan scholastic designation for what we would call philosophy, that is to say, logic and epistemology. Properly speaking, philosophy or the intellectual process of philosophical investigation belongs to the Sutra system. As with the Buddhist tradition in Tibet, there exist four systems of philosophical tenets (grub-mtha') that are studied in the philosophy colleges in both Buddhist and Bonpo the monasteries: the Vaibhashika, the Sautrantika, the Madhyamaka, and the Chittamatra. The pursuit of philosophical activity, in the spiritual context, leads to both the accumulation of merit and to the accumulation of wisdom, the latter principally indicating the understanding of Shunyata. Ritual activity and ethical conduct also lead to the accumulation of merit.

16. *Ge ma-sang gi bu'am/ sha zan srin-po'i bu'am/ khro-chu'i brag lha bu zhig bzhugs/ dbang ni sa-bdag rgyal-pos kyang begyur mi btub-pa/ bslu ru lha'i bu-mos kyang mi khugs-pa/ rdzas gtong phod che-ba ni yid-bzhin gyi nor-bu dang 'dra zhig bzhugs-so.* The *Ma-sang* were gods or spirits who inhabited Tibet before the coming of human beings and the flesh-eating Rakshasa demons (sha zan srin-po) were a race of cannibalistic evil spirits. They also once inhabited Tibet in prehistoric times and taught human beings to kill animals and eat their flesh. In terms of Indian mythology in general, these demons were also said to once have inhabited Lanka or Ceylon and are now thought by the Tibetans to inhabit a great island in the southern ocean, which some scholars would identify with Madagascar. The son of the god of the rock of melted bronze (khro-chu'i brag lha bu) might also refer to a local deity or spirit. Sadak (sa-bdag) is the general designation for earth spirits, the spirits of the soil.

17. *Las 'phro dang skal-bar ldan-pas/ bka' drin-can bla-ma dang ci ltar mjal na/ gyer-spungs chen-po snang-bzher lod-pos/ lo lnga ru phyi mtshams-bcad nas/ gro-ga'i sbu-gu la zhal gzugs nas snyan du dgongs-pas brgyud-do.* A disciple meets his teachers and the teachings, especially one's Root Guru, because of one's ripened good karma (las 'phro) and because of one's good fortune (skal-bar ldan-pa) in terms of secondary conditions. The master Gyerpungpa, during his five years in retreat (mtshams-bcad), literally "cutting off the boundaries", entered into a state of contemplation (dgongs-pa) and transmitted the intention of his teaching into the hearing (snyan du dgongs-pas) of his disciple Phawa Gyalzik Sechung. The implication is that, at the time, the latter was living elsewhere, together with his wife Rogshudza Gema (Rog-shud-za dGe-ma) and their two children. Gyerpungpa spoke to his disciple at a distance by causing the

image of his face to appear in a small hole in a piece of rolled birch bark (gro-ga'i sbu-gu la zhal gzugs nas). However, the Lopon explained matters as follows. The Guardians Nyipangse and Menmo would not allow Gyerpungpa to speak loudly when transmitting the Dzogchen precepts. Therefore, Gyerpungpa made a long tube of birch bark, set this so that it penetrated through the wall of his hermitage, and spoke in soft whispers directly into the ear of his disciple so that none of the local nature spirits might overhear the transmission. By using this method he communicated the complete instructions to his disciple. Thereafter the old man left his wife and family behind and went to the mountain of Megyud Karnak where he lived for a long time in solitude and at the end of his life of three hundred and seventy years, he realized the Rainbow Body.

18. His special place of practice for meditation where he resided (sa gnas khyad-par-can gang du bzhugs-pa) was at Megyud Karnak (Me-rgyud dkar-nag). This was a site of spiritual power or blessings (byin gyis brlabs-pa'i gnas) and here he displayed many signs of realization or success in practice (grub rtags) He became especially accomplished in certain aspects of Tantra. He realized the the original condition of the great bliss of the Dharmakaya (bon-sku bde-ba chen-po'i rang sa). And having received the Upadeshas of Dzogchen relating to the personal experiences of his master (bla-mas nyams kyi man-ngag), he displayed the realization of the Rainbow Body at the conclusion of his earthly career.

19. He became especially proficient in the practice of the Mantrayana (sngags kyi theg-pa), that is, the use of mantras in the Tantra system. In particular, he was expert in *gSang-sngags* or "the secret mantras" in general, in *This-sngags* or the mantras for magical rituals (this) associated with the cult of Meri, and in *Rigs-sngags* or mantras used for various different purposes.

20. *rTogs-pa mngon gyur thun-mong ma yin-pa ni/ bla-mas nyams kyi man-ngag btab nas/ lo gcig nas yar sangs-rgyas la re mi che-ba/ mar sems-can la dogs mi tsha-bar rtogs-so.* As the result of having received from Gyerpungpa the Upadeshas of the Experiences (nyams kyi man-ngag), that is to say, the Experiential Transmission (nyams rgyud), his extraordinary understanding of the Natural State became manifest within him and he realized enlightenment within only one year, transcending all thoughts with regard to Nirvana and Samsara. Thereupon he had no hopes nor expectations (re-ba) of ascending upward into the state of an enlightened Buddha (yar sangs-rgyas) and no fear nor anxiety (dogs-pa) of descending downward and falling once again into the state of an ordinary deluded sentient being (mar sems-can). He came to understand the Natural State as being the Primordial Base which is the source for both Nirvana and Samsara, it being prior to them and transcending them both, and while resting in this Natural State, there exists no ascending into spirituality and no descending into carnality.

21. The *g.Yen-khams* were a class of worldly gods.

22. Shardza Rinpoche gives the name of this master as *dMu Tso-stong* (Karmay, *Treasury*, p. 55), whereas the hagiography text has *dMu Tso-stangs*.

23. He received from his master the instructions for the Experiential Transmission (nyams brgyud) and retired to the crystal valley of Shang (Shangs shel-rong) in Tsang province in order to practice. Within one month he attained liberation due to his understanding of the Natural State (zla-ba gcig nas rtogs nas grol-ba lags-so).

24. *Sa gnas khyad-par-can gang du brten-pa'i tshe du bzhugs-pa ni/ gangs sta-rgo bya-ba byin gyis brlabs-pa'i gnas/ nyi-ma lung gi g.yon ngos/ pha-bong ngar-ba der bzhugs.* He resided in a cave on the glacial mountain of Targo (gangs rta-sgo, var. sta-rgo), just southwest of the Dang-ra lake (dang-ra mtsho) in Northern Tibet. According to Lopon Tenzin Namdak, this cave may still be seen even today. The cave, which the Lopon himself visited, consists of huge boulders and is capped with a large flat rock that is attributed to the work of the mountain god of Targo. This god had promised the master to build the walls of his retreat with boulders, if the master would supply a roof. The local nomads claim that this cave shelter was the result of the dice play of the mountain god and have forgotten all about the legends of the Bonpo Mahasiddhas. On the cult of this sacred mountain, see John Vincent Bellezza, *Divine Dyads: Ancent Civilization in Tibet*, Library of Tibetan Works and Archives, Dharamsala 1997.

25. Elsewhere it is said the name of his father was Gurub Tsugu (Gu-rub Tsu-gu) who belonged to the Gurub clan (gdung-rus gu-rub). One notices the special association of the *Gu-rib* clan, var. *Gu-rub*, with this native Zhang-zhung tradition of Dzogchen. Indeed, four out of these six Mahasiddhas belonged to this clan in Northern Tibet, as well as Gyerpungpa himself, namely, Mu Tsogge, Mu Tsotang, Mu Shodtram, and Gyalwa Lodro.

26. His principal places of practice were the cave of Rogchak Phuk (rog-lcag phug) near the Darok lake (da-rog mtsho) in Northern Tibet and a large secret cave (gsang phug chen-po) at Zang-zang lha-brag. He lived in these places where both humans and non-human spirits assembled (mi dang mi-ma-yin 'du-ba'i gnas der bzhugs-so). He subdued these non-human spirits (mi-ma-yin) and bent them to his will and had visions of his meditation deity (yi-dam lha), i.e., Zhang-zhung Meri.

27. *bLa-mas nyams kyi gdams-ngag btab nas.... mtshon-pa'i tshig phyir 'breng nas ma grol/ dpe don lung phyir 'breng nas ma grol.... snags-rgyas kyi dgongs-pa dang mnyam-pa lags-so.*

28. These Yantras ('phrul-'khor), or bodily positions and movements combined with breath control, are described in another text in the collection, *rDzogs-pa chen-po zhang-zhung snyan-rgyud las 'phrul-'khor zhal-shes man-ngag*, "The Upadeshas that give a Clear Explanation of the Yantras" [ff. 631], for which Ponchen Tsanpo is considered to be the author.

29. Ponchen Tsanpo (dPon-chen btsan-po) was born in the region of the rocks of Darok (yul da-rog gi brag ri na), which lie to the northwest of that lake (da-rog mtsho) in Northern Tibet according to Lopon Tenzin Namdak. Afterwards he went to *Zang-zang lha-brag* to receive the Dzogchen teachings from Mu Gyalwa Lodro (dMu rGyal-ca blo-gros). And according to the *'Bel gtam lung gi snying-po* of Lopon Tenzin Namdak, Ponchen Tsanpo practiced meditation at *Dwa-rog brag* and Gyalwa Lodro at *Dwa-rog lcags-phug* (f. 49).

30. *Nyams snang la nub kyi brag rong dkar-po'i gseb nas/ rin-po-che'i brum khrol-le-ba'i nang nas/ sprul-pa'i khye'u mtshan-ldan zhig yongs nas/ des mo la spyod-pa rmis tsam na/ phyi lo dus su sras gcig bltams-pa ni/ dpon btsan-po yin-no.* These three women, resembling the three witches or the three fates of folklore, were, no doubt, Dakinis, and they prophesized the birth of a son who would be a miraculous child, an emanation, possessing all the requisite marks (sprul-pa'i khye'u mtshan-ldan). This indicates that he was a Nirmanakaya (sprul-sku). Therefore, he was given the name of *bTsan-po* which means "the mighty one". The word *btsan-po* is also a title for a king. And because of his great learning and spiritual attainments, he recieved the title of *dpon-chen* meaning a great master. Another varient of his name is *dPon-rgyal btsan-po*.

31. *g.Yas-ru shangs kyi ri rtse 'grims kyin bzhugs/ bya rgyal rgod-po lta-bu'i rnal-'byor-pa yin-no.* He went to the Shang (shangs) region and lived on the mountain of *g.Yas-ru shangs*, dwelling there like a king of wild birds (bya rgyal rgod-po), that is, like a vulture (bya rgod), which is considered in Tibet to be the mightiest and highest flying of birds.

32. *brTen-pa'i tshe ni tshe la dbang-ba'i rig-'dzin yin-pas/ stong dang drug brgya rdzogs-pa dang/ gzhan don skye-ba rang dbang-can yin-pas/ gdul-bya 'dul-ba'i dus la bab ma bab kyis/ skye dang 'chi-bar snang-ba las/ 'di tsam-pa zhes bya-ba rang med-do.* There he realized the second of the higher stages of Tantric transformation, namely, the Vidyadhara stage of the power of long life (tshe la dbang-ba'i rig-'dzin), and thereby he was able to prolong his life for sixteen hundred years and to obtain the supreme body that is without pollutants (zag-med mchog gi sku), so that his physical body did not age or decay. This same power of long life realized through Tantric practice was attributed to Padmasambhava in the Nyingmapa tradition.

33. *Lus khams skye-gnas kyi zag-pa zad-pas/ khams kyi zas mi dgos-pa dang.* Because he had exhausted all pollutants or impurities (zag-pa zad-pas) in terms of his physical body (lus), constitution (khams), and birth condition (skye-gnas), it was no longer necessary for him to eat or partake of nourishment for his health (khams kyi zas). For this purpose, there exists Tantric practices known as *bcud-len* (Skt. rasayana), the preparation and partaking (len) of elixirs (bcud), that serve to extend and prolong one's life in the physical body. There exist external, internal, and secret aspects of these practices, which may be compared to Taoist alchemy and yoga.

34. *sKu-lus g.yu bya kh-byug tu sprul nas stag-gzigs su gshegs dang/ lho-nub tu srin-po'i kha-gnon mdzad-pa'o.* Transforming his physical body into the form of a turquoise cuckoo (g.yu bya khu-byug tu sprul-pas), he travelled to Tazik (stag-gzigs) in Central Asia to the northwest of Tibet. Then, like Padmasambhava, he departed from Tibet for a great island in the southern ocean in order to subdue the Rakshasa (sha zan srin-po) or cannibalistic demons there. This island was probably Madagascar which was well known to the Indian and the Indonesian seafarers of the time.

35. *rTogs-pa mngon gyur thun-mong ma yin-pa ni/ gdams-pa btab nas zhag bdun nas/ rtogs-pa shar-ba/ yid-ches-pa grub-pa brnyems-pa gsum byung nas/ sprul-pa'i sku dang gnyis su med-pa lags-so.* That is, he realized enlightenment or Buddhahood. All of these Mahasiddhas (grub-chen, grub-thob chen-po) from Zhang-zhung realized the Body of Light by way of the practice of Thodgal (thod-rgal), here called the practice of the Clear Light ('od-gsal). Cast in schematic form, these hagiographic notices resemble those of other Mahasiddhas, such as the Eighty-Four Mahasiddhas of the Indian tradition and the Twenty-Four Disciples of Padmasambhava. On the Eighty-Four Mahasiddhas, see Keith Dowman, *Masters of Mahamudra*, SUNY, Albany NY 1985, and on the Twenty-Four Disciples (rje 'bangs), see Tulku Thondup, *The Tantric Tradition of the Nyingmapa*, Buddhayana, Marion MA 1984.

36. *Legs-bshad mdzod*, ff. 190a-191a. See Karmay, *Treasury*, ibid., pp. 111-112.

37. *gNyis-pa sngags sems la gsum/ zhang-zhung/ rgya-gar/ yong lugs bon skor/ dang-po zhang-zhung gi bon skor ni.....* In this context, the Mantras (sngags) mean the Tantras, in particular the Tantric practice for the wrathful deity Zhang-zhung Meri, and the Mind Teachings (sems) indicate Dzogchen. In terms of the transmission by way of India, the Zhang-zhung prince Dranpa Namkha (Dran-pa nam-mkha') transmitted the Dzogchen precepts to his son Tsewang Rigdzin (Tshe-dbang rig-'dzin) who, in turn, transmitted them during a number of different encounters, probably visionary, to Lungbon Lhanyan (Lung-bon lha-gnyan). It is said that the latter received instructions from Tsewang Rigdzin for a number of important texts by Dranpa Namkha. As for the last cycle, the system of Yong (yong-lugs), these texts pertaining to the Tantric deity Walchen Rampa (dBal-chen Ram-pa) were loaded on to the backs of blue wolves by Khyungse Menyak (Me-nyag gi Khyung-gsas) and brought to Tibet from God (rGod) in Zhang-zhung. See Karmay, *Treasury*, ibid., p 115.

38. *Zhang-zhung gi bon skor sum brgya drug-cu.* The number 360 was sacred in the Zhang-zhung tradition and was associated with Mount Kailas in its mystic role as the sacred mountain at the center of the cosmos. Not only are there 360 teachings or doctrines within the Bon from Zhang-zhung, but there are 360 deities in the retinue of the great god Gekhod, the tutelary deity of the Kailas mountain and of the Zhang-zhung kingdom, of which it was the soul-mountain (bla-ri). Moreover, there are 360 knots, and therefore 360 prognostications, in the *Ju-thig* system of divination,

which also derives from Zhang-zhung. Tucci associated this sacred number in the Bonpo context with the 360 days of the year and suggested that, therefore, it could have an astrological significance. See Giuseppe Tucci, *The Religions of Tibet*, University of California Press, Berkeley 1980, pp. 217-220.

39. For the account of Gyerpungpa dispatching a magical missile of gold dust, here called *gser-dzwa* and elsewhere *btswo*, see the translation of the text known as the *Bon ma nub-pa'i gtan-tshigs* in Chapter Seven above. This rite included the hurling of an amount of gold dust, accompanied by fierce mantras (drag-sngags), in the direction of one's adversary whom one wishes to destroy. Gyerpungpa was an expert in this procedure and *btswo* represents a principal magical action ('phrin-las) associated with the practice of the Tantric deity Meri. Through accomplishing the sadhana of the deity, one may come realize a number of different siddhis of a practical as well as a spiritual nature. But even though the practice of *btswo* was transmitted to his successors, eventually knowledge of the rite died out with the Mahasiddha Lhundrub Muthur and it is no longer performed according to the Lopon.

40. On the *bKa' brgyud skor bzhi* or the Four Cycles for the Transmission of the Precepts of the Zhang-zhung Nyan-gyud, see Chapter Ten below. Here the lineages became separated not only in terms of geography as the Upper System (stod lugs), meaning the country to the west, and as the Lower System (smad lugs), meaning the country to the east, but also in terms of the teaching of the precepts (bka') as against the experiences (nyams) realized within the context of individual meditation practice.

41. Ponchen Tsanpo taught the extensive, the intermediate, and the condensed versions of the Experiential Transmission to his disciple Khyungjyid Muthur of Shang (shangs kyi khyung-byid mu-thur), otherwise known as dPon-chen Lhun-grub mu-thur, who was a Tibetan rather a Zhang-zhung-pa. See below. On the extensive, intermediate, and condensed versions of the experiential transmission (nyams brgyud rgyas 'bring bsdus gsum), see Chapter Ten below.

42. The oral transmission of the Mantras, including both the long and the short rites for Meri (sngags snyan-brgyud me-ri'i phrin-las che chung gnyis), refer to the Tantric ritual and meditation practices associated with the wrathful deity Zhang-zhung Meri, who was the personal meditation deity (yi-dam lha) of Gyerpungpa. In general, the lineages for the transmission of the Dzogchen teachings of the Zhang-zhung Nyan-gyud and those for the practice of Zhang-zhung Meri coincide. Here Khyungjyid Muthur of Shang obviously refers to Lhundrub Muthur, the first among the Five Masters of the System of the Lower Lineage. See below.

43. On *'Ol-sgom*, var. *'Or-sgom kun-'dul*, and on Yangton Chenpo, see Chapter Nine below.

44. *Tshig brgyud dang nyams brgyud gnyis-ka zung-'brel du brgyud-pas.*

45. Some among them attained the Body of Light and left no remainder behind ('od lus dang lhag-med grub-pa dang), whereas others obtained liberation afterwards in the Bardo or in a pure field into which they emanated naturally (bar-do dang rang-bzhin sprul-pa'i zhing). This refers to the methods of liberation (grol lugs) according to the spiritual capacities (dbang-po) of different practioners. The individual of an exceeding superior spiritual capacity (yang rab) attains liberation as the Body of Light of the Great Transfer ('pho-ba chen-po 'od lus) while in this present life and without any further necessesity to undergo the death process and the Bardo experience. The individual of a superior spiritual capacity (rab) can realize the Rainbow Body ('ja'-lus) at the point of physical death and does not need to pass into the Bardo experience. The individual of intermediate spiritual capacity ('bring-po) is able to realize liberation while in the Bardo. And the individual of inferior spiritual capacity (tha-ma) will realize liberation in a more fortunate rebirth, such as in a pure Buddha field (zhing-khams). See the discussion of this question of spiritual capacity and method of liberation in Part Three below in the subsequent volume in this series, *Space, Awareness, and Energy*, forthcoming..

46. *Bon gyi grub-thob lnga'i lo-rgyus bstan nas*.... For the translation of this portion of the *rNam-thar chen-mo* or great hagiography text by Paton Tan-gyal, see below. Here the terms "upper" (stod) and "lower" (smad) have referenece not to moral value, but to geography. "Upper" refers to the higher country to the west adjacent to Mount Kailas, which has a higher elevation. "Lower" refers to the lake country of Northern Tibet which stretches eastward and has a lower elevation. Both areas were included in the original kingdom of Zhang-zhung. Thus, the text says "into the lower country" (sa smad du) and that "the first was transmitted from the lower country" (dang-po sa smad nas brgyud de). It was in this lower country, the lake district of Zhang-zhung and Northern Tibet that Ponchen Tsanpo transmitted the Dzogchen teachings of the Experiential Transmission to his two Tibetan disciples Lhundrub Muthur and Shengyal Lhatse. Therefore, the Experiential Transmission (nyams rgyud) is also known as the Lower System or the System of Lower Zhang-zhung (smad-lugs). These two lines were again united in the person of Yangton Chenpo Sherab Gyaltsan. See Chapter Nine below. The location of these hagiographies in the collection are as follows:
sMad lugs kyi bla-ma lnga:
1) *dPon-chen Lhun-grub mu-thur* [38.2ff.]
2) *gShen-rgyal Lha-rtse* [40.5ff.]
3) *Lha-sgom dkar-po* [44.5ff.]
4) *dNgos-grub rgyal-mtshan ring-mo* [48.6ff.]
5) *'Or-sgom kun-'dul* [53.3ff.]
sTod lugs kyi bla-ma drug:
1) *Gu-ge Shes-rab blo-ldan* [55.6ff.]
2) *Kun-dga' ring-mo* [56.6ff.]

3) *rNal-'byor gsas-mchog* [57.5ff.]
4) *Khyung-byid mu-thur* [58.4ff.]
5) *rTsi bDe-ba ring-mo* 59.2ff.]
6) *rTog-med zhig-po* [59.6ff.]
Byang rgyud kyi bla-ma dgu:
1) *Shes-rab rgyal-mtshan* [60.5ff.], etc.

47. *dPon-chen Lhun-grub mu-thur* belonged to the *Khyung-po* clan (gdung-rus khyung-po). Shardza Rinpoche (Karmay, *Treasury*, ibid., p. 111) gives the master's name as *Shangs kyi khyung-byid mu-thur*. It was to this Tibetan disciple that Ponchen Tsanpo is said to have taught the extensive, medium, and condensed versions of the Experiential Transmission, as well as the Tantric practices of Zhang-zhung Meri. It would appear, as Lopon Tenzin Namdak indicates, that it was Ponchen Tsanpo, the last native-born Zhang-zhung master in the lineage, who translated the Experiential Transmission from his own language into Tibetan, although this does not necessarily prove that this transmission yet existed in the form of written texts. The transmission may have been entirely oral. At a later time, these redactions were organized into three divisions, probably by Orgom Kundul and his disciple Yangton Chenpo. This probably would have occurred in Northern Tibet in the so-called Dark Age of the 10th century before the revival of both Buddhism and Bon in the eleventh century.

48. It was customery for Bonpo sages at that time to wear blue, this being considered the sacred color of Bon, blue like the sky. Hence his meditration hat (sgom zhwa) was blue and also his robe was blue (sngo bem).

49. *sKu lus chung-ba dbu la sgom zhu chung-dun zhig mnabs-pa/ sku la sngo bem zhig mnabs-pa/ zhabs rjen-pa ru 'dug-pa/ dpe bum chung-dun zhig se-ral kha la bcug-pa/ phyag na lcags gtor theb chung-dun zhig snams-pa gcig dang mjal nas.....*

50. This initition or empowerment (dbang) would be that of Zhang-zhung Meri. On this initiation, see Reynolds, *The Cult and Practice of Zhang-zhung Meri: The Meditation Deity for the Zhang-zhung Nyan-gyud Tradition of Bonpo Dzogchen Teachings*, Bonpo Translation Project (privately printed), San Diego 1996.

51. *Der rta-pa'i zla-ba la tshogs re gtong gin thengs zhig gshegs-so.*

52. *g.Yas-ru shangs dang yon-po bya-ba'i gnas su bzhugs-so.*

53. The white goat (ra dkar) and the white female yak or dri ('bri dkar) were emanations (sprul-pa) of these two deities who were originally recruited by Gyerpungpa to be the special protectors of the Zhang-zhung Nyan-gyud tradition. On the guardian deities Nyipangse (Nyi-pang-sad) and Menmo Kuma (sMan Ku-ma), see Appendix Three below. Also see Reynolds, *The Invocations to the Guardian Deity Nyipangse and to the Goddess Menmo*, Vidyadhara Publications, Los Angeles 1999.

54. *Tso dmar nam-mkha' la mda' ltar 'phen-pa. Tso*, var. *btswo*, is a magical missile, a magical practice associated with the cult of Meri.

55. *Rang lus yi-dam gyi lhar rdzogs-pa'i sku dang gnyis su med-do.*
56. *bLa-ma de'i slob-ma'am mched grogs yin te.*
57. *sDang-ba'i dgra la tso dmar mda' ltar 'phen-pa yod.* This refers to the same magical art much practiced by Gyerpungpa.
58. *Tshe la dbang-ba'i rig-'dzin.*
59. *De dus bla-ma'i zhal nas/ khyod ri g.yung-drung lha-rtsa bya-ba'i dgon-pa zhig yod/ yon-dag skyid-'bar ram skyid gsum zer-ba zhig yod gsungs-so.*
60. *Dus der dpon btsan-po'i zhal nas gdams-ngag gsungs-pa/ rdzogs-pa chen-po'i don dam-pa yin ngo-shes-pa gcig yod/ yin-par 'dug ste gcig yod/ yin min cha med-pa gcig yod/ yin ngo-shes-pa ni grub-thob rnams kyis gdams-pa 'di rnams yin/ yin-par 'dug ste gter byon gyi bka'-rgyud zab-mo kun yin/ yin min cha med-pa ni de la yid bcos kyis bshad-pa byed-pa yin/ snyan-rgyud med-par gzhi lam gyi skad smra-ba ni/ gzhi skad bong-bu'i skad dang 'dra/ lam skad ni byi-ti byas tshang tshol-ba dang 'dra/ grub-thob rnams kyi nyams skad ni/ gser la nags tshur btab-pa dang 'dra gsungs....* Here the reference is to the *Nyams-rgyud* or the Experiential Transmission where the utterences of the Mahasiddhas of the past regarding their personal experiences in meditation practice were retained in memory. Ponchen Tsanpo communicated the *Nyams-rgyud* to his Tibetan disciples in Northern Tibet, but not the written texts in the Zhang-zhung language for the *bKa'-rgyud* or Precepts Transmission, which he conferred upon Sherab Lodro in Guge in Western Tibet. See below.
61. *bLa-ma ni sku lus g.yu khu-byug gcig tu sprul nas/ rtag-gzigs kyi yul du srin-po'i kha-gnan la gshegs-so.*
62. All phenomena, whether good or bad, beautiful or ugly, have for the practitioner but a single taste (ro-gcig). Just as the reflections in a mirror, whether they are good or bad, beautiful or ugly, in no way change or modify the nature of that mirror, so it is with the Nature of Mind of the practitioner.
63. *Nyams kyi mgur.* The composing of songs based on their experiences in meditation by these solitary hermits living in Northern and Western Tibet, as may be seen from the example of the well-known Songs of Milarepa (mgur 'bum). These songs were not only influenced by the Dohas composed by the Mahasiddhas of India in the vernacular, but equally by the Tibetan folk traditions of song.
64. This was the famous Bonpo hermitage known as *g.Yung-drung lha-rtse'i dgon-pa.* This site on the eastern shore of the Dang-ra lake was also visited by Lopon Tenzin Namdak during the time he was hiding in the Dang-ra region from the Chinese Communists after his monastery of Tashi Menri had been destroyed by the Red Guards.
65. Zurpoche Shakya Jyungne (Zur-po-che shakya 'byung-gnas, b. 954), was a famous early master of the Kama (bka'-ma) or continuous uninterrupted tradition of the Nyingmapa school. The other source for Dzogchen was Terma (gter-ma) or rediscovered treasure texts. He was said to have been

the greatest of the three Zur masters (zur rnam-pa gsum), the other two being Zurchungpa Sherab Dragpa (Zur-chung-pa shes-rab grags-pa, 1014-1074), and Zur Shakya Senge Drobugpa (Zur shakya seng-ge sgro-sbug-pa, 1074-1134). The former, Zurchungpa, was said to have realized the Rainbow Body of Light at the end of his earthly career. It is recorded that the Zur family originated in India and later settled in Eastern Tibet. As a famous Tantric master for the Mahayoga and the Anuyoga, Zurpoche had many masters, but he especially focused on the Tantric teachings of the *sGyu-'phrul drwa-ba* cycle (Skt. Mahajala), but also on the *rDzogs-chen sems-sde*. For the latter it would appear that he also had recourse to Bonpo masters, in this case Shengyal Yungdrung Lhatse. It was Zurpoche who first collected and classified the Old Tantras (rgyud rnying-ma), which now form the core of the Nyingmapa canon, the *rNying-ma'i rgyud-'bum*, where he grouped the root text Tantras together with their commentaries, sadhanas, and ritual manuals. Thereby he founded the scholastic tradition known as the Zur system (zur-lugs). This same transmission of Dzogchen from Ponchen Tsanpo is said here to have also come down to Rongzom Pandita (Rong-zom Pandita Chos kyi bzang-po, 1012-1131), another great Nyingmapa scholar of the *bKa'-ma* who founded his own scholastic tradition known as the Rong system (Rong-lugs). On Zurpoche, see Tarthang Tulku, *Masters of the Nyingma Lineage: Crystal Mirror* 11, Dharma Publishing, Berkeley CA 1995, pp. 79-80, and Tarthang Tulku, "A History of the Buddhist Dharma," in *Crystal Mirror* vol. 5, Dharma Publishing, Berkeley CA 1977, pp. 217-219. Also see Dudjom Rinpoche, *The Nyingma School of Tibetan Buddhism*, Wisdom Publications, Boston 1991, pp. 617-635.

According to Lopon Tenzin Namdak, it would appear that this transmission of the Dzogchen precepts from dPon-chen btsan-po was also incorporated in the 10th century into the Nyingmapa lineage of Zur-po-che (the Zur-lugs) and there it may have born the name of the *Rig-pa'i khu-byug*, "The Cuckoo of Awareness." Originally, this was the title of a small text of only six lines said to have been brought from India by Vairochana the translator in the eight century and it was, indeed, the first Dzogchen text translated by him. It has also been discovered in its Tibetan version in the Tun Huang library. See Reynolds, *The Golden Letters*, ibid., pp.230-236. But there exists another Bonpo Tantra of this same name describing in detail the instructions for Thodgal. According to the Lopon, although Zurpoche described these precepts for the *rDzog-chen sems-sde* as an oral tradition circulating in Northern and Western Tibet, they had already been set down in writing previously by Ponchen Tsanpo in the 9th century. Samtan Karmay in his book *The Great Perfection: A Philosophical and Meditative Teaching of Tibetan Buddhism*, Brill, Leiden 1988, asserts that Dzogchen was fabricated in the 10th and 11th centuries by certain unscrupulous Bonpo and Nyingmapa Lamas, here above named, and anachronistically attributed to certain illustrious figures in the 8th century, the Golden Age for Buddhism, as well as, in some respects, for Bon. However, the Lopon asserts that the Zhang-zhung Nyan-gyud lineages demonstrate that Dzogchen most certainly existed earlier than the 10-11th centuries, and it indeed existed in the 7-8th centuries with Tapihritsa and Gyerpungpa on the Bonpo side and with Padmasambhava, Vimalamitra, and Vairochana on the Nyingmapa Buddhist side. Karmay dismisses these Bonpo lineages as fabricated and unhistorical. However, the whole matter requires further research. Again, see the discussion in Reynolds, *The Golden Letters*, ibid.

66. *Kong-btsun de-mo dang sman ku-ma las sogs te/ srid-pa'i mo rigs thams-cad kyis lus 'bul bskar-ba byed las sogs-so/ gzhan yang byang-shar mtshams kyi rgyal-po ti-se lag-ring gis/ ma bsgrub-par bstan-pa'i las byed-par kha-blangs/ de las sogs srid-pa' pho rigs thams kyis kyang bstan-pa'i las byed-pa dang.....* On these guardian deities, Menmo Kuma (sMan-mo Ku-ma) and Nyipangse (Nyi-pang-sad), see Appendix Three below, as well as Reynolds, *The Invocations to the Guardian Deity Nyipangse and to the Goddess Menmo*,op. cit.

67. *gSer btso mda' ltar du 'phen-pa.* Elsewhere in the text it is said that this magical art associated with the deity Zhang-zhung Meri had been lost with death of Lhundrub Muthur.

68. *Lom-ting lha-sgom dkar-po* is also known as *Lom-ting sgom-chen* in other hagiographical lists of the Zhang-zhung tradition. He belonged to the Or clan (gdung-rus 'or) and was the son of Lomting Atsara (Lom-ting A-tsa-ra) who was a Lama very learned in the Bon of Causes and Apellations (rgyu tha-snyed kyi bon la mkhas-pa zhig yod de), that is to say, in the Causal Vehicles (rgyu'i theg-pa) among the Nine Ways of Bon. On them, see David Snellgrove, *The Nine Ways of Bon*, pp. 24-123, ibid.

69. *Ting-nge-'dzin dar gcig mdzad nas/ bcud dang ldan-pa'i slob-dpon gyis/ snod dang ldan-pa'i slob-ma/ phyag-rgya chen-po'i dbang bskur-ro.*

70. *bLa-ma'i zhal nas gdams-pa. 'di yi gzhung-lugs kyis/ sha mtsham la brtag-pa/ ming la brtag-pa/ sha mdangs la brtag-pa/ spyod-pa la brtag-pa/ rmi-lam la brtag-pa lnga-pa'o/ khyed la lnga-ka tshang-ngo.*

71. *sTong-nyid kyi don la phyogs-ris mi 'dug snyam nas/ rgyal-khams phyogs-med 'khyams-so gsungs.*

72. *Hag-khyu g.ya' skya'i ri..... spa-gro stag tshang seng-ge'i phug dang/ dang-ra'i brag phug gnam skas-can du byon.....*

73. *Phyi'i 'byung-ba dbang du 'dus-pa'i rtags/ nang mi dang mi min dbang du 'dus-pa'i rtags-so.... 'jig-rten gyi lha 'dre pho mo bran du khol-ba dang.....*

74. *bLa-mas nyams kyi gdams-ngag htab nas/ stag-tshang seng-ge'i phug tu grol-ba thob nas/ sangs-rgyas kyi dgongs-pa la 'gyur-ba med-par rtogs-pa lags-so.*

75. The father of *dNgos-grub rgyal-mtshan ring-mo* was *'Or bon lha-'bum*, elsewhere identified as the previous master, *Lom-ting lha-sgom dkar-po*, who belonged to the Or clan (gdun-rus 'or), and his mother was *Men-mo chos-se*. Among their four sons, *sTon-chung rgyal-mtshan* was the first, *dNgos-grub rgyal-mtshan* was the second, and *gSas kyi rgyal-mtshan* was the third.

76. *Chung-ma'i mtshan-nyid bra khal gcig/ bu-tsha'i mtshan-nyid 'gong-po gcig/ skye-ba 'di las mi len-pa'i sangs-rgyas bsgrub dka' 'di yin gsung nas ma gnang/ de bas sngags kyis gdams-pa de rnams nyams su longs/ de bas nga yis sog-pa mo ru btab-pa/ sog-pa pra ru dbab shes/ sgo rtsar rta-pa dkar dmar khra phung-ne-ba zhig bya yis slob gsungs-pas.....*
77. *Bon gyi snyam-rgyud..... chos kyi snyan-rgyud.*
78. Karmay identifies this figure as Gyaphugpa (rGya-phug-pa, 12th cen.). See George Roerich, *The Blue Annals*, Part I-II, Motilal Banarsidass, New Delhi reprint 1979, p. 727. With that master he studied (slob gnyer) Buddhist logic and epistemology (tshan-ma, Skt. pramana).
79. *Zhag-thag gi shangs-pa lce-chung-ba-can.* The Buddhist Dzogchen text refered to here is probably the Nyingmapa Tantra known as the *rDo-rje sems-dpa' nam-mkha'-che*, which is one of the principal Tantras belonging to the *rDzogs-cen sems-sde* class and it is said to have been revealed by *dGa'-rab rdo-rje* himself shortly after his birth in Uddiyana. See Reynolds, *The Golden Letters*, ibid., pp. 179-189. However, although he did not carry out his threat to seek out a Buddhist Dzogchen master, it appears that *dNgos-grub rgyal-mtshan* was sincerely interested in both spiritual traditions, the Bonpo and the Buddhist.
80. *g.Ya' skya'i pha-bong skyab leb tu.*
81. *Rong bya glag tshang gi phug.*
82. *Sangs-rgyas kyi gdangs-pa thugs su chud-pa lags-so.*
83. At the end of his life, the master thought to himself, "I have nothing to regret and I can conceive of nothing for which I should be ashamed in my sixty-three years. And I have realized the capacity within myself to work for the benefit of others. Now I will separate my Awareness from the materiality of my body by means of the Unification of the Four Primal Cognitions (ye-shes bzhi sbyor gyi gdams-pa)." These instructions are given in detail in the long version of the *Nyams rgyud smug-gu*, pp. 303-311. These cognitions may be described as follows:
    1) the primal cognition that is unattached to anything whatsoever (ci la yang ma chags-pa'i ye-shes), consisting of non-attachmnet to enemies, friends, nourishments, riches, Buddhas, gods, and so on;
    2) the primal cognition at the moment of passing away or dying ('da'-ka dus kyi ye-shes), which permits the vanquishing of the four demons (bdud bzhi), that is, the lord of death, the skandhas, the kleshas, and Devaputra;
    3) the primal cognition of liberating into the dimension of space (dbyings su grol-ba'i ye-shes), which represents the process of Thodgal— the residing of the inner light of Rigpa in the hollow space of the heart, the projecting of Rigpa along the translucent channel from the heart to the eyes, and so on; and
    4) the primal cognition of becoming like a vast expanse of space (klong du gyur-ba'i ye-shes), which is said to represent enlightenment itself, where the distinction between external and internal space dissolves in the realization of the Natural State of Kuntu Zangpo.

84. *Phyi-ba'i brus khung.*
85. *Nyams kyi mgur.*
86. *Ngas ni tshig don ma lus-par bstan-pa yin-no.... chud gsan nam mi gsan khyod-rang shes gsungs-so.*
87. *Me-ri'i sngags dang sems-phyogs.* The core of Tantric transformation practice is considered to be mantra (sngags) or the creative energy of sound, which calls manifestation into existence out of the infinite formless potentiality of Shunyata. Therefore, the Tantric system in general is often called the Secret Mantras (gsang-sngags). The Mind Teachings, literally "the side of mind" (sems-phyogs) refers to Dzogchen. Whereas, as the Path of Transformation, Tantra or Mantra especially relates to energy, including especially Speech or sound (gsung), Dzogchen, as the Path of Self-Liberation, is especially related to Mind (thugs).
88. *Chos kyi dge-bshes te-ra-ba bya-bas gsang gin rdzogs-chen 'dra phag tu spyad/ mar-sman kun-ne bya-bas spyad/ ru-stod kyi rnal-'byor gcig gis gser 'dra me-tog tu phul gin kyang spyad/ de rnams ni chos-pa'o.*
89. *sKu tshe'i gzhug la mdo-khams kyi khams-pa gnyis kyis dpe zhu byas-pas/ bla-ma'i zhal nas sgros 'dogs bcod-pa don gyi rgyud-pa la/ yig chung gi lhad ma zhugs-pa yin-pas/ bla yi-ge 'bru ru med-pa la/ yang-ston gyiszhu-ba phul nas/ nged gnyis kyis brjed tho bkod-pa ma yin-pa'i/ nga la yi-ge khyi lce tsam gcig yod red gsungs nas....* This passage clearly suggests that prior to the time of Orgom and Yangton in the 10th and 11th centuries the texts of the *Nyams-rgyud* or Experiential Transmission had not yet exist in written form, but remained an oral tradition only. They were now set down in writing for the first time through the efforts of Yangton Chenpo. However, the tradition suggests, and the Lopon also indicates this, the *bKa'-rgyud* did exist in some written form deriving from Zhang-zhung, if only as brief Upadeshas written on birch bark or yak horn, even from the time of Gyerpungpa in the 8th century and Ponchen Tsanpo in the next century.

These two Khampas (khams-pa gnyis), here unnamed, coming from *mDo-khams* in Eastern Tibet, requested the texts (dpe) for the Experiential Transmission. These were written down and edited by Yangton, to whom several texts in the Zhang-zhung Nyan-gyud cycle are attributed, notably the instructions entitled the *Byang-chub sems kyi gnad drug.* A translation of this text will be found in another volume of this series. With regard to this transmission, however, these three scribes cited above were commissioned to edit the entire draft manuscript of the instructions and establish a definitive version of the texts on paper. Thus, according to Lopon Tenzin Namdak, Orgom Kundul was a key figure in the lineage of transmission and superintended the fixing of the instructions in writing for the Experiential Transmission for the Zhang-zhung Nyan-gyud cycle.
90. *Khyad-par zhang-zhung me-ri'i sngags sems gnyis la grub-pa mngon du thob.*

91. *gLo-bur gyi dri-mas ma gos shing/ mngon-shes dang dgongs-pa gsal 'grib med-pas...*
92. *bLa-mas nyams kyi man-ngag btab nas... sangs-rgyas ngo-bo rang la rnyed-pa lags-so.*
93. *Yul gu-ge nang-khongs-pa/ gdung-rus snyel yin.*
94. *Ra rdzi kho na byas nas/ nyams snang dang rmi-lam la/ g.yu bya khu-byug cig yang yang du skad smra-ba bzhin 'dug byung.*
95. *Cog gis bzhag na bde yi gar song thong..... ngas de las ma rnyed kyi/ khyod-rang rtog dpyod thong.* Cog-bzhag, just leaving everything as it is when one finds oneself in the state of contemplation, is the principle involved in the *rDzog-chen man-ngag gi sde.* Leaving everything just as it is includes the position of one's body, one's gaze, one's breathing, and one's mind. One does not try to change or modify anything, but simply remains in the state of contemplation.
96. *Yul pu-hrang yul stod-pa/ gdung-rus stong-pa.*
97. *sPro bsdu dang bral nas/ rang so la bzhag-pas/ de bzhin 'dug gi nyams su longs.*
98. *Gangs ri mtsho gsum.*
99. *Phyi nang gi dngos-po thams-cad rang grol du zhig-pa bzhin..... de ltar yin-par thag-chod.*
100. *Yul gro-shod-pa zhig yin/ gdung-rus khyung-po.*
101. *sGo gsum gyi 'bad rtsol dang bral nas don la brtags-pas.... ngas de las 'chugs sa med-par go.*
102. *sNang stong dbyer-med du shes-pas/ gnyis-ka zil gyis non.*
103. *gDeng thob*, that is, he attained full confidence in his understanding of the Natural State of the Nature of Mind (sems-nyid gnas-lugs kyi rtogs-pa la gden chen thob-pa).
104. *Yul glo stod kyis cha yin/ gdung-rus rong-po.* This is Lo Mustang in modern day Nepal.
105. *bLo yis ched 'dzin dang bral nas rang rig-pa'i gdangs la gzhigs-pas/ yin-par thag-chod.*
   (*gLo stod bon 'khor gyi phu/ g.yas zur gyi rong la bzhugs-so.* According to the *mNga'-ris rgyal-rabs* of Ngawang Dragpa (Ngag-dbang grags-pa), the Tibetan king of Guge, Yeshe Od (Ye-shes 'od), expelled all Bonpos from his kingdom and permitted little contact of Buddhism and Bon. A number of leaders of the revival of Buddhism in the 11th century, such as Rinchen Zangpo the great translator and Kyungpo Naljor of the Shangpa Kagyudpa lineage came originally from Bonpo families before adopting Indian Buddhist Tantrism. The few Bonpos remaining in Western Tibet (mnga'-ris) and the Central Changtang region were largely isolated hermits practicing the Dzogchen tradition of Gyerpungpa. On the Upper Transmission (stod lugs) in Western Tibet and the Lower Transmission in Northern Tibet, see Chapter Eight. This is true of the 9th and 10th centuries. Only later with the Later Spreading of Buddhism (phyi dar) in the 11th century, did the Bonpos come to establish their own monasteries such as Yeru Wensakha as the result of the Terma discoveries of Shenchen

Luga in 1017. On the situation in Guge, see R. Vitali, *The Kingdoms of Gu.ge and Pu.hrang*, LTWA, Dharamsala 1996.

Chapter 9: The Later History of the Transmission

1. Yangton Chenpo is listed in the English Preface to the New Delhi edition of the text (p. 3) at the head of the Nine Masters of the Northern Lineage. But this is an error because in the Tibetan text (f. 64), although he is indeed the source for both lineages, his disciple Lung-sgom rtog-med is listed in this position.

2. *Yang-ston chen-po shes-rab rgyal-mtshan* belonged the *Ya-ngal* clan (gdung-rus ya-ngal) and so he became known as *Yang-ston chen-po*. *Yang-ston* is a title that represents an abbreviation for *Ya-ngal ston-pa*, "the teacher from the *Ya-ngal* clan." This clan became a line of hereditary Lamas of Dolpo in Northern Nepal, connected with the famous Bonpo temple of Samling (bSam-gling). Some of the Lamas in the lineage were monks, others were married and the succession passed from father to son or from uncle to nephew. Yangton Chenpo is said to have had two important sons who were also Lamas: *Dam-pa 'bum-rje 'od* and *kLu-brag-pa bkra-shis rgyal-mtshan*. On them, see below. The later, also known as *'Gro-mgon klu-brag-pa* is said to have been the founder of Ludrak (klu-brag) temple in Nepal. In the lineage found here he is named after his older brother. He is followed in turn by the name of Yangton Chenpo's grandson (dbon-po), namely, *rTogs-ldan dbon-po Ye-shes rgyal-mtshan* (var. Kun-bzang). *kLu-brag-pa* studied in Tsang province, taking vows and initiations from the Bonpo Lama *Ye-shes blo-gros*, who founded the academy (gtsug-lag khang) of *Dar-lding gser-sgo* in 1173, and *sMan-gong-pa*, b. 1123. See D. Snellgrove, *The Nine Ways of Bon*, ibid., p. 4, n. 4, and also D. Snellgrove, *Himalayan Pilgrimage*, Shambhala, Boston 1989, p. 127.

3. *Bru-chen g.Yung-drung bla-ma*, also known as *Bru bDag-nyid rje-btsun*, founded *Bru yi gdon-chen g.Yas-ru dben-sa-kha* monastery in 1072 and served as its first abbot (mkhan-po). This famous Bonpo monastery was located in Tsang province, not so far from Sakya (Sa-skya) monastery that soon became the greatest monastic university of its time in Tibet. *gYas-ru dben-sa-kha* still existed in 1387 when Nyammed Sherab Gyaltsan (mNyam-med Shes-rab rgyal-mtshan) entered it as a student at the age of thirty-one, but the monastery was destroyed in a great flood a few years later, since it had lost the protection of its guardian deity Srid-pa rgyal-mo. In 1405 Sherab Gyaltsan founded nearby the monastery of *bKra-shis sman-ri*, which continued the same lineage and high level of scholarship. According to Lopon Tenzin Namdak, in the early days, the Bonpo monks from the philosophy college at *g.Yas-ru'i dben-sa-kha* were often sent to Sakya for their post-graduate studies. *rMe'u-ston Lha-ri gnyen-po* 1024-1091, also known as *Gur-zhog-pa* and as *sMra-ba'i seng-ge*, "the lion of speech," was instrumental in formulating the *A-khrid* system of Bonpo

Dzogchen. On this, see Per Kvearne and Thubten Rikey, *The Stages of A-khrid Meditation: Dzogchen Practice of the Bon Tradition*, Library of Tibetan Works and Archives, Dharamsala 1996.

4. *Ba-ri Lo-tswa-ba*, born in 1040 in the same year as the illustrious Milarepa, was a famous translator (lo-tswa-ba) involved in the revival of Buddhism (phyi dar) in the 11th century, who visited both India and Nepal in search of Tantric transmissions and Sanskrit texts, and who was closely associated with Sakya monastery, founded in 1073. On Bari Lotsawa, see George Roerich, *The Blue Annals*, Part I-II, Motilal Banarsidass, New Delhi reprint 1979. Also see John Myrdhin Reynolds, *The Secret Book of Simhamukha*, forthcoming. Yangton Chenpo was pursuing his scholastic studies at Sakya in Pramana (tshad-ma) or logic and epistemology, Madhyamaka (dbu-ma), and the Prajnaparamita Sutras ('bum). It can be seen by this example, as well as others, that the Bonpos were very willing participants in the revival of Buddhist scholarship in Tibet in the 11th and 12th centuries that was especially connected with Sakya.

5. *Bon-po lce thang-ba bya-bar 'dug-pas khas mi len zer-pa yang byung.*

6. *bShad rgyud kyi gdams-pa gter-ma.*

7. *gTer-kha bcu-gsum tsam gyi bon.*

8. *sKabs don dang gnad don bcu-gsum gyi bon gtam byas.*

9. *bLa-ma lha'i rgyud 'dzin-pa'i 'or bon kun-'dul.* Se-bon khro-rgyal was a disciple of *'Or-sgon kun-'du*l, here called *'Or-bon kun-'dul.*

10. The Lower System for the Oral Transmission (snyan-rgyud smad lugs) and the Upper System for the Oral Transmission (snyan-rgyud stod lugs) both originated with dPon-chen btsan-po. The Mahasiddhas belonging to the latter were all very great adepts who lived in Western Tibet in regions such as Guge and Puhrang. According to the Lopon, it is conceivable that both the Upper System (stod-lugs) and the Lower System (smad-lugs) developed separately before their reunification with Yangton Sherab Gyaltsan.

11. *Nyams rgyud rgyas sdus yi-ge la thebs-pa lags-so.*

12. With his third wife in Western Tibet, he had two sons and a daughter. The two sons were *Dam-pa 'bum-rje 'od* and *bKra-shis rgyal-mtshan* and his daughter was *Jo-lcam* who gave birth to his grandson *Ye-shes rgyal-mtshan*, all of whom became his disciples.

13. *rDzogs-pa chen-po zhang-zhung snyan-rgyud la grub-pa thob-pa.*

14. *sPang-la nam-gshen gyi sprul-pa.*

15. *mKha'-'gro Ye-shes gsal bya-ba'i mthong snang la.*

16. *'Gyur med gyi dbyings.*

17. These names are given in a hand written list kindly provided by Lopon Tenzin Namdak.

The Northern Transmission Lineage (byang brgyud):

1) *sPa-ston bsTan-rgyal* (the above author),

2) *dBal-mchog bzang-po*,

3) *Khro-bo rgyal-mtshan*,

4) *Shar-pa tshul-dpal*,

5) *Tsha-sgang shes-rab 'od-zer,*
6) *Re-tshang shes-rab rgya-mtsho,*
7) *sGo-dzung blo-gros rgya-mtsho,*
8) *bsTan-pa 'od-zer,*
9) *Nyi-ma 'od-zer,*
10) *'Khrul-zhig g.yung-drung,*
11) *lDo-sgom bstan-po lhun-grub,*
12) *Nam-mkha' lhun-grub,*
13) *Mi-'gyur rgyal-mtshan,*
14) *mGron-ldog bsod-nams rgya-mtsho,*
15) *Nyi-ma rgyal-mtshan,*
16) *sMon-lam rgyal-mtshan,*
17) *mDzo tshul-khrims ye-shes,*
18) *sKyabs-'og Sangs-rgyas bstan-'dzin* (b 1928),
19) *sLob-dpon bstan-'dzin rnam-dag.*

The Southern Transmission Lineage is closely associated with Menri monastery (lho brgyud):
1) *rTogs-ldan sher-dpal,*
2) *Nam-mkha' 'od-zer,*
3) *g.Yung-drung ye-shes,*
4) *Rin-chen blo-gros* (the last Abbot of Yeru Wensakha).

Here follow the names of the Abbots of Menri monastery in numerical order:
1) *mNyam-nyid shes-rab rgyal-mtshan,* (founder of Tashi Menri monastery),
2) *Rin-chen rgyal-mtshan,*
3) *Nam-mkha' ye-shes,*
4) *Kun-bzang rgyal-mtshan,*
5) *Rin-chen rgyal-mtshan,*
6) *Tshul-khrims rgyal-mtshan,*
7) *bSod-nams ye-shes,*
8) *bSod-nams g.yung-drung,*
9) *She-tsu drung-mu,*
10) *Shes-rab 'od-zer,*
11) *g.Yung-drung rgyal-mtshan,*
12) *Shes-rab blo-gros,*
13) *Shes-rab 'od-zer,*
14) *gTsug-phud 'od-zer,*
15) *g.Yung-drung tshul-khrims,*
16) *Rin-chen 'od-zer,*
17) *Rin-chen lhun-grub,*
18) *Shes-rab bstan-'dzin,*
19) *Shes-rab dbang-rgyal,*
20) *g.Yung-drung dbang-rgyal,*
21) *Phun-tshogs rnam-rgyal,*
22) *Shes-rab dgongs-rgyal,*

Zla-ba rgyal-mtshan (founder of *g.Yung-drung gling* monastery),
23) *Nyi-ma bstan-'dzin,*
24) *Phyogs-las rnam-rgyal,*
25) *Shes-rab g.yung-drung,*
26) *Sangs-rgyas bstan-'dzin,*
27) *bsTan-'dzin tshul-khrims,*
28) *Phun-tshogs blo-gros,*
29 *rGyal-ba blo-gros,*
30) *bsTan-pa blo-gros,*
31) *Nyi-ma dbang-rgyal,*
32) *Shes-rab blo-gros,*
33) *Sangs-rgyas bstan-'dzin* (called *rtsa-ba'i bla-ma* in the *Tshig-bshad* text),
sLob-dpon bsTan-'dzin ranm-dag.
The present Abbot of Tashi Menri is H.H. *sMan-ri khri-'dzin Lung-rtogs bstan-pa'i nyi-ma.*
Lopon Tenzin Namdak provides a further list following also from *Rinchen rgyal-mtshan*:
Nyi-ma 'od-zer,
g.Yung-drung tshul-khrims,
bsTan-'dzin lhun-grub,
Nam-mkha' lhun-grub,
Mi-'gyur rgyal-mtshan,
bSod-nams rgyal-mtshan,
Nyi-ma rgyal-mtshan,
Nyi-ma bstan-'dzin,
bSod-nams phun-tshogs,
Shes-rab g.yung-drung, b. 1838
Sangs-rgyas bstan-'dzin,
bsTan-'dzin tshul-khrims,
Phun-tshogs blo-gros, b. 1876
Nyi-ma grags-pa,
g.Yung-drung tshul-khrims,
bsTan-'dzin blo-gros,
sKyabs-'og ljong-ldong Sangs-rgyas bstan-'dzin, 1928-1977
sLob-dpon bsTan-'dzin rnam-dag.

18. *'Dzin-pa phyogs 'dzin dang bral cing/ rtsa grub-rtags dpag tu med-pa.*
19. *Yid-ches kyi bde-ba shar/ rig-pa'i dmar thag-chod-do. Yid-ches* usually means belief, but in this context it has more a connotation of confidence or confident belief that lacks all doubt. *dMar* is an intensifier and *thag-chod* means to come to a definitive decision or discovery.
20. *Yul glo smad kyi shar-ri-ba zhig yin/ gdung-rus snyel.*
21. *gLo sha-ri'i dben gnas dang ri-khrod 'grims shing bzhugs.*
22. *bCos med rang sor bzhags-pas/ don gyi ngo-bor 'dug-pa/ de-ltar nyams su longs shes gsungs-pas.*

23. *bLo thag-bcod yid-ches kyi go-ba skyes nas/ ri-khrod 'grims shing bskyangs-pas/ lo gcig nas gdeng thob-bo.*
24. *Yul dwang-ra'i spyan dgon/ gdung-rus gnyag/ nang-tsho rgya.*
25. *Gangs chen sta-rgo dge-rgan gyi ri.... khyad-par dwang-ra'i spyan dgon gyi ze-phug bud sgo la bzhugs-so.*
26. *Yul ni bi-ri nang skor-ba/ gdung-rus ldang yin.*
27. *Gangs ri mtsho gsum.* The reference is to Mount Kailas (gangs-chen ti-se) and the nearby lakes, Lake Manasarovara (mtsho ma-pham, var. ma-pang g.yu-mtsho) and Lake Rakastal (la-ngag bsil-mo, var. la-ngar gser-mtsho). See Namkhai Norbu and Ramon Prats, *Gangs ti se'i dkar c'ag: A Bonpo Story of the Sacred Mountain Ti-se and the Blue Lake Ma-pang,* Is.M.E.O., Rome 1989.
28. *Zla-ba lnga nas dran shar gyi rnam-rtog thams-cad ci bzhin-pa'i ngang du/ sbrul mdud grol-ba bzhin du khrol gyis song nas/ rang rgyud la rtogs-pa'i ye-shes shar te mthar phyin-pa'o.*
29. *Yul dar-lding-pa/ gdung-rus snyel/ nang-mtsho snya yin.*
30. *bLo rang sor bzhag la rig-pa rten dang phrol.*
31. *Nyams su blangs-pas gnas-lugs kyi don brtan-pa thob-bo.*
32. Along with *dBal-gsas* and *Lha-rgod, Khro-bo gtso-mchog, dBal-phur nag-po,* and *Zhang-zhung Me-ri* or *dBal-chen Ge-khod* represent the five major cycles of the Bonpo Father Tantra (pha-rgyud).
33. These holy places or great sites (gnas chen) or places of realization (grub chen) had been sanctified by the presence of previous Siddhas who had attained realization there. He realized visionary experiences and displayed the signs of heat (nyams dang drod rtags), in this context "heat" means fervor in practice. This may be compared with the ancient Vedic notion of tapas or heat. On the question of heat or tapas in relation to the practice of yoga, see Mircea Eliade, *Yoga: Immortality and Freedom,* Princeton University Press, Princeton 1969.
34. The practice of Chudlen (bcud-len, Skt. rasayana) in the Tibetan context means the practice of fasting combined with a very sparse and light diet and partaking of certain alchemical preparations. It is said that the accomplished practitioner of *bcud-len* is able to live for long periods of time, without taking any food whatsoever, by absorbing the energies of the elements directly from the surrounding environment.
35. *gNas-lugs kyi don rtogs shing sangs-rgyas kyi dgongs-pa bsnyems-pa.*
36. *mDun gyi bar-sang 'od zer gyi dkyil na/ mi dkar-po shel dkar 'dra-ba/ phyi nang med-par gsal-bar ye-re dga'/ rje ta-pi-hri-tsa yin-par 'dug dgongs-pa zhig byung/ rje'i zhal nas man-ngag rnams gsungs-so.*
37. His *yi-dam lha* or meditation deity, *Kun-bzang A-skor,* is a special aspect of the Sambhogakaya *gShen-lha 'od-dkar.*
38. *bZung 'dzin gnyis bral rtog med lhun gyis grub-pa zhig 'dug-pas/ de dang 'du 'bral med-par bskyang-bas/ gnas-lugs ma dang mjal-ba yin-no.*
39. *'Khor 'das dbyer-med tha-mal byar-med chen-por grol-lo.*
40. *rGya-ston Ye-shes Rin-chen* was also known by the ephithet *rnam-grol,* "the completely liberated one."

41. *Gangs ri mtsho gsum. Ma-pang*, var. *ma-pham*; *Lag-ngar*, var. *la-ngar.* See Note 27 above.
42. *Ma bcos ma slad rang sar zhog la blo thag-chod-par nyams su langs.*
43. *sNya-nang gi bla-brang.... gdung-rus zangs tsha'i nang-tsho glan.*
44. *Cho-'phrul dang mthong snang mang-po byung/ rang sems su thag-bcad/ sgom 'byung gi shes-rab brdol nas.....*
45. *Khro-bo* is a major cycle among the Father Tantras (pha rgyud). This includes the text of the *Khro-bo dbang-chen*, which focuses on the wrathful meditation deity Tsochok (gtso-mchog) and the retinues of the Peaceful and Wrathful Deities (zhi-khro lha tshogs). This collection comprises the Tantric cycle of the Bonpo Book of the Dead. On the goddess and guardian deity Sidpa Gyalmo, see Reynolds, *The Healing Practice fror Sidpa Gyalmo*, Bonpo Translation Project (privately printed), San Diego 1996.
46. *bZang ngan thams-cad lhun gyis grub-pas/ de rnams don gcig ngang las mi 'da'.*
47. *De glan-ston gyis go nas/ 'khor 'das kyi bon thams-cad rang gi sems su gdeng thob-bo.*
48. The hagiography text places him at the head of the Northern Lineage (byang brgyud). The five masters from *Dam-pa 'bum-rje* to *Cig-chod Dad-pa shes-rab* (var. *Dad-shes*) are known as the Five Masters of the Mantras and the Mind Teachings (sngags sems bla-ma lnga) because they possessed both the teachings and the realization of the Tantric practice of Meri and the Mind Teachings of Dzogchen (sngags dang sems-phyogs).
49. *Gab mdzod gnyis kyi rnam-grangs..... sngags sems-phyogs mtshan-nyid gsum.* That is, he studied with this master the Dzogchen teachings of the *Gab-pa dgu skor* and the cosmological and Abhidharma teachings of the *Srid-pa'i mdzod-phug*. He also studied the Tantras or Mantras (sngags) and the Dzogchen teachings in general or Mind Section (sems-phyogs), as well as philosophy (mtshan-nyid), which was a speciality of the curriculum at the *Bru* clan foundation of *g.Ye-ru'i dben-sa-kha.*
Bru-ston Nyi-ma rgyal-mtshan, who belonged to the famous *Bru* clan which had come originally from the country of *Bru-sha* (Gilgit), was a master of both the Southern Treasures (lho gter lugs) and the Northern Treasures (byang gter lugs) and was a contemporary of *Bru g.Yung-drung bla-ma*, b. 1040, who founded *g.Yas-ru'i dben-sa-kha* monastery in 1072.
50. *Zag-med kyi bde-ba stong brgal la song ste... bu la da-dung sems-can gyi 'gro don bya dgos.*
51. *bKa' sgo'i gdams-pa 'thor-bu zhig gnang.... gdams-pa'i 'di'i pe bstan-par zhu byas.*
52. *mGon-po rnam gsum las sogs-pa'i gsang-sngags me-ri'i lha tshogs.... zhal bstan-pa 'dra yang rmis.* The mGon-po rnam gsum refer to A-ti mu-wer, Ku-byi mang-ke, and Ge-khod. See Reynolds, *The Cult and Practice of Zhang-zhung Meri*, Bonpo Translation Project (privately printed), San Diego 1996.
53. *mTshan bcas kyi dkyil-'khor mi dgos.*

54. *rDzogs-chen gyi don dbang...... snyan-rgyud gyi don dbang.* A *don dbang*, or an empowerment by way of the meaning alone, is conferred by meditation, visualization, and a few words only, in contrast to a *rdzas dbang*, where the empowerment is conferred by way of a ceremony utilizing various instruments and materials (rdzas). Such a transmission does not require any ritual elaboration as is usually the case with empowerments in the Tantra system.

55. *sNyan-rgyud rgyas-pa'i skor/ 'bring-po'i skor/ chung-ba 'thor-bu'i gdams-pa.*

56. From all the evidence available in the colophons, it would appear that it was Yangton Chenpo Sherab Gyaltsan, using Orgom Kundul as his principal source and informant, who was responsible more than any of the previous masters in the lineage for the Zhang-zhung Nyan-gyud collection as we have it today. He was greatly assisted in this task, of course, by his son Dampa Bumje.

57. This was a famous Bonpo monastic establishment supported by the *rMe'u* clan. See Karmay, *Treasury*, ibid., p. 110.

58. See Note 84 in Chapter Five above.

59. *kLu brag gi bdud srin.*

60. *Brag phug zhwa ru gyon...... ri lung rjes kyis bkang.*

61. *Kun tu bzang-po'i dgongs-pa mngon du 'char-ba'i gdams-pa.* That is to say, the practice of Thodgal.

62. *Khong spungs dran-pa'i dgongs-pa gnyis su med-par gyur.* On *Dran-pa nam-mkha'*, see Note 84 in Chapter Five.

63. *gLo dol 'brog gsum.*

64. *Yul gtsang stod stag-rtse.*

65. *gSang sngags phyi nang gi bsnyen bsgrub rnams rdzogs-par mdzad-do.*

66. *Thabs shes-rab kyis bde rlung nang chud-pa..... mnyam-nyid bde-ba chen-po'i don thugs su chud-pa lags-so.* That is to say, he became accomplished in the practice of psychic heat or *gtum-mo* according to the Tantras.

67. *Rig-pa rtsal chen*, literally he had great skill (rtsal) and intelligence (rig-pa). These are the ordinary meaning of these terms when not fuctioning as Dzogchen technical terms.

68. *Ma-mchog srid-pa'i rgyal-mo.* On this goddess, who is one of the principal Guardians of Bon, see Per Kvaerne, *The Bon Religion of Tibet*, ibid., and Reynolds, *The Healing Practice for Sidpa Gyalmo*, op. cit..

69. *Sangs-rgyas kyi dgongs-pa 'di rang sems yin-pa'i ye-shes thod-rgal shar.* "His own mind" (rang sems) in this context means not the thought process of the individual, but the Nature of Mind (sems-nyid).

70. *dBus gtsang ru bzhi.*

71. *mKha' klong dbyings gsum gyi dgongs-pa shar-bas/ sku-gsum gyi 'bras-bu mngon du gyur nas/ 'gro-ba'i don mthar phyin-par mdzad-do.* This refers to realization through the practice of vision or Thodgal.

72. *Zab-mo snyan-rgyud 'di'i mnga'-bdag tu gyur. Tshe-dbang rig-'dzin* was the elder son of the illustrious prince of Zhang-zhung, *Dran-pa nam-*

mkha'. Through the practice of the Tantras he acquired the Vidyadhara power of long life and so, it is said in Bonpo tradition, has has not died even until this day. His younger brother, *Padma mthong-grol*, is said to have later reappeared in the country of Uddiyana as Padmasambhava.

73. *bLa-mas nyams kyi man-ngag.*

74. *sNang-ba rang-grol du grol/ 'khrul-pa rang zhig tu zhig/ zhen-pa gcig chod du chod/ rgyu-med dngos-med rang-dag rtsa-bral du rtogs te/ tshe-dbang ri-khrod-pa chen-po nyid kyi dgongs-pa dang gnyis su med-par gyur-pa lags-so.*

75. *Bru-chen rGyal-ba g.yung-drung*, who belonged to the illustrious *Bru* clan, was the author of the famous *rGyal-ba phyag-khrid*, the practice manual for the Zhang-zhung Nyan-gyud system of Dzogchen. See Chapter Eleven below.

76. *Yul ni dol-po/ gdung-rus sangs.* Dolpo in located in modern Nepal.

77. Clear Light refers to the practice of vision (thod-rgal) and Tsalung to the practice of the internal yogas of the channels (rtsa) and the energies (rlung).

78. *Phyi 'jig-rten gyi bya-ba dgos-med rang sar dag/ nang nyams-len rig-pa shugs 'byung rang sar grol/ bar bzung 'dzin gnyis-med rang-rig mngon du gyur/ gnas-lugs 'gyur-med gdeng chen khong du chud-pa lags-so.*

79. *Yul ni gser ri'i ru rgyal gyi 'bum mtsho tsher-lung nang du 'khrungs gdung-rus khyung-po.*

80. *rGyal bsen.* Possession by the spirits and the ensuing madness which later abates follow the pattern of the typical shamanic vocation. See Mircea Eliade, *Shamanism: Archaic Techniques of Ecstasy*, Pantheon Books, New York 1964.

81. These are two major cycles of Bonpo Dzogchen teachings. See Chapter One above.

82. *Bya ri gtsug-ldan man-chod kyi gnas chen ri-khrod 'grims.*

83. *Zhu gshen spa dang rme'u.* On these four leading clans among the Bonpos and their monastic establishments, see Karmay, *Treasury*, ibid.

84. *rJe gTsong-kha-pa* (1357-1419), founder of the Gelugpa school of Tibetan Buddhism.

85. *Ye-shes dbal-mo* is the two-armed form of the goddess *Srid-pa'i rgyal-mo*. On her, see Per Kvaerne, *The Bon Religion of Tibet: The Iconography of a Living Tradition*, ibid. Also see Reynolds, *The Healing Practice for Sidpa Gyalmo*, ibid.

86. *Yul dben-sa-kha/ gdung-rus a-thog.*

87. *Rig-pa blo rtsal dang ldan.*

88. rGyal-po dang sman-mo. On these guardian deities, Nyipangse and Menmo, see Appendix Three below.

89. *rTsa thig rlung gsum la mnga' bsnyems/ las ldan gyi phyag-rgya ma bsten nas/ nyams rtogs kyi rtsal dang ldan-pas.....* Karmamudra (las ldan gyi phyag-rgya) refers to sexual yoga practice with a female consort. One of the desirable side affects of such practice would be rejuvenation and long life.

90. *rGyal-bas gcig-rgyud btab-pas/ a-thog 'khor 'das phye chu 'dres/ bon-nyid ma dang mjal/ spros-pa'i mtshan-ma las 'das-so.* The Mother (ma) is the Ultimatre Reality or Dharmata (bon-nyid).
91. *Yul ni mdo-smad kyi gyod-du bya-ba/ gdung-rus kar-tsa yin.*
92. *Mo dang sman dpyad las sogs rgyu tha-snyad kyi bon la mkhas-pa.*
93. These unsuitable activities (ma rung-ba'i spyod-pa) refer to the practice of black magic, for which purpose he relied on the wrathful Tantric deity Walse (dbal-gsas) and the Black Garuda (khyung nag). This gave him power over and the ability to command the eight classes of worldly spirits (sde brgyad). Thereby he could cure diseases and exorcise eveil spirits (nad dand gdon sel-ba).
94. *Khyod theg-chen bon gyis 'gro-ba mi 'dren-par/ sems-can re re tsam thar-par drongs-pas ci la phan gsungs.* Tsewang Rigdzin was the eldest son of Dranpa Namkha, the prince of Zhang-zhung. The latter attained an excessive longevity through long life practices (tshe sgrub).
95. *Nub cig nyams snang la/ rgyud-pa'i rtsa-ba'i kun-bzang thugs-rje-can yin zer-pa'i lha dkar-po gcig.....* This epiphany or visionary experience (nyams snang) would appear to refer to the Nirmanakaya Tapihritsa, who is at times called *Kun-bzang*, rather than to the Primordial Buddha.
96. According to Karmay, the *Shar-ba'i don 'grel* is a text by Sharwa Naljyor (Shar-ba rnal-'byor), *Treasury*, p. 172. The *Drung-mu'i bon gcod* is a text on Chod practice and Karmay attributes this probably to *Drung-mu ha-ra*, though it is not mentioned among his writings in *Treasury*, p. 108, n. 61.
97. That is to say, the Precepts Transmission (bka' brgyud), the Experiential Transmission (nyams brgyud), and the Single Transmission (gcig brgyud) to one disciple only. These three represent the complete transmission for the Zhang-zhung Nyan-gyud.
98. *......Zhag gsum nas spros-pa'i mtshan-ma dang bral/ 'dzin-pa'i mdud-pa las grol/ bdag-med chen-po'i don rtogs-pa lags-so.*
99. Nyams rgyud rgyas 'bring bsdud gsum, that is, the extensive (rgyas), the intermediate ('bring), and the abridged (bsdud) versions.
100. *gDams-pa rin-po-che 'di la gcig rgyud khyad-par-can gcig.*
101. *bDag la yang smug-mos lung-bstan cig byung.* This goddess was probably *sMan-mo Ku-ma.* On her, see Appendix Three below.
102. On this text, "The General Exposition of the View" (lta-ba spyi-gcod), see Part Two in *Space, Awareness, and Energy*, Snow Lion, forthcoming.
103. Gangs ti-se mtsho gsum. See Note 27 above.
104. *Ti-se la bya rgyal rgod du sprul nas bskor-ba.*
105. *rTogs-pa mngon gyur thun-mong ma yin-pa....... gang shar gnas-lugs kyi rang sgo dag nas/ yul med du rang ngo shes te/ blo sgom rang sar zhig nas/ sgom med chen-po mngon du thob-pa lags-so.* That is to say, he practiced Thodgal and realized all four or five stages in terms of the development of vision (snang-ba bzhi).

Chapter 10: Texts of the Menri Edition

1. For the translation of this text, the *Legs-bshad mdzod* by Shardza Rinpoche (Shar-rdza bKra-shis rgyal-mtshan, 1859-1935), see Samten G. Karmay, *The Treasury of Good Sayings: A Tibetan History of Bon*, Oxford University Press, London 1972; pp. 52-53.

2. This Terma tradition is often simply called *rDzogs-chen*. On this tradition and its principal text, the *rDzogs-chen yang-rtse'i klong gsal*, attributed to the Bonpo master *sNya-chen Li-shu stag-rings* in the 8th century, see Chapter One above. The treasure texts of the *bsGrags-pa skor gsum*, "The Three Cycles of Revelation," were discovered by *gZhod-ston dNgos-grub grags-pa* behind an image of Vairochana Buddha at the *Khom-thing* temple in *Lho-brag* in Southern Tibet around 1100 CE. These Three Cycles of Revelation are so-called because *'Chi-med gtsug-phud*, the celestial pre-existence of *sTon-pa gShen-rab*, revealed the Dzogchen teachings successively to three sages belonging to three different races of living beings, namely,

   1) *Lha-gshen Yongs su dag-pa*, the sage among the Devas (lha) who live in the heavens above (steng),
   2) *Mi-gshen Mi-lus bsam-legs*, the sage among human beings (mi) who live on the surface of the earth in between (bar), and
   3) *kLu-gshen Ye-shes snying-po*, the sage among the Nagas (klu) who live in the netherworld below ('og). These three correspond to the three zones of the world in ancient Bonpo cosmology.

3. The other tradition of Dzogchen, the *Gab-pa dgu skor*, "the Nine Cycles of the Secrets," discovered by *gShen-chen klu-dga'*, and also known as the Nine Cycles of the Lesser Mind Series of Teachings (sems smad sde dgu), consists principally of nine texts known as the *Byang-sems gab-pa dgu skor*, "the Nine Cycles of Secrets concerning the Bodhichitta or Nature of Mind." Also included here are the *Rig-pa'i khu-byug*, "the Cockoo of Awareness," and the *Sems phran sde bdun*, "the Seven Lesser Series concerning the Mind Teachings." The *Gab-pa dgu skor* was rediscovered by Shenchen Luga (gShen-chen klu-dga') in 1017 at a site in Tsang province, along with a large collection of other texts buried in two large wooden boxes.

4. Oral communication.

5. The System of the Southern Treasures (lho gter lugs), which represent what is generally called the Nine Ways of Bon (bon theg-pa rim dgu), were discovered by gShen-chen klu-dga' (996-1035) in 1017. See Chapter One above. On gShen-chen klu-dga', see Karmay, *Treasury*, op. cit., pp. 126-131.

   According to a number of hostile medieval Tibetan historians, it was *gShen-chen kLu-dga'* who plagiarized a large number of Buddhist texts in order to fabricate the Bonpo works he discovered. This accusation has often been repeated in Western works. However, according to Lopon Tenzin Namdak, *gShen-chen klu-dga'* was scarcely literate, certainly no scholar, and was in no way equipped to fabricate the *Khams-chen*, the Bonpo Prajnaparamita in sixteen volumes, let alone the many other works he discovered. It is more probable that *gShen-chen klu-dga'* did indeed discover the library that had belonged to the *gShen* clan, of which he was a descendent, and which was concealed in two large wooden boxes on their estate lands at the time of the persecutions in the eighth and ninth centuries. Very often the early finds of Bonpo Termas were made by individuals, such as illiterate farmers or hunters, who could not have possibly written the texts they discovered. Another prime example of this were the three Nepali *A-tsa-ras* or thieves who in 913 CE stole a heavy wooden box from Samye monastery, only to discover it was filled with Bonpo texts of little financial value to them. They sold their finds to a Bonpo village priest for some gold and a horse. On the three A-tsa-ras, see Karmay, *Treasury*, ibid., pp. 117-120.

6. This schema appears to be a later scholastic elaboration. However, in the Zhang-zhung Nyan-gyud tradition, Trekchod and Thodgal are mixed up together as practices that reinforce each other. After one has first been directly introduced to Rigpa by a Lama, then one practices fixation in order to develop Trekchod or contemplation. Once a certain degree of stability has been developed in contemplation, then one proceeds to the practice of vision in terms of the dark retreat. Thereafter one proceeds to space practice and sunlight practice, which represents Thodgal as such. This procedure is outlined in the *dngos-gzhi* or principal practices text in the *rGyal-ba phyag-khrid* of Druchen Gyalwa Yungdrung. The procedure of practice has also been explained in this way by Lopon Tenzin Namdak who points out that one does not have to have realized perfect Trekchod before engaging in vision practice. In fact, vision practice can help develop one's Trekchod. However, in the later Terma system of the Nyingmapas, the practices of Rushans, Trekchod, and Thodgal came to be rigidly separated and sequential, as for example in Jigmed Lingpa's *Khrid-yig ye-shes bla-ma*. Many Nyingmapa Lamas assert that a premature practice of Thodgal before Trekchod is sufficiently developed can actually impair one's success in practice. Oral communication.

7. There does exist a later edition of this Zhang-zhung Nyan-gyud collection, printed in pecha format, one containing three additional chapters discovered at Samling monastery in Dolpo in Nepal, and published by the Bonpo Monastic Centre in 1980. But unfortunately I have not had access to that edition for the preparation of the present volume.

8. *bKra-shis sman-ri* monastery in Tsang province was founded in 1405 by mNyam-med Shes-rab rgyal-mtshan, who became its first abbot (mkhan-po). It was the successor of an earlier foundation, g.*Yas-ru'i dben-sa-kha* monastery, which was closely associated with the *Bru* clan throughout its history. Menri monastery became the principal seat of Bonpo learning and scholarship in Central Tibet from its founding until its destruction in the mid 1950s by the Red Guards. Lopon Tenzin Namdak had been a student

at that same monastery and for a time he was the professor (slob-dpon) there as well. Due to the efforts of the Lopon, Menri was re-established at Dolanji in Himachal Pradesh, India, in the late 1960s and its first abbot was H.H. Sangye Tenzin (Yongs-'dzin ljong-ldong Sangs-rgyas bstan-'dzin, 1928- 1977). Its present abbot, H.H. Lungtok Tenpe Nyima (Lung-rtogs bstan-pa'i nyi-ma), has been recognized by the Tibetan Government in exile at Dharamsala in India as the head of the Bonpo school.

9. *Khyung-sprul 'Jigs-med nam-mkha' rdo-rje* was formerly the abbot of a Bonpo monastery at *Gu-ru gyam* near Mount Kailas in Western Tibet. According to recent editions of *The Voice of the Clear Light*, the newsletter of the Ligmincha Institute of Charlottesville, VA, the former abbot at Dolanji, *Yongs-'dzin Sangs-rgyas bstan-'dzin*, recognized his student Geshe Tenzin Wangyal (bsTan-'dzin dbang-rgyal), who now lives and teaches in the U.S., as the Tulku or reincarnation of Khyungtrul Rinpoche.

10. Included in the same publication is a second collection, the *rDzogs-chen gser-zhun-ma* precepts, rediscovered by the Terton Tsewang Gyalpo (gter-ston Tshe-dbang rgyal-po), but this is a later Terma tradition and is not directly connected to the ancient Zhang-zhung tradition.

11. The various masters (bla-ma) in these lineages practiced the precepts (bka') for Dzogchen and thereby gained personal experiences (nyams) in meditation, as well as understanding (rtogs-pa) of the Natural State. They transmitted these personal experiences, as well as the precepts themselves, to one special disciple who was a suitable vessel, in what is known as the Single Transmission (gcig rgyud). Only with Gyerpungpa did these precepts come to be written down in the Zhang-zhung language, albeit as brief Upadeshas, and only with Ponchen Tsanpo a generation later, the last native of Zhang-zhung in the lineage, were these precepts, as well as the personal meditation experiences of the previous masters, translated from the Zhang-zhung language and written down in Tibetan. Later redactors, principally Orgom Kundul and Yangton Chenpo, gathered these experiences of the masters into the three collections listed above, known as the extensive, the intermediate, and the condensed versions. The extensive collection (Zhang-zhung nyams rgyud rgyas-pa) included two divisions or separate volumes (skya smug gnyis) known as the Brown Volume because the outside cover of the book was originally painted the color brown (smug-gu) and the White Volume because the outside cover of the book was unpainted and so it remained white (skya-ru). In ancient times, Tonpa Shenrab gave instructions for the printing and covering of books in five different colors and these books were kept in copper caskets. Oral communication from Lopon Tenzin Namdak.

12. After the time of Ponchen Tsanpo, the transmission of the Zhang-zhung Nyan-gyud split into two separate lineages: the Transmission of the Precepts (bka' brgyud) as represented by the Six Masters of the System of Upper Zhang-zhung (stod lugs kyi bla-ma drug) and the Experiential Transmission (nyams brgyud) as represented by the Five Masters of the

System of Lower Zhang-zhung (smad lugs kyi bla-ma lnga). These two lineages were reunited by *Ya-ngal ston-pa Shes-rab rgyal-mtshan.* See Chapter Nine above.

13. *'Or-sgom kun-'dul,* 11th century, was the teacher of *Yang-ston chen-po Shes-rab rgyal-mtshan.* The later was also a disciple of *rMe'u-ston Lhari gnyen-po,* b. 1024. On *'Or-sgom,* see Chapter Eight above.

14. Patsun Tan-gyal (sPa-btsun bstan-rgyal seng-ge bzang-po) composed this work in 1299 at gTsang la-stod. For the translations of some of these hagiographies (rnam-thar), see above.

15. *'Jigs-med gling-pa,* 1729-1798. His commentary, the *Khrid-yig ye-shes bla-ma,* is part of his Terma cycle of the *kLong-chen snying-thig,* which is nowadays probably the most widespread and most popular of all Nyingmapa Terma traditions. According to his hagiography (rnam-thar), the 14th century Nyingmapa master *kLong-chen rab-'byams-pa* appeared to him three times in pure visions and bestowed upon him these teachings which complete the latter's own cycle of revelations.

16. The six realms (rigs drug) or the six destines of rebirth ('gro-ba drug) represent rebirth among the gods or Devas (lha) in the heaven worlds, rebirth among the Titans or Asuras (lha ma yin) in the nether regions, rebirth among human beings (mi) on earth, rebirth among the animals (dud-'gro), rebirth among the hungry ghosts or Pretas (yi-dwags) in the ghost realms, and rebirth among the denizens of the hot and cold hells (dmyal-ba). The Six Dulshen ('dul-gshen drug), corresponding to the Six Munis (thub-pa drug) of the Buddhist system, are emanations of *sTon-pa gShen-rab* that appear in these six destinies of rebirth in order to teach the beings there the spiritual path to liberation. These Six Dulshen are as follows:

1) Yeshen Tsugphud (Ye-gshen gtsug-phud) purifies the Deva realm,
2) Chegyal Parti (lCe-rgyal par-ti) purifies the Asura realm,
3) Drajin Pungpa (Gra-byin spungs-pa) purifies the human realm,
4) Tisang Rangzhi (Ti-sangs rang-zhi) purifies the animal realm,
5) Sangwa Ngangring (gSang-ba ngang-ring) purifies the Preta realm, and
6) Mucho Demdrug (Mu-cho ldem-drug) purifies the hell realms.

See Per Kvaerne, *Bon Religion: A Death Ritual of the Tibetan Bonpos,* Brill, Leiden 1985.

17. These Five Pure Deities (dag-pa'i lha lnga) represent the pure vision of the five skandhas (phung-po lnga) and their five consorts (yum lnga) represent the five elements ('byung-poi lnga) in their pure form as light. These deities are as follows:

1) Gawa Dondrub (dGa'-ba don-grub) and the goddess of the water element (chu'i lha-mo),
2) Jyedrag Ngomed (Bye-brag dngos-med) and the goddess of the fire element (me'i lha-mo),
3) Gelha Garchyuk (dGe-lha gar-phyug) and the goddess of the air element (rlung gi lha-mo),

4) Salwa Rangjyung (gSal-ba rang-byung) and the goddess of the earth element (sa'i lha-mo), and

5) Kunnang Khyabpa (Kun-snang khyab-pa) and the goddess of the space element (nam-mkha'i lha-mo). These deities correspond to the five Dhyani Buddhas (rgyal-ba rigs lnga) and Five Consorts (yum lnga) in the Buddhist system of the Tibetan Book of the Dead. On this system of correspondences in general, see Detlef Ingo Lauf, *The Secret Doctines of the Tibetan Books of the Dead*, Shambhala, Boulder 1977.

18. The distribution of these texts in this anthology amoung the four cycles of precepts was originally taken from Samten G. Karmay, *Catalogue of Bonpo Publications*, Toyo Bunko, Tokyo 1977, but here I have found it necessary to make some revisions in view of the contents of some of these texts.

19. Namkhai Norbu Rinpoche has proposed that this Tantra in twelve Upadeshas may represent the original communication from Tapihritsa to Gyerpungpa in the eighth century, all of the other texts in the collection being elaborations or commentaries composed by various later Bonpo masters. Oral communication.

20. Although the Outer Cycle is principally associated with the view of Dzogchen, after a direct introduction, the view is cultivated and realized by way of fixation practice, in particular, fixation on the white Tibetan letter A. See Appendix One. Fixation is used to develop stability in contemplation. So here the associated principal practice is the practice of contemplation or Trekchod. In terms of the Inner Cycle the practices of Trekchod and Thodgal are combined in terms of the dark retreat and space practice. The ability to remain in the state of contemplation is increased thereby. Only then would one proceed to sunlight practice. Without stability in contemplation, the practice of vision would be of no use, no different than watching television, as the Lopon said. See also Note 4 below.

21. This term *thod-rgal*, "immediate transition, leap over, surpassing the highest," the usual term employed in the literature of the Nyingmapas for the practice of vision with sunlight, is not found in the texts of the Zhang-zhung Nyan-gyud collection. Here the practice is called Odsal or Clear Light ('od-gsal). "Clear Light" refers to the visions that spontaneously occur while one is in the state of contemplation, whether the support of these visions is sunlight, empty space, or complete darkness.

Chapter 11: Practice Manual for the Zhang-zhung Nyan-gyud

1. *Bru-chen rgyal-ba g.yung-drung*, 1242-1290. He belonged to the famous Dru clan (gdung-rus bru), hence he was known as *Bru-chen*, "the great man of the Dru family." The Tibetan text of his *Phyag-khrid* or practice manual was published in *sNyan rgyud nam-mkha' 'phrul mdzod drang*

nges skor and *Zhang-zhung snyan-rgyud skor*, Tibetan Bonpo Monastic Centre, New Delhi 1972, ff. 539-726.

2. *g.Yas-ru'i dben-sa-kha* monastery was founded in 1072 by *Bru-chen g.Yung-drung bla-ma*, b. 1040. It soon became the most famous Bonpo monastery in Tsang provence and was the ancestral foundation to the Lopon's own monastery of Tashi Menri (bKra-shis sman-ri).

3. *Bru-chen nam-mkha' g.yung-drung* was head of the Dru clan (gdung-rus bru) that was said to have come originally from the country of Drusha (Bru-sha) lying to the west of Tibet. It is now identified as Gilgit in modern day Pakistan where the native language is Burushaski.

4. On *gShen-chen klu-dga'*, 996-1035, who discovered the largest single cache of old Bonpo texts, see Karmay, *The Treasury of Good Sayings*, ibid. pp.126-135.

5. The 10th and 11th centuries was the axial period for the revival of both Bon and Buddhism in Central Tibet. On the revival of Buddhism and the inception of the New Translations (phyi 'gyur), see Snellgrove and Richarson, *A Cultural History of Tibet*, ibid., pp. 111-143.

6. The *Srid-pa'i mdzod-phug*, in some ways, is considered to be a Bonpo Abhidharma, that is, a treatise on cosmology and cosmogony. However, there exist other Bonpo texts that may also be classified as Abhidharma, but the *mDzod-phug* is especially prominent. The root text exists in both the original Zhang-zhung language and in the Tibetan translation. There is a commentary in Tibetan attributed to Dranpa Namkha. A litho edition of the text has been published in India: *sNang srid mdzod-phug gi rtsa-ba dang spyi-don*, published as *mDzod-phug: Basic Verses and Commentary by Dran-pa Nam-mkha'*, Lopon Tenzin Namdak, Delhi 1966.

7. On *Dran-pa nam-mkha'*, also called *bLa-chen* or *gShen* or *dMu-gshen*, see Note 84 in Chapter Five above. See also Per Kvaerne, *The Bon Religion of Tibet*, ibid., p. 119, and S. Karmay, *Treasury*, ibid.

8. *mTshan-nyid bru la bka' bab tshul.* The Tibetan term *mtshan-nyid* (Skt. lakshana), "essential characteristic," may be loosely translated as "philosophy," the emphasis here being on logic and epistemology, rather than on metaphysics or ethics. When *Bru Nam-mkha' g.yung-drung*, the disciple of the great *gShen-chen klu-dga'*, founded the monastery of *g.Yas-ru dben-sa-kha*, he made philosophy (mtshan-nyid) the principal course of study there. This was because the master Shenchen had commissioned him to recopy the philosophical texts he had discovered. Also the proximity of Yeru Wensakha to Sakya (sa skya) monastery stimulated the development of logic and epistemology among the Bonpos, Sakya being at the forefront of the revival of Buddhist scholarship. According to the Lopon, Yeru Wensakha used to regularly send its Geshes (dge-bshes) to Sakya for their post-graduate studies.

9. *Bru-chen nam-mkha' g.yung-drung* and his son *Khyung gi rgyal-mtshan* together established the philosophical and exegetical tradition of this lineage (mtshan-nyid kyi bshad-srol). However, there also exist other

texts that the Bonpos consider to be Abhidharma, but the *Srid-pa'i mdzog-phug* is especially prominent.

10. The Bonpo term for a fully ordained monk is Drangsong (drang-srong, Skt. rishi), corresponding to the Buddhist term Gelong (dge-slong, Skt. bhikshu). Upon his ordination, he received his monastic name of *rGyal-ba g.yung-drung*, meaning "the indestructible victorious one.".

11. *bLa-ma gdan-sa bzung.*

12. *bLa-ma'i brgyud-pa'i rnam-thar*, ff. 98-104. *Bru-chen rgyal-ba g.yung-drung gi lo-rgyus la lnga/* (1) *gtsang-ma mi lus thob-pa yab dang yum gyi lo-rgyus ni/* (2) *bka'-drin-can gyi bla-ma dang ji-ltar mjal na/* (3) *sa gnas khyad-par-can gang du rten-pa tshe du bzhugs-pa ni/* (4) *thun-mong dang gnas-skabs kyi yon-tan dang grub rtags ni/* (5) *rtogs-pa mngon 'gyur thun-mong ma yin-pa ni.* Here we present the translation of that hagiography from the text.

13. Among his most important masters was *gCig-chod dad-pa shes-rab* whom he follows in the lineage of transmission for the Zhang-zhung Nyan-gyud. See the later lineages for the Zhang-zhung Nyan-gyud summarized in Chapters Eight and Nine above.

14. *Yul ni g.yas- ru'i dben-sa-kha/ gdung-rus bru yin/ yab bru-zha bsod-nams rgyal-mtshan la/sras sku mched bzhi yod-pa'i tha-ltag yin.*

15. *De nas 'dul-ba rin-po-che'i drung du dang-pa drang-srong gi sdom-pa blangs te/ tshul ming rgyal-ba g.yung-drung du mtshan gsol zhing/ bslab-pa tshul-khrims dan dang ldan-par mdzad.* His uncle mTshan-ldan 'dul-ba, as known as mTshan-ldan-pa, "the philosopher," is traditionally dated 1239-1293.

16. *Phyi nang gsang gsum gyi bon-sde la dbang lung byin-rlabs dang bcas zhus shing thugs rgyud sbyangs........ rtse gcig yengs-med du thugs-dam mdzad de.*

17. On *dByil-ston khyung-rgod-rtsal*, b. 1175, see Karmay, *Treasury*, ibid., pp. 173-174.

18. On *Lung-ston lha-gnyan*, 11 cen., see Karmay, *Treasury*, pp. 113-115.

19. On *rMa-ston srid-'dzin*, b. 1092, see Karmay, *Treasury*, pp. 167-168.

20. *dBang lung khrid byin-rlabs bcas.*

21. *La-stod gyi bLa-ma rtogs-ldan dad-pa shes-rab* had gone on pilgrimage (gnas bskor) to all the monasteries (grwa-sa), places of practice and realization (grub gnas), and great holy places (gnas chen) sacred to the Bonpos in Central Tibet (dbus gtsang) before he came to visit *dBen-sa-kha dgon-pa*. This master is also known as *bLa-ma rtogs-ldan*. The epithet *rtogs-ldan* means a yogin, literally "one who possesses understanding."

22. From *mTshan-ldan 'dul-ba*, otherwise known as *Bru-sha 'Dul-ba rgyal-mtshan*, he requested the scriptural authorizations (lung) of the *rDzogs-pa chen-po A-khrid dmar byang* and the *Dri-med lhan-skyes dbang ye dbang chen-mo*. On the *A-khrid* system of Dzogchen, see Per Kvearne, "Bonpo Studies: The A-khrid System of Meditation," Part One: "The Transmission of the A-khrid System," in *Kailash* v. I, n. 1, pp. 19-50, Part

Two: "The Essential Teachings of the A-khrid System, in Kailash v. I, n. 4, pp. 248-332, Kathmandu 1973. The second text is also known as the *sNyan-rgyud rig-pa gcer-mthong*. It has been republished as the *sNyan-rgyud rig-pa gcer-mthong gi skor* by the Tibetan Bonpo Monastic Centre, Dolanji, HP, India in 1972.

23. *sNyan-rgyud kyi lung*. A *lung* or scriptural authorization takes the form of the Lama reading the text aloud to the student; this the authorizes the student to read the text on one's own.

24. *gDams-pa 'di'i bka'-babs kyi rgyud-pa ya-ngal-ba yin zer-ba thos nas.....* *bLa-ma ya-ngal-ba* was *Yang-ston rgyal-mtshan rin-chen*, the master who transmitted the *Zhang-zhung snyan-rgyud* to *bLa-ma rtogs-ldan gcig-chod dad-pa shes-rab* and therefore preceded him in the lineage. See Chapter Nine above.

25. *bLa-ma gdan-sa-pa* refers to *Yang-ston rgyal-mtshan rin-chen* whose monastic seat or place of residence (gdan-sa) was Samling (bsam-gling) in Dolpo.

26. *Mi ma yin la bka'-bsgos*. These non-human spirits (mi ma yin) are presummably the guardian spirits of the Zhang-zhung tradition, *Nyi-pang-sad* and *sMan-mo*. See Appendix Three below.

27. As their dreams were auspicious and indicated that the non-human spirits would not cause disturbances, after requesting his two companions to leave the room, the Togdan conferred upon Lama Gyalwa the Single Transmission (gcig-brgyud), as recounted in section five below.

28. *Grub-chen gong-ma rnams la mos-gus byas-pa'i thugs-rjes/ yid-ches thag-chod spros mtha' chod-pa 'byung gsungs-pas......* In this context, *yid-ches* is "belief," *thag-chod* is "definitive decision," *mtha'* is "extreme," and *spros-pa* is "conceptual elaboration." Here "belief" is not just an opinion or just something intellectual; it involves one's whole being.

29. *De yang mi rtog ye-shes kyi bde-ba khong nas shar te/ bzung 'dzin mtshan-ma'i chu rgyun chad-pa dang*.

30. That is to say, the Trikaya becomes visible as Thodgal visions (mthar thug 'bras-bu sku gsum mngon du gyur-pas).

31. Thereby the Great Bliss remained in its own original condition of the Dharmakaya and he came to behold the face of his own Yidam Tsochok, whereupon the Generation Process (bskyed-rim) and the Perfection Process (rdzogs-rim), all emanating and reabsorbing, were liberated into their own original condition (bde-chen bon-sku'i rang sa zin-pa dang yi-dam gtso-mchog gi zhal gzigs/ bskyed rdzogs 'phro 'du rang sar grol). Thereafter immeasurable numbers of liberations of experience and understanding were born in his mind (myong rtogs kyi grol-ba dpag med-pa thugs la 'khrungs). Tsochok (gtso-mchog) is the central meditation deity (yi-dam lha) of the *Zhi-khro* cycle of the Bonpo Book of the Dead. Therefore, he is reminiscent of the Nyingmapa meditation deity *Che-mchog* who occupies much the same position. Tsochok is also one of the five principal Yidams of the the Bonpo system of the Father Tantras (pha

rgyud). Emanation and re-absorption ('phro 'du) is an importamt practice of the Generation Process (bskyed-rim), involving the emanating of rays of light from the seed syllable (sa-bon) that represents the essence of the meditation deity and the re-absorption of these same rays of light now baring the blessings of the Buddhas into the seed syllable once again. Thereupon the transformation into the deity occurs.

32. *'Khrungs nyid kyi mdzad-pa'i bka'-brten yang/ phyi nang gsang gsum bsdus nas.*

33. The scripture (gzhung) referred to here is the *Thun-mtshams bco-lnga-pa.* And the back-up literature (rgyab) refers to the *rGyab skor rin-chen gsal-'debs,* var. *Ngo-sprod rin-po-che'i gsal-'debs rgyab skor gyi gdams-pa,* pp. 117-185 in *A Tri Thun Tsham cho-na dan,* ibid.

34. *sPyang-'phags,* var. *rkyang-'phags,* otherwise unidentified.

35. *bLa-ma'i brgyud-pa'i rnam-thar,* f. 103. Bru-sha btsun indicates *Bru-chen rgyal-ba g.yung-drung.* His previous incarnation, *sNang-ba mdog-can,* was a great Bonpo sage in early times.

36. His younger brother was *Bru Nam-mkha' 'od-zer* and his nephew was *Bru-ston bSod-nams rgyal-mtshan.* The biography of this last master has also been translated by Kvaerne. See Per Kvearne, "Bonpo Studies: The A-khrid System of Meditation," Part One, ibid., pp. 41-46. As Kvaerne points out, there are some differences between the hagiographical text found in the collection that we have here and the one included in the *A-khrid* collection.

37. This importanda *A-khrid* text has been translated in part by Per Kvaerne. See the translation of the *Thun-mtshams bco-lnga-pa man-ngag khrid kyi rim-pa lag-len thun-mtshams dang bcas-pa* in Per Kvaerne and Thubten Rikey, *The Stages of A-khrid Meditation: Dzogchen Practice of the Bon Tradition,* Library of Tibetan Works and Archives, Dharamsala 1996. Also see Per Kvearne, "Bonpo Studies: The A-khrid System of Meditation," Parts One and Two, ibid.

38. The translation of the preliminary practice text (sngon-'gro), made in accordance with the oral commentaries by Lopon Tenzin Namdak, is found in Appendix Two below. According to the text of the principal practice (dngos-gzhi) composed by Druchen, "Second (that is, following after the first part consisting of the preliminary practices), in between (while one is on the spiritual path before attaining the goal), in terms of the stages of the principal practice that brings about the ripening and liberation of one's mind-stream, there are three parts:

1) at the beginning, without any grasping at thoughts, one fixates the mind (thog-mar sems ma zin-pa zin-par byed-pa),

2) in the middle, when mindfulness does not yet abide steadily, one employs (various methods) to bring about its abiding steadily (bar du dran-pa mi gnas-pa gnas-par byed-pa), and

3) and finally, when Self-Awareness is not yet clear, one employs (various methods) to make it clear (tha-mar rang-rig mi gsal-ba gsal-ba bya-ba)."

The first part outlines the practice of Trekchod by way of an explanation of how to fixate the mind (sems 'dzin gyi khrid), the second part explains the various methods of practice of the dark retreat, and the third part elucidates the various methods of the practice of Thodgal, that is, the practice of vision with sunlight.

39. A translation of this text will be found in Part One of *Space, Awareness, and Energy*, forthcoming.

40. For a translation of this text, together with a commentary based on Lopon Tenzin Namdak's oral instructions for making a dark retreat, see John Myrdhin Reynolds, *The Seven-fold Cycle of the Clear Light*, Bonpo Translation Project (privately printed), San Diego and Amsterdam 2001. Also see the second volume in this series.

Appendix One: The Guru Yoga for Tapihritsa

1. A short biographical note, or rather hagiography, of Tapihritsa is found in the hagiography section of the collection of the New Delhi edition: Lokesh Chandra, *History and Doctrine of Bon-po Nispanna-Yoga*, International Academy of Indian Culture, Introduction in English, Sata-Pitaka Series Indo-Asian Literatures, volume 73, New Delhi 1968. The text in question is entitled *brGyud-pa'i bla-ma'i rnam-thar*, "The Hagioigraphies of the Masters of the Lineage," composed by Paton Tan-gyal (sPa-ston bsTan-rgyal). A translation of this text will be found above in Chapter Five of Part One above.

2. *'Ja'-lus-pa*. The Rainbow Body ('ja'-lus) is ultimately realized by way of the practice of Thodgal (thod-rgal), where, at the time of death, the elements of the material body are dissolved back into pure radiant energy in the form of the clear colored lights of the rainbow. This phenomenon is an indication that the mind-stream of the individual has realized the Dharmakaya. By virtue of attaining this Rainbow Body, that same individual possesses the capacity to reappear as a Body of Light ('od-lus) in order to teach the Dharma to those disciples with whom there exists a previous spiritual karmic connection. This capacity is known in the Sutra system as the Rupakaya or Form Body. This Rainbow Body is realized through to the Dzogchen practice of Thodgal and should not be confused with the pure illusion body (sgyu-lus dag-pa) that is realized through the methods of Tantric transformation or Dzogrim (rdzogs-rim) and is also sometimes called a "Rainbow Body". Such an illusion body, whether pure or impure, is created by antecedent causes and by the functioning of the mind, whereas the Rainbow Body according to Thodgal occurs effortlessly and spontaneously, without causation intervening, immediately from the Nature of Mind upon the attaining of enlightenment.

3. *'Pho-ba chen-po'i 'od lus*. The process of realizing the Rainbow Body requires that the practitioner must enter into the actual process of dying, although one does not have to undergo the subsequent Bardo experience;

whereas, with the Great Transfer, one dissolves one's material body directly into empty space without the necessity for entering into the process of dying. In both cases, the phenomenon of the physical body fading away is an indication that the individual in question has attained enlightenment and realized the Dharmakaya, whereafter one has the capacity to re-manifest as a Rupakaya in the form of the Body of Light ('od-lus) in order to teach the Dharma and guide other beings to liberation.

4. On the life of Gyerpungpa, or *Gyer-spungs chen-po sNang-bzher lod-po*, see Chapter Five above. Also see David Snellgrove and Hugh Richardson, *A Cultural History of Tibet*, Geo Weidenfeld & Nicolson, London 1968.

5. The vital winds or psychic energies (rlung, Skt. vayu) are the mounts or horses upon which thoughts and mental processes ride like horsemen, enabling mind to interact with the physical body and the material environment. The five principal vital winds are Apana (thur-sel), concentrated in the lower part of the body, Vyana (khyab-'jug), concentrated throughout the muscles of the body, Samana (me-mnyam), concentrated in the belly, Udana (gyen-rgyu), concentrated in the throat, and Prana (srog-'dzin), concentrated in the heart. These are the same five principal vital winds spoken of in Hindu Yoga, Ayurvedic medicine, and Tibetan medicine. However, Prana (srog-'dzin) is only one of these vital winds and the general name for these current of psychic energy is not Prana but Vayu or "wind."

6. This description is found in the text of the *'Od-gsal bdun skor*, appended to the *rGyal-ba phyag-khrid*, (ff. 714-722), the practice manual for the Zhang-zhung snyan-rgyud. See chapter Eleven above.

7. In the Ngondro text (sngon-'gro) belonging to the Zhang-zhung Nyan-gyud cycle and translated below in Appendix Two, it is indicated that one should visualize the Sambhogakaya aspect Shenlha Odkar (gShen-lha 'od-dkar), together with the entire Tree of the Assembly (tshogs-shing), containing all of the masters of the lineages. But this is rather complicated and difficult outside of a genuine retreat situation, so Lopon Tenzin Namdak suggests that non-Tibetan practitioners might try to work with the much simpler visualization of Guru Tapihritsa alone in front of oneself..

8. On the Preliminary Practices, see Appendix Two below. Here we are following the oral explanation given by Lopon Tenzin Namdak for the Guru Yoga practice. The suggestions concerning the practice were taken from the oral instructions of the Lopon. The block-print edition of the *rGyal-ba phyag-khrid* lacks the explanation of the recitations (tshigs bshad), as well as the descriptions of the cycle of visualizations (dmigs skor) for the practices. These two texts, together with the preliminary practice text (sngon-'gro), the principal practice text (dngos-gzhi), and the four auxiliary texts on the view (lta-khrid), the meditation (sgom-khrid), the conduct (spyod-khrid), and the fruit (dmar-khrid) normally comprise the eight cycles or sections (skor brgyad) for the practice manual. This

lack has been supplemented by way of the oral explanations from the Lopon

9. The Tibetan text in transliteration is as follows:
spyi-gtsug bde-ba chen-po'i pho-brang du/
drin-can rtsa-ba'i bla-ma la gsol-ba 'debs/
sangs-rgyas sems su ston-pa rin-po-che/
rang ngo rang gis shes-par byin gyis rlobs//
This verse is known as the explanatory words of the prayer (gsol-'debs kyi tshig-bshad) and are used in the Guru Yoga. See below.
However, the original recitation text known as "the Exposition of the Words" (tshig-bshad) found in the rGyal-ba phyag-khrid provides a much longer liturgy for this practice. This followed by a detailed Lineage Prayer (brgyud-pa'i gsol-'debs), beginning with the Primordial Teacher (ye-ston) Kuntu Zangpo and coming down to our own time to Jongdong Sangye Tenzin, the thirty-third Abbot of Menri monastery and one of the principal masters of Lopon Tenzin Namdak.In the text, Sangye Tenzin is addressed as Tsawe Lama or the Root Master. The masters or Lamas occurring after Gyalwa Yungdrung in the lineage were, of course, added by later writers. Included in the list are the thirty-three Abbots (sMan-ri khri-'dzin) or Throne Holdes of Menri monastery. On this lineage, see Chapters Eight and Nine above and for the translation of the *Tsig-bshad* text, see Appendix 2, Section 4, below.

10. Here the text only mentions purification by way of the waters of wisdom or the luminous wisdom nectars (ye-shes kyi bdud-rtsi). But on a number of occasions, especially when practicing the Guru Yoga successively for each master of the Lineage of the Experiential Transmission (nyams brgyud), the Lopon has taught this purification practice by way of employing the powers of the three elements of fire, wind, and water. This method is also employed elsewhere in the Ngondro text. See "7. The Practice of Mantra Recitation," in Appendix 2, Section 3. This parallels the common method for the purification of puja offerings by way of reciting the mantras of the elements: RAM YAM KHAM. In Buddhist texts these three syllable evoke the purifying powers of these three elements respectively. However, in the Bonpo texts, the syllables employed are RAM YAM MAM, with their respective colors of red for fire, green for wind, and blue for water. In the Buddhist tradition, the color associated with water is usually white, whereas in the Bonpo tradition, it is blue. But these two colors are interchangeable, the sky being blue usually and clear water being transparent and colorless. In either case, the effect of the purification process is the same.
The practitioner should visualize that from the chest or heart center of the Guru seated in the sky above one emanates a ray or red light or a red syllable RAM, being of a fiery nature, which, when it enters one's body through the aperture at the crown of the head, transforms into the fires of wisdom (ye-shes kyi me), which burn up and utterly consume all the negative energies and pollutants found within one's being. In this way, all

of one's sins and obscurations are purified (sdig sgrib sbyang-ba). Next, a green ray of light or the green syllable YAM, having the nature of wind, emanates from the heart center of the Guru and enters into the crown of one's head. This transforms into the fierce winds of wisdom (ye-shes kyi rlung), which scatter and blow away all the remaining ashes. Finally, a blue ray of light or blue syllable MAM, having the nature of water, emanates from the heart center of the Guru and enters the crown of one's head. It transforms into water and these waters of wisdom (ye-shes kyi chu), washing and carrying away completely whatever traces remain behind of these pollutants. By means of the purification process with these three elements, the practitioner becomes a purified and suitable vessel for the receiving of the empowerments (dbang-bskur) and blessings (byin-rlabs) from the master in the sky above him. One should now visualize and think that one's physical body is thoroughly cleansed and purified, so that it is transparent like a crystal vase. When used as an adjective, the term "wisdom" (ye-shes) means that something belongs to a higher and a purer dimension of reality, one that is not afflicted by our impure karmic vision. In this usage, "wisdom" basically corresponds to our concept of "spiritual."

11. Note that, whereas the three syllables in the three places of the Guru in the usual Buddhist system are OM AH HUM, the Bonpo system has the syllables A OM HUM. Nevertheless, the procedure, its significance, and the colored rays of light are the same in both cases.

12. The Tibetan text in transliteration is as follows:
    sgo gsum dag-pa'i dge-ba gang bgyis-pa/
    khams gsum sems-can rnams kyi don du bsngo/
    dus gsum bsags-pa'i las sgrib kun byang nas/
    sku gsum rdzogs-pa'i sangs-rgyas myur thob shog//

13. This is known as the *'bum dgu*, that is nine times one hundred thousand.

14. Here I have followed the oral instructions from the Lopon regarding the practice of the Guru Yoga. Normally, any session of Dzogchen practice would begin with the Guru Yoga and conclude with the dedication of merit. This is in accord with Mahayana practice in general.

15. *sNgon-'gro gsol-'debs*, ff.23-28. This is suggested by the colophon. However, the rather scholastic nature of the Invocation would suggest otherwise. But perhaps the core of the six verses, commented on below, do derive from Gyerpungpa and the frame, consisting of the preface and the conclusion, were composed by later editors, such as Yangton Chenpo. This invocation has been recently reprinted as an appendix to the *sNgon-'gro'i gsol-'debs* in *rGyun khyer bon spyod phyogs bdus dang ldan thar lam 'dzogs-pa'i them-skes*, Bon Students Committee Central Institute of Higher Tibetan Studies, Sarnath, Varanasi, India 2001.

16. The transliteration of the text in Tibetan is as follows:
    EMAHO!
    kun-bzang thugs sprul-sku mdog shel dkar 'od/
    dri-med mdang gsal 'od zer phyogs bcur 'phro/

rgyan-med gcer-bu ye-nyid snying-po'i don/
mkhyen gnyis thugs-rje 'gro-ba'i don la dgongs/
bde-gshegs thugs bcud rdzogs-chen kun gyi mchog/
theg-pa'i yang rtse rgyud lung man-ngag snying/
gzhi yi gnas-lugs 'khor 'das grol 'khrul dang/
sgra 'od zer gsum skyon yon rab gsal zhing/
'gro-ba blo yi mun-pa kun gsal nas/
gzhi stong rtsa bral-ba lam gcig chod rtogs/
nyams rtogs mngon-gyur 'khor 'das sems su grol/
'bras-bu sku gsum dbyings su 'god mdzad-pa/
'gro-ba'i mgon-po ta-pi-hri-tsa la/
bdag blo rtse-gcig mos-pas gsol-ba 'debs/
bdag sogs 'gro la dbang-bskur byin gyis rlobs/
phyi nang gsang-ba'i bar-chad zhi-ba dang/
ma rig 'khrul-ba'i bdag-'dzin grol-bas kyang/
rang-rig mngon-gyur lta spyod mthar-phyin nas/
ye stong rtsa bral blo 'das chen-po'i don/
da-lta nyid du bdag la rtsal du gsol/
rje 'gro-ba'i mgon-po ta-pi-hri-tsa la/
gsol-ba 'debs-so 'gro drug thugs-rjes zungs la bdag rgyud khrol/
[ces sprul-sku ta-pi-hri-tsa la/ gyer-spungs snang-bzher lod-pos gsol-ba
phur tshugs su btab-pa'o/ bkra-shis/ dge'o//]

17. These are reminiscent of the six vajra verses known as the *Rig-pa'i khu-byug* or "The Cuckoo of Awareness" said to have been translated by Vairochana from a short text he obtained in India from his own master Shrisimha. This Tibetan text is said represent the first translation into Tibetan of a Dzogchen text from with Sanskrit or from the language of Uddiyana. Karmay, however, asserts this is not a translation from Sanskrit, but an original Tibetan composition. See Samten G. Karmay, *The Great Perfection: A Philosophical and Meditative Teaching of Tibetan Buddhism*, Brill, Leiden 1988. Verse four to six in this Bonpo text specifically refer to the Base, the Path, and the Fruit with reference to the practice of Thodgal and its final result, which is the attaining of the Rainbow Body of Light. Thodgal practice was the precise means by which the master Tapihritsa attained enlightenment as a Buddha and thereafter he re-appeared or re-manifested himself in a Body of Resurrection or Body of Light to his disciple Gyerpung Nangzher Lodpo. On these six vajra verses of Vairochana, see Samten G. Karmay, *The Great Perfection*, op. cit., and Reynolds, *The Golden Letters*, Snow Lion, Ithaca 1996.

18. The Tibetan text of these verses is as follows:
   1) *gZhi yi gnas-lugs 'khor 'das grol 'khrul dang/*
   2) *sgra 'od zer gsum skyon yon rab gsal zhing/*
   3) *'gro-ba blo yi mun-pa kun gsal nas/*
   4) *gzhi stong rtsa bral-ba lam gcig chod rtogs/*
   5) *nyams rtogs mngon-gyur 'khor 'das sems su grol/*
   6) *'bras-bu sku gsum dbyings su 'god mdzad-pa//*

19. This phenomenon of the dawning of the Clear Light after death is dealt with in more detail in Part Three of Reynolds, *Space, Awareness, and Energy*, Snow Lion, forthcoming. See also the translations and discussions in Reynolds, *Selections from the Bonpo Book of the Dead*, Bonpo Translation Project (privately printed), San Diego and Copenhagen 1997.

20. On the Base, see especially the translations and discussions regarding "the General Exposition of the View" in Reynolds, *Space, Awareness, and Energy*, Parts One and Two, Snow Lion, forthcoming.

21. Again, see the translations and discussions on Kunzhi and Rigpa in Reynolds, *Space, Awareness, and Energy*, forthcoming. See also Reynolds, *Selections from the Bonpo Book of the Dead*, op. cit.

22. The process of falling asleep each night and then entering into a dream state correspond to the process of dying and to the Bardo experience respectively.

23. These processes of evolution or the unfolding of Nirvana and Samsara from the primordial Nature of Mind are elaborated in much more detail in the translations of two texts, *'Khor-lo bzhi sbrag* and *'Od-gsal sems kyi me-long*, in Part Three of Reynolds, *Space, Awareness, and Energy*, forthcoming from Snow Lion.

24. On how fixation (sems-'dzin) is used in order to induce this state of contemplation, see Section Five below on the Guru Yoga and the Practice of Contemplation.

25. On the direct introduction (ngo-sprod) and the parallels here with the Three Statements of Garab Dorje, see Reynolds, *The Golden Letters*, ibid.

26. On the Son Clear Light (bu 'od-gsal), experienced in the practice of contemplation during one's lifetime, and the Mother Clear Light (ma 'od-gasl), experienced after death, see *Space, Awareness, and Energy*, Snow Lion, forthcoming.

27. All the phenomena or visions of Samsara and of Nirvana are liberated back into their original source, the Nature of Mind ('kor 'das sems su grol). Among the four stages in the development of vision (snang-ba bzhi) in the practice of Thodgal, this represents the final or culminating stage where all phenomena dissolve back into their source, the state of emptiness. This stage is known as the Exhaustion of Reality (bon-nyid zad-pa).

28. On the Dharmakaya and the Rupakaya, see the Appendix in Reynolds, *Self-Liberation through Seeing with Naked Awareness*, ibid.

29. On the *rGyal-ba phyag-khrid* text in general, see Chapter Eleven in Part One above and on the Preliminary Practices, see Appendix Two below. The suggestions regarding the practice were taken from the oral instructions of the Lopon. The translations of the texts of the Principal Practices and the Auxiliary Texts will be found in a future volume of this series. However, to actually engage oneself in the practices described, whether the preliminaries or the principal ones, the practitioner is well advised to seek out the personal instruction and guidance of a competent

Lama in the tradition because there exist certain oral instructions that are not written down in the texts. This is a living tradition. A book cannot be a substitute for personal instruction and guidance in one's spiritual development.

Appendix 2.1: The Introduction to Appendix Two

1. On the practice of the Guru Yoga, see Appendix One above.
2. Here we have repeated the instructions given orally by the Lopon.
3. These four meditations are generally known as the *blo-ldog rnam bzhi*, where *blo* means "mind or attitude", *ldog-pa* means "change or reversal", and *rnam bzhi* means "the four kinds".
4. This Buddhist idea of *blo-ldog* could almost be translated by the Greek *metanoia*, a notion that occupies a similar place in the Christian system.
5. For an example of an extended commentary on a Nyingmapa Ngondro text of this type, see the Padmakara Translation Group, *The Words of My Perfect Teacher*, Harper Collins Publishers, San Francisco 1994.
6. See Chapter Eleven above.
7. *rDzogs-pa chen-po zhang-zhung snyan-rgyud las lta-ba'i spyi-gcod kyi mnyam-bzhag sgom-pa'i lag-len.*
8. *Kun tu bzang-po rang-rig mnyam-par gnas la phyag 'tshal-lo.*
9. *sNgon-'gro phyi nang yul dang shes-pa sbyang.* Outer (phyi) and inner (nang) refer to the ordinary and the extraordinary preliminaries respectively.
10. *sNang-ba yul la sbyang-ba.*
11. *Phyi nang gsang gsum yang gsang gi skyabs-'gro*: the Outer Refuge consists of the Buddha, the Dharma, and the Sangha; the Inner Refuge consists of the Guru (bla-ma), the Meditation Deity (yi-dam), and the Dakini (mkha'-'gro-ma); the Secret Refuge consists of the channels (rtsa), the winds (rlung), and the bindus or energy quanta (thig-le); the Exceedingly Secret Refuge consists of the Essence (ngo-bo), the Nature (rang-bzhin), and the Energy (thugs-rje) of the Primordial State of Buddhahood.
12. *Nyon-mongs sdig sgrib sbyang-ba'i phyir.*
13. That is to say, one practices generosity impartially and indescriminately without being concerned of any benefit coming to oneself.
14. A Ganapuja (tshogs mchod) is a Tantric feast to which spiritual beings, as well as human beings, both male and female, are invited.
15. See the Mandala Offering described below in the translation.
16. *sGrib-pa byang-pa'i rim-pa.*
17. *Lan-chags gtor-ma*, that is, sacrificial offerings that pay off one's previous karmic debts to the sentient beings of the six destinies whom one has killed or otherwise injured in some previous lifetime.
18. *Lus sgrib sbyang.*
19. *Ngag sgrib sbyang.* The heart mantras (snying-po) used for this purpose are given below.

20. These seed syllables are located on the surface of the body at the forehead, at the throat, at the heart, at the navel, at the genitals, and on the soles of the two feet.

21. *Yid kyi sgrib-pa sbyang-ba.* For this process, see the translation below.

22. Translations of the text for the Principal Practices (dngos-gzhi) and of the Auxiliary Texts that form the Conclusion (rjes) will be found in the succeeding volumes of this series

Appendix 2.2: The Translation of the Ngondro Text

1. *'Dir kun bzang thugs kyi nying-khu/ bder-gshegs rgyal-ba'i bka' lung/ rig-'dzin 'phags-pa'i zhal-gdams/ gdams-pa kun gyi yang bcud/ snyan rgyud kun gyi zhe-phug/ dgongs-pa thams-cad kyi mthar-thug/ lta dgongs kun gyi yang rtse/ nyes don kun gyi mdo rtsa/ rgyud lung kun gyi gnad 'dus/ man-ngag kun gyi bcud dril/ gyer-spungs snang-bzher lod-po'i dngos-grub/ grub-chen gong-ma rnams kyi dgongs nyams/ las-ldan 'og-ma rnams kyi lam 'dren/ rdzogs-pa chen-po zab don gnad kyi mthar-thug 'khrul-pa'i phu thag gcod cing ye-shes gab bskung 'don-pa.*

2. *rGyu 'bras rdzun du btang nas sangs-rgyas btsan thabs su grub-pa.*

3. *Nyams-len rgyud la bkal nas yid-ches 'phral su ston-pa/ dmar thag nang du bcad nas grub rtags phyi ru ston-pa.*

4. *De dag kun gyi bcud phyung/ gnad bsdus/ dgongs-pa dril/ gab bskung bton nas.*

5. *'Dus byas thams-cad mi rtag/ dngos-po thams-cad 'gyur/ byas-pa thams-cad 'jig/ 'dus-pa thams-cad 'bral/ bsags-pa thams-cad 'dzad/ skyes-pa thams-cad 'chi.*

6. *sNying re rje snyams du bsam.*

7. *Mo 'debs rim-'gro sman dpyad byed.*

8. The four elements are air, fire, water, and earth, but these four actually represent the various modes in which energy manifests rather than being gross material substances. The Tibetan Books of the Dead describe how these elements progressively disintegrate and are reabsorbed into space during the process of dying. See the translations in Reynolds, *The Path of the Clear Light*, Snow Lion, forthcoming.

9. *Ci zhig la rang shugs kyis 'khor-ba blo ldog mi rtag-pa rgyud la skye...... snang-ba thams-cad sgyu-mar 'char bden zhen gyi 'khri-ba chod.*

10. The great master Dranpa Namkha (bLa-chen Dran-pa Nam-mkha') is said to have been a prince of ancient Zhang-zhung who was a famous practitioner of Dzogchen.

11. *sNgar byas-pa thams-cad ma shes-pa/ mo go-bas/ ma rig-pa'i rang-bzhin-can yin la/ de dag thams-cad gcig tu bsdoms nas/ mkhyen-pa-can rnams kyi thugs la sa-ler mnga'-bas..... de dag gi spyan lam du gnong zhing 'gyod-pa'i tshul gyis bshags-pa 'bul-lo.*

12. *Mi dge sdig-pa'i las rnams so-sor bshags/ dge-ba kun gyi rjes su 'breng-bar bya.*

13. Thre copy of the block print in my possession gives this mantra as OM NA-MA A-DKAR SHAG SA-LE SANG-NGE SWA-HA; the Lopon corrects the reading by adding the syllables GSHA' YA NI.
14. *Lar rang gis ma khrel-ba/ rang mgo rang gis ma bskor-ba zhig bya ste.*
15. *sTon-pa'i bka' 'di ma yengs dang du longs/ bden-pa'i tshig 'di ma brjed zung du zungs.*
16. This is explained from the standpoint of the conventional meaning (drang don las gsungs): *Rang gis rang bslus snying tshim rang la sdig.*
17. *De ltar sngon-'gro'i yan-lag rnams la spyod-pa'i dus su/ 'al 'ol sab sob bya lo tsam zhu lo tsam ma yin-pa/ sgo gsum rtse gcig tu dril.*
18. *Man-ngag yang snying rdzogs-chen dgongs-pa'i bcud.*
19. *sNod-ldan myong rtogs grol-ba thob 'gyur shog.*
20. *rDzogs-pa chen-po snyan-rgyud kyi rgyud dag cing sbyong-bar byed-pa sngon-'gro'i rim-pa rdzogs-so/ dge'o*

Appendix 2.3: The Commentary on the Ngondro Translation:

1. For the translation of this text, see Appendix One above. And on the contents of the *rGyal-ba phyag-khrid* and on the life of Druchen Gyalwa Yungdrung (Bru-chen rGyal-ba g.yung-drung), see Chapter 11 above.
2. On the meaning of the Primordial Buddha, see the discussion in Chapter Two above.
3. *dGongs rgyud nyams kyi man-ngag khyad-par-can.*
4. The signs of success or of realization (grub rtags) are also called the signs of heat with respect to the practice (nyams su len-pa'i drod rtags).
5. *Rig-pa gcer-bur 'byin cing snang sems ma bur sprod-pa.* And on the meeting of the Mother and the Son, see Reynolds, *The Path of the Clear Light,* forthcoming.
6. See Chapter Ten above.
7. Translations of these texts will be found in the succeeding volumes in this series.
8. *mTshan-ldan bla-ma dam-pa lta dgongs ldan la.* The Lopon cited the following verse known as "the method for relying upon the master as the support for the oral teachings of the Upadeshas" (man-ngag gi rten bla-ma bsten tshul):
e-ma byang-chub don-gnyer gang-zhig gis/
sgrub-pa'i zab lam sangs-rgyas rtsa-ba rje/
khyad gsum mtshan-nyid drug ldan bla-ma nyid/
go tshul bsam-sbyor dad-pas bsten-par bya//
And this verse translates as
"How wonderful! That someone who is the custodian of enlightenment Is the lord who is the root of Buddhahood and the profound path of practice;

The master himself should possess these three distinctions and the six essential characteristics;
As one's program and means for understanding, one should rely upon him with complete faith."
The distinctions and characteristics of an appropriate master or spiritual teacher have already been cited.

9. *Tshogs kyi 'khor-lo bskor cing gdams-pa'i dbang lung zhu/ tshogs gsangs rim-'gro'i yan-lag rgya-chen-po bya.*

10. *Phyi nang gi bar-chad zhi-ba dang/ bsam don 'grub-pa dang/ yul mchog rnams kyi skyabs 'og tu 'dus-par 'gyur.*

11. On the Guru Yoga practice in more detail, see Appendix One above.

12. The Tibetan text in transliteration is as follows:
spyi-gtsug bde-ba chen-po'i pho-brang du/
drin-can rtsa-ba'i bla-ma la gsol-ba 'debs/
sangs-rgyas sems su ston-pa rin-po-che/
rang ngo rang gis shes-par byin gyis rlobs//
The pronunciation of the verse is roughly as follows:
chyi-tsuk de-wa chen-po pho-drang du,
drin-chan tsa-we la-ma la sol-wa deb,
sang-gye sem su ton-pa rin-po-che,
rang ngo rang gi she-par jyin gyi lob.
This verse used for the concluding preliminary practice is known as "the exposition of the words for the prayer" (gsol-'debs kyi tshig-bshad). These expositions of the words (tshig-bshad) represent the actual liturgy to be recited aloud when performing the Ngondro exercises, but they were published separately and not included in the *sNgon-'gro 'bum dgu* text found in some editions of the *rGyal-ba phyag-khrid.* See the full translation of these texts in Appendix 2, section 4, below.

13. The Lopon also provided the following prayer of invocation to the master (bla-ma'i gsol-'debs) which may be used:
"Emaho! (How wonderful!)
O my benevolent master who possesses the nature of the Trikaya,
However your compassion and your blessings may be,
Please quickly bestow them upon my mind-stream!
And having pacified all hindrances outer, inner, and secret,
May I quickly come to realize my own mind as Kuntu Zangpo!
May the blessings of the master enter into my mind!
May the blessings of the master enter into my mind!
May the blessings of the master enter into my mind!"
The Tibetan text in transliteration is as follows:
e-ma-ho/ sku gsum don ldan bla-ma bka'-drin-can/
khyed kyi thugs-rje byin-rlabs ci-lta-ba/
bdag gi rgyud la myur du stsal du gsol/
phyi nang gsang-ba'i bar-chad kun zhi nas/
rang sems kun-bzang myur du grub gyur-cig/
bla-ma'i byin-rlabs sems la 'jug-par shog/

bla-ma'i byin-rlabs sems la 'jug-par shog/
bla-ma'i byin-rlabs sems la 'jug-par shog//
And the pronunciation is roughly as follows:
emaho! ku sum don dan la-ma ka-drin-chan,
khyed kyi thug-je jyin-lab chi-ta-wa,
dag gi gyud la nyur du tsal du sol!
chyi nang sang-we bar-chad kun zhi ne,
rang sem kun-zang nyur du drub gyur-chik!
la-me jyin-lab sem la jug-par shok!
la-me jyin-lab sem la jug-par shok!
la-me jyin-lab sem la jug-par shok!
And the second prayer is as follows:
"Emaho! (How wonderful!)
The blessings of the one who is known as the Teacher Kuntu Zangpo
Are the ultimate source of all the Buddhas of the three times.
I pray to the feet of my Root Guru to bestow upon me
The blessing that the primal cognition of Self-Awareness may arise within
me!"
The Tibetan text in transliteration is as follows:
e-ma-ho/ dus gsum sangs-rgyas ma lus 'byung-ba'i gnas/
byin-rlabs ston-pa kun tu bzang-po zhes/
rtsa-ba'i bla-ma'i zhabs la gsol-ba 'debs/
rang-rig ye-shes 'char-bar byin gyis rlobs//
And the pronunciation is roughly as follows:
emaho!
du sum sang-gye ma lu jyung-we ne,
byin-lab ton-pa kun tu zang-po zhe,
tsa-we la-me zhab la sol-wa deb,
rang-rig ye-she char-war byin-gyi lob.
14. The Tibetan text reads in transliteration:
dal brgyad 'byor bcu yon-tan bco-brgyad ldan/
thob dka' dpe grangs ngo-bos rab dpyad de/
da len lus rten rin-chen don yod du/
yang-dag dge-ba'i las la brtson-'grus bskyed//
The eight opportunities (dal-ba brgyad) afforded by a precious human
existence (mi lus rin-po-che) are as follows:
1) one has not been reborn among the denizens of the hells,
2) one has not been reborn among the Pretas or hungry ghosts,
3) one has not been reborn as an animal lacking articulate speech,,
4) one has not been reborn among the long-lived gods afflicted with sloth,
5) one has not been reborn among the barbarians in a border country,
6) one has not been reborn among the Tirthikas holding wrong views,
7) one has not been reborn in an age when no Buddhas have appeared,
and
8) one has not been reborn mentally deficient or with defective faculties.

Among the ten assets ('byor-ba bcu), first there are five assets due to oneself:

1. one is reborn as a human being,
2. one is reborn in a central country where the Dharma is taught,
3. one is reborn with all one's faculties intact,
4. one does not engage in extreme deeds or a lifestyle conflicitng with the Dharma, and
5. one possesses a faith in the Dharma.

Then there are five assets due to another (the Buddha and teachers):

1. a Buddha has appeared,
2. he has taught the Dharma,
3. his teaching has had a continuous existence until the present,
4. one has entered into that teaching of the Dharma, and
5. one meets with good spiritual friends who are teachers.

These eighteen are the definitive characteristics of this unique opportunity that should not be wasted.

15. *Bar-do'i snang-bar shar.* The dark retreat (mun-mtshams), which also represents a preparation for the Bardo experience after death, is one of the principal practices in this Zhang-zhung tradition of Dzogchen. A translation of the dark retreat text associated with the Zhang-zhung Nyan-gyud may be found in Reynolds, *The Seven-fold Cycle of the Clear Light* ('Od-gsal bdun skor), Bonpo Translation Project (privately printed), San Diego and Amsterdam 2001.

16. *sNang-ba thams-cad sgyu-mar 'char bden zhen gyi 'khri-ba chod.*

17. *Gang ltar btags-pa de ltar snang........ mi rtag rgyud la skyes-pas 'chi-ba dran gyur na/ ran no phyi-rabs rjes 'jug gshen-po kun.*

18. *bLa chen gyis gsungs.* Lachen (bla-chen), "the great master," refers to Dranpa Namkha (Dran-pa nam-mkha'). On him, see Note 84 in Chapter Five above.

19. *mDun gyi bar-sang/ bla-ma bder-gshegs bskyed tshim.*

20. *Tshe rabs nas tshe rabs thams-cad du sdig-pa'i las/ tshams med-pa lnga/ nye-ba bzhi/ lci-ba bzhi/ log-pa brgyad/ 'khrul-pa dgu/ mi dge-ba bcu......*

21. *Rang sems dri-ma med-pa dpang du btsug....... dge-ba'i rtsa-ba phra zhing phra-ba nas spyad-par bya.*

22. The Tibetan text in transliteration is as follows:

bdag dang 'gro-ba sems-can thams-cad kyis/
tshe-rabs thog-ma dpag tu med-pa nas/
tha-ma da-lta'i lus 'di blangs-pa yan-chad du/
sdig-pa mi dge'i las rnams ci bgyis-pa/
bder-gshegs khyed la mi 'chad mthol-lo bshags/
mi dge'i las rnams ci bgyis sgrib-pa ni/
khyed kyi thugs-rjes kun kyang byang-bar mdzad du gsol/
dge-ba kun gyi rjes su bdag yid-rangs bar bgyi'o//

The pronunciation of the text is roughly as follows:

dak dang dro-wa sem-chan than-chad kyi,

tse-rab thog-ma pak tu med-pa ne,
tha-ma dan-te lu di lang-pa yan-chad du,
dig-pa mi gei le nam chi gyi-pa,
der-shek khyed la mi chad thol-lo shak,
mi gei le nam chi gyi drib-pa ni,
khyed kyi thug-je kun kyang jyang-war dzad du sol,
ge-wa kun gyi jes-su dak yi-rang bar gyio.
See the translation of the entire text in Appendix 2, section 4, below.

23. The pronunciation of the mantra is approximately as follows: *swo mu-ra ta hen wer ni drum hrum/ mu-tre mu-tre mu-ra mu-tre/ mu-ye mu-ye ha-ra mu-ye/ mu-tro mu-tro wer-ro mu-tro/ mu ni gyer to ye chyab khar-ro/ tro dal hri hro wer ni wer-ro/ shud la wer-ro na hu ta ka/ shud-dho shud-dho du shud-dho-ya/ sa-le sa-le tri sa-le-ya/ snag-nge snag-nge su sang-ne-ya/ mu-ra ta hen tri tse drung mu ha-ha drum drum ho-ho lam lam/ hum hum phat phat! //*
Note that this hundred syllable mantra (yig brgya) is in the Zhang-zhung language, even though it includes a few Sanskrit words such as shuddho from shuddha, "pure, clear" and some Tibetan words such as *sa-le* from *sal-le-ba*, "clear" and *sang-nge* from *sang-nge-ba*, "clean". However, these may actually borrowings from Zhang-zhung into Tibetan. The meaning of some of these Zhang-zhung terms is known, for example:
dmu-ra -space, dimension (dbyings),
wer -king (rgyal-po),
wer-ro -victorious (rgyal-ba),
ha-ra -wisdom, gnosis, primordial awareness (ye-shes),
gyer -Bon, giving Tibetan *gyer-ba*, "to chant",
mu-tre -Dharmakaya (bon-sku),
mu-ye -Sambhogakaya (rdzogs-sku),
mu-spros -Nirmanakaya (sprul-sku).
As said, the seed syllable BRUM (Skt. BHRUM) evokes the celestial palace into being and the fierce mantra PHAT! expels negativities. On the Zhang-zhung language, see Erik Haarh "The Zhang-zhung Language: A Grammar and Dictionary of the Unexplored Language of the Tibetan Bonpos," in *Acta Jutlandica*, Vol. 40, no. 1, Universitetsforlaget i Aarhus, Copenhagen 1968, pp. 7-43.
Accordingly, the significance of the mantra may be roughly translated as follows:
hSwo dmu-ra ta han wer ni brum hrun: Swo! We do homage to the name of the Victorious One in the palace of the Shenrab who embodies the Trikaya!
Mu-tre mu-tre dmu-ra mu-tre: The Dharmakaya, the Dharmakaya, the Dharmakaya is the dimension of space!
Mu-ye mu-ye ha-ra mu-ye: The Sambhogakaya, the Sambhogakaya, the Sambhogakaya is the primordial awareness!
Mu-spros mu-spros we-ro mu-spros: The Nirmanakaya, the Nirmanakaya, the Nirmanakaya is victorious!

Mu ni gyer to ye khyab khar-ro: May the teacher of Bon illuminate the view of the disciples!
sPros bdal hri hro wer ni wer-ro: May the disciples attain the complete victory of knowledge!
Shud la wer-ro na hu ta ka: May we attain victory over all our sins, hindrances, and obscurations!
Shud-dho shud-dho du shud-dho-ya: Purify! Purify! May anger be purified!
Sa-le sa -le tri sa-le-ya: Clear! Clear! may attachments be cleared away!
Sang-nge sang-nge su sang-nge-ya: Cleanse! Cleanse! May confusion be cleansed!
dMu-ra ta han khri tse drung mu ha-ha brum brum ho-ho lam lam: By the power of one hundred-thousand Shenrabs, may we obtain the indestructible result of being reborn in his pure palace for the sake of benefitting beings!
Hum hum phat phat: Hum Hum! Expel! Expel!

24. On the significance of this mantra, see the section on the ritual service of mantra recitation below.
25. *sNgar byas kyi sdig sgrib thans-cad byang nas/ theg-pa chen-po'i snod du rung-par byed.*
26. *Gong ltar mdun gyi nam-mkha' la bskyed-pa'i skyabs gnas rnams kyi spyan lan du.*
27. *sNying-rje drag-po dung-dung-ba bcos ma yin-pa bskyed.*
28. The Tibetan of the text in transliteration is as follows:
    ji-ltar rgyal-ba 'phags-pa ji-bzhin du/
    'di sogs dus gsum dge-ba'i mthu dpal gyis/
    sems-can sangs-rgyas thob-par bya-ba'i phyir/
    bdag ni byang-chub mchog sems bskyed-do//
    The pronunciation of the verse is roughly as follows:
    ji-tar gyal-wa phag-pa ji-zhin du,
    di sok du sum ge-we thu pal gyi,
    sem-chan sang-gye thob-par jya-we chyir,
    dak ni jyang-chub chok sem kyed-do.
    This verse is taken from the *Tshig-bshad* text. See the translation below in Appendix 2, Section 4.
29. Nyammed Sherab Gyaltsan (mNyam-med Shes-rab rgyal-mtshan), 1356-1415, the first abbot of Tashi Menri (bKra-shis sman-ri) monastery, the successor of Yeru Wensakha (Ye-ru'i dben-sa-kha) monastery after its destruction in a disastrous flood, was one of the greatest schloars in the Bonpo tradition, comparable to Longchenpa (kLong-chen rab-'byams-pa) among the Nyingmapas, Sakya Pandita among the Sakyapas, and Tsongkhapa among the Gelugpas. The Lopon suggests the following prayer of invocation for this great Lama may be included among the Refuge formulae, or even with the Guru Yoga. This verse known as "the Prayer to the Lama who is the Lord without equal (rje mnyam-med bla-ma'i gsol-'debs)" is as follows:

bde-chen rgyal-po kun-bzang rgyal-ba 'dus/
mi brjed gzung ldan shes-rab smra-ba'i seng/
'dzam-gling bon gyi gtsug-rgyan mnyam-med-pa/
shes-rab rgyal-mtshan zhabs la gsol-ba 'debs//
"To Kuntu Zangpo, the king of great bliss, who is the embodiment of all the Victorious Ones,
To Mawe Senge, the lion of speech, whose wisdom apprehends without forgeting,
And to the Unequaled One, the head-ornament of Bon in this world,
I pray at the feet of Sherab Gyaltsan, the victory-banner of wisdom!"
In this prayer one invokes the Dharmakaya, the Sambhogakaya, and the Nirmanakaya aspects of the great Lama, whose name *mNyam-med Shes-rab rgyal-mtshan* means "the unequalled one, the victory-banner of wisdom." Mawe Sewnge (sMra-ba'i seng-ge) is the Bonpo equivalent of Manjushri, the great Bodhisattva of wisdom (shes-rab).

30. The Tibetan in transliteration is as follows:
gshen-rab bla-ma sku gsum 'byung-gnas dpal/
dus gsum bder-gshegs 'gro-ba yongs kyi mgon/
sku-gzugs zhal-skyin sku-gdungs gsung-rab brten/
phyogs bcu'i gshen-rab thar lam ston-pa'i sgron/
gnas bzhir phyag 'tshal 'gro kun skyabs su mchi//
The pronunciation of the verse is roughly as follows:
shen-rab la-ma ku sum jyung-ne pal,
du sum der-shek dro-wa yong kyi gon,
ku-zuk zhal-kyin ku-dung sung-rab ten,
chyog-chui shen-rab thar lam ton-pe dron,
ne zhir chyag-tsal dro kun kyab su chi.
This verse is found in the text of the *Tshig-bshad*. See the translation below in Appendix 2, Section 4. The Four Objects of Refuge (skyabs-yul bzhi) or Sources of Refuge (skyabs-gnas bzhi) are first the Lama or Guru (sTon-pa gShen-rab mi-bo), second the Buddhas or Sugatas (bder-gshegs) of the three times, third the Dharma or Bon as represented by images (sku-gzugs) or representations (zhal-skyin), scriptures and texts (gsung-rab) and stupas or reliquaries (sku-gdungs), which serve as the visible supports (rten) for the Body, Speech, and Mind of the Buddha respectively, and fourth the Sangha comprised of the great Bodhisattvas, here called Shenrabpas.

31. *rGyu dbyibs chags-tshad ldan-par bzo/ de la rgyan dang chas-pa grubs su bcug.* According to the text, the best materials for constructing the Mandala are gold and silver, while the next best is bell metal, *li 'khar-ba* or *li khra*, which is an alloy of gold, silver, zinc, and iron; *'khar-ba* meaning a gong made of bell metal). The inferior materials that may be employed are wood and clay.

32. *Dang-po phyi dus rang gzhan gyi bag sgrib thams-cad byang-bar bsam.*

33. In the block print edition, this mantra OM NAMA A DKAR GSHA' YA NI SHAG SA-LE SANG-NGE-YE SWAHA is lacking the syllables

GSHA' YA NI which the Lopon has added here. The pronunciation of the mantra, which like the other mantras found here is in the Zhang-zhung language, is approximately as follows: Om na-ma a-kar sha ya ni shak sa-le sang-nge-ye so-ha. The meaning of this mantra in the Zhang-zhung language is roughly as follows: "We do homage, and purifying our minds, we wipe away all our defilements, so that everything becomes clear and cleansed!"

34. The pronunciation of of the mantra BRUM RI TI GAR MA LA HO is as follows: drum ri-ti gar-ma la-ho. The significance of the mantra is "We make this celestial palace to be as great and delightful as the king of mountains itself!" The king of mountains is Sumeru at the center of the world in the ideal cosmology of the tradition.

35. The citation of this mantra in the block print edition is lacking the syllable for the Meru mountain, namely BRUM, which the Lopon adds here. In Buddhist texts this seed syllable or bija-mantra is usually spelled BHRUM, where its different components have the significance of the five primordial knowledges or cognitions (ye-shes lnga). The pronunciation of the mantra is as follows: A yam ram mam kham drum shak sa-le sang-nge so-ha. Roughly, the significance of the mantra is "The elements of space (A), air (YAM), fire (RAM), water (MAM), earth (KHAM), and the celestial palace itself (BRUM)— wiping our minds clear and clean, we destroy our obscurations!"

36. The mantra OM PHYOD PHUR SA-LE HA-LO SENG is pronounced as Om chyod phur sa-le ha-lo seng. The significance of this mantra is "And our minds become as clear and as clean as a flower!" The Mandala, the pure vision in one's mind, is compared to the flower that one offers to the enlightened ones.

37. *Man-tal ni rab nam-mkha'/ 'bring stong gsum/ tha-ma tshangs rgyud.*

38. The Tibetan text in transliteration reads:
NAMA A DKAR GSHA' YA NI SHAG SA-LE SANG-NGE-YE SWAHA/
BRUM RI TI GAR MA LA HO/
A YAM RAM MAM KHAM BRUM SHAG SA-LE SANG-NGE SWAHA/
PHYOD PHUR SA-LE HA-LO SENG/
e-ma /
'byung lnga'i steng du ri-rab ri bdun dang/
gling bzhi gling phran phyi nang 'dod-yon bcas/
nyi zlas brgyan-pa bye-ba phrag brgya 'di/
bdag gi blos blangs 'bul-lo bzhes su gsol/
OM A DA-DA DE-DE PHYOD PHUR SA-LE HA-LO SENG!
BSWO MU-YE SPROS KHYUNG YE LAM KRI KHRI TAR DAR/
gsal 'bar 'od dpag RAM SWAHA/
The pronunciation is roughly as follows:
Na-ma a kar sha ya ni shak sa-le sang-nge-ye so-ha,
drum ri ti gar ma la ho,

a yam ram mam kham drum shak sa-le sange-nge so-ha,
chyod phur sa-le ha-lo seng,
e-ma!
jyung nge teng du ri-rab ri dun dang,
ling zhi ling tran chyi nang dod-yon che,
nyi de gyan-pa jye-wa trak gya di,
dak gi lo lang bul-lo zhe su sol.
om a da-da de-de chyod phur sa-le ha-lo seng,
swo mu-ye tro khyung ye lam tri tri tar dar,
sal bar od pak ram so-ha!
The significances of the first four mantras have been given in the preceding footnotes. One should note that all of these mantras, like those in the confession formula, are presented in the Zhang-zhung language and not in the Sanskrit language of India. However, the seed syllables or bija-mantras for evoking the five elements and the celestial palace are the same as those in Sanskrit usage where this last syllable is spelled BHRUM. *E-ma* means "how wonderful!" The significance of the final mantra is "OM A DA-DA DE-DE— our minds become as clear and as clean as the flower!" In the next mantra, the sound of invocation BSWO! represents Nampar Gyalwa (rNam-par rgyal-ba) or Tonpa Shenrab, MU indicates the Dharmakaya (bon-sku), YE the Sambhogakaya, and SPROS the Nirmanakaya. The remaining syllables represent the attendant deities in the retinue. The final mantra literally states "Clear! Radiant! Light measured! RAM SWAHA!" but the significance is "May we receive the illumination of their wisdom!"

39. *gNas-lugs theg-pa chen-po'i nyams rtogs khyad-par-can rgyud la bskyed du gsol..... mchod-pa 'bul dang smon-lam gdab.*
40. *Khyad-par 'phags-pa'i sngon'gro gsum gyis rgyud dag-par bya-ba.*
41. *mDun gyi nam-mkha' la/ rtsa-ba'i bla-ma kun-bzang gshen-lha'i tshul du bzhugs-pa.*
42. *Sems-can thams-cad kyi gzugs phung gzha' 'od kyi rnam-par gyur.*
43. *bDag gi rnam-par shes-pa'i ngo-bo la phyogs mtshams steng 'og kun nas 'ub 'ub 'dus-par bsam.*
44. *Phyi snod thams-cad gzha' 'od du lhags te/ bdag gi sgyu-lus la phyogs bcu kun nas 'ub 'ub 'dus-par bsam.*
45. *bDag lus tshang rgyung gi zhing-khams grangs med-par gyur.*
46. *Sems-can thams-cad kun-bzang gi rang-bzhin du gyur.*
47. *mDzad spyod lha'i sku/ phyag-rgya chen-po la spyod-pa.*
48. *Thugs nyid spros-bral zab-mo'i dgongs-pa la dbang sgyur-ba.*
49. This mantra A A DKAR SA-LE 'OD A YAM OM 'DU is pronounced: A a-kar sa-le od a yam om du. The syllable of the first long A signifies Shenlha Odkar (gShen-lha 'od-dkar), whereas A-DKAR indicates the Dharmakaya (bon-sku). SA-LE 'OD means "the Clear Light" and A YAM mean "unborn wisdom." The syllable OM indicates the Five Bodies of the Buddha (bon-sku, rdzogs-sku, sprul-sku, ngo-bo nyid sku, mngon-par byang-chub kyi sku). The syllable 'DU indicates "so be it!"

50. In this mantra OM MA-TRI MU-YE SA-LE 'DU, each syllable corresponds to a manifestation of enlightened awareness:
OM is the Buddha Tonpa Shenrab represents skillful means and compassion;
MA is the Great Mother Sherab Jyamma (yum-chen Shes-rab byams-ma), represents wisdom and the vastness of space;
Then follow the six emanations of the Buddha, known as the Six Dulshen ('Dul gshen drug), who subdue and transform the six destinies of rebirth:
TRI is Mucho Demdruk (Mu-cho ldem-drug) transforms anger and hatred by means of total love and friendliness, thus purifying the various hell realms;
MU is Sangwa Ngangring (gSang-ba ngang-ring) transforms greed and desire by means of total generosity, thus purifying the realms of the Pretas or hungry ghosts.
YE is Tisang Rangzhi (Ti-sangs rang-zhi) transforms ignorance and confusion by means of total knowledge and wisdom, thus purifying the animal world.
SA is Drajin Pungpa (Gra-byin spung-pa) transforms envy and jealousy by means of total expansiveness, thus purifying the human world.
LE is Chegyal Parti (lCe-rgyal par-ti) transforms pride and arrogance by means of total peacefulness, thus purifying the realms of the Asuras.
'DU is Yeshen Tsugphud (Ye-gshen gtsug-phud) transforms indolence and sloth by means of total diligence and vigor, thus purifying the realms of the Devas.

51. The mantra A DKAR A RMAD DU TRI SU NAG-PO ZHI ZHI MAL MAL SWAHA is pronounced as A-kar a med du tri su nag-po zhi zhi mal mal so-ha. The significance of this mantra is roughly as follows:" May all misunderstandings be destroyed and may all negative actions of the three poisons be pacified; may the mind be peaceful in the light of wisdom!" The esoteric significance of the syllables of the mantra are explained in the Exposition of the Words (Appendix 2, Section 4) as follows:
A-DKAR means the Nature of Mind is completely pure,
A-RMAD means primordial awareness is clearly visible as light,
With DU TRI SU indicate that the evil destinies of rebirth in Samsara are purified, namely, the hells, the Preta realms, and the realms of the animals,
NAG-PO means the sins and obscurations of one's karma are purified,
ZHI ZHI indicates that the sufferings of Samsara are pacified,
MAL MAL means one comes to possess thoughts of happiness and
SWAHA indicates that one vanquishes Rudra, the demon of wrong views.

52. rJes dmigs-pas rgyas gdab cing byang-chub tu bsngo.

53. bLa-ma bder-gshegs yi-dam lha tshogs rgyal-sras sems-dpa'/ mkha'-'gro bon-skyong/ dpal-mgon sde brgyad ris drug dang bcas-pa.

54. gLo-bur du bdag gi thugs-kha'i thad-kar ye-shes kyi rang bug chen-po zhig thol gyis brdol-pa na tshur rang gi rnam-par shes-pa 'od kyi thig-ler gsal-ba.

55. *Khu-ba bdud-rtsi'i rgya-mtshor gyur-pas....... rtsigs-ma 'dod-yon sna-tshogs su gyur-bas.* In summary, the nutritious and excellent tasting nectars (dwangs-ma) are served to the enlightened beings, the juices and bodily fluids (khu-ba) are served to the Palgon (dpal-mgon) or Guardians, and the sediments and residues (rtsigs-ma) are served to the eight classes of spirits and the inhabitants of the six realms.
56. *sDe brgyad ris drug tshim.*
57. *rGyal-ba rnams mnyes/ dam-can rnams bskang/ lha srin rnams gdug sems zhi.*
58. *sGyu-lus mchod sbyin gyi tshogs su song-bar bsam.*
59. The Tibetan of these verses in transliteration is as follows:
    kye-ho/ bdag lus tshogs su 'bul-lo bzhes su gsol/
    yan-lag gzugs bzhi brtan brjid sgyed-pur btsugs/
    thod-pa rin-chen yangs-pa'i bzed-zhal du/
    sha khrag drod dbugs lpags tshil chu rgyus rkang/
    khams dang skye-mched rtsa dang yan-lag bcas/
    dbang-po dbang rten nang-khrol don snod dang/
    keng-rus so sen skra dang ba-spu'i tshogs/
    dwangs snyigs khu-ba (stong) gsum du rab spel nas/
    zag-bcas dman-pa'i lus 'di yon du 'bul/
    khyed kyi lta gdongs nyams rtogs khyad-par-can/
    da-lta nyid du bdag la stsal du gsol/
    bu-lon lan-chags ma lus 'dis byang nas/
    gnod byed kun kyang byang-sems mchog thob shog/
    dmigs-med rgya-cher bsngos-pa'i bsod-nams kyis/
    'gro rnams bdag ltas bcings-pa grol gyur-cig//
    The pronunciation of the text is roughly as follows:
    kye-ho!
    dak lu tsok su bul-lo zhe su sol,
    yan-lak zuk zhi tan jid gyed-pur tsuk,
    thod-pa rin-chen yang-pe zed-zhal du,
    sha trak drod uk pak tsil chu gyu kang,
    kham dang kye-ched tsa dang yan-lak che,
    wang-po wang ten nang-trol don nod dang,
    keng-ru so sen tra dang ba-pu tsok,
    dang nyik khu-wa sum du rab pel ne,
    zak-che man-pe lu di yon du bul,
    khyed kyi ta gong nyam tok khyad-par-chan,
    dan-ta nyid du dak la tsal du sol,
    bu-lon lan-chak ma lu di jyang ne,
    nod-jyed kun kyang jyang-sem chok thob shok,
    mik-med gya-cher ngo-we sod-nam kyi,
    dro nam dak te ching-pa drol gyur-chik.
    For a somewhat longer version of the liturgy for the Chod practice, see the translation of the Exposition of the Words in Appendix 2, Section 4.

60. See Appendix One above.
61. The Tibetan text may be transliterated as follows:
    spyi-gtsug bde-ba chen-po'i pho-brang du/
    drin-can rtsa-ba'i bla-ma la gsol-ba 'debs/
    sangs-rgyas sems su ston-pa rin-po-che/
    rang ngo rang gis shes-par byin gyis rlobs//
    Whereas the pronunciation is as follows:
    chyi-tsuk de-wa chen-po pho-drang du,
    drin-chan tsa-we la-ma la sol-wa deb,
    sang-gye sem su ton-pa rin-po-che,
    rang ngo rang gi she-par jyin gyi lob.
    For the recitation and the extensive lineage prayer, see Appendix 2, Section 4, below.
62. *'Al 'ol sab sob ma yin-pa.*
63. See Appendix One above.
64. In the text, only the purification by means of the wisdom waters emanating from the heart center of the Guru is indicated. At other times, the Lopon has taught the employing of the three elements for purification, namely, the wisdom fires, the wisdom winds, and the wisdom waters. See the section on the practice of the Guru Yoga above in Appendix One.
65. *dBang bskur byin gyis brlabs-pas/ de dag gi mkhyen-pa mdzad spyod nyams myong lta dgongs kyi yon-tan ci yod-pa thams-cad thob-par bsam......... rig-pa ngar bskyed/ mos-gus dung-dung-ba byas la gsol-ba gdab.*
66. *Bon spyod dgu rim thun-mong spyi dril tu nyams su len-pa........ lus gnad legs-par bcas te........ mi rtag-pa drag-po yang yang du sgom.*
67. *sDig-pa bshags-pa dang/ sems bskyed-pa skyabs 'gro/ man-tal/ bzlas brjod/ tshogs bsgyur/ gsol-'debs.*
68. The Tibetan may be transliterated as follows:
    sgo gsum dag-pa'i dge-ba gang bgyis-pa/
    khams gsum sems-can rnams kyi don du bsngo/
    dus gsum bsags-pa'i las sgrib kun byang nas/
    sku gsum rdzogs-pa'i sangs-rgyas myur thob shog//
    The pronunciation of the verse is as follows:
    go sum dag-pe ge-wa gang gyi-pa,
    kham sum sem-chan nam kyi don du ngo,
    du sum sag-pe le drib kun jyang ne,
    ku sum dzog-pe sang-gye nyur thob shok.
69. *Nyams su blangs-pa'i drod rtags......... dngos sam nyams snang rmi-lam la 'char........ yi-dam zhal mthong.*
70. *Rab 'bring tha-ma'i rtags te........ yid-ches ma skyes bar la gnad du bsnun-par bya.*
71. *g.Yung-drung sa la bsngo.*

Appendix 2.4: The Exposition of the Words

1. *Kun tu bzang-po bdag gzhan don gnyis la phyag-'tshal-lo.*
2. The Jinas or Victorious Ones (rgyal-ba) and the Exalted Ones or Aryas ('phags-pa) indicate the Buddhas and the great Bodhisattvas respectively.
3. The Shenrabpas (gshen-rab-pa) refer to the great Bodhisattvas that constitute the Arya Sangha or exalted community of practitioners of the Dharma.
4. On the use and meaning of these mantras employed for constructing and offering the mandala, see "The Practice of Offering the Mandala" in Appendix 2, Section 3 above.
5. The eight auspicious substances (rdzas brgyad) or rather emblems (bkra-shis rtags brgyad) are the wheel ('khor-lo), the conch shell (dung), the parasol (gdugs), the victory banner (rgyal-mtshan), golden fish (gser nya), the auspicious knot (dpal gyi be'u), the lotus (padma), and the vase (bum-pa). The seven precious jewels of royalty (rin-chen sna bdun) are the wheel ('khor-lo), the jewel (nor-bu), the elephant (glang-po-che), the thoroughbred horse (rta mchog), the queen (btsun-mo), the minister (blon-po), and the general (dmag-dpon).
6. The Jinaputras or spiritual sons of the Buddha (rgyal-sras) refer to the great Bodhisattvas, both male and female.
7. Note that a variant of this mantra is given in the Ngondro explanation given by the Lopon. See "The Practice of the Mantra Recitation" in Appendix 2, Section 3, above.
8. *bZlas lung 'phro 'du bya.* One should practice the emanating and reabsorbing ('phro 'du bya) the rays of light from the visualization and recite the Agama explaining the recitation (bzlas lung) of the mantra for purification. This Agama (lung) gives the esoteric meaning for the syllables in the mantra. In the Lopon's oral explanation, he suggested the reciting of three different mantras, but the text gives only this one mantra for purification. Note that the purification process is effected by way of the three elements: the wisdom fires, the wisdom winds, and the wisdom waters.
9. The practice of offering one's physical body (lus sbyin) is also known as Chod (gcod) the severing or cutting off of the ego or sense of self. On this, see "The Practice of Offering One's Body" in Appendix 2, Section 3, above.
10. The masters who became manifest as the Trikaya (sku gsum mngon du gyur-ba'i bla-ma) are the nine enlightened beings or Buddhas who represent the Direct Mind-to-Mind Transmission of the Victorious Ones (rgyal-ba dgongs rgyud dgu) or the nine-fold Mind-to-Mind Transmission of the Sugatas (bder-gshegs dgongs brgyud dgu). Both Jina (rgyal-ba) and Sugata (bder-gshegs) are synonyms for Buddha (sangs-rgyas). On this nine-fold Direct Mind Transmission, see Chapter Three above.
11. *Ma rtogs 'khor-ba'i gzung 'dzin grol nas kyang/ rang rig ye-shes 'char-bar byin gyis rlobs.*

12. Now we come to the Oral Transmission of the Siddhas (grub-thob snyan khung gi brgyud-pa) consisting of the Twenty- Four August Persons (gang-zag nyer-bzhi) or masters all of whom attained the Rainbow Body ('ja'-lus). These twenty-four are divided into four groups, the first being termed in the hagiography text translated above the Symbolic Transmission of the Bodhisattvas (sems-dpa' brda'i brgyud-pa). In the Lineage Prayer here, the masters who have totally transcended conceptions of the Natural State (gnas-lugs la chen bzla-ba'i bla-ma) are also known as the five Shenpos who subdued (and disciplined) all living beings ('gro 'dul gshen-po lnga). On the Oral Transmission of the Siddhas (grub-thob snyan-rgyud), see Chapter Four above.

13. In the hagiography text, the second group of Siddhas is termed the Awareness Transmission of the Vidyadharas (rig-'dzin rig-pa'i brgyud-pa), whereas in the present Lineage Prayer, the masters who penetrate directly into the essential points of the six meanings (don drug gnad du bsnan-pa'i bla-ma) are also called the six Bodhisattvas who are without equal (mnyam-med sems-dpa' drug). The six meanings (don drug) are those of the view (lta-ba), the meditation (bsgom-pa), the conduct (spyod-pa), the activity (phrin-las), the commitment (dam-tshig), and the attainment (dngos-grub).

14. In the hagiography text, the third group of Siddahs is termed the Oral Transmission of the August Persons (gang-zag snyan khungs kyi brgyud-pa), whereas in the present text the masters who teach abundantly the nine instructions (gdams dgu lhug-par ston-pa'i bla-ma) and also called the nine Siddhas who are Vidyadharas (grub-thob rig-'dzin dgu).

15. In the hagiography text, the four group of Siddhas among the twenty-four is termed the Transmission of the Learned Scholars and Translators (mkhas-pa lo-pan gyi brgyud-pa), whereas in the present text, the masters who were the four head-ornaments of the Upadeshas (man-ngag dbu-rgyan bzhi yi bla-ma) are also called the four Mahasiddas who were translators and scholars (lo-pan grub-chen bzhi). This concludes the lineage of the twenty-four masters who preceded Tapihritsa.

16. In the present text, Tapihritsa and Gyerpungpa are referred to as the masters who were the sources of the oral instructions and the precepts (gdams-ngag bka' yi byung-gnas bla-ma), but they are also called the two benevolent Nirmanakayas (sprul-sku drin-can gnyis), just as they are in the hagiography text. See Chapter Five above.

17. In the hagiography text, this group of is known as the six Mahasiddhas of Zhang-zhung Mar (zhang-zhung smar gyi grub-chen drug), whereas in the present text, the masters who possess the signs of realization (grub-pa rtags dang ldan-pa'i bla-ma) are also called the six (masters) who are holy and worthy (las-can dam-pa drug). See Chapter Eight above.

18. In the hagiography text, this group is known as the six masters of the Upper System, whereas in the present text, the masters who possessed experiences in meditation (bsgom-pa nyams dang ldan-pa'i bla-ma) are

also called the six Ascetics possessing understanding (rtogs-ldan 'khrul-zhig drug). This group represents the Precepts Transmission Lineage (bka' brgyud). See Chapter Eight above.

19. In the hagiography text, this group is known as the five masters of the Lower Transmission (smad lugs kyi bla-ma), whereas in the present text, the masters who possessed virtuous qualities without partialities (yon-tan phyog-med mnga'-ba'i bla-ma) are also simply called five Mahasiddhas (grub-chen lnga). They represent the Experiential Transmission (nyams brgyud). See Chapter Eight above.

20. In the hagiography text, this group is termed the masters of the Northern Lineage of Transmission (byang brgyud kyi bla-ma), whereas in the present text the masters who possessed the sources of the oral transmission (snyan-brgyud khungs dang ldan-pa'i bla-ma) are also called the nine Gurus who possess the source (khungs ldan bla-ma dgu). See Chapter Nine above.

21. Grouped together here as one are the two brothers (mched gnyis) Jyatang Tsultrim Zangpo (Bya-btang tshul-khrims bzang-po) and Sale-od Tsultrim Gyaltsan (Sa-le-'od tshul-khrims rgyal-mtshan). See Chapter Nine above.

22. The masters who taught the Mantras and the Mind of the Oral Transmissions (snyan-brgyud sngags sems ston-pa'i bla-ma) are also called the five Gurus of the Mantras and the Mind (sngags sems bla-ma lnga). The Mantras (sngags) refer to the teachings of Tantra and the Mind (sems) refers to the Dzogchen teachings.

23. In the hagiography text, this group is known as the masters of the Southern Lineage of Transmission (lho brgyud kyi bla-ma), whereas in the present text the masters who accomplished the benefit of living beings without any partialities ('gro don phyogs-med mdzad-pa'i bla-ma) are also called the nine Vidyadharas of the Precepts Transmission (bka' brgyud rig-'dzin dgu).

24. Druchen Gyalwa Yungdrung, one of the Abbots of Yeru Wensakha monastery was the author of the practice manual for the Zhang-zhung Nyan-gyud entitled the *rGyal-ba phyag-khrid*. See Chapter Eleven above.

25. The masters who liberated into the Primordial State that is like space (dgongs-pa mkha' ltar grol-ba bla-ma) are also called the eight (masters) who are the sovereigns of the profound path (zab lam mnga'-bdag brgyad).

26. The masters who have love in their hearts and benefit others (gzhan don thugs brtse ldan-pa'i bla-ma) are also called the two protectors of living beings ('gro-ba'i mgon-po gnyis).

27. The masters who hold the transmissions of the Precepts and the Upadeshas (man-ngag bka' brgyud 'dzin-pa'i bla-ma) are also called the three Gurus possessing the Lineages of Transmission (brgyud ldan bla-ma gsum).

28. The masters who demonstrated manifestly the profound meaning (zab don mngon du ston-pa'i bla-ma) are also called the eight who are the unequalled life-force of the teachings (mtshungs-med bstan srog brgyad).

29. Rinchen Lodro was the last Abbot of the old Yeru Wensakha monastery before it was destroyed in a disastrous flood in 1386. Nyammed Sherab Gyaltsan (mNyam-med shes-rab rgyal-mtshan, 1356-1415) rebuilt the monastery on higher ground, inaugurating it in 1405 and naming the new establishment Tashi Menri (bkra-shis sman-ri). He became its first Abbot or Menri Trizin (sman-ri khri-'dzin), the throne-holder of Menri. There now follows the list of the thirty-three successive Abbots of Menri.

30. The masters who hold the teachings of the Three Trainings (bslab gsum bstan-pa 'dzin-pa'i bla-ma) are also called the seven who are the Lords of the Three Trainings (bslab gsun dbang-phyug bdun). The three monastic trainings (bslab-pa gsum) are those in morality, meditation, and wisdom.

31. The masters who hold the Treasury of the Nine Vehicles (theg dgu bang-mdzod 'dzin-pa'i bla-ma) are also called the eight (masters) who possessed confidence without equal (mnyam-med gdeng ldan brgyad).

32. The masters who exhibited nakedly the Natural State (gnas-lugs rjen-par ston-pa'i bla-ma) are also called seven who liberated everything without partialities (phyogs-med kun grol bdun).

33. Nyima Tenzin was the author of the famous *bsTan-rtsis* or chronology of Bonpo history. See Per Kvaerne, "A Chronological Table of the Bon-po: The bsTan rcis of Nyi-ma bstan-'jin," in *Acta Orientalia*, vol. 33, Copenhagen 1971, pp. 205-282. His friend and colleague Dawa Gyaltsan (Zla-ba rgyal-mtshan) founded Yungdrungling monastery in 1834, which soon became the second most famous Bonpo monastery in Central Tibet.

34) The masters who had pride in their realization of the Secrets and the Mind (gsang sems grub-pa'i snyems-pa'i bla-ma) are also called the four supreme individuals who are most worthy (las-can skyes-mchog bzhi). The Secrets (gsang) refer to Tantra and the Mind (sems) refers to Dzogchen.

35. Sherab Lodro, the last Abbot to reside at Menri in Tibet, died in exile in India in 1963. Jongdong Sangye Tenzin (lJong-ldong Sangs-rgyas bstan-'dzin, 1928-1977), a former Lopon or professor at Menri, was chosen by lot in 1969 to become the thirty-third Abbot of Menri, now re-established at Dolanji in India. After the latter's death in 1977, he was succeeded by H.H. Lungtog Tenpai Nyima (Lung-rtogs bstan-pa'i nyi-ma) as the thirty-fourth holder of the throne of Menri, who has been recognized by the Tibetan Government in Dharamsala as the Head of the Bonpo School.. See Appendix Four below.

36. The masters for whom there arise in their mind-streams a sure and certain knowledge (nges-shes rgyud la 'char-ba'i bla-ma) are the Mother, the Son, and the Energy (ma bu rtsal gsum), otherwise known as Kunzhi or the state of Shunyata, Rigpa or intrinsic awareness, and Tsel or the inherent energy of the Nature of Mind. On these three and their interrelations, see Reynolds, *Space, Awareness, and Energy*, Parts One and Two, Snow Lion, forthcoming.

37. Druchen Gyalwa Yungdrung composed this lineage prayer only up to his own master Chigchod Dadshe. The invocations for the remaining masters were added by later authors, probably at Menri monastery.

Appendix Three: The Invocations of Nyipangse and Menmo

1. On the guardian deities of Tibet, the Dharmapalas, in general, see Rene de Nebesky-Wojkowitz, *Oracles and Demons of Tibet: The Cult and Iconography of the Tibetan Protective Deities*, Mouton, The Hague 1956.
2. In which case *Srid-pa'i rgyal-mo* is known as *Srid-rgyal dre'u-nag* and *Srid-rgyal dre'u-dmar* respectively. On this guardian goddess, see Per Kvaerne, *The Bon Religion of Tibet: The Iconography of a Living Tradition*, Serindia Publications, London 1995. See also my privately printed monograph, John Myrdhin Reynolds, *The Healing Practice for Sidpa Gyalmo from the Bonpo Terma Tradition*, Bonpo Translation Project (privately printed), San Diego 1996.
3. On the conflict between indigenous shamanism and Buddhism in Nepal over this question of blood sacrifice, the killing of living beings as offerings to the gods and spirits, see Stan Royal Mumford, *Himalayan Dialogue: Tibetan Lamas and Gurung Shamans in Nepal*, University of Wisconsin Press, Madison 1989. And on this issue in relationship to Mongolia, see Walther Heissig, *The Religions of Mongolia*, University of California Press, Berkeley CA 1980.

    The ancient Greeks called the lower spirits who inhabit the atmosphere *daimones*, which is the origin of the English word "demon", meaning nowadays an exclusively evil spirit. But in the original Greek usage of the term, these *daimones* or spirits were not necessarily evil, but could be good spirits (agathodaimon) or evil spirits (kakodaimon). These spirits of the atmosphere, near to the earth and to humanity, were contrasted with the higher gods or *theoi*, more distant and remote, dwelling in the heavens. However, in the ancient Greek religion, both among the peasants in the country side, as well as among the populations of the towns and the city states themeselves, the *theoi* and the *daimones* were both propitiated with blood sacrifices. This was also true of the Celtic, Germanic, and Slavic peoples of old Europe. On this aspect of ancient Greek folk religion, see Jane Harrison, *Prolegomena to the Study of the Greek Religion*, Meridian Books, New York 1955. The Christian Church, in its turn, set all these hosts of *daimones* or pagan spirits into opposition to their own angels (angeloi) that were thought of as messengers from the great Creator God above, and strove to reduce and "demonize" these nature spirits in the historical process of the Church's supplanting innumerable pagan cults. One finds the expression of this attitude, for example, in St. Augustine's *De Civitate Dei*, "On the City of God".
4. Oral communication from Lopon Tenzin Namdak. Also see Tarthang Tulku, *Ancient Tibet*, Dharma Publishing, Berkeley 1986.

5. Furthermore, Tonpa Shenrab first fulfilled the same role that was later undertaken by Zarathrushtra (Zoroaster) in Iranian Central Asia, by Shakyamuni Buddha in India, and by Jesus Christ in the West, in terms of guiding humanity to a higher morality and a higher spiritual religion that went beyond the mere propitiation of the lower spirits with blood sacrifices in order to secure worldly benefits. The teachings and work of these spiritual masters of the higher ethical religions or Dharma all led to an abandoning of blood sacrifice as the principal religious rite observed by both individuals and tribal communities. And this was accompanied by a corresponding shift from a concern with the collective and its relationship to the Otherworld of the spirits to a concern with the salvation of the individual soul. There existed this same spiritual thrust in Zoroastrianism, later Judaism, Buddhism, Jainism, later Hinduism, Islam, and Christianity, where individual ethical responsibility came to take precedence over the collective.

6. For the discussion in terms of cultural anthropology, see Mumford, *Himalayan Dialogue*, op. cit.

7. See the account summarized from the *gZer-myig* in Hoffmann, *The Religions of Tibet*, ibid., pp. 90-92.

8. The Lopon refers to the reign of the non-human spirits (mi ma yin) over human beings and the introduction of meat eating among humans in his *g.Yung-drung bon gyi bstan-pa'i 'byung khungs nyung bsdus*, Kalimpong 1962. But see also Tarthang Tulku, *Ancient Tibet*, op. cit., pp. 107-111.

9. The Dralha (dgra-lha, var. sgra-bla) are an important class of warrior gods, and nowadays they are often associated with the cult of the epic hero Gesar. On the Dralha in general, see Rene de Nebesky-Wojkowitz, *Demons and Oracles of Tibet*, op. cit., pp. 318-339. On the Dralha in their Bonpo context, see Snellgrove, *The Nine Ways of Bon*, ibid. pp. 42-97.

10. On the old Bonpo cosmology, see Samten G. Karmay, "A General Introduction to the History and Doctrines of Bon," ibid.

11. See the account from the *gZer-myig* summerized in Hoffmann, *The Religions of Tibet*, ibid.

12. For the story of the conversion of Nyipangse, see below.

13. See Erik Haarh, "The Zhang-zhung Language: A Grammar and Dictionary of the Unexplored Language of the Tibetan Bonpos," in *Acta Jutlandica*, Vol. 40, no. 1, Universitetsforlaget i Aarhus, Copenhagen 1968, pp. 7-43.

14. *mNyam-med Shes-rab rgyal-mtshan*, 1356-1415, founded *bKra-shis sman-ri* monastery in 1405 where, according to the colophon to the text of this Rite of Invocation (bka' bsgo), he composed this short liturgy. See the translation below. The Lopon agrees with this identification of Nyipangse with Tshangs-pa dkar-po.

15. On Tshangs-pa dkar-po, see Nebesky-Wojkowitz, *Demons and Oracles of Tibet*, ibid., pp. 145-153, and also Ladrang Kalsang, *The Guardian Deities of Tibet*, Little Lhasa Publications, Dharamsala 1996, pp. 86-90.

16. The title srog-bdag means the owner (bdag-po) of the life-force (srog). Labrang Kalsang in his book *The Guardian Deities of Tibet*, op. cit., recounts three stories of the origin of Tsangpa Karpo, pp. 86-90. In them, the deity is variously subdued by Vajrapani, Hayagriva, and Ekajati. In one of these stories an account is given of how the deity acquired the name of *Tshangs-pa dung gi thor-tshugs-can*. According to the text of the *Srog-bdag gser gyi ga-phur*, long ago the deity *rGyal-po bde-ba* and his wife *bDe-ba'i glog phreng-ma* had a son, who soon grew up to be very intelligent, possessing many manly attributes, and accomplished in all fields of learning, especially the Vedas and the Brahmanical sciences. Because he became swollen with pride, he later went to the summit of the Himalaya mountains and challenged the Bodhisattva Vajrapani to a contest of their magical powers. But no matter what he did, he was not able to vanquish the mighty Vajrapani. In despair he asked why his Brahmanic powers could not prevail against the Bodhisattva and proved so useless. Vajrapani explained that he himself is an enlightened being who, as a Bodhisattva, remains engaged in the world in order to help lead sentient beings to liberation and enlightenment. Much astonished, the Brahman youth inquired how he could acquire this Bodhichitta, the enlightened mind of the Bodhisattva. Whereupon Vajrapani gave him instructions in the Bodhichitta and conferred upon him the name of *Tshangs-pa dung gi thor-tshugs-can*, prophesying that he also would become an enlightened Bodhisattva. As a sign of this, Vajrapani crowned him with a tiara made of a precious conch shell lined with pearls and gold. He told him never to take this headdress off and gave him further instructions in the Dharma. Since that time, this deity also became known by the name of *Li-byin ha-ra*. As the result of his initiation by Vajrapani, his magical powers and capacities multiplied ten fold.

17. *Tshangs-pa dkar-po dung gi thor-tshug-can* represents the peaceful form of Tsangpa (tshangs-pa zhi-ba), while as *bSe'i khrab-can*, "the one wearing a cuirass of leather (bse-khrab)," he represents the fierce aspect of the deity (tshangs-pa drag-po). He is called a Yaksha (gnod-byin) and the great wild *bTsan rgod-po*. Being red in color and attired in armor, his manifestation is that of a *bTsan* spirit.

18. When he founded Menri, *mNyam-med Shes-rab rgyal-mtshan*, invited six deities to be the six patron guardian deities of his new monastery, these being

1) *Srid-pa'i rgyal-mo* in her four-armed black form riding on a black mule (Srid-rgyal dre'u nag);

2) *Yum-sid* (yum srid), a guardian from the Bonpo Terma tradition;

3) *sGra-bla-ma*, the goddess consort of dBal-chen Ge-khod, the patron deity of Mount Kailas, where her presence is symbolized by a lesser mountain;

4) *Mi-bdud 'byams-pa*, a wrathful spirit who belongs to the retinue of great Tantric deity dBal-gsas who first subdued him; he was later subdued by Sherab Gyaltsan;

5) *bTsan Hur-pa*, a powerful spirit of the bTsan class;

6) *rGyal-po bSe'i khrab-can.*
   It is said that when the latter was in India, he was a guardian at the great
   monastic university of Nalanda. Later he came to Tibet and was installed
   as a guardian at *bSam-yas* monastery. He was later subdued by *g.Yung-
   drung bla-ma* who founded *g.Yas-ru dben-sa-kha* monastery. This
   establishment was later destroyed in a flood and succeeded by *bKra-shis
   sman-ri* monastery. Oral comminication from Lopon Tenzin Namdak.

19. The Ging or Ging-chen are a kind of spirit. More commonly he is called
    Lha-chen Tsang-pa dkar-po. This clearly indicates that, in general, he is
    not ranked as a *rGyal-po* spirit, but as a Lha.

20. Also on Tshangs-pa dkar-po, see Ladrang Kalsang, *The Guardian Deities
    of Tibet*, ibid., pp. 86-89.

21. *dPal rta-mchog rol-pa'i gsung.*

22. The *Khra-'brug lha-khang* temple in the Yarlung valley, the home country
    of the kings of Tibet. According to Hugh Richardson, who visited the
    area, this temple is the largest and most important of the royal foundations
    in the Yarlung region. He and Snellgrove accept the traditional ascription
    of the erection of this temple to *Srong-btsan sgam-po*, even though on the
    verandah of the temple there is found a bell bearing an inscription with
    the name of king *Khri-srong lde'u-brtsan.* On these old Buddhist temples
    in Yarlung and Lhasa, see Snellgrove and Richarson, *A Cultural History
    of Tibet*, ibid., pp. 73-74.

23. And so, it is said, the successive kings of Tibet also relied upon him as a
    protective deity.

24. *Khrag 'thung rol-pa'i dkyil-'khor.* Padmasambhava incorporated a
    number of the indigenous pagan deities of Tibet into the retinues of
    attendent deities now found in the mandalas of the *bKa'-brgyad*, the
    Tantric practices of the Eight Herukas.

25. *rNam-dag khrims khang gling.* The *sBa-bzhed*, the early historical records
    of the sBa clan, is an invaluable source on the time of the Tibetan
    monarchy.

26. The great Fifth Dalai Lama, *Ngag-dbang blo-bzang rgya-mtsho*, b. 1617,
    became the spiritual and temporal ruler of Tibet in 1642 when Gushri
    Khan, his patron and chief of the Qoshot Mongols, defeated in battle
    Karma bstan-skyong who had reigned as the last native king of Tibet
    (1623-1642). This king was overthrown by the Mongols at the instigation
    of the Fifth Dalai Lama because, being allied with the Karma Kagyudpa
    sect, he had begun persecuting the growing Gelugpa sect in the Lhasa
    region. Thereupon Gushri Khan recognized the Dalai Lama as the ruler of
    Tibet and the latter set up his Gandan Phodrang goverment, making
    Tsangpa Karpo one of its chief protective deities. This governement
    continued to rule Tibet until Tibetan independence was finally
    extinguished by the Chinese Communists in 1959, whereupon the
    Fourteenth Dalai Lama, together with his government, was forced to flee
    into exile in India.

27. The oracle (lha-pa, srung-ma) functions as a medium or mouth-piece for a spirit that takes possession of that individual and utters prophecies and advice through him or her. At La-mo monastery near the village of *La-mo lcog* resides the *La-mo byang-chub lcog gi chos-skyong* oracle through whom *Tshangs-pa dkar-po* speaks. The oracle at *gNas-chung* monastery is, however, the one most closely connected with the Tibetan Government. It is through this oracle that the guardian deity Pehar usually speaks

28. See Nebesky-Wojkowitz, *Demons and Oracles of Tibet*, ibid., 153.

29. On the question of Pehar in general, see Nebesky-Wojkowitz, *Demons and Oracles of Tibet*, ibid. pp. 94-133. And on *Tshangs-pa*, see Nebesky-Wojkowitz, ibid., pp. 145-153.

30. *Bi-har rgyal-po* would be in Sanskrit vihara-raja, where vihara means monastery and raja (rgyal-po) means king, here indicating the chief protective deity of the monastery or temple. On the other hand, some scholars have speculated that the name could come from Middle Persian *patkar* or Avestan *paitikara*, both meaning "war."

31. Zahor or Zahora was a famous Buddhist district in Northern India, now identified by the Tibetans with Mandi in Himachal Pradesh and with the nearby lake of Riwalsar or Tso Pema. The whole area is closely associated with the activities of Padmasambhava and his consort, the princess Mandarava.

32. Pehar resided at the meditation school (sgom grwa) at temple of Bhata Hor which lay in the country of the Uighur Turks (Yu-gur) in Central Asia to the north of Tibet. To the Tibetans, the Uighurs were also known as Hor, a term later applied to the non-Turkic Mongols. At Bhata Hor the deity was also known as *Pho-lha gnam-theb dkar-po*, "the ancestral male god of the white clouded sky" and as *gNam-lha dkar-po*, "the white sky god." This indicates his celestial nature.

33. *Pe-har* is sometimes spelled in the texts as *Pe-dkar*, where the syllable *dkar* is interpreted as *dkar-po*, "white."

34. On the name *Tshangs-pa dung gi thor-tshugs-can,* see above. Apparently, in this account Pehar is being assimilated to Indra, the king of the Trayatrimsha Devas who dwell on the summit of the cosmic mountain Meru. Therefore, this deity is being identified with both Brahma (Tshangs-pa) and Indra Shatakratu (brGya-sbyin) as the king of heaven. This suggests an interesting correspondence between the cult of Pehar and that of the old Hebrew mountain god and sky deity Yahweh. This was first pointed out to me by Philip Hemley in an oral communication.

35. His parents were *gNam gyi dkar-po*, "the white one of heaven," and *Shugs-ldan rgyal-mo*, "the powerful queen." His name *brGya-byin dkar-po*, "the white Shatakratu," refers to his assuming the office of Indra Shatakatu, the king of the gods on the summit of the Meru mountain. He was known as *gNam-lha dkar-po*, "the white god of the sky," among the Uighurs (Hor) and as *Srog-bdag dkar-po*, "the white owner of the life-force," at Bhata Hor. These are also all epithets of Nyipangse as well.

36. *kLu'i rgyal-po Zur-phud lnga-pa.* This Nagaraja is sometimes identified with the mountain god gNyan-chen thang-lha. This account is found in Giuseppe Tucci, *Tibetan Painted Scrolls,* vol II, IsMEO, Rome 1949, p. 735, 745, n. 62.

37. *rGyal-po,* literally "king," is a type of restless spirit, usually of a deceased warrior or of a monk who has died a violent death. Therefore, the Gyalpos are exceedingly temperamental and dangerous.

38. *Srid-pa'i pho rigs thams-cad dbang du bsdus.*

39. *dBang chen gyi rgyal-po nyi-pang-sad kyis srog snying phul.*

40. The five principal meditation deities (yi-dam lha) of the Father Tantras (Pha rgyud) are also known as the Five Supreme Ones of the Divine Citadel (gsas-mkhar mchog lnga). They are as follows:
    1) *dBal-gsas* who represents the Body Aspect (sku),
    2) *Lha-rgod* who represents the Speech Aspect (gsung).
    3) *gTso-mchog* who represents the Mind aspect (thugs),
    4) *dBal-chen Ge-khod* who represents the Quality Aspect (yon-tan), and
    5) *Phur-pa* who represents the Activity Aspect (phrin-las).

41. This event occurred with *Lhun-grub mu-thur* in the 10th century, the first native Tibetan in the lineage, who was also a great Tantrika and practitioner of the Secret Mantras. See Chapter Five in Part One above.

42. Nebesky-Wojkowitz, *Demons and Oracles of Tibet,* ibid., p. 147.

43. Also on the iconography of Nyipangse, see Per Kvaerne, *The Bon Religion on Tibet,* ibid. pp. 109-111. Here he also provides a translation of the invocation of Nyipangse which will be found below.

44. The order of progression here is according to the Bonpo style (bon skor), that is, counter-clockwise:
    1) in Zhang-zhung at the center, he is *Shel 'gying dkar-po nyi-pang-sad,* "the mighty white crystal sun god,"
    2) in Phrom in the north, he is *Srog-bdag srid-pa rgyal-po,* "the owner of the life force, the king of existence,"
    3) in Tazik in the west, he is *Shel 'gying dkar-po,* "the mighty white crystal,"
    4) in India in the south, he is *Tshangs-pa dung gi thor-tshug-can,* "the Brahma having a white conch shell in his plaited hair,"
    5) in China in the east, he is *rGyal-po Zla-pang-sad,* "the king, the moon god," and
    6) in Tibet also in the center, he is *sKya-hrang chen-po,* "the great sKya-hrang."
    Tazik is in the west, India is in the south, China is in the east, and both Zhang-zhung and Tibet are in the central region of the Himalayas. Tazik was the ancient name for the Iranian speaking part of Central Asia to the northwest of Tibet. The term survives in the modern name of the country of Tajikistan. The name Trom (phrom, khrom) appears to come from Middle Iranian *Phrom,* the Turkish *Rum,* the name for the Roman empire in the west, especially in its Byzantine form. In the Gesar Epic, *Phrom* is the home of the hero Gesar whose name may derive from Kaisar or

Caesar. But in the epic itself, which dates from a later period, Phrom came to be located to the northeast of Tibet. Even today, the royal family of Ling in Kham claims descent from Gesar. Pu (spu) is an ancient name for a portion of Central Tibet or its ruling dynasty.

45. The five classes of great kings (rgyal-po chen-po sde lnga) include various magical apparitions of Nyipangse (rdzu-'phrul sna-tshogs), such as Nyipangse and Dapangse (nyi-pang-sad dang zla-pang-sad), Zhapangse and Werro Gyalpo (gzha'-pang-sad dang wer-ro rgyal-po), Namkha Gyalpo, Yacho Gyalpo, and Gyalpo Chenpo Tsugphudchan (nam-mkha' rgyal-po yo-co rgyal-po/ rgyal-po chen-po gtsug-phud-can), together with the retinues of Gyachen Nyipangse (rgya-chen nyi-pang-sad 'khor bcas).

46. The races of the female spirits of existence whom he gathered under his power (srid-pa mo rigs thams-cad dbang du bsdus) refer to all the feminine energies of nature, those energies which manifest to humanity in female forms. *sMan-mo* is a general archaic term for a goddess. *sMan-mo Ku-ma-ra-dza* offered the prana of her heart (snying srog) as a token of her submission to Gyerpungpa. Thereby the Mahasiddha came to hold power (dbang du bsdus) over the goddess and her retinues of goddesses.

47. *sMan-mo Ku-ma-ra-dza*, var. *Ku-ma*, is identified as the sky goddess (gnam sman). The name Ku-ma-ra-dza is probably from Sanskrit Kumanaraja, or more properly Kumari-rajni, "the maiden queen." According to the Lopon, *sMan-mo* is an emanation of the great sky goddess gNam-phyi gung-rgyal. Her entourage includes the glacial mountain goddesses (gangs sman), the slate mountain goddesses (g.ya' sman), the rock cliff goddesses (brag sman), the pasture goddesses (spang sman), the forest goddesses (nag sman), the river goddesses (chu sman), the lake goddesses (mtsho sman), and the island goddesses (do gling sman). The myth of her bringing medicine to earth will be found translated in Namkhai Norbu, *Drung, Deu, and Bon: Narratives, Symbolic Languages, and the Bon Tradition of Ancient Tibet*, ibid., pp. 113-117. Also on sMan-mo, see Per Kvaerne, *The Bon Religion of Tibet*, ibid., pp. 109-111.

48. This originally Bonpo goddess also became the chief guardian deity of the Drigung Kagyudpa school, having once incarnated in their leading family. Known as Achyi (A-phyi), she is the patroness of a form of dice divination known as *A-phyi mo*.

49. *dBal-chen ge-khod gnod-sbyin 'dul la phyag 'tshal-lo*. His title *dbal-chen* means "the great flaming one" *gnod-sbyin 'dul* means "he who subdues or tames ('dul-ba) those spirits who cause harm" (gnod-sbyin). The name *Ge-khod* in the Zhang-zhung language means "he who subdues the demons", or in Tibetan *bdud 'dul*. On the dichotomy in Tibetan folk culture between *rgod-pa*, "wild, uncivilized, chaotic," and *'dul-ba*, "tamed, civilized, ordered," see Geoffrey Samuel, *Civilized Shamans: Buddhism in Tibetan Societies*, Smithsonian Institution Press, Washington DC 1993.

50. *gShen gyi drang-srong Shes-rab rgyal-mtshan.* The name *bKra-shis sman-ri* means the monastery of "the auspicious medicine mountain." This monastery in Tsang province, founded in 1405, which soon became the chief center of learning among the Bonpos in Central Tibet, replaced the earlier foundation, Yeru Wensakha, which had been destroyed in a great flood a decade before.

Appendix Four: Lopon Tenzin Namdak

1. The personal name Tenzin Namdak means in Tibetan the completely pure (rnam-dag) holder of the teachings (bstan 'dzin). In general, the title Lopon (slob-dpon, Skt. acharya) designates the head teacher or professor in a monastic institution. He is principally in charge of educating the new monks both in terms of the Dharma and the Vinaya, whereas the Abbot or Khanpo (mkhan-po, Skt. upadhyaya) is, in general, the chief religious administrator of the monastery and the senior monk who administers the monastic vows to the novices and other monks. The honorific title Yongdzin (yongs 'dzin) usually designates the tutor and philosophy instructor superintending the education of high incarnate Lamas. Rinpoche (rin-po-che), does not necessarily mean a Tulku (sprul-sku) or recognized reincarnate Lama; it is the honorific term meaning "the most precious one" extended to religious personages worthy of great respect for their extensive learning and/or accomplishments in meditation practice. The Lopon belongs to the tradition of Menri monastery, the Abbots of which, known as Menri Trizin (sman-ri khri-'dzin) or the throne-holders of Menri, are selected by lot, rather than by reincarnation. Thus, the institution of Tulkus is not very prevalent in the tradition of Old Bon, although there do exist some Bonpo Tulkus or recognized reincarnations in this school.

2. According to Tibetan convention, an individual is one year old as soon as one is born and so in the view of the Lopon and his family, he was eight years old when he entered Tengchen monastery, the legal age for doing so as a novice.

3. Bonpo monasteries and practitioners predominate in the Khyungpo district of Eastern Tibet or Kham. The area of Tengchen (steng-chen) consists of the valleys of the southward flowing Gachu and Ruchu tributaries of the great Selween river and those of the northwest flowing feeder rivers known as Dakchu and Kyilkhorchu. In Tibetan the word *chu* means river as well as "water" in general. The capital of the district is called Tengchen, also known as Gyamotang. Tengchen town is situated in a wide cultivated valley hemmed in by sandstone hills. The old Tibetan village of Tengchen-kha and the modern district town of Tenchen (altitude 3750) face each other across the Dakchu river. When visiting the village of Tengchen-kha, Gyurme Dorje found the people to be extremely hospitable and tolerant. Bonpos, Nyingmapas, and Gelugpas all participated together in the Tsechu or tenth day festival for Guru

Padmasambhava. Most of the monasteries in the region are Bonpo rather than Buddhist. The two most important monasteries are on the northern ridge that overlooks the river and is across from Tengchen-kha. These are Tengchen (steng-chen) monastery and Ritro Lhakang (ri-khrod lha-khang). Tengchen monastery is also called Namdak Pema Long-yang (rnam-dag padma klong-yangs). It was founded in 1110 by Sherab Gyaltsan and Monlam Gyaltsan. The third lineage holder after these two greatly expanded the community of yogis around Tengchen and established Rito Lhakhang hermitage above the temple in 1180. These two monasteries have close connections with the Bonpo monasteries in Central Tibet of Menri and Yungdrung Ling, as well as with the Ngawa region and Nangzhik monastery in particular. Repairs to Tengchen monastery were made possible by the donations of Lopon Tenzin Namdak on his visit to Tengchen in 1986 and these renovations continue under the direction of Lama Sherab Gelek, who was enthroned as the abbot of the monastery by the Lopon. Particularly notable at Tengchen is Nampar Gyalwa Lhakhang (rnam-par rgyal-ba lha-khang) with many wall-paintings of deities and mandalas. Ritro Lhakhang also has an abbot's residence (bla-brang) and many notable wall-paintings, including a chamber containing the reliquary of Monlam Gyaltsan, and also other early lineage holders: Nyima Gyaltsan, Kunga Gyaltsan, Jimpa Gyaltsan, Tsultrim Gyaltsan, Yungdrung Gyaltsan, and Tsultrim Nyima. Formerly both monasteries had about three hundred monks each, but nowadays (1999) Tengchen has eighty-five and Ritro Lhakhang has only twenty-three. See Gyurme Dorje, *Footprint Tibet Handbook*, Footprint Handbooks, Bath 1999, p. 388-389.

4. On the distinction between Old Bon and New Bon, see Chapter One above.

5. The three river valleys of Oyuk, Thobgyal, and Shang in Tsang province are now known as Namling (rnam-gling) district. Through these valleys flow the Nam-gung-chu, the Thobpu-chu, and the Shang-chu, respectively. Their tributaries all rise amid the southern slopes of the Nyenchen Thanglha mountain range to the north and flow southward to converge with the Tsangpo or Brahmaputra river. This is an important region in Bonpo history. Menri monastery lies in the Thobgyal valley and Yungdrung Ling, founded in 1834 by Dawa Gyaltsan (Zla-ba rgyal-mthsan), a colleague and friend of the Abbot of Menri, Nyima Tenzin, lies in the lower Oyuk valley to the east of Thobgyal. See Gyurme Dorje, *Footprint Tibet Handbook*, Footprint Handbooks, Bath 1999, p. 249.

6. For example, the Lopon did all the line drawings in the study of Bon published by the Tibetologist David Snellgrove. See David Snellgrove, *The Nine Ways of Bon*, ibid.

7. According to the Nepali Buddhist text, the *Svayambhu Purana*, seven Buddhas in succession have visited this hill and graced it with their presence, namely, Vipashyin, Shikhin, Vishvabhu, Krakucchanda, Kanakamuni, Kashyapa, and the historical Buddha Shakyamuni.

According to local legend, the great stupa of Baudhanath at the eastern end of the valley contains the relics of the Buddha Kashyapa. An inscription of the Buddhist emperor Ashoka found on a pillar in the Tarai asserts that he once restored a stupa in this location that was said to have contained the relics of the Buddha Kanakamuni. At the time of the visit of the Buddha Vipashyin, the Kathmandu valley was still a large Naga lake, but on a lotus growing from a small island, he saw a self-originated light (svayamabhu-jyoti). Later the great Bodhisattva Manjushri came to this lake from China, and intrigued by this same self-originated light, cut a cleft in the southern hills bounding the lake at the Chobar Gorge and drained the lake. Thus, the hill of Swayambhu became visible. It is said in the Bonpo tradition that in the same way as these other six prehistoric Buddhas visited the sacred hill, Tonpa Shenrab did so as well.

8. When one follows the Thobpu-chu river northward upstream from its confluence with the Tsangpo or Brahmaputra river, one finds that the valley splits in two and the village of Thobgyal (thob-rgyal) is located near this dividing of the valley. Then when one continues following the eastern branch upstream, now known as the Zhungchu river, by way of Gangpa one comes to the sites of the Bonpo monasteries of Yeru Wensakha, Menri, and Kharna. Yeru Wensakha (g.yas-ru dben-sa-kha) was founded in 1072 by Druje Yungdrung Lama (Bru-rje g.yung-drung bla-ma), a disciple of the famous Bonpo Terton Shenchen Luga (gShen-chen klu-dga', 996-1035), who discovered the great collection of Bonpo texts known as the Southern Treasures (lho gter lugs). This master especially entrusted his disciple Yungdrung Lama with the preservation of *mtshan-nyid* or the philosophical texts he had recovered. For centuries thereafter this monastery was closely connected with the Dru clan (bru rigs) and many of its Geshes were sent for their post-graduate studies to Sakya monastery, the greatest monastic university in Tibet in its time. Yeru Wensakha monastery was destroyed in a disastrous flood in 1386, leaving little remaining. However, the ruins of this foundation are still visible. According to local legend, at that time a Sadhu came from India and felt that he was not treated respectfully at the monastery. Therefore, he performed some black magic and sent down a flood that destroyed the monastery entirely. However, the monks were able to save the library and this was preserved at the later Menri monastery and the villagers from nearby Thobgyal were also able to save some other things from the monastery. Rebuilding higher up the slopes of the Zhungchu valley, Tashi Menri monastery (bkra-shis sman-ri), "the auspicious medicine mountain," was founded in 1405 by Nyammed Sherab Gyaltsan (mNyam-med Shes-rab rgyal-mtshan), the greatest scholar in the Bonpo tradition, ranking with Longchen Rabjampa among the Nyingmapas, Sakya Pandita among the Sakyapas, and Je Tsongkhapa among the Gelugpas. It is said that this event had been predicted by the Buddha Tonpa Shenrab himself. For centuries Menri monastery was the most important Bonpo teaching center for Old Bon in all of Tibet. Menri would attract monk students,

such as the Lopon himself, from Tengchen, Ngawa, and Gyarong districts in Eastern Tibet. Prior to its destruction in the 1960s in the Cultural Revolution, it housed more than three hundred monks. Now there are only about fifty monks living among the extensive ruins. There has been some rebuilding done. In former times, there were four colleges including a dialectics school or Shedra (bshad-grwa) and a large assembly hall. The oldest extant building is known as red hermitage (grub-khang dmar-po). Further upstream are the Kharna caves where Bonpo hermits and yogis had practiced for centuries. A new monastry was founded there in 1838 by Sherab Yungdrung. See Gyurme Dorgye, *Footprint Tibet Handbook*, ibid., p. 249-250.

9. See David Snellgrove, *The Nine Ways of Bon*, Oxford University Press, London 1967.

10. When the Lopon escaped from Tibet, he was able to bring two valuable texts with him. The first was an anthology of texts from the *Zhang-zhung snyan-rgyud* cycle, printed from blocks carved at Menri monastery in Tibet, probably in the 1950s. This block-print edition later republished in New Delhi and serves as the basis for the translations in this volume and in the forthcoming volume. For the contents of this collection, see Chapter Ten above. The second was an *dbu-med* (headless script) hand-written copy of the *Ma rgyud thugs-rje nyi-ma*, including the three root texts or Tantras and their commentarties from the cycle of the Bonpo Mother Tantra. These texts were also later reprinted by photo offset in India.

11. Lokesh Chandra and Lopon Tenzin Namdak, *History and Doctrine of Bon-po Nispanna-Yoga*, International Academy of Indian Culture, New Delhi 1968.

12. Although the number of Bonpo refugees was small in proportion to the total flood of Tibetan refugees, according to the official Chinese Government census of Tibet and China, the Tibetan followers of the Gelugpa school form the largest single group in the ethnic Tibetan population. However, as the second largest group among the ethnic Tibetans, the Nyingmapas and the Bonpos are tied. The various Kagyudpa groups are smaller and the Sakyapas constitute the smallest group in the Tibetan population among the five schools. Oral communication from Lopon Tenzin Namdak.

13. See Tadeusz Skorupski, "Tibetan gYung-Drung Bon Monastery in India", Kailash, vol. VIII, nos. 1-2, Kathmandu 1981; reprinted separately by gYung-Drung Bon Monastic Centre, Solan, India 1983.

14. See Tadeusz Skorupski, "Tibetan gYung-Drung Bon Monastery in India", op. cit. At the time when Skorupski visited the monastery, the monastic community consisted of three groups of monks. The first group consisted of twenty older monks who had come from Tibet. Their main activities were to perform puja ceremonies at the houses of lay people, private religious practices, and participate in all the rituals in the temple at the monastery. The second group consisted of thirty-five young monks who

had taken their monastic vows at the new monastery. They were being educated by the Lopons in traditional Bonpo studies and trained to live according to the Vinaya. The monastery provided these students with a mid-day meal of rice and dal, afternoon tea, and soup (thug-pa) in the evening. As for their clothing and their morning tea and bread, they had to provide these items for themselves. Their syllabus consisted of philosophy (mtshan-nyid), epistemology and logic (tshad-ma), Prajnaparamita (phar-phyin), the paths and stages (sa-lam), Madhyamaka (du-ma), cosmology (mdzod-phug), monastic discipline ('dul-ba), Tantra (rgyud), Dzogchen (rdzogs-chen), religious history (bon-'byung), poetry (sdeb-sbyor), astrology (rtsis), and grammar (sgra). The third group consisted of boys between seven and fourteen years of age. They received a primary education in the Central Government School in the village near the monastery. The normal school syllabus included Hindi and English, and in addition they were taught Tibetan grammar and history. These boys had a separate kitchen and took responsibility for collecting firewood and preparing their own meals. All boys, whether or not orphans, were maintained by the monastery. Parents were not obliged to pay for their sons' upkeep, but contributions were welcome. When a boy joins the monastic community, he has his head shaved (symbolic of renouncing the world) and receives a new name in a short ceremony called *tshe-ring*, "long life." Therafter he wears monastic robes when he attends puja ceremonies and ordinary clothes when he attends the government school. They do not take monk's vows until age eighteen, although they can take them earlier if they wish. At this age, if they fail to take the full monasticd vows, they must leave the monastery and enter the worldly life.

15. On the Mahasiddha and Tantric adept Gyerpungpa, see Chapter Five above and on the empowerment or initiation (dbang bskur) for Zhang-zhung Meri, see the translation of the Ngondro text in Appendix 2, Section 2, above. On the meditation deity of Meri in general, see Per Kvaerne, *The Bon Religion of Tibet: The Iconography of a Living Tradition*, Serindia Publications, London 1995, and John Myrdhin Reynolds, *The Cult and Practice of Zhang-zhung Meri: The Meditation Deity for the Zhang-zhung Nyan-gyud Tradition of Bonpo Dzogchen Teachings*, Bonpo Translation Project (privately printed), San Diego 1996.

16. For the curriculum in more detail, see Krystyna Cech, "History, Teaching, and Practice of Dialectics according to the Bon Tradition," in *Tibet Journal* 11, no. 2, 1986, pp. 3-28.

17. The refers to the practice of the eight syllable mantra OM MATRI MUYE SALE 'DU, particularly from the tradition of Lodan Nyingpo (bLo-ldan snying-po), the Terton of the 14th century. On this mantra, see the Commentary on the Ngondro translation, "7. The Practice of Mantra Recitations," especially Footnote 50 in Appendix 2, Section 3, above.

18. The district in Amdo called Ngawa (rnga-ba) is named after the Ngachu tributary of the Marchu river, which flows south to Mt. Nyenpo Yurtse. Just east of Ngawa town lie the Bonpo monasteries of Nangzhik and Thobgyal, both representing the traditions of Old Bon or Yungdrung Bon and thus they did not become involved in the Rimed Movement of the 19th century in Eastern Tibet. Nangzhik Gonpa is the larger of the two and the monks are well schooled in dialectics, some of them having visited Triten Norbutse monastery in Nepal. See Gyurme Dorgye, *Footprint Tibet Handbook*, ibid., p.613. Nangzhik was established in 1766 and became one of the biggest and most active Bonpo monasteries in Tibet. The spiritual lineage of this monastery is said to descend from Zhugom Trulzhik (Zhu-sgom 'khrul-zhig), who belonged to the famous Zhu clan, on of the six clans in Tibet entrusted with the preservation and dissemination of the Bonpo teachings, the others being *dMu-gshen, Bru, sPa, rMe'u,* and *Khyung.* See Karmay, *Treasury*, ibid., pp.3-13. He was born in the year 964 at the Yardrok (yar-'brog) lake in South Tibet when his father, the Bonpo master Zhu Kyese Chenpo (Zhu skye-se chen-po), was residing there. According to Shardza Rinpoche, Zhu Trulzhik received the Dzogchen teachings from Zhu Kyidpo (Zhu skyid-po) and transmitted them in turn to his own son Zhu Yelegpo (Zhu g.yas leg-po) born in the year 1002, who became a disciple of the famous treasure-text discoverer Shenchen Luga (996-1035), who entrusted his disciple with the preservation of the *Sems-phyogs* or Dzogchen teachings. See Karmay, *Treasury*, ibid., p.122, 137. It is said that when Zhu Trulzhik was born, he had a vision of Shenlha Odkar and looking into the sky, he began to sing. In later life, he traveled on pilgrimage to Mt. Kailas in West Tibet and there met Lama Nyima Gyaltsan (bLa-ma nyi-ma rgyal-mtshan), who belonged to the Ya-ngal clan, and received from him the transmission for the *Zhang-zhung snyan-rgyud.* Then, because of a prophecy he received from the goddess Sidpa Gyalmo, saying that the eighteen Zhigpos would become his disciples, he returned to Amdo. Among these eighteen was Nangzhik Lodro Gyaltsan (sNang-zhig blo-gros rgyal-mtshan, 11 cen.), for whom the monastery was eventually named. Thus, the origin of this monastic lineage is ascribed to the Zhu clan. On this lineage, see Donatella Rossi, "The Monastic Lineage of sNang zhig dgon pa in Amdo rNga ba," in *The Tibet Journal*, vol. 23, no. 4, Dharamsala 1998, pp. 58-71. On Nangzhik monastery in general, as well as its lineage, also see the two articles by Per Kvaerne, "The Monastery of sNang-zhig of the Bon Religion in the rNga-ba District of Amdo", in *Studi in Onore di Luciano Petech*, P. Daffina (ed), *Studi Orientali*, vol. 9, Rome 1990, pp.207-222, and "The Succession of Lamas at the Monastery of sNang-zhig in the rNga-ba District of Amdo," in *Les Habitants du Toit du Monde: Tibet et Himalaya*, Samten Karmay and Philippe Sagant (eds), *Recherches sur la Haute Asie* 12, Societe d'ethnologie, Nanaterre 1997, pp. 155-157.

19. The original Triten Norbutse (khri-brten nor-bu-rtse) was founded in the 14th century by the great Bonpo master Shen Nyima Gyaltsan (gShen Nyi-

ma rgyal-mtshan, b.1360), who belonged to the Shen (gshen) clan when claims descent from Tonpa Shenrab himself, the founder of the Bon religion. Triten Norbutse became one of the four principal monastic institutions that provided Bonpo education from the 14th century until the Chinese Communist occupation in the later 1950s. Known for its rich cultural and academic heritage, the monastery was destroyed in the Cultural Revolution in the 1960s.

It was re-established by Lopon Rinpoche in Kathmandu in 1987, whith the able assistance of Geshe Nyima Wangyal who became its first abbot or Khenpo. The monastery is at present headed by Khanpo Tenpa Yungdrung. Located on the slopes of Nagarjun Hill below the king's forest at the western end of the valley, it faces the famous great stupa of Swayambhunath to the east, a site that had been miraculously blessed by the presence in the past of Tonpa Shenrab himself. At present there are about one hundred and fifteen monks, both Tibetan refugees and others from the Bonpo areas of Nepal such as Dolpo and Mustang, residing and receiving their education at the monastery. The monastery was founded with the purpose to provide a complete education in Bonpo tradition and practice. This is embodied in the nine year program in academic studies for the Geshe degree and the four year program of meditation practice in Dzogchen. The monastery is, therefore, essentially an educational institution, and not a residential one for monks.

The education at the monastery falls into two principal sections, as was the case at Menri itself in Tibet:

1) The first system of education is known as the system of the learned scholar (mkhas-pa pandita yi lugs). This represents the nine year program in academic studies, culminating in the Geshe (dge-bshes) degree, and including Sutra, Tantra, and Dzogchen, entailing a curriculum of Bonpo philosophy (here the emphasis is on Madhyamaka) and the principal canonical texts, as well as the secular sciences of astrology, medicine, poetics, grammar, and so son. There is also the learning of ritual practices, chanting of various liturgies and the accompanying music, religious art and architecture, and so on. But the emphasis is on scholarly academic studies by way of study and debating, rather than meditation practice. But later this knowledge can be applied in practice, including meditation retreats, as well as ordinary life outside the monastery. Ordinarily, unless engaged in retreat or further studies, the monk must leave the monastery after successfully completing the Geshe degree.

2) The second system of education is known as the system of the ascetic yogis (ku-sa-li-pa'i lugs), where a four year program focuses on Dzogchen practice in order to realize the Nature of Mind. The four major traditions of Bonpo Dzogchen texts are studied and practiced in order to develop experiential understanding in terms of meditation practice. In this system, one goes to a qualified Lama, receives

instructions in the preliminary practices and does them, from anywhere from three to six months. Then one returns to the Lama, receives instruction on fixating the mind (sems 'dzin) and thereafter a direct introduction to the Natural State (rig-pa'i ngo-sprod). This understanding is then developed with further retreat practices. The Sanskrit term Pandita means a scholar well versed in book learning and intellectual knowledge, whereas a Kushali (v. ku-sa-li, ku-su-li) indicates a practitioner who has attained high spiritual realization by way of meditation practice.

In the year 2001, six students had completed their academic studies and passed their oral examination and were awarded their Geshe degrees. Today they are teaching other monks and take part in various monastic and community activites for the benefit of the Bonpo people of Nepal. This included setting up schools in remote regions like Dolpo. Also a Tibetan medical school was started in Western Nepal under the guidance of the monastery in 2001. Three students from this school have been awarded medical diplomas.

The library at the monastery, build with financial aid from Germany, possesses a complete collection of Bonpo canonical texts, both the Kangyur (bka'-'gyur) and the Katen (bka'-brten), recently reprinted in Changdu, China. In Central Tibet itself, all wood-blocks and the books printed from them had been destroyed in the Cultural Revolution. At present, there is a program to catalogue and index all these Bonpo texts as well as putting them on to computer diskettes.

20. On the view of Dzogchen, especially with regard to the philosophical views of Madhyamaka, Chittamatra, and Mahamudra, see John Myrdhin Reynolds, *Bonpo Dzogchen Teachings*, op.cit.

21. Shardza Tashi Gyaltsan (Shar-rdza bkra-shes rgyal-mtshan), was born in 1859 in the village of Da (brda) in the region of Dagang (zla-gang) or Dzakhog (rdza-khog) between the two rivers of Ngulchu and Dzachu. His father belonged to the Hor clan. When he was still a boy of nine, at the urging of Lama Tenzin Wangyal (rDza-sprul bsTan-'dzin dbang-rgyal), with great reluctance his parents allowed him to become a monk. The Lama ordained him and gave him the name Tashi Gyaltsan (bKra-shis rgyal-mtshan). With this Lama, he studied Sutra, Tantra, and Dzogchen, receiving his education at Dza Tengchen (rdza stcng-chen) monastery. He took all the Vinaya and Bodhisattva vows as well as Tantric vows from his Root Lama, Dzatrul Tcnzin Wangyal. In terms of Tantra, there five root vows and twenty-five branch bows for the visualization process (bskyed-rim), five root vows and one hundred branch vows for the perfection process (rdzogs-rim) and thirty vows for Dzogchen. He kept all of these vows carefully. He began his Tantra studies with the empowerment for the meditation deity Walse Ngampa (dBal-gsas rngam-pa) where he was introduced to the Nature of Mind. In total, he had twenty-four masters, among them Tenzin Wangyal, Dechen Lingpa, Duddul Lingpa, Samten Yeshe, Shengyal Tenzin, and so on.

At the age of thirty-four, he became disgusted with the world, and he decided to spend the rest of his life in retreat, going to the remote site of Yungdrung Lhunpo on the border of his native district of Shardza or Eastern Dza. Here he built a small hut, planning to be in permanent retreat and live in solitude. In his district, the people practiced mainly New Bon, but he saw also the value of Old Bon as preserved by the five clans of Dru (bru), Zhu, Pa (spa), Meu (rme'u) and Shen (gshen), but he personally mainly followed the system of Dru (bru-lugs), because this was the lineage of Menri monastery. He practiced both Yeshen Tantra and Yeshen Chenpo Tantra, as well as Dzogchen. He composed commentaries on all the Nine Ways of Bon, was well as many rituals and prayers.

Among his disciples was Sang-ngak Lingpa (gSang-sngas gling-pa) and his successor was his nephew Lodro Gyatso bLo-gros rgya-mtsho). Below his master's meditation hut, Sang-ngak Lingpa built a meditation center called Gethang (dge-thang) which had a small temple. Soon this became a major teaching center for Bon in Kham. Here also wood-blocks were carved for some three hundred and thirty volumes, including Shardza Rinpoche's own works in thirteen volumes. Many Bonpo Lamas and also some Buddhist ones such as Changchub Dorje, the Dzogchen master of Namkhai Norbu Rinpoche, came hear to receive his teachings. When he grew older, he turned over the running of the center to his nephew. When he was seventy-six, he warned his disciples that his time had come, and he went to a solitary place called Rabzhiteng (rab zhi steng) and put up a small tent where he practiced Thodgal. In the fourth Tibetan month in 1933, he had himself sewn up in the tent. His successor Lodro Gyatso and his younger brother Tsultrin saw that his property was distributed to both Bonpo and Buddhist monasteries as he had requested. His students, who had assembled outside, saw rainbows about the tent and observed other signs such as earthquakes. Fearing that their master would disappear completely, they opened the tent and found that his physical body, wrapped in rainbow lights, had shrunk to the size of one cubit and was suspended in the air. Many hundreds of people saw this phenomenon. His disciple made a large stupa of gilded copper and what remained of his body was placed inside. See Lopon Tenzin Namdak, *Heart Drops of Dharmakaya: Dzogchen Practice of the Bon Tradition*, Snow Lion, Ithaca 1993, pp. 17-29.

22. Lopon Tenzin Namdak, *Heart Drops of Dharmakaya: Dzogchen Practice of the Bon Tradition*, Snow Lion Publications, Ithaca 1993. However, as useful as this book may be, it is not actually a literal translation of the Tibetan text, but a paraphrase and explanation by the Lopon given orally, recorded and then transcribed and edited, of what is contained in the text. The text, *'Od-gsal rdzogs-pa chen-po'i lam gyi rim-pa khrid-yig kun tu bzang-po'i snying-tig shes bya-ba bzhugs*, belongs to a cycle of teaching and practice by Shardza Rinpoche known as the *Kun-bzang snying-tig*, was given the title by the editor of "Heart Drops of Dharmakaya," which is not the actual meaning in Tibetan. The translation "heart drops" makes

no sense in the context. The word *thig-pa* means "drop," but *snying-thig* is an abbreviation for *snying-po'i thig-le* meaning "the Essence of the Mind," in this case, of Kuntu Zangpo, who is indeed the Dharmakaya (bon-sku) in the Bonpo system like the Nyingmapa. The word *thig-le* (Skt. bindu) in Tantra means a tiny sphere of luminous energy resembling a ball of liquid mercury. It is spherical in shape, not like a raindrop. Also, for example, Guru Tapihritsa is visualized sitting within a rainbow *thig-le* or sphere of rainbow light. In the context of Dzogchen, however, the term very often means "essence" as it does here. In its ordinary usage, *snying-po* means the physical heart, and by extension the core or essence of something. But here in the Dzogchen context, *snying-po* means "Mind", not the thought process but the Nature of Mind (sems-nyid). In any event, Kuntu Zangpo does not have a "mind" in the ordinary sense of discursive thoughts (rnam-rtog), since He is primordially enlightened, but rather non-dual primal cognitions of reality or *ye-shes*. See the discussion of the Primordial Buddha in Chapter Two above. Therefore, the above title should be translated "here is contains the Essence of the Mind of Kuntu Zangpo, being the explanatory text for the stages of the path of the Clear Light Great Pefection."

23. The short article "The Condensed Meaning of an Explanation of the Teachings of Yungdrung Bon" was published as an appendix in John Myrdhin Reynolds, *Yungdrung Bon—The Eternal Tradition*, Bonpo Translation Project (privately printed), New York and Freehold 1992. The article was subsequently reprinted with other material as a booklet with the same title by the Bonpo Foundation, Kathmandu 1993.
24. See John Myrdhin Reynolds, *Bonpo Dzogchen Teachings according to Lopon Tenzin Namdak: Dzogchen Teachings from the Retreats in Austria, England, Holland, and America*, Bonpo Translation Project (privately printed), Freehold and Amsterdam 1992.
25. This account of the Lopon"s activities in Tibet were published on the website of the Association Yungdrung Bon in France: www.yungdrung-bon.org.
26. The curriculum, following the traditions of Menri in Tibet, is more or less the same as that at Dolanji. See Krystyna Cech, "History, Teaching, and Practice of Dialectics according to the Bon Tradition," op.cit.
27. This information comes from Lopon Tenpa Yungdrung in the brochure "Triten Norbutse Bonpo Monastery Monk Sponsorship Project," n.d.
28. Geshe Tenzin Wangyal Rinpoche (dge-bshes bsTan-'zin dbang-rgyal) was born in Amritsar, India, his 1960, his father being Nyingmapa and his mother Bonpo. He received his religious education at Dolanji with Lopon Sangye Tenzin and Lopon Tenzin Namdak, eventually in the Dialectics School. From there he graduated in 1986 with a Geshe degree. He was employed for a time at the Library of Tibetan Works and Archives in Dharmsala and in 1988 he was invited by Namkhai Norbu Rinpoche to the latter's retreat center at Merigar north of Rome in order to teach on the Bonpo tradition of Dzogchen. After a brief time engaging in research at

universities in Norway and Sweden, he taught extensively in Italy and elsewhere in Europe. For 1991 and 1992, he was a Rockefeller Fellow at Rice University, Houston, Texas, and in 1994-1995 he held a grant from the National Endowment for the Humanities for research into the logical and philosophical aspects of the Bon tradition. Before that, he had established the Ligminche Institute, at first in Charlottesville and later in Serenity Ridge, Virginia. Since that time, Rinpoche has traveled extensively in America and Europe presenting teachings from the Bonpo tradition. Ligmincha Institute publishes a newsletter, The Voice of the Clear Light, and to date, Rinpoche has published three books in English, drawn from his many lectures and course: *Wonders of the Natural Mind*, Station Hill Press, Barrytown 1993, and reprinted Snow Lion, Ithaca 2000; *The Tibetan Yogas of Dream and Sleep*, Snow Lion, Ithaca 1998; and *Healing with Form, Energy, and Light*, Snow Lion, Ithaca 2002.

Bibliography

Works in English

Beckwith, Christopher, *The Tibetan Empire in Central Asia*, Princeton University Press, Princeton 1987.

Bellezza, John Vincent, "Pre-history of Tibet," *Himal*, December 1999, Kathmandu, pp.42-43.

Bellezza, John Vincent, "A Preliminary Archaeological Survey of gNam mtsho and Dang ra g.yu mtsho," in *The Tibet Journal*, vol. 21, Dharamsala 1996, pp. 58-84

Bellezza, John Vincent, *Divine Dyads: Ancient Civilization in Tibet*, Library of Tibetan Works and Archives, Dharamsala 1997.

Bellezza, John Vincent, "High-Country Culture: A Civilization Flourished in the Himalayas before Buddhism Reached Tibet," *Discovering Archaeology* v.1 n.3, May-June 1999, pp. 78-83.

Berglie, Per-Arne, "Preminary Remarks on Some Tibetan Spirit Mediums in Nepal," in *Kailash: A Journal of Himalayan Research* 4 (1) Kathmandu 1976, pp. 85-108.

Bernbaum, Edwin, *The Way to Shambhala: A Search for the Mythical Kingdom beyond the Himalayas*, Anchor Press/ Doubleday, New York 1980.

Cech, Krystyna, "History, Teaching, and Practice of Dialectics according to the Bon Tradition," in *Tibet Journal* 11, no. 2, 1986, pp. 3-28.

Chandra, Lokesh, *History and Doctrine of Bon-po Nispanna-Yoga*, International Academy of Indian Culture, Introduction in English, Sata-Pitaka Series Indo-Asian Literatures, volume 73, New Delhi 1968.

Conze, Edward, *Buddhist Thought in India*, George Allen & Unwin, London 1962.

Conze, Edward, *Thirty Years of Buddhist Studies: Selected Essays*, University of South Carolina Press, Columbia 1968.

Corbin, Henry, *Spiritual Body and Celestial Earth; From Mazdean Iran to Shi'ite Iran*, Princeton University Press, Princetion NJ 1977..

Dalai Lama, H.H. The, *The Buddha Nature: Death and Eternal Soul in Buddhism*, Bluestar Communications, Woodside CA 1997.

Dargyay, Eva, "The Concept of a Creator God in Tantric Buddhism," in *Journal of the International Association of Buddhist Studies*, vol. 8, no. 1, Madison 1985, pp. 31-47.

Dargyay, Eva, "A Nyingmapa Text: The *Kun-byed rgyal-po'i mdo*," in Barbara Aziz and Matthew Kapstein (eds), *Soundings in Tibetan Civilization*, Manohar Manushiram, Delhi 19985, pp. 282-293.

Dargyay, Eva, *The Rise of Esoteric Buddhism in Tibet*, Motilal Banarsidass, Delhi 1977.

Das, Sarit Chandra, *Contributions on the Religion and History of Tibet*, Manjusri Publishing House, New Delhi 1970; reprinted from *Journal of the Asiatic Society of Bengal*, 1881.

Das, S.C., *A Tibetan-English Dictionary*, Calcutta 1902

David-Neel, Alexandra, *The Superhuman Life of Gesar of Ling*, Claude Kendall, New York 1934.

Doresse, Jean, *The Secret Books of the Egyptian Gnostics*, The Viking Press, New York 1960.

Dorje, Gyurme, *Footprint Tibet Handbook*, Footprint Handbooks, Bath 1999.

Dowman, Keith, *The Legend of the Great Stupa*, Dharma Press, Berkeley CA 1973.

Dowman, Keith, *Masters of Mahamudra*, SUNY, Albany NY 1985.

Dudjom Rinpoche, *The Nyingma School of Tibetan Buddhism*, vols. I & II, Gyurme Dorje and Matthew Kapstein (eds), Wisdom Publications, Boston 1991.

Dumezil, Georges, *Mitra-Varuna*, Zone Books, New York 1988.

Eliade, Mircea, *The Sacred and the Profane: The Nature of Religion*, Harcourt, Brice & World, New York 1957.

Eliade, Mircea, *Shamanism: Archaic Techniques of Ecstasy*, Pantheon Books, New York 1964.

Eliade, Mircea, *Yoga: Immortality and Freedom*, Princeton University Press, Princeton 1969.

Francke, A.H., "gZer Myig: a Book of the Tibetan Bonpos," in *Asia Major* I, 1924; N.s. I, 1949.

Gard, Richard, and Sangye Tandar, *The Twelve Deeds: A Brief Life Story of Tonpa Shenrab, the Founder of the Bon Religion*, Library of Tibetan Works and Archives, New Delhi 1995.

Goldstein, Melvyn C., and Cynthia M. Beall, *Nomads of Western Tibet: The Survival of a Way of Life*, University of California Press, Berkeley 1990.

Grant, Robert, *The Gnostic Gospel of Thomas*, Doubleday, Garden City NY 1960.

Guenther, Herbert V., *The Life and Teachings of Naropa*, Oxford University Press, Oxford 1963.

Haarh, Erik, "The Zhang-zhung Language: A Grammar and Dictionary of the Unexplored Language of the Tibetan Bonpos," in *Acta Jutlandica*, Vol. 40, no. 1, Universitetsforlaget i Aarhus, Copenhagen 1968, pp. 7-43.

Harrison, Jane, *Prolegomena to the Study of Greek Religion*, Meridian Books, New York 1955.

Heissig, Walther, "A Mongolian Source to the Lamaist Suppression of Shamanism in the 17th Century," in *Anthropos* 48, pp. 493-533.

Heissig, Walther, *The Religions of Mongolia*, University of California Press, Berkeley CA 1980.

Hoffmann, Helmut, *The Religions of Tibet*, George Allen & Unwin, London 1961.

Hopkins, Jeffrey, *Meditation on Emptiness*, Wisdom Publications, London 1983.

Jackson, David, "Birds in the Egg and New-Born Lion Cubs: Metaphors for the Potentialities and Limitations of 'All-at-once" Enlightenment," IATS, Narita Conference, Japan 1990, pp. 1-23.

Jackson, David, *Enlightenment by a Single Means: The Tibetan Controversies on the "Self-Sufficient White Remedy" (dkar po chig thub)*, Der Ostereichischen Akademie der Wissenschaften, Vienna 1994.

Jonas, Hans, *The Gnostic Religion: The Message of the Alien God and the Beginnings of Christianity*, Beacon Press, Boston 1963.

Kalsang, Ladrang, *The Guardian Deities of Tibet*, Little Lhasa Publications, Dharamsala 1996.

Karmay, Samten G., *Catalogue of Bon-po Publications*, Toyo Bunko, Tokyo 1977.

Karmay, Samten G., "A Discussion of the Doctrinal Position of the rDzogs-chen from the 10th to the 11th Centuries, in *Journal Asiatique* 1-2, Paris 1975, pp. 147-155.

Karmay, Samten G., "A General Introduction to the History and Doctrines of Bon," in *The Memoirs of the Research Department of the Toyo Bunko*, No. 33, Tokyo 1975, pp. 171-218.

Karmay, Samten G., *The Great Perfection: A Philosophical and Meditative Teaching of Tibetan Buddhism*, Brill, Leiden 1988.

Karmay, Samten G., *The Little Luminous Boy: The Oral Tradition from the Land of Zhangzhung depicted on two Tibetan Paintings*, Orchid Press, Bangkok 1998.

Karmay, Samten G., *The Treasury of Good Sayings: A Tibetan History of Bon*, Oxford University Press, London 1972.

Kuznetsov, B.I., "Who was the Founder of the Bon Religion," in *Tibet Journal*, Vol. I, No. 1, Dharamsala 1975.

Kvaerne, Per, "Aspects of the Origin of Buddhist Tradition in Tibet," in *Numen* 19, 1972, pp.30-40.

Kvearne, Per, "Bonpo Studies: The A-khrid System of Meditation," Part One: "The Transmission of the A-khrid System," in *Kailash* v. I, n. 1, pp. 19-50, Part Two: "The Essential Teachings of the A-khrid System, in Kailash v. I, n. 4, pp. 248-332, Kathmandu 1973.

Kvaerne, Per, *Bon Religion: A Death Ritual of the Tibetan Bonpos*, Brill, Leiden 1985.

Kvaerne, Per, *The Bon Religion of Tibet: The Iconography of a Living Tradition*, Serindia Publications, London 1995.

Kvaerne, Per, "A Bonpo Version of the Wheel of Existence," in *Tantric and Taoist Studies in Honour of R.A. Stein*, Vol. I, Michel Strickmann (ed),

Melanges chinois et bouddhiques vol. XX, Institut Belge des Hautes Etudes Chinoises, Bruxelles 1981, pp. 274-289.

Kvaerne, Per, "A Chronological Table of the Bon-po: The bsTan rcis of Nyima bstan-'jin," in *Acta Orientalia*, vol. 33, Copenhagen 1971, pp. 205-282.

Kvaerne, Per, "The Great Perfection in the Tradition of the Bonpos," in Whalen Lai and Lewis Lancaster (eds), *Early Ch'an in China and Tibet*, Asian Humanities Press, Berkeley CA 1983, pp. 367-392.

Kvaerne, Per, "The Monastery of sNang-zhig of the Bon Religion in the rNga-ba District of Amdo", in *Studi in Onore di Luciano Petech*, P. Daffina (ed), *Studi Orientali*, vol. 9, Rome 1990, pp.207-222.

Kvaerne, Per, and Thubten Rikey, *The Stages of A-khrid Meditation: Dzogchen Practice of the Bon Tradition*, Library of Tibetan Works and Archives, Dharamsala 1996.

Kvearne, Per, "The Succession of Lamas at the Monastery of sNang-zhig in the rNga-ba District of Amdo," in *Les Habitants du Toit du Monde: Tibet et Himalaya*, Samten Karmay and Philippe Sagant (eds), *Recherches sur la Haute Asie* 12, Societe d'ethnologie, Nanaterre 1997, pp. 155-157.

Lamotte, Etienne, *History of Buddhism from the Origins to the Saka Era*, Universite Catholique de Louvain, Peeters Press, Louvain-Paris 1988.

Lauf, Detlef Ingo,*The Secret Doctines of the Tibetan Books of the Dead*, Shambhala, Boulder CO 1977.

Lopez, Donald S., and Steven C. Rockefeller, *The Christ and the Bodhisattva*, SUNY, Albany NY 1987.

Mack, Burton, *The Lost Gospel: The Book of Q and Christian Origins*, Harper Collins, San Francisco 1993.

Martin, Daniel, *Mandala Cosmology. Human Body Good Thought and the Revelation of the Secret Mother Tantras of Bon*, Asiatische Forschungen Band 124, Harrassowitz Verlag, Wiesbaden 1994.

Mumford, Stan Royal, *Himalayan Dialogue: Tibetan Lamas and Gurung Shamans in Nepal*, University of Wisconsin Press, Madison 1989.

Murti, T.R.V., *The Central Philosophy of Buddhism: A Study of the Madhyamika System*, George Allen & Unwin, London 1955.

Namdak, Lopon Tenzin, "The Condensed Meaning of an Explanation of the Teachings of Yungdrung Bon," in John Reynolds, *Yungdrung Bon; The Eternal Tradition*, Bonpo Translation Project, New York 1994.

Namdak, Lopon Tenzin, *Heart Drops of Dharmakaya: Dzogchen Practice of the Bon Tradition*, Snow Lion, Ithaca 1993.

Namdak, Lopon Tenzin, and John Reynolds (tr), *The Condensed Meaning of an Explanation of the Teachings of Yungdrung Bon*, Bonpo Foundation, Kathmandu n.d.

Nebesky-Wojkowitz, Rene de, *Oracles and Demons of Tibet: The Cult and Iconography of the Tibetan Protective Deities*, Mouton, The Hague, 1956.

Neumaier-Dargyay, E.K., *The Sovereign All-Creating Mind, the Motherly Buddha*, SUNY, Albany NY 1992.

Norbu, Namkhai, *The Crystal and the Way of Light: Sutra, Tantra, and Dzogchen*, Arkana Penguin Books, London 1993.

Norbu, Namkhai, *Drung, Dreu and Bon: Narrations, Symbolic Languages, and the Bon Tradition in Ancient Tibet*, Library of Tibetan Works and Archives, Dharamsala 1995.

Norbu, Namkhai, *The Necklace of gZi: A Cultural History of Tibet*, Library of Tibetan Works and Archives, Dharamsala 1981.

Norbu, Namkhai, and Ramon Prats, *Gangs ti se'i dkar c'ag: A Bonpo Story of the Sacred Mountain Ti-se and the Blue Lake Ma-pang*, Is.M.E.O., Rome 1989.

Padmakara Translation Group, *The Words of My Perfect Teacher*, Harper Collins Publishers, San Francisco 1994.

Peters, Larry G., *Ecstasy and Healing in Nepal*, Udena Publications, Malibu CA 1981.

Peters, Larry G., "The Tibetan Healing Rituals of Dorje Yudronma: A Fierce Manifestation of the Feminine Cosmic Force," in *Shaman's Drum* 45, Ashland OR 1997, pp. 36-47.

Reynolds, John Myrdhin, *Bonpo Dzogchen Teachings*, Bonpo Translation Project (privately printed), Freehold and Amsterdam 1992.

Reynolds, John Myrdhin, *The Cult and Practice of Zhang-zhung Meri: The Meditation Deity for the Zhang-zhung Nyan-gyud Tradition of Bonpo Dzogchen Teachings*, Bonpo Translation Project (privately printed), San Diego 1996.

Reynolds, John Myrdhin, *The Golden Letters*, Snow Lion Publications, Ithaca NY 1996.

Reynolds, John Myrdhin, *The Healing Practice for Sidpa Gyalmo*, Bonpo Translation Project (privately printed), San Diego 1996.

Reynolds, John Myrdhin, *The Instructions of Shardza Rinpoche for the Practice of Vision and the Dark Retreat*, Bonpo Translation Project (privately printed), Freehold and Amsterdam 1992.

Reynolds, John Myrdhin, *The Invocations to the Guardian Deity Nypangse and to the Goddess Menmo*, Bonpo Translation Project (privately printed), Los Angeles 1999.

Reynolds, John Myrdhin, *Namkhai Norbu: The Cycle of Day and Night*, Station Hill Press, Barrytown NY 1987.

Reynolds, John Myrdhin, *Practices from the Zhang-zhung Nyan-gyud*, Bonpo Translation Project (privately printed), Freehold and Amsterdam 1992.

Reynolds, John Myrdhin, *Selections from the Bonpo Book of the Dead*, Bonpo Translation Project (privately printed), San Diego and Copenhagen 1997.

Reynolds, John Myrdhin, *Self-Liberation through seeing with Naked Awareness*, Station Hill Press, Barrytown 1989; second edition: Snow Lion Publications, Ithaca NY 1998.

Reynolds, John Myrdhin, *The Seven-fold Cycle of the Clear Light*, Bonpo Translation Project (privately printed), San Diego and Amsterdam 2001.

Reynolds, John Myrdhin, *Yungdrung Bon: The Eternal Tradition*, Bonpo Translation Project (privately printed), New York 1991.

Rock, Joseph, "Contributions to the Shamanism of the Tibetan-Chinese Borderland", in *Anthropos* LIV (1959), pp. 796-818.

Roerich, George,*The Blue Annals* by George Roerich, Part I-II, Motilal Banarsidass, New Delhi reprint 1979.

Rossi, Donatella, "The Monastic Lineage of sNang zhig dgon pa in Amdo rNga ba," in *The Tibet Journal*, vol. 23, no. 4, Dharamsala 1998, pp. 58-71.

Samuel, Geoffrey, *Civilized Shamans: Buddhism in Tibetan Societies*, Smithsonian Institution Press, Washington DC 1993.

Sharma, D.D., *A Discriptive Grammar of Kinnauri*, Studies in Tibeto-Himalayan Languages 1, Mittal Publications, Delhi 1988.

Skorupski, Tadeusz, "Tibetan gYung-Drung Bon Monastery in India", Kailash, vol. VIII, nos. 1-2, Kathmandu 1981; reprinted separately by gYung-Drung Bon Monastic Centre, Solan, India 1983.

Snellgrove, David, *Himalayan Pilgrimage: A Study of Tibetan Religion by a Traveller through Western Nepal*, Shambhala, Boston 1989.

Snellgrove, David, *Indo-Tibetan Buddhism: Indian Buddhists and Their Tibetan Successors,* Serindia Publications, London 1987.

Snellgrove, David, *The Nine Ways of Bon*, Oxford University Press, London 1967.

Snellgrove, David, and Hugh Richardson, *A Cultural History of Tibet*, Geo Weidenfeld & Nicolson, London 1968.

Stein, R.A., *L'epopee tibetaine de Gesar dans a version Lamaique de Ling*, Annales du Musee Guimet, Bill. d'Et. LXI, Paris 1956.

Stein, R.A., *Recherches sur l'epopee et le barde au Tibet*, Annales du Musee Guimet, Paris 1959.

Stein, R.A., *Tibetan Civilization*, Faber and Faber, London, 1972.

Tarthang Tulku, *Ancient Tibet*, Dharma Publishing, Berkeley 1986.

Tarthang Tulku, "A History of the Buddhist Dharma," in *Crystal Mirror* vol. 5, Dharma Publishing, Berkeley CA 1977.

Tarthang Tulku, *Masters of the Nyingma Lineage: Crystal Mirror 11*, Dharma Publishing, Berkeley CA 1995.

Thar, Tsering, "The Ancient Zhang Zhung Civilization," in *Tibet Studies: Journal of the Tibetan Academy of Social Socciences*, Lhasa 1989, pp. 90-104.

Thondup, Tulku, *Hidden Teachings of Tibet: An Explanation of the Terma Tradition of the Nyingmapa School of Buddhism*, Wisdom Publications, London 1986.

Thondup, Tulku, *The Tantric Tradition of the Nyingmapas*, Buddhayana, Marion MA 1984.

Tucci, Giuseppe, *The Religions of Tibet*, University of california Press, Berkeley 1980.

Tucci, Giuseppe, *Tibetan Painted Scrolls*, vol II, IsMEO, Rome 1949.

Tucci, Giuseppe, *Travels of Tibetan Pilgrimes in the Swat Valley*, The Greater India Society, Calcutta 1940.

Trungpa, Chogyam, *Born in Tibet*, George Allen & Unwin, London 1966.

Upasak, C.S., *History of Buddhism in Afghanisthan*, Central Institute of Higher Tibetan Studies, Sarnath Varanasi 1990.

Uray, Geza, "The Old Tibetan Verb Bon," in *Acta Orientalia Academiae Scientarium Hungaricae*, Budapest 1964, vol. 17, no. 3, pp. 323-334.

Valantasis, Richard, *The Gospel of Thomas*, Routledge, London 1997.

van Renterghem, Tony, *When Santa was a Shaman*, Llewellyn Publishers, St. Paul MN 1995.

Vitali, R., *The Kingdoms of Gu.ge and Pu.hrang*, LTWA, Dharamsala 1996.

Wangyal Rinpoche, Tenzin, *The Wonders of the Natural Mind: The Essence of Dzogchen in the Native Bon Tradition of Tibet*, Station Hill Press, Barrytown NY 1993.

Wayman, Alex, "Analogical Thinking in the Buddhist Tantras", in *The Buddhist Tantras*, Samual Weiser, New York 1973.

Wayman, Alex, *The Buddhist Tantras: Light on Indo-Tibetan Esotericism*, Samual Weiser, New York 1973.

Wayman, Alex, *The Yoga of the Guhyasamajatantra*, Motilal Banarsidass, New Delhi 1977.

Zaehner, R.C., *The Dawn and Twilight of Zoroastrianism*, G.P. Putnam, New York 1961.

Works in Tibetan

rGyun khyer bon spyod phyogs bdus dang ldan thar lam 'dzogs-pa'i them-skes, Bon Students Committee Central Institute of Higher Tibetan Studies, Sarnath, Varanasi, India 2001.

sNyan-rgyud rgyal-ba'i phyag-khrid by Bru-chen rGyal-ba g.yung-drung in *sNyan rgyud nam-mkha' 'phrul mdzod drang nges skor* and *Zhang-zhung snyan-rgyud skor*, Tibetan Bonpo Monastic Centre, New Delhi 1972.

sNyan rgyud nam-mkha' 'phrul mdzod drang nges skor and *Zhang-zhung snyan-rgyud skor*, Tibetan Bonpo Monastic Centre, New Delhi 1972, ff. 539-726.

sNyan-rgyud rig-pa gcer-mthong gi skor, Tibetan Bonpo Monastic Centre, Dolanji, HP, India in 1972.

Thun-mtshams bco-lnga-pa man-ngag khrid kyi rim-pa lag-len thun-mtshams dang bcas-pa, Tibetan text in Kvaerne and Thubten Rikey, *The Stages of A-khrid Meditation: Dzogchen Practice of the Bon Tradition*, Library of Tibetan Works and Archives, Dharamsala 1996.

sNang srid mdzod-phug gi rtsa-ba dang spyi-don, published as *mDzod-phug: Basic Verses and Commentary by Dran-pa Nam-mkha'*, Lopon Tenzin Namdak, Delhi 1966.

dBal-gsas las rim, Tibetan Bonpo Monastic Centre, New Delhi 1973.

'Bel gtam lung gi snying-po, by Lopon Tenzin Namdak, n.d.

Ma rgyud thugs-rje nyi-ma'i rmi-ba lam du khyer-ba'i 'grel-pa (ff. 621-654) and *Ma rgyud thugs-rje nyi-ma'i gnyid-pa lam du khyer-ba'i 'grel-pa* (ff. 721-755) in the *Ma rgyud sangs-rgyas skor gsum*, New Delhi 1985.

rDzogs-chen yang-rtse klong-chen gyi khrid gzhung cha-lag dang bcas, Bonpo Monastic Centre, New Delhi 1973.

Zhang-zhung snyan-rgyud in *History and Doctrine of Bonpo Nispanna Yoga*, Sata-Pitaka Series Indo-Asian Literatures, Volume 73, International Academy of Tibetan Culture, New Delhi 1968; Introduction in English by Lokesh Chandra.

Zhang-zhung snyan-rgyud kyi bla-ma'i nyams rgyud 'bring-po sor bzhag-pa dang bsdus-pa 'thor-bu bcas, Tibetan Bonpo Monastric Centre, Solan HP 1973.

Zhang-zhung snyan-rgyud kyi bla-ma'i nyams rgyud rgyas-pa skya smug gnyis, Tibetan Bonpo Monastric Centre, Solan HP 1973.

Zhang-zhung snyan-rgyud kyi bla-ma'i nyams rgyud rgyas-pa skya smug gnyis, Tibetan Bonpo Monastic Centre, New Delhi 1973.

Zhang-zhung snyan-rgyud kyi bla-ma'i nyams rgyud 'bring-po sor bzhag-pa dang bsdus-pa thor-bu, Tibetan Bonpo Monastic Centre, New Delhi 1973.

g.Yung-drung bon gyi bstan-pa'i 'byung khungs nyung bsdus by Namdak, Lopon Tenzin, Kalimpong 1962.

Legs-bshad rin-po-che'i mdzod dpyod-ldan dga'-ba'i char by Shardza Tashi Gyaltsan, Romanized Tibetan text in Samten G. Karmay, *The Treasury of Good Sayings: A Tibetan History of Bon*, Oxford University Press, London 1972.

Sangs-rgyas kyi bstan rtsis ngo-mtshar nor-bu'i phreng-ba by Nyi-ma bstan-'dzin, in *Tibetan Zhang-zhung Dictionary*, Tibetan Bonpo Foundation, New Delhi 1966.

Srid-pa rgyud kyi kha-byang chen-mo, Bonpo Monastic Centre, New Delhi 1976.

Glossary of Tibetan Terms

ka-dag	primordial purity, primordially pure
ka-dag chen-po	total primordial purity
kun-rtog ma rig-pa	ignorance that conceptualizes everything
kun-gzhi	Alaya, the basis of everything
kun tu zang-mo	Kuntu Zangmo, pn. of the Primordial Wisdom
kun tu bzang-po	Kuntu Zangpo, pn. of the Primordial Buddha
kun-bzang dgong-pa	primordial state of the individual
bka'	precept
bka' brgyud	Precepts Transmission
bka' brgyud skor bzhi	the Four Cycles of the Precepts Transmission
bskyed-rim	Generation Process, visualization process
khrid	guiding explanation
khregs-chod	Trekchod, releasing all tensions and rigidities
'khrul gzhi	the basis of delusion
'khrul-lugs	system of delusion, the evolution of Samsara
gyer	1. chant, 2. Bon, Dharma (ZZ)
gyes tshul	the process of separation (of Samsara and Nirvana)
grub brgyud	Practice Lineage
grub rtags	signs of realization, signs of success in one's practice
grub-thob snyan-brgyud	Oral Transmission of the Siddhas
grub-mtha'	philosophical tenet
grol-lugs	system of liberation, the unfolding of Nirvana
grol gzhi	the basis of liberation
dgongs brgyud	Mind Transmission, direct transmission mind-to-mind
dgongs-pa	1. intention, 2. Mind, 3. Primordial State
rgyal-ba'i dgongs brgyud	the Mind Transmission of the Victorious Ones
sgo gsum	the three gates (of body, speech, and mind)
sgom-pa	meditation, to meditate
bsgrags-pa skor gsum	the Three Cycles of Revelation
ngo-sprod	direct introduction

ngo-bo rang-bzhin thugs-rje	Essence, Nature, and Energy
ngo-shes	recognition, to recognize
dngos-gzhi	principal practice, principal section
sngon-'gro	preliminary practice, preliminary section
co-bzhag	leaving it just as it is
gcig brgyud	Single Transmission
chod rtogs	adefinitive understanding
'ja'-lus	rainbow body
nyams	experience, experience in meditation
nyams brgyud	Experiential Transmission
nye brgyud	short lineage of transmission
nyon-mongs-pa	emotional defilement, negative emotion, passion, klesha
mnyam-bzhag	state of contemplation
snyan brgyud	Oral Transmission
ting-nge 'dzin	samadhi, contemplation
gti-mug	confusion
rtogs-pa	understanding, to understand
stag-gzigs	Tazik, ancient name for Central Asia
stong-cha	on the side of emptiness
stong-pa nyid	Shunyata, emptiness
stod brgyud	Upper Lineage of Transmission
ston-pa	Teacher, the founder of a spiritual tradition
thig-le	bindu, tiny sphere of light, energy droplet
thig-le nyag-gcig	the Unique Sphere
thun	meditation session
theg-pa rim dgu	the nine successive vehicles to enlightenment
thod-rgal	Thodgal, instantaneous transition
bdag-'dzin	grasping at a self, ego identity
bder-gshegs, bde-bar gsegs-pa	Sugata, a title of the Buddha
nam-mkha' ar-gtad	fixation on space
gnas-lugs	Natural State
rnam-rtog	thought, discursive thought
rnam-shes	consciousness
snang stong	empty forms
snang stong dbyer-med	inseparability of appearance and emptiness
snang yul	visible object
sprul-sku	Nirmanakaya, Emanation Body
sprul-pa	emanation, to emanate
sprul-pa'i khye'u-chung	the little boy who is an emanation
pha rgyud	Father Tantra
'pho-ba chen-po	the Great Transfer
'pho-ba chen-po 'od sku	Body of Light of the Great Transfer

bon	1. Dharma, the ultimate reality, teaching of the Buddha, 2. dharmas, phenomena
bon-sku	Dharmakaya, Body of the Ultimate Reality
byang brgyud	Northern Transmission
byin-rlabs	blessings, spiritual energy of inspiration
bla-ma'i rnal-'byor	Guru Yoga, unification with the master
blo	thought process, intellect
blo 'das chen-po	totally beyond the intellect
blo 'das brjod-med chen-po	totally inconceivable and inexpressible
dbang	empowerment, initiation
dbus gter lugs	system of the Central Treasures
dbyer-med	inseparable, inseparability
'bras-bu'i sku gsum	Trikaya of the Fruit
ma 'gag-pa	unceasing
ma rig-pa	ignorance
man-ngag	upadesha, secret oral instruction
mi rtog-pa	without thoughts, state of having no thoughts
mun-mtshams	dark retreat
dmigs-bcas	meditation with an object
dmigs-pa	visualization, imagination, to visualize
dmigs-med	meditation without an object
smad brgyud	Lower Lineage of Transmission
tsi-ta	the physical heart (ZZ)
btswo	a magical missile
rtsa 'dul	training the breathing
rtsa dbu-ma	the central channel, Avadhuti
rtsa rlung	yoga of the channels and the winds
rtsa gsum 'dus mdor	the junction of the three channels
rtsal	energy
rtse-gcig	one-pointed concentration
tshang-pa'i bu-ga	the aperture of Brahma (at the crown of the head)
tshig bshad	exposition of the words (that are to be recited)
mtshan-nyid	1. essential characteristics, 2. philosophy
mtshams-bcad	securing the boundaries, making a retreat
rdzogs-sku	Sambhogakaya, Body of Perfect Enjoyment
rdzogs-chen, rdzogs-pa chen-po	Dzogchen, the Great Perfection
rdzogs-rim	Perfection Process
rdzogs sangs-rgyas-pa	Perfect Buddhahood
gzhan snang	manifestation due to another (extrinsic cause)
gzhi	the Base, basis, foundation
gzhi'i sku gsum	Trikaya of the Base
gzhi'i gnas-lugs	Natural State of the Base
'od kyi khye'u-chung	the little child of light, the little luminous boy

'od-gsal	Clear Light, the practice of the Clear Light (Thodgal)
'ol-mo lung-ring	Shambhala, an ancient country in Central Asia
yid	the discursive or functional mind, manas
yid kyi khye'u-chung	the little child of the mind
yid kyi rnam-shes	mental consciousness, manovijnana
ye-nyid	Primordial State
ye-nyid snying-po	the essence of the Primordial State
ye nas rig stong dbyer-med	inseparability of awareness and emptiness from the very beginning
ye gzhi	Primordial Base
ye-shes	primal cognition, primal awareness, primordial awareness, gnosis
ye-shes kyi bdud-rtsi	wisdom nectar
ye-shes kyi rlung	wisdom winds
ye sangs-rgyas-pa	Primordial Buddhahood
rang snang	self-manifestation
rang-byung ye-shes	self-originated primal awareness
rang-byung rig-pa'i sku	Body of Self-Originated Awareness
rang rtsal	inherent energy
rang-bzhin	nature, natural, Nature
rang-rig	self-awareness
rang-rig mngon gyur	self-awareness becomes manifest
rang-rig ye-shes	primal cognition of self-awareness
rig-cha	on the side of awareness
rig-pa	Awareness, intrinsic awareness
rig-pa gcer mthong	awareness seeing nakedly (without conceptions)
rig-pa ngo-sprod	direct introduction to intrinsic awareness
rig-pa'i rang rtsal	the inherent energy of intrinsic awareness
rig-pa'i rang gsal	the inherent clarity of intrinsic awareness
rig-pa'i ye-shes	primal cognitions of intrinsic awareness
ring brgyud	long lineage of transmission
ru-shan dbye-ba	exercises making discrimination (between mind and Nature of Mind)
rlung	breath, vital winds (of which prana is the chief)
rlung-ro	stale air (in the lungs)
lam gyi sku gsum	Trikaya of the Path
lung	scriptural authorization (by reading aloud), scripture, Agama
lung-bstan	prophecy, prophetic saying
lung ma bstan	neutral dull state of mind without thoughts
shes-rab	wisdom, discriminating wisdom
gshen	1. practitioner, 2. pn. of an ancient clan
gshen-rab mi-bo	Nirmanakaya Buddha who appeared in Olmo Lungring in ancient times

gshen-lha 'od dkar	Sambhogakaya Buddha
bshad brgyud	Exposition Transmission
sems	mind, thought
sems-nyid	the Nature of Mind
sems-nyid gnas-lugs	Natural State of the Nature of Mind
sems dang sems 'byung	states of consciousness and contents of consciousness
sems smad sde dgu	the Nine Lower Sections of the Mind Transmission
sems-'dzin	exercises for fixating the mind (on some object of meditation)
so-mtshams	the Boundary (between death and the onset of the Bardo experience)
gsal-cha	on the side of luminous clarity
gsal-ba	clear, clarity, clear luminosity
gsal stong dbyer-med	inseparability of clarity and emptiness
gsas	god, deity
gsas-mkhar	temple, divine citadel
gsas-mkhar mchog lnga	the Five Supreme Ones of the Divine Citadel (in Father Tantra)
gsol-'debs	prayer, invocation, to pray
lhan-skyes	co-emergent, spontaneously born
lhan-skyes ma rig-pa	co-emergent spontaneously born ignorance
lhug-pa	alertly relaxed
lhun-grub	spontaneous perfection, spontaneously perfected
lhun-grub chen-po	total spontaneous perfection
lho gter lugs	system of the Southern Treasures
lho brgyud	Southern Lineage of Transmission
lhod-pa chen-po	total relaxation
ag-tse	the joint of the spine and the skull (ZZ)

[ZZ=Zhang-zhung word]

Index

MASTERS AND DEITIES

TOPICS AND PLACES